T0392809

THE ROUTLEDGE HANDBOOK OF TRANSATLANTIC RELATIONS

The Routledge Handbook of Transatlantic Relations is an essential and comprehensive reference for the regulation of transatlantic relations across a range of subjects, bringing together contributions from scholars, policy makers, lawyers and political scientists. Future oriented in a range of fields, it probes the key technical, procedural and policy issues for the US of dealing with, negotiating, engaging and law-making with the EU, taking a broad interdisciplinary perspective including international relations, politics, political economic and law, EU external relations law and international law and assesses the external consequences of transatlantic relations in a systematic and comprehensive fashion.

The transatlantic relationship constitutes one of the most established and far-reaching democratic alliances globally, and which has propelled multilateralism, trade regulation and the EU-US relationship in global challenges. The different contributions will propose solutions to overcome these problems and help us understand the shifting transatlantic agenda in diverse areas from human rights, to trade, and security, and the capacity of the transatlantic relationship to set new international agendas, standards and rules.

The Routledge Handbook of Transatlantic Relations will be a key reference for scholars, students and practitioners of Transatlantic Relations/EU-US relations, EU External Relations law, EU rule-making, EU Security law and more broadly to global governance, International law, international political economy and international relations.

Elaine Fahey is Professor of Law at the City Law School, City, University of London.

ROUTLEDGE INTERNATIONAL HANDBOOKS

Routledge International Handbook of Multidisciplinary Perspectives on Descendants of Holocaust Survivors
Edited by Judith Tydor Baumel-Schwartz and Amit Shrira

Routledge International Handbook of Visual-motor skills, Handwriting, and Spelling
Edited by Yanyan Ye, Tomohiro Inoue, Urs Maurer, and Catherine McBride

Routledge Handbook of Environmental Policy
Edited by Helge Jörgens, Christoph Knill and Yves Steinebach

The Routledge Handbook of Soft Power (2nd Edition)
Edited by Naren Chitty, Lilian Ji, Gary D Rawnsley

The Routledge Handbook of Urban Logistics
Edited by Jason Monios, Lucy Budd and Stephen Ison

The Routledge Handbook of Comparative Global Urban Studies
Edited by Patrick LeGalès and Jennifer Robinson

The Routledge Handbook of Transatlantic Relations
Edited by Elaine Fahey

THE ROUTLEDGE HANDBOOK OF TRANSATLANTIC RELATIONS

Edited by Elaine Fahey

LONDON AND NEW YORK

Designed cover image: Alberto Masnovo / Getty Images

First published 2024
by Routledge
4 Park Square, Milton Park, Abingdon, Oxon OX14 4RN

and by Routledge
605 Third Avenue, New York, NY 10158

Routledge is an imprint of the Taylor & Francis Group, an informa business

© 2023 selection and editorial matter, Elaine Fahey; individual chapters, the contributors

The right of Elaine Fahey to be identified as the author[/s] of the editorial material, and of the authors for their individual chapters, has been asserted in accordance with sections 77 and 78 of the Copyright, Designs and Patents Act 1988.

All rights reserved. No part of this book may be reprinted or reproduced or utilised in any form or by any electronic, mechanical, or other means, now known or hereafter invented, including photocopying and recording, or in any information storage or retrieval system, without permission in writing from the publishers.

Trademark notice: Product or corporate names may be trademarks or registered trademarks, and are used only for identification and explanation without intent to infringe.

British Library Cataloguing-in-Publication Data
A catalogue record for this book is available from the British Library

ISBN: 978-1-032-25534-7 (hbk)
ISBN: 978-1-032-25556-9 (pbk)
ISBN: 978-1-003-28391-1 (ebk)

DOI: 10.4324/9781003283911

Typeset in Bembo
by MPS Limited, Dehradun

CONTENTS

FIGURES

TABLES

CONTRIBUTORS

Gabriella Bolstad is a junior research fellow in the Norwegian Institute of International Affairs' (NUPI's) Research Group on Security and Defence. Bolstad's research focus on transatlantic relations, China in international politics, geopolitics and the Arctic.

Martin T. Braml served as research economist at the World Trade Organisation until 2022. Since 2021, Braml is also lecturer in trade policy at the University of Passau, Germany. His main expertise lies in international economics, trade policy, and macroeconomics. In these fields, he has contributed to economic policy debates in Germany.

Simon Dekeyrel is a policy analyst in the Sustainable Prosperity for Europe Programme at the Brussels-based think tank European Policy Centre, Belgium. He recently completed his PhD on the contemporary evolution of EU energy policy at the University of Nottingham, UK, where he was part of the EU Horizon 2020 Marie Skłodowska-Curie research project 'EU Trade and Investment Policy'. His primary research interests are EU internal and external energy and climate policy.

Albert Didriksen is a research assistant at the Innlandet University, Norway. Since September 2022, he is a PhD student in political science, more specifically political theory and political philosophy at the Central European University, Vienna, Austria. Previously, he was also a seminar teacher, teaching on research design, qualitative and quantitative methods, as well as political theory at the University of Oslo, Norway.

Joseph Dunne is director of the European Parliament (EP) Liaison Office in Washington DC, which was set up to foster and develop relations between the

EP and the US Congress, since 1 October 2019. Earlier, Dunne was a senior resident fellow at the German Marshall Fund in Washington DC and a visiting fellow at the Schar School of Policy and Government at George Mason University. Up to that time, he was a director in the European Parliament Research Service.

Michelle Egan is professor and Jean Monnet Chair Ad Personam in the School of International Service American University DC, US. Egan focuses on comparative politics and political economy. She works on Europe and the United States, with a focus on issues of federalism, trade, governance and law. Egan is co-director of the Transatlantic Policy Center with Professor Garret Martin.

L. Johan Eliasson is professor of political science at the East Stroudsburg University, US. He teaches European politics, trade, international relations, international law, a simulation on the European Union and research methods. Elliasson's research focuses on European mobilisation around trade policy, transatlantic trade and European Union economic integration.

Elaine Fahey is professor of law at City Law School, City, University of London, UK and visiting professor at American University, Washington College of Law. She held a Jean Monnet Chair in Law and Transatlantic Relations from 2019-2022. She is co-director of the Institute for the Study of European Law (ISEL). Her research interests include the relationship between EU law and global governance, international relations, trade and technology and transatlantic relations.

Gabriel J. Felbermayr is director of the Austrian Institute of Economic Research (WIFO). He specialises in international economics, international trade agreements, economic policy and environmental economics. Previously, Felbermayr was a professor of economics at the University of Munich and director of the Ifo Institute for Economic Research, Munich. From 2019 to 2021, he was the President of the Kiel Institute for the World Economy.

Robert G. Finbow is Eric Dennis Memorial Professor of Political Science and deputy director of Jean Monnet European Union Centre of Excellence, Dalhousie University, Canada. Finbow's current research focuses on the socially responsible elements of trade agreements, especially labour and social issues in NAFTA and the EU. His focus recently has been on the Canada-European Economic and Trade Agreement (CETA), especially the implications for social policy and federalism.

Karsten Friis is a senior research fellow and head of the Norwegian Institute of International Affairs' (NUPI's) Research Group on Security and Defence. Friis' main area of expertise is security and defence policies, international military operations, civilian-military relations, Nordic security, cyber security, as well as the Western Balkans.

Jenya Grigorova is dispute settlement lawyer at the WTO. Her research interests include international trade law, in particular WTO law, issues related to energy regulation on both international and regional levels, international investment law and environmental law. Grigorova has published on various pressing issues in international trade relations, concerning trade in the energy sector, as well as on specific aspects of EU law, relating to EU restrictive measures and to EU environmental policy measures.

Peter Holmes is Emeritus Reader at the University of Sussex Business School. He is now a fellow of the UK Trade Policy Observatory (UKTPO) and a director of InterAnalysis. He is a specialist in European Economic Integration and other global public policy issues, including the EU's relations with the WTO. Holmes is interested in the relationship among the complex of policies on trade, competition, regulation and technology.

Davor Jancic is senior lecturer in law at Queen Mary University of London, UK. His research interests include EU institutional law and governance, comparative regional integration and regional organisations, democracy and legitimacy beyond the state. He has dedicated a large portion of his research output to national parliaments in the EU, the European Parliament and EU foreign affairs (e.g. with the US and China), parliamentary diplomacy and so forth.

Maria Kendrick is senior lecturer in law at City, University of London, UK. Her research areas cover tax law and EU law, including integration, differentiated integration and tax. Dr Kendrick's research also covers the subject of Brexit. Maria is also, by invitation, on the Editorial Board of Kluwer Law International's Regulating for Globalization Blog and *Global Trade and Customs Journal.*

Giulio Kowalski is doctoral researcher at City, University of London, UK. His research revolves around the impact of the digitisation of the economy on the Competition and Data Protection Law frameworks. In particular, Kowalski looks into the interrelation between these two fields of law in the present digital age and endeavours to address the different issues that arise from incorporating privacy as a qualitative parameter into the competition and merger assessment by domestic and supranational competition authorities.

Mark Ledwidge is a Senior Research Fellow within International Politics City University London, and an independant educational consultant and researcher. He is an expert on race pertaining to US foreign policy and International Relations. He was previously also on the Organising Commitee of the AHRC-Funded Research Network on the Presidency of Barack Obama.

Minako Morita-Jaeger is senior research fellow in International Trade of University of Sussex Business School and a Policy Research Fellow of the UK Trade Policy Observatory (UKTPO). Prior to her research work, she was intensively engaged in trade policy in practice as an economic affairs officer at the UNCTAD in Geneva, a WTO services trade negotiator at the Japanese delegation in Geneva and a principal trade policy analyst at the Japan Business Federation (Keidanren) in Tokyo.

Akasemi Newsome is associate director of the Institute of European Studies at the University of California, Berkeley, US. Her research on the politics of labour, immigration and comparative racialisation in Europe addresses topics at the forefront of international and comparative political economy, including rights and global governance, institutions, capitalist development and social movements.

David O'Sullivan is a senior counsellor at Steptoe & Johnson LLP, Brussels, Belgium and former EU Ambassador to the US. O'Sullivan oversaw the EU's bilateral relationship with the US, including political, economic and commercial affairs. A long-time EU official, he has served in several senior official posts in the European public service. In these roles, he developed a deep understanding of the trade and diplomatic relationships of the EU and its member countries and the full range of transatlantic business relationship issues.

Inderjeet Parmar is Professor of International Politics at City, University of London, UK. Parmar's research interests focus on the history, politics and sociology of Anglo-American foreign policy elites over the past 100 years, specifically embodied in organisations such as philanthropic foundations, think tanks, policy research institutes, university foreign affairs institutes and state agencies.

Ernst-Ulrich Petersmann is an Emeritus Professor at the Department of Law at European University Institute (EUI) Florence, Italy. He taught constitutional law at the Universities of Hamburg and Heidelberg and was a professor of international law and European law at the Universities of St. Gallen, Fribourg, Geneva, the Geneva Graduate Institute of International Relations and the EUI. He has published more than 30 books and 350 contributions to books and journals focusing on international law, European law and comparative constitutional law.

Sara Poli is professor of EU law at University of Pisa, Italy. She is currently member of the Jean Monnet networks EUDIPLO and EUCTER. She has held a Jean Monnet Chair between 2013 and 2016. She has carried out research with the support of the DAAD short term fellowship, Robert Schuman fellowship (EUI), the Marie Curie fellowship (EUI), the Fulbright-Schuman fellowship and the Belgian 'Vlac fellowship'.

Kenneth Propp is an adjunct professor of EU law at the Georgetown University Law Center, US, and a non-resident senior fellow at the Atlantic Council, Europe Center, and consults for technology companies on transatlantic digital and privacy law and policy issues. Privously, he was director of trade policy for The Software Alliance (also known as BSA), an association of major software companies and served as legal counsellor at the US Mission to the EU, where he led US government's engagement with the EU on digital and privacy law and policy, and participated in US-EU trade negotiations.

Marianne Riddervold is a research professor at the Norwegian Institute of International Affairs' (NUPI's) Research Group on Security and Defence. She is also professor of political science/international relations at the Inland School of Business and Social Sciences and a senior fellow at the UC Berkeley Institute of European Studies. Riddervold's research interests include EU foreign and security policies, international relations and security, maritime security, transatlantic relations and theory development within the fields of international relations and European integration.

Charles B. Roger is an associate professor and Ramón y Cajal Research Fellow at the Institut Barcelona d'Estudis Internacional, Spain. His research explores the transformations occurring in our system of global governance and how these are shaping our ability to address cross-border problems.

Viktor Szépis a postdoctoral researcher at the University of Groningen, Netherlands. His research mirrors his interdisciplinary background and focuses on the legal and political dimensions of EU foreign and sanctions policy. At present, he devotes most of his time to the Horizon 2020 ENGAGE project that examines the possibilities to create a more coherent and effective EU external action.

Fabien Terpan is Jean Monnet Chair in EU Law & Politics and senior lecturer at Sciences Po GrenobleUGA, France. He is the deputy director of the Centre d'Etudes de la Sécurité Internationale et des Coopérations Européennes (CESICE). His research focus lies on the EU's common foreign and security policy, international security policy and the interplay between law and politics in the European Union.

Maria Tzanou is a senior lecturer in Law at Keele University Law School, UK. Tzanou's research focuses on European constitutional and human rights law, privacy, data protection, surveillance, the regulation of new and emerging technologies and the inequalities of data privacy law and how these affect vulnerable groups.

Peter Van Elsuwege is Jean Monnet Chair in EU Law at Ghent University, Belgium, where he is co-director of the Ghent European Law Institute (GELI). He is also visiting professor at the College of Europe (Natolin Campus) and board member of the Centre for the Law of EU External Relations (CLEER) at the Asser Institute in The Hague. His research activities focus on the law of EU external relations and EU citizenship.

Thomas Verellen is assistant professor of EU Law, Utrecht University, Netherlands, and visiting assistant professor, University of Michigan Law School, Ann Arbor, US. He is an expert in EU and comparative foreign relations law and has a particular interest in the impact of geopolitical change on the governance of EU trade and investment policy. At Michigan, Verellen does a comparative research project on legal and political accountability mechanisms in EU and US trade and investment policy.

Alasdair R. Young is a Professor **of International Affairs** and Neal Family Chair at Georgia Institute of Technology (Georgia Tech), US. He co-directs the Center for European and Transatlantic Studies, a Jean Monnet Center of Excellence, and the Center for International Strategy, Technology, and Policy. His research interests include environment, globalisation and localisation, international trade and investment, regulation with geographic focus on Europe, Europe – United Kingdom, and the United States.

ACKNOWLEDGEMENTS

This publication was produced with the support of the Erasmus+ Jean Monnet Chair grant (2019–2022) Decision No. 2019- 1794-001-001. I am very grateful to Ivanka Karaivanova for stellar research assistance and support for the project at various stages and to Eve Poyner for research support.

Special thanks are due to Andrew Taylor for his support to the project and patience with its development and thanks also to Sophie Iddamalgoda and Meghan Flood.

Thanks to all of the authors of this project who participated in multiple events online and eventually in person in preparation for this project over a number of years.

Thanks to the following who graciously read draft chapters and supplied many useful comments and suggestions or inputted into the publication in other ways of significance to merit acknowledgements: David Collins, Sabrina Cuendet-Robert, Daniel Francis, Mauro Gatti, Anna-Louise Hinds, Szilárd Gaspar-Szilagyi, Leigh Hancher, Kristina Irion, Imelda Maher, Isabella Mancini, Eva Pander Maat, Jed Odermatt, Wyn Rees, Ryan Stones, Martin Trybus, Guillaume Van de Loo, Eva Van der Zee, Declan Walsh and Philippa Watson.

Elaine Fahey
London, 26 September 2022

INTRODUCTION

Elaine Fahey

CITY LAW SCHOOL, CITY, UNIVERSITY OF LONDON

A landmark relationship

The relationship between the European Union (EU) and United States (US), as will be developed in this handbook), tends to be complex and multifaceted. Relations are variously depicted as cyclical, intergovernmental and fundamental to multilateralism and crisis-driven. They are driven also by and tend to 'ignite' geopolitics, as much as complex domestic issues and themes. EU-US relations are the foundation of the theoretical 'West'. In practical terms, they form the key plank currently and for some time of international economic law, culture and finance. More recently, they are centrally placed in the regulatory playing-field of big tech and global data flows (Gardner, 2020). As will be explored here, a broad range of attempts at transatlantic governance have been characterised as unsuccessful in scholarship. They raise the seemingly eternal question as to what the history of transatlantic governance indicates to us in terms of the expectations and realities of transatlantic cooperation in view of its breadth and distinctiveness, as much as the reach of the cooperation (Nicolaidis, 2005; Pollack, 2005; Young, 2009; Petersmann, 2015; Smith, 2019). Views on transatlantic cooperation and their potential have arguably retreated substantially in the post–World War II (WW2) years from calls for communities of law and transatlantic institutions (e.g. Stein and Hay, 1963).

The transatlantic partnership may well be an iconic partnership for a long time, fundamental to the global economy and world security. Yet, it has long been one of the 'problem children' of international economic law for over decades (Petersmann, 2003). Moreover, the EU and US have consistently shaped international approaches to public international law, albeit distinctively and differently (Dunoff and Pollack, 2013). The role of the US in crafting the global order after WW2 was decisive, including the active promotion of European integration yet patterns of change thereafter a complex to map. Over the next 60 or so years, the transatlantic partnership was central to global events through the building of the Western liberal order and all the institutions that went with it. It has for many years been evidenced by the un-equalness or un-equilibrium of power. For much of the 20th Century, the US was evidently the stronger partner both militarily and economically. Even as Europe grew into a larger and more cohesive economic and normative power, its heavy reliance on the US security umbrella gave the US the upper hand particularly

DOI: 10.4324/9781003283911-1

post 9/11 (O' Sullivan, in this volume). In contemporary times, however, the EU and US constitute two of the leading global figures in trade, economics, agriculture, security and as bulwarks of the liberal global legal order post-WW2, at least until recently. The EU supported fully the US pivot to mega-regionals to exclude China and pivot away from the World Trade Organization (WTO) framework, in particular, the Transatlantic Trade and Investment Partnership (TTIP), which quickly stalled with the advent of a new administration but which afforded the EU the change to align its post-Lisbon Trade agenda with more gusto (De Ville and Siles-Brügge, 2015; Griller et al., 2017). It spurned a subsequently complex period for EU trade policy, which has framed itself as being based upon 'free and open' trade and competition but has been stymied by a defensive turn to a lexicon of strategic autonomy, digital sovereignty and multiple trade defence instruments. The Ukraine crisis has strengthened relations between the allies. At the same time, however, both structural (the rise of China) and domestic (eg 'America first' policy or the strategic autonomy of the EU) factors suggest that the EU-US relationship will weaken over time due to the impact of such factors, in particular on US foreign policy preferences, especially where the EU is strengthening its own foreign policy, including in the area of security and defence (Riddervold and Newsome, 2019). Yet the metrics of the relationship are often shifting across political scientists, political theory and political economy trade and data lawyers and governance scholarship, where the calibration between convergence and divergence has been complex. Within a political cycle, significant variations on the state of transatlantic relations have also followed as well as their analysis. Transatlantic relations as a regional genre have undoubtedly shown themselves to be a vibrant source of dynamic theorisation. The place of actors, powers, competences and institutions form pivotal concepts but also far from objective ideals, imbued often with constructivism. Conflict as much as contestation and convergence is easily overplayed or overanalysed. Although a thirst for international cooperation, standards and institutionalisation is seen globally as pivotal to the success of the international economic order, such efforts arguably have often been stymied at transatlantic or domestic level. This handbook explores many of these themes, isolating these questions in this landmark relationship.

A history of failing to cooperate and disputes

The transatlantic partnership is significant for its regular, high-profile and many experiments in transnational governance, mainly failed ones, often failed through components thereof rather than the sum of its parts (Nicolaidis and Shaffer, 2005; Petersmann, 2015). A recent and highly significant transatlantic digital trade cooperation, EU-US Privacy Shield Agreement, arguably was not adequately 'policed' by the US Federal Trade Commission and viewed with much distrust by the Court of Justice of the EU (CJEU) (Terpan, 2018; Fahey and Terpan, 2021). Other disputes constitute some of the longest ongoing of all time between WTO members and the transatlantic partnership has also not sufficed to stop the WTO Dispute Settlement body collapsing into failure (Pollack and Shaffer, 2009; Scott, 2009; Krisch, 2010; Bradford, 2020). The US and EU conduct relations pursuant to more than 35 bilateral treaties and other international agreements on subjects as diverse as trade and investment, transport, and law enforcement – a scale of cooperation comparable to the extensive network of US agreements with individual EU member states (Propp, in this volume). At the same time, the failed negotiation of TTIP and the invalidation of commercial data transfer agreements such as the Privacy Shield Framework attests to the unique legal and political challenges that the EU poses for US government negotiators and how US federal law, agencies and actors are not aligned on EU law, values or policy (Propp, in this volume). A new era of transatlantic relations appears rather easily reset from US administration to the next (Fahey, 2021). Crucially though, key EU-US attempts to address global challenges at the outset of the Biden administration, evolving into a Transatlantic Trade and Technology Council, appeared to place WTO reform down the menu of an extensive agenda. In the background, the EU has had to develop a range of controversial measures and ultimately a new industrial policy of defensiveness and strategic autonomy to deal with a new era of foes from the US to China and develop the autonomy of EU law against a recent backdrop of several hostile third countries refusing to recognise its esoteric organisational and diplomatic credentials, i.e. the UK recently and US initially. To a degree, the US has also engaged in this agenda, leading the way for the EU but also aligning and synthesizing to a high degree.

Traditionally, political science accounts have contended that EU-US relations are law-light institution-light. These descriptions need certain health warnings and time limitations as to their accuracy (Fahey, 2014). At the time of writing, there were a number of high-profile and longstanding disputes between the EU and US at the WTO only recently resolved, *outside* of the multilateral institutional system, that is, the WTO. Many landmarks in the history of EU-US relations in trade and technology and other areas date to the Transatlantic Declaration of 1990, expanded through the New Transatlantic Agenda (NTA) in 1995 (Pollack, 2005), have been through soft law and been evolved somewhat ironically through international organisations and a commitment to light touch commitment to multilateralism. The advent of the Trump administration appeared to give effect to an unprecedented shift in Transatlantic relations since before WW2 – but mostly – from institutions. Prior to this, the Obama-era TTIP negotiations had brought the EU and US closer to much deeper forms of cooperation (Bartl and Fahey, 2014). Countless trade wars ensued which already appears to have changed to a high degree with the Biden administration, for example, already with the Transatlantic Trade and Technology Council (TTC) proposed immediately by the European Commission to the new Biden administration and swiftly implemented could mark a new change. Yet its law-light, institution-light characteristics are beyond dispute, and it evidences a new era of negotiation, law, policy and governance of trade and technology. Equally, the Biden administration has publicly and internationally endorsed 'soft law' trade solutions and non-binding framework agreements as the future of international economic law, scorning conventional 'binding' trade agreements, arguably distinctly at odds with the EU commitment to the rule of law and binding dispute settlement.

Transatlantic relations are, however, no stranger to a series of innovative hybrid governance or soft law engagement on law-making and soft law outcomes of note, including many so-called transatlantic dialogues over the years (Pollack and Shaffer,

2001). Whether they generate higher standards for the other party or not is arguably less of the focus for some time, more the conflict, convergence and contestation processes (Bermann et al., 2000; Scott, 2009). Whether they have contributed to the worsening of global governance through, for example, the dominance of big business instead of civil society concerns remains to be proven, but increasingly sensitive in the era of big tech. Many other *formal* law-making processes take place against this difficult backdrop (Fahey, 2014; Jančić, 2015). It can be easily suggested that the history of transatlantic relations shows a fine line between cooperation and conflict, although the forum for both is similar. One of the most significant sites of transatlantic 'law-making' has been until recently at the WTO. Yet it is here also where the EU and US have displayed their starkest differences as to the rule of law, interpretive legitimacy and the place of dispute settlement and courts. Most disputes between the EU and US have taken place before the WTO Dispute Settlement Body (DBS) in recent times, until at least the demise of the WTO DSB in late 2020 (Pollack and Shaffer, 2009; Petersmann, 2015). There, the EU and US have historically been involved in most disputes and have arguably contributed to its legalization, downfall and legitimacy deficit.

Framing shifts in the landmark relationship

Often, the policy shifts of EU-US relations are complex to discern. As Riddervold and Newsome (2019) state, at a first glance, the EU-US relationship seems stronger than ever. At the time of writing, the two stand firmly together in a strong and coordinated response to Russia's invasion of Ukraine and the crimes against humanity that has followed. But does this suggest that transatlantic relations are back to normal after the tumultuous Trump years and the US' pivot to Asia? Lately, the EU and US may be embarking on a new period of policy and in particular regulatory cooperation, one less focused on the technical differences between their rules and more focused on what shared objectives they have, particularly in relation to China (Young, in this volume).

The failings and failures of transatlantic cooperation through law are plentiful, doomed to failure through non-compliance, plagued with sub-optimal remedies (Pollack and Shaffer, 2009; Petersmann, 2003; 2015; Petersmann and Mayr, 2017; Gardner, 2020). The EU-US Joint Agenda for Global Change included a Transatlantic Trade and Technology Council (EU-US TTC), putatively developing a loose institutionalisation of key global challenges, which is focussed upon in many chapters of this Research Handbook. The EU proposed as part of its global change agenda a TTC – centered upon multiple working groups. The span of areas of policy and the prominence of international law instruments therein indicates the vast ambitions of the transatlantic partnership in global policy-making, explored well in this handbook. Yet it is couched in soft law as much as multilateralism and these parallel legal tracks evidence its lack of convergence and limited institutionalisation to convergence further.

EU-US relations have generated multiple complex data transfer agreements that have spawned many esoteric formulations of governance and several struggles between the EU and US as to the balance between security, surveillance and privacy (Cole et al., 2017; Terpan, 2018; Farrell and Newman, 2019; Fabbrini et al., 2021). In the post-9/11 period, the place of civil liberties in Europe have been understood to have been adversely affected by the transatlantic relationship and the norm promotion it generated (Cremona et al., 2011; Mitsilegas and Vavoula, 2021). Transatlantic relations may have entered a new era after the CJEU decision in *Schrems II* (CJEU, 2020) propelling a new Transatlantic Privacy Framework resulting in a Transatlantic Data Review Court and binding standards, yet its execution will be far from straightforward.

Chapters in this handbook across sections traverse directly and indirectly a vast scholarship on the mutual and external influence of transatlantic standards and of the directions of transatlantic law-making, also demonstrating global effects and significance for law and governance scholarship as well as the study of integration and transnationalism (e.g. Shaffer, 2000; Scott, 2009; Vogel, 2012; Bradford, 2020).

The project views 'framing' here thus also as a multidisciplinary exercise in order to frame shifts in law-making, governance and norms.

Framing actors and institutions in EU-US relations

The *place, actors and structures of a particular* time are thus of much significance also. 'The Transatlantic Declaration (TAD)' was adopted in 1990 at the Paris CSCE Summit with then US President Bush, Prime Minister Andreotti of Italy and Commission President Delors which established an institutional framework for transatlantic consultations. In, 1995 the EU-US Biannual Summit took place in Madrid with US President Clinton, Prime Minister Gonzales of Spain and President Santer of the European Commission adopted the New Transatlantic Agenda (NTA) together with a Joint EU-US Action Plan. The Agenda and Plan codified the mechanics and the substance of the transatlantic relationship and demonstrated Europe's progress toward unity and the US commitment to a 'Europe whole and free' following the fall of the Berlin wall on 9 November 1989, the first 'réalisation concrète' in Schuman/Monnet language since President Kennedy's speech of 4 July 1962 at Philadelphia's Independence Hall when he proposed a 'transatlantic partnership of equals' and a 'Declaration of Interdependence' between the New World and the New Europe (Burghardt, 2015).

The WTO has arguably subsequently operated as the most centralised and focus point of transatlantic engagement at multilateralism at least until the collapse of the dispute settlement system through the (in)action of the US, in part at least.

Members of the US Congress and the European Parliament have been meeting regularly since 1972. Nevertheless, it was only in 2010 that one side established a dedicated structure with the explicit task of channelling and deepening ties between the two legislatures – a European Parliament Liaison Office (Dunne, in this volume). Operating *outside* of legal strictures and structures or on the margins thereof, for example, as to extraterritoriality is also a key hallmark of transatlantic engagement on certain fronts (see Poli; Van Elsuwege; Szep, in this volume). Historically, many have sought an 'Atlantic Community of Law', a 'Transatlantic Marketplace' or a

'Transatlantic Civil Society' to be forged between the EU and US. Such entities have been mooted with a view to creating a transatlantic polity of sorts, inter alia for economic, political and even socio-cultural reasons (Fahey and Curtin, 2014). The lack of Transatlantic Institutions, from a court to a legislature or political union or sorts has long been a lament of many commentators (Stein and Hay, 1963). The possibility of a Transatlantic Data Review Court or Transatlantic Parliament or Political Union is discussed by many in this handbook (Fahey and Terpan, in this volume; Dunne, in this volume; Jančić, in this volume, who consider in part how these developments link to past and present institutional and other actors).

In the early 2000s when the EU and US appeared disinterested in alternatives to dispute settlement outside of the WTO and form of judicalisation or oversight, Petersmann wrote:

> Since EU and US politicians may have no self-interest in limiting their policy discretion by additional judicial restraints, how can EU and US citizens defend their constitutional interests in judicial protection of maximum freedom and other human rights across frontiers? What can academics do to promote rule of law, judicial dialogue, and co-operation between national and international courts in transatlantic relations?
>
> *(Petersmann, 2003)*

They constitute prescient observations as to the challenges of transatlantic institutions and institutionalisation. Temporal evolutions are significant however in EU-US relations. As Dunne outlines in this handbook, Transatlantic Declaration on EC-US Relations of 1990 and the NTA of 1995. Both explicitly mentioned parliamentary cooperation As early as 1984, in the first term of the directly elected Parliament, the EP adopted a resolution oping that the Parliament could arrange to 'be represented in its own right at [the Commission's] delegation in Washington'. Nearly two decades later, in 2006, the idea then secured full EP approval, for the idea of a permanent EP presence in Washington DC, fully achieved and operationalised at the time of writing as his account explains further. Indeed, subsequently, it can be said now that the European Parliament (EP) and Congress aim not only to influence their executive branches but also to act autonomously in the transnational arena through parliamentary diplomacy. They seek to secure concessions both formally by scrutinizing transatlantic international agreements, and have created capacities for internal scrutiny and trans-national interparliamentary dialogue to gain greater presence, visibility and influence in international affairs (Jančić, 2016).

State of the art problems

This research handbook considers the state of the art of transatlantic relations, broadly conceived. In some subjects, it transpires that this can be more discreet or policy-specific and descriptive, whereas in others, a longer-term view on a subject, discipline or genre is taken. The deliberately broad 'take' of this handbook can hopefully be 'forgiven' with this caveat or open misdemeanor in mind, to allow for a broader disciplinary engagement and include as many contributions as possible, from academia, practice, policy-makers, think-tanks to former diplomats and policy-makers. This research handbook moreover takes a broad view of the concept of the transatlantic (including its broader formulations as to North American and the Anglo-American spheres for example) and EU-US relations and considers a diverse, lively and multifarious grouping of subjects across contributors and fields and reflections upon a range of questions as to the actors of transatlantic relations.

From politics, to international relations (IR), to economics to political economy and more, there are a host of backgrounds and disciplines captured in this handbook. It considers the direct and indirect engagement of transatlantic actors with global governance, as to international organizations, international law, regional development, multilateral policy making and initiatives to ignite transatlantic law-making, growth and evolve its place in transnational standard-setting. The handbook themes thus consider the transatlantic impetus to evolve trade and technology as much as its output – and beyond, to wider fields such as security and defiance. The handbook across contributions reflects upon the externalities of transatlantic trade and technology, economics, politics, security and defence in global governance. The handbook draws many perspectives of law, politics and economics, including EU law, international law, international relations, global governance and transnational rule-making scholarship to frame contemporary transatlantic relations. Leading new research on interactions between the EU and US legal orders is thus captured. This handbook considers how the transatlantic relationship constitutes one of the most established and far-reaching democratic alliances globally, which has propelled multilateralism, trade regulation and the EU-US relationship in global challenges. The handbook probes the key technical, procedural and policy issues for the US of dealing with, negotiating, engaging and law-making with the EU that challenge and evolve existing international organisations law and EU external relations, marking key shifts in its actorness. Key themes also include EU and US cooperation in the digital age, the EU-US relationship inside and outside of international organisations and a new institutional infrastructure for EU-US trade and technology. The EU and US have been pivotal historically in developments towards convergence in international law and the institutional frameworks underpinning them. The book reflects upon these sites of EU and US engagement. These debates have resonance with how we understand the shifting transatlantic agenda in diverse areas from human rights, trade, security and the capacity of the transatlantic relationship to set new international agendas, standards and rules.

We hope that the reader finds a stimulating set of accounts of a past, present and vibrant future research agenda.

Next, a brief outline of the handbook text is set out.

Overview of the main fields and themes considered

The handbook is organised in 24 chapters around four core themes: (I) EU-US intra-organization relations, (II) Trade, Investment and Cooperation in Transatlantic relations, (III) Norm promotion practices of the EU and US in the digital age and

(IV) The political and economic character of transatlantic relations. The span of the chapters thus takes into account a vast array of fields. The selection thus of four themes is also rather arbitrary but hopefully the reader will agree that the themes span the conceptual and practical core functioning and locus of the transatlantic partnership – a complex study of global governance; also a study of the world's largest economic area and key drive of the digital economy.

In Part I, EU-US intra-organization relations, the section takes a span of policymakers and theorists, which is 'structuralist' in its focus but also focusing on how the EU and US have addressed global challenges separately and also together.

Dunne in 'Connecting the US Congress and the European Parliament: The Work and Role of the EP Liaison Office in Washington DC' outlines the evolving role and historical context of the European Parliament Liaison Office (EPLO) in Washington DC as a vivid work in progress from the perspective of a policy-maker. He shows how the EPLO has added an important 'hard' dimension to institutionalising the EU-US inter-parliamentary relationship. An array of factors – the huge boost given to EU-US relations as a result of the Ukraine crisis, which slowed down the policy 'pivot to Asia' and brought the European Union into sharper focus; a new realisation of the importance of the European Parliament in influencing and delivering privacy, climate, digital, antitrust and online platform regulation emanating from the EU, the exponential development of virtual interactions during and since the COVID-19 pandemic, and the increasing intensity of parliamentary contacts – are all combining to change traditional attitudes in the Congress. O' Sullivan in 'EU-US Relations in a Changing World' drawing from practice outlines the many diplomatic challenges of the diplomatic organisation, content and actions of the EU engaging with the US. When it speaks and decides with one voice, it can have huge influence, such as when it adopted EU regulations on data privacy which have become the de *facto* global standard. But, as often as it speaks with one voice, the EU can end up speaking with the voices of its 27 members. This is confusing for friends and adversaries alike. He argues that few in Washington, beyond specialists and policy wonks, really understand how the EU works and how to deal with it and yet the legal and policy outcomes have evolved immeasurably across administrations, at least until the Trump administration. Propp exposes deftly in 'Negotiating with the European Union – A US Perspective' the complexity of negotiating with the EU from a US perspective in practice. Relations between the US and the EU on law enforcement and security matters have come to be grounded in a series of binding international agreements. US negotiators, he maintains, remain frustrated by the obscurity of mixed competence, but they have persevered where the practical benefits of proceeding with Brussels are clear. A lingering US preference for bilateralism nevertheless sometimes comes to the fore.

In 'Transatlantic Parliamentary Cooperation at Fifty', Jancic outlines how the transatlantic relationship furnishes an enduring space for parliamentary diplomacy, norm entrepreneurship and coalition building. It enables EU and US parliamentarians to discuss legislative, regulatory and general political developments; debate their respective approaches to bilateral initiatives (like the TTC) and shared international challenges (like Russia's invasion of Ukraine); and to identify divergences and consider ways to address them. Roger in 'The Rise of Informal International

Organizations' using a substantial data set argues that the shift towards informality in international organisations has primarily been a product of changing cooperation problems and two major domestic shifts that have subsequently projected outwards and reshaped the Transatlantic order. Van Elsuwege and Szep then in 'The Revival of Transatlantic Partnership? EU-US Coordination in Sanctions Policy' show how both the EU and US increasingly use sanctions as an important foreign policy tool and aim to reinforce the impact of their measures on the basis of close coordination. Significantly, this coordination is not based on formal legal or institutional structures but is essentially informal and political. Whereas the existence of geopolitical threats such as Russia's military aggression against Ukraine and new security challenges from emerging powers such as China and India stimulates a revival of the transatlantic partnership, leading to increased sanctions coordination, frictions about the extra-territorial application of unilateral sanctions cannot be excluded. Poli in 'The EU and US Global Human Rights Sanction Regimes: Useful Complementary Instruments to Advance Protection of Universal Values? A Legal Appraisal' outlines how the EU has been far more selective in using restrictive measures than the US in the case of human rights breaches. In contrast to the US Global Magnitsky Programmes, the EU scheme can be considered residual with respect to third country sanctions regimes. Poli shows how the two Global Human Rights Sanction programmes are useful legal instruments that complement other diplomatic tools used by the US and EU to reinforce respect of human rights. Finally, in Part I, Bolstad and Friis argue persuasively in 'NATO and Transatlantic Security Relations' that a combination of strong US engagement and leadership with a broadly shared threat perception among Allies (primarily towards Russia) is the combination that continues to make NATO a significant embodiment of transatlantic security relations.

Part II sets out many key questions of the partnership relating to trade, arguably, the high-water mark of cooperation.

Petersmann in 'Transatlantic Economic and Legal Disintegration? Between Anglo-Saxon Neo-Liberal Nationalism, Authoritarian State-Capitalism and Europe's Ordo-Liberal Multilevel Constitutionalism' argues that path-dependent value-conflicts among Anglo-Saxon neo-liberalism, authoritarian state-capitalism, Europe's multilevel constitutionalism and 'third world conceptions' of regulation will continue to distort 'regulatory competition'. The geopolitical rivalries impede transatlantic leadership for protecting the universally agreed sustainable development goals. Thereafter, Grigorova in 'Reverberations of the CJEU *Achmea B.V.* Decision in The Transatlantic Space' analyses and categorises the different approaches adopted. Focusing on the cases recently decided by US courts, the chapter also tentatively assesses the issues raised before these courts, as well as the potential relevance of the practice on this issue in other jurisdictions. Through this analysis, the chapter aims at drawing more general conclusions as to the relevance accorded to EU law by investment tribunals and by US courts, and as to the potential theoretical and practical implications of these decisions. Verellen next in 'Executive Accountability in Unilateral Trade Policy. A Transatlantic Perspective', by means of a comparative analysis of executive accountability in unilateral trade policy in the US and the EU, describes this transformation of executive power in the EU and the accountability gaps it risks amplifying. Dekeyrel in a highly topical piece 'Transatlantic Energy Relations: A Brief History and a Tentative Outlook' analyses the evolving dynamic of EU-US energy relations through the lens of securitisation theory. It considers how transatlantic energy realities diverged in the 2000s as the American shale revolution transformed the US from the world's largest importer of oil into an energy-exporting powerhouse, while the EU's supply picture gradually worsened as its relations with Russia deteriorated. Secondly, it studies transatlantic energy relations during the 2010s, analysing Europe's attempt to emulate the US shale boom, the birth and expansion of transatlantic gas trade as well as US support for EU diversification and opposition to Nord Stream 2. Thereafter, it analyses the securitisation and paradigm shift in EU energy policy following Russia's invasion of Ukraine, and explores its implications for transatlantic energy relations. Next, Egan in 'Taking Back Control: The Political Economy of Investment Screening in US and EU' highlights the sectoral and geographic scope of foreign direct investment, the different investment policy responses across two economic crises, and the efforts to work together through the new Transatlantic Trade and Technology Council. It assesses whether there is an opportunity to further align the U.S.-EU partnership and learn to cooperate to deal with threats posed to both their national security and strategic economic interests.

In Part III, the handbook considers a range of themes as to the digital area and cooperation in this context, often plighted by complex global governance.

Terpan and Fahey in 'The Future of the EU-US Privacy Shield' outline how soft law and its complex enforceability, construction and classification is a thorny one and EU-US relations have contributed to many of these challenges through an evolving variety of increasingly complex, novel or simply hybrid transatlantic instruments. The chapter discusses whether a solution is possible to frame and stabilise the transfer of data between European Union and the US. For this, we will come back to the Safe Harbour and the Privacy Shield, in a first section, to get a clear view of why these arrangements were deemed inadequate. A second section will explain the situation created by the ruling in *Schrems II* while a third one will explore the possible evolutions of the data transfer regime, considering the ongoing discussions between EU and US authorities. Kendrick in 'The EU and US Transatlantic Agendas on Taxation' considers both EU and US transatlantic agendas on 'fair' corporate taxation in a digitalised economy. What will become apparent is that both the EU and the US are trying to ensure that their own transatlantic agendas on taxation become the basis of the new norms of the digital age. Both the EU and US transatlantic agendas on taxation therefore demonstrate a desire to harmonise corporate tax to make it 'fair' in order to facilitate new norm promotion practices in the digital age, but according to their own agendas. Kowalski in 'Transatlantic Regulation of Digital Platforms' Anticompetitive Unilateral Behaviours: The "beneficial" Divergence between EU and US Antitrust Law' explores the concept of 'beneficial divergence' between EU and US antitrust and whether at least some of these features can serve as a 'development platform' to improve EU antitrust law. The chapter examines recent case law concerning digital platforms and looking features characterising the different analytical frameworks and, therefore, convergence and divergence between the EU and US legal system of competition. Tzanou in 'Who Occupies the Transatlantic Data Privacy Space? Assessing the Evolving Dynamics, Underlying Reasons and the Way Forward' argues that the EU-US data privacy relations are complex, multifaced, constantly evolving and rooted on a combination of different underlying reasons, some of which are unrelated to the transatlantic space. It explores the evolving dynamics of the EU-US data privacy relations by focusing on their different layers of complexity, examines the potential justifications of these troubled relations, and offers some suggestions regarding the potential ways forward in light of recent developments.

Finally in Part IV, the handbook takes a broader perspective on the characterization of the transatlantic relationship, looking beyond trade issues.

In Young' chapter 'The Transatlantic Regulatory Relationship: Limited Conflict, Less Competition and a New Approach to Cooperation', the EU and the US are considered the world's two regulatory great powers. As they both have relatively open economies and their economic relationship is very complex, regulatory differences are the primary grit in the transatlantic economy. These differences sometimes result in high-profile trade disputes and contribute to perceptions of regulatory competition. Regulatory differences have also prompted extensive efforts to mitigate their adverse economic effects through cooperation. The chapter surveys transatlantic regulatory conflict, competition and cooperation. Morita-Jaeger and Holmes in 'Bilateral, Trilateral or – Quadrilateral? The UK-US Relationship in a Global Context' look at a range of data and consider the economic facts by analysing UK-US trade and investment relations and examine economic and political factors that shape the UK's government aims in promoting the UK-US bilateral trade relationship from pre-Brexit to post-Brexit since domestic politics plays an important part in analysing foreign policy. They explore key factors that affect the relationship in the international context and provide some reflections on how the UK-US bilateral trade relationship could evolve. Parmar and Ledwidge in a rich and thought-provoking piece, 'Anglo-American Power in the Wake of Brexit and America First: A Crisis at the Heart of the Liberal International Order', argue that the Anglosphere is an *imperial transnational historic bloc* of powers rooted in 19th-century racialised Anglo-Saxonism, British imperialism and the white dominions of the Commonwealth. After 1945, the Anglo-American alliance forged in WW2 consolidated in the 'rules-based liberal international order'). They argue that realist and liberal-internationalist theories legitimise the liberal order, characterise the Anglosphere as a force for good, as an equally elite and mass-led hegemonic project, or a mixture of both. It aims contributes to a deeper understanding of Anglo-American power, regarding their declining position in the global system, and their anxieties about decline that is prevalent in Anglospheric discourses about America First, Global Britain and attitudes to non-white powers like China, in addition to the EU. Felbermayer and Braml in 'The Measurement, Structure and Dynamics of the Transatlantic Current Account' argue from an economics perspective – and drawing from significant data – that the success of transatlantic trade policy cannot and should not be measured by the sign of the bilateral trade balance or the growth of exports. The current account – with all its sub-accounts on goods trade, services trade, primary and secondary income – is far better suited to assess economic ties between countries than the sole focus on merchandise goods trade including all its sub-accounts. Transatlantic trade policy is characterized by notable attempts to liberalize trade in the 1990s and 2010s, which ultimately have failed. Recent developments such as the set-up of the Transatlantic Trade Council (TTC) suggest that EU-US trade policy is increasingly shaped by geopolitical considerations. Next, Finbow in 'Asymmetry and Civil Society Backlash: Changing European Calculations in Trans-Atlantic Investment Relations from CETA to TTIP and Beyond' examines the recent history of EU's transatlantic investment relationships with Canada and the US. It compares the provisions in the Canada-European Union Comprehensive Economic and Trade Agreement (CETA) with the EU's proposals for a TTIP with the US. It is based on background interviews, official policy statements, ratified agreements, draft texts, and academic analyses. It considers stakeholder and official views of the benefits, costs, and controversies of an investment chapter. Last but not least, Riddervold, Newsome and Didriksen in 'Transatlantic Relations in a Changing World' drawing from a range of studies discuss the factors that contribute to explain a stable or changing relationship in the transatlantic context and synthesise well the broader debates that the final section of the handbook seeks to capture. It finds that EU-US relations are robust in many contexts and settings. It is obvious that the Russian invasion of Ukraine has helped to enhance relations between the allies. However, at difference to previous periods in the relationship, domestic and structural factors suggest a longer-term weakening of the relationship.

References

Bartl, M. and Fahey, E. 2014. A Postnational Marketplace: Negotiating the Transatlantic Trade and Investment Partnership (TTIP). *In:* Fahey, E. and Curtin, D. (eds.), *A Transatlantic Community of Law: Legal Perspectives on the Relationship between the EU and US legal orders*. Cambride: Cambridge University Press.

Bermann, G., Lindseth, P., and Herdegen, M. (eds.). 2000. *Transatlantic Regulatory Cooperation*. Oxford: Oxford University Press.

Bradford, A. 2020. *The Brussels Effect: How the European Union Rules the World*. Oxford: Oxford University Press.

Burghardt, G. 2015. New Transatlantic Agenda Celebrates 20th Anniversary! [online]. 3 December. *AmCham EU*. https://www.amchameu.eu/news/new-transatlantic-agenda-celebrates-20th-anniversary. Accessed 30 September 2022.

CJEU. 2020. Judgement in Case C-311/18 Data Protection Commissioner v Facebook Ireland Limited, Maximillian Schrems (Schrems II) EU:C:2020:559.

Cole, D., Fabbrini, F., and Schulhofer, S. (eds.). 2017. *Surveillance, Privacy and Trans-Atlantic Relations*. Oxford: Hart Publishing.

Cremona, M. et al. (eds.). 2011. *The External Dimension of the European Union's Area of Freedom, Security and Justice*. Brussels: P.I.E. Peter Lang.

De Ville, F. and Siles-Brügge, G. 2015. *TTIP: The Truth about the Transatlantic Trade and Investment Partnership*. Oxford: Wiley.

Dunoff, J. and Pollack, M. 2013. *Interdisciplinary Perspectives on International Law and International Relations: The State of the Art*. New York: Cambridge University Press.

Fahey, E. 2014. On The Use of Law in Transatlantic Relations: Legal Dialogues Between the EU and US. *European Law Journal*, 20, 368.

Fahey, E. and Curtin, D. (eds.). 2014. *A Transatlantic Community of Law: Legal Perspectives on the Relationship between the EU and US legal orders*. Cambridge: Cambridge University Press.
Fahey, E. and Terpan, F. 2021. Torn between Institutionalisation and Judicialisation: The Demise of the EU-US Privacy Shield. *Indiana Journal of Global Legal Studies*, 28, 205.
Fabbrini, F., Celeste, E., and Quinn, J. (eds.). 2021. *Data Protection Beyond Borders: Transatlantic Perspectives on Extraterritoriality and Sovereignty*. Oxford: Hart Publishing.
Farrell, H. and Newman, A. (eds). 2019. *Of Privacy and Power: The Transatlantic Struggle over Freedom and Security*. Princeton: Princeton University Press.
Gardner, A. 2020. *Stars with Stripes: The Essential Partnership between the EU and US*. Cham: Palgrave Macmillan.
Griller, S., Obwexer, W., and Vranes, E. (eds). 2017. *Mega-Regional Trade Agreements: CETA, TTIP, and TiSA: New Orientations for EU External Economic Relations*. Oxford: Oxford University Press.
Jančić, D. 2016. Transatlantic Regulatory Interdependence, Law and Governance: The Evolving Roles of the EU and US Legislatures. *Cambridge Yearbook of European Legal Studies*, 17, 334. https://onlinelibrary.wiley.com/doi/full/10.1111/jcms.12345
Krisch, N. 2010. Pluralism in Post-national Risk Regulation: The Dispute over GMOs and Trade. *Transnational Legal Theory*, 1, 1–29.
Mitsilegas, V. and Vavoula, N. 2021. *Surveillance and Privacy in the Digital Age: European, Transatlantic and Global Perspectives*. Oxford: Hart Publishing.
Nicolaidis, K. 2005. A Compact Between The United States and Europe. *Brookings Institute*.
Nicolaidis, K. and Shaffer, G. 2005. Transnational Mutual Recognition Regimes: Governance without Global Government. *Law and Contemporary Problems*, 68, 263.
Pollack, M. and Shaffer, G. (eds). 2001. *Transatlantic Governance in the Global Economy*. Lanham, MD: Rowman & Littlefield.
Pollack, M. 2005. The New Transatlantic Agenda at Ten: Reflections in an Experiment in International Governance. *Journal of Common Market Studies*, 43, 899.
Pollack, M. and Shaffer, G. 2009. *When Cooperation Fails: The International Law and Politics of Genetically*. Oxford: Oxford University Press.
Petersmann, E.-U. and Pollack, M. (eds). 2003. *Transatlantic Economic Disputes: The EU, the US, and the WTO*. Oxford: Oxford University Press.
Petersmann, E.-U. 2015. Transformative Transatlantic Free Trade Agreements without Rights and Remedies of Citizens? *Journal of International Economic Law*, 18, 579.
Petersmann, E.-U. and Mayr, S,. 2017. CETA, TTIP, TiSA, and Their Relationship with EU Law. *In*: Griller, S., Obwexer, W. and Vranes, E. (eds.), *Mega-Regional Trade Agreements: CETA, TTIP, and TiSA: New Orientations for EU External Economic Relations*. Oxford: Oxford University Press.
Riddervold, M. and Newsome, A. 2019. Introduction: Transatlantic Relations in Times of Uncertainty: Crises and EU-US Relations. *In:* Riddervold, M. and Newsome, A. (eds.), *Transatlantic Relations in Times of Uncertainty Crises and EU-US Relations*. Abingdon, Oxfordshire: Routledge.
Scott, J. 2009. From Brussels with Love: The Transatlantic Travels of European Law and the Chemistry of Regulatory Attraction. *American Journal of Comparative Law*, 57, 897.
Shaffer, G. 2000. Globalization and Social Protection: The Impact of EU and International Rules in the Ratcheting Up of U.S. Privacy Standards. *Yale Journal of International Law*, 25, 1.
Smith, M. 2019. The EU, the US and the Crisis of Contemporary Multilateralism. *In:* Riddervold, M. and Newsome, A. (eds.), *Transatlantic Relations in Times of Uncertainty Crises and EU-US Relations*. Abingdon, Oxfordshire: Routledge.
Stein, E. and Hay, P. 1963. Cases and Materials on the Law and Institutions of the Atlantic Area. *In*: Stein, Eric and Hay, Peter (eds.), Ann Arbor: The Overbeck pany.
Terpan, F. 2018. EU-US Data Transfer from Safe Harbour to Privacy Shield: Back to Square One? *European Papers*, 3, 1045.

Vogel, D. 2012. *The Politics of Precaution: Regulating Health, Safety, and Environmental Risks in Europe and the United States*. Princeton: Princeton University Press.
Young, A.R. 2009. Confounding Conventional Wisdom: Political not Principled Differences in the Transatlantic Regulatory Relationship. *The British Journal of Politics and International Relations*, 11(4), 666.

SECTION I

EU and US Intra-Organisations Relations

1

CONNECTING THE US CONGRESS AND THE EUROPEAN PARLIAMENT

The Work and Role of the EP Liaison Office in Washington DC

Joseph Dunne

DIRECTOR, EUROPEAN PARLIAMENT LIAISON OFFICE IN WASHINGTON D.C.

The European Parliament Liaison Office in Washington DC (EPLO) was created to facilitate and deepen ties between the European Parliament (EP) and the US Congress. It supports parliamentary diplomacy between the EU and the US, the longest-lived and most resilient of all of the EP's relationships with other parliamentary bodies. EPLO is the spearhead for EP-Congress parliamentary cooperation, particularly for the Transatlantic Legislators' Dialogue (TLD), the flagship structure between the EP and the US House of Representatives. By virtue of its location, EPLO enjoys a unique position for outreach and for projecting the work of the EP in the US. It reaches out to congressional members and staff to explain the EP's positions, and works with partner organisations, stakeholders and citizens, think tanks and academia to provide a platform for Members of the European Parliament (MEPs) to express their views, making sure the voice of Parliament is heard.

Parliamentary cooperation between the EU and the US has a low public profile and is a perpetual 'work-in-progress'. At the same time, there is undoubtedly a generally positive view of the European Union or the EP among Members of Congress.

The paradox of weak institutionalisation, a 'soft' connecting structure embedded in an overall favourable attitude, of positive perception without engagement, appears characteristic not only of the TLD but also of the broader EU-US relationship (Fahey and Terpan in Chapter 15). Transatlantic relations are indeed 'institution-light' but they sit on a stable bedrock of shared empathy, even if surface political manifestations have ebbed and flowed. It is not, however, a relationship of equals. Members of Congress have tended not to view MEPs as their parliamentary

DOI: 10.4324/9781003283911-3

equivalents, although attitudes are evolving as their awareness and understanding of the EU and the EP deepens.

The EPLO has added an important 'hard' dimension to institutionalising the EU-US inter-parliamentary relationship. Its story is one of overcoming the disconnects in the relationship, counteracting the lack of awareness of parliamentary cooperation, making new connections and attaining greater buy-in from US Congressional actors by more successfully linking the legislators in these two continental democracies. I will argue in this chapter that changing attitudes in the Congress, deriving from a combination of factors – the huge boost given to EU-US relations as a result of the Ukraine crisis, which slowed down the policy 'pivot to Asia' and brought the EU into sharper focus; a new realisation of the importance of the EP in influencing and delivering privacy, climate, digital, antitrust and online platform regulation emanating from the EU, the new possibilities afforded by virtual meetings during and since the COVID-19 pandemic, and the increasing intensity of parliamentary contacts – have all positively transformed the prospects for deeper cooperation in the future.

A house in Washington

As early as 1984, in the first term of the directly elected Parliament, the EP adopted a resolution[1] tabled by the MEP, and later President, Klaus Hänsch, whose para. 42 'hoped' that the Parliament could arrange to 'be represented in its own right at {the Commission's] delegation in Washington'.

The landmark reports tabled by Elmar Brok MEP and Erika Mann MEP in 2006 (European Parliament 2006a, 2006b) went a step further and secured full EP approval, with 470 votes in favour out of 617 votes cast, for the idea of a permanent EP presence in Washington DC. The plenary resolution called for 'the necessary funds for establishing a permanent EP official post in Washington DC that ensures proper institutionalisation of Parliament's own activities and allows for improved liaison between the EP and the US Congress'. The Internal Market Committee (IMCO) input specified that 'the opening of a permanent EP liaison office in Washington is overdue, as it would provide a key means of strengthening contacts between the EP and TLD on the one hand, and Congress, on the other'. (IMCO, 2006) Progress in creating the office was nonetheless slow, and in 2009, the Parliament invited its secretary general to proceed 'as a matter of the utmost urgency' with the deployment of an official to Washington as Liaison Officer (European Parliament 2009).

The EPLO Washington DC office was duly established on 29 April 2010 with a small staff - three policy professionals and two administrative staff – 'co-located' in the EU Delegation, the EU's Embassy to the US. The creation of the liaison office has been interpreted by some observers (Farrell and Newman 2019) as being linked to the then-prevailing conflict over privacy and data protection as well as being a way of combatting the perception that 'structural inequalities between the power and political role of EU parliamentarians and US members of Congress meant that the latter did not really recognize the former as peers'. It was, at the very least, felicitous that the creation of the office coincided with the Parliament's new co-legislative powers under the

Lisbon Treaty, including on data protection and consent to international agreements. The new Treaty profoundly changed the setting for EU external relations (Propp in Chapter 3, Fromage 2019; Szép 2022) and provided a compelling practical case for closer legislative cooperation (CRS 2013).

Members of the US Congress reacted quickly to the establishment of EPLO. Bills were submitted in September 2010 and January 2011 by Congressman Darrel Issa, along with Rep. Bart Gordon and Rep. Alcee Hastings, to provide for a statutory Congressional Commission on the EU, including the establishment of an office in Brussels to mirror the EPLO in Washington DC. The CRS (2013) noted that despite support for the idea in a Hearing of the House Foreign Affairs Committee's Europe Subcommittee, the lead Congressional body responsible for EU relations, 'Congress as a whole has not demonstrated significant interest in or enthusiasm about establishing a reciprocal liaison office in Brussels'. On the EP side, the secretary general indicated his openness to hosting a US Congress liaison office in Brussels (CRS 2013).

A clear motive in establishing EPLO, as Farrell and Newman suggest, was to correct the perception of lack of equivalence between the members of the EP and Congress. It is undeniable that, just as there are fundamental differences between the EU and the US as political entities, each of the respective legislatures has a distinct shape, function and culture. These structural and procedural differences provide a basis for some to argue that effective cooperation between the EP and the US Congress on legislation is close to impossible. The CRS (2014, 2022) observes that 'structural and procedural differences between Congress and the EP likely would impede more extensive legislative cooperation'. The real difficulty of legislative cooperation, however, resides less in the different - but nonetheless comparable - structures and procedures, than in the level of interest and buy-in of the legislators themselves, the 'issue areas' which correlate with congressional behaviour (Henehan 2000). The experience of EPLO has shown that transatlantic legislative cooperation seems to have the best chance of success when dialogue can be initiated early, on essentially the same policy challenge at the same time: when both chambers are confronted by a need to legislate on a new, usually global, issue.

Kreppel (2006) notes that 'when compared across three characteristics' – internal organization and committee structure, voting patterns and legislative influence – 'the two legislatures are surprisingly similar'. Meanwhile, both legislatures are constantly in evolution and roles can shift (Kreppel 2005). The gradual erosion of Congress' place in the US constitutional system of divided powers and competing branches (Davidson, Oleszek 2022) contrasts with the EP's gradual adjustment of the institutional balance in its favour through informal institution-building (Hecke and Wolfs 2015; Jančić 2016) and its strengthening position in interparliamentary cooperation and diplomacy (Raube 2022). Comparisons are therefore not inevitably favourable to Congress: for example, the House of Representatives was unable to act on the Swift and PNR issues, whereas the EP was able to leverage its power of consent to block and influence outcomes on these agreements (Propp, in this volume).

We can better understand the dynamics of today's EP-Congress relationship, the reality and the perception of both houses, as well as the role of EPLO, if we first retrace the developments that began some 40 years ago. The first steps in inter-parliamentary contacts were in fact taken at the initiative of the US Congress in January 1972. A Congressional Delegation ('CoDel') led by the Chair of the Europe Subcommittee, Rep. Benjamin Rosenthal, visited Luxembourg, and, coincidentally, a delegation of the Ways and Means Committee visited Brussels at the same time. According to the Congressional reports, with the arresting titles 'The European Community and the American Interest' and 'A Growing Bond: the European Parliament and the Congress', these visits marked 'the beginning of an effort to establish parliamentary ties with an institution representing the increasingly effective economic and political integration of Europe'. The Congressmen were 'greatly impressed by the development of a European political consciousness' and by 'the political development at the European Parliament and by its important future role in the European Community' (Tulli 2017). The US side hoped to set 'a style and pattern of meetings' twice a year, alternately in Washington and in Europe, for 'carefully planned and comprehensive' political and economic discussions, 'conducted with informality and candor'.

The two visits from the US House of Representatives triggered an immediate and enduring response from MEPs in May 1972, led by EP Vice-President Schuijt. The vice-President reported to the plenary on 31 May:

> Above all, we wish to open a dialogue that will not end when we leave the United States but may be continued at regular intervals and developed further in a spirit of mutual understanding. This is not merely a diplomatic or even a governmental concern. But it should be … a matter of permanent preoccupation for the elected representatives of our peoples.
>
> *(Tulli 2017)*
>
> A United States – European Community Interparliamentary Group was created.

The foundational documents for the EU-US inter-parliamentary relationship are the Transatlantic Declaration on EC-US Relations of 1990 and the New Transatlantic Agenda (NTA) of 1995. Both explicitly mentioned parliamentary cooperation. The NTA stressed the importance of 'enhanced parliamentary links'. Parliamentary frustration at the lack of progress on this NTA commitment (CRS 2013) gave rise to the TLD. Thus, on 15 January 1999, during the 50th inter-parliamentary meeting in Strasbourg, 27 years after the bi-annual meetings set in train by Rep Rosenthal and EP Vice-President Schuijt, the EP and the US House of Representatives formalised their institutional cooperation in a 'Strasbourg Declaration', into a framework they named the 'Transatlantic Legislators' Dialogue'.

In order to overcome the difficulty of maintaining in-person contact caused by the cost, time and effort of travelling and organising the bi-annual meetings, early and pioneering recourse was had to video conferences. This was one of the practical measures enumerated in the 'Strasbourg declaration' creating the TLD, along with the convening of a Steering Group and special working groups on subjects of mutual interest. The EP delegates had in fact 'jumped the gun' in terms of top-level support for the initiative, announcing the initiative before securing the full agreement of the leadership, but the necessary authorisations were nevertheless duly granted. Despite these good intentions, and political endorsement, however, video-conferenced meetings never really caught on and remained an occasional exception to the regular in-person meetings. The COVID-19 pandemic later brought about a major, albeit temporary, change.

Parliament's continued frustration at the lack of progress in EU-US relations, and particularly at its weak institutionalisation, came to a head in the early 2000s. A reflection paper of the Transatlantic Policy Network (TPN 2003) with EP and Congressional, as well as academic and think tank input, noted that 'Americans are seen to value institutions for what they can do, Europeans for their durability and continuity'. The TPN report saw the solution to the slow pace of transatlantic cooperation in deeper political dialogue, and advocated building on the TLD and 'active consideration' of a 'Transatlantic Assembly' of legislators.

Impatient at the lack of 'the necessary conviction and determination' on the part of other EU institutions, the EP adopted the 2006 resolutions referenced earlier, on 'improving EU-U.S. relations'. As well as providing the mandate for the creation of EPLO, as we have seen, they echoed the TPN recommendations, calling for an upgrade of the TLD and for a Transatlantic Assembly. The advent of the Obama administration brought new hope for closer cooperation. In 2009, the EP called yet again for a Transatlantic Assembly, making far-reaching proposals on deepening the institutional structures to harness 'the current momentum' and 'to improve and renew the framework of the transatlantic relationship'. The Transatlantic Assembly itself would serve 'as a forum for parliamentary dialogue, identification of objectives and joint scrutiny'. It 'should meet in plenary twice a year and be comprised on an equal basis of both Members of the European Parliament and Members of both Houses of the US Congress'. The resolution was followed by the publication in 2009 of a study by the Atlantic Council and other think tanks, putting forward even wider-ranging recommendations on 'forging a strategic US-EU partnership'. These proposals were then reprised and strengthened in a TLD Joint Statement in December of that year.

The momentum was channelled into the negotiations on the Transatlantic Trade and Investment Partnership (TTIP) and eventually dissipated by its failure in 2016. The demise of TTIP and the new Trump administration in the White House did not however cause the EP to abandon its calls for 'a structured and strategic dialogue on foreign policy at transatlantic level, also involving the European Parliament and the US Congress'. Its 2018 resolution recalled an earlier 'suggestion to create a Transatlantic Political Council (TPC) for systematic consultation and coordination on foreign and security policy'. It welcomed 'the ongoing and uninterrupted work of the TLD in fostering EU-US relations through parliamentary dialogue and coordination on issues of common interest', and welcomed 'the relaunch of the bipartisan Congressional EU Caucus for the 115th Congress', asking 'the European Parliament Liaison Office (EPLO) and the EU delegation in Washington to liaise more closely with [the Caucus]'.(European Parliament 2018).

Following the change of administration in the US with the election of President Biden, the EP adopted a new report on EU-US relations in 2021, with rapporteur

Tonino Picula MEP. This resolution echoed the approach of the 2009, Obama-era, report, seeking to harness the favourable impetus generated by the successful EU-US Summit of 15 June 2021. It returned to the idea of a Transatlantic Assembly, albeit *sotto voce*. Instead, it focussed on the possibly more achievable goal of greater institutionalisation of the TLD, noting: 'that raising the awareness of structures such as the Transatlantic Legislators' Dialogue and organising more regular meetings and visits ... would restore confidence in and the durability and efficiency of transatlantic cooperation'. The resolution even went as far as urging the US Congress to 'enhance the Transatlantic Legislators' Dialogue by authorising it as a formal body with permanent membership', that is, with the appointment of designated members, as opposed to the *ad hoc* membership of the US delegation to the TLD (European Parliament 2021).

There is a marked difference in institutional structure between the EP and the House of Representatives in how they deal with delegations in the context of foreign relations. As Šabič (2015) notes, interparliamentary groups for the UK, Canada, Mexico and the Organization for Security and Co-operation in Europe (OSCE) exist in statute,[2] and include both House and Senate membership. The NATO PA Parliamentary Group, on the other hand, has a separate legal base,[3] as does the Security and Cooperation in Europe, or 'Helsinki', Commission.[4] A variant is the bipartisan 'House Democracy Partnership', a House-only entity, which is not a statutory body but features in the Rules of the House of Representatives.[5]

Congress has shown little receptivity to the EP's calls to give such a statutory or Rules-based foundation to the TLD, despite - so far unsuccessful - efforts on the part of Co-Chair Rep Jim Costa (H.R. 4105 in the 116th Congress and H.R. 6624 in the 117th) to include the Senate in the TLD and to give the TLD a basis in statute.

While the House is thus highly selective in the number of interparliamentary bodies, the EP, by contrast, has a comprehensive, worldwide network of delegations covering every region provided for in its Rules of Procedure (Title VIII, Chapter 2). The EP delegation to the TLD is part of this organisational structure, led by its Delegation for relations with the United States of America (D-US), comprising 64 members and currently chaired by Radosław Sikorski MEP, a former Polish defence and foreign minister who is well-known and widely respected in Washington. Their US counterparts are the TLD co-chairs appointed by the Speaker of the House in a bipartisan arrangement, currently Congressman Jim Costa (Democrat-California) and Congresswoman Ann Wagner (Republican-Missouri). The US meeting participants are chosen on a volunteer basis.

The asymmetric nature of this TLD structure stems, at least in part, from a traditional reluctance on the part of the Congress to go beyond the small number of existing formal and institutionalised relationships with other parliamentary bodies, detailed above, some of which were created in the late 1950s and the most recent (the British-American Interparliamentary Group) in 1991. In 2013, the assessment of the CRS was that there were enough skeptics that doubted the utility or need to establish a stronger relationship between the U.S. Congress and the European Parliament ... that Congress as a whole seems to be at best ambivalent to such efforts and has not demonstrated as much enthusiasm as the EP about forging closer relations.

Above and beyond the question of willingness or enthusiasm is undoubtedly the fact that, as Marcy (Marcy 1959) points out, 'Members from Congress.. attend [interparliamentary meetings] in their individual capacities'. The Members of Congress are thus not formally expected to speak solely on behalf of the institution they represent, unlike their European counterparts from the EP.

EPLO and developing parliamentary connection: 'A bridge between two houses'

As the lead player in the EP with responsibility for US relations, the D-US has always had the ambition of coordinating the gamut of legislative cooperation activities, including the transatlantic contacts made at committee level. The Steering Committee created with the establishment of the TLD brought together the chairs of legislative committees. In this way, the D-US sought to complement the largely external, security, defence and trade policy orientation of the bi-annual TLD meetings (Lazarou 2020) and to integrate the work being done in the EU-US committee-to-committee dialogues. In practice, the field has proved too wide, and the two streams have co-existed rather than converged. The legislative committees of the EP have pursued their own policy-specific channels and actively maintain their own contact network and longer-term connections through annual visits. In fact, the TLD members are rarely the key players in legislation of transatlantic interest. As is well-illustrated by Jančić (2015) in the case of the Emission Trading Scheme (ETS) Directive, recourse was not taken to the TLD to enable transatlantic dialogue on the disputed legislation.

EPLO has managed to act as a channel for the committee-to-committee dialogues, giving it a wider range of action than the TLD dialogue alone. The committees are interested in coordinating regulatory regimes in their legislative areas, and have been consistently active in the efforts described by Young in Chapter 19. In the early days, from EPLO's inception to the TTIP negotiations, these efforts focussed largely on trade, financial services and product safety. More recently, as new momentum was generated by the change in the US administration at the end of 2020 and then the sudden closeness produced by Russia's war on Ukraine, the palette of issues became the global challenges facing both the US and the EU: the climate transition and the instruments to fight climate change such as the Carbon Border Adjustment Mechanism (CBAM), energy policy and regulating the digital economy and online platform services.

EPLO has taken the lead in facilitating committee-to-committee meetings across the spectrum of policy issues. Human rights has always been an area where EU and US views were broadly convergent. As Szép suggests in his work on sanctions, human rights protection is a policy field where the EP is consistently expanding its reach. The EP has sought out Congressional support, and, equally, the Congress has looked to the EP for support. The preferred instruments, increasingly resorted to, are the use of joint statements (Lazarou 2020) and letters jointly signed by members from both parliaments, to give them extra weight and legitimacy. With the added formation of ad hoc networks like the Interparliamentary Alliance on China (IPAC), which involves members from national parliament, EP and Congress, parliaments are in fact generating layers of 'legislative networks' of the kind envisaged by Šabič (2016).

A joint virtual meeting, mediated by EPLO, between the Helsinki Committee in Congress (the joint Congressional/Executive commission for the Organization for Security and Cooperation in Europe, OSCE) and the EP's Human Rights Subcommittee in September 2020, was a high-water mark in inter-parliamentary cooperation on human rights during the COVID-19 pandemic. The unanimity of viewpoints was striking.

Issues touching on trade and economic relations are more complicated and controversial. It might appear self-evident that the EU and US, with the largest trade-flow in the world, and with the largest combined market and investment pool, would want to align or converge legislation, regulatory policy and standards so as to avoid the creation of non-tariff barriers and obstacles to mutually-reinforcing economic growth. This was the avowed purpose of legislative cooperation called for in the EP resolutions described earlier, and the 'early warning system' so earnestly wished for, to alert legislators to legislation or draft legislation which would negatively affect the transatlantic market and common interest. The hope was that an early warning system would obviate unpleasant surprises like the disagreements over privacy legislation, and develop a 'barrier-free' internal market between the EU and the US.

Even if the push for regulatory convergence ultimately failed with the demise of TTIP, the concept certainly incentivised committee-to-committee cooperation from 2008 onwards, with a noticeable intensification after the establishment of EPLO. In 2010, alone there were visits to the US by delegations from the Special Committee on the Financial Crisis and from a majority of the legislative committees – the Committees on Civil Liberties, Transport (twice), Internal Market and Consumer Protection, Legal Affairs and Economic and Monetary Affairs (twice). The Committee on Foreign Affairs (AFET), the subcommittees on Security and Defence (SEDE) and Human Rights (DROI), and the Committee on Industry, Research and Energy (ITRE) were equally active. So marked was the development that the 2013 CRS report 'Evolving Transatlantic Legislative Cooperation' focussed on improving direct committee-to-committee contact and strongly suggested a coordination role for the TLD as the best achievable outcome from the European perspective.

Parliamentary Committees have thus always accounted for the majority of interactions between the EP and the US Congress, while the TLD meetings have taken centre-stage as the 'official' locus of EP-Congress relations. As Table 1.1 shows, the intensity of the relationship has remained surprisingly stable over the years, with only a loose link to the political 'colour' (red or blue) of the US Administration.

Once reduced travel opportunities in EP election years, and the pause caused by the COVID-19 pandemic, are factored in, the level of engagement can be considered fairly constant, with a slight rise as the overall long-term trend.

An average of 100 MEPs have visited the US Congress each year since the establishment of EPLO. The large number of virtual meetings in 2020/2021, when in-person meetings were not possible, is particularly noticeable, and reinforces the

Table 1.1 Overview of European Parliamentary Visits to Washington DC

YEAR	*Committee and US Delegation Visits*	*Individual MEP Visits*	*Meetings of the Transatlantic Legislators' Dialogue (TLD) in US*	*'Parliamentary Conversations' & Virtual Meetings*
2010	10	5	1	
2011	5	14	1	
2012	9	21	1	
2013	13	22		
2014*	1	15	1	
2015	10	15	1	
2016	11	17	1	
2017	19	16	1	
2018	17	7		
2019*	6	9	1	
2020-(pre-Covid)	3	1		
2020 (Lockdown)				14
2021 (post-Covid)	7	2		33
2022 (end July)	10	17	1	4
TOTAL:	121**	161	9***	51

Sources: European Parliament; Figure 1.

Notes

* Travel by parliamentary delegations is curtailed in election years (2014, 2019).

** Committee delegations comprise, on average, 7 Members. This number of delegations corresponds to approx. 847 individual members.

*** A typical TLD Interparliamentary meeting will comprise delegations of 8 to 10 members from the EP side.

impression of a long-term rise in engagement on legislative issues of mutual interest, focussed on trade, digital economy, artificial intelligence and the climate transition.

A peak in the number of visiting parliamentarians in 2017 demonstrated that the cooler transatlantic diplomatic relations of the Trump era had, at least initially, little impact on the intensity of parliamentary contacts (Vandeputte 2022), and that a substantial level of EP-Congressional cooperation was maintained. A high influx of MEPs can again be expected in 2022, as European members seek to capitalise on the new openness to the European Union, and to multilateral fora, on the part of the Biden administration.

Although the availability of members of Congress in Washington DC has decreased somewhat in recent years, in favour of presence in their districts, the number of congressional meetings organised by EPLO for incoming EP delegations has steadily increased. For the most part, the meetings are with individual members of Congress, but often they can take the form of in-person, committee-to-committee meetings, notably for the International Trade Committee (INTA) in 2020 and 2022, but also for other committees, such as the Committee on Culture and Education (CULT) in 2022. In 2021, a visit from the Special Committee on Artificial Intelligence in a Digital Age (AIDA) prompted a first meeting of the Congressional Caucus on AI.

While the larger flow has been in the direction of Europe to America, traffic has not been one-way only. Congressional delegations, or 'CoDels', visiting the EP, are a regular feature and are increasing in frequency (Lazarou 2020). A delegation of the Select Committee on Modernization and the Rules Committee in 2022, which, rather unusually, dedicated its full visit to the EP, presages greater exchange in the future.

With a helping hand from the pandemic lockdown, and the new acceptability of 'zoom' meetings, the number of committee-to-committee dialogue streams, or 'parliamentary conversations' mediated by EPLO has increased exponentially. Some twenty-one parliamentary dialogues during the lockdown held out the promise of genuine transatlantic parliamentary exchange on legislative issues before respective positions have solidified. The end of the pandemic brought a restoration of the primacy of in-person meetings but virtual meetings can add the consistency of contact that the TLD always sought (and failed) to obtain with video-conferencing.

The depth of the virtual dialogue and the intensity of the in-person contacts since the pandemic has coincided with, and been framed by, the era of global challenges. The EU has forged ahead with attempts to regulate the digital economy, manage the climate transition and energy crisis and to restore multilateral trade mechanisms. EP-Congress dialogue has brought a new level of understanding, but it is not an inevitably convergent process: the objections of the House of Representatives and the Senate to what they perceived as discrimination against US companies by European legislators in the Digital Markets Act (DMA)[6] is a case in point, as one legislature realises the risk of being subjected to a 'Brussels' or a 'Washington effect' from the other. At the same time, members of parliament borrow concepts and regulatory ideas from each other in a symbiotic process.

Common ground is also being found on the need to deal with the increasing assertiveness of authoritarian actors and on how to deal with existential threats to parliamentary and democratic legitimacy. The way has opened for transatlantic parliamentary cooperation to boost democracy at home and abroad, a priority of the Biden administration and a key concern that now lies at the base of EU-US relations. The EP and the Congress have a new opportunity to work together and learn from each other, this time to unravel and disarm the developing threats posed by cyberattacks, disinformation and dark money, all intertwining with the regulation of online platforms.

It was always understood that, important as the step was, the establishment of an EP office in Washington DC could never, of itself, comprehensively cater for the dynamic, multi-dimensional, multi-stakeholder information flow across the Atlantic. EPLO accordingly partners with bodies channelling stakeholder and business views, such as the Transatlantic Business and Consumer Dialogues, many of which were created in the lead up to the TTIP negotiations as contributors to the Transatlantic Economic Council, active from 2007 to 2016. As the momentum for regulatory cooperation has receded, the associated bodies have lost salience. Nevertheless the work with stakeholders continues, and involves business interests, non-governmental organisations, consulting groups and the Chambers of Commerce. Among these stakeholder organisations, the Transatlantic Policy Network retains its specificity of seeking to blend and synergize the business-oriented and the parliamentary dialogues. Most recently, the US-EU Trade and Technology Council (TTC), launched at the June 2021 U.S.-EU Summit, holds out the promise of successful executive-to-executive cooperation in key areas.

In this respect, the question posed by Raube (2022), and Thiel (2022) of the complementarity of 'EP diplomatic action', including the establishment of EPLO, and the public diplomacy of EU delegations, is relevant to Washington DC. EPLO works in close coordination with the EU Delegation at all operational levels, and all incoming parliamentary delegations are systematically briefed by the EU Ambassador.

A parliamentary vehicle intended to support the EP-Congress relationship, created largely at the initiative of EPLO, is the EU Caucus in the House of Representatives. The first Caucus was officially launched in the 115th Congress by Rep. Gregory Meeks (Democrat-New York) and Rep. Joe Wilson (Republican-South Carolina), with the message that 'the European Union plays a significant role in safeguarding and promoting our shared values of freedom and … Our shared aspiration for enduring European peace and prosperity is undoubtedly in the interests of the United States'. The EU Caucus has been renewed in each Congressional session since even if it has not, like many others, been noticeably active.

Outlook

EPLO has developed an increasingly influential role over the years. As the involvement with Congress widens and deepens, there can be at least a modest expectation of sooner or later reaching the critical mass and leading the Congress to adapt its structures, thereby achieving greater balance in the TLD relationship. At the same time, by connecting the committees on new legislative challenges, the traditional conundrum of where to look for the 'early warning' appears to have resolved itself.

Legislators on both sides of the Atlantic understand that regulatory approaches to global problems (from climate change and a form of Cross Border Carbon Adjustment Mechanism (CBAM) to antitrust and 'big tech' regulation, to whether and how to converge on the regulation of the digital economy; to the taxation of multinational firms, how to regulate cryptocurrency, to artificial intelligence) could clearly benefit from a common or concerted approach. The US is holding back and has been generally unwilling to go down the regulatory path in some of these areas. Attempts at dialogue have been driven from the European side but are recognised on the US side to be necessary. Non-traditional and difficult areas of policy are no longer exempt from discussions, as women's' issues, gender equality and agriculture policy become subjects of open dialogue.

The Members of Congress involved now range across many committee formations, a far cry from the limited pool of the past. Closer cooperation brings 'socialisation' and mutual trust, building up over time as the broader legislative partnership is strengthened and a wider cross-section of Members of Congress become involved in the committee-to-committee dialogue.

Despite the Congressional leadership's reluctance to date to endorse a more permanent or embedded status to parliamentary dialogue with the EU, it seems conceivable that the US-EU convergence brought about by the war in Ukraine will, in due course, bring new impetus to proposals for a dedicated body in Congress. It could take the form of a Congressional Commission on the EU, as originally proposed in 2010, or more diffuse or specialised arrangements such as a Congress-Parliament Working Group on China to complement the IPAC network, as was suggested in a Hearing of the Europe Subcommittee in the House of Representatives.[7]

Both legislatures, EP and Congress, are searching for broader forms of cooperation and parliamentary diplomacy in support of democracy. EPLO is seeking to play its part in facilitating a new and higher level of connection. Changing attitudes in the Congress and a growing understanding of the global nature of legislative challenges and of the need to keep the executive accountable, enabled by the new possibilities afforded by vsirtual meetings, have transformed the prospects for future cooperation for the better.

Notes

1 Official Journal C 127/94 of 14 May 1984.
2 Title 22, Chapter 7 of the U.S. Code.
3 Title 22 § 1928a, U.S. Code.
4 Title 22 §3001 to 3009, U.S. Code.
5 § 1125 f., Rules of the House of Representatives of the United States, 117th Congress.
6 Hon Suzan DelBene Letter dated February 23, 2022 to President Joseph R. Biden. https://delbene.house.gov/uploadedfiles/eu_digital_markets_act_letter.pdf
US Senators Ron Wyden, Mike Crapo, Letter dated February 1 to President Joseph R. Biden. https://www.finance.senate.gov/imo/media/doc/2022.02.01%20Wyden-Crapo%20Letter%20to%20POTUS%20on%20DMA%20DSA.pdf
7 Statement of Dr. Karen Donfried President, German Marshall Fund of the United States, to the Subcommittee on Europe on 'The Importance of Transatlantic Cooperation During the COVID-19 Pandemic' July 14, 2020.

References

Congressional Research Service (CRS) 29 July 2013 The US Congress and the European Parliament: Evolving Transatlantic Legislative Cooperation.

Congressional Research Service (CRS) 2014 The European Parliament and U.S. Interests, K Archick, last updated May 6, 2022.

Davidson, R. and Oleszek, W. et al. 2022 'Congress and its Members' 18th Edition, CQ Press, SAGE Publications.

European Parliament resolution (P6_TA(2006)0238) of 1 June 2006 on improving EU-US relations in the framework of a Transatlantic Partnership Agreement.

European Parliament resolution (P6_TA(2006)0239) of 1 June 2006 on EU-US Transatlantic Economic Relations.

EP: Opinion of the Committee on the Internal Market and Consumer Protection (IMCO) adopted on 21 March 2006.

European Parliament resolution (P6_TA(2008)0192) of 8 May 2008 on the Transatlantic Economic Council.

European Parliament resolution (P6_TA(2009)0193) of 26 March 2009 on the state of transatlantic relations in the aftermath of the US election.

European Parliament resolution (P8_TA(2018)0342) of 12 September 2018 on the state of EU-US relations.

European Parliament resolution (P9_TA(2021)041) of 6 October 2021 on the future of EU-US relations.

Farrell, H. and Newman, A. 2019 'Of Privacy and Power: The Transatlantic Struggle over Freedom and Security', Princeton.

Fonck, D. 2019 'The Emergence of the European Parliament as a Diplomatic Mediator: Conceptualising, Exploring and Explaining Parliamentary Diplomacy in EU Foreign Policy' PhD Thesis, KU Leuven.

Fromage, D. 2019 The European Parliament in inter-parliamentary cooperation, in Raube op cit

Hecke, S. and Wolfs, W. (2015). *The SAGE Handbook of European Foreign Policy: Two Volume Set.* London: SAGE Publications Ltd. Available at: [Accessed 8 Mar 2023].

Henehan, M. 2000 Foreign Policy and Congress: An International Relations Perspective, The University of Michigan Press.

Hon Benjamin, S. Rosenthal and Hon Donald, S. Fraser 1972a "The European Community and the American Interest': Report of Special Study Mission to Europe', January 1972, *Committee on Foreign Affairs pursuant to H. Res.* 109.

Hon Benjamin, S. Rosenthal and Hon Donald, S. Fraser 1972b 'A Growing Bond: The European Parliament and the Congress' Report on the First Official Visit to Congress by a Delegation from the European Parliament', May 1972, *Committee on Foreign Affairs pursuant to H. Res.* 109.

Jančić, D. 2014 'The European Parliament and EU–US Relations: Revamping Institutional Cooperation', in Elaine Fahey and Deirdre Curtin (eds.), *A Transatlantic Community of Law: Legal Perspectives on the Relationship between the EU and US Legal Orders.* Cambridge University Press, pp. 35–68.

Jančić, D. 2015a 'Transatlantic Regulatory Interdependence, Law and Governance: The Evolving Roles of the EU and US Legislatures', *Cambridge Yearbook of European Legal Studies.* 17(1), pp. 334–359.

Jančić, D. 2015a 'The Transatlantic Connection: Democratizing Euro-American Relations through Parliamentary Liaison', in Stelios Stavridis and Daniela Irrera (eds.), *The European Parliament and its International Relations.* London: Routledge, pp. 178–196.

Jančić, D. and Stavridis, S. 2016 'Introduction: The Rise of Parliamentary Diplomacy in International Politics', *The Hague Journal of Diplomacy.* 11(2–3), pp. 105–120.

Karns D. A. 1970 'The Effect of Inter-parliamentary Meetings on the Foreign Policy Attitudes of United States Congressmen', *International Organization.* 31(3), pp. 497–513.

Kreppel, A. 2006 'The Environmental Determinants of Legislative Structure: A Comparison of the US House of Representatives and the European Parliament', in Poweer and Crae (eds.), *Exporting Congress? The Influence of the US Congress on World Legislatures.* University of Pittsburgh Press.

Kreppel, A. 2005 'Understanding the European Parliament from a Federalist Perspective: The Legislatures of the United States and the European Union in Comparative Perspective', in A. Menon and M. Schain (eds.), *Comparative Federalism: THe European Union and the United States in Comparative Perspective.* Oxford University Press.

Lazarou, E. 2020 'Transatlantic Parliamentary Diplomacy: Contributing to the future of Transatlantic relations', *Turning the Tide: How to Rescue Transatlantic Relations*, pp. 60–74.

Marcy C. 1959 'A Note on American Participation in Interparliamentary Meetings', *International Organization.* 13(3), pp. 431–438.
Raube, K. 2022 *Parliamentary Cooperation and Diplomacy in EU External Relations: An Essential Companion.* Edward Elgar Publishing.
Šabič, Z. 2016 Parliamentary Diplomacy and the US Congress: The Case of the NATO Parliamentary Assembly, *The Hague Journal of Diplomacy.* 11(2–3), pp. 235–252.
Szép V. 2022 'Transnational Parliamentary Activities in EU Foreign Policy: The Role of Parliamentarians in the Establishment of the EU's Global Human Rights Sanctions Regime', *Journal of Common Market Studies.* 60(6), 1741–1757.
Thiel, M. 2022 EU Public Diplomacy in the United States: Socio-political Challenges & EU Delegation Agency, *Journal of Contemporary European Studies*, DOI: 10.1080/14782804.2022.2084049
Transatlantic Legislators' Dialogue, 67th Interparliamentary Meeting, Joint Statement, New York, 4-7 December 2009.
Transatlantic Policy Network (TPN) 'A Strategy to Strengthen Transatlantic Partnership' Washington/Brussels, 4 December 2003.
Tulli, U. 2017 'Challenging Intergovermentalism and EPC. The European Parliament and Its Actions in International Relations, 1970–1979', *Journal of Contemporary European Research.* 13(2), pp. 1076–1089.
US House of Representatives H.Con.Res.322-111th Congress (2009-2010): Establishing the Congressional Commission on the European Union, and for other purposes.
US House of Representatives H.Con.Res.2-112th Congress (2011-2012): Establishing the Congressional Commission on the European Union, and for other purposes.
US House of Representatives H.R.4105 - 116th Congress (2019-2020) To authorize the Transatlantic Legislators' Dialogue (United States-European Union Interparliamentary Group), and for other purpose.
Vandeputte S. 2022 'Bridging the Atlantic: An Exploration of EU-US Parliamentary Diplomacy', Unpublished thesis. KU Leuven.
Wagner, W. M. and Raunio, T. 2017 "Challenging Executive Dominance'. Legislatures and Foreign Affairs. West European Politics', *Special Issue.* 40(11–19.
Willem Schuijt, Report on behalf of the Committee on External Economic Relations on parliamentary relations between the European Community and the United States of America Document 82/72, PE 30.399 def.

2

EU-US RELATIONS IN A CHANGING WORLD

David O'Sullivan

The role of the US in crafting the global order after World War II was decisive, including the active promotion of European integration. Over the next 60 or so years, the transatlantic partnership was central to global events through the building of the Western liberal order and all the institutions that went with it. It was never an equal partnership. For much of the period, the US was by far the stronger partner both militarily and economically. Even as Europe grew into a larger and more cohesive economic and normative power, its heavy reliance on the US security umbrella gave the US the upper hand. Although the US was generally supportive of greater integration in Europe, it often found the emerging structures and institutions bewildering.

The EU is an unusual political animal in international relations, an 'unidentified political object', as President Jacques Delors (1985) once said. It is not a country. But neither is it a mere international organisation. In some areas (trade, market regulation) it has real federal powers. It has (for 19 countries at least) a single currency. It has a consolidated legal order. When it speaks and decides with one voice, it can have huge influence, such as when it adopted EU regulations on data privacy which have become the de facto global standard. But, as often as it speaks with one voice, the EU can end up speaking with the voices of its 27 members. As Kenneth Propp points out in his excellent chapter 'Negotiating with the European Union – A U.S. Perspective', this can be very confusing for friends and adversaries alike (Propp in this volume).

Few in Washington, beyond policy wonks, really understand how the EU works and how to deal with it. There is a strong lobby for NATO in Congress. The significance of the EU for US security, economic and value interests has yet to find a coherent voice. However, in the coming great power confrontation of the 21st century, the EU arguably holds more of the levers than NATO. Kinetic military power will remain important, but the real challenges will be economic, technological, cyber, and informational. In these areas, it is the EU as a bloc rather than individual member states which yields the real power.

DOI: 10.4324/9781003283911-4

One of the greatest challenges of future transatlantic relations is how to reflect this new reality in both policy formulation and execution. The degree of economic interpenetration is staggering, both in terms of trade in goods and services and investment (Congressional Research Services 2021). The scale dwarfs that of any other relationship for either of us.

But the Trump years wrought great damage: questioning the value of NATO, withdrawing from the Paris climate deal and the JCPOA, but, perhaps more worryingly, questioning whether the EU was a partner or a 'foe' (Reuters Staff 2018). The arrival of Biden represents a very welcome change not just of style and tone but also of policy. But many have pointed out that elements of America First remain. The fact is the US is changing. Trump was on one level a radical break with the past but on another a not illogical development along a spectrum of policy visible even in the Obama era. America is not only more politically polarised than almost at any time in its history, crucially, its demographics are changing. By 2045, Americans of European origin will be in the minority (Frey 2018).

There has been a growing disillusionment with the way the world works, and specifically America's role in it, which Trump was able to exploit very skilfully: a fatigue in the American body politic with the seemingly endless wars from Korea and Vietnam through to the Gulf, Afghanistan, and Iraq, combined with a pervasive sense that the US was being systematically taken advantage of not only by adversaries but (possibly even more so) by allies. The election of Biden was a defeat for Trump personally but not a resounding rejection of the thrust of his policies. Hence, the very understandable early focus of the new administration on domestic priorities until the war in Ukraine changed everything.

It is impossible to overestimate the damage that the Trump years did to transatlantic relations. There was not a single area of policy where was not disagreement and frequently confrontation. Trump's particular dislike of alliances seemed to find a special focus in the EU, which he believed was created in opposition to the US and which he even once characterised as a 'foe' (though in fairness he probably meant 'rival').

There was an early clash over his withdrawal from the Paris Agreement on climate change. His withdrawal from the Iran nuclear deal (the JCPOA) came after extensive lobbying by both Macron and Merkel to keep the US on board. He openly questioned the value of NATO and seemed at one point to wobble on the issue of America's commitment to Article 5 (the co-belligerency clause). And he fuelled trade disputes by using an arcane provision relating to national security to impose punitive tariffs on European steel and aluminium exports, even as he claimed that the real problem was China. In fact, Chinese exports had been radically reduced by a battery of trade defence measures and the main burden of the new tariffs fell on allies, such as the EU, Canada, and Mexico. He vociferously threatened to use the same measure on car exports. This threat never materialised mainly because it would have been hugely counter-productive for US industry, but the constant aggressive brandishing of the option seriously poisoned the atmosphere.

In addition, Trump's trade representative, Bob Lightheizer, followed through on his wish to see an end to the WTO Appellate Body by refusing to approve the nomination of new judges, eventually bringing the system to a complete halt.

But perhaps the most corrosive aspect of Trump's approach was his open hostility to the EU as such. He was the first American President to express outright opposition to the very idea of European integration. Trump's personal animus was instinctive and visceral. He owned a golf course in Ireland and had had a planning application to build a sea wall turned down on environmental grounds, linked to the existence of an EU law. The decision was entirely down to the local authorities, but he remained convinced that Brussels was responsible. More generally, he found that the EU was an obstacle to his more transactional approach to international relations. With the exception of China – and to a lesser extent – Russia, almost any premier, or President who entered the Oval office to engage with Trump did so on unequal terms. The US always held more cards and could hope to prevail. However, when EU leaders talked to Trump about trade, they simply referred him to the President of the Commission, Jean-Claude Juncker. Trump found this infuriating, though he did eventually have to come a deal with EU through the auspices of Juncker. When he was dealing with the EU, the interlocutor on the other side had almost as much weight as the US. This explains Trump's enthusiastic embrace of Brexit (Holland 2019). In his conversations with EU leaders after his election, his first question was often, 'tell me when are you going to leave the EU?' No matter how many times leaders explained that they liked the EU and had no intention to leave, he would continue to ask the question. He really believed that the UK departure would be the beginning of the end of the EU.

Trump's visceral dislike of European integration reflected a more considered, intellectual view of many around him that, somehow, the EU was a threat to national identity and culture. Advisors like Steve Bannon and Sebastian Gorka deeply disliked any multilateral organisation which they saw as somehow enfeebling the nation state from which they believed all authority should flow. Their philosophy was best captured in the book *The Virtue of Nationalism* by the Israeli author, Yoram Hazony (2018). Several State Department officials told me that was considered a key reference text for the Trump administration. Hazony argues that the nation state is the optimum unit of governance in contrast with structures such as the EU where 'liberal internationalism is not merely a positive agenda (…) It is an imperialist ideology that incites against (…) nationalists, seeking their delegitimization wherever they appear' (Hazony 2018).

I used to try in vain to convince Trump acolytes that, far from seeking the destruction of the nation state, the EU provided a framework in which countries could retain a high degree of autonomy over their national life while giving them the benefits of collective action where this would produce better outcomes for citizens. My speeches increasingly reminded American audiences that our member states continued to have strong national identities which were complemented, and not threatened, by membership of the EU. I frequently used the example of Ireland which, I argued, never had a higher international profile as a country than since it joined the EU. I used also to remind that the last thing Europe was likely to suffer from was a shortage of nationalism, paraphrasing Churchill about the Balkans to argue that, as a continent, Europe had too often produced more nationalism than it could consume.

So, the arrival of Biden was a very welcome relief. Not only was there a radical change in the tone and content of the messaging about allies in general and Europe in particular, but there was real change on substance. Biden immediately proposed to re-join the Paris Accord; he indicated willingness to re-join the Iran deal; he re-affirmed America's firm commitment to NATO; and he renewed strong links between his administration and the EU. In terms of his team, he surrounded himself with people very well versed in European affairs, Tony Blinken as Secretary of State, Wendy Sherman as his Deputy, Toria Nuland and Karen Donfried working under her, Jake Sullivan and Amanda Sloat in the National Security Council. There can rarely have been a team of presidential advisors so experienced on Europe.

And, yet, the first year was actually distinctly bumpy.

It quickly became clear that Biden was not going quickly to reverse Trump's trade policies. This was not necessarily a surprise, but the reality did come as a disappointment. There was no early move to dismantle the steel and aluminium tariffs and clearly no urgency at all to try to unblock the WTO even if Biden did at least allow the selection of a new DG to proceed. In addition, the long brewing Airbus/Boeing litigation came to ahead in Geneva with both sides moving towards retaliation.

However, the new team did engage and by the end of the first year, the trade news was not so bad. There was agreement to create a new consultative forum, the Trade and Technology Council (European Commission 2022). A work around was found for the steel tariffs (even if this meant the EU essentially swallowing a deal with Biden which it had refused with Trump!) and the aircraft subsidies dispute was kicked down the road with both sides withdrawing from tariff retaliation.

Year 2021 was of course the time of COVID-19 and the US completely blind-sided European partners by proposing early on an international waiver of intellectual property rights on vaccines. There were few details, but the Europeans were left to pick up the pieces in Geneva during increasingly acrimonious debates with developing countries while the US did not really engage. There was a strong sense that America had grandstanded without any real intention to follow through. Indeed, the US took a very restrictive view about vaccine sharing as it tried to grapple with the mess on the virus that Biden had inherited from Trump.

In the summer, there was the disastrous withdrawal from Afghanistan, where, once again, the Europeans felt hung out to dry by a unilateral US decision to stick to the withdrawal date in August, notwithstanding the fact that no plans for an orderly withdrawal had been put in place. The Europeans were left to scramble to withdraw their forces and the chaos, which ensued played out very badly on television screens around the world. Afghanistan had been an example of solid US-NATO-EU strategic cooperation out of the European theatre. There was deep disappointment at the way it ended.

The almost final blow seemed to come in September when the US, Australia and the UK announced the AUKUS submarine deal. Several years previously, France had signed a large defence contract to provide Australia with submarines. Australia did not want nuclear powered vessels, so the French agreed to build conventionally powered ones. The US basically stole the contract from France with Australia now claiming they needed nuclear vessels. This was wrapped up in what was announced a new strategic Pacific pact, AUKUS, which was heralded as a new strategic alliance between the US, the UK and Australia to push back against China.

Dirty tricks around defence procurement are common and, on one level, this could just be seen as yet another bit of sharp commercial practice. However, it was clearly a stab in France's back, and it was announced with little or no prior consultation with Macron who found himself caught off guard, despite the fact that France is actually the European country most engaged in the pacific region, with two overseas territories there, and a significant military and naval presence (Pajon 2021). It was hard to understand how the Biden administration, with such a complement of Europe experts, could have so badly mishandled the communication around this issue.

All of this combined to create a certain European disillusionment with Biden in his first year. One newspaper reported that he was seen as 'Trump with manners' (NRC Handelsblad 2021).

The game changer has, of course, been the Russian invasion of Ukraine.

Initially at least, this also seemed again like an area where the US and the Europeans would not be entirely on the same page. When the US began, in the autumn of 2021, to push out intelligence warnings about a likely Russian invasion, there was initial scepticism, not helped by vivid memories of the Iraq WMD debacle in 2003. Nobody – not even the Ukrainians – really believed that Putin would be crazy enough to start a real war. The US reaction this time was much smarter. They continued to share in an unprecedented way, increasingly compelling evidence that the military build-up was real.

The initial European reaction, led by Macron, was to try to reach out to Putin and seek some kind of diplomatic outcome. In hindsight, the futility of these efforts is clear. However, it would have been reprehensible not to try.

The Biden team then began a major effort of diplomatic outreach to prepare for the coming war. They mobilised large numbers of diplomats to spend time in Europe, both with individual countries, with NATO and, very tellingly, with the EU. This was genuine consultation with a genuine willingness to adjust the US position to take account of the European perspective. Very often consultation with the Americans consists of saying 'here is our position, wouldn't you like to agree with it?'

The Biden administration deserves huge praise for the unprecedented degree of transatlantic consultation and coordination, and for the very skillful way, they have managed to build a coalition of support for Ukraine, through sanctions and other measures, and to maintain that coalition using a technique of American diplomacy that we have not seen for a very long time.

The fundamental difference between Trump and Biden is that Trump thinks alliances are things that drag you down, while Biden believes that they build you up. Hence, he understood that, in dealing with this crisis, you needed a broad-based coalition, primarily with, but not only, the Europeans. He has also worked with the

Europeans to bring on board the Japanese and the South Koreans and other like-minded countries.

Another big difference was the focus on the EU as such. The Biden people quickly understood that sanctions, the main weapon of retaliation against Putin, is an EU competence.[1] So, they invested heavily in working with EU Commission to prepare the ground for the deployment of an unprecedented array of sanctions designed to punish Russia hard. This was reflected in the language. Blinken wrote, 'The U.S.-EU relationship stands on a foundation of shared values, including democratic governance, fair competition based on market principles, rule of law, respect for human rights, and inclusive growth. The Trade and Technology Council supports these values' (2022b), and 'We celebrate the European Union as a friend and a partner of first resort. Through the strength and vibrancy of the relationship, we are working together the challenges of the present and the future' (Blinken 2022a). Biden said, 'The idea ultimately grew into the—what is now a 27-nation European Union—an economic powerhouse and a global force for peace and close partners of all—on all the issues we face' (2022). So, there has been a real renaissance in the US-EU relationship, forged by the furnace of Putin's war in Ukraine.

The immediate focus continues to be on the war and the West's response. The key question is whether this will translate into greater cooperation across the full range of policies where profound differences still remain.

The Trade and Technology Council offers an interesting platform for discussion of the pressing economic issues, but it is not really a negotiation forum, and it is unclear what concrete outcomes it can produce. The need to agree on standards, supply chain issues, digital policies and how much state intervention is needed on all these questions is obvious. If the EU and the US cannot find common ground on at least some of these thorny matters, then precious energy will be wasted in transatlantic disputes which could be better used for addressing the challenge posed by China. If we are condemned to a new division of the global economy into three main blocs, China, the US and the EU, then it will be important to preserve as much of the current transatlantic openness as possible.

And, of course, how to deal with China itself is one of the biggest issues. For the US, important though pushing back against Putin's aggression in Ukraine may be, the new focus on Russia is an unwelcome diversion from what both Republicans and Democrats see as American's biggest threat – China's seemingly inexorable rise. It can only be a matter of time before the US make a clear request of Europe to join their cause, something which the EU and its member states have, until now at least, been hesitant to do.

On top of all this, comes the issue of US politics. The Biden administration has just over two years to run. What happens if they lose control of Congress in the mid-terms? What happens if Trump himself or a surrogate with similar views returns to the White House in 2024?

The new flourishing of transatlantic relations, and in particular, the much-improved relations between the US and the EU institutions risked being severely tested in the coming years.

Note

1 Article 29 Treaty on European Union (TEU) [2012] O.J. C 326/13, and Article 215 Treaty on the Functioning of the European Union (TFEU) [2012] O.J. C 326/47.

References

Biden, J. 2022. Remarks by President Biden. 9 May. Available from: https://ua.usembassy.gov/remarks-by-president-biden-at-signing-of-s-3522-the-ukraine-democracy-defense-lend-lease-act-of-2022/ [Accessed 30 September 2022].

Blinken, A. 2022a. Tweet of 9 May 2022. Available from: https://twitter.com/secblinken/status/1523674149457055745 [Accessed 30 September 2022].

Blinken, A. 2022b. Tweet of 15 May 2022. Available from: https://twitter.com/secblinken/status/1525932781653606401 [Accessed 30 September 2022].

Congressional Research Services. 2021. *U.S.-EU Trade and Economic Relations*. 21 December. Available from: https://sgp.fas.org/crs/row/IF10931.pdf [Accessed 30 September 2022].

Delors, J. 1985. Speech. 9 September, Luxembourg. Available from: https://www.cvce.eu/content/publication/2001/10/19/423d6913-b4e2-4395-9157-fe70b3ca8521/publishable_en.pdf [Accessed 30 September 2022].

European Commission. 2022. EU-US Trade and Technology Council: strengthening our renewed partnership in turbulent times. Statement, 16 May. Available from: https://ec.europa.eu/commission/presscorner/detail/en/IP_22_3034 [Accessed 30 September 2022].

Frey, W. H. 2018. The US will become 'minority white' in 2045, Census projects [online]. *Brookings*. 14 March. Available from: https://www.brookings.edu/blog/the-avenue/2018/03/14/the-us-will-become-minority-white-in-2045-census-projects/#:~:text=The%20new%20statistics%20project%20that,populations%20(see%20Figure%201) [Accessed 30 September 2022].

Hazony, Y. 2018. *The Virtue of Nationalism*. New York: Basic Books.

Holland, S. 2019. Trump adviser Bolton: U.S. would enthusiastically support a UK choice for no-deal Brexit [online]. *Reuters*, 12 August. Available from: https://www.reuters.com/article/uk-usa-britain-idUSKCN1V20W3 [Accessed 30 September 2022].

NRC Handelsblad. 2021. For world trade, Biden is a Trump with manners [online]. *NRC Handelsblad*, 2 February. Available from: https://www.nrc.nl/nieuws/2021/02/02/voor-de-wereldhandel-is-biden-een-trump-met-manieren-a4030279 [Accessed 30 September 2022].

Pajon, C. 2021. AUKUS, the Indo-Pacific, and France's Role: Fluctuat Nec Mergitur [online]. *IRFI*, 22 September. Available from: https://www.ifri.org/en/publications/publications-ifri/articles-ifri/aukus-indo-pacific-and-frances-role-fluctuat-nec [Accessed 30 September 2022].

Reuters Staff. 2018. Trump calls EU a 'foe' on trade: CBS News interview [online]. *Reuters*, 15 July. Available from: https://www.reuters.com/article/us-usa-trump-eu-foe-idUSKBN1K50R6 [Accessed 30 September 2022].

3

NEGOTIATING WITH THE EUROPEAN UNION – A U.S. PERSPECTIVE

Kenneth Propp

Introduction

The United States and the European Union conduct relations pursuant to an extensive network of international agreements, more than 35 in all (U.S. Department of State 2020, pp. 140–141). Many address trade and other commercial issues, as befits the EU's origins as an economic entity. The United States maintains as many international agreements with the EU and its components as it does with many sizeable EU member states. Indeed, the Washington-Brussels legal relationship is arguably of greater weight, since in areas like trade the EU acts exclusively for its member states.

A significant number of the more recent agreements relate to transatlantic dimensions of newer, shared competences acquired by Brussels, notably justice and home affairs. Over the past two decades, accords with Washington have been concluded on extradition, police and judicial cooperation, and transfers of personal data relating to airline passengers and to financial transactions.[1] High-profile negotiating failures like the planned Transatlantic Trade and Investment Partnership have sometimes overshadowed these practical achievements in the Justice and Home Affairs realm, however.

EU officials who have negotiated these agreements can attest that the United States is no easy international partner. It is often rigid, wedded to negotiating texts developed in Washington, and loath to make changes that might require legislative action by the U.S. Congress. An EU veteran once confessed to me that the Commission had resorted to organizing simulated negotiating sessions in order to train its officials on how to deal with the recalcitrant Americans.

The converse, of course, is also true. For the U.S. government, negotiating with Brussels poses unique legal and political challenges. Washington is not so systematic, however, in training its negotiators in the mysteries of Brussels in which they regularly become tangled. This chapter therefore is intended as a brief guide to the numerous

 DOI: 10.4324/9781003283911-5

ways in which the EU is no ordinary international partner for the United States (or, for that matter, other third countries). It does so by tracing lessons learned – rewards, pitfalls, and surprises – through a series of transatlantic JHA negotiations.

Three sets of issues illustrate the uniqueness of the European Union as a negotiating partner for third countries such as the United States. One is the identification of the European negotiator when the subject-matter implicates both Union and member state competences. In addition, even when it is clear that competence lies with Brussels, there have been occasions – at least before the advent of the Lisbon Treaty –when questions have arisen about which EU institution properly served as negotiating agent. Finally, a foreign country must be cognizant of the activist roles of the European Parliament and the Court of Justice in evaluating EU international agreements.

These topics often are entangled with the EU's doctrine of "mixity." "Mixity is a hallmark of the EU's external relations," a leading scholar has observed (Eeckhout 2011, p. 212). The EU pursues mixed agreements – those to which member states as well as the Union become party – not only where the EU treaties so require but "also where the substance of the agreement falls partly within the competence of the Union and partly within the competence of the Member States" (Chalmers et al. 2010, p. 648). As a result, "conclusion of the agreement therefore requires joint action by the EU and its Member States, the latter complementing, as it were, the otherwise insufficient power of the EU" (Eeckhout 2011, p. 213). As a U.S. observer has explained, "mixity allows the reassembling of divided sovereignty" (Olson 2011, p. 333).

The EU pursues mixed agreements for a variety of reasons. Including member states as parties enables them to remain visible actors internationally, thus avoiding tension between the Council and Commission. Substantively, resort to a mixed agreement avoids the complex task of exactly delimiting the scope of EU and member states' powers. Mixed agreements have the further advantage that they reflect unanimity among members, since they must be approved domestically in each member state (Eeckhout 2011, p. 221).

Whatever their virtues from an EU perspective, the reality of mixed agreements is often quite different for third countries. From the perspective of the U.S. government, "mixity is experienced ... as a seemingly endless series of practical problems" (Olson 2011, p. 331). The United States first confronted mixity in multilateral negotiations, but, more recently, JHA agreements have amply illustrated the challenges.

Who negotiates – EU or member states?

A basic question asked by a third country is who sits on the other side of the negotiating table. The United States traditionally concluded law enforcement and security agreements with individual European countries, but over the past two decades, it has begun to regard the European Union instead as the preferred negotiating partner. The first major – though not complete – step in that direction came with the 2003 Extradition and Mutual Legal Assistance Agreements.

Agreements with the EU on transfers of personal data relating to airline passengers and to financial transactions soon followed. The United States does not necessarily see the EU as its exclusive treaty partner in the JHA area, however. It chose to conclude agreements on Preventing and Combating Serious Crime with member states, despite the existence of an EU negotiating mandate, and it may consider a similar stance for projected agreements on access to electronic evidence in criminal matters.

EU-US extradition and mutual legal assistance agreements

Before the September 11, 2001, attacks on the United States, the U.S. government had never considered the European Union an important partner for law enforcement and security matters. In the immediate aftermath, however, that perception changed radically – and was reciprocated in Brussels.

Following the attacks, Congress enacted the PATRIOT Act,[2] granting the Executive widespread new powers in the intelligence and security realms. Officials from the U.S. Department of Justice and the Council Secretariat began to consider whether transatlantic cooperation against terrorism could be expanded beyond traditional bilateral law enforcement channels to include the European Union as well.[3]

Council representatives first suggested negotiating an agreement with the United States on counter-terrorism cooperation, but discussions later evolved towards consideration of possible extradition and mutual legal assistance agreements. In Washington, there was initial skepticism. The EU had no investigators or prosecutors, and little operative criminal justice responsibility, so what would be the point of the United States entering into formal legal assistance relationships with the Union itself? The United States already had mutual legal assistance treaties (MLATs) with the major EU member states where evidence needed for criminal matters tended to be located, as well as a comprehensive network of bilateral extradition treaties.

The United States, however, soon realized potential benefits in regulating transatlantic judicial assistance matters with the European Union. It recognized that "by concluding agreements with the European Union, the United States could achieve uniform improvements and expansions in coverage across much of Europe,"[4] not only under existing bilateral MLATs but also by creating legal assistance relationships with newer members with which it had no existing relations.[5]

The agreements had novel dimensions under EU and U.S. external relations law, as well as international law. The EU chose to base the extradition and mutual legal assistance agreements on the authority of Articles 24 and 38 of the Treaty on European Union, which empowered the Presidency to negotiate "third pillar" (i.e., justice and home affairs) international agreements with binding effect on the Union and all member states, pursuant to mandates granted by the Council of the European Union. Indeed, the resulting agreements, completed in 2003, constituted the EU's first use of Articles 24 and 38 legal authority.

For the United States, these negotiations were an even deeper venture into legal *terra incognita*. Never previously had it concluded a law enforcement agreement with the European Union as an entity.[6] The overwhelming majority of previous U.S. agreements with European institutions had been with the Community or the Commission, even in the law enforcement area.[7] Nor did the European Union at the time enjoy international legal personality, a defect that would not be remedied until the advent of the Treaty of Lisbon.[8] However, Council lawyers identified several international agreements that the Union had concluded with the successor states of ex-Yugoslavia in the late 1990s as evidence of its already-extant "effective" legal personality. Ultimately, State Department treaty lawyers accepted this argument, and concluded that the Union was an appropriate actor under international law.

There was also, for the United States, the delicate question of assuring itself that the European Union in fact enjoyed substantive external competence to conclude these agreements. At that time, the EU lacked an express competence for this purpose. Ultimately, the United States accepted the Council's view that it could act on the basis of the doctrine of implied external competence resulting from the Court of Justice's landmark 1970 *ERTA* judgment.[9]

At the same time, U.S. negotiators insisted that since the effect of the new EU-US agreements on mutual legal assistance and extradition would be to make changes in existing treaties that the United States maintained not with the European Union itself but rather with individual EU member states, each member state should provide its sovereign consent to those changes.[10] EU negotiators contended that member state approval of the EU-level agreement would suffice for this purpose, but the United States was not content to rely on the effect of internal EU law. Consequently, it was agreed that each member state would conclude separate bilateral instruments with the United States acknowledging the manner in which the new EU-level extradition and mutual legal assistance obligations would apply to their existing bilateral treaties.[11] The bilateral instruments, while time-consuming to negotiate,[12] have had the practical advantage of being easier for U.S. judges to interpret in often-contentious extradition and mutual assistance proceedings.

The U.S.-EU Extradition and Mutual Legal Assistance Agreements thus represented a hybrid approach. The United States accepted the value of the EU as a treaty partner in the JHA area. As the U.S. President explained to the Senate, "the U.S.-EU Agreements will enable the strengthening of an emerging institutional relationship on law enforcement matters between the United States and the European Union, during a period when the EU is actively harmonizing national criminal law procedures and methods of international cooperation."[13] Yet the United States also sought additional certainty for international law and domestic criminal law purposes by insisting on maintaining direct extradition and mutual legal assistance relationships with individual member states.

The EU-US extradition agreement[14] contained several significant substantive innovations. It replaced outdated exhaustive lists of extraditable offenses with a dual criminality approach that covers significant newer offenses such as those relating to terrorism, cybercrime, money-laundering, and sexual exploitation.[15] The United States secured a provision establishing that a U.S. extradition request to an EU member state would not be disadvantaged in relation to a further request for the same individual received from another member state pursuant to the European Arrest Warrant.[16] A corresponding achievement, from the EU perspective, was allowing a member state to decline to extradite to the United States a person facing a criminal charge for which the death penalty could be imposed.[17] Previously, such a provision was not universal in member state extradition treaties with the United States. Questions about the comprehensiveness of this provision have been noted by a leading European scholar, however (Mitsilegas 2003, p. 526).

The EU-US mutual legal assistance agreement[18] also had practical law enforcement value. It enabled criminal investigators and prosecutors better to obtain information on criminal bank accounts located in the territory of the other party.[19] It also facilitated the use of video transmission technology, so that a prosecutor could remotely take the statement of a witness or expert located in the territory of the other party and have the testimony admitted in the prosecutor's home state courts. Remote video depositions became especially important during the COVID-19 pandemic.

Preventing and combating serious crime agreements

The United States has chosen not to negotiate with the European Union in law enforcement-related contexts where member states retain principal authority, however. A prime example is police information-sharing, governed instead by a network of bilateral Agreements Enhancing Cooperation in Preventing and Combating Serious Crime (PCSC Agreements).

Under U.S. law,[20] foreign countries whose residents enjoy visa-free travel to the United States must execute a PCSC agreement. The agreement allows U.S. border agencies to query the other country's biometric fingerprint database in respect of an individual seeking to enter the United States. If a match is found, additional information on persons suspected of involvement in terrorist or other serious criminal offenses may be conveyed, resulting in the person's exclusion or arrest at the U.S. border.

When the United States in 2008 began its PCSC negotiating initiative, EU member states including Germany asked the Council of the European Union to issue a negotiating directive authorizing the Commission to pursue such an agreement with the United States (Brand 2007). The U.S. Department of Homeland Security, the lead agency, was reluctant to engage with the EU on this subject, however, since authority over visa issuance and the relevant fingerprint databases rested with member states, not Brussels. DHS also believed that it could achieve a result closer to its model negotiating text if it pursued member states one by one. The Commission objected strenuously to U.S. approaches to individual member states on a subject it wished to negotiate collectively with the United States.

The United States nevertheless persevered, stressing to member states that their status as Visa Waiver Program beneficiaries could be endangered absent a bilateral agreement. In November, 2008, the conservative Czech government of President Vaclav Klaus was the first to break ranks with EU brethren and sign a PCSC agreement with the United States.[21] In the years since, the other EU member states that are part of the Visa Waiver Program also have done so.

CLOUD Act agreements

Mutual legal assistance treaties enable prosecutors to make requests to foreign governments for information located in their territory that is needed for a domestic criminal proceeding; a foreign central authority and its courts are responsible for obtaining and transferring the requested information. This system respects foreign judicial sovereignty, but it was devised at a time when requests for foreign-located evidence were relatively rare. Today, however, communications relevant to the most local of criminal prosecutions are often stored by a cloud service provider in another country (Christakis et al. 2018). The volume of MLAT requests, correspondingly, has expanded exponentially. A 2018 report by the European Commission found that "more than half of all investigations involve a cross-border request to access [electronic] evidence" (European Commission 2018). Long delays in fulfilling requests have been the result, to prosecutors' great frustration.

In 2018, the United States became the first government to respond systematically to the problem, enacting the Clarifying Lawful Overseas Use of Data Act (CLOUD Act).[22] One provision authorizes the U.S. executive branch to conclude agreements with "foreign governments" that would enable prosecutors to obtain foreign-located electronic data, in cases involving serious crimes, directly from cloud service providers without outgoing requests first being subject to individualized government review.[23] Absent such an agreement, the Electronic Communications Privacy Act (ECPA) prohibits U.S.-based companies from disclosing communications content directly to a foreign government.[24]

The U.S. government thus far has concluded two CLOUD Act agreements, with the UK[25] and Australia.[26] Additionally, in September 2019, the United States announced that it would pursue such an agreement with the European Union, noting that the Council of the European Union had adopted a negotiating mandate authorizing the negotiations.[27]

U.S. negotiations with the EU soon stalled, however, over a variety of issues. One difficulty reportedly is the Commission's insistence that the United States renounce the possibility of resorting to unilateral criminal process in deference to CLOUD Act-based requests (Christakis and Propp 2020). A second problem is that the EU, unlike the United States, had yet to adopt a law like the CLOUD Act regulating foreign access to electronic evidence.[28] Commission negotiators reportedly were unwilling to continue negotiations with the United States until the EU's own legislation on e-evidence is completed. Some U.S. officials even privately questioned whether the EU satisfied the "foreign government" criterion in the CLOUD Act, notwithstanding the formal Department of Justice announcement committing to work with the EU.

If U.S.-EU negotiations remain stalled, the United States eventually may be tempted instead to pursue CLOUD Act agreements with individual EU member states, as it did previously with PCSC Agreements. The EU doubtless would strongly resist such a U.S. effort to circumvent its competence for data protection matters. The current standstill over electronic evidence thus illustrates that the United States, at least in the law enforcement and security area, still approaches certain decisions on its European negotiating partner as tactical and pragmatic ones.

Who negotiates for the EU – commission or council?

In an ordinary international negotiation, the United States finds itself across the table from the foreign government's executive branch officials. In seeking an agreement with the European Union, however, the question of who occupies the opposing chair is not necessarily simple to answer, since the executive power is dispersed among Brussels institutions. Even where the Commission presents itself as the counterpart, however, there may be legal uncertainty about this role – as the United States learned to its surprise and consternation in the case of the 2004 Passenger Name Record (PNR) agreement. The Lisbon Treaty, however, has served to clarify the question. Under Article 218 of the Treaty on the Functioning of the European Union (TFEU), the Commission typically acts as negotiator for the EU, subject to negotiating mandates developed in the Council of Ministers with input from the European Parliament.

Passenger name record agreement

The impetus for the first U.S. PNR agreement with the European Union was the September 11, 2001, terrorist attacks in the United States. One provision of the PATRIOT Act requires airlines systematically to collect passenger name record (PNR) data on all international flights to and from the United States, and to provide the data to the U.S Department of Homeland Security.[29]

PNR consists of the data an individual provides to an airline electronic reservation system, including address, telephone, and credit card numbers, as well as potentially sensitive information such as meal preferences or special needs. DHS reviews this data before departure of an international flight to assess whether anyone on board might be involved in terrorist or other criminal activity, and in that case to deny them permission to travel or arrange for detention upon arrival.

Airlines flying from Europe to the United States welcomed this additional U.S. security measure but also realized that complying with it could put them in violation of European data protection law. Civil libertarians objected that the U.S programme required transfer of data on large numbers of innocent travelers, with the goal of finding a few previously unidentified criminals. Airlines therefore urgently petitioned the Brussels to address this potential conflict of laws with the United States.

Negotiating an international accord reconciling the security benefits of PNR transfer to the United States with privacy protections meeting EU standards proved complex. Beginning in 2002, the European Commission, acting pursuant to Council authorization, took up the task. In 2004, a deal was struck: the United States issued a set of unilateral undertakings to accord specific protections to transferred EU-origin PNR,[30] and, in return, the Commission, utilizing its implementing powers, issued a decision under Article 25(6) of Directive 95/46[31] finding these protections "adequate" for European data protection purposes. The Commission then submitted both documents to the European Parliament. The Parliament, however, expressed doubts that the agreement fulfilled fundamental rights requirements and, in April 2004, sought the opinion of the Court of Justice.

Two years later, in May 2006, the CJEU issued its opinion.[32] The Court never reached the merits of the Parliament's application, however. Instead, it focused on the choice of Article 95 of the then-operative Treaty Establishing the European Community[33] as the legal basis for the Commission's adequacy finding pursuant to Directive 95/46. The Commission contended that reliance on this legal basis was appropriate since PNR data was collected by airlines for commercial purposes and utilized within the scope of the internal market. The Court disagreed. It noted that "Article 3(2) excludes from the Directive's scope the processing of personal data … concerning public security, defence, State security and the activities of the State in areas of criminal law."[34] The purpose of the agreement with the United States is "to make lawful processing of personal data that is required by United States legislation"[35] relating to counterterrorism. As a result, the Commission had acted *ultra vires* in negotiating with the United States, and the Court accordingly annulled the Agreement.

The European Commission was duly embarrassed by having misjudged the legal basis under the TEC. The U.S. government was surprised and dismayed to discover that its erstwhile negotiating partner in Brussels in fact lacked competence for that task. The Parliament, for its part, was disappointed that the Court of Justice had failed to issue a ringing declaration of fundamental rights. The result was unsatisfactory to all – except perhaps the Council of the European Union. Early in 2007, it authorized the Council Presidency – not the Commission – to open new negotiations with the United States, relying on member states' national competences for security and law enforcement. A successor agreement – largely similar in content – was hastily concluded later that year.[36]

Approval issues

The advent of the Lisbon Treaty in 2009 expanded the European Parliament's powers in relation to EU international agreements. Under Article 218(6) TFEU, the Council now may conclude many types of international agreements only after obtaining the consent of the Parliament. The Parliament has wielded this power effectively to influence the content and progress of EU data transfer agreements with the United States. The Court of Justice also may play a significant role in the ultimate validation of EU international agreements, through its power to issue opinions, at the request of an EU institution or member state, on compatibility with EU law.[37]

Role of the European Parliament

The Court's rejection of the Commission's chosen legal basis for the 2004 EU-US PNR Agreement, discussed earlier, was one early manifestation of this institutional interplay experienced by the United States. The successor 2007 PNR agreement never entered into force definitively, as the Parliament continued to object to the sufficiency of its data protection provisions. The EU applied it provisionally for several years, but eventually persuaded the United States that it required revision.

A durable PNR agreement with the United States was concluded only in 2012. The Parliament consented to it, and the agreement continues in force a decade later.[38]

Parliament's earliest – and perhaps most dramatic – exercise of its power to withhold consent to an international agreement involved another data transfer agreement with the United States, the Terrorist Finance Tracking Program (TFTP) Agreement. TFTP, conducted by the Department of Treasury, analyses the global flow of banking transactions believed to be connected to the financing of terrorism. It relies on data collected by the Society for Worldwide Interbank Financial Telecommunication (SWIFT), a Belgium-based company that enjoys a near-monopoly on messaging services for international financial transactions.

Late in 2009, the Council reached an agreement with the United States permitting transfer of SWIFT data located within the EU to the U.S. Treasury for counter-terrorism analysis purposes, in return for U.S. commitments to afford a set of privacy protections modelled on EU law. A Council attempt hurriedly to adopt the agreement in the final days before the Treaty of Lisbon took effect met with disaster, however, when several member state parliaments balked at ratification. The Parliament perceived an end-run around its incipient consent power. Consequently, early in 2010, the European Parliament formally refused consent to the EU-US TFTP agreement, in a defiant first exercise of its new power under Article 218 TFEU. Later that year, the Commission and the United States concluded an adjusted second agreement.[39]

The EU assumed an unusual dual role in implementing the TFTP agreement. Each Treasury request to SWIFT for data is first reviewed by Europol to verify that it properly falls within the counter-terrorism scope of the agreement.[40] In addition, the EU as party to the agreement undertook to "ensure" that SWIFT complies with Treasury requests, lending its sovereign weight to compliance by a private company.[41] Treasury in turn agreed to put its analytical capabilities at the disposal of European law enforcement agencies seeking analysis of data that had been transferred to the United States, and to cooperate with any future TFTP of its own that the EU might devise.[42] Despite these additions to the failed 2009 agreement, the 2010 TFTP Agreement proved controversial in the European Parliament, and received consent only by a narrow margin.

Since then, the agreement has proved its worth for both sides. Indeed, more than 40% of the database searches performed by Treasury during the last three-year period examined by the Council were on behalf of EU member states or Europol. The EU and its members accounted for nearly 75% of all TFTP leads disseminated to foreign governments. In effect, then, TFTP, in addition to benefitting U.S. counter-terrorism analytical efforts, "resembles an outsourcing arrangement, with the US Treasury Department effectively serving as an offshore service provider for the EU and European governments," as Adam Klein, the former chairman of the U.S. Privacy and Civil Liberties Oversight Board, has observed (2020).

The European Parliament's power to give or withhold consent to a broad swathe of EU international agreements contrasts markedly with the more limited counterpart role played by the U.S. legislature for U.S. international agreements. The U.S. Constitution grants to the President the "Power, by and with the Advice and

Consent of the Senate, to make Treaties, provided two thirds of the Senators present concur."[43] The United States chose to conclude the Extradition and Mutual Legal Assistance Agreements with the EU as treaties, because they served to modify corresponding treaties that the United States maintained with member states.

Today, however, most U.S. international agreements are not denominated as treaties subject to Senate advice and consent. Instead, the vast majority – more than 90% – are categorized by the U.S. Department of State as executive agreements rather than treaties (2013, p. 544). The President concludes executive agreements on the basis of his own, constitutionally assigned powers. Congress is not formally consulted, although in practice the executive branch consults with it informally, as it did in the cases of the PNR, TFTP, and "umbrella" law enforcement data protection agreements.[44] In most cases, therefore, U.S. executive branch negotiators enjoy greater discretion than their EU counterparts, who are aware that every choice they make could become a reason for the European Parliament subsequently to refuse consent.

Role of the Court of Justice of the European Union

We have already seen, in the case of the 2004 EU-US PNR agreement, how the European Parliament invoked its power under TFEU 218(11) to obtain the opinion of the CJEU on the agreement's conformity to EU fundamental rights law. Although the Parliament did not seek the CJEU's view before approving the 2011 PNR Agreement with the United States, in 2015 it did challenge a similar agreement that the Commission had struck with Canada. Two years later, the court ruled that portions of the draft Canada agreement were incompatible[45] with EU fundamental rights law.

The Commission recently conceded that the U.S.-EU PNR Agreement is "not fully in line" with the court ruling in the Canada PNR case (European Commission 2021). Topics addressed in the U.S.-EU agreement and cited by the Commission as problematic include "the retention of PNR data, the processing of sensitive data, notification to passengers, prior independent review of the use of PNR data, rules for domestic sharing and onward transfers, [and] independency of oversight" (European Commission 2021). The Commission has yet to ask the United States to renegotiate the 2011 PNR Agreement, which continues in force. Instead, it decided first to renegotiate its draft PNR agreement with Canada along the lines required by the CJEU – a process that is still ongoing – before essaying a new one with the United States. Nonetheless, the 2011 U.S.-EU PNR agreement eventually will have to be renegotiated, an indirect casualty of the CJEU *Canada PNR* opinion.

The CJEU's not infrequent scrutiny of EU international agreements contrasts with the rarity of U.S. Supreme Court review for U.S. ones. There is a long tradition in the United States of judicial deference to executive action in the foreign affairs area, best expressed in the "political question" doctrine. When presented with a case raising a foreign affairs issue, the U.S. Supreme Court, relying on longstanding precedent, first asks whether the U.S. Constitution commits the issue to executive decision and whether prudential considerations counsel against judicial intervention.[46] The result is almost always judicial abstention.

The CJEU, on the other hand, must issue opinions on draft EU international agreements when requested to do so. It has not hesitated to examine the details of a text and sometimes to demand substantial revisions. EU negotiators of JHA agreements thus must reckon with the likelihood of judicial scrutiny by the Luxembourg court.

Conclusion

Relations between the United States and the European Union on law enforcement and security matters have come to be grounded in a series of binding international agreements. U.S. negotiators remain frustrated by the obscurity of mixed competence, but they have persevered where the practical benefits of proceeding with Brussels are clear. The Extradition and Mutual Legal Assistance Agreements, for example, were the most efficient means to achieve uniform improvements in existing bilateral treaties and to establish new relations with smaller member states. Nonetheless, the U.S. government insisted on the reinforcing step of implementing those improvements bilaterally with member states. A lingering U.S. preference for bilateralism nevertheless sometimes comes to the fore. Washington chose to ignore an EU negotiating mandate for a PCSC Agreement, successfully inviting member states to defy Brussels, and conceivably could attempt the same in the e-evidence area.

The United States also has had to reckon regularly with the impact on negotiations that complex EU -inter-institutional relations can have. The Commission may present itself as the EU negotiating partner, only to be told by the Court of Justice that it has erred in its assertion of competence, as happened with the 2004 PNR Agreement. The Parliament has not hesitated to wield its consent power, forcing renegotiation of two data transfer agreements, the 2007 PNR Agreement, and the 2009 TFTP Agreement. The United States also has felt the effects of the Court of Justice's activism on the fundamental rights implications of JHA agreements. Washington may be an especially difficult partner for Brussels in reaching international agreements, but the EU also is no ordinary sovereign for the United States to face across the table.

Notes

1 Agreement on Extradition between the European Union and the United States, O.J. L181, 19.07.2003, p. 27; Agreement on Mutual Legal Assistance between the European Union and the United States, O.J. L 181, 19.07.2003, p. 34; Agreement between the European Union and the United States of America on the use and transfer of passenger name records to the United States Department of Homeland Security, O.J. 2012 L 215, 11.08.2012 (hereinafter "2012 PNR Agreement"); Agreement between the European Union and the United States of America on the processing and transfer of Financial Messaging Data from the European Union to the United States for the purposes of the terrorist Finance Tracking Program, O.J. L 195, 27.07.2010, p. 5 (hereinafter "2010 TFTP Agreement").

2 USA Patriot Act, Public Law 107-56, 115 Stat. 272, 26 October 2001.

3 Message from the President of the United States transmitting the Mutual Legal Assistance Agreement with the European Union, Senate Treaty Doc. 109-13, letter of submittal, p. VI, 28 September 2006.

4 *Id.*, p. V.

5 *Id.*

6 A US agreement with the European Police Office (Europol), a specialized EU law enforcement entity, was already in place. Agreement to Enhance Cooperation in Preventing, Detecting, Suppressing, and Investigating Serious Forms of International Crime, with Annex, TIAS 01-1207, 6 December 2001; Supplemental Agreement on the Exchange of Personal Data and Related Information, with Exchange of Letters, TIAS 01-1207, 20 December 2002.
7 See, *e.g.,* Agreement with the European Community on Customs Cooperation and Mutual Assistance in Customs Matters, 1997 O.J. L 222, 12.08.1997, p. 17.
8 This provision is now codified as Article 47 of the Treaty on European Union (TEU).
9 Case 22/70, *Commission* v. *Council (European Road Transport Agreement)*, [1971] ECR 263.
10 Message from the President of the United States transmitting the Mutual Legal Assistance Agreement with the European Union, Senate Treaty Doc. 109-13, letter of submittal, p. VII, 28 September 2006.
11 Message from the President of the United States transmitting the Mutual Legal Assistance Agreement with the European Union, *supra,* p. II.
12 As a result of this decision, the United States eventually concluded 56 bilateral instruments with the (then-)28 EU member states, all of which had to be approved through national constitutional processes before the entire package, including the EU-US Agreements, could take effect in 2010.
13 Message from the President of the United States transmitting the Mutual Legal Assistance Agreement with the European Union, *supra,* p. II.
14 Agreement on Extradition between the European Union and the United States, *supra.*
15 *Id.*, Art. 4.
16 *Id.*, Art. 10.
17 *Id.*, Art. 13.
18 Agreement on Mutual Legal Assistance between the European Union and the United States, *supra.*
19 *Id.*, Art. 4.
20 Section 217, Immigration and Nationality Act, 8 U.S.C. 1187(c)(2)(F).
21 Agreement between the Government of the United States of America and the Government of the Czech Republic on Enhancing Cooperation in Preventing and Combating Serious Crime, TIAS 10-501, 12 November 2008.
22 The Clarifying Lawful Overseas Use of Data Act [hereinafter CLOUD Act], contained in Consolidated Appropriations Act, 2018, P.L. 115–141, div. V. Available from: https://www.crossborderdataforum.org/wp-content/uploads/2018/07/Cloud-Act-final-text.pdf [Accessed 30 April 2022], codified at 18 U.S.C. 2713 *et seq.*
23 18 U.S.C. 2523(b).
24 Section 104 of the CLOUD Act amends ECPA to permit such disclosures pursuant to a CLOUD Act agreement.
25 Agreement between the Government of the United Kingdom of Great Britain and Northern Ireland and the Government of the United States of America on Access to Electronic Data for the Purpose of Countering Serious Crime, October 3, 2019. Available from: https://assets.publishing.service.gov.uk/government/uploads/system/uploads/attachment_data/file/836969/CS_USA_6.2019_Agreement_between_the_United_Kingdom_and_the_USA_on_Access_to_Electronic_Data_for_the_Purpose_of_Countering_Serious_Crime.pdf [Accessed 30 April 2022].
26 Agreement between the Government of the United States of America and the Government of Australia on Access to Electronic Data for the Purpose of Countering Serious Crime, December 15, 2021. Available from: https://www.justice.gov/dag/cloud-act-agreement-between-governments-us-and-australia [Accessed 30 April 2022].
27 Joint US-EU Statement on Electronic Evidence Sharing Negotiations, September 26, 2019. Press Release. Available from: https://www.justice.gov/opa/pr/joint-us-eu-statement-electronic-evidence-sharing-negotiations [Accessed 30 April 2022]. The EU was acting pursuant to a Recommendation for a Council Decision proposed by the

Commission on May 2, 2019. See Recommendation for a Council Decision authorising the opening of negotiations in view of an agreement between the European Union and the United States of America on cross-border access to electronic evidence for judicial cooperation in criminal matters, COM (2019)70, final.

28 For a fuller discussion of the European law difficulties presented by CLOUD Act agreements, see Christakis 2019.

29 USA Patriot Act, *supra*. Implementing regulations are found at 19 Code of Federal Regulations § 122.49d.

30 Agreement between the European Community and the United States of America on the processing and transfer of PNR data by air carriers to the United States Department of Homeland Security, Bureau of Customs, 2004 O.J. L 183, 20.05.2004, p. 84 (no longer in force).

31 Directive 95/46/EC of the European Parliament and of the Council on the protection of individuals with regard to the processing of personal data, 1995 O.J. L 281, 24.10.1995, p. 31 (no longer in force).

32 Joined Cases C-317 & 318/04, *European Parliament v. Council and Commission*, EU:C:2006:346.

33 This provision now is Article 114 of the Treaty on the Functioning of the European Union.

34 Joined Cases C-317 & 318/04, *supra*, at I-4830.

35 *Id.*

36 Agreement between the European Union and the United States of America on the processing and transfer of PNR data by air carriers to the United States Department of Homeland Security, 2007 O.J. L 2004, 26.07.2007, p. 18 (no longer in force).

37 Art. 218(11), Treaty on the Functioning of the European Union.

38 2012 PNR Agreement,*supra*.

39 2010 TFTP Agreement, *supra*.

40 *Id.*, Art. 4.

41 *Id.*, Art. 3.

42 *Id.*, Arts. 10, 11. The European Commission developed options for a counterpart EU TFTP analysis but never introduced a legislative proposal.

43 Constitution of the United States, Article II, Section 2(2).

44 Agreement on the Protection of Personal Information Relating to the Prevention, Investigation, Detection and Prosecution of Criminal Offenses 2016 O.J. L 336, 12 October 2016, p. 3. Article 19 grants citizens of the other party the right to judicial review of government handling of their personal information. This provision required the United States Congress to amend the Privacy Act, which previously had extended such redress only to US citizens.

45 Opinion 1/15, *Draft Agreement between Canada and the European Union on Transfer of Passenger Name Record Data, Opinion of the Court (Grand Chamber)*, EU:C:2017:592.

46 *See, e.g.*, *Goldwater v. Carter*, 444 U.S.996, 998 (1979).

References

Brand, C., 2007. EU Pushing Toward Shared Police Database. *Associated Press*, 16 January.

Chalmers, D., Davies, G. and Monti, G., 2010. *European Union Law*. 2nd ed. Cambridge: Cambridge University Press.

Christakis, T., Daskal, J. and Swire, P., 2018. *The Globalization of Criminal Evidence* [online]. International Association of Privacy Professionals. Available from: https://iapp.org/news/a/the-globalization-of-criminal-evidence/ [Accessed 30 April 2022].

Christakis, T., 2019. *21 Thoughts and Questions about the US-UK CLOUD Act Agreement* [online]. European Law Blog. Available from: https://europeanlawblog.eu/2019/10/17/21-thoughts-and-questions-about-the-uk-us-cloud-act-agreement-and-an-explanation-of-how-it-works-with-charts [Accessed 30 April 2022].

Christakis, T. and Propp, K., 2020. *The Legal Nature of the UK-US CLOUD Agreement* [online]. Cross Border Data Forum. Available from: https://www.crossborderdataforum.org/the-legal-nature-of-the-uk-us-cloud-agreement/ [Accessed 30 April 2022].

Eeckhout, P., 2011. *EU External Relations Law*. 2nd ed. Oxford: Oxford University Press.

European Commission, 2018. Commission Staff Working Document Impact Assessment accompanying the document Proposal for a Regulation of the European Parliament and of the Council on European Production and Preservation Orders for electronic evidence in criminal matters, *SWD* (2018) 118, final.

European Commission, 2021. Report from the Commission to the European Parliament and the Council on the Joint Evaluation of the Agreement between the United States of America and the European Union on the Use and Transfer of Passenger Name Records to the United States Department of Homeland Security, *COM* (2021) 18, final.

Klein, A. (Chairman, US Privacy and Civil Liberties Oversight Board), 2020. *Statement on the Terrorist Finance Tracking Program* [online]. Available from: https://documents.pclob.gov/prod/Documents/EventsAndPress/ff62d017-c241-4dfd-a164-7cda92bd8395/TFTP%20Chairman%20Statement%2011_19_20.pdf [Accessed 30 April 2022].

Mitsilegas, V., 2003. *New EU-USA Cooperation on Extradition, Mutual Legal Assistance and the Exchange of Police Data*. European Foreign Affairs Review.

Olson, P., 2011. Mixity from the Outside: the Perspective of a Treaty Partner. *In:* Hillion, C. and Koutrakos, P., eds. *Mixed Agreements Revisited: The EU and its Member States in the World*. London: Bloomsbury, 331–348.

U.S. Department of State, 2013. *The Constitution of the United States of America: Analysis and Interpretation* [online]. U.S. Government. Available from: https://www.govinfo.gov/content/pkg/GPO-CONAN-2013/pdf/GPO-CONAN-2013.pdf [Accessed 30 April 2022].

U.S. Department of State, 2020. *Treaties in Force: A List of Treaties and Other International Agreements of the United States in Force on January 1, 2020.*

4
TRANSATLANTIC PARLIAMENTARY COOPERATION AT FIFTY

Davor Jancic

Introduction

The election of Joseph Biden as President in November 2020 allows the US not only to move away from the unilateralist and inward-looking approach of the previous administration but also to reinvigorate the transatlantic relationship between the US and the EU (Blockmans 2021; O'Sullivan in this volume). This is all the more salient given that the two polities have long shared fundamental political and societal values, as well as their commitment to addressing global challenges, such as maintaining international peace and security, combating terrorism, managing pandemics, addressing democratic backsliding, facilitating human rights protection, curbing climate change, regulating the digital economy and fostering global trade.

The hallmark of the post-Trump transatlantic rapprochement was the establishment of the EU-US Trade and Technology Council (TTC) at the EU-US summit in Brussels on 15 June 2021. Although this initiative has been viewed as 'too timid' for not addressing the key contentious issues like data protection and food safety (Chase 2021: 85 and 87), the TTC created a formal platform for intergovernmental and regulatory dialogue. Nevertheless, an important, albeit not always politically prominent, component of the transatlantic relationship is that between the two polities' respective parliaments: the European Parliament (EP) and the US Congress (Jancic 2015a). It has been argued that transatlantic inter-parliamentary relations have proven relevant as a 'second level of diplomacy' (Lazarou 2020: 61) during the Trump administration. This was necessary because of the latter's often antagonistic attitude towards the EU, seen not least in the unannounced temporary downgrading in 2018 of the EU Ambassador in Washington from the rank enjoyed by state ambassadors to that of an envoy of an international organisation, and in the travels bans from the Schengen area to the US introduced during the COVID-19 pandemic. The relevance of inter-polity

DOI: 10.4324/9781003283911-6

dialogues, including interparliamentary cooperation, lies in discussing mutual policy outcomes, negotiating bilateral agreements and seeking recognition of an institution's or polity's very identity (Blanc 2023).

This chapter analyses transatlantic relations from the perspective of the EP. The objective is to develop the existing literature on EU-US parliamentary cooperation by demonstrating how EP action in the transatlantic space contributes to transnational political contestation and public discourse shaping through policy legitimisation and delegitimisation in a variety of contexts ranging from dialogue to the adoption of formal instruments of pronouncement. To do so, the chapter takes stock of the current state of affairs in the transatlantic interparliamentary relationship, 50 years after their commencement, through an examination of the empirical material consisting of parliamentary resolutions, reports, public hearings, statements and other sources.

The analysis is structured as follows. In the next section, the chapter situates the EP in the context of wider EU external relations, emphasising its growing diplomatic role in international relations. The third section presents the institutional, legal and policy framework for the EP's diplomatic relations with the US, before delving into the political practice. The latter analyses different types of EP engagement: (a) plenary resolutions on the state of transatlantic relations and on EU-US agreements; (b) US-bound missions by EP standing committees, subcommittees and special committees; and (c) activities of the EP Delegation for Relations with the US (D-US) acting alone and within the Transatlantic Legislators' Dialogue (TLD). The last section concludes by assessing the advantages and disadvantages of transatlantic parliamentary cooperation.

The European Parliament's growing parliamentary diplomacy engagement

Often lauded in the literature as the leading parliamentary institution in international affairs which inspired other regional integration projects (Dri 2010), the EP proactively pursues an agenda of value promotion and norm entrepreneurship in line with thesis that describes the EU as a normative power (Whitman 2011). With limited powers in certain areas of EU external action, particularly concerning foreign, security and defence policies (Kleizen 2016: 42), the EP has sought to assert itself as an important player by maintaining autonomous international relations (Stavridis and Irrera 2015), thus bringing foreign affairs closer to the citizens and increasing the legitimacy of EU external action (Eckes 2014).

Parliamentary diplomacy plays a central and increasing part in this dynamic, with the EP seeking greater influence beyond EU borders through interactions with numerous partner countries and regions (Stavridis and Jancic 2017; Moraes 2018). In the broader sense, parliamentary diplomatic activism encompasses the more classic constitutional function of scrutinising EU foreign policy. In the stricter sense, it centres on the establishment of direct links with state and non-state actors through dialogues, mutual visits and the creation of formal transnational interparliamentary forums or alliances. The EP thereby contributes to the implementation of Article 21 TEU. This requires the Union's action on the international scene to be guided by the principles that have inspired its own creation – above all democracy, rule of law and human rights protection. It also mandates that the Union shall seek to develop relations and build partnerships with third countries and international organisations that share these principles. The conduct of EU-US relations at both intergovernmental and interparliamentary levels is the epitome of this Treaty commitment, owing to a shared understanding of the need to advance the said values in bilateral relations and global governance.

However, this does not mean that transatlantic relations are immutable and invulnerable to erosion. After all, in its 2022 resolution on the Common Foreign and Security Policy, the EP strongly supported the development of transatlantic relations as a partnership of equals, but did so warning, first, of the necessity for the Union to 'swiftly adapt to the changing role of the US on the global stage in order to safeguard its vital interests and pursue its foreign policy goals'; and, second, of the need to develop a European sovereignty and an ability to act autonomously if needed.[1]

Neither are transatlantic relations frictionless. That disagreements exist is demonstrated not only by trade disputes (Petersmann and Pollack 2003) and regulatory divergences (Young in this volume) but also by the EP's well-documented opposition to EU-US international agreements – such as the ACTA, SWIFT and PNR agreements (Meissner 2016) – or to bilateral arrangements such as the EU-US Privacy Shield (Fahey and Terpan 2021: 218).[2] Yet, such opposition does not necessarily equate with influence, as the EP has not always been able to shape the content of these agreements. In the case of the SWIFT agreement, for instance, the EP has been argued to have been a norm taker, due to its inability to exert substantial concessions (Servent and MacKenzie 2012). Despite this, the EP is sufficiently impactful to be regularly lobbied by foreign diplomats, as former US Ambassador in Brussels, Anthony Gardner, did on matters like data privacy, Transatlantic Trade and Investment Partnership (TTIP) negotiations and the digital economy (Gardner 2020: 19).

There is also no absolute convergence on the EU's founding values and human rights in particular. This is shown by the EP's condemnation in October 2021 of the de facto total abortion ban in the State of Texas,[3] and by its criticism of the overturning of *Roe v Wade* by the US Supreme Court.[4] Nonetheless, the near-total abortion ban in Poland demonstrates that gender equality and women's rights are not a settled matter within the EU either. The common EU-US goal of global values promotion is hence more nuanced than the invocation in official documents of the 'shared values' would suggest.

All of this makes interparliamentary dialogue ever more important and valuable, so that bilateral legislative and regulatory decision making is not carried out in mutual isolation but in a collaborative fashion. A telling example of this was the use of a whole gamut of instruments by the EP's plenary and its committees during TTIP negotiations (Roederer-Rynning 2017: 517), including the organisation of sessions and hearings with US delegation representatives and direct meetings with US officials in Washington (Meissner and Schoeller 2019: 1086). This enables European and American approaches to be discussed and differences to be accommodated (Jancic 2015b). In relation to this, it has correctly been argued that intergovernmental transatlantic cooperation is insufficient to address the rising number of challenges, because

> unless elected representatives of the public, who set the rules and fund politically sensitive issues such as climate change, privacy, digital taxation, and government subsidies are fully engaged in transatlantic regulatory cooperation, fears over the loss of national sovereignty and domestic prerogatives will consign such collaboration to a legislative graveyard. (Stokes 2021)

That parliaments can indeed be significant actors in EU-US diplomatic relations is demonstrated by the fact that the EP only began denouncing the CIA's alleged use of so-called enhanced interrogation techniques over Guantánamo Bay detainees after the US Senate published a report of over 6,700 pages about it (Jancic 2016).[5] Interparliamentary dialogue can also contribute to addressing multilateral challenges by voicing support or criticism within formal international parliamentary institutions and by seeking to build more informal transnational coalitions of like-minded parliamentarians with the aim of engagement on common causes and issues of shared concern, such as China's human rights record and the situations in Hong Kong, Tibet and Xinjiang (Brattberg 2020: 12).[6]

Institutionalisation and political practice of EU-US parliamentary relations

Institutionalisation

As I described elsewhere in greater detail, the impetus for the formalisation of EP-Congress ties lay in the 1990 Transatlantic Declaration and the 1995 New Transatlantic Agenda. The former document welcomed the two parliaments' action to 'improve their dialogue' and the latter attached 'great importance to enhanced parliamentary links' (Jancic 2014: 49). The establishment in 1999 of the TLD made official the informal interparliamentary meetings which began 27 years earlier, when members of the EP (MEPs) first met with US senators.

Besides the President, the plenary and the committees, the EP's most specialised entity for transatlantic affairs is D-US. Among the EP's 45 standing interparliamentary delegations, D-US is the largest one and one that contributes members to the TLD. It consists of 64 members and 64 substitute members, and is currently presided over by Radosław Sikorski, who was previously foreign and defence minister in different Polish governments. This is the first time a Polish MEP heads D-US, as the previous 13 chairpersons were predominantly from the UK (6) and Germany (5), and only one each from the Netherlands and Denmark.[7]

On the American side, the Congress' TLD delegation is far less institutionalised and does not include senators, although MEPs regularly meet with them when TLD meetings are organised in the US. The US TLD co-chair is elected by the Speaker of the House of Representatives, while TLD delegation members are chosen by the co-chair on a voluntary but bipartisan basis (Lazarou 2020: 64). An attempt to achieve a more permanent structure of the TLD's congressional component has hitherto failed. The Transatlantic Legislators' Dialogue Enhancement Bill, introduced in the House of Representatives in July 2019 by the current US TLD Co-Chair Jim Costa (D-CA), did not progress in the legislative procedure.[8] In February 2022, he introduced a new Transatlantic Legislators' Dialogue Act Bill, aiming to formalise a 24-member US-EU Interparliamentary Group within Congress that would be composed of 12 Representatives and 12 senators and from which the TLD delegation would be drawn.[9] Although the chances of this bill being adopted are low, the number of co-sponsors has risen from 7 in 2019 to 10 in 2022.

These developments show that the driver of transatlantic interparliamentary relationship is the EP, with much larger, more stable and official parliamentary infrastructure in place. While the Congress has exhibited awareness of the need for greater balance both within Congress and towards the EP, the political will to effect this has been wanting. To date, the only formal interparliamentary groups and delegations within the Congress are for relations with Canada, Mexico, the UK, Organization for Security and Co-operation in Europe and NATO Parliamentary Assemblies, China, Russia and Japan.[10]

Political practice

For both the EU and the EP, the transatlantic relationship remains central. This flows from the Parliament's resolutions, committees' diplomatic missions to the US and D-US' engagements within the TLD. These three aspects are examined in turn below.

Since lawmaking is not always available as a means of action in foreign affairs, ***resolutions*** adopted by the plenary voice the EP's stance on the state of transatlantic relations and on the relevance of the transatlantic partnership for wider international affairs. Although not legally binding, resolutions can carry political weight because they reveal the Parliament's prevailing understanding of the EU-US relationship and global developments, and because they often announce the institution's future plans regarding bilateral and multilateral matters.

Regarding *bilateral relations*, the EP's periodic resolutions on EU-US relations consistently emphasise the importance of further institutionalising and upgrading the structures and scope of transatlantic interparliamentary cooperation. The October 2021 resolution highlights this prominently, while providing a sense of the Biden-era transatlantic aspirations.[11]

First, it acknowledges a certain degree of decline in the overall transatlantic relationship, underlining that the EU-US parliamentary cooperation can serve to 'restore confidence in and the durability and efficiency of transatlantic cooperation' not least through the raising of the awareness of the TLD and through more regular bilateral meetings at committee level.[12]

Second, the resolution stresses the need for deeper legislative cooperation and a more inclusive interparliamentary dialogue, such as through the establishment of a transatlantic legislators assembly. This is a long-standing EP request, which it has repeatedly made since the TLD's creation.[13] On the occasion of the first EU-US summit of the Biden Administration in June 2021, a group of 21 MEPs from the European People's Party – including prominent political figures like Antonio Tajani, Roberta Metsola and Radosław Sikorski – reiterated the call for a transatlantic assembly, which would serve as an 'idea lab for new impetus carrying the relationship between Washington and Brussels' (Caspary et al. 2021), but what this lab would do is unclear. While the assembly proposal has been welcomed by some commentators (Stokes 2021), it has hitherto not materialised due to the lack of political will, particularly on the American side (Howorth 2009: 13), and poor identification of the potential roles, structure and added value of such an assembly compared to the existing TLD. Relatedly, the resolution urged the US Congress to elevate the TLD to the level of a formal body with permanent membership, while the re-establishment of the Congressional EU Caucus was welcomed.

Third, interparliamentary coordination sought by the EP is of a multilevel nature and is pursued through the exchange of best practices on sub-national, national and global challenges not only between the EP and Congress but also with EU national parliaments and US State legislatures.[14] On the EU's side, national parliaments occasionally scrutinise transatlantic affairs, especially where their Member State's interests are adversely affected and where the matter is highly salient, the way TTIP negotiations were (Jancic 2017). Substantively, interparliamentary coordination concerns regulatory and legislative approximation, such as on bilateral trade, the taxation of technology companies, human-centric artificial intelligence and oversight over online platforms. However, MEPs also encourage collaboration on the more political issues of foreign policy. The resolution thus advocates a joint transatlantic approach to China and emphasises the need for a 'strong parliamentary dimension' of the EU-US high-level strategic dialogue on China.[15] It also advocates EP-Congress cooperation regarding the persecutions and incarcerations of human rights defenders and civil society representatives.[16]

Interparliamentary cooperation is also addressed in sector-specific EP resolutions, which sometimes recommend institutional adjustments. Importantly, the May 2022 resolution on artificial intelligence proposed the reinforcement of the TTC by an interparliamentary dimension given the Council's strategic potential.[17] The EP also engages on the TTC through debriefing meetings between its International Trade Committee and the EU's TTC Co-Chairs, Commission Executive Vice-Presidents Margrethe Vestager and Valdis Dombrovskis. The first such debrief was held in October 2021 and was joined by the chairs of committees devoted to the internal market, industry and artificial intelligence. This allowed MEPs to raise the issue of transparency in the TTC's work and to recommend using the TTC to learn from American legislation banning products made using forced labour, to expand international partnerships in resolving supply chain bottlenecks, and to reform the World Trade Organization.[18] On the Congress' side, no decision has yet been made as to whether a parliamentary component of the TTC should be created, and if so, whether through the US TTC delegation or through a congressional advisory council, then how such a component should operate, and what its relationship with the TLD should be. The Congressional Research Service nevertheless recognises room for parliamentarians to 'weigh in' on the structure, priorities and scope of the

TTC and for them to use this forum to pronounce on bilateral and global issues, and devise parameters by which to assess the success of the TTC's outcomes (Akhtar et al. 2022: 28–29). The idea of parliamentary cooperation on technology governance has further support. It has been argued that the EP and Congress should spearhead the creation of a Democratic Digital Technology Caucus, which would be open to other democratic countries and which would discuss regulatory philosophies, share draft proposals and facilitate inter-committee cooperation in this field (Barker 2021: 11). However, neither the inaugural nor the second TTC meeting addressed the proposal for a parliamentary TTC component, despite emphasising the necessity of consultations on legislative and regulatory developments in areas such as dual-use export controls and investment screening, and despite acknowledging the importance of consulting with diverse business and non-profit stakeholders and enabling them to provide common proposals to the TTC.[19]

Regarding *multilateral relations*, the EU-US partnership within NATO continues to be critical for the Union's security and defence. The EP recognised this in its July 2021 resolution on EU-NATO cooperation, hailing over 70 years of the enduring 'transatlantic bond' that needs deepening, enhancement and adaptation to the evolving global threats.[20] MEPs also emphasised the importance of parliamentary diplomacy, calling for a stronger role of the NATO Parliamentary Assembly (NATO PA), for the upgrading of the EP's delegation to full status within it, and for a joint meeting of the EP's and Congress' foreign affairs committees to discuss common security threats and how EU-NATO cooperation could address them.[21] Conversely, a resolution on NATO adopted by the US Senate in April 2019 did not mention parliamentary cooperation and diplomacy,[22] suggesting lower salience of the NATO PA. This corresponds to academic findings that although it has supported the creation of the NATO PA in 1955 and was instrumental to the setting up of parliamentary training through Rose-Roth seminars in 1990, Congress has a 'very selective approach' to interparliamentary activities (Šabič 2017: 229).

The EP's ***committees*** for external and internal EU policies also contribute to parliamentary diplomacy.[23] They do so through the dispatch of missions, the organisation of hearings and workshops with representatives of the civil society and business and thematic experts, and other forms of correspondence with Congress members.

Among the *committees focusing on external policies*, AFET periodically leads missions to Washington DC to discuss the most topical issues on the EU-US agenda. These enable MEPs to meet with members and officials from both houses of Congress, from various Administration departments and agencies (such as the State Department, the National Security Council, the Cybersecurity and Infrastructure Security Agency, the US Trade Representative Office, and the US Treasury), and from leading think tanks and human rights organisations. To maximise opportunities for exchange, these missions can incorporate members from SEDE and DROI, and can involve other trips, such as SEDE members' visit to the NATO Joint Force Command in Norfolk, Virginia, in October 2019 to discuss EU-NATO cooperation.[24] Jointly with DROI, AFET also traditionally sends an annual delegation to the UN General Assembly in New York, which often meets with the ambassador or deputy ambassador from the US permanent representation to the UN.[25] Back in Brussels, AFET holds exchanges of views with relevant US representatives, principally the US Ambassador to the EU.[26] Some of its public events are specifically devoted to transatlantic affairs too, such as hearings on EU-US relations in May 2018 and December 2020.

AFET's subcommittees can organise activities of their own, such as DROI's exchange of views with the US Special Envoy on North Korea Human Rights Issues (January 2015), and the inclusion of the US Deputy Assistant Secretary in the State Department as one of the speakers at the hearing on LGBTI rights outside the EU (September 2017).

For its part, INTA occasionally dispatches missions to Washington DC, during which MEPs meet not only with Congress and Administration members but also with those from EU and US businesses, trade unions and the civil society. The mission conducted in early November 2021 was important because, as the first post-Biden mission, it revealed a 'renewed sense of transatlantic engagement' on both sides, despite Biden's continuation of the Buy American policy and other differences.[27] These missions can be an 'indispensable tool' in aiding political and technical network-building and facilitating the committee's scrutiny of the TTC.[28] INTA also sends delegations to the WTO Ministerial and Parliamentary Conferences, where MEPs can organise meetings with the US delegation, as they did in November 2017, when they discussed the US position on the blocking of the nomination of judges on the WTO Appellate Body with trade staffers from the House Ways and Means Committee and the Senate Finance Committee.[29] INTA has also held numerous US-related hearings, workshops and exchanges of views. These were especially relevant during TTIP negotiations from 2012 to 2016 (Coremans and Meissner 2018: 571) – when they were often co-organised with other interested committees such as EMPL, JURI, ITRE, IMCO and DEVE – but extend beyond this as shown by the hearing on US trade policy (September 2021) and the workshop on the US withdrawal from the Trans-Pacific Partnership (November 2017). Relatedly, INTA used to have a very productive monitoring group on the US during TTIP negotiations (Coremans 2017: 34–35), which contributed to improvements in administrative and political capacities of this committee (Coremans and Meissner 2018).

Among the *committees focused on internal EU policies*, many engage in transatlantic parliamentary diplomacy too. As one of the most active committees, LIBE periodically sends missions not only to Washington DC to discuss policy and legislation on issues like data protection, law enforcement, counterterrorism, the US Visa Waiver scheme and artificial intelligence, but also to other places, like Boston or Sillicon Valley, to debate with academics or big tech representatives.[30] Other committees that dispatch US-bound missions include INGE, AIDA, REGI, JURI and AFCO, while FEMM's attendance at the UN Commission on the Status of Women in New York allow MEPs to meet with American officials and civil society organisations.

Although missions by committees and individual MEPs are the key platforms for interparliamentary cooperation (Dunne in this volume), the ***EP's D-US and TLD*** also provide important spaces for transatlantic policy debates. Ordinary D-US meetings are held on average nine times a year and are devoted not only to preparing for interparliamentary meetings (IPMs) within the framework of the TLD and discussing its outcomes, but also to the organisation of exchanges of views with EU, US and other officials and thematic experts. IPMs are intended to be held twice-yearly. One of the key recent IPM discussions concerned the recognition of the importance of scrutinising the TTC, including by creating a 'TLD TTC transatlantic platform'.[31] Like committee missions, the Delegation's visits to Washington DC for the purposes of TLD meetings are also used to meet with US government officials and stakeholders. Beyond this, the Delegation feeds into the EP's work through the TLD Steering Committee, in which a number of committees are represented, and through post-mission reporting to AFET.

Parliamentary diplomacy in action: Russian invasion of Ukraine

When it comes to international conflict, a prime domain for diplomatic action, Russia's invasion of Ukraine is exemplary of vigorous transatlantic parliamentary diplomacy. As with previous crises involving Ukraine (Fonck 2019; Redei and Romanyshyn 2019; Nitoiu and Sus 2017), the invasion demonstrates how the different layers of parliamentary engagement can combine to try and shape public discourse about a cause as fundamental as peace. This engagement is presented below in a chronological and more granular fashion to showcase the diversity of some of the EP's and Congress' key diplomatic initiatives in this matter.

On the EP's side, before the invasion began, an AFET-SEDE fact-finding mission was sent to Kyiv, Zaporyzhzhya and Mariupol (30 January–1 February 2022) to show solidarity with Ukraine concerning Russia's military build-up on Ukraine's borders. The delegates met with Ukraine's prime minister, deputy prime minister, defence minister, and the Speaker and prominent members of Ukraine's Parliament *Verkhovna Rada*.[32] On 16 February, D-US held an exchange of views with the director of the Centre for European Policy Analysis on relations with Russia regarding Ukraine. Then, on 26 February, two days after the invasion started, the TLD co-chairs issued a joint statement expressing 'complete support and solidarity' with Ukraine's people and government.[33] On 1 March, Ukraine's President, Volodymyr Zelensky, began addressing parliaments worldwide to plead support, starting with a speech before the EP delivered remotely during an extraordinary plenary session on the Russian invasion of Ukraine.[34] This session adopted a resolution insisting that 'all future sanctions must continue to be closely coordinated with transatlantic allies and like-minded international partners in order to maximise their effectiveness'.[35] On 10 March, D-US exchanged views with the US Ambassador to the EU, Mark Gitenstein, on transatlantic cooperation regarding the invasion. AFET organised a hearing on the same topic four days later.[36] An executive transatlantic response only came a month after the invasion began, when on 24 March, Presidents Von der Leyen and Biden issued a joint statement strongly condemning it.

On 1 April, the EP President, Roberta Metsola, the first high EU official to visit invaded Ukraine, delivered a speech in Kyiv before the *Verkhovna Rada*.[37] Soon after, on 6 April, D-US exchanged views with a European External Action Service representative on invasion-focused cooperation with the US. This was followed by the adoption of three Ukraine-related plenary resolutions–on the EU's protection of children and young people fleeing the war (7 April), on the war's impact on women (5 May) and on the fight against impunity for war crimes (19 May) – albeit that none mentioned transatlantic cooperation. Subsequently, on 22 May, the 84th TLD meeting, attended by a Ukrainian parliamentarian, deplored the invasion.[38] Another two exchanges of views were held in D-US thereafter: one on the American vision and transatlantic dialogue regarding NATO's future after Russia's invasion of Ukraine with a German Marshall Fund representative (9 June); and another on transatlantic cooperation in support of Ukraine with a US Army Lieutenant General (7 July). Ukraine's Statehood Day (28 July) saw another speech delivered by Metsola before the *Verkhovna Rada*.

On the Congress' side, beyond legislating to impose sanctions on Russia and provide military, economic and humanitarian aid to Ukraine, American parliamentarians were very diplomatically active. Like the EP, acting on Russia's military build-up, a seven-member Senate delegation visited Zelensky and Ukrainian government officials in Kyiv on 17 January to express firm support for Ukraine,[39] followed by a similar Kyiv visit on 28 January by an 11-member House of Representatives delegation, led by its Foreign Affairs Committee Chairman, Gregory Meeks (D-NY).[40] Both houses of Congress proceeded to pass Ukraine-related resolutions, with the Senate supporting an independent and democratic Ukraine against Russia's invasion (17 February);[41] the House of Representatives demanding a cease-fire, the withdrawal of the Russian forces, the continuation of sanctions against Putin's regime, and the provision of defensive security assistance to Ukraine (2 March);[42] and the Senate condemning Putin and other Russian officials 'for committing atrocities, including alleged war crimes' and calling for the International Criminal Court's involvement (15 March).[43] Zelensky then remotely addressed both houses of Congress on 16 March, while the House Speaker, Nancy Pelosi (D-CA) – together with four other Democrat members including chairmen of the House foreign affairs, intelligence and rules committees – reciprocated with an unannounced visit to Zelensky in Kyiv on 30 April as the highest US official to do so since the invasion began.[44] Pelosi then received the Order of Princess Olga, a medal awarded for outstanding contribution to the state of Ukraine.[45]

Other examples of congressional diplomatic visits include: a four-member delegation of Senate Republicans visiting Zelensky in Kyiv, led by minority leader Mitch McConnell (R-KY) (14 May);[46] a bipartisan visit to Zelensky in Kyiv by senators Lindsey Graham (R-SC) and Richard Blumenthal (D-CT) to promote the idea of Russia as a state sponsor of terrorism (7 July);[47] a five-member bipartisan House delegation visiting Zelensky and Defence Minister Reznikov in Kyiv led by the chairman of the Armed Services Committee, Adam Smith (D-WA) (23 July);[48] and a bipartisan visit to Zelensky and Reznikov in Kyiv and to Bucha, Irpin and Hostomel Airport by senators Amy Klobuchar (D-MN) and Robert Portman (R-OH), co-chair of the Ukraine Caucus and member of the Foreign Relations Committee (30 August), both of whom then received an Order of Merit of 1st Degree from Zelensky.[49]

Finally, Congress has pressured the Secretary of State, Anthony Blinken, to designate Russia as a state sponsor of terrorism. To this end, the Senate passed a resolution co-sponsored by senators Graham and Blumenthal (27 July),[50] while the House introduced a mirroring resolution (12 May)[51] and a legislative bill co-sponsored by a bipartisan group of six Representatives (28 July).[52] At the time of writing, only Cuba, North Korea, Iran and Syria feature on the US government list of states sponsors of terrorism.

Concluding remarks

Analysing the institutional and empirical aspects of the EP-Congress relationship, this chapter has sought to demonstrate that transatlantic relations furnish an enduring space for parliamentary diplomacy, norm entrepreneurship and coalition building. It enables EU and US parliamentarians to discuss legislative, regulatory and general political developments; debate their respective approaches to bilateral initiatives (like the TTC) and shared international challenges (like Russia's invasion of Ukraine); and to identify divergences and consider ways to address them.

One of the main *advantages* of transatlantic parliamentary cooperation is the breadth of the platforms and institutional actors involved (above all Speakers, plenaries, committees, delegations, missions, caucuses and dialogues) and the variety of the instruments deployed (chiefly resolutions, reports, statements and, in some cases, legislation). Flexibility is another asset, seen in the widespread use of videoconferencing and in both legislatures' ability to shape the composition of the delegations sent abroad in order to maximise impact. To this should be added relative regularity and frequency of meetings, and, perhaps most importantly, the restoration of enthusiasm for collaboration under the Biden Administration.

The *disadvantages* are equally salient. The most tangible one concerns asymmetry in the institutional arrangements. While the EP has an intricate set of rules and bodies devoted to transatlantic relations, Congress has no Europe-focused inter-parliamentary group, no liaison office in Brussels, and no senators among its TLD delegation. More significantly, many transatlantic diplomatic activities, whether conducted jointly or separately, suffer from insufficient public visibility, follow-up and influence. There is also little consensus over future EP-Congress cooperation and over its projection onto the global arena, which many TLD statements call for. Given the importance of the EU-US relationship, the involvement of non-central legislatures is also unclear.

Lastly, the example of Russia's invasion of Ukraine at once exhibits EU and US parliamentarians' eagerness to engage in diplomacy and utilise foreign policy to express their party political and collective positions, render value judgments, inform their domestic decisions, shape policies and steer political processes. Yet, it also shows the scarcity of mutual coordination, which could otherwise add weight to their efforts and translate into greater clout and effectiveness. Although room for fine-tuning remains, transatlantic interparliamentary cooperation has therefore significantly evolved in the last half a century.

Notes

1 Resolution of 17 February 2022 on the implementation of the Common Foreign and Security Policy–annual report 2021, points 55 and 30.
2 Resolution of 5 July 2018 on the adequacy of the protection afforded by the EU-US Privacy Shield.
3 Resolution of 7 October 2021 on the state law relating to abortion in Texas, USA.
4 Resolution of 9 June 2022 on global threats to abortion rights: the possible overturning of abortion rights in the US by the Supreme Court.
5 Resolution of 8 June 2016 on follow-up to the EP resolution of 11 February 2015 on the US Senate report on the use of torture by the CIA.
6 Resolution of 12 September 2018 on the state of EU-US relations, recital B.
7 See www.europarl.europa.eu/cmsdata/196440/Chairs-D-US-2019.pdf.
8 H.R.4105—116th Congress (2019–2020).
9 H.R.6624—117th Congress (2021–2022).
10 22 U.S. Code §§276d-276p and §1928a.
11 Resolution of 6 October 2021 on the future of EU-US relations.
12 Ibid, point 6.
13 See the intervention by James Elles MEP in the EP debate on the EU-US summit on 13 Dec 2000 and the EP Resolution of 15 May 2002 on the Commission Communication to the Council on Reinforcing the Transatlantic Relationship: Focusing on Strategy and Delivering Results.
14 Ibid, point 8.
15 Ibid, point 95.
16 Ibid, point 25.
17 Resolution of 3 May 2022 on artificial intelligence in a digital age, point 265.
18 Press release, 'MEPs welcome EU-US cooperation in the Trade and Technology Council, call for transparency', 26 October 2021.
19 TTC, Inaugural Joint Statement, 29 September 2021 (Pittsburgh, US); TTC, 2nd Meeting Joint Statement, 16 May 2022 (Paris-Saclay, France).
20 Resolution of 7 July 2021 on EU-NATO cooperation in the context of transatlantic relations.
21 Ibid, point 64.
22 S.Res.123—116th Congress (2019–2020) of 4 April 2019 supporting the North Atlantic Treaty Organization and recognizing its 70 years of accomplishments.
23 The committee name abbreviations used are: Committee on Foreign Affairs (AFET), Subcommittee on Security and Defence (SEDE), Subcommittee on Human Rights (DROI), Committee on International Trade (INTA), Committee on Development (DEVE), Committee on Employment and Social Affairs (EMPL), Committee on Legal Affairs (JURI), Committee on Industry, Research and Energy (ITRE), Committee on Internal Market and Consumer Protection (IMCO), Committee on Civil Liberties, Justice and Home Affairs (LIBE), Committee on Regional Development (REGI), Committee on Constitutional Affairs (AFCO), Committee on Women's Rights and Gender Equality (FEMM), Special Committee on Foreign Interference in all Democratic Processes in the European Union, including Disinformation (INGE), and Special Committee on Artificial Intelligence in a Digital Age (AIDA).
24 AFET-DROI-SEDE, Mission Report (New York & Washington DC, 27–31 October 2019).
25 AFET-SEDE, Mission Report (UN Headquarters, New York, 1–2 November 2021), 7.
26 AFET, Activity Report 2014–2019, 16.
27 INTA, Mission Report (Washington DC, 1–5 November 2021), 2.
28 Ibid, 5 and 2.
29 INTA, Mission Report (Buenos Aires, Argentina, 9–13 December 2017), 5.

30 LIBE, Mission Report (Washington DC & Boston, 24–28 Feb 2020); LIBE, Mission Report (Washington DC & San Francisco/Silicon Valley, 16–20 May 2016).
31 84th TLD, Joint Statement (Paris, France, 22 May 2022), 7.
32 AFET-SEDE, Mission Report (Kyiv, Zaporyzhzhya & Mariupol, 30 January-1 February 2022).
33 TLD, 'Co-Chairs Costa, Sikorski Issue Statement following the Russian invasion of Ukraine', 26 February 2022.
34 EPRS, Briefing 'Russia's war on Ukraine: Speeches by Ukraine's President to the European Parliament and national parliaments', April 2022.
35 Resolution of 1 March 2022 on the Russian aggression against Ukraine, point 21.
36 AFET, Hearing 'Transatlantic cooperation following Russian aggression on Ukraine', 14 March 2022.
37 Press release, 'Metsola: Courage and Hope to the People of Ukraine', 1 April 2022.
38 Supra n 31.
39 'Bipartisan Senate delegation meets with Ukrainian leaders amid Russia tensions', *Washington Post*, 17 January 2022.
40 'Meeks leading bipartisan trip to Ukraine amid Russia tensions', *The Hill*, 25 January 2022.
41 S.Res.519—117th Congress (2021–2022).
42 H.Res.956—117th Congress (2021–2022).
43 S.Res.546—117th Congress (2021–2022).
44 'Nancy Pelosi leads surprise delegation to Kyiv and Poland, and vows US support', *CNBC*, 1 May 2022.
45 'Zelensky awards Pelosi the Order of Princess Olga, a Ukrainian civil honor', *Washington Post*, 1 May 2022.
46 'McConnell leads delegation of Republican senators to Kyiv', *Politico*, 14 May 2022.
47 'US senators visit Kyiv to promote Russia "state sponsor of terrorism" bill', *Reuters*, 7 July 2022.
48 'Bipartisan House delegation meets with Zelensky in Kyiv', *The Hill*, 23 July 2022.
49 'Volodymyr Zelenskyy met with US Senators Robert Portman and Amy Klobuchar', 30 August 2022, www.president.gov.ua/en/news/volodimir-zelenskij-zustrivsya-z-senatorami-ssha-robertom-po-77425.
50 S.Res.623—117th Congress (2021–2022).
51 H.Res.1113—117th Congress (2021–2022).
52 H.R.8568—117th Congress (2021–2022).

References

Akhtar, S. I. et al. (2022) 'US-EU trade relations', *CRS Report R47095*.
Barker, T. (2021) 'The hidden G2 for democratic tech governance is the EU-US relationship: A starter kit', *DGAP Analysis no. 2*.
Blanc, E. (2023) 'Recognition through dialogue: how transatlantic relations anchor the EU's identity', *The British Journal of Politics and International Relations* 25(1).
Blockmans, S. (2021) 'EU-US relations: reinventing the Transatlantic Agenda', *Intereconomics* 56(1): 5–7.
Brattberg, E. (2020) 'Reinventing transatlantic relations on climate, democracy, and technology', *Carnegie Endowment for International Peace Working Paper*.
Caspary, D. et al. (2021) 'Biden in Brussels–what's in the "in-tray"?', *EUobserver*, 15 June.
Chase, P. (2021) 'Reframing and energizing transatlantic regulatory cooperation', *Revue Européenne du Droit* 3: 85–90.
Coremans, E. (2017) 'From access to documents to consumption of information: the European Commission transparency policy for the TTIP negotiations', *Politics and Governance* 5(3): 29–39.

Coremans, E. and Meissner, K. L. (2018) 'Putting power into practice: administrative and political capacity building in the European Parliament's Committee for International Trade', *Public Administration* 96(3): 561–577.

Dri, C. (2010) 'Limits of the institutional mimesis of the European Union: the case of the Mercosur Parliament', *Latin American Policy* 1(1): 52–74.

Eckes, C. (2014) 'How the European Parliament's participation in international relations affects the deep tissue of the EU's power structures', *International Journal of Constitutional Law* 12(4): 904–929.

Fahey, E. and Terpan, F. (2021) 'Torn between institutionalisation and judicialisation: the demise of the EU-US privacy shield', *Indiana Journal of Global Legal Studies* 28(2): 205–244.

Fonck, D. (2019) Servants or rivals? Uncovering the drivers and logics of the European Parliament's diplomacy during the Ukrainian crisis. *In:* K. Raube, M. Baç, and J. Wouters (eds), *Parliamentary cooperation and diplomacy in EU external relations: an essential companion*. Cheltenham: Edward Elgar, 306–322.

Gardner, A. L. (2020) *Stars with stripes: the essential partnership between the European Union and the United States*. Cham: Palgrave Macmillan.

Howorth, J. (2009) 'A new institutional architecture for the transatlantic relationship?', *IFRI Europe Visions no. 5*.

Jancic, D. (2014) The European Parliament and EU-US relations: revamping institutional cooperation?. *In:* E. Fahey and D. Curtin (eds), *A transatlantic community of law: legal perspectives on the relationship between the EU and US legal orders*. Cambridge: Cambridge University Press, 35–68.

Jancic, D. (2016) 'The role of the European Parliament and the US Congress in shaping transatlantic relations: TTIP, NSA surveillance and CIA renditions', *Journal of Common Market Studies* 54(4): 896–912.

Jancic, D. (2015a) The transatlantic connection: democratising Euro-American relations through parliamentary liaison. *In:* S. Stavridis and D. Irrera (eds), *The European Parliament and its international relations*. London: Routledge, 178–196.

Jancic, D. (2015b) 'Transatlantic regulatory interdependence, law and governance: the evolving roles of the EU and US legislatures', *Cambridge Yearbook of European Legal Studies* 17: 334–359.

Jancic, D. (2017) 'TTIP and legislative-executive relations in EU trade policy', *West European Politics* 40(1): 202–221.

Kleizen, B. (2016) 'Mapping the involvement of the European Parliament in EU external relations–a legal and empirical analysis', *CLEER Papers 4*.

Lazarou, E. (2020) Transatlantic parliamentary diplomacy: contributing to the future of transatlantic relations. *In:* S. R. Soare (ed.), *Turning the tide: how to rescue transatlantic relations*. Paris: EU Institute for Security Studies, 60–74.

Meissner, K. (2016) 'Democratizing EU external relations: the European Parliament's informal role in SWIFT, ACTA, and TTIP', *European Foreign Affairs Review* 21(2): 269–288.

Meissner, K. L. and Schoeller, M. G. (2019) 'Rising despite the polycrisis? The European Parliament's strategies of self-empowerment after Lisbon' *Journal of European Public Policy* 26(7): 1075–1093.

Moraes, C. (2018) The European Parliament and transatlantic relations: personal reflections. *In*: E. Fahey (ed.), *Institutionalisation beyond the nation state–transatlantic relations: data, privacy and trade law*. Cham: Springer, 31–38.

Nitoiu, C. and Sus, M. (2017) 'The European Parliament's diplomacy: a tool for projecting EU power in times of crisis? The case of the Cox-Kwasniewski mission', *Journal of Common Market Studies* 55(1): 71–86.

Petersmann, E.-U. and Pollack, M. A. (eds) (2003). *Transatlantic economic disputes: the EU, the US, and the WTO*. Oxford: Oxford University Press.

Redei, L. and Romanyshyn, I. (2019) 'Non-parliamentary diplomacy: the European Parliament's diplomatic mission to Ukraine', *European Foreign Affairs Review* 24(1): 61–80.

Roederer-Rynning, C. (2017) 'Parliamentary assertion and deep integration: the European Parliament in the CETA and TTIP negotiations', *Cambridge Review of International Affairs* 30(5–6): 507–526.

Servent, A. R. and MacKenzie, A. (2012) 'The European Parliament as a "norm taker"? EU-US relations after the SWIFT agreement', *European Foreign Affairs Review* 17(2): 71–86.

Šabič, Z. (2017) Parliamentary diplomacy and the US Congress: the case of the NATO Parliamentary Assembly. *In:* S. Stavridis and D. Jancic (eds), *Parliamentary diplomacy in European and global governance*. Leiden: Brill, 213–229.

Stavridis, S. and Jancic, D. (eds) (2017) *Parliamentary diplomacy in European and global governance*. Leiden: Brill.

Stavridis, S. and Irrera, D. (eds) (2015), *The European Parliament and its international relations*. London: Routledge.

Stokes, B. (2021) 'A new transatlantic era needs new institutions', *GMF Insights*.

Whitman, R. (ed.) (2011) *Normative power Europe: empirical and theoretical perspectives*. Basingstoke: Palgrave Macmillan.

5

THE RISE OF INFORMAL INTERNATIONAL ORGANIZATIONS

Charles B. Roger

IBEI

Introduction

Global governance has been shifting in new directions. Whereas in the past, international cooperation primarily occurred through diplomacy, international treaties, and formal international organizations (IOs), like the United Nations and the World Bank, it has increasingly been achieved via informal means, like transgovernmental networks, soft law, and informal IOs. These varieties of governance differ from their predecessors in several ways, but primarily because they occur outside of traditional diplomatic channels and through instruments that are non-binding in nature. Previously, interactions between officials were heavily mediated by professional diplomats with well-established relationships governed by a complex system of customary international law, and agreements were legally "binding." IOs were constituted by treaties and underpinned by a host of legal privileges and immunities. Now, officials within states interact on a regular basis, states sign numerous non-binding agreements, and policymakers conduct their relations within institutions that fall outside of the traditional boundaries of international law (Kennan 1997; Abbott and Snidal 2000; Slaughter 2000; Roger 2020; Vabulas and Snidal 2021).

This "move" to informality is a global trend. Yet it has been especially pronounced within the Transatlantic area. To some, this claim may seem puzzling. Usually, it has been states in other regions, like the Asia-Pacific, that have typically been said to hold a strong preference for informal cooperation (Kahler 2000). There, we see institutions like APEC, ASEAN, and the Quad, which have been noted for their informality. They have often been contrasted with the highly "legalized" institutions that exist in the Transatlantic area—the European Union (EU), the North Atlantic Treaty Organization (NATO), the Organisation for Economic Co-operation and Development (OECD), and so on. But the contrast is misleading. While Transatlantic states are certainly knitted together via numerous treaties and

DOI: 10.4324/9781003283911-7

formal IOs—arguably, far more than elsewhere—they have also been significant creators of informal arrangements. Indeed, in relative terms, informal bodies now comprise a significant share of the governance portfolios of states in the Transatlantic area. And it is here, interestingly, where the largest number of informal IOs have appeared—where the "move" has gone the furthest.

Why has the Transatlantic area embraced informal governance to such an extent? Despite the region's prominence in political discourse, we have surprisingly few answers. In recent years, numerous studies have appeared to explain why states rely on informal institutions in specific contexts (Stone 2011; Vabulas and Snidal 2013; Roger 2020). These have called attention to a range of factors, including the nature of the cooperation problems states confront, the distribution of power and the scope for conflict between them, as well as political dynamics that occur within their domestic political arenas. Together, these have told us much about what drives states to create informal IOs. Yet, most of these studies explain why states opt for informality in specific cooperative contexts and only a handful have asked why certain *regions* have embraced informality to a greater or less or extent. Of these, the Asia-Pacific has been the primary focus (Kahler 2000; Jetschke 2009; Kahler and MacIntyre 2013; Pakkanen 2016). Since the region has historically been noted for the degree to which it has embraced informal governance, as described, it makes sense that efforts have concentrated there. Yet this narrow focus has meant that our understanding of others remains limited. Further, because Transatlantic relations have frequently been regarded as especially legalized, the area has been particularly neglected.

In this chapter, I close this gap in our understanding by exploring the drivers of informality in this region. I begin, in the next section, by first presenting evidence on the shifting patterns of governance within the Transatlantic area, comparing it with the Asia-Pacific case in particular. In doing so, I show that Transatlantic states are indeed the most significant users of informal IOs. In the third section, I discuss the different causal logics underlying the main arguments that have been advanced by scholars to explain why states create informal institutions, focusing especially on cooperation problems, state power, and domestic politics—in particular, growing polarization and the rise of the regulatory state. I show that each offers insights into patterns in the Transatlantic area, but their relative impacts remain unclear. In the fourth section, I then conduct a quantitative analysis that draws on a novel dataset of formal and informal IOs created by OECD states to evaluate and weigh the different roles these factors have played. I show that while all are important, changing cooperation problems and changing domestic political dynamics within powerful states have been the most significant drivers of informality. In the conclusion, I reflect on what this means for Transatlantic relations more generally. I point, specifically, to some of the more worrying implications this study has for the robustness of cooperation in the region.

Informal IOs in the Transatlantic area

The move to informality is now a well-document trend in international relations (IR; Roger 2020; Roger and Rowan 2022a; Vabulas and Snidal 2021). Increasingly, around the world and across a range of issue areas, states are relying less on highly legalized cooperative instruments, like international treaties and formal IOs, and relatively more on institutions that deliberately avoid creating legal obligations between states (Abbott and Snidal 2000; Shaffer and Pollack 2010; Pauwelyn, Wessel, and Wouters 2012). These new modes of governance include informal international agreements, or "soft law," which go by a variety of names in practice but are more generally referred to as "memorandums of understanding" (Lipson 1991; Aust 2012). Perhaps most prominently, though, they include a variety of informal IOs—defined as international organizations, created by states, that lack a firm legal basis in international law (Roger and Rowan 2022b). At the global level, well-known examples include bodies like the Group of Twenty (G20), the BRICS Summits, and the Financial Stability Board (FSB). But these are, in fact, only the tip of a vast "iceberg" of informal institutions that have been of increasing interest to scholars of IR. In recent years, a range of studies have been published on these entities seeking to measure their frequency in international politics, explain their growth, explore how they work, and understand their broader impacts.

These efforts have reached several important descriptive findings. First, while informal IO have clearly grown over time, there is significant variation in their prevalence across issue areas. Vabulas and Snidal (2021) have shown that informal IOs appear to be disproportionately involved in areas of "high politics," like security, political affairs, and many economic issues. Leading examples include security institutions, like the Nuclear Suppliers Group, the Proliferation Security Initiative, and the Wassenaar Arrangement; political institutions, like the BRICS and the Group of Seven (G7); and economic institutions, like the Basel Committee on Banking Supervision and the Financial Action Task Force. Second, there is significant regional variation in the distribution of informal bodies. This had, in fact, long been a presupposition of scholars. Miles Kahler (2000) and others have observed, for instance, that Asia-Pacific states have revealed a strong preference for informal governance (see also Kahler and MacIntyre 2013; Pakkanen 2016). This was thought to contrast sharply with the supposedly opposing preference for legalized cooperation elsewhere, especially among states in Western Europe and North America. However, subsequent research has shown that the contrast between Asia-Pacific and European states at the heart of these studies is not as sharp as it seems.

Indeed, if we look closely at data from Roger (2020) and Roger and Rowan (2022b), informal IOs have become a prominent fixture of cooperation in the Transatlantic area. Figure 5.1 presents both the absolute numbers of informal IOs that Transatlantic and Asia-Pacific states have created since 1945, and the changing relative share of informal IOs in their overall governance portfolios. It shows, first, that informal IOs have become important governance instruments for states in both regions. In relative terms, Asia-Pacific states appear to have created many informal IOs early on—a fact that may account for the widespread perception that that they are particularly disposed to informal cooperation. But, across both Transatlantic and Asia-Pacific states, informal IOs have become crucial tools of governance, constituting nearly 45% of all the IOs they have created. In this sense, the two regions are much more comparable than earlier studies have suggested. However, the shift in the

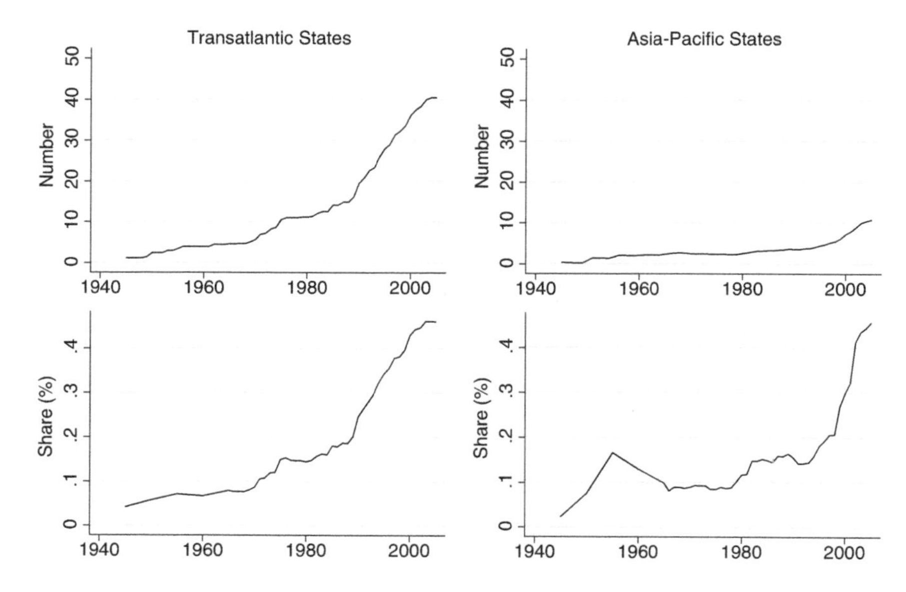

Figure 5.1 Governance Portfolios

Transatlantic area is even more pronounced if we consider the absolute number of informal IOs these states have established. While the average Asia-Pacific state had, by 2005, created around 10 informal IOs, a typical Transatlantic state was involved in creating over 40. This is a significant difference and reveals the prominent role that Transatlantic states have been playing in the overall growth of informality in world politics. While formal institutions have undoubtable been important for these states—representing a major part of their approach to cross-border governance, as other studies have shown—in no other region has informal governance become so important in both absolute and relative terms.

Why informality? Theorizing problems, power, and politics

The growing prominence of informal IOs raises the inevitable question of why this has occurred. On this front, as explained already, scholars have highlighted several causal mechanisms. Most of these have broad applicability and may apply anywhere that informality appears. Further, there is already evidence that each has played a role. However, their importance may vary to some degree depending on the region or issue area we consider, and some are likely to be particularly relevant to answering the specific question that this chapter deals with: why has informality grown in the Transatlantic area? In what follows, therefore, I outline these mechanisms—focused on 1) cooperation problems, 2) the distribution of interests and power, and 3) domestic politics—which have already achieved some prominence in the literature. I discuss the causal logic of the arguments and some of the basic evidence for each. In the following section, I then weigh the importance of these explanations through a quantitative analysis.

The first and perhaps most common approach to understanding the growth of informal IOs is one that emphasizes the nature of the problems states face. Often, such arguments have been couched in the language established by the "rational design" tradition of IR, which suggests that different problems create incentives for states to opt for contrasting designs (Koremenos 2016). Along these lines, scholars such as Vabulas and Snidal (2013) have advanced arguments suggesting that informal IOs have distinct properties that make them better or worse at solving certain kinds of cross-border challenges. They are, for instance, hypothesized to be better at addressing issues where speed is essential to success, where agility is needed, or where greater confidentiality is important—all qualities that informal IOs are thought to possess. Formal IOs, by contrast, are believed to be advantageous when speed, agility, and confidentiality are less important—and, especially, when there is high potential for opportunism. If correct, we can then expect to find a strong correlation between different institutional designs and the specific problems states confront. Of course, such arguments are not unique to Vabulas and Snidal and their theory of informality is not limited to these factors alone; other scholars have advanced similar ideas. In some cases, the specific hypotheses are different—occasionally, even contradictory. But, in each, the basic argumentative logic is virtually identical.

Although the arguments advanced by these scholars are not typically extended in this way, they do suggest a common narrative about the rise of informal IOs, which may well apply to Transatlantic states. In particular, they suggest that if the type of cooperation problem that states face is a major driver of institutional design, then the rise of informal IOs is likely to be a product of changes in the character of the issues that states have confronted over time. If informality is more likely to be chosen when cooperation problems require greater agility, flexibility, confidentiality, and so on, then states must be confronting problems with these characteristics more frequently. Such a shift in the nature of the problems states face is often linked to the deepening of interdependence. Tony Porter has, for instance, located the causes of the shift toward what he refers to as "transnational institutions"—a broad category that includes informal bodies—in a number of broader systemic changes, primarily related to the process of globalization (Porter 2012, p. 26). The current world economy, he notes, is distinguished by an accelerated pace of events, more frequent crises, and growing uncertainty about the future, which are jointly responsible for larger changes in the nature of international institutions. "With acceleration," he argues, "formal law and traditional bureaucratic international organizations can be too slow" (Ibid, p. 26.). The growth of uncertainty and systemic risks is, in turn, associated with more flexible, more informal, and less centralized institutions. Given the extent of interdependence in the Transatlantic area, this is a highly probable explanation of the pattern we see.

Such accounts are not the only explanations on offer, of course. Another group has advanced quite different arguments that focus primarily on state interests and the distribution of power. Randall Stone's work is exemplary in this regard. In his book *Controlling Institutions* and elsewhere, he has argued that informality tends to increase when the preferences of states conflict and when power is more unequal (Stone 2011; 2013). When preferences are at odds with one another, powerful states may reasonably expect that they will want to intervene more frequently in political affairs in a more ad hoc manner; and, when power is unevenly distributed, that they can act quite freely and do not need to bring smaller states—who generally prefer greater formality, given its ability to "bind" stronger states—on board. At the global level, the relevance of these dynamics for the growth of informality has been demonstrated in work by Prantl (2014) and Vabulas and Snidal (2020). Empirically, their arguments have focused on the impact of rising powers, like China, India, and Brazil, who have increasingly challenged the liberal international order. But power-based explanations may, equally, help to explain patterns of governance in the Transatlantic area. With a host of small and large states with vastly different resources—from Portugal and Luxembourg to "great powers," like Germany and the United States—power differentials are fairly high; and, in the postwar period, the region has been characterized by both cooperation and high levels of conflict (Drezner 2007; Pollack and Shaffer 2009; Farrell and Newman 2019).

The final set of causal mechanisms that I focus on locate the drivers of informality squarely within the domestic political arenas of powerful states—where internal changes have projected outward to shape the global political landscape. Specifically, building on Roger (2020), I argue that two domestic "shifts" can be linked to the rise of informal IOs. The first is the rise of the regulatory state. In recent years, numerous studies have observed that a major revolution has taken place over the past century, as states have shifted away consistently, if unevenly, from direct interventions in markets and toward indirect rule by independent agencies (Jordana, Levi-Faur, and Fernández-i-Marín 2011). This has transformed governance within states, but has also been shown to have international repercussions since these agencies generally prefer to avoid legalization, like to act with greater autonomy in the international arena, and generally aim to limit the scope for domestic interventions in their affairs (Damro 2006; Bach 2010; Roger 2020). The rise of informal IOs in the Transatlantic area can, accordingly, be regarded as an extension of this trend. States embracing such an approach to domestic issues—which are particularly common in the region—tend to prefer "lite" institutions, since they more closely correspond with the prevailing logic of governance and are strongly preferred by the growing number of agencies that have been increasingly drawn into international affairs. The character of the dominant institutions in the regional system would then mirror those prevalent within the political arenas of the states involved, especially those with the power to control the institutional design process.

The second shift behind the rise of informal IOs is the growth of polarization and divided government within the domestic political arenas of powerful states, which has generally made policymaking more difficult over time. Today, for instance, many lament the extent to which American legislative politics has been hindered by political partisanship—caused by growing economic inequality, conflicting ideologies, interest group politics, and years of gerrymandering (McCarty, Poole, and Rosenthal 2006). The problem seems particularly acute at present, but it is actually a long-term trend. Since the end of the Second World War, polarization and legislative gridlock have steadily increased (Binder 2003). This has extended to and limited the United States' ability to ratify formal agreements and created an additional incentive for informal institutions, which can be used as a substitute. In recent years, as David Kaye has put it, "the U.S. Senate [has rejected] multilateral treaties as if it were a sport" and this has increasingly forced policymakers to search for alternative forms of international cooperation that do not rely upon these formal instruments—what he calls "stealth multilateralism" (Kaye 2013, p. 113). While the trend is most apparent within the United States, it has affected a host of other powerful Transatlantic states as well. France, Germany, and the UK, for instance, have seen more divided and minority/coalition governments since the 1970s and 1980s (Elgie 2001). The dynamics behind this trend are likely to be different in each case, but the overall effect is very much the same: policymaking has become more difficult, and has been leading policymakers to rely upon informal governance as a way of bypassing domestic opposition.

Before moving on to the empirical analysis, it is important to note that these hypotheses are not mutually exclusive. Indeed, it is possible that the growth of informal IOs in the Transatlantic area—and the global system, more generally—has been a function of several overlapping dynamics. Existing studies certainly provide evidence that each is operating, to a degree. However, if this is the case, a second-order question—noted earlier—naturally follows: what are the relative effects or weights of these different factors? If all have played a role in the governance shift that we see in Transatlantic relations, have domestic politics or global shifts been more important? The following section attempts to disentangle the dynamics at work to provide an answer to this question.

Analyzing the drivers of informality

The statistical analysis in this chapter uses a sample of 90 formal and informal IOs drawn from the larger database created by Roger (2020) and Roger and Rowan (2022a; 2022b). It contains virtually all of the formal and informal IOs created exclusively by OECD states between the years 1950 and 2005. Formality is measured dichotomously, reflecting the contrasting legal bases of each type, with formal IOs receiving a score of 0 and informal IOs receiving a score of 1. Of course, OECD states have created many formal and informal IOs with countries from beyond the Transatlantic area, and many have been created in other regions. This naturally limits what we can say about the drivers of trends in other regions, like the Asia-Pacific, where dynamics may be different. But this focus does allow us to speak directly to the question of what has been occurring within the Transatlantic area. Further, since these states are some of the most significant creators of formal and informal IOs in quantitative terms, this does have important implications for our overall understanding of the move to informality as well.

The first independent variable that I develop, *Agencies*, is designed to measure the idea that a group of states are more likely to create an informal IO if powerful states in that group have embraced new modes of governance domestically. The signature institutions exemplifying such new modes of governance are, as mentioned earlier, independent agencies, such as the Securities and Exchange Commission (SEC) and the Federal Trade Commission (FTC) in the United States (Levi-Faur 2005; Pollitt et al. 2005). Given this, it is reasonable to think that when there are many such agencies within the most powerful states involved in creating an IO, we should expect the creation of an informal IO to be more likely, if the theory is correct. On the basis of this insight, I develop a measure that relies on the database created by Jordana at al., which measures the number of independent agencies across a set number of issue areas within (mainly) OECD states (Jordana, Levi-Faur, and Fernández-i-Marín 2011). The variable is created by recording the value that this measure takes for each "founding" state in the year that each IO in the database is established, weighting this value by GDP to take into account the fact that it is the preferences of the most powerful states that matter most, and summing these values.[1] In this way, the variable provides us with an estimate of the extent to which new modes of governance have been embraced by the most powerful states involved in creating each IO in the database. If the theory is right, we should expect this to have a positive relationship with the dependent variable.

The second variable, *Constraints*, is intended to evaluate the idea that informal IOs should become more likely as powerful states are subject to greater domestic constraints over time. *Constraints* is modeled on a similar variable utilized in the analysis in Roger (2020). It uses data from the Henisz's (2002) veto players database to measure the extent of domestic constraints within the states involved in creating each of the IOs in the dataset across different periods of time. As with *Agencies*, I record the value that the measure takes for each state in the year that an IO is established. Again, to take into account the idea that it is the constraints in the most powerful states that should matter most for questions of institutional design, I also weight these values by each state's GDP in that year. After summing these values, we then have a measure of the domestic constraints faced by policymakers in the most powerful states involved in creating each of the IOs in the sample. If the expectation I have articulated in the last section is correct, states should be more likely to create an informal IO when *Constraints* takes a high value.

Next, to test the central functionalist hypothesis, I have developed a third main variable, *Interdependence*, which measures the extent of globalization between states. Globalization is, of course, a multidimensional phenomenon that encompasses economic, social, and political forms of integration. A number of scholars have, therefore, developed measures of globalization that aim to capture the overarching concept with a great deal of subtlety (Held et al. 1999; Dreher, Gaston, and Martens 2008). However, these are generally not suitable for our purposes here, since they tell us about the degree to which a state is globalized but not the particular ties that link states together. For this reason, I have developed a variable modeled on the one used by Haftel and Thompson (2006), which measures the average level of intra-IO trade relative to overall levels of international trade, relying on data from the Correlates of War Bilateral Trade Database (Barbieri, Keshk, and Pollins 2009). This variable is limited in that it does not capture all of the relevant dimensions of globalization, but it does provide a valuable indication of how tightly integrated a particular group of states is at the time that an IO is established. A higher value indicates that a group of founding states trades more with each other than they do with the rest of the world. And, if functionalist drivers are important, this should make it more likely that an IO will be informal.

Finally, in order to assess power-based explanations I develop two variables, *Interests* and *Power*. To create *Interests*, I followed a similar approach to Koremenos (2016) who uses the Affinity of Nations index (Gartzke 2006)—based on UN General Assembly voting—to assess whether state preferences are more or less aligned. In that database, the individual dyadic values are positively valued when states vote alike. Here, the dyadic values for all the states involved in creating an IO are recorded and averaged, and I have inverted the measure to ease interpretation. The resulting variable indicates the degree to which a founding group of states have divergent preferences at the time that an IO is established. If the first power-based hypothesis is right, then, this should increase the probability that an IO will be informal. The second power-based variable I create is intended to test the second main hypothesis emerging from these studies: that more or less equal groups of states are likely to opt for informality less (or more) frequently. To test this idea, *Power* is a measure of economic inequality across the states involved in creating each IO in the dataset. Specifically, it is created by calculating a Gini-coefficient (ranging from 0 to 1) using GDP data for each group of founding states.

Table 5.1 presents results from a probit analysis that employs these variables. The first four models report the basic relationships between the main variables and the

Table 5.1 Regression Results

VARIABLES	*1*	*2*	*3*	*4*	*5*	*6*
Agencies	0.182***				0.163***	0.148***
	(0.0461)				(0.0466)	(0.0507)
Constraints		9.560***			9.172**	11.51**
		(3.105)			(4.100)	(4.587)
Interdependence			1.445*		2.316**	2.330**
			(0.754)		(1.035)	(1.160)
Interests				1.851**	2.665**	2.917**
				(0.883)	(1.165)	(1.284)
Power				−0.0490	−1.919	−2.175
				(0.944)	(1.309)	(1.557)
Environment						−6.704***
						(0.729)
Security						−5.637***
						(0.418)
Economic						−6.287***
						(0.729)
Scientific						−6.891***
						(0.889)
Constant	−1.351***	−0.196	−0.746**	1.195	0.905	7.763***
	(0.286)	(0.139)	(0.301)	(0.835)	(1.209)	(1.491)
Observations	90	90	90	89	89	89

Robust standard errors in parentheses, *** p<0.01, ** p<0.05, * p<0.1.

outcome: *Informality*. Models 1 and 2 show that the two domestic politics variables, *Agencies* and *Constraints*, are statistically significant at the 0.001 confidence level and indicate that both are positively associated with informality. In Model 3, *Interdependence* is statistically significant at the 0.1 level, and also tends to increase the likelihood that states will create an informal IO. Finally, in Model 4, *Interests* and *Power* are included but only the former is statistically significant and indicates that there is a positive relationship between conflicting interests and informality. These results remain broadly the same when each of the variables is included in the same model, as shown in Model 5. All the coefficients maintain their signs and significance levels. Finally, Model 6 includes several additional controls for the different issue areas that organizations are active in to address any unobserved heterogeneity at this level. The central results, again, maintain their signs and significance levels. The controls are also, notably, significant suggesting that there are some baseline differences across organizations active in different issue areas.

This analysis suggests that all the main mechanisms—with the exception of inequalities of power—are important for determining whether an IO is likely to be formal or informal. However, the results do not tell us anything about the relative size of these effects, and whether one or the other causal mechanism seems to play a more significant role, overall, in driving informality in the Transatlantic area. To gain some insight into the magnitudes of each variable's impact, I first present the semi-standardized coefficients for each in Figure 5.2, which enables easy comparisons of their relative impacts. These estimates are derived from Model 5 and show how the (logged) odds that an IO will be informal shift in response to similar one-standard deviation changes in the main independent variables. Here, we see that *Agencies* has the largest effect on the outcome. A one-standard deviation increase in *Agencies* tends to increase the odds that states will create an informal IO by roughly 0.7. *Constraints* has the second-largest effect. A one-standard deviation increase in the variable raises the odds that states will create an

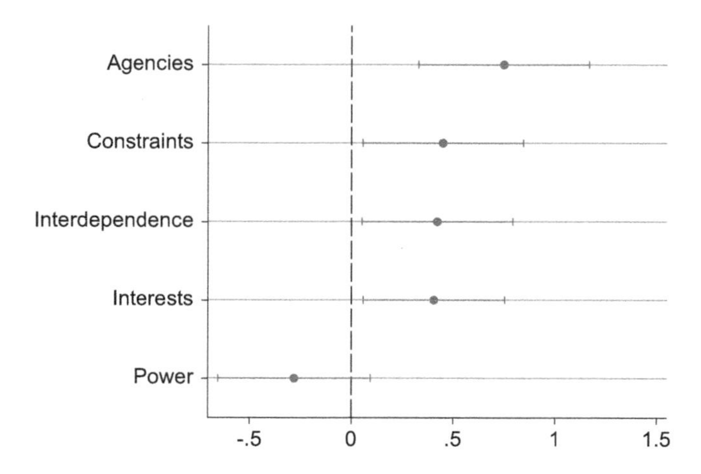

Figure 5.2 Semi-standardized Coefficient Plot

informal IO by about 0.5. Finally, one-standard deviation increases in *Interdependence* and *Interests* tend to increase the probability of informality by somewhat smaller amounts.

These findings suggest that the two domestic political factors—domestic constraints and the embrace of new modes of domestic governance—have had the largest impact on informality across Transatlantic states. Cooperation problems and conflicting interests have been important as well, although their impact appears to have been somewhat smaller by comparison. And, if anything, inequalities of power seem to have had a negative effect. To illustrate the different historical impacts of each variable, I also generate predicted probabilities that show the likelihood of the IOs states create being informal at specific points in time. These are displayed in Figure 5.3. Each prediction is calculated using the actual values for each variable in the years that each IO in the dataset was created—holding all others at their means—and the coefficients from Model 6 to generate estimates of how the overall likelihood of informal IOs emerging has changed between 1950 and 2005. In this way, we can attempt to isolate, to some degree, the hypothetical effect of the real changes that took place over the period of analysis.

Confirming but expanding upon the marginal effects estimates displayed in Figure 5.3, the top-left panel shows that the growing embrace of new modes of governance in powerful states made it much more likely that states would create informal IOs over time. The fitted line shows that, given the actual changes we see in this variable alone, the average probability that states would create informal IOs rose from about 0.2 in the 1950s to about 0.65 in 2005. The top-right panel shows

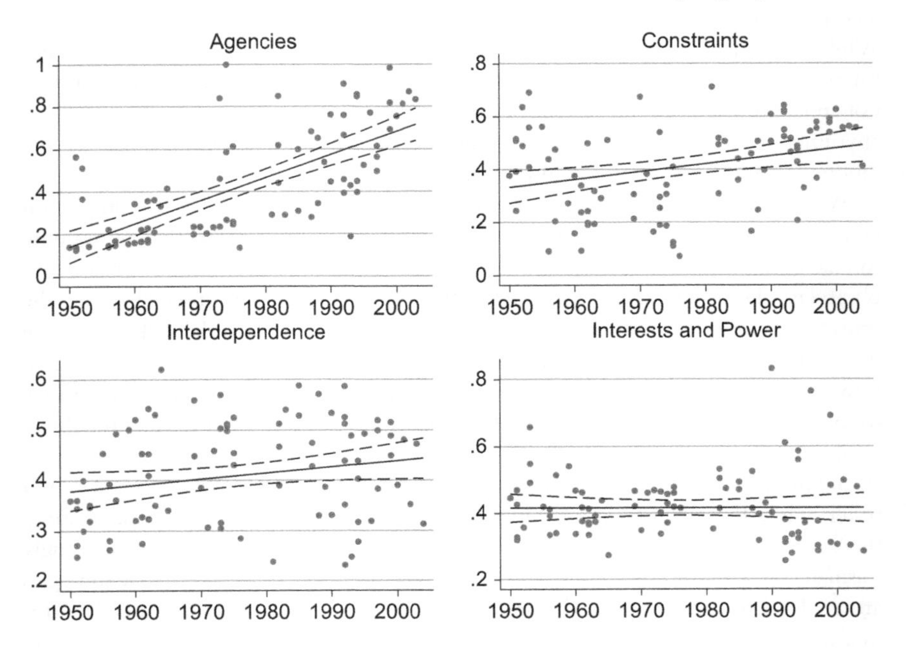

Figure 5.3 Predicted Probabilities, 1950–2005

similar estimates for *Constraints* and reveals a somewhat smaller overall effect. Growing domestic constraints in powerful states tended to marginally increase the likelihood that states would create informal IOs from about 0.37 in 1950 to 0.51 over the same period. The effect of deepening interdependence on institutional design, visualized in the bottom-left panel, shows that globalization may have increased the likelihood that IOs would be created informally, with the average probability of them emerging rising from about .39 in 1950 to only .48 in 2005. Interestingly, conflicting *Interests* and *Power* inequalities appear to have modestly reduce the likelihood that states would create informal IOs, with the trend line falling somewhat from 1950 to 2005.

Conclusion

This chapter has aimed to develop two important insights into patterns of governance in the Transatlantic area. First, in contrast with past work that has juxtaposed the highly legalized institutions created by Transatlantic states with the less legalized ones created by Asia-Pacific states, it has demonstrated that states in the region have rapidly become prominent creators of informal institutions. Second, it has explored the reasons for this growth by drawing on and adapting existing theories of informality and weighing the relative roles of each causal mechanism. It showed, specifically, that domestic political factors—growing polarization and the rise of the regulatory state—appear to have had the largest impact overall. Deepening independence and conflicting preferences were also shown to be important, if somewhat secondary factors, yet only the first appears to have played a major historical role. While conflicting interests do appear to increase the probability that states will opt for an informal design in specific instances, the preferences of Transatlantic states do not appear to have become noticeably more conflictual over the period of analysis. If anything, they became less so, and this may have modestly worked against the "move" to informality we see in the region.

What does all this mean for Transatlantic governance? Perhaps the most important take-away is that the growth of informal IOs has not simply been an efficient response to changing problems, as some have supposed. In line with functionalist arguments, observers like Anne-Marie Slaughter (2000, p.179) have, for instance, seen the growth of informal institutions as a welcome change from the "slow-moving dinosaurs"—formal IOs—of the postwar era. The arguments presented here suggest, however, that while changing cooperation problems have been important, the move to informality has primarily occurred for reasons that are unrelated to the underlying issues institutions are asked to address—because they help bureaucrats to operate more autonomously and help policymakers to bypass domestic constraints, for instance. As a result, while the quantity of institutions in the Transatlantic area may be increasing, there is evidence of a decline in their quality, as institutions have become increasingly mismatched with the problems states face (Roger 2020, pp. 203–211). While strategies are available to supplement and thereby improve their designs (see Roger 2022), it is unclear that these are sufficient on their own to fully compensate for the deficiencies inherent within the informal order that has appeared.

Note

1 All the GDP data in this article comes from Gleditsch (2002).

References

Abbott, Kenneth W., and Duncan Snidal. 2000. "Hard and Soft Law in International Governance." *International Organization* 54 (3): 421–456.

Aust, Anthony. 2012. "Alternatives to Treaty-Making: MOUs as Political Commitments." In *The Oxford Guide to Treaties*, edited by Duncan B. Hollis. Oxford: Oxford University Press.

Bach, David. 2010. "Varieties of Cooperation: The Domestic Institutional Roots of Global Governance." *Review of International Studies* 36 (3): 561–589.

Barbieri, Katherine, Omar M. G. Keshk, and Brian Pollins. 2009. "Trading Data: Evaluating Our Assumptions and Coding Rules." *Conflict Management and Peace Science* 26 (5): 471–491.

Binder, Sarah A. 2003. *Stalemate: Causes and Consequences of Legislative Gridlock*. Washington, DC: The Brookings Institution.

Damro, Chad. 2006. *Cooperating on Competition in Transatlantic Economic Relations: The Politics of Dispute Prevention*. London: Palgrave Macmillan.

Dreher, Axel, Noel Gaston, and Pim Martens. 2008. *Measuring Globalization: Gauging Its Consequences*. New York: Springer.

Drezner, Daniel. 2007. *All Politics Is Global: Explaining International Regulatory Regimes*. Princeton: Princeton University Press.

Elgie, Robert. 2001. *Divided Government in Comparative Perspective*. Oxford: Oxford University Press.

Farrell, Henry, and Abraham L. Newman. 2019. *Of Privacy and Power: The Transataltic Struggle over Freedem and Security*. Princeton: Princeton University Press.

Gartzke, Erik. 2006. *The Affinity of Nations Index, 1946–2002 (Version 4.0)*. https://pages.ucsd.edu/~egartzke/data/affinity_codebook_03102006.pdf.

Gleditsch, Kristian S. 2002. "Expanded Trade and GDP Data." *Journal of Conflict Resolution* 49 (5): 712–724.

Haftel, Yoram Z., and Alexander Thompson. 2006. "The Independence of International Organizations: Concept and Applications." *Journal of Conflict Resolution* 50 (2): 253–275.

Held, David, Anthony McGrew, David Goldblaatt, and Jonathan Perraton. 1999. *Global Transformations: Politics, Economics and Culture*. Cambridge: Polity Press.

Henisz, Witold J. 2002. "The Institutional Environment for Infrastructure Investment." *Industrial and Corporate Change* 11 (2): 355–389.

Jetschke, Anja. 2009. "Institutionalizing ASEAN: Celebrating Europe through Network Governance." *Cambridge Review of International Affairs* 22 (3): 407–426.

Jordana, J., D. Levi-Faur, and X. Fernández-i-Marín. 2011. "The Global Diffusion of Regulatory Agencies: Channels of Transfer and Stages of Diffusion." *Comparative Political Studies* 44 (1): 1343–1369.

Kahler, Miles. 2000. "Legalization as Strategy: The Asia-Pacific Case." *International Organization* 54 (3): 549–571.

Kahler, Miles, and Andrew MacIntyre. 2013. *Integrating Regions: Asia in Comparative Context*. Stanford: Stanford University Press.

Kaye, David. 2013. "Stealth Multilateralism: U.S. Foreign Policy Without Treaties - or the Senate." *Foreign Affairs* 92 (5): 113–124.

Kennan, George F. 1997. "Diplomacy without Diplomats?" *Foreign Affairs* 76 (5): 198–212.

Koremenos, Barbara. 2016. *The Continent of International Law: Explaining Agreement Design*. Cambridge: Cambridge University Press.

Levi-Faur, D. 2005. "The Global Diffusion of Regulatory Capitalism." *The Annals of the American Academy of Political and Social Science* 598 (1): 12–32.

Lipson, Charles. 1991. "Why Are Some International Agreements Informal?" *International Organization* 45 (4): 495–538.
McCarty, Nolan, Keith Poole, and Howard Rosenthal. 2006. *Polarized America: The Dance of Ideology and Unequal Riches*. Cambridge, MA: MIT Press.
Pakkanen, Saadia M. 2016. *Asian Designs: Governance in the Contemporary World Order*. Ithaca: Cornell University Press.
Pauwelyn, Joost, Ramses Wessel, and Jan Wouters. 2012. *Informal International Lawmaking*. Oxford: Oxford University Press.
Pollack, Mark A., and Gregory Shaffer. 2009. *When Cooperation Fails: The International Law and Politics of Genetically Modified Foods*. Oxford: Oxford University Press.
Pollitt, Christopher, Janice Caulfield, Amanda Smullen, and Colin Talbot. 2005. *Agencies: How Governments Do Things through Semi-Autonomous Organizations*. Basingstoke: Palgrave Macmillan.
Porter, Tony. 2012. "The Relevance of Temporality to Transnational Institutions." *Institute on Globalization and the Human Condition Working Papers* 12 (3): 25–29.
Prantl, Jochen. 2014. "Taming Hegemony: Informal Institutions and the Challenge to Western Liberal Order." *The Chinese Journal of International Politics* 7 (4): 449–482.
Roger, Charles. 2016. "Soft Governance: Why States Create Informal Intergovernmental Organizations, and Why It Matters." *Dissertation, University of British Columbia*. University of British Columbia.
Roger, Charles B. 2020. *The Origins of Informality: Why the Legal Foundations of Global Governance Are Shifting, and Why It Matters*. Oxford: Oxford University Press.
Roger, Charles B. 2022. "The Coral Reefs of Global Governance: How Formal IOs Make Informality Work." *Journal of European Integration* 44 (5): 657–675.
Roger, Charles B., and Sam Rowan. 2022a. "Analyzing International Organizations: How the Concepts We Use Affect the Answers We Get." *Review of International Organizations* 17 (3): 597–625.
Roger, Charles B., and Sam S. Rowan. 2022b. "The New Terrain of Global Governance: Mapping Membership in Informal IOs." *Journal of Conflict Resolution*.
Shaffer, Gregory C, and Mark a Pollack. 2010. "Hard vs. Soft Law: Alternatives, Complements and Antagonists in International Governance." *Minnesota Law Review* 94: 706–799.
Slaughter, Anne-Marie. 2000. "Governing the Global Economy Through Government Networks." In *The Role of Law in International Politics: Essays in International Relations and International Law*, edited by Michael Byers, 177–205. Oxford: Oxford University Press.
Stone, Randall W. 2011. *Controlling Institutions: International Organizations and the Global Economy*. Cambridge: Cambridge University Press.
Stone, Randall W. 2013. "Informal Governance in International Organizations: Introduction to the Special Issue." *The Review of International Organizations* 8 (2): 121–136.
Vabulas, Felicity, and Duncan Snidal. 2013. "Organization Without Delegation: Informal Intergovernmental Organizations (IIGOs) and the Spectrum of Intergovernmental Arrangements." *The Review of International Organizations* 8 (2): 193–220.
Vabulas, Felicity, and Duncan Snidal. 2020. "Informal IGOs as Mediators of Power Shifts." *Global Policy* 11 (S3): 40–50.
Vabulas, Felicity, and Duncan Snidal. 2021. "Cooperation under Autonomy: Building and Analyzing the Informal Intergovernmental Organizations 2.0 Dataset." *Journal of Peace Research* 58 (4): 859–869.

6

THE REVIVAL OF TRANSATLANTIC PARTNERSHIP? EU-US COORDINATION IN SANCTIONS POLICY

Peter Van Elsuwege[1] *and Viktor Szép*[2,*]

[1]GHENT UNIVERSITY
[2]UNIVERSITY OF GRONINGEN

Introduction

In a context of waning multilateralism, there is a significant increase of unilateral sanctions in contemporary world politics (Moret, 2021). Such sanctions are adopted outside the framework of the United Nations (UN) in response to a variety of challenges to international peace and security. Traditionally, the United States (US) is known as "the most prolific user of sanctions at the world stage" (Moret, 2021: 23). This can be attributed to the strong role of the dollar in the world economy and the American ambition to play a leadership role in the international arena (Mulder, 2022).

Over the past decades, the European Union (EU) also increasingly used the sanctions instrument to promote the objectives of its Common Foreign and Security Policy (CFSP), making it "the second most prolific user of unilateral sanctions in the world" (Moret, 2021: 23). The ambition to improve its so-called 'strategic autonomy' only reinforces this tendency. Through the adoption of sanctions – formally defined as 'restrictive measures' – the Union aims to project and defend its own norms and values without being dependent upon other actors. This requires, on the one hand, a strengthening of the mechanisms for the implementation and enforcement of EU sanctions and, on the other hand, an effective safeguarding policy against the unlawful extraterritorial application to EU operators of sanctions imposed by third countries (European Commission, 2021a; Council of the EU, 2022a). With respect to both dimensions, the role of the US is crucial. It is well-known that sustained coordination with a close ally and like-minded partner such as the US is essential to improve the

DOI: 10.4324/9781003283911-8

effectiveness of the EU's sanctions (De Vries, Portela and Guijarro-Usobiaga, 2014). At the same time, the extra-territorial application of US sanctions on EU economic operators is a long-term irritant in EU-US relations (Ruys and Ryngaert, 2020).

Against this background, it is not surprising that cooperation on the use of sanctions figures high on the agenda of the renewed Transatlantic Partnership. On the occasion of the 2021 EU-US Summit, both partners expressed their intention "to enhance cooperation on the use of sanctions to pursue shared foreign policy and security objectives, while avoiding possible unintended consequences for European and US interests" (White House, 2021). Proceeding from this observation, the aim of this chapter is to analyse the legal and political framework for cooperation in sanctions matters and to examine how this translates into practice. After a brief introduction to the increased use of sanctions as a foreign policy tool by the EU and the US, the existing mechanisms for transatlantic sanctions coordination are scrutinised. Subsequently, the practice of sanctions coordination in the cases of Iran and Russia is addressed. Finally, the challenges in relation to the extraterritorial application of US sanctions are discussed.

In love with sanctions: EU and US approaches to sanctions

The EU has become a major sanctions actor in international relations. It has addressed several international crises through the use of sanctions and targeted individuals and entities from all around the world. The evolution of its sanctions regime peaked in reaction to Russia's actions against Ukraine, which was unprecedented in the sense that no state of Russia's size had been subject to major EU sanctions with such economic and financial repercussions before. Paul James Cardwell has convincingly argued that "the extent to which sanctions have been imposed [in the EU], or at the very least discussed in the Council, means that it is little exaggeration to say that the CFSP has become oriented towards sanctions as an appropriate response to global or regional problems" (Cardwell, 2015: 288). Similarly, Ramses Wessel and others have found that approximately 80% of CFSP decisions are either about establishing or amending sanctions regimes based on Articles 29 and 31(2) of the Treaty on European Union (TEU) respectively (Wessel et al., 2021).

Indeed, over time, the EU has constantly increased the number of its sanctions regimes. Currently, it runs more than 30 country specific and 4 horizontal sanctions regimes, the latter being also able to target individuals and entities irrespective of their geographical locations, including for reasons of terrorism, cyberattacks, the use of chemical weapons and human rights violations (Portela, 2020a: 3). The Union has so far designated individuals and entities from Asia (33%), Africa (26%) and Europe (25%), followed by the Americas (6%) (Giumelli, Hoffmann and Książczaková, 2021: 12). It is noteworthy that the Americas is the region where most divergences can be observed in the transatlantic space: while Washington has traditionally targeted Latin American individuals and entities more frequently, Brussels has refrained from joining these measures and only blacklisted its first Venezuelan targets in 2017 (Portela, 2020b: 122).

Similarly, the US relies heavily on sanctions to tackle global challenges. The global reach of US foreign policy is manifested in the extensive use of economic sanctions. Even if their effectiveness is sometimes questioned, US economic sanctions are imposed in almost every foreign policy challenge. The reason for the increased use of sanctions is twofold. On the one hand, the strong role of the dollar in global economic relations enhances the US' abilities to use economic coercion against adversaries, even against the will of its European and other allies. On the other hand, US leaders generally see sanctions as low cost tools to project US power without confronting enemy forces (Fishman, 2020; Mulder, 2022).

This development is confirmed by the numbers of sanctions imposed in the last couple of decades. Twice as many sanctions were imposed between 1990s and 2000s compared to the period between 1950 and 1985. By the 2010s, the number of US sanctions doubled again (Mulder, 2022). Also in recent times, sanctions designations have increased considerably: whereas in 2014, the US had 6,000 sanctions in place, five years later, it further increased by almost 2,000 sanctions. Interestingly, when the Trump administration decided to withdraw from the Iranian nuclear deal, the US imposed 700 fresh sanctions on a single day (Gilsinan, 2019). As a new record, almost 1,500 individuals, companies and entities were listed in 2018 and almost 800 listings were recorded in 2019 (Portela, 2020b, p. 123).

The 2022 war in Ukraine triggered further sanctions by the US, the EU and other like-minded states. Since late February 2022, the Biden administration has imposed sanctions over approximately 800 Russian targets, and almost 1,000 foreign companies decided to leave the Russian market as part of their "self-sanctioning" strategy (Kilcrease *et al.*, 2022). Similarly, half a year after the war started, the EU has adopted six rounds of restrictive measures against Russia. The EU's targeted sanctions in response to Russia's actions to undermine the territorial integrity, sovereignty, and independence of Ukraine now apply to more than 1,200 individuals and approximately 108 entities (Council of the EU, 2022b). All these actions required a strong coordination by the EU and the US whose framework and practice are detailed in the next sections.

The framework for transatlantic sanctions coordination

The Transatlantic Partnership lacks an overarching legal framework governing the alignment of different sanctions regimes. This does not mean that the two sides would not coordinate their measures in certain cases. As High Representative of the Union for Foreign Affairs and Security Policy/Vice-President of the Commission (HR/VP) Josep Borrell emphasised: "the EU regularly discusses issues related to restrictive measures with the [US] government as well as with the US Congress. These discussions are guided by considerations such as the value of transatlantic unity as well as the need to avoid unintended consequences for European economic actors" (European Commission, 2020a). After the election of Joe Biden in 2020, the European Commission and the HR/VP also stressed that the EU and the US "will seek to enhance coordination on the use of sanctions including in the pursuit of shared objectives, while avoiding unintended consequences for European and US economic interests and the unilateral use of extraterritorial sanctions" (European Commission and High Representative, 2020: 10).

After the election of Joe Biden, the US re-established the Office of Sanctions Coordination. This office, which is mainly responsible to coordinate sanctions measures with like-minded states, was first established in 2013 by then-US Secretary of State Hillary Clinton but was abandoned in 2017 when Rex Tillerson was nominated US Secretary of State. In 2013, the office was headed by Daniel Fried who had been very active in coordinating the sanctions against Russia with EU allies already in 2014 (Gramer, 2017; Fried and Fishman, 2021). Since April 2022, James O'Brien operates as the Coordinator for Sanctions Policy with the rank of Ambassador. The new Office of Sanctions Coordination "will oversee work on sanctions and further strengthen cooperation with allies and partners in the use of this critical tool" (US Department of State, 2022). In May 2022, the two sides also agreed to launch a Transatlantic Task Force "to ensure the effective implementation of [the] financial sanctions by identifying and freezing the assets of sanctioned individuals and companies that exist within our jurisdictions" (European Commission, 2022).

The willingness of coordination, however, does not translate automatically into complete synergies. Perfect alignment of transatlantic sanctions is impossible and full harmony between sanctions regimes should not be expected (Fishman, Kendall-Taylor and Stent, 2022: 5). In general, the extent to which the EU and the US can agree on different measures largely depends on the (foreign and commercial policy) interests of the respective parties. In the EU, this is further complicated by the fact that the establishment of sanctions regimes requires a unanimous agreement of 27 Member States that have all sorts of different relations with third countries. For instance, the Ukrainian crisis of 2014 illustrated the limits of what the EU can agree on and has painfully demonstrated the exposure of certain EU states to the Russian economy. Especially in the energy sector, EU Member States were careful in their approach in the sense that in 2014 they sought to avoid major interruption in their energy supply. The situation changed significantly following Russia's military intervention in Ukraine in February 2022. German Chancellor Olaf Scholz quickly announced the halting of certifying the Nord Stream 2 gas pipeline, a long-standing source of conflict between the EU and the US. This decision must be seen against the background of a Joint Statement of the US and Germany, adopted in July 2021 in a context of a growing Russian military build-up around the Ukrainian borders. On this occasion, it was agreed:

> Should Russia attempt to use energy as a weapon or commit further aggressive acts against Ukraine, Germany will take action at the national level and press for effective measures at the European level, including sanctions, to limit Russian export capabilities to Europe in the energy sector, including gas, and/or in other economically relevant sectors. This commitment is designed to ensure that Russia will not misuse any pipeline, including Nord Stream 2, to achieve aggressive political ends by using energy as a weapon.
>
> *(US Department of State, 2021)*

This statement may be regarded as a compromise implying that the US did not impose any sanctions regarding Nord Stream 2 at that stage in return for a German commitment to halt the certification of the pipeline in case of Russian aggression. This explains the immediate German reaction when the situation escalated in February 2022. Hence, the US-German Joint Statement may be regarded as an example of informal and political sanctions coordination outside any formal US-EU legal framework.

In addition, the EU and the US coordinate their measures both multilaterally and bilaterally. At the multilateral level, the G7 is one of the most important fora for coordination. The European Commission recently acknowledged the importance of G7 partners in this regard and underlined the prominence of "sustained close coordination with allies and like-minded partners to align sanctions regimes to the largest possible extent". It also held that "regular dialogue and cooperation on sanctions with third partners, in particular G7 partners will be pursued by the [HR/VP] and the Commission" (European Commission, 2021a:18). Indeed, the G7 has proven to be an effective forum for sanctions coordination, both with respect to Russia's actions against Ukraine in 2014 and 2022 as with respect to Belarus in 2021 (European Council, 2021: 20).

Between convergence and divergence: The practice of sanctions coordination in relation to Iran and Russia

Transatlantic sanctions cooperation was very intense in the Iranian and Russian cases, which ironically also caused significant frictions between the two sides. In the Iranian case, the EU and the US went beyond UN Security Council Resolutions. They imposed an unprecedented level of pressure on the Iranian regime to give up its nuclear weapons programme. This included, amongst others, the introduction of a new series of oil sanctions in 2011 and 2012. The impact on Iran's oil export revenues was much larger than initially anticipated. It has been argued that this effect was not so much the result of the respective unilateral oil embargoes put in place by the US and the EU but, rather, a consequence from the coordinated flanking measures in the financial and shipping-insurance markets (Smith, 2019; Van de Graaf, 2013).

Whereas the transatlantic coordination of sanctions against Iran worked remarkably well, the US voiced concerns about the implications of Iranian appeals before the EU Courts. A key problem was that only very limited information about the reasons for the adoption of the sanctions was shared with the courts. Taking into account that the EU Courts must be able to review the lawfulness and merits of restrictive measures in the EU legal order, the Council cannot simply refer to the confidential or secret nature of such information (Court of Justice, 2013). Hence, the General Court annulled the listing of several companies and individuals in the absence of concrete evidence about their engagement with nuclear proliferation in Iran (Eckes, 2014: 893). An interesting example is the case of Fulmen, an Iranian company active in the electrical equipment sector and Mr. Mahmoudian, the chairman of its board of directors. The General Court (2012) annulled their inclusion in the EU sanctions lists due to a lack of sufficient evidence. The Fulmen company also challenged the validity of the US Office of Foreign Assets Control (OFAC) before the US District Court for the District of Columbia. The latter dismissed the action and explicitly rejected the claim that the EU's decision to delist Fulman required OFAC to do the same (Lester, 2020).

The divergence of targeted sanctions and judicial review did not prevent the EU and the US to adopt a common approach in preparation of the Joint Comprehensive Plan of Action (JCPOA). This agreement, commonly known as the 'Iranian nuclear deal', was adopted in July 2015 between Iran and the five permanent members of the UN Security Council plus Germany (P5+1) together with the EU. The JCPOA resulted in a coordinated commitment to lift the nuclear-related sanctions. However, under the Trump administration, the US withdrew from the JCPOA and adopted secondary sanctions forcing EU operators to cease business relations with Iranian companies or to face the possibility of exclusion from US markets (see *infra*). This led some EU Member States to establish the 'Instrument in Support of Trade Exchanges' (INSTEX), which created channels for transactions with Iran notwithstanding the existence of US sanctions. INSTEX had only modest economic benefits but, as Pierre Vimont, former secretary-general of the EEAS, emphasised, "INSTEX was never thought of as economically efficient" but rather as "a political answer to underline to Iran that we, like Russia and China, are still committed to the nuclear deal" (Portela, 2021: 4).

After the election of Joe Biden as the new US President, a revival of the Iran nuclear deal was again on the agenda. HR/VP Josep Borrell coordinated the negotiations for a new compromise text which could open the door to the lifting of the US sanctions. However, in late August 2022, the US administration was dissatisfied with the progress so far, implying that the prospects for a rapid revival of the JCPOA looked grim (Guerrero, 2022). Hence, the Iranian case illustrates how the coordination of EU and US sanctions cannot be disconnected from the broader (geo)political context. This is further confirmed with the case of sanctions against Russia.

A first high point of cooperation was reached in 2014–2015 (Fishman, Kendall-Taylor and Stent, 2022: 3). John E. Smith, former OFAC director, who was in charge of preparing US sanctions in 2014, told that coordination was so intense that those days were the "first all-nighters since university life" (Smith, 2019). Communications between the two sides were more intense than ever which manifested in the sheer number of exchanges of information in every hour, either by phone or e-mail, complemented by regular in-person working group meetings led by Dan Fried, former coordinator for Sanctions Policy at the State Department. John E. Smith even added that "we shared our respected targeting list, something we had never done before so that each side at the end of the Atlantic knew generally what the other side intended to do next" (Smith, 2019). However, the Russian case also demonstrated divergences: the US was disappointed with the EU's relatively low level of engagement and criticised it for not adopting further measures. The EU, on its part, was frustrated that the US was unable to understand some European countries' historical and economic relations with Russia which seriously affected the EU's abilities to adopt harsher measures without inflicting pains in the European markets. One of the main differences was that EU sanctions targeted loans and investment only to oil producers, while the US also included the gas producer Novatek. Moreover, the EU exempted pre-existing contracts in a number of areas, such as arms trade or oil projects. At the same time, there was a widespread agreement that both sides needed to go beyond mere asset freezes. US and EU economists worked together to develop sectoral sanctions that targeted particularly vulnerable areas of the Russian economy.

The Russian military aggression against Ukraine in February 2022 intensified the cooperation and triggered an almost never seen transatlantic coordination to impose sanctions again Russia (Szép, 2022). The EU and US coordinated their efforts remarkably well and these sanctions regimes were much better aligned than sceptics expected. US President Joe Biden said "over the last few months, we have co-ordinated closely with our NATO Allies and partners in Europe and around the world to prepare that response" (White House, 2022a). President Biden also added that he "spent countless hours unifying our European allies. We shared with the world in advance what we knew Putin was planning and precisely how he would try to falsely justify his aggression" (White House, 2022a). A senior State Department official also confirmed that between December 2021 and February 2022, top Biden administration officials spent "an average of 10 to 15 hours a week on secure calls or video conferences with the EU and member states" to coordinate the sanctions against Russia. An EU official acknowledged that the intensity of cooperation was exceptional: "we have never had in the history of the [EU] such close contacts with the Americans on a security issue as we have now – it's really unprecedented" (Financial Times, 2022a).

The measures adopted by the transatlantic community and especially by the EU went beyond most of the expectations in terms of the pace of decision-making and the content of the measures. On the one hand, the unanimity requirement in EU foreign and sanctions policy often slows down the EU to adopt the necessary measures even if it faces pressing challenges. For instance, in the case of the sanctions against Belarus in 2020, Cyprus blocked EU sanctions regimes because of its view that the EU did not take all the necessary measures vis-a-vis Turkey. In February 2022, however, the EU was faster than ever which is partly explained by the intensity of EU-US coordination that took place between December 2021 and February 2022 (Szép, 2022). This does not mean that no debate occurred in the EU. For instance, Poland sought to exclude more Russian banks from the SWIFT system than the rest of the Member States. However, on the other hand, even if some disagreements took place between the Member States, sanctions are also unprecedented in the sense that the measures have far-reaching financial and economic consequences. For instance, the Russian Central Bank is also on sanctions lists which is unprecedented in the sense that central banks are rarely, if ever, targeted by the EU.

Coordination on the prohibition of oil import from Russia turned to be particularly challenging. While the US banned the import of Russian oil already in March 2022 (White House, 2022b), the question of energy interdependence from Russia and its potential large-scale implications on the European economy prompted serious debates in the EU. While some Member States such as the Baltic States and Poland advocated a ban on Russian oil already during Spring 2022, others were more concerned about their potential to find alternatives. Hungary in particular voiced concerns that a total ban on Russian oil would jeopardise its industry and economy. After weeks of negotiations, an agreement was reached on a complete ban on all Russian seaborne crude oil and petroleum products covering 90% of all oil imports from Russia. Hungary, Slovakia and the Czech Republic, three landlocked Central European states, secured exemptions for the pipeline imports they rely on (Financial Times, 2022b). Throughout the summer of 2022, G7 finance ministers continued their work to set a price limit on Russian seaborne oil and petroleum products that would allow service providers to continue to do business with Russia if these products are sold at or below a certain level. In September 2022, the G7 agreed on a price cap on Russian oil that forces importers to abide by the ceiling if they want G7 shipping insurance to transport the fuel (Preussen, 2022). Hence, the Russian war against Ukraine triggered an unprecedented level of sanctions coordination among allied and like-minded states.

US' secondary sanctions and the EU's strategic autonomy: a challenge for the Transatlantic Partnership

The adoption of sanctions not only provides a platform for translatlantic cooperation. It is also an area with a huge potential for frictions in EU-US relations. This is particularly the result of the US' practice of adopting so-called secondary sanctions. The latter target economic operators outside of the US which are doing business with targeted entities. The objective is to increase the effectiveness of the 'primary sanctions', which are limiting the economic relations between the US and the target state. In other words, secondary sanctions aim to prevent that third states and their economic operators compensate or 'backfill' the negative effect of primary sanctions on the target. They are, therefore, often perceived as 'anti-circumvention measures' or instruments to avoid sanctions evasion (Ruys and Ryngaert, 2020: 8).

Whereas the political logic behind the adoption of secondary sanctions is clear, they are contested from a legal point of view. In particular, the extraterritorial effect of secondary sanctions is difficult to reconcile with key principles of international law such as the principle of non-intervention and the prohibition of abuse of rights (Ruys and Ryngaert, 2020: 10). Moreover, the introduction of civil and financial penalties for engaging in economic transactions with sanctions targets is problematic under the customary international law of jurisdiction when there is only a tenuous link with the US. This is, for instance, the case when a contract between an operator from a third country and a sanctions target is subject to transactions in US dollars, implying an exposure to the US financial system with US dollar SWIFT payment messages sent to US financial institutions. Accordingly, the mere dollar denomination of international business transactions may bring foreign financial institutions in a difficult situation. A clear example is the case of the French bank PNB Paribas, which was sentenced to pay nearly 9 $bn for transactions in dollars on behalf of Sudanese, Iranian and Cuban entities subject to US economic sanctions (US Department of Justice, 2015). This US practice has been heavily criticised in legal doctrine (Bismuth, 2015; Kerbrat, 2021). The mere routing of financial messages via US servers without any other link with the US is deemed in violation of international law (Emmenegger, 2016).

From the perspective of the EU, the practice of secondary US sanctions is highly problematic. As observed by the European Commission (2021a), "These measures threaten the integrity of the Single Market and the EU's financial systems, reduces the effectiveness of the EU's foreign policy and puts strain on legitimate trade and investment in violation of basic principles of international law". Moreover, they generate substantial economic losses for the EU. According to figures from the European Council on Foreign Affairs (2019), the re-introduction of US extra-territorial sanctions against Iran cost EU companies more than USD 22.5 billion.

Sustained coordination may help to prevent the adoption of divergent sanction regimes and, therefore, also the negative implications following from the extra-territorial application of third country sanctions. This explains the EU's ambition to reinforce its coordination efforts with allies and like-minded countries, in particular within the G7 context. At the same time, the elaboration of additional policy options to deter and counteract the unlawful extra-territorial application of unilateral sanctions by third countries to EU operators is also on the agenda (European Commission, 2021a: 19). Back in 1996, in response to secondary US sanctions against Cuba, Iran and Libya, the EU already adopted the so-called Blocking Statute (Regulation 2271/96). This is the main legal instrument to defend the EU's interests against measures with extraterritorial effects by prohibiting EU actors to comply, in principle, with those sanctions (Regulation 2271/96, article 5). The Blocking Statute nullifies the effect of any foreign decisions, including court rulings and arbitration awards, in the EU. Moreover, the EU operators are legally entitled to seek compensation for their losses (Regulation 2271/96, article 6).

However, in reality, EU companies often find themselves between a rock and hard place: they either comply with the Blocking Statute or face the threat of being excluded from US markets. The central role of the dollar in the global economy allows Washington to threaten non-US actors, including European entities, to restrict their access to American markets if they engage with partners that are subject to US sanctions. The Blocking Statute, on the other hand, prohibits compliance with such measures. The two different and directly opposing legal regimes result in a 'catch-22 situation' where European companies either sacrifice their access to the US market or face substantial damages and penalties in the EU (De Vries, 1998: 348).

The challenges surrounding the application of the Blocking Statute in practice can be illustrated with the *Bank Melli* case (C-124/20), involving the termination of a contract between a German company and an Iranian Bank which was subject to US secondary sanctions. The latter were re-introduced following the decision of (then) US President Trump to withdraw from the JCPOA (United Nations, 2015), and the activation of Title III of the Helms-Burton Act. Taking into account the extraterritorial application of those measures and their adverse effects on EU operators, the European Commission included them in the annex to the Blocking Statute (European Commission, 2018).

When the German company Telekom unilaterally terminated all its contracts with Bank Melli Iran (BMI) – an entity included in the US sanctions list – without express reasons and without authorisation from the Commission under Article 5, paragraph 2 of the EU Blocking Statute, BMI challenged the legality of this action in Germany. In this context, the Hamburg High Regional Court referred a set of preliminary questions to the Court of Justice, essentially seeking clarification regarding the precise scope of the prohibition to comply with secondary sanctions under Article 5, paragraph 1 of the EU Blocking Statute and the implications of non-compliance.

The Grand Chamber judgement of the Court of Justice pointed at the broadly defined objectives of the EU Blocking Statute to conclude that the prohibition on complying with secondary sanctions also applies in the absence of an order or instruction by a foreign administrative or judicial authority (Court of Justice, 2021: para. 51). The prohibition is drafted in "clear, precise and unconditional terms", implying that a sanctioned entity such as BMI may rely on Article 5, paragraph 1 against an EU operator such as Telekom (Court of Justice, 2021: para. 60). The latter can still terminate contracts without providing reasons on the condition that it can prove, in the context of civil proceedings concerning the alleged breach of the Blocking Statute, that this termination did not seek to comply with the foreign legislation (Court of Justice, 2021: para. 68). Hence, the burden of proof is on the side of the EU operator. This reversal of the burden of proof from the applicant to the defendant is important and derives from a concern to ensure the effectiveness of the Blocking Statute (Challet, 2022). Whereas the Court of Justice did not provide any further guidance about the required level of proof, Advocate General Hogan referred to a company's right to make ethical choices in the conduct of its business activities. Accordingly, a company's engagement in "a coherent and systematic corporate social-responsibility policy (CRS)" may provide an acceptable ground for cutting ties with entities having links with the Iranian regime (AG Hogan, 2021: para. 87–88).

Whereas the Court's judgement thus brought more clarity with respect to the scope of the Blocking Statute and its procedural requirements, its substantive application and the implications in case of non-compliance remain controversial. Article 9 of Regulation 2271/96 only generally provides that the sanctions which Member States impose in the event of an infringement of its relevant provisions must be "effective, proportional and dissuasive". This is to be determined by national courts, having regard to all the circumstances of a particular case (Court of Justice, 2021: para. 74). In the case at stake, an application of this provision implied that the termination act of Telekom would be null and void and, therefore, devoid of any legal effect. As the Court of Justice observed, such an annulment would entail a limitation on the freedom to conduct a business enshrined in Article 16 of the EU Charter of fundamental rights (Court of Justice, 2021: paras 76–77). This freedom is, however, not absolute and may be limited in the public interest (Court of Justice, 2021: para. 81). Whereas the objectives of Regulation 2271/96, which are to protect the established legal order and the interests of the EU, may indeed be regarded as a possible limitation to the fundamental rights of economic operators, it is for the national courts to assess its proportionality in light of the potential losses to which the operator will be exposed when it is unable to terminate a contract with an entity included in the US sanctions list (Court of Justice, 2021: para. 92).

Arguably, the Court's judgement does not solve the dilemmas and legal uncertainties for EU operators confronted with US secondary sanctions (Challet, 2022; Shipley, 2022). In particular, it does not solve the inherent tension between the EU's interest to ensure the effectiveness of the Blocking Statute as an instrument to deter and counteract the unlawful extraterritorial application of third country sanctions, on the one hand, and the legal protection of EU operators facing the negative implications on their freedom to conduct business, on the other hand. An amendment of the Blocking Statute may help to bring more clarity on this matter, as suggested by AG Hogan (2021: para 5).

The European Commission launched the process for a revision of Regulation 2271/96 as part of a more comprehensive EU policy against extraterritoriality and in the context of its ambition to become a strategically autonomous actor (European Commission, 2021a). The aim is to include additional deterrence and counteracting mechanisms and to streamline the application of the Regulation, amongst others through a reduction of the compliance costs for EU operators. The outcome of the public consultation, launched in the first stage of the revision process, revealed an interest in legal support for operators entangled in foreign legal proceedings and financial compensations for the cost of operating in a sanctioned environment (European Commission, 2021b). Moreover, the European Commission (2021c) also initiated a proposal for an anti-coercion instrument and envisages the strengthening of alternative mechanisms such as the Instrument in Support of Trade Exchanges (INTEX) launched in reaction to the US secondary sanctions against Iran (see *infra*). Whereas a detailed analysis of the various instruments would go beyond the scope of this chapter, the EU's ambition to foster its strategic autonomy implies a more assertive approach in response to the extraterritorial application of US sanctions. It may, therefore, be regarded as a significant challenge for the renewed Transatlantic Partnership.

Conclusion

The start of the Biden administration as well as the outbreak of the Russian war against Ukraine provided the context for an unprecedented level of EU-US sanctions coordination. Both partners increasingly use sanctions as an important foreign policy tool and aim to reinforce the impact of their measures on the basis of close coordination. Significantly, this coordination is not based on formal legal or institutional structures but is essentially informal and political. It takes place at the bilateral level or even between the US and individual Member States as has been illustrated with the US-German joint statement in relation to the Nord Stream pipeline project. At the multilateral level, the G7 is an increasingly important format for the coordination of sanctions with like-minded countries.

At the same time, the coordination of EU-US sanctions cannot conceal the continued existence of important challenges. Proceeding from the EU's ambition to enhance its 'strategic autonomy', a more assertive strategy to counter the extraterritorial application of US secondary sanctions is on the agenda. Moreover, the domestic political context in both the EU and the US largely determines the scope for cooperation and convergence of the respective unilateral sanctions regimes. The example of the Trump administration and its unilateral decision to withdraw from the JCPOA with Iran illustrates the consequences of divergence in the respective sanctions regimes of the US and the EU. It triggered an amendment of the EU Blocking Statute and new initiatives such as INSTEX in order to overcome the negative consequences for the EU's own strategic interests. Whereas the existence of geopolitical threats such as Russia's military aggression against Ukraine and new security challenges from emerging powers such as China and India stimulate a revival of the Transatlantic Partnership, leading to increased sanctions coordination, frictions about the extraterritorial application of unilateral sanctions cannot be excluded.

Note

* This project has received funding from the European Union's Horizon 2020 research and innovation programme under grant agreement no. 962533.

References

Bismuth, R. (2015) 'Pour une apprehension nuancé de l'extraterritorialite´ du droit américain – Quelques réflexions autour des procédures et sanctions visant Alstom et BNP Paribas' (2015) 61 *Annuaire Français de Droit International Law* 785–807.

Cardwell, P. J. (2015) 'The Legalisation of European Union Foreign Policy and the Use of Sanctions', *Cambridge Yearbook of European Legal Studies*, 17; 287–310, doi:10.1017/cel.2015.11.

Challet, C. (2022), 'Judgment in *Bank Melli Iran*: The Court of Justice, Too, is Between a Rock and a Hard Place' at: https://eulawlive.com/op-ed-judgment-in-bank-melli-iran-the-court-of-justice-too-is-between-a-rock-and-a-hard-place-by-celia-challet/ (accessed: 14 September 2022).

Council of the EU (2022a), Conclusions on the EU's economic and financial strategic autonomy: one year after the Commission's Communication, doc. 6301/22.

Council of the EU (2022b), 'Russia's Aggression against Ukraine: the EU targets additional 54 individuals and 10 entities', at: https://www.consilium.europa.eu/en/press/press-releases/2022/07/22/russia-s-aggression-against-ukraine-the-eu-targets-additional-54-individuals-and-10-entities/ (accessed: 18 February 2022).

Court of Justice (2013), Case C-218/12 P, *Council v. Fulmen and Mahmoudian*, EU:C:2013:775.

Court of Justice (2021), Case C-124/20, *Bank Melli Iran v. Telekom Deutschland*, EU:C:2021:1035.

De Vries, A. Portela, C. and Guijarro-Usobiaga, B. (2014) 'Improving the Effectiveness of Sanctions: A Checklist for the EU', *CEPS Special Report No. 94*, at: https://www.ceps.eu/ceps-publications/improving-effectiveness-sanctions-checklist-eu/

De Vries, A. (1998), 'Council Regulation (EC) No 2271/96 (the EU Blocking Regulation)', *International Business Lawyer* 26(8): 345–353.

Eckes (2014), 'EU Restrictive Measures against Natural and Legal Persons: From Counterterrorist to Third Country Sanctions', *Common Market Law Review* 51:3, 869–905.

European Commission (2018), Delegated Regulation (EU) 2018/1100 of 6 June 2018 amending the Annex to Council Regulation (EC) No 2271/96 protecting against the effects of extra-territorial application of legislation adopted by a third country, and actions based thereon or resulting therefrom, OJ (2018) L 199I/1.

European Commission (2020a) 'E-002880/2019 Answer given by Vice-President Borrell on behalf of the European Commission (4.2.2020)'. Available at: https://www.europarl.europa.eu/doceo/document/E-9-2019-002880-ASW_EN.pdf

European Commission and High Representative of the Union for Foreign Affairs and Security Policy (2020) 'Joint Communication to the European Parliament, the European Council and the Council: A new EU-US agenda for global change', JOIN (2020) 22.

European Commission (2021a) *The European economic and financial system: fostering openness, strength and resilience*, COM (2021) 32 final.

European Commission (2021b), Summary of results of the open public consultation on the review of the Blocking Statute, at: https://ec.europa.eu/info/law/better-regulation/have-your-say/initiatives/13129-Unlawful-extra-territorial-sanctions-a-stronger-EU-response-amendment-of-the-Blocking-Statute-/public-consultation_en (accessed: 14 September 2022).

European Commission . (2021c). Proposal for a Regulation of the European Parliament and of the Council on the protection of the Union and its Member States from economic coercion by third countries, COM (2021) 775 final.

European Commission (2022), Joint Statement on further restrictive economic measures', at: https://ec.europa.eu/commission/presscorner/detail/en/statement_22_1423 (accessed: 8 September 2022).

European Council (2021) 'Carbis Bay G7 Summit Communiqué: Our Shared Agenda for Global Action to Build Back Better'. Available at: https://www.consilium.europa.eu/media/50361/carbis-bay-g7-summit-communique.pdf

Emmenegger, S. (2016) 'Extraterritorial Economic Sanctions and their Foundation in International Law' 33 *Azirona Journal of International and Comparative Law* 3, 632–660.

European Council on Foreign Affairs (2019), 'Strategic Sovereignty. Meeting the Challenge of Secondary Sanctions', available at: https://ecfr.eu/wp-content/uploads/4_Meeting_the_challenge_of_secondary_sanctions.pdf

Financial Times (2022a) 'Weaponisation of finance: how the west unleashed "shock and awe" on Russia', *Financial Times*, 6 April.

Financial Times (2022b), 'EU leaders agree to ban majority of Russian oil imports', *Financial Times*, 31 May.

Fishman, E. (2020) *How to Fix America's Failing Sanctions Policy, Lawfare*. Available at: https://www.lawfareblog.com/how-fix-americas-failing-sanctions-policy (Accessed: 18 February 2022).

Fishman, E., Kendall-Taylor, A. and Stent, A. (2022) *Toward a New Transatlantic Approach to Russia Sanctions: A Report to Russia Sanctions*. CNAS Transatlantic Forum on Russia? Available at: https://www.cnas.org/publications/reports/toward-a-new-transatlantic-approach-to-russia-sanctions (Accessed: 22 February 2022).

Fried, D. and Fishman, E. (2021) 'The rebirth of the State Department's Office of Sanctions Coordination: Guidelines for success', *Atlantic Council*, 12 February. Available at: https://www.atlanticcouncil.org/blogs/new-atlanticist/the-rebirth-of-the-state-departments-office-of-sanctions-coordination-guidelines-for-success/ (Accessed: 22 February 2022).

General Court (2012), Joint cases T-439/10 and T-440/00, *Fulmen and Mahmoudian v. Council*, EU:T:2012:142.

Gilsinan, K. (2019) *A Boom Time for U.S. Sanctions, The Atlantic*. Available at: https://www.theatlantic.com/politics/archive/2019/05/why-united-states-uses-sanctions-so-much/588625/ (Accessed: 18 February 2022)

Giumelli, F., Hoffmann, F. and Książczaková, A. (2021) 'The when, what, where and why of European Union sanctions', *European Security*, 30(1): 1–23, doi:10.1080/09662839.2020.1797685.

Gramer, R. (2017) *State Department Scraps Sanctions Office – Foreign Policy*. Available at: https://foreignpolicy.com/2017/10/26/state-department-scraps-sanctions-office/ (Accessed: 22 February 2022).

Guerrero, C. (2022), 'Little room left for further Iran nuclear negotiations, says Borrell', at: https://www.euractiv.com/section/politics/short_news/little-room-left-for-further-iran-nuclear-negotiations-says-borrell/

Hogan, A. G. (2021), Opinion in Case C-124/20, *Bank Melli Iran v. Telekom Deutschland*, EU:C:2021:386.

Kerbrat, Y. (2021) 'Unilateral/extraterritorial sanctions as a challenge to the theory of jurisdiction' in: Beaucillon, C. (ed.) *Research Handbook on Unilateral and Extraterritorial Sanctions*, Cheltenham: Edward Elgar, pp. 165–185.

Kilcrease, E. *et al.* (2022) *Sanctions by the Numbers: Economic Measures against Russia Following Its 2022 Invasion of Ukraine, Center for a New American Security*, at: https://www.cnas.org/publications/reports/sanctions-by-the-numbers-economic-measures-against-russia-following-its-2021-invasion-of-ukraine

Lester M. (2020), 'US court dismisses Fulmen's Iran sanctions listing challenge', at: https://www.europeansanctions.com/2020/04/us-court-dismisses-fulmens-iran-sanctions-listing-challenge/ (accessed: 14 September 2022).

Moret, E. (2021) 'Unilateral and extraterritorial sanctions in crisis: implications of their rising use and misuse in contemporary world politics', in: Beaucillon, C. (ed.) *Research Handbook on Unilateral and Extraterritorial Sanctions*, Cheltenham: Edgar Elgar, pp. 19–36.

Mulder, N. (2022) 'How America Learned to Love (Ineffective) Sanctions', *Foreign Policy*. Available at: https://foreignpolicy.com/2022/01/30/us-sanctions-reliance-results/ (Accessed: 18 February 2022).

Portela, C. (2020a) 'A blacklist is (almost) born: Building a resilient EU human rights sanctions regime, *EUISS Brief* 5, at: https://www.iss.europa.eu/sites/default/files/EUISSFiles/Brief%205%20HRS.pdf (Accessed: 18 February 2022).

Portela, C. (2020b) 'Transatlantic Cooperation on Sanctions in Latin America: From Convergence to Alignment', in Soare, S. R. (ed.) *Turning the Tide: How to Rescue Transatlantic Relations*, Paris: EUISS.

Portela, C. (2021) *Creativity wanted: Countering the extraterritorial effects of US sanctions*, available at: https://www.iss.europa.eu/sites/default/files/EUISSFiles/Brief_22_2021_0.pdf (accessed: 18 February 2022).

Preussen, W. (2022), 'G7 finance ministers agree to Russian oil price cap', *Politico*, 2 September.

Ruys, T. and Ryngaert, C. (2020) 'Secondary Sanctions: A Weapon out of Control? The International Legality of, and European Responses to, US Secondary Sanctions', *British Yearbook of International Law*, pp. 1–116. doi:10.1093/bybil/braa007.

Shipley T. (2022), 'The EU Blocking Statute after *Bank Melli*', EU Law Live Weekend Edition, January 29.

Smith, J. E. (2019) *Iran, Russia, and the Future of EU-US Sanctions Cooperation*. Available at: https://www.americanacademy.de/videoaudio/iran-russia-and-the-future-of-eu-us-sanctions-cooperation/ (Accessed: 18 February 2022).

Szép, V. (2022) 'Unmatched Levels of Sanctions Coordination', *Verfassungsblog*. Available at: https://verfassungsblog.de/unmatched-levels-of-sanctions-coordination/ (Accessed: 13 May 2022).

United Nations (2015), Security Council resolution 2231 on the Joint Comprehensive Plan of Action (JCPOA) on the Islamic Republic of Iran's nuclear programme.

US Department of Justice (2015), 'BNP Paribas sentenced for Conspiring to Violate the International Emergency Economic Powers Act and the Trading with the Enemy Act, at: https://www.justice.gov/opa/pr/bnp-paribas-sentenced-conspiring-violate-international-emergency-economic-powers-act-and (accessed: 9 September 2022).

US Department of State (2021), Joint Statement of the United States and Germany on Support for Ukraine, European Energy Security and our Climate Goals, at: https://www.state.gov/joint-statement-of-the-united-states-and-germany-on-support-for-ukraine-european-energy-security-and-our-climate-goals/ (accessed: 8 September 2022).

US Department of State (2022), Head of the Office of Sanctions Coordination, at: https://www.state.gov/head-of-the-office-of-sanctions-coordination/ (accessed: 9 September 2022).

Van de Graaf T. (2013), 'The "Oil Weapon" Reversed? Sanctions against Iran and U.S.-EU Structural Power', *Middle East Policy* 20(3): 145–163.

Wessel, R. A. *et al.* (2021) 'The future of EU Foreign, Security and Defence Policy: Assessing legal options for improvement', *European Law Journal*, 26 (5–6): 71–390, doi:10.1111/eulj.12405

White House (2021), EU-US Summit Statement, at: https://www.whitehouse.gov/briefing-room/statements-releases/2021/06/15/u-s-eu-summit-statement/

White House (2022a) *Remarks by President Biden Announcing Response to Russian Actions in Ukraine, The White House.* Available at: https://www.whitehouse.gov/briefing-room/speeches-remarks/2022/02/22/remarks-by-president-biden-announcing-response-to-russian-actions-in-ukraine/ (Accessed: 23 February 2022).

White House (2022b), United States bans imports of Russian oil, liquified natural gas and coal, 8 March 2022, at: https://www.whitehouse.gov/briefing-room/statements-releases/2022/03/08/fact-sheet-united-states-bans-imports-of-russian-oil-liquefied-natural-gas-and-coal/ (Accessed: 23 February 2022).

7

THE EU AND US GLOBAL HUMAN RIGHTS SANCTION REGIMES

Useful Complementary Instruments to Advance Protection of Universal Values? A Legal Appraisal

Sara Poli

PROFESSOR OF EU LAW, UNIVERSITY OF PISA

Introduction

The EU and US share common values, including respect for human rights, and seek to promote them outside their borders. In recent times, these two subjects of international law have enacted two horizontal 'sanctions regimes' to counter human rights abusers in the world.

The first is the so-called Global Magnitsky Human Rights Accountability Act, which has been in force since 2016 (hereinafter 'Global Magnitsky Act' or 'GMA'). This piece of legislation expands the reach of a previous Statute named after a Russian lawyer, Sergei Magnitsky, who was killed in prison in 2009 after having discovered a tax fraud scheme involving high-level state organs (Wilson and Sheppard II 2019).[1] The GMA was later implemented by Executive Order (EO) 13818 of 20 December 2017, entitled 'Blocking the Property of Persons Involved in Serious Human Rights Abuse or Corruption', adopted on the basis of emergency powers enjoyed by the government in line with the International Emergency Economic Powers Act (IEEPA).[2] The language of this Executive Order broadens the scope of the GMA and makes it easier to impose sanctions.[3]

The second act is the EU Global Human Rights Sanctions Regime (EUGHRSR),[4] inspired by the GMA, as is the case for the Canadian[5] and UK legislation,[6] respectively, developed in 2017 and 2020.[7] The EUGHRSR was

 DOI: 10.4324/9781003283911-9

adopted in 2020 upon a proposal of the High Representative of the Union for Foreign Affairs and Security Policy ('HR'); the Dutch government[8] took the initiative to discuss the adoption of this new regime at Council level in 2018 (Russel 2021);[9] shortly afterwards, the European Parliament supported the creation of the new instrument with a resolution of 2019 where it went as far as to advocate the use of qualified majority voting within the Council to facilitate the adoption of restrictive measures against human rights abusers.[10]

The purposes of this chapter are to examine whether the two Global Human Rights Sanction programmes are useful legal instruments to promote respect for human rights and the extent to which criticism of the two measures is founded. In order to address these issues, the major differences between the EU and US legal regimes will be identified; in particular, in section 2, attention is drawn to: (a) divergences with respect to the material scope of the sanctions regimes and to the evidentiary standards to be satisfied in order to list a person responsible for breaches of human rights; and (b) the right of the addressees of the sanctions to seek judicial review. Section 3 comments on the way the two legal instruments have been applied in practice to situations of human rights abuses and on the criticism addressed against them. Finally, in the concluding remarks, an assessment is made of whether the two regimes, despite some pitfalls, could be considered useful.

The scope of the EU and US sanctions regimes and the major differences between them

The common aim of the Global Human Rights Sanctions programmes is to make those who abuse human rights accountable for their acts and to deter individuals (often state organs) from committing breaches of human rights. In both jurisdictions, the sanctions take the form of measures of an economic nature consisting of the blocking of property (US), 'asset freezes' and prohibitions to make economic resources available to the targeted natural persons or entities owned by them[11] and other categories of non-state entities. The prohibitions are imposed on EU or US operators/entities, respectively, subject to EU or US law. For this reason, the sanctions regimes do not apply extraterritorially. The targets of US financial sanctions are placed on a list of specially designated persons ('SDP') administered by the Department of Treasury's Office of Foreign Assets Control (OFAC) while individuals and other state entities who are the object of EU restrictive measures are listed in Council CFSP Decisions and Regulations, under Article 215 TFEU. Both the EU Council and the US Department of State may also impose visa restrictions (EU) or suspension of entry (US).[12]

Under EO 13818, the President is allowed to impose the mentioned forms of sanctions upon declaring a national emergency with respect to an 'unusual and extraordinary threat to the national security, foreign policy, or economy of the United States'.[13] The decision on who should be sanctioned is made by the Secretary of the Treasury, in consultation with the Secretary of State and the

Attorney General. Congress may recommend that the President impose financial sanctions but the exercise of this power is discretionary (Booth 2020–2021).[14]

In the EU, the listing decision, that is, the inclusion of the addressees of the sanctions in the annexes of CFSD Decisions and Regulations instituting restrictive measures, under Article 215 TFEU, is adopted by the Council, acting by unanimity upon a proposal from a Member State or from the HR, taking into consideration the objectives of the CFSP and the gravity or impact of the abuses. In contrast to the GMA, in the EUGHRSR, the European Parliament does not have a formal right of initiative.

Regarding the persons who can be listed, the EU sanctions regime makes it possible to impose restrictive measures on a broad range of targets, including natural persons who are responsible for human rights breaches or those who support these persons or are associated with them, such as those doing business with them;[15] in addition, restrictive measures can be imposed on individual state organs, non-state organs, and 'other actors exercising effective control or authority over a territory', such as rebels. The Council has special discretion in designating 'non-state entities': they can be listed taking into consideration (a) the objectives of the common foreign and security policy; and (b) the gravity and impact of the abuses. Executive Order 13818 uses different wording but can be applied to the same broad categories of targets. Indeed, it applies to 'any foreign person determined by the Secretary of the Treasury' who is responsible for or complicit in, or has directly or indirectly engaged in, serious human rights abuse.[16]

As for the scope *ratione materiae* of the two sanctions regimes, this is quite different.

Under the GMA, restrictions may be imposed in two situations. The first concerns persons who are responsible for extrajudicial killings, torture, or other gross violations of internationally recognised human rights against an individual in any foreign country who seeks to expose illegal activity carried out by government officials or obtain, exercise, defend, or promote internationally recognised human rights and freedoms, such as the freedoms of religion, expression, association, and assembly, and the rights to a fair trial and democratic elections.[17] An open-ended list of gross human rights violations was included in the Statute. EO 13818 has 'reduced the threshold of sanctionable conduct from responsibility for "gross" human rights violations to being "responsible or complicit in, or to have directly or indirectly engaged in serious human rights abuse" (Hamer 2021; Booth 2020–2021).[18] The second situation concerns persons who are government officials or senior associates of government officials responsible for, or complicit in, ordering, controlling, or otherwise directing, acts of significant corruption, including the expropriation of private or public assets for personal gain, corruption related to government contracts or the extraction of natural resources, bribery, or the facilitation or transfer of the proceeds of corruption to foreign jurisdictions complicit in acts of significant corruption.[19]

In the EU, the trigger of sanctions is, on the one hand, genocide and crimes against humanity. In these situations, breaches of *erga omnes* obligations for States are committed. On the other hand, a non-exhaustive list of other violations may be included. In particular, these are the following: (a) serious human rights violations or abuses (torture and other cruel, inhuman or degrading treatment or punishment, slavery, extrajudicial, summary or arbitrary executions and killings, the enforced disappearance of persons, arbitrary arrests or detentions); (b) other human rights violations or abuses, 'in so far as those violations or abuses are *widespread, systematic* or are otherwise of serious concern as regards the objectives of the common foreign and security policy set out in Article 21 TEU'. The latter category includes: (a) trafficking in human beings, as well as abuses of human rights by migrant smugglers, sexual and gender-based violence, violations or abuses of freedom of peaceful assembly and of association, violations or abuses of freedom of opinion and expression, violations or abuses of freedom of religion or belief.

Thus, there are two important differences between the EUGHRSR and the GMA. The first is that the possibility to institute restrictive measures on those who engage in corruption is not provided for in the EU sanctions regime and there seem to be no plans to expand its scope. In the EU, the Council has chosen to counter specific forms of corruption (the misappropriation of State funds) in relation to three countries in the EU neighbourhood (Ukraine, Tunisia and Egypt[20]). According to a study of the European Parliament Research Service, one of the reasons behind this choice is that the Council struggled to maintain EU restrictive measures on the misappropriation of funds which were struck down by the ECJ in various cases between 2017 and 2020 (Russel, 2021)[21] The EU decision not to tackle corruption through the adoption of restrictive measures is wise, given the difficulties of demonstrating the actual violation of human rights as a result of corruption (Peters 2018; Davis 2018).[22]

The second difference is that the EU is concerned with a broader range of human rights breaches than the US; in addition, the EU seeks to ensure respect of the most important human rights conventions listed in Article 1(2), while the US adopts sanctions in the case of breaches of 'internationally recognized human rights'. Given that there are no references to EU human rights treaties included, this provision gives broad discretion to the President as to when the GMA can actually be used. In the EU, CFSP Decision no. 2020/1999 states that the Council lists persons who breach human rights having regard to 'customary international law and widely accepted instruments of international law'. Therefore, in principle, the EU's regime could be said to reinforce compliance with the mentioned international conventions having a multilateral nature. This is a positive aspect of the regime considering that the EUGHRSR has not been adopted to implement a UN Security Council Resolution. However, the mentioned provision essentially leaves the EU Council free to autonomously determine when the EUGHRSR can be used in situations where human rights protected by the listed Human Rights Treaties are breached. In principle, the Council's sanctions should be enacted as a reaction to findings or statements, released by the bodies entrusted to oversee compliance with the Human Rights Conventions listed in Article 1(2), that human rights were breached. This is one of the reasons the EUGHRSR has been criticised (Editorial 2021).[23] It is true that the EU's or the US's legitimacy in enacting sanctions would be greater in the case where an international body had pre-identified breaches of human rights;

otherwise, global human rights sanctions programmes run the risk of imposing sanctions in an arbitrary fashion. Even if the Council or the US President is entitled to institute sanctions for breaches of human rights obligations on the basis of autonomous foreign affairs concerns, it is submitted that there should be clear evidence, which could be provided by non-governmental organisation (NGO) reports or by other legal sources (i.e. the reports of an independent commission of enquiry or even the rulings of the European Court of Human Rights), that in a third country there have been breaches of human rights in order for the person identified as responsible to be sanctioned. Turning to the evidentiary burden required to impose restrictive measures, under the GMA, there must be credible evidence of breaches of human rights; in this respect, the role of NGOs and that of foreign governments is important.[24] In contrast, in the EUGHRSR regime, no evidentiary standards are set. The Council is bound to follow the directions provided on evidence by the ECJ. In particular, the Court requires this institution to have a set of indicia that are sufficiently specific, precise, and consistent to establish that there is a sufficient link between the person subject to a measure freezing his or her funds and the regime being combated.[25] Where possible, internet-based sources must be used for the listing but closed evidence in the Court may also be used. Failure to comply with these principles will lead to the annulment of the contested restrictive measure. In practice, the Court has been at times deferential to the Council since, for example, it has considered that it may be difficult for the Council to produce evidence because of the state of war in Syria.[26] However, there are also cases concerning the same third country regime in which the GC held that the Council had not discharged its obligation to provide evidence that the addressee of a certain sanction fulfilled the designation criteria.[27]

Turning to victims of human rights violations, the EU does not mention who they should be for the listing decision to be made; as a result, any serious breach of human rights that falls within the scope *ratione materiae* of the regime may trigger the sanctions. As for the US legislation, whistleblowers and human rights defenders have been the primary victims to be protected on the basis of the Magnitsky Act of 2012. This is understandable considering the history of the Statute. However, EO 13818 deviates from this choice and generalises the possibility to enact sanctions against any kinds of 'foreigners'.

Finally, while under the GMA it is clear when sanctions can be terminated,[28] the EU Council does not detail in its guidelines on the application of restrictive measures in what circumstances the latter will be abolished. For example, it is not clearly stated (as would be required for human rights to be respected) that human rights abusers will be de-listed if the designee 'has been prosecuted appropriately' for the activity, as in the case of the US legislation. Under the EUGHRSR, the list of designated persons is reviewed every year.

It is now necessary to examine the right to challenge restrictive measures or sanctions in the EU and the US.

Under the GMA, every year the US President[29] must present a report to Congress describing the individuals who have been sanctioned and the type of sanctions imposed.[30] It should be noted that these documents lack important pieces of information: while it is possible to identify the number of persons subject to sanctions, neither the full list of the designated persons nor the reasons for imposing such measures can be found. A database, including the names of all listed individuals or entities under the GMA or the EO 13818, is publicly available; however, the reasons for listing are lacking. In contrast, the EU Council lists in the annexes of the CFSP Decisions and Regulations the names of the persons and entities who are subject to restrictive measures and details the reasons why they fulfil the designation criteria. For this reason, it may be argued that the EU regime is more transparent than that of the US.

Under the GM Programmes, persons who are listed may ask the OFAC to delete their names from the list and are entitled to challenge the decisions of this agency before the courts. However, as was noted, 'courts apply the "arbitrary and capricious" standard under the Administrative Procedures Act, analysing whether the agency had reasonable basis for its action. This standard is "exceedingly deferential" to the agencies'.[31] To date, there seem to have been no cases of Magnitsky sanctions challenged before the US courts.[32]

Before the EU sanctions regime was enacted, Eckes argued that: 'The EU HRSR [...] cannot and should not be followed too closely [the US model of Global Magnitsky] as it does not offer judicial protection to those sanctioned in a way that would meet due process guarantees under the [EU] Charter of Fundamental Rights' (Eckes 2022).[33] This concern can be shared.

Turning to the EU context, since the entry into force of the Lisbon Treaty, the CFSP Decision instituting restrictive measures with respect to natural and legal persons and other state entities can be reviewed, under Article 275(2) TFEU. Annulment actions and a preliminary ruling on validity are legal remedies available for the addressees of sanctions. It is noteworthy that there is no case-law regarding challenges of designations under the EUGHRSR since so far none of the few persons listed under the authority of this horizontal regime has introduced any annulment actions with respect to the listing Decisions. However, looking at the way the ECJ has interpreted the right to legally challenge EU restrictive measures in general, it can be argued that, in the EU context, due process rights are respected and broad access to justice is offered to those who are listed. Due to space constraints, it is not possible to expand on the case-law on restrictive measures. However, we can say that Article 275(2) TFEU has been interpreted by the Court of Justice in light of the value of the rule of law and the right to effective judicial protection enshrined in Article 47 of the EU Charter of Fundamental rights (Poli 2023).[34] Recently, the ECJ has also enabled an Iranian bank with a branch in Germany designated in the US sanctions list to rely on the EU Blocking Regulation, prohibiting compliance with the US secondary sanctions, in order to bring civil proceedings concerning the alleged breach of the prohibition laid down by the regulation.[35]

It is now time to turn to how the sanctions programmes under examination have been applied in practice.

The application of the Global Magnitsky programmes and the EUGHRSR in practice and contestations over them

When the EUHRSR was enacted, Clara Portela aptly noted that the EU sanctions regime was 'unfinished business' since it was not clear how listings decisions might be turned into tools to promote human rights (Portela 2021).[36] Let us now consider the way the two Global Human Rights sanctions regimes have been applied in practice.

The US has widely used its GM programmes. According to the government, the US pursues a policy of rough balance between targets designated for human rights abuse and those listed for corruption (Congressional Research Service 2021).[37] In the first year of the application of EO 13818, the US designated 101 foreign persons (individuals or entities) for human rights abuses or corruption. In particular, persons who were responsible for, or complicit in, or having directly or indirectly engaged in, serious human rights abuse were designated in the following countries: Myanmar, Cambodia, the Democratic Republic of Congo, the Dominican Republic, Nicaragua, Saudi Arabia and Turkey. At the end of 2020, there were 243 persons or entities that filled the Special designation Lists.[38] By way of example, targeted persons include: Chinese officials for breaches of the human rights of Muslim minority groups in northwest China's Xinjiang province; corrupt actors in South Sudan involved in draining the country of critical resources; and Ugandan officials engaged in an adoption scam that victimised Ugandan-born children.[39] At the end of 2021, the number of designated persons was substantially the same as in 2020: a total of 148 individuals and 189 entities were listed; most of them were targets sanctioned because they were owned or controlled by a sanctioned individual.[40] According to the numbers quoted in a report of the Congressional Research Service, 89 were designated primarily for human rights abuses and 56 were listed primarily for corruption (only three persons were designated in relation to both human rights abuses and corruption).[41] As of 29 August 2022, about 400 persons or entities designated under the authority of the GM Programmes can be counted in the database which is publicly available; the sanctioned persons are spread over 40 countries.[42] Recently, the US has relied on the GMA to sanction perpetrators of gross human rights violations carried out in 2017–2018 against the Russian human rights defender Oyub Titiev, leader of the Chechen branch of the Memorial, an organisation that documents human rights violations and which was banned in 2021.[43] The latest listing concerns Liberian officials whose property and interests were blocked, since 'through their corruption these officials have undermined democracy in Liberia for their own personal benefit'.[44] Designations under the authorities of the Global Magnitsky programme for human rights abuses were even made in the context of the conflict provoked by Russia in Ukraine.[45]

In the US, the vast majority of persons are subject to financial sanctions rather than visa bans.[46] In the EU, targeted persons are usually the object of both forms of sanctions; visa bans are implemented by Member States.

Turning to the EU, the Council relied on the EUGHRSR for the first time in March 2021. Three different CFSP Decisions were adopted to fill the EU lists: 17 persons were the target of financial measures and entry restrictions (in addition, five entities were the object of asset freezes). This shows a tendency to use only sparingly the EUGHRSR instead of third country sanctions regimes.[47] For example, restrictive measures for human rights violations carried out after the coup d'état of 1 February 2021 by officials in Myanmar were made under the country specific sanctions regime.[48] The EU has also relied on the existing Ukrainian sanctions regime of 2014[49] to impose asset freezes and visa bans on 65 persons and 18 entities involved in human rights abuses in the context of the conflict started in 24 February 2022. The specific reasons to institute restrictive measures was to 'ensure accountability for human-rights violations and violations of international humanitarian law in Ukraine by the Armed Forces of the Russian Federation'.[50] In particular, Russian nationals were sanctioned for 'the reported atrocities committed by the Armed Forces of the Russian Federation in Bucha and other Ukrainian towns'.[51] Members of the Federal Service of the National Guard of the Russian Federation (Rosgvardia) were also included in the EU restrictive measures for taking part in the killing, rape and torture of civilians in Bucha.[52] The EU could have used the EUGHRSR to impose sanctions on account of these mentioned breaches but it refrained from doing so.

In principle, one of the advantages of using thematic sanctions regimes is their flexibility (Borrell Fontelles 2021);[53] indeed, imposing an asset freeze or a visa ban on human rights abusers should be politically easier than imposing global sanctions on a certain third country. The EU's reluctance to make use of its horizontal sanctions regime that addresses human rights abuses is not easy to explain.

Turning to the persons actually included in the EU lists, the first targeted persons in March 2021 were four officials involved in the arbitrary arrests and detention of Alexei Navalny, as well as widespread and systematic repression of freedom of peaceful assembly and of association, and freedom of opinion and expression in Chechnya.[54] It should be emphasised that the ECtHR in various rulings against Russia confirmed that Navalny's arrest breached the obligations of the European Convention of Human Rights and Fundamental Freedoms. In particular, the Strasbourg Court found that Russian authorities had deprived the Russian political leader of his freedom in an arbitrary manner.[55] When this person was re-arrested in 2021, the ECtHR upheld his request for interim measures, under Rule 39, and required the Russian government to release him with immediate effect. This decision was grounded on this country's inability to protect Navalny's life. Russia refused to implement the Court's ruling.[56] In this context, there is little doubt that serious breaches of human rights were committed by Russian officials in relation to Navalny's arrest in 2021. Listing those who were responsible for the arrest in a situation in which the Strasbourg Court had recognised that Russia had breached its obligations is to be welcomed. As a result of the rulings of the ECtHR, there was certainly credible evidence that the rights of the mentioned person were violated.

A few days after the first listing of early March 2021, the EU Council imposed restrictive measures on a number of other persons and entities. These were four Chinese individuals and one entity responsible for large-scale arbitrary detentions and degrading treatment of Uighurs and other minorities and were thus included on the EU 'blacklists'. It is noteworthy that there are no country-specific sanctions regimes in place in the EU for breaches of international law committed by China (with the exception of an arms embargo).[57] Further targeted persons were high-level officials and entities of the DPRK, members of the militia in Libya, Russian officials operating in the Chechen Republic, members of the security forces of South Sudan, and one entity in Eritrea (the National Security Office of the Government of Eritrea). In all cases, persons were designated for repressive policies[58] with respect to members of the opposition or civil society or gender-based minorities.

The third group of persons listed in December 2021 is represented by the Wagner Group and three of its members. This is a Russia-based unincorporated private military entity, active in Ukraine, Syria, Libya, the Central African Republic (CAR), Sudan and Mozambique. This entity was established in 2014 as a successor organisation of the Slavonic Corps. It is led by Dimitriy Utkin, who was also included on the blacklist together with an advisor to the President of the Central African Republic (CAR), who is defined 'as a key figure in the Wagner Group's command structure and keeps close links with the Russian authorities'.[59] What is striking is that three members of the Wagner Group were included in the EUGHRSR while other participants of the same Group feature in third country sanctions regimes such as those concerning the situation in Ukraine, Libya and Syria. It is noteworthy that the founder of this Group appears in both the Syrian and the horizontal sanctions regimes.[60] It is not clear what the reasons are for this duplication of listings.

Serious human rights violations such as torture, extrajudicial, summary or arbitrary executions and killings in Syria are the grounds for the listing of this Group and of its members which is formed by officials of the intelligence service or Russian state security.[61] The EU justifies its action on the basis of the objectives of the Common Foreign and Security Policy, in particular the consolidation and support for democracy, the rule of law, human rights and the principles of international law in accordance with point (b) of Article 21(2) TEU.[62] Overall, the EU has listed persons, groups and entities responsible for many of the situations of gross or serious human rights violations envisaged in CFSP Decision 1999/2000. One may note that so far none of the listings has designated persons for the trafficking of human beings.

The way the two Global Human Rights Sanctions Regimes have been implemented reveals the following trends. The first is that although both the EU and the US seek to consolidate respect of human rights abroad, the EU has been far more selective[63] than the US in its sanctions practice.[64] A few high-profile cases of human rights abuses have been the object of restrictive measures. However, in contrast to the US, no persons were listed either for violations of human rights in Tigray[65] or for the murder of the Saudi journalist Jamal Khashoggi. The European Parliament unsuccessfully asked the EU and its Member States to consider imposing sanctions through the Human Rights Sanctions mechanisms in both cases.[66] The US listed members of the Cuban political leadership for the repression of peaceful demonstrations in July 2021 while the EU refrained from doing so.

The second trend is that neither in the EU nor in the US do the authorities enacting the sanctions justify the adoption of the restrictive measures for breaches of specific Treaties obligations. Therefore, the sanctions are autonomously determined by the EU Council and the US President, which is a reason for criticism. We will return to this issue in section 4.

The third trend is that to the extent the EU decides to rely on the EUGHRSR, the persons or entities included in the EU list also mostly appear in the SDL of the US[67] or at least were sanctioned on the same day in both jurisdictions, as in the case of three Chinese officials who were targeted in both countries on 22 March 2022. However, the US followed the EU's lead in imposing sanctions on seven Russian officials who were involved in Navalny's arrest. In one case involving an army general, Lokujo, who was responsible for extrajudicial, summary or arbitrary executions and killings in South Sudan, the EU included his name on the list independently of the US. As for the Wagner Group, the US has neither imposed sanctions on this entity, nor on all those on the EU listing decision of December 2021. In sum, there is a certain degree of coordination between the EU and the US (as well as with Canada and the UK) in listing human rights abusers (Poli 2021).[68] However, there is no systematic alignment of the EU sanctions decisions with those of the US.

Both the EU and US sanctions regimes have been contested on two grounds: first, being unilateral coercive measures, they are not in line with international law, as it is emphasised by a resolution of the UN Human rights Council of 2021 adopted with a recorded vote of 30 to 15 (with 2 abstentions);[69] second, human rights sanctions regimes and in particular those available in the US would not respect human right standards of the addressees (Ruys 2017).[70]

As for the former criticism, one of the points which is made is that unilateral coercive measures interfere in the domestic affairs of a sovereign country. However, Bjorge argues: Human rights are examples of matters that fall outside the State's *domaine réservé*. The principle of State sovereignty does not allow States to decide freely on matters relating to fundamental human rights. For that reason, unilateral sanctions imposed with a view to inducing a State to cease breaches of human rights do not concern matters in which the State is permitted, by the principle of State sovereignty, freely to decide (Bjorge 2022).[71]

The author shares the view that the EU and US human rights regimes are compatible with international law; in particular, even if the US or EU does not act to implement a UNSC Resolution, they may lawfully adopt restrictive measures to dissuade abusers of human rights from continuing their breaches of *erga omnes* obligations which are binding on the States in whose territories these persons operate. Having said this, it should be acknowledged that the EU is sometimes ambiguous with respect to the objectives of the EUHRSR; for example, the EEAS has described the human rights sanctions regime as an instrument to give the EU 'more leverage to support democracy worldwide'.[72] While the promotion of democracy is an EU and US value and qualifies as an objective of EU external action and US security strategy,[73] it cannot be said that it is an *erga omnes* obligation for a state to be ruled on the basis of democratic principles. In addition, it should be acknowledged that measures against corrupted officials cannot be justified in the name of breaches of *erga omnes* obligations by third countries. However, as Ruys notes, restrictive measures against corrupted officials are not contrary to international law.[74]

Turning to the second criticism, the EUHRSR is contested since it has the potential of having a punitive character without having been enacted in full respect of the guarantees associated with acts of a criminal nature. This criticism may be extended to the GMA, which is the source of inspiration of the EU measures. Some scholars note that asset freezes may qualify as being punitive in nature if the so-called

Engels[75] criteria are met. Without it being necessary to delve into a full legal analysis of these criteria, suffice it to say that the decisive one is that asset freezes tend to last for an indefinite period of time, thus making these measures 'resemble a *de facto* appropriation of property akin to permanent criminal confiscation' (Al-Nassar, Neele, Nishioka and Luthra 2021).[76] These scholars argue that restrictive measures gravitate toward being more punitive than preventive when they are addressed to persons for their past behaviour and when they are no longer in a position of power. In these cases these measures should guarantee respect to principles related to criminal proceedings, including the presumption of innocence.[77]

The present author takes the view that listings under the EUGHRSR are not punitive in nature since they are temporary (and subject to review every 12 months); in any case, it is too early to say that asset freezes enacted on the basis of the EUGHRSR are permanent, given that they have been in place only since 2021. In addition, the addressees of restrictive measures can submit observations to the Council after these measures are enacted and can challenge the listing Decisions before the ECJ. Although the Council enjoys great discretion in imposing restrictive measures, the ECJ has upheld annulment actions brought by targeted persons. In recent times, some have been upheld on the ground that the Council has not complied with the right to effective judicial protection protected under Article 47 of the Charter, as hinted at in section 2. All these elements contribute to lessen concerns regarding the failure of EU sanctions to respect the human rights of the addressees of the sanctions.

The contribution of the EUGHRSR and GMA to the protection of human rights: concluding remarks

We have seen that the US has often used its GM programmes to address human rights abuses as well as corruption: in contrast, the EU has been far more selective in using restrictive measures in the case of human rights breaches, despite its sensitivity towards these kind of violations.[78] The Council has targeted persons or entities responsible for gross violations of human rights from a core group of countries such as China, the Democratic People's Republic of Korea (DPRK), Libya, Eritrea, South Sudan, and Russia.[79] The addressees of restrictive measures include high-ranking officials and other state entities, members of military bodies and also military groups such as the Wagner Group.

In contrast to the GMA, the EU scheme can be considered residual with respect to third country sanctions regimes. While the deterrent effect has been overall modest, it has been a useful signalling instrument in the following situations: (a) to react to gross violations of human rights when there are no third country specific sanctions regimes; (b) when a member of the UNSC with veto power is responsible for these breaches (as in the case of China and Russia).[80]

It is now time to assess whether the two Global Human Right Sanctions Programmes should be maintained. Economic sanctions are optimistically defined by an American NGO as 'an effective resource to publicly repudiate and impose repercussions for human rights abuses, providing leverage in countries where accountability strategies are otherwise limited'.[81] The author takes the view that both the US and EU Global Human Regimes serve to react to human rights abuses in situations where silence over serious or even gross human rights violations would be tantamount to considering similar breaches acceptable. The added value of these regimes is that they send a political signal of disapproval to the third country in which the concerned violations were committed. The enactment of a collection of unilateral coercive measures between 2016 and 2020 to deter State officials from committing human rights abuses shows that a number of states are willing to stigmatise gross breaches of human rights through sanctions so as to deter human rights abusers from continuing to act as they do. It is certainly unsatisfactory that this has been done from a single component of the international community (Western countries); this weakens the importance of universal values such as the protection of human rights. Despite the disappointing number of countries wishing to rely on sanctions to counter human rights abuses, in the opinion of this author, the two sanction regimes are useful legal instruments that complement other diplomatic tools such as statements on the human rights situations that require the attention of the US government and the Council used by the EU and the US to reinforce respect of human rights. It is necessary to resort to unilateral measures particularly when UN-organisms such as the Human Rights Council are dominated by countries tolerating or committing through their state organs human rights abuses.[82] In a comparison between the two horizontal regimes, the EUGHRSR emerges as less contestable than the GM programmes for its legality, given that it does not address corruption and it has been used in practice in a few cases of well-documented situations of human rights abuses.

Notes

1 The research at the basis of the essay is updated to end September 2022. The Sergei Magnitsky Rule of Law Accountability Act of 2012, Public Law No. 112–208, § 402, 126 Stat. 1496, 1503. As a reaction to Magnitsky's death, the US Congress enacted the Statute mentioned above and targeted individuals involved in the detention, abuse, or death of Sergei Magnitsky, or were involved in the criminal conspiracy uncovered by Magnitsky. Press Release, U.S. Department of Treasure, Treasury Targets Individuals Involved in the Sergei Magnitsky Case and Other Gross Violations of Human Rights in Russia (20 December 2017), https://home.treasury.gov/news/press-releases/sm0240. Financial sanctions and visa bans were imposed on 18 persons. See Thomas H. Wilson & J. Robert Sheppard II, 2019. In memory of Sergei Magnitsky: A lawyer's role in promoting and protecting international human rights *Hous J Int'l L*, 41, 343–349. In 2014 the European Parliament recommended that the Council adopt visa bans against the Russian officials responsible for the killing of Sergei Magnitsky. However, this request was not accommodated. See European Parliament recommendation to the Council of 2 April 2014 on establishing common visa restrictions for Russian officials involved in the Sergei Magnitsky case, OJ 2017, C 408/43.

2 International Emergency Economic Powers Act, 91 Stat. 1625 (1977), P.L. 95–223, 91 Stat. 1626.

3 See section 2.

4 Council Decision (CFSP) 2020/1999 of 7 December 2020 concerning restrictive measures against serious human rights violations and abuses, OJ 2020, L 410I/13; Council Regulation 2020/1998/EU of 7 December 2020 concerning restrictive measures against serious human rights violations and abuses, OJ 2020, L 410 I/1.

5 Justice for Victims of Corrupt Foreign Officials Act S.C. 2017, c.21 ('Sergei Magnitsky Law').
6 The Global Human Rights Sanctions Regulations 2020, no. 680, https://www.legislation.gov.uk/uksi/2020/680/made.
7 For comparative remarks on the way the sanction regimes work, see M. Russel, 2020. EU human rights sanctions-towards a European Magnitsky Act, European Parliament research Service, https://www.europarl.europa.eu/italy/resource/static/files/import/seminario_per_giornalisti_sakharov/eprs-briefing-659402-eu-human-rights-sanctions-final.pdf.
8 In 2018 the Dutch Parliament adopted a motion that urged the government to propose the creation of the new regime at the EU level.
9 M. Russel, 2020. Global human rights sanctions – Mapping Magnitsky laws: The US, Canadian, UK and EU approach, European Parliament Research Service, 5.
10 European Parliament resolution of 14 March 2019 on a European human rights violations sanctions regime, 2019/2580(RSP), point 6. The Parliament's request with respect to adopting listing decisions by qualified majority was not accepted.
11 In both jurisdictions, these entities include those owned by more than 50% by the designated human rights abusers.
12 For the legal framework on the basis of which visa restrictions may be imposed, see Department of State: Notices: Global Magnitsky Human Rights Accountability Act Annual Report, Federal Register vol. 83, no. 248 (2018), 18 December 2018, 67460, 67463.
13 https://home.treasury.gov/system/files/126/12212017_glomag_faqs.pdf.
14 Taylor Booth, 2020–2021. The Global Magnitsky Act: U.S. leadership or lip service in the fight against corruption? *Journal of Global Rights and Organizations*, 11, 1, 17.
15 Commission guidance note on the implementation of certain provisions of council regulation (EU) 2020/1998, COM (2020) 9432, 2.
16 Art. 1(a) ii).
17 Section 1263(a)(1) of P.L. 114–328.
18 David I. Hamer, 2021. Commentary: The European Union joins the global Magnitsky movement. *N.Y.U.J. Int'l L. & Pol*, 53, 1003, 1009. According to Booth, the EO makes it possible to punish acts of 'corruption' rather than 'significant corruption'; in addition, the Executive Order of 20 December 2017 does not seek to punish only those who expose illegal activity by the government or promote human rights. Booth, n. 14, 15.
19 Section 1263(a)(3).
20 The "misappropriation regime" in Egypt was abolished in 2020. For more information on the three sanction regimes see https://www.sanctionsmap.eu/#/main, accessed on 7 September 2022.
21 M. Russel, 2021. Global human rights sanctions – Mapping Magnitsky laws: The US, Canadian, UK and EU approach, European Parliament Research Service, https://www.europarl.europa.eu/thinktank/en/document/EPRS_BRI(2021)698791, 6.
22 On this issue, see Anne Peters, 2018. Corruption as a violation of international human rights. *European Journal of International Law*, 29, 1251, 1287. For scholars who take a different view, see Kevin E. Davis, 2019. Corruption as a violation of international human rights: A reply to Anne Peters (1 November 2019). *European Journal of International Law*, 29, 1297 ff.
23 More precisely, it is argued that the EUGHRSR makes no reference to breaches of specific human rights instruments and no trial or any process of adjudication is foreseen by the EU restrictive measures. It is not clear on what factual basis the listing decision rests. See Editorial, 2021. *CMLRev,* 621, 630.
24 GMA, sec 1263(a) & (c).
25 Case C-630/13 P *Anbouba v Council*, ECLI:EU:C:2015:247, para 53.
26 Case C-193/15 P *Akhras v Council*, ECLI:EU:C:2016:219, para 61.
27 Case T-249/20, *Abdelkader Sabra v Council*, ECLI:EU:T:2022:140.
28 These circumstances are the following: a) the designee does not engage in the activity for which sanctions were imposed; the designee 'has been prosecuted appropriately' for the activity; the designee has significantly changed his or her behaviour, 'paid an appropriate

consequence', and credibly committed not to engage in future sanctionable activity; or the termination is in the interest of U.S. national security. Congressional Research Service, The Global Magnitsky Human Rights Accountability Act, 3 December 2021, 8, available at https://crsreports.congress.gov.

29 In contrast, EO 13818 imposes the obligation to draw the report on the Departments of State and Treasury.

30 GMA, 1264(a), (b).

31 International Corporate Accountability Roundtable (ICAR), U.S. *Sanctions regimes & human rights accountability strategies*, 2018, 14, https://enoughproject.org/wp-content/uploads/2018/06/ToolsofTrade_Enough_ICAR_June2018.pdf.

32 Hamer, n. 18, 1014–1015.

33 C. Eckes, 2022. EU global human rights sanctions regime: is the genie out of the bottle?, *Journal of Contemporary European Studies*, 30, 255, 263.

34 S. Poli, 2022. Article 47 of the Charter of Fundamental Rights in the Common Foreign and Security Policy: Does it afford adequate protection of the right to effective judicial protection to private parties? in Eliantonio, M. Bonelli, G. Gentile, eds. *Article 47 of EU Charter and effective judicial protection: The Court of Justice's perspective, I,* 2022 173 ff.

35 Case C-124/20 *Bank Melli Iran v Council*, ECLI:EU:C:2021:1035.

36 C. Portela, 2021. The EU human rights sanctions regime: Unfinished business? *Revista General de Derecho Europeo* 54, 19, 44.

37 Congressional Research Service, n. 28, 9.

38 Department of State: Notices: Global Magnitsky Human Rights Accountability Act Annual Report, Federal register vol. 86 (2021) n. 1, 4 January 2022, 174, 175, accessed on 10 August 2022.

39 *Id.*

40 Congressional Research Service, n. 28, 10.

41 Ib.

42 For more information, see https://sanctionssearch.ofac.treas.gov/, accessed on 29 August 2022.

43 https://home.treasury.gov/news/press-releases/jy0654, accessed on 15 August 2022.

44 https://home.treasury.gov/news/press-releases/jy0921, accessed on 16 August 2022.

45 See Office of Foreign Assets control changes to the Specially Designated Nationals and Blocked Persons List since 1 January 2022, 114–117. However, the US has enacted the bulk of its sanction against Russia on the basis of EO 14024 of 15 April 2021, 'Blocking Property with Respect to Specified Harmful Foreign Activities of the Government of the Russian Federation'.

46 These are enacted under authorisation through Section 7031(c) of the annual appropriations bill for the Department of State, Foreign Operations, and Related Programs (SFOPS).

47 These are the following: Burma, Belarus, Burundi, Democratic Republic of Congo, Democratic Republic of North Korea, Iran, Libya, Nicaragua, Russia, Syria and Venezuela.

48 Council Decision (CFSP) 2021/482 of 22 March 2021 amending Decision 2013/184/CFSP concerning restrictive measures against Myanmar/Burma, OJ 2021, L 99/I/13.

49 Council Decision 2014/145/CFSP of 17 March 2014 concerning restrictive measures in respect of actions undermining or threatening the territorial integrity, sovereignty and independence of Ukraine, OJ 2014, L 78/16.

50 Council Decision (CFSP) 2022/883 of 3 June 2022 amending Decision 2014/145/CFSP concerning restrictive measures in respect of actions undermining or threatening the territorial integrity, sovereignty and independence of Ukraine, OJ 2022, L 153/92, recital 3.

51 Id.

52 Council Decision (CFSP) 2022/1272 of 21 July 2022 amending Decision 2014/145/CFSP concerning restrictive measures in respect of actions undermining or threatening the territorial integrity, sovereignty and independence of Ukraine, OJ 2022, L 193/219.

53 J. Borrell Fontelles, 2021. European foreign policy in times of COVID-19, Brussels, 145.
54 Council Decision (CFSP) 2021/372 of 2 March 2021 amending Decision (CFSP) 2020/1999 concerning restrictive measures against serious human rights violations and abuses, OJ 2021, L 71I/6.
55 ECtHR, Navalny v. Russia, application no. 29580/12, 36847/12, 11252/13, 12317/13 and 43746/14, judgement of 15 November 2018. The Court found that Russia had breached Articles 5.1, 6.1 and 11 ECHR.
56 Parliamentary Assembly of the Council of Europe, Report, The arrest and detention of Alexei Navalny in January 2021, Doc. 15270, 19 April 2021, https://assembly.coe.int/nw/xml/XRef/Xref-XML2HTML-en.asp?fileid=29161&lang=en, accessed on 15 August 2022.
57 https://ec.europa.eu/commission/presscorner/detail/en/MEMO_16_2258.
58 These include torture and other cruel, inhuman or degrading treatment or punishment, extrajudicial, summary or arbitrary executions and killings, enforced disappearance of persons, and arbitrary arrests or detentions, as well as widespread forced labour and sexual violence against women.
59 Council Decision (CFSP) 2021/2197 of 13 December 2021 amending Decision (CFSP) 2020/1999 concerning restrictive measures against serious human rights violations and abuses, OJ 2021, LI 445/17, annex.
60 https://www.consilium.europa.eu/en/press/press-releases/2021/12/13/eu-imposes-restrictive-measures-against-the-wagner-group/pdf (accessed on 10 September 2022).
61 Council Decision (CFSP) 2021/2197, n. 59, recital 5.
62 Ib., recital 6.
63 According to the NGO Human Rights First, the US Administration ignored credible evidence of sanctionable conduct in Azerbaijan, Bahrain, Egypt, the Philippines, Tajikistan, the United Arab Emirates, and Uzbekistan. Booth, n. 14, 19.
64 However, as of 2021, about 56/145 designations concerned cases of corruption.
65 The U.S. Department of the Treasury's Office of Foreign Assets Control (OFAC) sanctioned General Filipos Woldeyohannes (Filipos), the Chief of Staff of the Eritrean Defence Forces (EDF), for being a leader or official of an entity that is engaged in serious human rights abuse committed during the ongoing conflict in Tigray (August 2021).
66 P9_TA(2021)0421 Humanitarian situation in Tigray, European Parliament resolution of 7 October 2021 on the humanitarian situation in Tigray (2021/2902(RSP)), OJ 2022, C 132/L 205, para 23; P9_TA(2021)0357, The death penalty in Saudi Arabia, notably the cases of Mustafa Hashem al-Darwish and Abdullah al-Howaiti European Parliament resolution of 8 July 2021 on the death penalty in Saudi Arabia, notably the cases of Mustafa Hashem al-Darwish and Abdullah al-Howaiti (2021/2787(RSP)), OJ 2022, C 99/85, para. 20.
67 On 22 March 2021, the EU imposed restrictive measures against persons or entities who already featured in the US sanction lists. These were officials from China, North Korea, one Chinese entity, one entity from North Korea (the Central Public Prosecutor's Office), one Libyan militia member (Kaniyat Militia), one governmental entity from Eritrea, two members of the ISIS who operated in Libya, and Russians who conducted persecutions in the Chechen Republic.
68 S. Poli, 2021. The UK as a third country: The current model of cooperation with the European Union in the adoption of restrictive measures. *European Papers*, 6, 141–154.
69 Resolution n. 46/5, The negative impact of unilateral coercive measures on the enjoyment of human rights, 23 March 2021, Report of the Human Right Council to the UN General Assembly, A/76/53, 42.
70 T. Ruys, 2017. Reflections on the global Magnitsky Act and the use of targeted sanctions in the fight against grand corruption *Revue Belge de Droit International*, 50 492, 507–508.
71 E. Bjorge, 2022. Unilateral and extraterritorial sanctions symposium: The human rights dimension of unilateral sanctions, https://opiniojuris.org/2022/03/03/unilateral-and-extraterritorial-sanctions-symposium-the-human-rights-dimension-of-unilateral-sanctions/.

72 Borrell Fontelles, n. 53, 141.

73 See National Security Strategy of the Unites States of America, December 2017, 4, available at https://history.defense.gov/Historical-Sources/National-Security-Strategy/.

74 Ruys, n. 69, 501.

75 ECtHR, *Engel and Others v the Netherlands*, Application no. 5100/71 (8 June 1976).

76 Hanine Al-Nassar, Eveline Neele, Shingo Nishioka and Vedika Luthra, 2021. Guilty until proven innocent? The EU Global Human Rights Sanctions Regime's potential reversal of the burden of proof. *Security and Human Rights* 1, 13.

77 Id., 17.

78 See the full range of the EU's concerns over human right abuses in the Joint Communication to the European Parliament and the Council, EU Action Plan on Human Rights and Democracy 2020–2024, JOIN (2020) 5.

79 Council Decision (CFSP) 2021/481 of 22 March 2021 amending Decision (CFSP) 2020/1999 concerning restrictive measures against serious human rights violations and abuses, OJ 2021, L 99I/25.

80 It would be politically difficult to establish a sanctions regime in view of the human right breaches in China due to the importance of this third country for EU trade relations.

81 International Corporate Accountability Roundtable (ICAR), n. 31, 18.

82 For example, the EU has made statements at the UN Human Right Council to urge China to allow meaningful access to the Xinjiang Uighur Autonomous Region for independent observers, including the UN High Commissioner for Human Rights. The EU also calls for the release of human rights defenders. See https://www.eeas.europa.eu/delegations/un-geneva/hrc43-item-4-human-rights-situations-require-councils-attention-eu-statement_en of 10 March 2020, accessed on 16 August 2022.

References

Al-Nassar, H., Neele, E., Nishioka, S., Luthra, V., 2021. Guilty until proven innocent? The EU Global Human Rights Sanctions Regime's potential reversal of the burden of proof. *Security and Human Rights* 1, 25.

Bjorge, E., 2022. Unilateral and extraterritorial sanctions symposium: The human rights dimension of unilateral sanctions. https://opiniojuris.org/2022/03/03/unilateral-and-extraterritorial-sanctions-symposium-the-human-rights-dimension-of-unilateral-sanctions/.

Borrell Fontelles, J., 2021. *European foreign policy in times of COVID-19*, Brussels.

Booth, T., 2020-2021. The Global Magnitsky Act: U.S. leadership or lip service in the fight against corruption? *Journal of Global Rights and Organizations*, 11, 1, 34.

Congressional Research Service. (2021). he Global Magnitsky Human Rights Accountability Act, 3 December 2021, 8, available at https://crsreports.congress.gov'

Davis, K. E., 2018. Corruption as a violation of international human rights: A reply to Anne Peters (1 November 2019). *European Journal of International Law*, 29, 1289–1296.

Eckes, C., 2022. EU global human rights sanctions regime: Is the genie out of the bottle? *Journal of Contemporary European Studies*, 30, 255–269.

Editorial, 2021. *CMLRev*, 58, 621–634.

Hamer, D. I., 2021. Commentary: The European Union joins the global Magnitsky movement. *N.Y.U. J. Int'l L. & Pol*, 53, 1003–1015.

Peters, A., 2018. Corruption as a violation of international human rights. *European Journal of International Law*, 1251, 1287.

Poli, P., 2022. Article 47 of the Charter of Fundamental Rights in the Common Foreign and Security Policy: Does it afford adequate protection of the right to effective judicial protection to private parties? in Eliantonio, M., Bonelli, M., Gentile, G., (eds). *Article 47 of EU Charter and effective judicial protection: The Court of Justice's perspective, I*, 2022, 177,192.

Poli, P., 2021. The UK as a third country: The current model of cooperation with the European Union in the adoption of restrictive measures. *European Papers*, 6, 141–154.

Portela, C., 2021. The EU human rights sanctions regime: Unfinished business? *Revista General de Derecho Europeo* 54, 19,44.

Russel, M., 2021. *Global human rights sanctions – Mapping Magnitsky laws: The US, Canadian, UK and EU approach*, European Parliament Research Service, https://www.europarl.europa.eu/thinktank/en/document/EPRS_BRI(2021)698791.

Russel, M., 2020. EU human rights sanctions-towards a European Magnitsky Act, European Parliament Research Service, https://www.europarl.europa.eu/italy/resource/static/files/import/seminario_per_giornalisti_sakharov/eprs-briefing-659402-eu-human-rights-sanctions-final.pdf.

Ruys, T., 2017. Reflections on the global Magnitsky Act and the use of targeted sanctions in the fight against grand corruption. *Revue Belge de Droit International*, 50, 492,512.

Wilson, T. H., & Sheppard II, J., 2019. In memory of Sergei Magnitsky: A lawyer's role in promoting and protecting international human rights. *Hous J Int'l L*, 41, 343,386.

8

NATO AND TRANSATLANTIC SECURITY RELATIONS

Gabriella Bolstad and Karsten Friis

NORWEGIAN INSTITUTE OF INTERNATIONAL AFFAIRS (NUPI)

Introduction

Since the Second World War, the North Atlantic Treaty Organization (NATO) has by many been considered the most important embodiment and symbol of what is often referred to as the 'West'. NATO has represented an institutionalisation of transatlantic relations through decades of shifting challenges, and remains to be the backbone of Western security, even if transatlantic relations as such has rapidly evolved encompassing numerous sectors and industries. As argued by several authors in this volume (see e.g. Jancic, 2023, in this Handbook), the United States and Europe share many fundamental political and societal values – and democratic principles are also the foundation of NATO's solidarity rests on. A defence alliance cannot be purely instrumental – the mutual security commitments and alliance solidarity require constant maintenance. If not, the political commitment cannot be taken for granted in situations of crisis and war. Hence, in this chapter, we ask how NATO has managed to remain relevant throughout all these years, and in particular how have the recent turbulent years in Washington D.C. and the renewed tensions with Russia have impacted the organisation?

The NATO-in-crisis literature represents a rather pessimistic narrative by overstating NATOs internal disputes thus impending that the Alliance has seemed ineffectual and on the verge of internal collapse on several instances (see Cox, 2005; Menon, 2007). On the other hand, there are numerous scholarly explanations of why NATO has indeed endured and demonstrated to be resilient throughout many decades – despite many crisis-prone situations. Adapting its policies and reforming its institutional and military structures has been important (Jordan, 1967; 1987; Smith, 1990; Michta and Hilde, 2014; Krüger, 2014; Lindley-French, 2015), but the US leadership and the deterrent effect of its nuclear arsenal are perhaps stronger explanations (Efjestad and Tamnes, 2020). Furthermore, NATO has become a crucial venue for developing shared threat assessments and responses, which has contributed to keeping the ever-larger family of allies united (see e.g. Riddervold and Newsome, 2018; Riddervold et al, 2023, in this handbook).

DOI: 10.4324/9781003283911-10

This chapter will build on several of these analyses and offer a brief discussion of NATO's key historical moments and turning points set in the Cold War phase; the post–Cold War phase; and the post-9/11 phase. Each of these periods witnessed different kinds of challenges for NATO, and therefore also distinct kinds of responses. With this background, we will turn to the post-2014 phase where Russian warfare has served to strengthen NATO cohesion and resolve focussed on collective defence. We will argue that in today's critical situation, the combination of strong US engagement and leadership with a broadly shared threat perception among Allies (primarily towards Russia) is the combination that continues to make NATO a significant embodiment of transatlantic security relations.

The Cold War phase

Since its founding in 1949, NATO's primary purpose has consisted of its allies' shared commitment to defend common interests and liberal-democratic values through collective defence. During the Cold War, the geopolitical tensions between the Western and Eastern blocs defined this transatlantic relationship. NATO contributed to a greater sense of West European cohesion and provided a mechanism for the United States to participate in European economic and military recovery (McCalla, 1996). While allies differed in their attitudes over tactical means, strategy, burden-sharing and US leadership, unity continued to be fostered by the overarching raison d'être, threat of Soviet expansionism (Webber et al., 2012).

In the 1950s, the analogy between the Korean War and the division of Germany acted as an impetus for the institutional expansion and the reconstruction of NATO's architecture. The growing emphasis on military preparedness due to the anxiety of a potential full-scale Soviet incursion in Western Europe led to the formal adoption of NATO's Massive Retaliation doctrine working as a deterrent and concurrently allowing European allies to focus on economic and political recovery. Shortly after, US General Dwight D. Eisenhower was appointed as the first Supreme Allied Commander Europe (SACEUR) and the Supreme Headquarters Allied Powers Europe (SHAPE) was established.

The 1962 Cuban Missile Crisis and the Soviet achievement of nuclear parity raised concerns about the credibility of US nuclear guarantee through extended deterrence (Johnston, 2017; Stoddart, 2012). While Britain accepted US leadership, the French government decided to withdraw from NATO's integrated military structure in 1966, following President Charles de Gaulle's refusal to accept the collective control over French armed forces (Krüger, 2014). In the aftermath, NATO became a political instrument for détente, seeking to ease strained relations with the Soviet bloc (Krüger, 2014; Schmidt, 2014). This was reflected in the Harmel report which introduced a dual-track policy comprising both deterrence and détente. The Flexible Response doctrine was formally adopted in 1967 as a triad of conventional, tactical nuclear and strategic nuclear deterrence (Hartley and Sandler, 1999). According to Stoddart (2012) and Thies (2009), the Flexible Response worked as a compromise strategy with the attempt to couple American and European strategic preferences.

During the 1970s, NATO continued to be based on the concepts of deterrence and détente. The US preoccupation with the war in Vietnam and the Soviets achievement of parity in strategic nuclear forces led to increasing US dissatisfaction over undue share of the transatlantic security calling for Europe to do more for their defence (Stoddart, 2012). Concurrently, European statesmen raised concerns over US troop reductions on the European continent. According to Stoddart (2012), the declining confidence in US military commitment raised questions over whether a US President would sacrifice the American homeland for the sake of Europe.

The growing rift between the United States and Europe concerning burden-sharing in conjunction with declining credibility of US nuclear protection led to the Dual-Track approach in 1979 to stive for a US-USSR arms control agreement, while simultaneously planning to deploy new US intermediate-range nuclear forces (INF) in Western Europe (Thies, 2009). The Dual-Track approach proved to be another hardship test for NATO due to large anti-nuclear protests in Europe. The disputes over United States increased defence spending and Europeans' preference for arms control and détente were possibly the most significant transatlantic challenge since the Second World War.

Nevertheless, as Thies (2009) argues, the general support of the transatlantic Alliance remained stable broadly in the premise that NATO-benefits outweighed the negatives for both sides of the Atlantic.

The post-Cold War phase

Following the fall of the Berlin Wall in 1989 and the collapse of the Soviet bloc, the Cold War came to an end and many analysts predicted the collapse of NATO consequently (see Mearsheimer, 1990; Wallander, 2000). NATO during the 1990s struggled to articulate a new raison d'être (Hallams et al., 2013) after the collapse of the Soviet Union which had dominated its existence for more than 40 years. Concurrently, the NATO-EU relationship developed and the search for a 'new identity' came to dominate the decade. The initiative became known under the Security and Defence Identity (ESDI), which led to considerable disagreements within the transatlantic relationship. In essence, the EU sought to develop a defence identity following the Maastricht Treaty, and there was a lack of clarity about how the two organisations would interact with one another. The 1991 Strategic Concept demonstrated 'a shift from NATO's focus on the Soviet threat to a wider conception of security threats that the Alliance would be expected to deal with' (Flockhart, 2014: 78).

NATO in the post–Cold War period is the subject of significant debate in the academic literature and can be defined by two central pillars. The first is the Alliance's membership enlargement and engagement with non-member partnerships, and the second is its willingness to take on military activities. With the violent breakup of Yugoslavia from 1991 on, NATO intervened in 1995, not as an act of self-defence, but as a force for peace and stability, seeking to prevent former foes of the Cold War from fighting each other (Flockhart, 2014).

In the lead-up to the Balkan Wars, NATO had become somewhat of a wider collective security institution (Hallams et al., 2013). By the late 1990s, NATO troops fought in what Flockhart (2014: 80) claims to be the 'Balkan tragedy', culminating in the air campaigns Operation Deliberate Force in Bosnia 1995 and the Operation Allied Force in Kosovo 1999. NATO's involvement in the Balkans challenged the utility of the Alliance and demonstrated the profound 'capability gap' between US and European allies (Terriff, 2013; Flockhart, 2014).

The legacy of NATO in the Balkan Wars is controversial. On the one hand, the outcome of the Kosovo operation was considered a success as Serbian forces were driven out of Kosovo. On the other hand, the operations were considered questionable since it did not have a UN Security Council mandate, and some asked whether or not NATO should be engaged in sovereign conflicts. Nonetheless, the genocide in Srebrenica in 1995 (together with the Rwanda genocide in 1994) had profound political impact among Western policy makers. They would no longer stand idle and allow such things to happen, so the use of force for humanitarian reasons was considered both a right and a plight. Hence, the principle that the protection of universal human rights shall trump national sovereignty (later labelled Responsibility to Protect - R2P - in the UN-system), emerged out of these wars.

In sum, NATO proved capable of adapting to a new reality by transforming its bureaucratic structure and acting as a military peacekeeping instrument. The Partnership for Peace (PfP) programme launched in 1994 and the 1997 NATO-Russia Founding Act enabled the Alliance to reach out to former adversaries. In 1999, the enlargement of the Alliance to the first three former Warsaw Pact states took place: Poland, Hungary, and the Czech Republic. Bulgaria, Estonia, Latvia, Lithuania, Romania, Slovakia, and Slovenia joined in 2004. As Flockhart (2014: 82) suggests, 'even though the decision to undertake enlargement and go out-of-area was fiercely contested, the practice of consensus decisions was not compromised'. Furthermore, NATO constructed a convincing narrative portraying the Alliance as 'an agent of democratic change in central and Eastern Europe' (Flockhart, 2014: 83).

The post-9/11 phase

Shortly after the 11 September 2001 terror attacks on the United States, NATO invoked the collective defence provisions of Article 5 for the first time in history. The out-of-area dilemma which had kept NATO tied to act within the north Atlantic area during the Cold War and the 1990s had come to an end. Although it was a US-led invasion of Afghanistan in 2001, NATO provided the International Security Assistance Force (ISAF) that took over the stabilisation of Afghanistan in 2003 and implemented the UN Security Council Resolution (Rühle, 2013). ISAF continued until 2014. Over this decade ISAF morphed from a primarily counter-terrorism mission to a nation-building mission, with high ambitions of building security through development (Auerswald and Saideman, 2014). This 'softer' dimension of ISAF was primarily a European initiative, whereas the US emphasised its new counterinsurgency doctrine (Friis, 2012). Various European operational caveats, unequal burden sharing, different rules of engagement, diverging principles for cooperation with civilians, were among many issues that created tensions within

ISAF and NATO (Fairweather, 2014; Friis, 2020). The failures, set-backs and internal disputes in ISAF became a source of transatlantic tension.

But the main source of dispute came in 2003, when the Bush administration decided to attack Iraq. Except for the United Kingdom, European allies were deeply sceptical about the legitimacy and necessity of a war in Iraq. Thus, the United States decided not to work through NATO in conducting Operation Iraqi Freedom (OIF). The Bush administration stated that US corroboration with NATO would be on US terms and not hamper US ability to act in response to the Global War on Terrorism (Webber et al., 2012). Consequently, the US pattern of behaviour in the aftermath of 9/11 left Europeans feeling sidelined, hence crumbled European trust in the transatlantic relationship (Rühle, 2003; Terriff, 2013).

Some analysts argue that fighting transnational terrorism unified NATO and assured the Alliance's continued relevance after a decade of clashing interests during the Balkan Wars (Efjestad and Tamnes, 2020). The more pessimistic set of commentaries claim the so-called Global War on Terror and President Bush's decision to declare war against Iraq led NATO to the verge of collapse and that the Alliance would be 'ill-advised to contemplate future large-scale operations' (Burns, 2003; Rühle, 2013). Thies (2009: 3) describes this as 'exaggerated claims of NATO in crisis' but political relations across the pond were far from rosy.

The Bush administration was at odds with Europe also when it came to further enlargement of NATO. In the run-up to the NATO Summit in Bucharest in 2008, the U.S. wanted the Alliance to express a firm commitment to Ukraine and Georgia about future membership. Germany, France and others resisted this, out concern of antagonising Russia (Marsch and Dobson, 2013; German, 2017). After a fierce diplomatic struggle over formulations, the final wording in the Summit communiqué was that these countries 'will become members of NATO' (NATO, 2008). No date for membership was set, but the commitment was there, even if few really believed this was in any way imminent.

The NATO-led Libyan 'Operation Unified Protector' (OUP) in 2011 turned NATO into a military actor in Northern Africa. This operation had a UN Security Council mandate to protect civilians in the ongoing war, but the mission soon turned, at least tacitly, to a fight in support for regime change. It was primarily a British-French initiative, with the U.S. as a reluctant supporter. President Obama' description of the U.S. role as 'leading from behind' is telling. According to Terriff (2013: 106), the OUP was an operational success, however, the Libyan operation, much as had been the case with the Kosovo campaign, once again demonstrated the European's lackluster military capability and European dependence on American military resources. The disastrous end-result in Libya also makes the term 'success' ill fit. As some cynical commentators put it: 'the operation was successful, but the patient died'.

The incidence of 9/11 gave birth to the 'war on terror' and a strong emphasis on international operations. The slogan 'out-of-area or out-of-business' depicted a NATO adapting to a new political reality, but this period also put serious strains on NATO's internal cohesion. Uneasiness about the utility and legitimacy of international operations such as ISAF among several European allies, combined with the absence of a broadly shared perception of a conventional military threat, contributed to this. In this phase, NATO was perhaps more fragmented than ever before – but at the same time, there were no signs of collapse or breakdown of the Alliance.

The post-2014 phase

The illegal Russian annexation of Crimea and warfare in eastern Ukraine from 2014 became a watershed moment in NATO. After a period of growing frustration with lack of progress with the war in Afghanistan, and the closure of the ISAF mission, Putin's intervention gave the Transatlantic Alliance a new momentum. Allies previously unconvinced about the threat from the east – which was repeatedly stressed by members such as Poland and the Baltic states – became much more willing to turn NATO around and making it capable and relevant to respond to Russia. The transatlantic security relations got a boost, not only in NATO, but also in the broader sense. The United States increased its defence spending in Europe, comprehensive sanctions against Russia were agreed between the EU and the United States, and all bilateral military cooperation between NATO-countries and Russia was cancelled. Several economic and financial relations were also cut or reduced.

The joint transatlantic response to the Russian warfare in Ukraine in 2014 was most clearly demonstrated at the NATO Wales Summit 3–4 September the same year. Even before the Summit, President Obama paid a visit to the Baltics as a symbolic gesture of solidarity and Alliance commitment. Addressing an audience in Tallinn, Estonia, ha said: 'We will defend our NATO allies, and that means every ally … In this Alliance, there are no old members or new members, no junior partners or senior partners. They're just allies, pure and simple' (Ramirez, 2014).

The decisions made in Wales represented a new/old direction of NATO. Collective defence was to again become the primary focus of the Alliance. This required both new forces which could react quickly in case of a crisis, and more long-term restructuring of the Alliance away from international operations and towards the defence of Europe. To achieve this, Allies agreed to a Readiness Action Plan (RAP), with an enhanced NATO Response Force (NRF) and a new spearhead force, the so-called Very High Readiness Joint Task Force (VJTF) consisting of about 1,000 troops which could be deployed on short notice (NATO, 2014). New plans for the territorial defence of Europe were also drafted, a task which had been more or less ignored since NATO enlarged to encompass eastern European countries in 2004.

In addition to this, the allies agreed to spend more on defence. At the Summit they committed to the Defence Investment Pledge where European member-states recognised recognised the need to stop cutting defence budgets, and to 'aim to move towards' spending 2% of gross domestic product (GDP) on defence by 2024 (NATO, 2014: para 14). Inadequate defence spending in Europe, as seen from Washington, had been a thorn in transatlantic relation for many years, and even if the Europeans now agreed to turn the tide, it was formulated in such vague terms that the commitment was not as reassuring as the United States wanted.

Nonetheless, the United States increased its engagement in Europe. From 2015 President Obama earmarked $1 billion in emergency response to Russian aggression, under the name of European Reassurance Initiative. It was a military programme supporting the activities of the US military and its allies in Europe. The following year the budget increased to $3.4 billion.

Transatlantic solidarity was also demonstrated when NATO at its Warsaw Summit 8–9 July 2016, decided to deploy permanent rotational troops in the Baltics and Poland, the Enhanced Forward Presence (EFP). These relatively modest battalion-sized battle groups were multinational and served as a 'tripwire': too small to prevent a military attack, but its multinational makeup would make allied nations comprising the battlegroups involved from the first moment, should they be attacked (Friis, 2017). This would increase the chances of triggering Article 5 and involve all NATO in response. The United States committed to lead the EFP in Poland, while Canada took responsibility in Latvia. Since 2014, the USA had quadrupled the budget for its European forces and deployed a brigade rotating in Eastern Europe with equipment for yet another brigade pre-located in Europe.

The Trump administration

The election of Donald Trump as President of the United States in 2016 sent shockwaves into this new harmonious transatlantic relationship. During the campaign, he had repeatedly questioned the necessity and utility of NATO and spoken favourably about Russia's President Putin. At his first appearance at NATO at the Brussels meeting in 2017, he failed to declare his administration's commitment to NATO's mutual security guarantees – leaving question marks in allied capitals about this very core of the Alliance. As former U.S. ambassador to NATO Nicholas Burns wrote on Twitter, 'Every US President since Truman has pledged support for Article 5–that US will defend Europe. Not so Trump today at #NATO. Major mistake' (Gramer, 2017).

Instead, Trump used the opportunity to criticise European allies for spending too little on defence. While that criticism was in line with what the United States had repeatedly complained about, Trump lifted it to the top of his NATO agenda. The following years became turbulent in NATO, as Trump continued his unpredictable and critical approach towards the Alliance. It climaxed at the 2018 Brussels Summit, when Trump reportedly was at the brink of revoking the US security guarantees unless allied defence spending met his demands. Last-minute diplomatic brinkmanship apparently saved the alliance at this juncture, but the turbulence continued (Schuette, 2021). Trump was again about to discredit NATO at his State of the Union address in early 2019, but an interview that NATO Secretary-General Stoltenberg gave on Fox News, crediting Trump for making allies add 100 billion extra U.S. dollars on defence, apparently made Trump change his mind (ibid.; Gregg, 2019). From late 2019 onwards, the transatlantic security relations eased somewhat, as Trump made less critical remarks and seemed pleased with his apparent success in increasing allied defence spending.

It is worth noting though, that even in these difficult years, the U.S. European Deterrence Initiative continued as before. The Trump administration actually increased the budget by 40% in 2017. The budget grew year by year, and in 2017, it was renamed the European Deterrence Initiative (EDI) to reflect the US' strategy towards Russia. The budget peaked in 2020 at almost $6 billion, and funded activities such as training of forces, multinational exercises and development of military capabilities and equipment (Department of Defense, 2021).

Furthermore, even if President Trump had a critical stance towards NATO, the Alliance had broad bipartisan support in the US Congress throughout his presidency. In a gradually more divided political landscape in the United States, support for NATO has remained significant from both sides of the isle. Also, among top officials at the Pentagon and the State Department, NATO had broad support. Observers used terms such as 'the adults in the room' to depict the Secretaries of Defence, State, the National Security Adviser who, even if they were replaced one by one, continued to play a moderating effect on Trump's impulses. NATO therefore travelled through dire straits those years but survived.

The Biden administration

The election of Joe Biden as U.S. President in 2020 was nonetheless met with broad relief in most European capitals. Much of this had to do with transatlantic tensions in other sectors than security, but also in security and defence communities the atmosphere was optimistic. As credible deterrence and unwavering solidarity are fundamental ingrediencies in security and defence policies – in these circles, even minor political flickering or vague signals are considered risky and unsafe. Biden was very clear and firm in stating the commitment of the United States to NATO from the moment he took office.

However, he quickly ran into troubles. The exit of the remaining NATO troops in Afghanistan in the summer of 2021 became a disastrous operation – and allies complained that the Biden administration had failed to consult and involve them in the planning. There are different versions of what did and did not take place internally in NATO at this time, but the end result was a feeling in Europe that Biden's team had not lived up the standards the President had promised when it came to mending the transatlantic security relations after the Trump years (Warrell et al., 2021; Erlanger, 2021).

Biden's team got a chance to prove their commitment, however. In late fall 2021, they began sharing intelligence with their allies about a new Russian military build-up around Ukraine. This way the alliance gradually built a shared situational awareness of the dramatic developments around Ukraine. Soon the United States also began making its concerns public, sharing intelligence with the media and warning Russia that the world was watching. As none of this seemed to stop Putin, allies begun developing counter-measures. Comprehensive sanctions against Russia and its elites were developed in close tandem with the EU, ready to be launched if and when Russia invaded Ukraine. In parallel, NATO planners began drafting plans to reinforce the eastern flank of the alliance, specifically those countries bordering Russia, Belarus, and Ukraine. This time around Europeans hailed the Biden administration for its openness and unprecedented willingness to engage and consult.

The Russian invasion of Ukraine in February 2022 introduced a new phase of transatlantic relations, not because of the Russian action as such, which in many ways was a continuation of the path taken in 2014, but because the Western response changed. Transatlantic security cooperation became more intense and detailed, both in the months with diplomatic activity prior to the Russian attack, and afterwards when the sanctions were introduced. NATO functioned as a forum for policy exchanges – as well as a military defence organisation which triggered its collective defence plans, reinforced the eastern flanks, and revised its force structure (NATO, 2022). The Biden administration's renewed commitment to European security was also substantial (Department of Defense, 2022). Furthermore, the invasion incentivised Europeans to commit more on defence spending. Particularly Germany's decision to spend 2% of GDP on defence is by itself the most important change in European NATO in decades, and will positively impact transatlantic security relations.

Finland's and Sweden's NATO membership applications were also a direct result of Russia's aggression, and will also serve to further strengthen the transatlantic bonds. Both countries already had bilateral defence cooperation agreements with the United States, but with NATO membership, this cooperation will be brought to new levels.

The embodiment of this 'new-old' NATO can be found in the 2022 Strategic Concept, adopted at the Madrid Summit (NATO, 2022). Here Russia is described as 'the most significant and direct threat to Allies' security', and the core principle of collective defence is highlighted. In many ways it is full circle, with an Alliance more focussed on one overarching threat than the last 30 years.

Hence, the post-2014 period witnessed a NATO returning to its root of collective defence. Even if South European allies remained more concerned with international terrorism, they fully recognised the danger Russia now represented to Europe and supported both sanctions through EU and the reconfiguration of NATO. Despite the very challenging four years with Trump in the White House, NATO not only survived but also came out stronger and more united. Russia's renewed aggression in 2022 reinforced this transatlantic unity further. Besides the politically unifying effects of aggression, the NATO military branch worked resolutely since 2014 to ramp up collective defence. Strong US leadership – in particular from 2021 onwards – also contributed to this.

Conclusion

The transatlantic relationship is the fundamental pillar of NATO, and the strength of this bond is rooted in the shared interests, common values, togetherness, and institutional robustness of the Alliance. A strong US commitment is a prerequisite for NATO to prosper, but it cannot be taken for granted. Without US economic and military power, NATO's security guarantee is likely to diminish (Efjestad and Tamnes, 2020). Since 1949, NATO has faced critical commentaries about its ability to remain relevant. In his 2011 speech, former U.S Secretary of Defence Robert Gates criticised European allies for not prioritising military spending and the lack of political willingness to preserve transatlantic security, warning of a 'dim if not dismal future for the Alliance' (Gates, 2011). European allies remain anchored as a regional Alliance, whose ambition remains limited to security and stability within the North Atlantic, while the US has appealed repeatedly for the Europeans to take leadership responsibility in military operations beyond this scope (Vershbow et al., 2020; Terriff, 2013).

NATO serves as the most important mechanism of transatlantic security and has proven remarkably adaptable to a continually changing security environment for more than 70 years. Until this day, no member state has terminated its membership under Article 13 of the Treaty. On the contrary, the numbers of NATO's member states and partnerships have consistently increased and NATO as an organisation has radically changed in terms of size, scope, and missions since 1949 (Johnston, 2017; Efjestad and Tamnes, 2020). Nevertheless, NATO continues to face a number of political and military challenges. Key among these is the debate over burden-sharing, a tension between northern and southern European allies over priorities, and Turkey, about which space does not allow us to discuss here. However, disagreement among allies is not a new phenomenon and the perennial dilemmas on political unity and military capability are likely to range in the years to come.

Nonetheless, despite the recent significant strengthening of transatlantic security and defence cooperation, there is a fear in Europe that in the longer run, the United States' security orientation towards Asia and China will prevail. The question of how that will impact the transatlantic security relations remains open.

References

Auerswald, D. P., and Saideman, S. M. 2014. *NATO in Afghanistan - Fighting Together, Fighting Alone*. Oxford: Princeton University Press.

Burns, R. N. 2003. 'NATO has Adapted: An Alliance with a New Mission'. *The New York Times*. 24 May. Available at: https://www.nytimes.com/2003/05/24/opinion/IHT-nato-has-adapted-an-alliance-with-a-new-mission.html.

Cox, M. 2005. Beyond the West: Terrors in Transatlantia. *European Journal of International Relations*, 11(2), 203–233.

Department of Defense, 2021. *European Deterrence Initiative. Department of Defense Budget Fiscal Year (FY) 2022*, June 2021. Available at: https://comptroller.defense.gov/Portals/45/Documents/defbudget/FY2022/FY2022_EDI_JBook.pdf

Department of Defense, 2022. *Fact Sheet - U.S. Defense Contributions to Europe*, June 29, 2022. Available at: https://www.defense.gov/News/Releases/Release/Article/3078056/fact-sheet-us-defense-contributions-to-europe/

Efjestad, S. and Tamnes, R. 2020. NATO's Enduring Relevance' *in* Olsen, A. ed. *Future NATO Adapting to New Realties*. Abingdon: Routledge Journals, 8–26.

Erlanger, S. 2021. 'NATO Chief Backs Biden, Saying Europe Was Consulted on Afghanistan', *The New York Times*, 10 September 2021. Available at: https://www.nytimes.com/2021/09/10/world/europe/afghanistan-europe-stoltenberg.html

Fairweather, J. 2014. *The Good War. The Battle for Afghanistan 2006–14*. London: Jonathan Cape.

Flockhart, T. 2014. 'Post-Bipolar Challenges: New Visions and New Activities', *in* Mayer, S. ed. *NATO's Post-Cold War Politics: The Changing Provision of Security*. London: Palgrave Macmillan, 71–88.

Friis, K. 2012. Which Afghanistan? Military, Humanitarian, and State-building Identities in the Afghan Theater. *Security Studies*, 21(2), 266–300.

Friis, K. ed. 2017. *NATO and Collective Defence in the 21st Century: An Assessment of the Warsaw Summit*. London: Routledge.

Friis, K. 2020. *Civil-Military Relations in International Interventions: A New Framework for Analysis*, Oxon: Routledge.

Gates, R. 2011. *The Security and Defense Agenda*, as delivered by Secretary of Defense Robert Gates, Brussels, Belgium, 10 June. Available at: http://www.acus.org/natosource/text-speech-robert-gates-future-nato

German, T. 2017. NATO and the Enlargement Debate: Enhancing Euro-Atlantic Security or Inciting Confrontation? *International Affairs*, 93(2), 291–308

Gramer, R. 2017. 'Trump Hands Putin a Win at First NATO Meeting.' *Foreign Policy*. 25 May. Available at: https://foreignpolicy.com/2017/05/25/trump-nato-meeting-brussels-defense-spending-transatlantic-alliance/

Gregg, R.. 2019. 'NATO head: Trump's tough talk has added $100B to alliance, helped deter Russia', Fox News, 27 January. Available at: https://www.foxnews.com/politics/nato-head-says-trumps-tough-talk-has-helped-alliance.

Hallams, E., Ratti, L., and Zyla, B. 2013. 'Introduction – A New Paradigm for NATO?', *NATO Beyond 9/11: The Transformation of the Atlantic Alliance*. 1st ed. London: Palgrave Macmillian.

Hartley, K. and Sandler, T. 1999. Burden-Sharing: Past and Future. *Journal of Peace Research*. 36(6), 665–680.

Hodge, C. C. 2013. 'A Sense of Return: NATO's Libyan Intervention in Perspective' *in* Hallams, E., Ratti, L., and Zyla B. eds. *NATO Beyond 9/11: The Transformation of the Atlantic Alliance*. London: Palgrave Macmillan, 67–90.

Jancic, D. 2023 'Transatlantic Parliamentary Cooperation at Fifty' *in* Fahey, E. ed. *Handbook on Transatlantic Relations*. Routledge.

Johnston, A. S. 2017. *How NATO Adapts: Strategy and Organisation in the Atlantic Alliance since 1950*. Baltimore, MD: Johns Hopkins University Press.

Jordan, R. S. 1967. *The NATO International Staff/Secretariat 1952–1957*. London: Oxford University Press.

Jordan, S. R. 1987. *Generals in International Politics: NATO's Supreme Allied Commander Europe*. Lexington: University Press of Kentucky.

Krüger, D. 2014. Institutionalising NATO's Military Bureaucracy: The Making of an Integrated Chain of Command' *in* Mayer, S. ed. *NATO's Post-Cold War Politics: The Changing Provision of Security*. London: Palgrave Macmillan, 50–68.

Lindley-French, J. 2015. *The North Atlantic Treaty Organisation: The Enduring Alliance* 2nd ed. London: Routledge.

Marsh S. and A. P. Dobson. 2013. Fine Words, Few Answers: NATO's "Not So New" New Strategic Concept *in* Hallams, E. Ratti, L. and Zyla B. ed. *NATO Beyond 9/11: The Transformation of the Atlantic Alliance*. Location: Palgrave Macmillan, 155–177.

McCalla. B. R. 1996. NATO's Persistence after the Cold War. *International Organisation*, 50(3), 445–475.

Mearsheimer, J. J. 1990. Back to the Future: Instability in Europe after the Cold War. *International Security*. The MIT Press, 15(1), 5–56.

Menon, R. 2007. *The End of Alliances*. Oxford : Oxford University Press.

Michta, A. and Hilde, P. S. ed. 2014. *The Future of NATO: Regional Defense and Global Security*. Ann Arbor: University of Michigan Press.

NATO, 2008. *Bucharest Summit Declaration*. Available at: https://www.nato.int/cps/en/natolive/official_texts_8443.htm

NATO, 2014. *Wales Summit Declaration*. Available at: https://www.nato.int/cps/en/natohq/official_texts_112964.htm

NATO, 2022. *Strategic Concept*. Available at: https://www.nato.int/strategic-concept/index.html

Ramirez, L. 2014. 'Obama Stresses NATO Commitment to Baltics', *Voanews*. 3 September. Available at: https://www.voanews.com/a/president-obama-baltic-nations-ukraine/2436881.html

Riddervold, M. and Newsome, A. 2018. Transatlantic Relations in Times of Uncertainty: Crisis and EU-US Relations. *Journal of European Integration*, 40(5), 505–521.

Riddervold, M., Newsome, A., and Didriksen, A. 2023. 'A Weakening EU-US Relationship?' *in* Fahey, E. ed. *Handbook on Transatlantic Relations*. Routledge.

Rühle, M. 2003. NATO after Prague: Learning the Lessons of 9/11. *The US Army War College Quarterly: Parameters*. 33(2), 89–93.

Rühle, M. 2013. Reflections on 9/11: A View from NATO' *in* Hallams, E., Ratti, L., and Zyla, B. eds. *NATO Beyond 9/11: The Transformation of the Atlantic Alliance*. London: Palgrave Macmillan, 54–66.

Schmidt, G. 2014. From London to Brussels: Emergence and Development of a Politico-Administrative System *in* Mayer, S. ed. *Nato's Post-Cold War Politics: The Changing Provision of Security*. London: Palgrave Macmillan, 31–49.

Schuette, L. A. 2021. Why NATO Survived Trump: The Neglected Role of Secretary-General Stoltenberg. *International Affairs*, 97(6), 1863–1881.

Smith, J. 1990. ed. *The Origins of NATO*. Exeter: University of Exeter Press.

Stoddart, K. 2012. *Losing an Empire and Finding a Role: Britain, the USA, NATO and Nuclear Weapons 1964–70*. New YorkPalgrave Macmillan.

Terriff, T. 2013. Déjà vu all over again? 11 September 2001 and NATO Military Transformation *in* Hallams, E., Ratti, L., and Zyla, B. eds. *NATO Beyond 9/11: The Transformation of the Atlantic Alliance*. London: Palgrave Macmillan, 91–117.

Thies, J. W. 2009. *Why NATO Endures*. New York: Cambridge University Press.

Vershbow R. A. and Breedlove, M. P. 2020. Permanent Deterrence and the US Military Presence in Europe in Olsen, A. ed. *Future NATO Adapting to New Realties*. Abingdon: Routledge Journals, 26–41.

Wallander, A. C. 2000. Institutional Assets and Adaptability: NATO After the Cold War. Cambridge University Press, 54(4), 705–735.

Warrell, H., Chazan, G., and Milne, R. 2021. 'Nato allies urge rethink on alliance after Biden's 'unilateral' Afghanistan exit'. *Irish Times*, 17 August 2021.Available at: https://www.irishtimes.com/news/world/asia-pacific/nato-allies-urge-rethink-on-alliance-after-biden-s-unilateral-afghanistan-exit-1.4649515

Webber, M., Sperling, M., and Smith, J. 2012. *NATO's Post-Cold War Trajectory Decline or Regeneration?* Houndmills, Basingstoke, Hampshire: Palgrave MacMillan.

SECTION II

Trade, Investment and Cooperation in Transatlantic Relations

9

TRANSATLANTIC ECONOMIC AND LEGAL DISINTEGRATION? BETWEEN ANGLO-SAXON NEO-LIBERAL NATIONALISM, AUTHORITARIAN STATE-CAPITALISM AND EUROPE'S ORDO-LIBERAL MULTILEVEL CONSTITUTIONALISM

Ernst Ulrich Petersmann

Overview

This contribution explains why – in contrast to the cold war with the dysfunctional Soviet Union – the current ideological differences between neo-liberal nationalism (as illustrated by the Brexit and by business-driven 'Washington protectionism'), totalitarian state capitalism (e.g. in China) and Europe's ordo-liberal, multilevel constitutionalism are rooted in diverse, cultural and constitutional traditions that are likely to persist. Russia's illegal invasions of Ukraine have reinforced military cooperation in NATO and 'democratic alliances' assisting Ukraine in its defence against Russia's war against human rights and democratic governance. Yet, the regulatory competition disrupts UN and World Trade Organization (WTO) governance of the universally agreed Sustainable Development Goals (SDGs) and risks impeding transatlantic and global trade, investments and environmental cooperation.

DOI: 10.4324/9781003283911-12

From the 'old' to a 'new' Washington consensus?

The drafting of the 1944 Bretton Woods Agreements establishing the International Monetary Fund (IMF) and the World Bank, of the 1945 UN Charter, the 1947 General Agreement on Tariffs and Trade (GATT 1947) and of the 1979 Tokyo Round Agreements was dominated by Anglo-Saxon democracies prioritizing civil and political liberties, economic liberalization, deregulation, privatization and 'financialization' of international relations based on the US dollar as global reserve currency and competition as decentralized information, coordination and sanctioning mechanisms for enhancing economic welfare. The underlying pursuit of 'welfare economics' prioritized macro-economic 'Kaldor-Hicks efficiencies' rather than 'Pareto efficiency gains' for all citizens; business-driven economic regulation and financing of democratic elections promoted 'regulatory capture' limiting trade and competition (e.g. by protecting domestic producers through discriminatory 'trade remedies', subsidies, regulatory standards and intellectual property rights), lobbying against US ratification of UN agreements protecting public goods (like the Framework Convention on Tobacco Control elaborated in the context of the World Health Organization [WHO]) and increasing social inequalities (e.g. inside the USA). Process-based constitutionalism (e.g. favoring business- and money-driven political decision-making) and constitutional nationalism (e.g. in Anglo-Saxon countries like Australia, Britain, Canada, New Zealand, the USA) contributed to import protection (e.g. for domestic agricultural, textiles and steel producers), to only limited participation in free trade agreements (FTAs), and to an increasing number of transatlantic economic disputes (Petersmann and Pollack 2003).

Under the US Trump administration (2017–2021), the 'regulatory capture' of US trade policies (e.g. on import protection for steel and aluminum industries), the US withdrawal from various multilateral treaties by executive orders of President Trump, and the illegal US destruction of the WTO Appellate Body (AB) revealed some of the systemic conflicts between US neo-liberalism and Europe's ordo-liberal, rights-based economic constitutionalism. USTR Lighthizer, his deputy ambassador Shea and US secretary of commerce Ross had all been long-standing business lobbyists who, like President Trump himself, identified US business interests (e.g. in rejecting WTO judicial findings limiting US executive policy discretion) with the national US interest. President Trump's decisions to withdraw the USA from UN agreements (e.g. on the WHO, the 2015 Paris Agreement on climate change mitigation) and regional trade agreements (like the 2016 Trans-Pacific Partnership, the draft agreement for a Transatlantic Trade and Investment Partnership) were taken unilaterally without requesting approval by the US Congress. The 2020 USTR Report criticizing the AB jurisprudence perceived WTO law as an instrument of US power politics; it ignored the (quasi)judicial mandates of WTO dispute settlement bodies and their (quasi)judicial methodologies by insisting on business-driven US interpretations of WTO rules without identifying violations by the AB of the customary law rules of treaty interpretation (Petersmann 2022, chapter 3).

Anglo-Saxon commentators described the WTO as 'the paradigmatic product of Geneva School neoliberalism' (Slobodian 2018, at 25), and the 'creation of the

WTO (as) a crowning victory of the neoliberal project of finding an extra-economic enforcer for the world economy in the twentieth century' (at 23). Yet, they neglect categorical differences between Anglo-Saxon neo-liberalism and European ordo-liberalism: US neo-liberalism and Chicago School economists prioritize liberalization of market access barriers, deregulation, privatization and financialization of markets to empower utilitarian market actors (*homo economicus*) to pursue their self-interests and enhance the self-regulating forces of market competition. The German, European and Virginia Schools of ordo-liberalism perceive markets as legal constructs (rather than as gifts of nature), which cannot maximize general consumer welfare without legal limitations of market failures, governance failures and 'constitutional failures' (e.g. as defined in European constitutional law). The methodological individualism underlying ordo-liberal 'constitutional economics' (i.e. deriving values from individual informed consent) defines 'efficiencies' not only in terms of utilitarian cost-benefit analyses (like macro-economic 'Kaldor-Hicks-benefits' greater than related social costs) but also in terms of mutually beneficial legal and economic agreements (e.g. on rules-based liberal trade and third-party adjudication of disputes). GATT/WTO jurisprudence (e.g. on interpreting GATT/WTO rules as protecting non-discriminatory conditions of competition) emphasized the systemic, ordo-liberal functions of states and of the GATT/WTO legal and dispute settlement systems as 'guardians' of non-discriminatory conditions of competition. The USTR Report on the WTO AB of February 2020 justified the Trump administration's illegal 'blocking' of WTO AB nominations by insisting on US interpretations of WTO rules and US criticism of AB findings without any evidence that legal interpretations by the AB violated the customary rules of treaty interpretation or the (quasi)judicial AB mandate for impartial, independent and prompt third-party adjudication through quasi-automatic adoption of WTO panel and AB reports by the Dispute Settlement Body (DSB). The USTR Report – notwithstanding its valid criticism of some WTO rules and dispute settlement practices (e.g. that the AB stopped consulting with the parties when deciding to disregard the Article 17.5 deadline) – suffers from legal biases and incorrect claims such as:

- US denial of (quasi)judicial functions of WTO third-party adjudication, even though numerous WTO publications and WTO dispute settlement reports over more than 20 years acknowledged the (quasi)judicial mandates of WTO dispute settlement bodies (i.e. WTO panel and AB reports as adopted by the DSB);
- US disregard for judicial AB arguments in the performance of the Dispute Settlement Understanding (DSU)'s mandate 'to clarify the existing provisions of those agreements in accordance with customary rules of interpretation of public international law' (Article 3 DSU), for instance whenever the AB found compliance with the time limit of 90 days (Article 17.5 DSU) – which was imposed by US negotiators in 1993 notwithstanding the widespread criticism that no other court seems to be limited by such an unreasonably short time limit – impossible to reconcile with the other AB tasks (e.g. due to illegal US blocking of the filling of AB vacancies);

- contradictory USTR claims that AB legal findings against the US violated the DSU prohibition to 'add or diminish the rights and obligations in the covered agreements' (Article 3.2 DSU) – even if the AB had justified these legal findings on the basis of the customary rules of treaty interpretation and its (quasi)judicial mandate – notwithstanding the USTR's regular support of AB reports accepting 'creative WTO interpretations' advocated by the USTR as a legal complainant;
- US description of US 'zeroing practices' as a 'common-sense method of calculating the extent of dumping' (p. 2) even if their biases had been consistently condemned by the AB and DSB as violations of the WTO obligations of 'fair price comparisons' (which are hardly mentioned in the USTR report);
- one-sided focus on WTO texts as interpreted by US negotiators without regard to the customary law and DSU requirements to clarify the meaning of the (often indeterminate) WTO provisions with due regard also to WTO legal texts revealing the 'context, object and purpose' of WTO provisions and the explicitly recognized 'systemic character' of what the WTO Agreement calls 'this multilateral trading system' (Preamble) and its 'dispute settlement system' (Article 3 DSU);
- denigration of AB members as 'three unelected and unaccountable persons' (pp. 8, 13) whose 'overreaching violates the basic principles of the United States Government' (idem, Introduction), notwithstanding the election of AB members through consensus decisions of 164 DSB member governments (including the USA), their (quasi)judicial mandate, and the approval of WTO agreements (including the DSU) by the US government and US Congress;
- insulting claims that the AB Secretariat has weakened the WTO dispute settlement system by not respecting WTO rights and obligations (p. 120).

Neither the US Trump administration nor the Biden administration proposed any compromise solutions for reforming the DSU. Most WTO members rejected protectionist US proposal for exempting trade remedies and unilateral invocations of WTO 'security exceptions' (e.g. for justifying the US trade war against China) from WTO third-party adjudication. The disruption of the WTO dispute settlement system by a dysfunctional AB led to the non-adoption of ever more WTO panel reports due to their 'appeal into the void' of a no longer functioning AB system (Petersmann 2021). The 'Economic and Trade Agreement' signed by the Chinese and US governments on 15 January 2020 provided for discriminatory Chinese commitments to buy US products, discriminatory US import tariffs and US trade restrictions (e.g. targeting Chinese technology companies) without third-party adjudication. This bilateral 'opt-out' – by the two largest trading nations – from their WTO legal and dispute settlement obligations seems to be the policy option preferred by USTR officials in order to better use power asymmetries in rebalancing bilateral US trade deficits through bilateral reciprocity negotiations.

Without a multilateral WTO dispute settlement system, the UN sustainable development goals, climate change mitigation, future WTO negotiations, and also US efforts at inducing market-oriented reforms in China's totalitarian state-capitalism are unlikely to succeed. The recent support by the Biden administration – and also by the

IMF and World Bank – of activist fiscal, economic, health and environmental policies in response to the global health pandemic, climate change, security and food crises illustrates how distinctions between 'neo-liberalism', 'state-capitalism' and 'ordo-liberalism' refer to policy trends that elude precise definitions and continue to evolve. Also in the USA, government spending, budget deficits, central bank interventions, welfare payments and corporate bailouts have increased over the past decades. The neo-liberal focus on business efficiency in terms of consumer prices is now challenged by focusing also on the welfare of workers, farmers, house owners, and citizens adversely affected by media concentration, rising health and housing costs, and environmental harm. President Trump's arbitrary destruction of the WTO AB, the lack of majority support in the US Congress for restoring the WTO AB system, for concluding new FTAs, and for introducing carbon taxes as the most efficient policy instrument for carbon reductions aimed at climate change mitigation, illustrate some of the continuing differences between US neo-liberalism (e.g. US preferences for power-oriented trade protectionism unrestrained by impartial adjudication), compared with EU ordo-liberalism (like leadership for introducing Multi-Party Interim WTO arbitration in 2020, for adopting the European climate law in June 2021, and publishing on 14 July 2021, 13 legislative EU Commission proposals aimed at making Europe the first carbon-neutral continent by 2050, thereby exercising EU leadership inside and beyond Europe for implementing the Paris Agreement on climate change mitigation).

The multilevel constitutional 'Brussels consensus'

German and European ordo-liberal conceptions of a 'competitive social market economy' (Article 3 Treaty on European Union (TEU)) are embedded into multilevel guarantees of human and constitutional rights protected by multilevel democratic, judicial and science-based governance institutions (Petersmann 2022, chapter 5). They prioritize civil, political, economic, social and cultural human and constitutional rights and the need for systemic limitations of 'market failures', 'governance failures' and 'constitutional failures' based on 'constitutional economics' (cf Petersmann 2022, chapter 4). This EU focus on protecting fundamental rights (e.g. in EU common market law, data protection and digital services regulations, environmental litigation enforcing human and constitutional rights against greenhouse gas (GHG) emissions provoking climate change) and greater social equality (e.g. by limiting tax avoidance, threatening services taxes on US tech giants) through multilevel, constitutional and judicial remedies underlies numerous transatlantic economic disputes. As EU law prescribes (e.g. in Arts 3, 21 TEU) protecting human rights, democratic governance and rule-of-law in both internal and external EU policies, citizens and democratic institutions insist on EU leadership for protecting transnational rule-of-law (e.g. through the EU initiative for appellate arbitration based on Article 25 DSU, reforms of investor-state arbitration), human rights conditionality of EU external policies (e.g. in FTAs with less-developed countries) and unilateral introduction of carbon border adjustment mechanisms (CBAMs) aimed at preventing 'carbon leakage' (e.g. by transferring carbon-intensive production of aluminum, cement and steel abroad to countries with lower environmental standards).

Anglo-Saxon neo-liberalism prioritizes constitutional nationalism (as illustrated by the 'Brexit') compared to the EU's multilevel constitutional protection of the common market and of multilevel democratic and judicial institutions embedded into regional human rights law and multilevel constitutional law. Europe's regional economic constitutionalism has no equivalent in North America and is rejected by 'Brexiters' pursuing a 'Singapore at Thames' as a deregulated competitor for the EU. Business-driven economic regulation and related 'regulatory capture' are today more restrained inside the EU (e.g. due to its more public financing of political election campaigns) than in the USA, where business- and money-driven presidential and congressional elections often lead to appointment of business leaders (like US President Trump, his Secretary of Commerce W.Ross), business lobbyists (like USTR R.Lighthizer, his deputy USTR D.Shea) and congressmen financed by business interests (like coal and steel industries).

Anglo-Saxon process-based constitutional nationalism

The Biden administration has temporarily settled some of the long-standing EU-US trade disputes (like the long-running disputes over subsidies for aircraft makers Airbus and Boeing, European digital taxes on US tech groups, the US Section 232 tariffs on EU aluminum and steel). The EU-US cooperation in the Transatlantic Trade and Technology Council did, however, not prevent the illegal trade discrimination in the 2022 Inflation Reduction Act (like tax credits for electric vehicles and their batteries produced in North America subject to local content requirements); it may also prove incapable of preventing the reintroduction of discriminatory US steel tariffs if the EU remains unwilling to accept the US proposals for imposing 'carbon tariffs' on 'dirty steel products' produced in China. A comparison of the EU's environmental constitutionalism and 'EU climate law' of June 2021 with the protectionist, economic and environmental rules and trade discrimination in the 2022 US Inflation Reduction Act of August 2022 suggests that the EU's multilevel 'environmental constitutionalism' – specifying environmental principles, rights and duties in EU constitutional law and legislation, and offering also citizens multilevel judicial remedies for enforcing human and constitutional rights to protection of the environment and climate change mitigation – differs fundamentally from the process-based traditions of Anglo-Saxon constitutionalism.

Anglo-Saxon constitutional nationalism prioritizes the regulation of legislative, executive and judicial procedures, for instance based on the view that the people and their elected representatives - rather than citizens and courts of justice invoking human and constitutional rights for social change - should define the nation's political identity and make its most important policy decisions (Loughlin 2022). The unwritten constitutional conventions (e.g. in the United Kingdom) and the traditionally short constitutional texts tend to lack references to transnational PGs (like protection of the SDGs) as a task of modern democratic constitutionalism. The 'Brexit' confirms that rights-based, multilevel constitutionalism requiring all branches of government to protect international PGs (like UN human rights law, regional common markets, global environmental protection) – and international rules of a higher legal rank (like Arts 9–12 TEU) prescribing transnational constitutional, parliamentary, participatory and deliberative democracy are distrusted by Anglo-Saxon people. The focus in US courts on 'negative freedoms' from coercion by government – and on judicial deference to 'political questions' to be decided by Congress (like the regulatory powers of the US Environmental Protection Agency) – impedes judicial recognition of 'positive constitutional rights' (e.g. to health and environmental protection) if they have not been explicitly recognized in legislation. European courts perceive their judicial mandates as 'constitutional guardians' differently in view of the multilevel guarantees of human and constitutional rights and related PGs in Europe's multilevel, democratic constitutionalism and 'European' democratic cultures. EU citizens tend to perceive democratic constitutions as expressing dynamically evolving 'higher laws of societies' for responding to changing regulatory challenges and democratic needs of citizens through multilevel democratic legislation, administration and adjudication; EU citizenship enables EU citizens to serve as 'constitutional guardians' of adjusting laws and policies for protecting PGs in a globalized world, where no state can protect the SDGs without international law and multilateral cooperation. Such 'progressive democratic constitutionalism' supporting 'affirmative constitutional obligations' of both legislative and judicial institutions and citizens (e.g. to prevent oligarchic domination of the US economy resulting in socially unjust inequalities and failures to protect PGs) remains deeply contested by US conservatives using 'originalist constitutional interpretation' for opposing social reforms (cf. Fishkin and Forbath 2022). Given the Supreme Court's conservative view of the US Constitution and the difficulties of amending the US Constitution, US advocates of the SDGs (like climate mitigation) often avoid 'constitutional interpretations' and human rights arguments in support of the SDGs (like the human right to a healthy environment recognized by the UN Human Rights Council in 2021). For example, the US Inflation Reduction Act – as the most important climate change mitigation legislation in US history – could be adopted in August 2022 only in exchange for numerous protectionist discriminations (like tax credits, local content requirements) favoring US industries in clear violation of WTO law – and without responding to the 2022 US Supreme Court ruling limiting the regulatory powers of the US Environmental Protection Agency. Without judicial and congressional recognition of human and constitutional rights to climate change mitigation inside the USA, democratic support and judicial remedies for climate change mitigation rest much weaker inside the USA than in Europe, where national and European courts are increasingly protecting claims by citizens and non-governmental organizations that failures to limit public and private GHG emissions are violating human and constitutional rights and corresponding duties of governments and corporations.

Authoritarian and state-capitalist regulation

The 'Beijing consensus' prioritizes the power monopoly of China's communist party, which is not effectively constrained by China's national constitution (e.g. as citizens cannot enforce human and constitutional rights in independent Chinese courts). Similarly, Russia's President Putin and his kleptocratic oligarchs dominate Russia's de facto governance without effective 'constitutional checks and balances', for instance by executive orders suspending human and democratic rights inside Russia (e.g. of the political opposition and public media) and outside Russia (e.g. through illegal invasions into Ukraine). Authoritarian power politics – like China's totalitarian 'surveillance capitalism', health-lockdowns, 'social credit system', disregard for minority rights and non-transparent power struggles inside China's communist party - challenges the UN human rights system and the market-oriented, neo-liberal 'Bretton Woods system' by state-capitalist and totalitarian conceptions of regulation. Russia's political domination of the Eurasian Economic Community, China's bilateral and regional domination of 'Belt & Road agreements' on financial, trade and infra-structure networks with more than 80 countries, and related Eurasian agreements on regional Asian institutions and on 'China-Russia strategic cooperation' offer alternative rules and institutions for power-oriented, economic cooperation among authoritarian governments suppressing human rights and democratic constitutions. This focus on national self-interests of rulers prompts also 'populist governments' in less-developed countries – like the other BRICS countries Brazil, India and South-Africa – to prioritize 'populist strongmen politics', particular third world interests (e.g. in preferential treatment, exceptions from climate change mitigation disciplines) and economic needs (like intellectual property rights waivers for local production of generic vaccines), for instance in WTO negotiations and in their abstention from UN General Assembly resolutions condemning Russia for its illegal invasion of Ukraine and related violations of UN law. The diversity of neo-liberal, state-capitalist, ordo-liberal and 'third world' conceptions of UN and WTO politics is bound to continue and to complicate also transatlantic cooperation.

Increasing geopolitical rivalries and regulatory competition

The increasing regulatory competition among neo-liberal, state-capitalist, ordo-liberal constitutional and authoritarian paradigms of economic regulation reveals incoherent conceptions of the existing UN and WTO 'world order treaties'. For instance, Russia's suppression of human rights at home and abroad (as currently in Ukraine) undermines the most basic principles of UN law. Russia's disregard for judicial orders in 2022 by the International Court of Justice and the European Court of Human Rights to suspend Russia's illegal invasion of Ukraine, China's disregard for the judicial finding of 2016 under the Law of the Sea Convention of the illegality of China's unilateral claims over large areas in the South China Sea, and the illegal US blocking of the nomination of WTO AB members disrupt the international rule-of-law. The constructive EU responses – like the EU initiatives for introducing WTO appellate arbitration based on Article 25 DSU, for reforming investor-state arbitration procedures through negotiations in the UN Commission on International Trade Law and in the International Center for the Settlement of Investment Disputes, and for introducing WTO-consistent CBAMs as of 2023 – have, so far, not been supported by the USA in view of its reluctance to accept international adjudication and additional WTO legal disciplines on US carbon emissions. The EU's efforts at strengthening its 'strategic autonomy' reflect a lack of trust in the global UN and WTO legal and political systems.

The 2015 UN Sustainable Development Agenda emphasizes the importance of human rights, democratic governance and rule-of-law for protecting the universally agreed SDGs. Yet, UN General Assembly resolutions on promoting 'UN constitutionalism' and respect for human rights by stronger 'corporate responsibilities' remain widely disregarded in the legal practices of many UN member states and of the more than 10,000 transnational corporations participating in the 'UN Global Compact' on business and human rights (cf. Petersmann 2022, chapter 2). The declining effectiveness of peaceful settlement of disputes contributes to an increasing number of 'trade wars' (e.g. by China and the USA) and collective sanctions (e.g. by more than 30 democracies against Russia's arbitrary violations of UN law). The 'polarization politics' by populist 'strongmen' (like Presidents Putin, Trump and Xi Jinping) contribute also to a rise in the number of authoritarian governments (e.g. in the 'illiberal' EU member states Hungary and Poland) and to a declining number of democracies, thereby rendering collective protection of the SDGs more difficult also among democracies (e.g. Hungary refusing to participate in certain collective EU sanctions against Russia's military aggression).

Disintegration of multilevel UN and WTO governance?

The geopolitical rivalries among US neo-liberalism, China's state-capitalism and Russian imperialism have led to trade wars and economic sanctions disrupting WTO negotiations and the WTO legal and dispute settlement systems. For instance, WTO negotiations on electronic commerce and on internet governance are impeded by competing regulatory paradigms of authoritarian countries (e.g. prioritizing censorship and alleged state interests), neo-liberal countries (e.g. US support for business-driven 'cyber empires' controlled by US technology companies) and ordo-liberal constitutionalism (e.g. EU regulation of services markets protecting privacy and other fundamental rights and judicial remedies in Internet governance); the quip – 'in the US, data belongs to the big companies; in China; to the state; in Russia, to the secret services; and in Europe, to the individuals' – illustrates the mutually conflicting conceptions of regulation. The UN security system fails to protect human rights and 'democratic peace', for instance due to regular abuses of veto-powers by permanent members of the UN Security Council and illegal cyber-attacks. Russia's wars of aggression against neighboring countries undermine also Europe's security order based on respect for human rights and democratic self-determination. Thanks to US President Biden, the security and defense cooperation among NATO countries has overcome previous challenges by the Trump administration and remains the strongest pillar of transatlantic cooperation.

China's insufficient cooperation with the WHO in controlling the COVID-19 health pandemic provoked President Trump to withdraw the USA from WHO membership; 'vaccine nationalism' and insufficient reconciliation of the property rights of pharmaceutical industries with human rights of access to affordable medicines prevented supply of vaccines to all countries and people in need. The insufficient greenhouse gas (GHG) reduction commitments made at the 'COP 26' of the UN Framework Convention on Climate Change in Glasgow in November 2021 reinforced the EU's determination to unilaterally introduce CBAMs as of 2023; yet, CBAMs – and their consistency with the non-discrimination principles of WTO law and with the preferential treatment of less-developed countries (as acknowledged also in the Paris Agreement) – are bound to provoke further trade conflicts and trade retaliation unless additional multilateral disciplines can be agreed (e.g. for calculating the carbon content of traded products like cement and steel). The insufficient UN responses to environmental disasters (like over-fishing, plastic pollution of the oceans, biodiversity losses, climate change) entail economic regulatory challenges (like de-carbonizing and de-plastification of economies) that risk further undermining social welfare (e.g. of the ca 140 million climate refugees predicted by the UN for 2050). The successful, albeit modest results of the WTO Ministerial Conference in June 2022 confirm the need for global cooperation in protecting the SDGs. Yet, the coalition of only some 40 democracies assisting Ukraine in its collective self-defense against *erga omnes* violations of UN law illustrates how power politics risks disintegrating UN and WTO treaty systems and global cooperation. If plurilateral and regional cooperation among like-minded countries – rather than global economic integration also among geopolitical rivals – should become the new security policy paradigm, UN and WTO governance will become even less capable of protecting the SDGs.

Disintegration of transatlantic leadership?

Whether industrialized countries can realize their policy commitments to carbon-free 'circular economies' by 2050 will depend on transatlantic cooperation and leadership. The latter will be easier with democratic US presidencies than in case of a return of Donald Trump as US President denying climate change. The increasing challenges (e.g. by China and Russia) of the post-1945/1989 hegemonic US liberal world order (like the US dollar as global reserve currency, the US nuclear umbrella protecting liberal democracies and safe transport connections, IMF/GATT rules protecting liberal trade, freedom of payments and monetary stability) are related also to crises of democratic governance and business-driven 'regulatory capture' of economic legislation, administration and adjudication inside the USA. Populist demagogy – for instance polarizing societies through tribal identity politics, distorting deliberative democracy by public disinformation, undermining constitutional democracy by manipulating election results, judicial appointments weakening constitutional checks and balances, abusing executive powers and promising simple solutions to complex global governance problems (cf. Naim 2022) – is undermining democratic constitutionalism. The tribalism and nationalist protectionism of the Republican party entails that – beyond NATO – the USA can no longer be relied as a partner in protecting multilateral rule-of-law: systemic diversity has become a permanent fixture not only in relations with China and Russia but also in transatlantic relations. The decline of US global leadership for UN/WTO economic policies reinforces power-oriented domination of regional economic cooperation regimes (e.g. Russia dominating the Eurasian Community among formerly Soviet republics; China dominating bilateral economic cooperation with 'Belt & Road' partner governments; the US dominating the protectionist transformation of the

North American Free Trade Area into the USMCA). The US withdrawal from Trans-Pacific and Trans-Atlantic FTAs, 'home shoring' of global supply chains and politically motivated relocation of industries to the USA (e.g. as envisaged in the 2022 US Chips Act) reinforce departures from globalization of economies. Geopolitics and global governance crises politicize economic regulation; they render mutually incoherent, regional and national responses more likely (like Russian power politics vis-a-vis neighboring countries, unilateral EU introduction of CBAMs, competing regional systems of Internet governance). Western insistence on higher environmental, social and governance standards reinforces China's move toward a more self-sufficient, inwardly focused 'dual circulation economy' and China's politicization of external supply chains (e.g. restricting imports from Australia and Lithuania for political reasons). The diverse 'political economies' governing authoritarian Eurasian countries, Anglo-Saxon constitutional nationalism and Europe's multilevel constitutionalism promote 'systemic competition' (e.g. among China and Europe) also in their external cooperation with third countries in Africa, Asia and Latin-America (like competition between China's non-transparent, sometimes non-conditional financial assistance to foreign sovereign debtors compared with the transparent and conditional assistance by the Bretton Woods institutions and the 'Paris club' member states). President Putin's aggressive use of military aggression and threats of nuclear wars illustrate why power politics is unlikely to lead to a post-neoliberal world economy responding more effectively to climate change and other regulatory challenges of global PGs. Europe's capacity as 'global market regulator' (e.g. 'Brussels effects' of EU common market standards) remains fragile and contested also by the USA in view of Europe's comparatively weaker military, technological and financial power.

The historical EU experience was that the legal and democratic legitimacy, economic efficiency and social acceptability of European integration depend on multilevel constitutionalism promoting overall coherence of multilevel governance of PGs in Europe. EU law requires (e.g. in Arts 3 and 21 TEU) to promote the EU's internal constitutional principles (like human rights, democratic governance, rule-of-law) also in the EU's external relations in conformity with the worldwide recognition of human rights, democratic governance and rule-of-law in UN law and in the 2030 UN Sustainable Development Agenda. Yet, due to the diverse neo-liberal and authoritarian traditions in other states, the EU conceptions of ordo-liberal, multilevel constitutionalism remain contested by many third states (like 'human rights conditionality' of EU trade policies, 'security screening' of foreign investments, prohibition of investor-state arbitration in relations among EU states, EU anti-coercion measures and politically motivated economic sanctions, unilateral CBAMs). Similarly, what EU law requires the EU institutions to consider 'transnational governance failures' (like competitive distortions resulting from foreign violations of labor and worker rights, illegal Russian use of military force, Chinese 'economic coercion' vis-à-vis Lithuania, illegal US blocking of the nomination of WTO AB members, carbon leakage undermining the goals of the 2015 Paris Agreement on climate change mitigation), justifying EU countermeasures, remains often contested by third countries. The illegal blocking of compulsory third-party adjudication of trade disputes in the WTO risks provoking additional, unilateral countermeasures further disrupting the rules-based trading system. Past efforts at elaborating transatlantic FTAs and promoting stronger cooperation between the US Congress and European parliamentarians failed due to insufficient political support from the USA. New transatlantic institutions among government executives (like the Trade and Technology Council) are no substitute for citizen-driven, transatlantic economic integration and environmental co-operation agreements (e.g. on linking emission trading systems and carbon border adjustment measures). If Donald Trump should return to the US presidency in 2025 and continue undermining the credibility of democratic, trade and environmental US policies by 'big lies' (e.g. about democratic election outcomes, the multilateral WTO legal and trading system, climate change), transatlantic cooperation will become even more difficult.

Knowledge problems and constitutional problems of market regulation

Similar to the dissolution of empires following World War I and to decolonization during the post–World War II period, the emergence of a multipolar world (e.g. with China expected to replace the USA as the largest economy, and India to replace Japan as the second-largest economy in the 2030s) raises existential questions of how the peaceful coexistence and coherence of the interdependent social, political, economic, legal and cultural orders – and their efficient coordination – can be promoted in ways that respect human and democratic rights of citizens without ignoring the changing environmental and power realities. EU rules limiting market failures and governance failures (e.g. as defined in EU competition law, environmental law, social, human and constitutional rights) evolved progressively in response to economic and governance crises among European states and often remain contested outside Europe; the term 'governance failure' refers to non-compliance with EU law rather than to scientific knowledge (e.g. about market competition as decentralized, cybernetic information, coordination- and sanctioning mechanisms). The unwillingness of the Biden administration and the US Congress to limit US trade policy discretion by compulsory WTO AB adjudication was described as 'governance failure' in terms of non-compliance with WTO law (e.g. Article 17.2 DSU and IX.1 WTO Agreement). In other areas like competition and monetary policies, the US continues respecting the need for cooperation among regulatory authorities in Europe and the USA (e.g. based on the 1991 EU-USA cooperation agreement providing for 'negative' and 'positive comity' among EU and US competition authorities). The current US unwillingness to conclude new FTAs is a lawful, albeit politically contested exercise of US sovereignty rather than a 'governance failure' as defined in WTO law. The entry into force, on 1 January 2022, of the Regional Comprehensive Economic Partnership (RCEP) between China and 14 Asia-Pacific countries, and its regulatory competition with the Comprehensive and Progressive Agreement for Trans-Pacific Partnership (CPTPP)[1], illustrates how Asian countries – similar to African countries participating in the Pan-African FTA; American countries participating in regional FTAs in Southern, Central and North America; and European countries participating in the EU, EFTA and EEA – remain determined to protect the advantages of rules-based, liberal trading systems at regional levels of governance in view of the increasing challenges of the global WTO system for multilateral trade regulation, dispute settlement, trade negotiations, multilateral surveillance of trade policies and legal security.

The UN's 'constitutional governance model' (as recommended in UN resolutions on human rights, democratic governance, rule-of-law and the SDGs) and Europe's integration experiences are reminders that transnational PGs (like the SDGs) cannot be effectively protected for the benefit of all citizens without empowering citizens through human and democratic rights and parliamentary and judicial protection of transnational rule-of-law. Yet, notwithstanding the adoption of national constitutions (written or unwritten) and of at least one UN human rights convention by all UN member states, constitutional reforms of UN and WTO governance remain limited to a few policy areas (like compulsory adjudication in WTO law, investment law and in the UN Convention on the Law of the Sea). Without compulsory judicial remedies, UN HRL cannot be effectively enforced inside and among UN member states. Only in exceptional situations did the UN Security Council (SC) assert 'legislative powers', for example to establish international criminal courts and respond to international health pandemics by adopting, for instance, UN SC Resolutions 2532 and 2565 (2020) acknowledging that 'the unprecedented extent of the COVID-19 pandemic is likely to endanger the maintenance of international peace and security'[2] and calling 'upon all parties to armed conflicts to engage immediately in a durable humanitarian pause' to provide humanitarian assistance to the world's most vulnerable in conflict zones.[3] Many other proposals for strengthening the UN security and rule-of-law systems were blocked by the veto powers provided for in the UN Charter, just as the compulsory WTO dispute settlement system was disrupted by illegal veto practices since 2017. The more UN and WTO member states disregard human rights, rule-of-law, undistorted market competition and 'environmental constitutionalism' as decentralized steering mechanisms for protecting global PGs like the SDGs, the less are national and intergovernmental power politics ('America first') capable of preventing unnecessary poverty (SDG1) and protecting food security (SDG2), public health (SDG3), public education for all (SDG4), gender equality (SDG5), access to water and sanitation for all (SDG6), and many other SDGs like combatting climate change (SDG13) and 'access to justice' (SDG16). As the geopolitical rivalries between China, Russia and the USA undermine transnational rule-of-law and the needed global cooperation in pursuit of the SDGs, reasonable citizens must resist international power politics as lacking democratic and social legitimacy.

Notes

1 The CPTPP is an FTA between Australia, Brunei Darussalam, Canada, Chile, Japan, Malaysia, Mexico, Peru, New Zealand, Singapore and Vietnam, which entered into force in 2018 after US President Trump withdrew the USA in spite of the earlier signing of the agreement under the Obama administration.

2 SC Res. 2532 (July 1, 2020) pmbl. para 11; SC Res. 2565 (Feb. 26, 2021) pmbl. 17.

3 SC Resolution 2532 para 2.

References

Fishkin, J. and Forbath, W. E. (2022). *The Anti-Oligarchy Constitution: Reconstructing the Economic Foundations of American Democracy*. Harvard University Press.

Loughlin, M. (2022). *Against Constitutionalism*. Harvard University Press, pp. 124–35.

Naim, M. (2022). The Dictator's New Playbook: Why Democracy is Losing the Fight, in *Foreign Affairs*. March/April 2022.

Petersmann, E. U. and Pollack, M. A. (eds. 2003). *Transatlantic Economic Disputes. The EU, the US and the WTO*. Oxford University Press.

Petersmann, E. U. (2021). Neo-liberal, State-Capitalist and Ordo-liberal Conceptions of World Trade: The Rise and Fall of the WTO Dispute Settlement System, in: China (Taiwan) Yearbook of International Relations 38 (2020), 1–41 (Brill).

Petersmann, E. U. (2022). *Transforming World Trade and Investment Law for Sustainable Development*. Oxford University Press.

Slobodian, Q. (2018). *Globalists. The End of Empire and the Birth of Neoliberalism*. Harvard University Press.

10

REVERBERATIONS OF THE CJEU *ACHMEA B.V.* DECISION IN THE TRANSATLANTIC SPACE

*Jenya Grigorova**

WORLD TRADE ORGANIZATION

Introduction

In March 2018, the Court of Justice of the European Union (CJEU) issued its decision in *Slovak Republic v. Achmea B.V.*[1] (*Achmea*). It ruled that the Treaty on the functioning of the European Union (TFEU) precludes dispute settlement provisions in bilateral investment treaties (BIT) concluded between two European Union (EU) Member States (intra-EU BITs). This and several subsequent decisions by the CJEU set the ground for a new type of arguments raised by host States in the context of investor-State dispute settlement (ISDS) proceedings based on intra-EU BITs.

This chapter addresses the reverberations of the *Achmea* decision in the Transatlantic space.[2] It starts with a brief summary of the *Achmea* decision and subsequent developments surrounding the general trend of asserting the incompatibility of dispute settlement provisions of intra-EU BITs with EU law, before briefly summarizing the reactions by some arbitral tribunals to *Achmea*-related arguments raised by host States. The chapter then focuses on analyzing the ways in which US courts have approached *Achmea*-related arguments, raised when enforcement of arbitral awards is sought in the United States. It examines the issues raised in the cases recently decided by US courts, and aims to tentatively draw more general conclusions as to the relevance accorded to the CJEU decision by investment tribunals and by US courts, and as to the potential theoretical and practical implications of these decisions.

The *Achmea* decision and subsequent developments in the European Union

In *Achmea*, the CJEU addressed a request for a preliminary ruling by the *Bundesgerichtshof* (German Federal Court of Justice). The Slovak Republic had brought

DOI: 10.4324/9781003283911-13

an action before the German courts to set aside an award rendered by an arbitral tribunal on the basis of a BIT concluded between the the Netherlands and the Czech and Slovak Federative Republic. The Slovak Republic had 'expressed doubts as to the compatibility of the arbitration clause in Article 8 of the BIT with Articles 18, 267 and 344 TFEU'.[3]

The CJEU noted three points of fundamental importance:

- investment arbitral tribunals may be called on to interpret or to apply EU law (particularly the provisions concerning the fundamental freedoms);[4]
- investment arbitral tribunals are not part of the EU judicial system and are not entitled to make a reference to the CJEU for a preliminary ruling, i.e., are not subject to mechanisms capable of ensuring the full effectiveness of the rules of the EU;[5]
- there are limited means of review of investment arbitral awards by national courts (such review ensuring that the questions of EU lawwhich the tribunal may have to address can be submitted to the CJEU by means of a reference for a preliminary ruling).[6]

Accordingly, the CJEU found that by concluding BITs and including in those BITs dispute settlement provisions, EU Member States establish a mechanism for settling disputes between an investor and a Member State which could prevent those disputes from being resolved in a manner that ensures the full effectiveness of EU law, even though they might concern the interpretation or application of that law.[7] For that reason, the CJEU considered that the TFEU precludes dispute settlement provisions in BITs concluded between EU Member States.

In subsequent decisions, the CJEU continued on the path of asserting the inconsistency of investor-State dispute settlement provisions in intra-EU BITs with the EU treaties. In *PL Holding*, it ruled that EU Member States are required to challenge the validity of arbitration clauses contrary to EU law.[8]

In *Komstroy*[9], it addressed a request for a preliminary ruling from the *Cour d'Appel de Paris* (Paris Court of Appeals). The Republic of Moldova had brought an action for annulment against an award rendered in Paris by an ad hoc arbitral tribunal established on the basis of the Energy Charter Treaty (ECT). The ECT is a multilateral investment treaty to which the EU, its Member States and non-Member States are parties.

With respect to the issues addressed in this chapter, the CJEU decision in *Komstroy* is notable to the extent that it extended the logic developed in *Achmea* to the ECT (see Böhme, 2022). The CJEU noted that

- the ECT constitutes an 'act of EU law' and, consequently, an arbitral tribunal under Article 26 ECT (Investment dispute settlement) is required to interpret, and even apply, EU law[10] (see Dashwood, 2022; Odermatt, 2021);
- ad-hoc arbitral tribunals under the ECT do not constitute components of the judicial system of a Member State;[11]
- to the extent that judicial awards rendered by ad hoc tribunals established on the basis of the UNCITRAL arbitration rules are subject to judicial review by national courts, such review can only be carried out in so far as the domestic law permits it.[12]

Accordingly, the CJEU found that Article 26(2)(c) of the ECT is not applicable to disputes between a Member State and an investor of another Member State.[13] Article 26 of the ECT can thus no longer serve as a legal basis for initiating intra-EU investment disputes relating to the energy sector (Declève, 2021), even if EU Member States remain under an international obligation to comply with the arbitration mechanism provided for by Article 26 of the ECT in their relations with each other, as well as in relations with the third country parties (Dashwood, 2022). In practice, this would complicate the enforcement of awards in EU Member States and open the door to potential set aside proceedings before their domestic courts. This naturally promotes investors seeking the enforcement of those arbitral awards in non-EU Member States (Dashwood, 2022).

Following the *Achmea* decision, on 5 May 2020, EU Member States signed an Agreement for the termination of Bilateral Investment Treaties between the Member States of the European Union.[14] Annex A of the Agreement lists intra-EU BITs that are 'terminated according to the terms of this Agreement' (Article 2). The Contracting Parties 'confirm that Arbitration Clauses are contrary to the EU Treaties and thus inapplicable' (Article 4.1) As of the date on which the last of the parties to a BIT became a Member State of the European Union, 'the Arbitration Clause in such a Bilateral Investment Treaty cannot serve as legal basis for Arbitration Proceedings' (Article 4.2). The Agreement also establishes a clear path as to any future disputes brought on the basis of dispute settlement provisions in intra-EU BITs and addresses extensively some issues pertaining to pending disputes. In a comparable trend, in June 2022, the Contracting Parties to the ECT announced an agreement in principle on the modernization of the ECT, including the introduction of an article clarifying that Article 26 does not apply among parties that are members of the same Regional Economic Integration Organisation, such as the EU, in their mutual relations.[15]

EU Member States and the Commission (as *amicus curiae*) have raised before investment tribunals, as a challenge to their jurisdiction, the general argument that EU law precludes ISDS provisions in intra-EU BITs. More specifically, EU Member States have argued that

- the tribunal has no jurisdiction because an EU investor is not entitled to bring an investment arbitration proceeding against an EU Member State, and that tribunal should reach this conclusion either because it should interpret the BIT/ECT in line with EU law[16] or because it is bound by *Achmea* as part of the applicable law to its jurisdiction;[17]
- the tribunal has no jurisdiction because there is no valid offer to arbitrate (the host State's offer to arbitrate could not validly have extended to intra-EU disputes);[18] or
- the tribunal should refrain from exercising jurisdiction on the basis of judicial propriety and the fact that enforcement of the award would be impossible within the EU.[19]

Most investment tribunals, as well as some domestic courts, have – in different ways and for different reasons – rejected these *Achmea*-related arguments. This section provides several examples. An extremely thorough and useful analysis of the practice of investment tribunals constituted under intra-EU BITs and the ECT is provided in Gáspár-Szilágyi and Usynin (2019).

In *Masdar Solar & Wind Cooperatief U.A. v. Kingdom of Spain*, the arbitral tribunal, composed on the basis of Article 26 of the ECT, found that *Achmea* had no bearing on the case, and that it was 'of limited application and cannot be applied to multilateral treaties to which the EU is a party'.[20]

In *UP (formerly Le Chèque Déjeuner) and C.D Holding Internationale v. Hungary*, the arbitral tribunal noted that that case differed in determinative aspects from *Achmea*. First, the jurisdiction of the arbitral tribunal was based on the Convention on the Settlement of Investment Disputes between States and Nationals of Other States (ICSID Convention) and not on UNCITRAL rules, like the arbitral tribunal in *Achmea*. Second, the place of arbitration was London and arbitration proceedings were governed by the ICSID Convention, not by German law. Third, judicial review of the award was possible through an annulment procedure. And fourth, an annulment decision would not have been subject to further review.[21]

In *Vattenfall AB and others v. Federal Republic of Germany*, the arbitral tribunal, composed on the basis of Article 26 of the ECT, found that EU law (and the *Achmea* judgment) were not part of the law applicable to the assessment of the tribunal's jurisdiction. The tribunal noted that Article 26 of the ECT has no carve-out concerning the applicability of ECT's dispute settlement provisions to EU Member States inter se.[22]

In *Greentech Energy Systems A/S, et al v. Italian Republic*, an arbitral tribunal, again composed on the basis of Article 26 of the ECT, found that *Achmea* had no preclusive effect such as to remove the tribunal's jurisdiction, because (i) the tribunal's jurisdiction derived from the ECT; (ii) the tribunal was not called upon to apply EU law; (iii) and *Achmea* did not extend to ECT.[23]

In *Eskosol S.p.A. in liquidazione v. Italian Republic*, the arbitral tribunal noted that EU law was not part of the applicable law for determining the scope of the tribunal's jurisdiction. According to the tribunal, *Achmea* did not disturb the tribunal's jurisdiction because: (i) it did not extend to ECT cases; (ii) it did not bind the tribunal; (iii) it could not invalidate the ECT.[24]

In *Infracapital v. Kingdom of Spain*, the arbitral tribunal had issued a decision on jurisdiction, liability and directions on quantum. After the issuance of the *Komstroy* ruling, Spain submitted a request of reconsideration of the tribunal's decision, arguing that the tribunal lacked jurisdiction to hear the intra-EU dispute. The arbitral tribunal considered that EU law was not applicable to jurisdiction, and as a result, the Komstroy Judgment was irrelevant to the question of jurisdiction. In addition, the arbitral tribunal expressed concerns with respect to the possibility that there be a separate treatment for intra-EU disputes and non-intra-EU disputes, noting that nothing in the ECT allowed arbitral tribunals to decline jurisdiction on the basis of a party's status or its 'obligations under a different legal order'.[25]

In *Green Power v. Kingdom of Spain*, an arbitral tribunal established on the basis of Article 26 of the ECT, under the Stockholm Chamber of Commerce (SCC) rules and seated in Stockholm, analysed the validity of the arbitration agreement under the law applicable to its jurisdiction, which included certain EU norms applicable both as a matter of international law and of domestic law. Relying on the *Achmea* and *Komstroy* judgments, the arbitral tribunal considered that Spain's offer to arbitrate under the ECT was not applicable in intra-EU relations. Accordingly, the tribunal concluded that it had no jurisdiction to hear the claims.[26]

Interestingly, after the issuance of the award in *Green Power*, Spain requested the tribunal in *Infracapital* to reconsider its decision on jurisdiction, liability and directions on quantum. The tribunal rejected the request, noting that the *Green Power* arbitration was substantially different, as it had been brought under the SCC rules and the seat of arbitration was Stockholm, these two elements attracting the application of EU law. The *Infracapital* tribunal, on the other hand, was set up under the ICSID rules and was seated in Washington, D.C.[27]

On an increasing number of occasions, investors have sought the enforcement of arbitral awards issued by arbitral tribunals on the basis of dispute settlement provisions in intra-EU BITs, or the ECT, before the US domestic courts. One explanation of this phenomenon are the expected consequences of the *Achmea* decision, that is, domestic courts in EU Member States not allowing for the enforcement of such arbitral awards.[28]

After a brief summary of the enforcement procedures before US domestic courts, this section surveys the *Achmea*-related arguments raised by host States in most cases where investors have sought the enforcement of arbitral awards before the US domestic courts, and those courts' decisions, comparing them to those of other non-EU domestic courts and drawing some general conclusions.

The involvement of US courts

In the United States, the enforcement of investment arbitral awards is sought mostly before the United States District Court for the District of Columbia (D.D.C.) which has original jurisdiction over cases involving foreign states. The enforcement of arbitral awards issued by an ICSID arbitral tribunal is governed by the ICSID Convention, whereas the enforcement of arbitral awards issued by ad hoc tribunals under other rules (e.g., under the Rules of Arbitration of the Arbitration Institute of the Stockholm Chamber of Commerce [SCC]) is governed by the New York Convention on the Recognition and Enforcement of Foreign Arbitral Awards (New York Convention).

In the first scenario, Article 54(1) of the ICSID Convention requires all Contracting States to recognize an award rendered pursuant to the Convention as binding and enforce the pecuniary obligations imposed by that award 'as if it were a final judgment of a court in that State'. In the United States, the ICSID Convention was given domestic effect through the Investment Disputes Act (Enabling Statute), which provides that the 'pecuniary obligations imposed by such an award shall be enforced and shall be given the same full faith and credit as if the award were a final judgment of a court of general jurisdiction of one of the several states'.[29] In addition, the Foreign Sovereign Immunities Act (FSIA), which governs the enforcement and recognition of awards against a sovereign State, provides that 'subject to existing international agreements to which the United States is a party, [...] a foreign state shall be immune from the jurisdiction of the courts of the United States and of the States', subject to a list of exceptions, in particular when the foreign state has 'waived its immunity either explicitly or by implication' (28 U.S.C. § 1605(a)(1)), and actions to 'confirm an award made pursuant to [...] an agreement to arbitrate, if [...] the agreement or award is or may be governed by a treaty or other international agreement in force for the United States calling for the recognition and enforcement of arbitral awards' (28 U.S.C. § 1605(a)(6)).[30] The FSIA is the sole source of subject matter and personal jurisdiction in actions to enforce ICSID arbitration awards.[31] This means that host States, as foreign sovereigns, have the right to assert procedural defenses to enforcement.

In the second scenario, the enforcement of arbitral awards not issued by ICSID tribunals is governed by the New York Convention. Pursuant to its Article III, '[e]ach Contracting State shall recognize arbitral awards as binding and enforce them'. In the United States, enforcement can be sought through a summary proceeding. Article V sets out a limited list of grounds on which host States can rely to request that the recognition and enforcement be refused (see Gaillard and Siino, 2021).

Achmea-*related arguments before US courts*

EU Member States have relied on *Achmea* before US courts in support of motions to dismiss the petitions and deny enforcement of the awards, arguing (in general terms) that the arbitration agreement underlying the award is not valid, and – consequently – the D.D.C. lacks subject matter jurisdiction under the FSIA to recognize the award. Table 10.1 reflects how this general argument was developed in most cases, with a focus on some nuances.[32]

Decisions by US courts

Host States have requested that the confirmation and enforcement proceedings before US courts be dismissed or, at least, stayed.

So far, the D.D.C. has accepted to stay several proceedings. For most, the D.D.C. stayed the proceedings until an ICSID *ad hoc* Committee has issued its ruling.[49] On several, rarer occasions, the D.D.C. granted a motion to stay in relation to annulment or set aside proceedings in the national courts of the seat of arbitration. For instance, in *Novenergia II v. Spain,* the D.D.C. stayed proceedings, on the basis of the New York Convention, until resolution of the set-aside proceedings before the Swedish Svea Court of Appeal. Interestingly, the D.D.C. noted that 'comity' considerations favored a stay, inter alia because the issue was of importance to the EU and 'better suited for initial review in their courts'.[50] The D.D.C. followed a similar logic in *Greentech v. Italy* and *CEF v. Italy,* regarding requests by Italy to stay the proceedings while annulment or set-aside proceedings were ongoing in Sweden. In *Foresight v. Spain*, the US District Court for the Southern District of New York granted a motion to transfer the case and referred the application to stay to the D.D.C.

Table 10.1 *Achmea*-related arguments before US courts

Case	*Arbitration rules*	*Investment treaty*	Achmea-*related arguments by EU Member State*	*European Commission* amicus *brief*
Micula v. Romania[33]	ICSID	Sweden – Romania BIT	general challenge to the D.D.C's subject matter jurisdiction	*Achmea* rendered the arbitration agreement in the BIT invalid and unenforceable and the D.D.C. lacks subject-matter jurisdiction under the FSIA, because the award was not issued pursuant to a valid arbitration agreement.[34]
Masdar v. Spain[35]	ICSID	ECT	D.D.C. lacks subject-matter jurisdiction because the action does not satisfy any of the exceptions to immunity outlined in the FSIA. Spain never entered into a valid agreement to arbitrate before an ISCID tribunal, because Article 26 of the ECT does not apply to disputes between EU Member States and investors from other EU Member States. The arbitral tribunal never enjoyed the jurisdiction necessary to issue the award, and the D.D.C. consequently does not have jurisdiction to enforce it.	i The proper application of customary international law rules of treaty interpretation compels the conclusion that the ECT does not apply intra-EU; ii Even if it were possible to interpret Article 26 of the ECT as encompassing intra-EU disputes, such an interpretation would conflict with the EU Treaties, and that conflict, as a matter of international law, must be resolved in favor of EU law; iii Principles of international comity and due respect for foreign sovereigns counsel in favor of denying enforcement.[36]

(*Continued*)

Table 10.1 (Continued)

Case	*Arbitration rules*	*Invest-ment treaty*	Achmea-*related arguments by EU Member State*	*European Commission* amicus *brief*
Novenergia II v. Spain[37]	SCC Arbitration Institute	ECT	D.D.C. lacks subject-matter jurisdiction to hear the merits under the FSIA because no arbitration agreement exists	Same as in *Masdar v. Spain*[38]
Foresight v. Spain[39]	SCC Arbitration Institute	ECT	ECT does not have intra-EU application because EU law precludes investor-state arbitration for intra-EU disputes. Following this logic, there was no offer to arbitrate from Spain and thus the underlying arbitration is invalid. As a result, the US Court lacks subject matter jurisdiction.	Same as in *Masdar v. Spain* and *Novenergia II v. Spain*[40]
Greentech v. Italy / CEF v. Italy[41]	SCC Arbitration Institute	ECT	D.D.C lacks jurisdiction over the petitions and the award is not enforceable.	
9REN v. Spain[42]	ICSID	ECT	D.D.C. lacks subject matter jurisdiction under the FSIA because there is no arbitration agreement.	
NextEra v. Spain[43]	ICSID	ECT	several grounds for dismissal including *forum non conveniens* and lack of subject matter jurisdiction of the D.D.C. under the FSIA because no arbitration agreement exists	

RREEF v. Spain[44]	ICSID	ECT	several grounds for dismissal including lack of subject matter jurisdiction of the D.D.C. under the FSIA	
InfraRed v. Spain[45]	ICSID	ECT	There was no agreement to arbitrate because EU law precludes Spain from making an offer to arbitrate with any national of an EU Member State over any matters that may require the interpretation or application of EU law. In addition, binding EU caselaw precludes Spain's purported consent to arbitrate disputes with EU- based investors arising under the ECT, rendering the entire ICSID arbitration void *ab initio* and divesting the D.D.C. of subject-matter jurisdiction.	Same as in *Masdar v. Spain, Novenergia II v. Spain* and *Foresight v. Spain*[46]
Hydro Energy v. Spain[47]	ICSID	ECT	i D.D.C. lacks jurisdiction under the FSIA because Spain is presumptively immune to the jurisdiction of US courts, and none of the exceptions to the FSIA applies because there was no agreement to arbitrate;	The CJEU has directly answered the question at the heart of the case, i.e., whether Spain's offer of arbitration in Article 26 of the ECT extended to EU companies. The D.D.C. has the authority and obligation to consider this question in determining whether it has subject-matter jurisdiction under the FSIA to entertain the

(*Continued*)

Table 10.1 (Continued)

Case	*Arbitration rules*	*Investment treaty*	Achmea-*related arguments by EU Member State*	*European Commission* amicus *brief*
			ii granting the complaint would violate the foreign sovereign compulsion doctrine; iii the award is not entitled to 'full faith and credit' since the arbitral tribunal lacks jurisdiction over Spain because there is no agreement to arbitrate, and the award is unenforceable; iv if there were any question about the EU law above, the D.D.C. should dismiss the petition under the doctrine of *forum non conveniens*.	action. The CJEU's answer to that question warrants the highest degree of deference as a matter of international comity.[48]

Note: Compiled by author.

The requests for stay and the ensuing decisions do not discuss the *Achmea*-related arguments raised by host States in support of their motions to dismiss (alternative to the motions to stay the proceedings). For that reason, these decisions will not be the focus of this section. There are, however, a handful of cases where the D.D.C. has addressed some *Achmea*-related arguments.

The first such case, and to date the one that discusses these issues to the fullest extent, is *Micula v. Romania.*[51], The D.D.C. rejected Romania's *Achmea* objection and confirmed the award. It held that Romania had failed to carry its burden of showing that *Achmea* forecloses the D.D.C.'s jurisdiction under the FSIA's arbitration exception (28 U.S.C. § 1605(a)(6)). According to the D.D.C, the CJEU's reasoning in *Achmea* turned on protecting the autonomy of EU law, and Romania had not shown that the concern that animated *Achmea* (un-reviewability of an arbitral tribunal's determination of EU law by an EU court) was present in the *Micula* case. The D.D.C. highlighted three reasons for that:

- The facts in *Micula* were materially different than the ones in *Achmea*. In *Achmea*, the challenged government action and the arbitration proceeding commenced after the Slovak Republic had entered the European Union. In *Micula*, all key events (i.e., the entry into force of the Sweden – Romania BIT, the challenged government action, and the commencement of the arbitral proceedings) had occurred before Romania acceded to the European Union, and therefore at a time when Romania was 'subject, at least primarily, to its own domestic law'.
- The dispute before the arbitral tribunal did not relate to the interpretation or application of EU law. The arbitral tribunal considered EU for factual context, not as a source of controlling law – and therefore did not decide a question of EU law 'in a way that implicates the core rationale of *Achmea*'.
- In a ruling concerning a state aid decision in *Micula*, the General Court of the EU had specified that the arbitral tribunal was not bound to apply EU law to events occurring prior to the accession, and had therefore explicitly refuted Romania's position that *Achmea* nullified the arbitration agreement contained in the Sweden – Romania BIT.

In other words, the D.D.C. distinguished the *Micula* case from *Achmea* without necessarily rejecting the relevance of EU law. As some commentators observed, the decision in *Micula* shows that awards based on intra-EU BITs are potentially enforceable before US courts, although at the same time, the D.D.C. did not foreclose the relevance of the CJEU's decision in future proceedings to enforce intra-EU investor-state awards before US courts (Yanos and Ramos-Mrosovsky, 2021). The *Micula* judgment was affirmed by US Court of Appeals for the District of Columbia Circuit.[52]

In several other cases, while granting the host States' petitions to stay, the D.D.C. briefly mentioned the potential complications of addressing directly *Achmea*-related arguments. In *Masdar v. Spain*, it noted that 'deciding this case may eventually demand resolving a thorny dispute over the implications of multiple treaty obligations and a shifting legal landscape in the European Union', and considered it 'wiser to leave those intricate issues for another day".[53] In *9REN v. Spain*, it observed that Spain's motion to dismiss raised 'intricate questions regarding the validity of arbitration agreements with EU member states under EU law' and that the Court was 'loath to wade into this territory unnecessarily".[54] In *InfraRed v. Spain*, it noted that to decide on Spain's motion to dismiss, it would 'need to come down on one side or the other of an extremely high-stakes war of interpretation between the EU and several of its member states on one side and several ICSID tribunals and investors on the other'.[55]

The D.D.C. recently addressed *Achmea*-related arguments in the context of motions for preliminary injunction in proceedings to confirm two arbitral awards (*NextEra v. Spain* and *9REN v. Spain*)[56]. While the proceedings were pending, Spain initiated legal action in the District Court of Amsterdam (against *NextEra*) and the District Court of Luxembourg (against *9REN*) seeking orders requiring the investors to withdraw the proceedings before the US domestic courts and to cease enforcement of the awards. In response, the investors asked the D.D.C. to issue preliminary injunctions preventing Spain from pusuing the actions before the Dutch and Luxembourg courts. Addressing Spain's arguments, the D.D.C. reached two important conclusions regarding *Achmea*-related issues. First, the D.D.C. found that it has jurisdiction over Spain under the FSIA's arbitration exception, and this despite Spain's submission that, based on *Achmea* and *Komstroy*, there was no arbitration agreement because 'any such agreement would violate core tenets of EU sovereignty as set out in the EU Treaties'. To reach this conclusion, the D.D.C. considered Spain's *Achmea*-related arguments no different than any other assertion that a party lacked a legal basis to enter or invoke an arbitration agreement. Such assertions go to arbitrability and, therefore, are an issue of the award's merits rather than 'a backdoor challenge to FSIA jurisdiction'. Second, the D.D.C. found that the investors had a strong likelihood of succeeding on the merits of their petitions, and this despite Spain's submission that the awards were not entitled to full faith and credit because the tribunals lacked jurisdiction. Since the arbitral tribunals had determined that they had jurisdiction after hearing Spain's arguments, the D.D.C. considered that the question had been fully and fairly litigated and finally decided at that stage. The awards were therefore entitled to full faith and credit. In its attmpt to not directly address *Achmea*-related arguments, the D.D.C. thus appears to have relegated such discussions to the arbitral tribunals. To the extent that those tribunals have proven reluctant to accept that they do not have jurisdiction, the D.D.C.'s practice could de facto have far-reaching effects.

Comparison with non-EU national courts

The D.D.C.'s approach is comparable – to a certain extent – to those adopted by other non-EU national courts, particularly Switzerland's *Tribunal Fédéral*, Australia's Federal Court and the UK Supreme Court.

Switzerland's *Tribunal Fédéral* has so far been faced twice with *Achmea*-related arguments, and – similarly to the D.D.C. – has so far avoided substantive discussions on the issue. In *Natland et al. v. Czech Republic*, the *Tribunal Fédéral* rejected the

Czech Republic's application to set aside an arbitral award.[57] The *Tribunal Fédéral* dismissed *Achmea* argument because the Czech Republic had not raised it during the arbitration proceedings and recognized that it could not raise it during the proceedings before the *Tribunal Fédéral*. In *PV Investors v. Spain*, the *Tribunal Fédéral* rejected Spain's application to set aside an arbitral award.[58] The *Tribunal Fédéral* did not discuss *Achmea*, but noted that Spain did not seek annulment on the basis of lack of jurisdiction, but that its arguments were based solely on procedural rights.

In *Eiser Infrastructure v. Spain*, Australia's Federal Court found that the applicants were entitled to recognition and enforcement of an arbitral award The Federal Court noted, however, that Spain had failed to comply with the award for reasons that may be related to the controversy arising from *Achmea*.[59]

Finally, in *Micula v.* Romania, the Supreme Court of the United Kingdom lifted a stay on enforcement of the arbitral award that had been decided by the lower courts pending an appeal decision from the CJEU on whether payment of the award would violate Romania's EU law obligations. The Supreme Court found the stay contrary to the United Kingdom's treaty obligations under the ICSID Convention. It noted that 'the principle of comity and the two-way application of the principle of sincere co-operation would be likely to lead the Court of Justice to leave the interpretation of the Convention, to which the EU is not a party, to the domestic courts of the United Kingdom as a Contracting State'. The Supreme Court found that 'it would not be appropriate for this court to stay enforcement in deference to the EU courts on this issue, which is not one of EU law'.[60]

Reverberations in the transatlantic space - issues raised or to be expected

Some practical issues remain pending. The ways in which the US domestic courts have so far addressed and may in the future address *Achmea*-related objections may have a direct effect on choice of seat of arbitral tribunals. They may also encourage claimants to seek enforcement in the United States or other jurisdictions outside the EU (to the extent that such enforcement is possible). Finally, set-aside proceedings clearly might delay such enforcement.

Arguably more importantly, the US domestic courts' approach (and its potential evolution) raises several conceptual issues. The most obvious one is related to the fate of awards already issued by arbitral tribunals. Those awards would not be enforceable in EU Member States but may be enforceable in the United States.

Related is the more theoretical question whether international law provides for tools to deal with situations involving the interaction of three legal 'regimes': EU law, intra-EU BITs, and US law. On the one hand, from the perspective of US courts, the enforcement of an investment arbitral award is an issue of US domestic law (and of the US obligations under international treaties such as the ICSID Convention and the New York Convention), which takes into consideration elements of the legal regime underlying the award, that is, the investment treaty serving as the basis for the agreement to arbitrate. It is hard to fit into that intellectual structure the relevance of EU law, that is, a legal regime containing obligations for one of the parties in the arbitration proceedings. On the other hand, one cannot ignore the specific nature of intra-EU BITs and the role that EU law plays with respect to the international obligations of EU Member States. More specifically, the arbitral awards for which enforcement is sought are based on international agreements (intra-EU BITs) between States that subsequently concluded another international agreement (the TFEU). At the same time, and to complicate things further, the EU legal system is an integral part of the Member States' legal systems.

Those different concerns are somewhat difficult to reconcile with the traditional tools available in private international law or public international law. The latter comes closer to providing some insights into possible approaches through the debates surrounding the relationship between international courts (see Fontanelli, 2009).

In an attempt to reconcile those different concerns, the D.D.C. appears to employ two techniques.

On a more subtle level – and one that has its limits – the D.D.C. notes the chronological sequence of the host states' international commitments, that is, the fact that those states concluded the underlying investment treaties and adopted the challenged measures *before* their accession to the European Union. The D.D.C. thus appears to suggest that a conflict may be avoided by simply situating the events on the two sides of the controlling temporal factor that is the host State's accession to the European Union.

On a less subtle, but probably more enduring, level, the D.D.C has recourse to the concept of 'comity', referring to 'the spirit of cooperation in which a domestic tribunal approaches the resolution of cases touching the laws and interests of other sovereign states'.[61] US courts have justified, under the rubric of comity, a deference as a sign of respect for foreign sovereignty, as a means of protecting the parties' expectations in the interest of international commerce, and as a mechanism of avoiding conflict with the management of foreign relations (Paul, 1991). As Fontantelli puts it, comity 'has something to do with institutional loyalty and good faith', as on its basis, courts may be willing spontaneously to grant wider acknowledgment and higher credit to the case law of other courts (Fontanelli, 2009). Thus, to the extent that public international law provides limited devices to address the complicated interrelation of three legal regimes, comity seems to be a safe, albeit probably unsatisfactorily vague, choice.

Conclusion

All things considered, the *Achmea* decision has had – and will continue to have for a while – important repercussions in the Translatlantic space. So far, US courts have managed to avoid directly addressing the question of the relevance of *Achmea* before them but have been deferential to the specificities of the EU legal order (relying on concepts such as *comity*). It remains, however, to be seen, whether such deference is sustainable or – sooner or later – US domestic courts might have face a situation where they have to directly address the relevance of the CJEU's decision in *Achmea* in the US legal order.

Notes

* The opinions presented in this article are those of the author and are not binding on either the WTO Secretariat or WTO Members. Mistakes are those of the author only.

1 CJEU, *Slovak Republic v. Achmea B.V.* (Case C-284/16).

2 The issues discussed in this chapter concern the enforcement in the United States of arbitral awards concerning investment operations by EU companies in EU Member States. For that reason, international cooperation *fora*, such as the EU-US Trade and Technology Council or the project of Transatlantic Trade and Investment Partnership are only marginally relevant as examples of transatlantic cooperation in the area of international investment.

3 CJEU, *Achmea B.V.*, para. 14.

4 CJEU, *Achmea B.V.*, para. 42.

5 CJEU, *Achmea B.V.*, paras. 43–49.

6 CJEU, *Achmea B.V.*, paras. 50–55.

7 CJEU, *Achmea B.V.*, para. 56.

8 CJEU, *Poland v. PL Holding Sàrl* (Case C-109/20).

9 CJEU, *Republic of Moldova v. Komstroy LLC* (Case C-741/19).

10 CJEU, *Komstroy*, paras. 23, 49 and 50.

11 CJEU, *Komstroy*, para. 52.

12 CJEU, *Komstroy*, para. 58.

13 CJEU, *Komstroy*, para. 66.

14 Agreement for the termination of Bilateral Investment Treaties between the Member States of the European Union, SN/4656/2019/INIT, OJ L 169, 29.5.2020, p. 1–41.

15 See Public Communication Explaining the Main Changes Contained in the Agreement in Principle, 24 June 2022 (available here).

16 *Masdar Solar & Wind Cooperatief U.A. v. Kingdom of Spain* (ICSID, ARB/14/1) (16 May 2018).

17 *UP (formerly Le Chèque Déjeuner) and C.D Holding Internationale v. Hungary* (ICSID, ARB/13/35) (9 October 2018).

18 *Eskosol S.p.A. in liquidazione v. Italian Republic* (ICSID, ARB/15/50) (7 May 2019).

19 *UP and C.D. v. Hungary*; *Vattenfall AB and others v. Federal Republic of Germany* (ICSID, ARB/12/12) (31 August 2018); and *Eskosol S.p.A. in liquidazione v. Italian Republic* (ICSID, ARB/15/50) (7 May 2019).

20 *Masdar Solar & Wind Cooperatief U.A. v. Kingdom of Spain* (ICSID, ARB/14/1) (16 May 2018).

21 *UP (formerly Le Chèque Déjeuner) and C.D Holding Internationale v. Hungary* (ICSID, ARB/13/35) (9 October 2018).

22 *Vattenfall AB and others v. Federal Republic of Germany* (ICSID, ARB/12/12) (31 August 2018).

23 *Greentech Energy Systems A/S, et al v. Italian Republic* (SCC, 2015/095) (23 December 2018).

24 *Eskosol S.p.A. in liquidazione v. Italian Republic* (ICSID, ARB/15/50) (7 May 2019).

25 *Infracapital F1 S.à r.l. and Infracapital Solar B.V. v. Kingdom of Spain* (ICSID, ARB/16/18), Decision on Respondent Request for Reconsideration regarding the Intra-EU Objection and the Merits (1 February 2022).

26 *Green Power K/S and Obton A/S v. Spain* (SCC, V 2016/135), Award (16 June 2022).

27 *Infracapital F1 S.à r.l. and Infracapital Solar B.V. v. Kingdom of Spain* (ICSID, ARB/16/18), Second decision on Reconsideration (19 August 2022).

28 Where the recognition, execution, enforcement, or payment related to arbitral awards rendered on the basis of dispute settlement provisions in intra-EU BITs have been sought before the national courts of EU Member States, those courts have followed the directions of the CJEU. In Germany, in the context of subsequent litigation in *Achmea v. Slovak*

Republic, the German Federal Court of Justice set aside the arbitral award following the CJEU judgment (Federal Court of Justice, *Achmea v. Slovak Republic*, Decision of 31 October 2018). In *Raiffeisen Bank International AG v. Croatia*, the Higher Regional Court Frankfurt declared arbitral proceedings (seated in Frankfurt) inadmissible because the conclusion of an effective arbitration agreement is precluded by the fact that the arbitration provision of the BIT is contrary to EU law and cannot form the basis of an obligation to arbitrate (Higher Regional Court Frankfurt, *Raiffeisen Bank International AG v. Croatia*, Decision of 11 February 2021.). In Sweden, the Svea Court of Appeal in *Greentech v. Italy* and *CEF v. Italy*, found that the enforcement of the awards may not take place "until further notice" (Svea Court of Appeal, Stay of execution, Decisions of 28 March 2019 and 24 April 2019).

29 22 U.S.C. § 1650a.

30 28 U.S.C. §§ 1330, 1332, 1391(f), 1441(d), 1602–1611. As the D.D.C. explained in *Masdar Solar v. Spain*, courts appear to be unanimous in their assessment that petitions brought against foreign sovereigns seeking to enforce ICSID awards qualify for either the arbitral exception or the waiver exception. (D.D.C., Memorandum Opinion, *Masdar Solar & Wind Cooperatief U.A. v. Kingdom of Spain*, Civil Action No. 18–2254 (JEB), 18 September 2019).

31 863 F.3d 96, 100 (2d Cir. 2017). Until recently, several New York federal courts recognized and enforced arbitral awards through summary *ex parte* proceedings, whereas some courts of the District of Columbia considered that a plenary proceeding was necessary. In *Mobil Cerro Negro, Ltd. v. Bolivarian Republic of Venez.*, the US Court of Appeals for the Second Circuit held that the FSIA is the sole source of subject matter and personal jurisdiction in actions to enforce ICSID arbitration awards.

32 Table 1 does not reflect cases where the US domestic courts' decisions do not reflect *Achmea*-related arguments raised by the host states (see, for instance, D.D.C., Memorandum Opinion, *Infrastructure Services Luxembourg S.A.R.L. and Energia Termosolar B.V. v. The Kingdom of Spain*, Civil Action No. 18–1753 (EGS), 28 August 2019; D.D.C., Memorandum Opinion, *Eiser Infrastructure Limited and Energia Solar Luxembourg S.A.R.L. v. Kingdom of Spain*, Civil Action No. 18–1686 (CKK), 13 February 2020).

33 D.D.C., Memorandum Opinion, *Ioan Micula, et al., v. Government of Romania*, Case No. 17-cv-02332 (APM), 11 September 2019.

34 European Commission *amicus* brief in *Micula v. Gov't of Romania*, D.D.C (available here).

35 D.D.C., Memorandum Opinion, *Masdar Solar & Wind Cooperatief U.A. v. Kingdom of Spain*, Civil Action No. 18–2254 (JEB), 18 September 2019.

36 European Commission *amicus* brief in *Masdar v. Spain*, D.D.C (available here).

37 D.D.C., Memorandum Opinion, *Novenergia II – Energy & Environment (SCA) v. The Kingdom of Spain*, Civil Action No. 18-cv-01148 (TSC), 27 January 2020.

38 European Commission *amicus* brief in *Novenergia II v. Spain*, D.D.C. (available here).

39 United States District Court Southern District of New York, Opinion & Order, *Foresight Luxembourg Solar 1 S.A.R.L. et al. v. Kingdom of Spain*, 19 Civ. 3171 (ER), 30 March 2020.

40 European Commission *amicus* brief in *Foresight v. Spain*, D.D.C (available here).

41 D.D.C., Memorandum Opinion, *CEF Energia, B.V.*, et al. v. Kingdom of Spain, No. 19-cv-3443(KBJ), 23 July 2020.

42 D.D.C., Memorandum Opinion, *9REN Holding S.A.R.L. v. Kingdom of Spain*, Civil Action No. 19-cv-07187 (TSC), 30 September 2020 and D.C., Memorandum Opinion, *9REN Holding S.A.R.L. v. Kingdom of Spain*, Civil Action No. 19-cv-07187 (TSC), 15 February 2023.

43 D.D.C., Memorandum Opinion, *NextEra Energy Global Holdings B.V., et al. v. Kingdom of Spain*, Civil Action No. 19-cv-01618 (TSC), 30 September 2020 and D.D.C., Memorandum Opinion, *Next*Era Energy Global Holdings B.V., et al. v. Kingdom of Spain, Civil Action No. 19-cv-01618 (TSC), 15 February 2023 .

44 D.D.C., Memorandum Opinion, *RREEF Infrastructure (G.P.) Limited, et al. v. Kingdom of Spain*, Civil Action No. 1:19-cv-03783 (CJN), 31 March 2021.
45 D.D.C., Memorandum Opinion, *InfraRed Environmental Infrastructure GP Limited, et al. v. Kingdom of Spain*, Civil Action No. 20-cv-817(JDB), 29 June 2021.
46 European Commission amicus brief in *InfraRed v. Spain*, D.D.C (available here).
47 D.D.C., Memorandum Opinion, *Hydro Energy 1, S.A.R.L., et al. v. Kingdom of Spain*, Civil Case No. 21–2463 (RJL), 28 June 2022.
48 European Commission *amicus* brief in *Hydro Energy v. Spain,* D.D.C. (available here).
49 This was the case in *Masdar v. Spain, NextEra v. Spain, InfraRed v. Spain, Hyrdo Energy v. Spain, RREEF v. Spain, Eiser v. Spain* and *Infrastructure Services v. Spain.*
50 2020 WL 417794 (D.D.C.) (27 January 2020).
51 D.D.C., Memorandum Opinion, *Ioan Micula, et al., v. Government of Romania*, Case No. 17-cv-02332 (APM), 11 September 2019.
52 United States Court of Appeals for the District of Columbia Cirguit, *Ioan Micula, et al., v. Government of Romania*, No. 19–7127, 19 May 2020.
53 D.D.C., Memorandum Opinion, Masdar Solar & Wind Cooperatief U.A. v. Kingdom of Spain, Civil Action No. 18–2254 (JEB), 18 September 2019.
54 D.D.C., Memorandum Opinion, 9REN Holding S.A.R.L. v. Kingdom of Spain, Civil Action No. 19-cv-07187 (TSC), 30 September 2020.
55 D.D.C., Memorandum Opinion, InfraRed Environmental Infrastructure GP Limited, et al. v. Kingdom of Spain, Civil Action No. 20-cv-817(JDB), 29 June 2021.
56 D.D.C., Memorandum Opinion, 9REN Holding S.A.R.L. v. Kingdom of Spain, Civil Action No. 19-cv-07187 (TSC), 15 February 2023 and D.D.C., Memorandum Opinion, NextEra Energy Global Holdings B.V., et al. v. Kingdom of Spain, Civil Action No. 19-cv-01618 (TSC), 15 February 2023.
57 *Tribunal Fédéral,* Judgment of 7 February 2020, 4A_80/2018.
58 *Tribunal Fédéral,* Judgment of 23 February 2021, 4A_187/2020.
59 Federal Court of Australia, Judgment of 24 February 2020, NSD 601 of 2019 / NSD 602 of 2019.
60 Supreme Court of the United Kingdom, Judgment of 19 February 2020, Hilary Term [2020] UKSC 5, on appeals from: [2018] EWCA Civ 1801 and [2019] EWHC 2401 (Comm)
61 *Société Nationale Industrielle Aérospatiale v. U.S. District Court for the Southern District of Iowa*, 482 U.S. 522, 543 n.27 (1987).

References

Böhme, B. (2022), "The future of the Energy Charter Treaty after Moldova v. Komstroy", *Common Market Law Review* 59: 853–870.

Dashwood, A. (2022), "Republic of Moldova v Komstroy LCC: Arbitration under Article 26 ECT outlawed in Intra-EU Disputes by Obiter Dictum", *European Law Review* 1: 127–140

Declève, Q. (2021). Can EU Member States Replicate Plurilateral Agreement on Intra-EU BITs to Implement Komstroy Judgment?International Litigation Blog (http://international-litigation-blog.com/can-eu-member-states-replicate-plurilateral-agreement-on-intra-eu-bits-to-implement-komstroy-judgment/).

Fontanelli, F. (2009), "Yuval Shany. Regulating Jurisdictional Relations between National and International Courts", *European Journal of International Law* 20: 1263–1331.

Gáspár-Szilágyi, S. and Usynin, M. (2019), "The Uneasy Relationship between Intra-EU Investment Tribunals and the Court of Justice's Achmea Judgment", *European Investment Law and Arbitration Review Online*, 4(4): 29–65.

Gaillard, E. and Siino, B. (2021), "Enforcement under the New York Convention", *Global Arbitration Review* (https://globalarbitrationreview.com/guide/the-guide-challenging-

and-enforcing-arbitration-awards/2nd-edition/article/enforcement-under-the-new-york-convention).

Odermatt, J. (2021), "Is EU Law International? Case C-741/19 Republic of Moldova v Komstroy LLC and the Autonomy of the EU Legal Order", *European Papers* 6(3): 1255–1268.

Paul, J. (1991), "Comity in International Law", *Harvard International Law Journal*, 32: 1–79.

Tribunals and the Court of Justice's Achmea Judgment", *European Investment Law and Arbitration Review Online*.

Yanos, A. and Ramos-Mrosovsky, C. (2021), Intra-EU Investment Treaty Disputes in US Courts: Achmea, Micula and Beyond, *Global Arbitration Review* (https://globalarbitrationreview.com/review/the-arbitration-review-of-the-americas/2022/article/intra-eu-investment-treaty-disputes-in-us-courts-achmea-micula-and-beyond).

11

EXECUTIVE ACCOUNTABILITY IN UNILATERAL TRADE POLICY

A Transatlantic Perspective*

Thomas Verellen

UTRECHT UNIVERSITY, UTRECHT, THE NETHERLANDS

Introduction

Faced with a changing geopolitical environment, the European Union (EU) started upgrading its unilateral trade instruments toolbox.[1] In 2017, the EU modernized its anti-dumping and anti-subsidy rules to better equip the European Commission to deal with state-induced trade distortions (Hoffmeister, 2020). In 2020, the EU established a framework to screen foreign direct investment in the EU.[2] In May 2021, the Commission proposed an instrument to tackle foreign subsidies – thereby filling a perceived gap between the EU's state aid and anti-dumping rules.[3] Also in 2021, the EU revised its Enforcement Regulation to enable the Commission to retaliate against violations of international trade agreements in the absence of a final WTO dispute settlement report.[4] In the Spring of 2022, Parliament and Council reached an agreement to make access to procurement markets in the EU dependent on reciprocity (Bounds, 2022). And in December 2021, the Commission proposed an 'anti-coercion' instrument, which – if adopted – will grant the Commission broad powers to retaliate against acts of 'coercion.'[5] All of these initiatives fit in the Commission's ambition to strengthen the EU's 'open strategic autonomy'[6] and to put in place a trade policy that is 'open, sustainable, and assertive.'[7]

The list of measures is impressive, leading Politico, a news organization, to speak of a 'trade bazooka' (Hanke, 2019). The combined effect of these initiatives is a significant strengthening of executive power in EU trade policy – an area in which the EU holds exclusive competence and in which Member States are thus constitutionally precluded from acting on their own.[8] Moreover, these legislative initiatives have to be looked at in conjunction with the increased use in recent years of sectoral economic sanctions adopted by the Council within the framework of the

DOI: 10.4324/9781003283911-14

EU's Common foreign and security policy (CFSP). Most recently, in response to the Russian invasion of Ukraine, the Council restricted imports of a wide range of Russian and Belarussian goods into the EU, including coal, iron, steel and wood. This return to economic sanctions represents a policy change as in recent decades CFSP restrictive measures have typically been targeted at individuals rather than economic sectors or entire economies. Taken together, this makes for a picture of a heavily armed EU trade power: a Union that is increasingly capable of deploying and leveraging its large internal market as an instrument of economic statecraft (Meunier and Nicolaidis, 2019). And a Union that is increasingly willing to deploy trade policy instruments not only in pursuit of trade liberalization but also in pursuit of non-trade related objectives, including, most significantly in this moment: security.[9]

In this chapter, I look at how executive power in the unilateral trade policy sphere is held to account in the EU. I will do so in light of the abovementioned reforms to the EU's trade defence toolbox, and I will do so from a comparative perspective by contrasting the allocation of executive power in the EU in the area of unilateral trade policy with that in the United States. The chapter's argument is primarily descriptive, but has a normative tinge: I argue that executive power in unilateral trade policy in the EU is going through a transformation. Taken together, the various instruments I referred to earlier significantly strengthen the position of the Commission. This is the case as most of these instruments will be – or already are – deployed by the Commission. The Commission both proposes and adopts measures, and in the process exercises a growing amount of discretion. At the same time, it remains difficult for the Member States, and very challenging for the European Parliament, to oppose measures. As I will describe, this state of affairs is not as different from that in existence in the United States as one might expect at first glance, given the important structural differences between the EU and U.S. executives. Indeed, the U.S. experience in this area can be understood as a cautionary tale of how growing executive power leads to accountability challenges that over time become increasingly difficult to surmount. Given this observation, a question arises: are existing accountability mechanisms up to the task to ensure that unilateral trade policy in the EU are fully under democratic control?

The chapter has two parts. I first take a comparative detour to look at how executive accountability works in the United States, and at how the perceived shortcomings of the U.S. arrangements have led to calls for reform. I then turn to the EU and further unpack how executive power is allocated in the EU when it comes to unilateral trade instruments – a category that covers the instruments adopted in the context of both the EU's common commercial policy (CCP) and the CFSP. The two substantive sections are followed by a conclusion.

Unilateral trade measures in the United States: Taming the imperial presidency

The imperial presidency in unilateral trade policy

In his 1973 book, Arthur Schlesinger referred to the U.S. Presidency as 'imperial' in nature (Schlesinger, 1973, pp. 9–10). As Schlesinger himself noted, the Imperial

Presidency was not a novel phenomenon in the United States of the early 1970s. What *was* new, he argued, was its extension from *foreign* to *domestic* affairs. For indeed, in the foreign affairs realm, the President's powers have traditionally been expansive. Domestically, the President is bound by numerous checks and balances – not in the least the fact that the President does not control Congress and depends on it to pass legislation. By contrast, in the foreign affairs realm the President has more leeway to act independently from the other branches of government, be it by making executive agreements that do not require Congressional approval (Claussen, 2021a; Hathaway et al., 2020, pp. 639–641), by making use of his own constitutional powers as commander-in-chief, or by making use of the unilateral trade powers delegated to him by Congress (Koh, 1988).

In the trade policy sphere broadly considered, Congress has delegated important responsibilities to the President (Irwin, 2017). As is well known, the United States Trade Representative (USTR) negotiates trade agreements on behalf of the President. In the narrower context of *unilateral* trade policy, Congress delegated important powers to both the President and the USTR. For example, under Section 232 of the Trade Expansion Act 1962, the President can undertake 'action … to adjust the imports of [an] article and its derivatives so that such imports will not threaten to impair the national security.'[10] This includes the raising of import tariffs or the introduction of import quotas.[11] 'National security' is left undefined by Congress, leaving it to the President to give meaning to the concept. And perhaps unsurprisingly, the President has interpreted the concept expansively as essentially encompassing the entire national economy.[12] In other words: Congress empowered the President to take trade measures against imports that threaten to impair U.S. national security, and it left the assessment of when measures do so to the President's own discretion. Similar points can be made about other unilateral trade powers, such as the President's authority to take measures – including import bans – under the International Emergency Economic Powers Act (IEEPA)[13], or the USTR's power to take measures under Section 301 of the Trade Act 1974. For each of these instruments, Congress has delegated a power to the President or an agency or cabinet department that he controls such as the USTR. This power is subject to relatively undemanding substantive checks in the form of broadly framed, open-ended conditions.[14]

Crucially, the executive has the final say on whether those conditions are met in a specific case. Relevant in this regard is that federal courts in the United States have in the recent past been deferential towards the executive in their own assessment of whether the executive had complied with the conditions.[15] And further upstream, U.S. courts have not questioned the constitutionality of the broad delegations of powers.[16] In similar vein, while section 232 measures are reviewable in light of the GATT security exception following the World Trade Organization (WTO) panel report in *Russia-Measures Concerning Traffic in Transit,*[17] the paralysis of the WTO appellate body undermines the effectiveness of the WTO dispute settlement mechanism and thus of the international legal disciplines imposed on the discretion of the President in this area (Galbraith, 2018; Hoekman and Mavroidis, 2019).

Congressional checks on presidential power

When delegating powers to the President or any other part of the executive branch, Congress tries to retain a degree of control over how the executive exercises those powers. Historically, the legislative veto was an important instrument for Congress to do so. Under the legislative veto, depending on how the veto was set up, either both houses of Congress or a single house could veto a presidential order taken on the basis of such delegated authority. It could do so by means of, respectively, a concurrent or a simple resolution. Each chamber could act by an ordinary majority. In contrast to the ordinary legislative process, no presidential signature was required to veto an executive measure. Commentators have argued that this was an effective tool for Congress to exercise oversight over the executive. It was effective, in particular because in the field of trade policy many of the administrative safeguards of the Administrative Procedure Act (APA) – for example, the requirement that the public has the opportunity to comment – do not apply (Claussen, 2021b, p. 850). In this area, some delegations of authority to the President – notably IEEPA sanctions and section 232 sanctions on oil and oil-related products – are subject to the legislative veto.[18] However, in 1983 in the case of *INS v Chadha,* the Supreme Court declared the one-house and the two-house legislative veto without presentment to the President unconstitutional.[19] As a consequence of this ruling, it was no longer possible for a single house of Congress to terminate unilateral trade measures taken by the President on the basis of, for example, Section 232 by means of an *ordinary* majority. Instead, a *two-third* majority in *both* houses was required to insulate the resolution against a potential presidential veto. As a result, to the regret of some (Biden, 1984; Strauss, 1983) and the delight of others (McGowan, 1977, p. 1149), the legislative veto became ineffective as a means to keep a check on the President's exercise of delegated trade powers (Schütze, 2011, pp. 666–669).

The fate of the legislative veto is symptomatic of the wider state of executive accountability in unilateral trade policy in the United States. Congress has other instruments at its disposal to exercise oversight over the President, but it faces collective action problems in deploying those instruments effectively (Koh, 1988). To be clear, existing trade delegations are subject to some procedural checks. Sections 232 and 301 impose specific executive decision-making procedures,[20] and Section 232 imposes time limits on presidential action[21] – limits which federal courts have recently enforced in response to President Trump's failure to comply with them when imposing tariffs on steel imports.[22] Section 232 also still contains a legislative veto provision, although the statute now expressly provides Congress can only exercise the veto by means of a joint resolution, which must be presented to the President.[23] Similarly, IEEPA requires the President to first declare a national emergency before taking action; he must consult with Congress for as long as the national emergency continues;[24] he must submit a report to Congress whenever he adopts a measure in the framework of the IEEPA;[25] and he must periodically report to Congress about the actions he has undertaken and changes that have occurred since the previous report.[26] Similar consultation requirements exist for Section 232 measures,[27] but not for Section 301 measures.[28] However, more far-reaching mechanisms such as sunset provisions or report-and-wait requirements have not been used in the unilateral trade policy context (Goithein, 2020). Likewise, Congress has not tried to frame existing delegations more narrowly (Claussen, 2018). Bills have been introduced to grant Congress an *ex ante* veto power over individual measures as opposed to an *ex post* power to terminate measures as currently exists under the legislative veto, but such bills have not been adopted.[29]

The scarcity of alternative procedural checks, coupled with the demise of the pre-*Chadha* legislative veto, makes it difficult for Congress to meaningfully impact Presidential unilateral trade policy. It is difficult for Congress, a collective body, to act – even by ordinary majority (Meyer and Sitaraman, 2019, p. 609). To raise the bar further and to require a two-thirds majority to oppose presidential actions means Congress can act only if there is a quasi-complete bipartisan consensus that the President's actions were ill advised. In a two-party system in which the President is a member of one of the two parties represented in Congress, it is difficult to assemble that broad a coalition. At least when it comes to unilateral trade capabilities, then, procedural checks on an Imperial Presidency endowed with significant trade powers remain limited. While this may have been appropriate in an era in which presidents felt constrained not only by legal limits but also by non-legal conventions and informal codes of conduct (Goldsmith, 2012), it is worth considering whether the Trump experience does not call for legal guardrails to be introduced to ensure executive accountability moving forward (Bauer and Goldsmith, 2020; Hillman, 2019).

Unilateral trade measures in the European Union: A fragmented yet increasingly powerful executive

A fragmented executive to engage in unilateral trade policy

How does the EU compare to the United States when it comes to executive accountability in the realm of unilateral trade policy? It is important to acknowledge at the outset how very different the EU is structured compared to the United States. Contrary to the constitutional arrangements in the United States, the EU Treaty framers (the Member States) did not establish a directly elected executive with important constitutional powers of its own, including the power to deploy the military. Instead, as described by Deirdre Curtin, executive power in the EU is more dispersed, more fragmented (Curtin, 2009, p. 65). The Commission exercises important *administrative* executive powers (Curtin, 2009, pp. 4, 5), but so does the Council. (This is the case in particular in the framework of the CFSP, where the Council can impose restrictive measures.) As far as the *political* aspects of executive power are concerned (i.e. the power to exercise political leadership and to determine the course of the 'ship of state'), the European Council is the main player (van Middelaar, 2013), with the Commission trying to steer a course between loyalty towards the European Council (of which the Commission President is a member) and steering its own, independent course as the EU institution charged with the responsibility of defending the general EU interest (Bocquillon and Dobbels, 2014). That being said, executive dominance is very much a feature of the EU decision-making landscape, and the question of how to ensure that executive power is held democratically accountable is a key challenge for the EU moving forward (Curtin, 2014). This certainly holds true for unilateral trade policy, where EU executive bodies – in particular Council and Commission – exercise meaningful discretionary authority and are likely to do so to an even greater extent as the EU legislature upgrades the EU's unilateral trade instruments toolbox (Verellen, 2021).

How then, is executive accountability ensured in this area of EU policy making? A first observation: the executive power to deploy unilateral trade instruments in the EU is fragmented. Two decision-making set-ups live side by side. On the one hand, the Council can adopt restrictive measures with little Commission involvement. It must do so by unanimity. On the other hand, the Commission plays a central role in the deployment of the CCP unilateral trade instruments listed in the introduction to this chapter. Most of these instruments are adopted by means of implementing acts. Bar exceptional cases in which the EU legislature empowers the Council rather than the Commission to enact implementing acts,[30] such acts are adopted on the basis of the so-called Comitology system.[31] In this system, the Commission proposes measures, and a committee consisting of Member States – technically not a Council committee – has the opportunity to oppose measures the Commission proposes. However, it can only do so by means of a qualified majority of its members.[32] This is a high threshold, which makes it hard for Member States to stop the Commission in its tracks. Crucially, in neither decision-making set-up does the Parliament play a meaningful role. The Parliament only needs to be informed of the general developments in the CFSP. And in the context of CCP-implementing acts it can let the Commission know that it believes a proposed measure to be *ultra vires* the Commission's powers.[33] In such a case, the Commission has to reconsider the measure, but it cannot be stopped from adopting the measure the second time around.[34] In addition, the Commission must in many instances keep the parliament informed of general developments by sending it an annual report.[35]

CCP unilateral trade instruments have traditionally been subject to more demanding substantive conditions compared to their U.S. counterparts. Classic trade defence measures such as anti-dumping and anti-subsidy measures need to comply with the requirements set out in the WTO agreements on the same topic as implemented in the EU's legal order. Many of the proposed instruments are – or will be, if they get adopted – subject to fairly stringent substantive conditions as well. For example, under the Foreign Subsidies Regulation, redressive measures could be adopted only in the presence of foreign subsidies that 'distort the internal market.'[36] Foreign subsidies distort the internal market 'where a foreign subsidy is liable to improve the competitive position of the undertaking concerned in the internal market and where, in doing so, it actually or potentially negatively affects competition on the internal market.'[37] And to make that determination, the Commission proposal lists a number of criteria that the Commission may take into account, including the amount and nature of the subsidy, and the level of economic activity of the undertaking concerned on the internal market.[38] In similar fashion, under the International Procurement Instrument, measures can be adopted in the presence of 'third-country measures or practices' that 'result in a serious and recurrent impairment of access of Union goods, services and/or economic operators to the public procurement or concession markets.'[39] The substantive conditions in both of these instruments reflect the *defensive* finalities of the CCP unilateral trade instruments: they are intended to better equip the EU to withstand unfair trade practices by third countries; not to empower the EU to actively pursue (geo)political objectives other than trade liberalization.

Procedural checks on the European Commission

That said, the substantive conditions will only have teeth when embedded in an institutional framework that provides for meaningful procedural checks on the decision-maker. At this level, the differences between the EU and the United States are less pronounced than they appear at first glance. In both systems does the power to *propose* and the power to *adopt* often rest in the hands of a single institution: the President in the United States, the Commission in the EU. Certainly, anti-dumping and anti-subsidy investigations are typically launched following a complaint brought by industry. The same will hold true for the International Procurement Instrument.[40] However, both of these instruments also empower the Commission to launch investigations *ex officio*.[41] By contrast, under the Foreign Subsidies Regulation, there will not be a complaint mechanism, and the Commission will always start investigations on its own initiative.[42] The same will hold true for the Anti-Coercion Instrument if it is adopted in its current form.[43] For all of these instruments, the Commission can thus propose measures and also adopt them. Coupled with the reverse qualified majority voting rule in the Comitology committee, this makes for a particularly weak procedural check on the Commission.

Furthermore, if the Anti-Coercion Instrument is adopted in its current form, the Commission will find itself in the peculiar position of being able to circumvent the unanimity requirement that governs the adoption of restrictive measures in the CFSP. Under the Anti-Coercion Instrument, the Commission would be able to propose and adopt measures 'where a third country seeks, through measures affecting trade or investment, to coerce the Union or a Member State into adopting or refraining from adopting a particular act.'[44] This would be the case when that third country

> interferes in the legitimate sovereign choices of the Union or a Member State by seeking to prevent or obtain the cessation, modification or adoption of a particular act by the Union or a Member State by applying or threatening to apply measures affecting trade or investment.[45]

Here as well, the Commission proposal lists a number of indicators to guide that assessment. These indicators include the intensity, severity, frequency, duration, breadth and magnitude of the third country's measure and the pressure arising from it, as well as the extent to which the third-country measure encroaches upon an area of the Union's or Member States' sovereignty.

Despite these efforts at further determining what constitutes 'economic coercion,' the notion remains nebulous. The concept of 'coercion' is known in international law, but it remains unclear whether coercion can exist outside of the context of the use of (military) force (Raju, 2022). The concept as defined in the proposed anti-coercion regulation also contains a subjective element: for there to be economic coercion, there must be an *intention* on behalf of the third country to practice coercion. This subjective element raises evidentiary hurdles as it will be difficult – if not impossible – for the Commission to get watertight evidence of what the third country's intentions really are. At the same time, there may be pressure on the Commission to act, especially in the face of gridlock within the Council making it impossible for the EU to adopt restrictive measures.

Indeed, absent procedural checks, the Commission may be quick to conclude that economic coercion is indeed present, as drawing this conclusion would enable the EU to impose measures very similar to restrictive measures but without the need for unanimity among the Member States. The situation would be different if the EU legislature were to empower the Council rather than the Commission to adopt the necessary implementing acts to retaliate against coercive practices by third countries. In this scenario, a qualified majority of Member States would have to *approve* the measure before it gets enacted.[46] This is a higher threshold compared to the negative qualified majority requirement in the Comitology process. It is, however, still a lower threshold compared to CFSP restrictive measures, which are adopted by unanimity in the Council. The risk that unanimity in CFSP decision-making will be circumvented through a broad interpretation of the substantive conditions to impose anti-coercion measures thus exists also, albeit to a lesser extent, in the scenario that the Council rather than the Commission has the final say on such measures.

Such 'slippery slope' dynamics have played out in the United States, where Congress has found it difficult to operate as a check on presidential power. One example outside of the unilateral trade policy context is the practice of concluding executive agreements. The U.S. Constitution prescribes that the Senate is to give its 'advice and consent' to treaties by means of two-thirds of its members. Yet since the late 1930s, over 90% of international agreements concluded by the United States are made by the President, often in tandem with Congressional legislation adopted by ordinary majorities (Hathaway et al., 2020, p. 632). This practice is premised on a distinction maintained by the President between 'treaties' in the meaning of Article II of the U.S. Constitution and other international agreements. Yet there is reason to question the distinction as nowhere in the text of the Constitution is any mention made of executive agreements as an alternative way of concluding international agreements (Tribe, 1995). A similar phenomenon has occurred in the context of the use of military force. In 2011, President Obama insisted that military operations such as imposing a no-fly zone over Libya did not constitute 'war' in the meaning of the War Powers Resolution, and that therefore no Congressional approval of the operation was needed (Fisher, 2012). Similarly, in the unilateral trade policy context, 'national security' has been interpreted so broadly that it encompasses the entire national economy,[47] and 'national emergencies' – the presence of which is required for the President to be able to adopt IEPPA sanctions – have become so common that in July 2020 there were no fewer than 33 national emergencies ongoing (Casey et al., 2020, pp. 48–66).

Could similar erosions of the substantive conditions governing the use of unilateral trade instruments materialize in the EU? The risk should not be dismissed out of hand. For various reasons, EU institutions, including the Commission, may feel compelled to stretch the text of the secondary legislation empowering it to act. Examples of such efforts are not hard to find. For example, in response to President Trump's unilateral Section 232 import tariffs, the Commission imposed retaliatory measures on the basis of the Enforcement Regulation.[48] The legality of such measures under WTO law and under the Enforcement Regulation was premised on the U.S. tariffs being safeguard measures. It is doubtful, however, whether they really were safeguard measures. (The U.S. itself maintained that they were national security measures (Lee, 2019, pp. 492–496).) Or a second example: in 2020, the Commission imposed countervailing duties on imports of glass fibre fabrics from Egypt following an investigation that established that a Chinese state-owned company had set up shop in Egypt, from which it subsequently exported subsidized fabrics to EU markets.[49] On this occasion, the Commission could be criticized for stretching the Anti-Subsidy Regulation – and the Agreement on Subsidies and Countervailing Measures which it implements into EU law – beyond what its text can bear (Crochet and Hegde, 2020). Yet, there is little that other EU institutions could do to prevent the measures from being adopted as these measures too are subject to the abovementioned reverse qualified majority requirement.

To be clear, the Court of Justice as well as international bodies such as the WTO dispute settlement mechanism continue to play an important role in holding the Commission to account. At the time of writing in the summer of 2022, a challenge against the Commission's decision in the abovementioned trade defence case involving glass fibre fabrics was pending before the General Court of the EU. And in other recent trade defence cases as well, the General Court has not shied away from taking a deep dive into the Commission's calculations and from ultimately concluding that those calculations were not in conformity with the applicable legislation.[50] If the trade defence context is of any guidance, the General Court and the Court of Justice likely will not shy away from scrutinizing Commission decisions under the Foreign Subsidies Regulation, the International Procurement Instrument or the Anti-coercion Instrument either. In so doing, both EU courts will ensure that the limits of the delegations of authority are complied with and the Commission does not act *ultra vires.*

That said, in so far as executive decision-making has a meaningful discretionary component, ex ante institutional checks may be needed to properly legitimize the executive's actions as it is not the Court's task to second-guess exercises of political discretion. Moreover, if we take seriously the Treaty requirement that the 'functioning of the Union shall be founded on representative democracy' set out in Art. 10(1) TEU, the Commission must be answerable for its actions not only to the Court of Justice, but also to those institutions that endow the EU decision-making process with input legitimacy so as to ensure that all discretionary actions undertaken by the EU are subject to democratic control (Schmidt, 2013). This imperative becomes all the more salient as EU trade policy involves increasingly complex trade-offs between public and private interests – often with redistributive implications. (To name but one example in the context of the proposed Anti-Coercion Instrument: Would it be in the Union interest to take measures to tackle economic coercion practiced by China against Lithuania if, by doing so, German exports to China will suffer?) As discussed, today such input legitimacy is ensured primarily through the involvement of the Member States in the adoption of implementing acts. It is worth considering whether Member State oversight is sufficient to ensure proper executive accountability in the EU's unilateral trade policy. Greater parliamentary involvement may be needed as well.

Conclusion

In this chapter, I looked at the allocation of executive power in unilateral trade policy in the United States and the EU. I discussed how on both sides of the Atlantic executive power leads to accountability challenges. With reference to the U.S. experience, I showed how in the EU a risk for abuse of power by the executive as it deploys an increasingly powerful set of unilateral trade instruments should be taken seriously. The existence of such risk should be taken into consideration in the design of the governance framework of unilateral trade instruments. As trade policy becomes more political and indeed geopolitical, the stakes increase and the balancing of interests and values becomes more difficult. Such decision-making should be subject to meaningful procedural checks. At present, and in addition to judicial review by the Court of Justice, Member States can operate as a check on the Commission through their involvement in the Comitology process. In a polity that draws its legitimacy both from states and individual citizens, it is worth considering whether the Parliament should not have a role to play in the process of adopting unilateral trade measures as well.

Notes

* Special thanks to the Belgian American Educational Foundation for their financial support which allowed me to conduct the research necessary to write this chapter. This chapter is based on an article that will be published in the first half of 2023 in the German Law Journal under the title 'Imperial Presidency versus Fragmented Executive? Unilateral Trade Measures and Executive Accountability in the European Union and the United States'.

1 Unilateral trade instruments are unilateral instruments that affect economic and financial relations with one or more third countries. In this chapter, I specifically look at unilateral trade instruments that *restrict* rather than *expand* market access, and I limit the inquiry to instruments that directly or indirectly pursue foreign policy and security-related goals.

2 Regulation (EU) 2019/452 of 19 March 2019 establishing a framework for the screening of foreign direct investments into the Union, OJ L 79I, 21.3.2019, p. 1–14.

3 Proposal for a regulation on foreign subsidies distorting the internal market, 5.5.202, COM(2021) 223 final (the 'Foreign Subsidies Instrument Proposal').

4 Regulation (EU) 2021/167 of 10 February 2021 amending Regulation (EU) No 654/2014 concerning the exercise of the Union's rights for the application and enforcement of international trade rules OJ L 49, 12.2.2021, p. 1–5 (the 'Enforcement Regulation').

5 Proposal for a regulation on the protection of the Union and its Member States from economic coercion by third countries, 8.12.2021, COM/2021/775 final (the 'Anti-Coercion Instrument Proposal').

6 Communication from the Commission, *Europe's moment: Repair and Prepare for the Next Generation*, COM(2020) 456 final, 27.5.2020, 12–13.

7 Communication from the Commission, *Trade Policy Review - An Open, Sustainable and Assertive Trade Policy*, COM(2021) 66 final, 18.2.2021.

8 Art. 2(1) TFEU.
9 Art. 21(2)(a) TEU.
10 19 U.S.C. § 1862 (c) (1) (A).
11 *Fed. Energy Admin. v. Algonquin SNG, Inc.*, 426 U.S. 548, 96 S. Ct. 2295, 49 L. Ed. 2d 49 (1976), at 561.
12 15 CFR § 705.4 (b) (3).
13 IEEPA empowers the President to impose sanctions on individuals and – perhaps – also import tariffs. To adopt such measures, the President must declare a national emergency. He can do so when he considers there to be 'any unusual and extraordinary threat ... to the national security, foreign policy, or economy of the United States.'
14 See e.g. 50 U.S.C. § 1701 or 50 U.S.C. § 411(b).
15 *PrimeSource Bldg. Prod., Inc. v. United States*, 505 F. Supp. 3d 1352 (Ct. Int'l Trade 2021), 1304.
16 In the domestic context, the Supreme Court has indicated a willingness to review the limits and constitutionality of delegations of power to executive agencies. See recently *Nat'l Fed'n of Indep. Bus. v. Dep't of Lab., Occupational Safety & Health Admin.*, 142 S. Ct. 661, 211 L. Ed. 2d 448 (2022).
17 Panel Report, *Russia-Measures Concerning Traffic in Transit*, 30, WTO Doc. WT/DS512/R (adopted Apr. 26, 2019).
18 50 U.S.C. § 1703 (b) and 19 U.S.C. § 1862 (f).
19 *I.N.S. v. Chadha*, 462 U.S. 919 (1983).
20 50 U.S.C. § 1862 (b) and 50 U.S.C. § 2414 (a) (1).
21 19 U.S.C. § 1862 (c) (1), requiring the President to take action within 105 days following receipt of a report prepared by the Commerce Secretary.
22 See e.g. *PrimeSource Bldg. Prod., Inc. v. United States*, 505 F. Supp. 3d 1352 (Ct. Int'l Trade 2021).
23 19 U.S.C. § 1862 (f).
24 50 U.S.C. § 1703 (a).
25 50 U.S.C. § 1703 (c).
26 *Id.*
27 50 U.S.C. § 1862 (d).
28 Section 301 measures do not have to be reported to Congress; Congress plays no direct role in the Section 301 decision-making process at all.
29 See e.g. H.R.2618 - Global Trade Accountability Act of 2021.
30 Art. 291(2) TFEU.
31 Regulation (EU) No 182/2011 of 16 February 2011 laying down the rules and general principles concerning mechanisms for control by Member States of the Commission's exercise of implementing powers, OJ L 55, 28.2.2011, p. 13–18.
32 Ibid, Art. 5.
33 Ibid, Art. 11.
34 Ibid.
35 See e.g. Regulation (EU) 2016/1036 of 8 June 2016 on protection against dumped imports from countries not members of the European Union, OJ L 176 30.6.2016, p. 21., Art. 23.
36 Foreign Subsidies Instrument Proposal, Art. 1(1).
37 Ibid., Art. 3(1).
38 Ibid.
39 Consolidated proposal for a regulation on the access of third-country economic operators, goods and services to the Union's public procurement market and procedures supporting negotiations on access of Union economic operators, goods and services to the public procurement markets of third countries (International Procurement Instrument - IPI), 2012/0060 (COD) (the 'International Procurement Instrument Proposal'), Art. 2(f).
40 Ibid., Art. 6(1).
41 Ibid for the International Procurement Instrument, and in the trade defence context see e.g. Art. 5(6) of Regulation (EU) 2016/1036 of 8 June 2016 on protection against dumped

imports from countries not members of the European Union, OJ L 176, 30.6.2016, p. 21–54.
42 Foreign Subsidies Instrument Proposal, Art. 8(2).
43 Anti-Coercion Instrument Proposal, Art. 3(1).
44 Ibid., Art. 1(1).
45 Ibid., Art. 2(1).
46 Art. 16(4) TEU.
47 15 CFR § 705.4 (b) (3).
48 Commission Implementing Regulation (EU) 2019/159 of 31 January 2019 imposing definitive safeguard measures against imports of certain steel products, OJ L 31, 1.2.2019, p. 27–74.
49 Implementing Regulation 2020/776 imposing definitive countervailing duties on imports of certain woven and/or stitched glass fibre fabrics originating in the Chinese mainland and Egypt, OJ L 189, 15.6.2020, p. 1–170.
50 See in particular Case T-383/17, *Hansol Paper Co. Ltd v European Commission*, EU:T:2020:139, para. 77, pending on appeal (Case C-260/20 P).

References

Bauer, B., Goldsmith, J. L., 2020. *After Trump: Reconstructing the Presidency*. Washington DC: Lawfare Press.

Biden, J. R. J., 1984. Who Needs the Legislative Veto?. *Syracuse Law Review* 35, 685–701.

Bocquillon, P., Dobbels, M., 2014. An Elephant on the 13th Floor of the Berlaymont? European Council and Commission Relations in Legislative Agenda Setting. *Journal of European Public Policy* [online] 21, 20–38. Available from: 10.1080/13501763.2013.834548

Bounds, A., 2022. Brussels to Bring in Powers to Handicap Foreign Bids for State Contracts. *Financial Times*, 15 March.

Casey, C. A., Fergusson, I. F., Rennack, D. E., Elsea, J. K., 2020. The International Emergency Economic Powers Act: Origins, Evolution, and Use, CRS Report for Congress. Congressional Research Centre – Library of Congress, Washington DC.

Claussen, K., 2018. *Trade War Battles: Congress Reconsiders Its Role*. [online]. Washington DC, Lawfare. Available from: https://www.lawfareblog.com/trade-war-battles-congress-reconsiders-its-role [Accessed: 12 July 2020].

Claussen, K., 2021a. Trade's Mini-Deals. *Virginia Journal of International Law* [online] 62(2). Available from SSRN: https://ssrn.com/abstract=3836909 [Accessed xxx].

Claussen, K., 2021b. Trade Administration. *Virginia Law Review* [online] 107, 845–917. Available from: 10.2139/ssrn.3602190 [Accessed xxx].

Crochet, V., Hegde, V., 2020. China's "Going Global" Policy: Transnational Subsidies under the WTO SCM Agreement (Working Paper No. 220). Leuven Centre for Global Governance Studies, Leuven.

Curtin, D., 2014. Challenging Executive Dominance in European Democracy. *The Modern Law Review* [online] 77(1), 1–32. Available from: 10.1111/1468-2230.12054 [Accessed xxx].

Curtin, D., 2009. *Executive Power of the European Union: Law, Practices, and the Living Constitution*. Oxford: Oxford University Press.

Fisher, L., 2012. The Law: Military Operations in Libya: No War? No Hostilities? *Presidential Studies Quarterly* 42(1), 176–189.

Galbraith, J., 2018. U.S. Tariffs on Steel and Aluminum Imports Go into Effect, Leading to Trade Disputes. *The American Journal of International Law* 112(3), 499–504.

Goithein, E., 2020. *Good Governance Paper No. 18: Reforming Emergency Powers*. [online] New York: Just Security. Available from: https://www.justsecurity.org/73196/good-governance-paper-no-18-emergency-powers/ [Accessed: 30 May 2022].

Goldsmith, J., 2012. *Power and Constraint: The Accountable Presidency After 9/11*. 1st ed. New York: W. W. Norton.

Hanke, J., 2019. *EU builds anti-Trump trade bazooka.* [online] Politico. Available from: https://www.politico.eu/article/eu-builds-anti-trump-trade-bazooka/ [Accessed xxx].

Hathaway, O. A., Bradley, C. A., Goldsmith, J. L., 2020. The Failed Transparency Regime for Executive Agreements: An Empirical and Normative Analysis. *Harvard Law Review* 134, 629–725.

Hillman, J. A., 2019. How to Stop Trump's Trade War Madness. *The New York Times.* 11 August.

Hoekman, B., Mavroidis, P. C., 2019. Burning Down the House? The Appellate Body in the Centre of the WTO Crisis (No. 56), *EUI Working Papers.*

Hoffmeister, F., 2020. The Devil Is in the Detail: A First Guide on the EU's New Trade Defence Rules. *In:* Weiß, W., Furculita, C. (Eds.), *Global Politics and EU Trade Policy: Facing the Challenges to a Multilateral Approach, European Yearbook of International Economic Law.* Berlin: Springer International, 211–230.

Irwin, D. A., 2017. *Clashing over Commerce: A History of US Trade Policy.* University of Chicago Press.

Koh, H. H., 1988. Why the President (Almost) Always Wins in Foreign Affairs: Lessons of the Iran-Contra Affair. *The Yale Law Journal* [online] 97(7), 1255–1342. Available from: 10.2307/796442 [Accessed xxx].

Lee, Y.-S., 2019. Three Wrongs Do Not Make a Right: The Conundrum of the US Steel and Aluminum Tariffs. *World Trade Review* [online] 18(3), 481–501. Available from: 10.1017/S147474561900020X [Accessed xxx].

McGowan, C., 1977. Congress, Court, and Control of Delegated Power. *Columbia Law Review* [online] 77(8), 1119–1174. Available from: 10.2307/1121832 [Accessed xxx].

Meunier, S., Nicolaidis, K., 2019. The Geopoliticization of European Trade and Investment Policy. *Journal of Common Market Studies* [online] 57, 103–113. Available from: 10.1111/jcms.12932 [Accessed xxx].

Meyer, T., Sitaraman, G., 2019. Trade and the Separation of Powers. *California Law Review,* 107, 583–672.

Raju, D., 2022. *Proposed EU Regulation to Address Third Country Coercion – What Is Coercion?* EJIL: Talk!. Available from: https://www.ejiltalk.org/proposed-eu-regulation-to-address-third-country-coercion-what-is-coercion/ [Accessed: 19 January 2022].

Schlesinger, A. M., 1973. *The Imperial Presidency.* Boston, MA: Houghton Mifflin Harcourt.

Schmidt, V. A., 2013. Democracy and Legitimacy in the European Union Revisited: Input, Output and 'Throughput.' *Political Studies* [online] 61(1), 2–22. Available from: 10.1111/j.1467-9248.2012.00962.x [Accessed xxx].

Schütze, R., 2011. "Delegated" Legislation in the (new) European Union: A Constitutional Analysis. *The Modern Law Review* [online] 74(5), 661–693. Available from: 10.1111/j.1468-2230.2011.00866.x [Accessed xxx].

Strauss, P. L., 1983. Was There a Baby in the Bathwater? A Comment on the Supreme Court's Legislative Veto Decision. *Duke Law Journal* 1983(4),789–819. Available from: 10.2307/1372466 [Accessed xxx].

Tribe, L. H., 1995. Taking Text and Structure Seriously: Reflections on Free-Form Method in Constitutional Interpretation. *Harvard Law Review* [online] 108(6), 1221–1303. Available from: 10.2307/1341856 [Accessed xxx].

van Middelaar, L., 2013. *The Passage to Europe: How a Continent Became a Union.* New Haven, CT: Yale University Press.

Verellen, T., 2021. *Unilateral Trade Measures in Times of Geopolitical Rivalry* [online]. Verfassungsblog Available from: https://verfassungsblog.de/unilateral-trade-measures-in-times-of-geopolitical-rivalry/ [Accessed: 13 June 2021].

12

TRANSATLANTIC ENERGY RELATIONS

A Brief History and a Tentative Outlook*

Simon Dekeyrel

EUROPEAN POLICY CENTRE, BRUSSELS, BELGIUM

Introduction

In the 1970s, the first gas contracts were signed between member states of the European Community and the Soviet Union. For the member states in question – West Germany, Italy and France – this was seen as a way to diversify their energy supply (Perović, 2017). In the context of an all-powerful Organisation of the Petroleum Exporting Countries (OPEC) and successive oil shocks, "red gas" appeared an excellent alternative to Middle Eastern oil, which had become the dominant source of energy after a meteoric rise in the Western European energy mix in the preceding decades.

Arguably, at that time, the start of Soviet gas trade genuinely increased Europe's energy security. The Soviet Union appeared a remarkably dependable supplier, and did not exhibit a propensity for intentional supply disruptions. The Soviets were in fact so preoccupied with demonstrating their reliability as a supplier that they prioritised their Western European over their domestic customers, quite literally leaving the latter in the cold when facing shortfalls in production (Högselius 2013). As such, the trans-European gas trade was not a source of contention, conflict or division as it palpably is today, but instead a source of rapprochement and one of the very few domains where mutually beneficial cooperation beyond the Iron Curtain was established in a period characterised by such stark division as the Cold War (ibid.).

The only ones more sceptical about the increasing European dependence on red gas were the Americans. In the context of reignited Cold War tensions in the early 1980s, the Yamal pipeline project became the focal point of contention. Proposed by the Soviets in the late 1970s as a dedicated export pipeline from Siberia to Western Europe, Yamal would be able to effectively double Soviet gas exports and consolidate the position of red gas in the Community's energy mix. Not as inclined to adopt such a "pragmatic" position vis-a-vis the continuously expanding East-West

 DOI: 10.4324/9781003283911-15

gas trade, newly elected President Reagan quickly presented himself as a fierce opponent of the Yamal pipeline, labelling it as a threat to Western European security. Therefore, he and his administration persistently attempted to persuade their allies in Western Europe to drop the project. In a speech before Congress in 1981, Richard Perle, President Reagan's assistant secretary of defence, expressed the American objections as follows:

> We believe Europe will incur dangerous vulnerability to the interruption of supplies of natural gas from the Soviet Union. [...] But even in the absence of crisis severe enough to lead to a Soviet cut-off, there is the day-to-day influence that must flow, like the gas itself, through a pipeline to which there will be no practical alternative.
>
> *(Perle 1981)*

These pleas fell on deaf ears on the other side of the Atlantic. Western European governments called attention to the limited capacity of Yamal and contended that the pipeline would contribute to, rather than undermine, the security and diversification of their energy supply (Högselius 2013). They were joined by the Commission of the European Communities, which similarly argued that American concerns were unsubstantiated, stating that a complete disruption of Soviet gas to the Community would only lead to minimal problems even "in the most extreme circumstances" (Commission of the European Communities 1982 cited Högselius 2013, p. 193). Despite continuous American opposition and even an embargo on technology and equipment necessary for the construction of the pipeline (which was strongly condemned in Western Europe), Yamal was eventually inaugurated in 1983.

The US would seemingly remain the sole concerned about the ever-growing European reliance on Soviet/Russian gas over the next 25 or so years. Only after the second Russo-Ukrainian gas crisis in 2009, which lasted longer and wreaked much more havoc than the first gas crisis in 2006, the EU began to take its dependence on Russian energy imports more seriously as well. Nevertheless, even after the Ukraine crisis in 2014, the share of Russian gas in the EU's energy mix increased (Eurostat 2022).

Against the backdrop of the war in Ukraine, the sentiment voiced by President Reagan and consistently repeated by later US administrations has now become almost universally professed in Europe as well. In the REPowerEU Communication released in the beginning of March, the European Commission (hereinafter: the Commission) proposed to completely phase out Russian fossil fuels in the EU's energy mix "well before" the end of the decade (European Commission 2022a, p. 1). Shortly after, EU heads of state collectively affirmed their commitment to this objective in the Versailles Declaration (European Council 2022).

This chapter analyses the impact of the Russo-Ukrainian war on EU-US energy relations through securitisation theory. Specifically, it relies on Corry's distinction between riskification and securitisation to highlight the new security logic that has been introduced in European energy policy and, by extension, in transatlantic energy relations following Russia's invasion of Ukraine. It will be argued that, whereas the gas crisis in 2009 and the Ukraine crisis in 2014 instigated a process of riskification in European energy policy, the war in Ukraine has "securitised" European energy policy. That is to say, the dependence on Russian gas/energy is no longer understood as what Corry (2012) calls a *risk* or *constitutive cause of harm* (i.e. something that makes harmful events possible or more probable) to be managed or mitigated via precautionary measures. Rather, it has become understood as an *existential threat* or *direct cause of harm* to be eliminated through "no-holds barred action" (Corry 2012, p. 249). This, in turn, has wide-ranging policy implications; while the intersubjective understanding of the energy dependence on Russia as a risk prompted changes *within* the market-oriented policy paradigm of the EU, the intersubjective understanding of the energy dependence on Russia as an existential threat is instead causing a wholesale shift *of* the EU's policy paradigm. This securitisation is set to transform the dynamic of transatlantic energy relations in radical fashion.

The divergence and convergence of EU-US energy realities

In the early 2000s, rising oil and gas prices and a resurgence of resource nationalism in major energy-producing countries brought energy security back on the Western political agenda. At that time, the energy realities of the EU and the US looked remarkably alike; both were highly dependent on the import of fossil fuels to satisfy their energy needs, and this dependence was expected to increase for the foreseeable future.

Around the mid-2000s, these realities would start to diverge. In the US, a combination of tight energy markets and technological advances in hydraulic fracturing ("fracking") and horizontal drilling techniques transformed enormous amounts of previously unprofitable gas and oil reserves trapped within shale formations into commercially viable assets, leading to a veritable boom in energy production: the American shale revolution. This abruptly halted the uptrend in US import dependence that started in the mid-1950s. Total net imports of energy reached their peak in 2005 and then entered a period of rapid decline (which continues up until this day, with the US becoming the biggest natural gas producer in the world in 2011, the biggest oil producer in 2018, and a net exporter of energy in 2019) (US Energy Information Administration 2019; 2022). This triggered a renewed sense of energy abundance, which soothed American concerns over resource scarcity and security of supply.

Across the Atlantic, the polar opposite happened as the EU's relations with Russia started to deteriorate. At the beginning of the decade, the high reliance on supplies from its Eastern neighbour did not yet factor into the EU's elevated concerns over energy security. In the 2000 Green Paper "Towards a European strategy for the security of energy supply", the Commission described the growing import dependence of the EU as one of its "structural weaknesses regarding energy supply" (European Commission 2000, p. 2) and dramatically portrayed the European continent as a "Gulliver in chains" (ibid. p. 19) – European households, services and the transport sector were "held hostage by oil" (ibid. p. 13). Nevertheless, the Green Paper asserted that "the continuity of supplies from the Soviet Union, and then Russia, over the last 25 years is testimony to an exemplary stability" (ibid. p. 44).

A succession of episodes, incidents and crises would erode this image of trustworthiness and reliability in the course of the decade. With Putin's rise to power in the early 2000s, the "early post-Soviet openness to foreign investment and the neo-liberal agenda of economic liberalisation, deregulation and privatisation" (Dannreuther 2015, p. 475) made place for an increasingly vehement rejection of the EU's market-oriented approach to the energy sector. The limited privatisation of the 1990s was overturned and a gradual renationalisation of the Russian energy industry ensued (Dannreuther 2015). In January 2006, Russian-Ukrainian disputes regarding gas prices led Gazprom to cut off supplies to Ukraine, which disrupted gas flows to Europe for three days and resulted in shortfalls in the gas supply of many EU member states (Stern 2006). This put a first serious dent in the European perception of the gas trade with Russia as a manifestation of "exemplary stability", but the true turning point would be the second Russo-Ukrainian gas crisis three years later.

In January 2009, a new round of pricing and other contract-related disputes between Gazprom and Ukrainian gas company Naftogaz led to a complete cut-off of Russian gas to Europe via Ukraine, lasting for a total of 13 days (Pirani et al. 2009). This painstakingly revealed many of the weaknesses and infrastructural bottlenecks in the European gas system. Available supplies in Western Europe were unable to reach Eastern European markets due to insufficient bidirectional capacity, which prevented a reversal of flows from an east-west to a west-east direction. Whereas the first gas crisis in 2006 still strengthened member states' resolve in retaining a national prerogative over their energy supply and did little in terms of the establishment of a common energy policy (Natorski and Herranz-Surrallés 2008), the severity and specific features of the 2009 dispute underlined that the existing division of competences between member states and the EU was no longer working. This, in combination with the institutional developments under the Lisbon Treaty which finally provided European energy policy with a formal basis in EU treaty law, enabled the Commission to successfully frame Europe's import dependence as a risk making the EU vulnerable to supply disruptions, which required a degree of supranational management to ensure that the Internal Energy Market would effectively deliver security of supply (see also Maltby 2013).

This triggered certain changes within the EU's market-oriented mode of energy governance, where the move towards liberalised markets was now supplemented by a variety of precautionary measures to reinforce the resilience of the European gas system. In the internal dimension, Regulation 994/2010 concerning measures to safeguard security of gas supply repealed "the notoriously benign Directive 2004/67/EC" (Noël 2010), and required the installation of bi-directional capacity on all cross-border interconnections in the EU and laid down stricter standards to prevent/mitigate supply disruptions. Another instance was the European Energy Programme for Recovery (EEPR), established by Regulation 663/2009. This €4 billion funding scheme for energy infrastructure allowed the EU to intervene in the construction and implementation phases of priority projects, whereas low budgets previously restricted EU financial intervention to funding feasibility studies

(Prontera 2019). The EEPR would prove an important stepping stone for further supranational involvement in the area of energy infrastructure. It served as the foundation for the Connecting Europe Facility - Energy (CEF-E) programme and a new revision of the guidelines for trans-European energy infrastructure, which institutionalised the more interventionist role of the EU in network development that started with the EEPR.

In the external dimension, the Commission embarked on a more proactive search for diversification of the European gas supply and engaged in direct negotiations with alternative (non-Russian) suppliers. As such, the energy realities of the EU and the US would once again intersect.

Attempt at a European shale revolution and the birth and expansion of the transatlantic gas trade

Before 2009, attempts by the EU and the US to create a structured venue for a transatlantic energy dialogue were unsuccessful. At the 2006 EU-US Summit, both parties agreed to an annual strategic review of EU-US energy cooperation and the establishment of the EU-US High Level Dialogue on Climate Change, Clean Energy and Sustainable Development (The White House 2006). These fora, however, failed to develop into more stable frameworks for discussion and cooperation (Conley et al. 2016).

In the wake of the second gas crisis, they were replaced by the EU-US Energy Council. This initiative was envisaged as "a new framework for deepening the transatlantic dialogue on strategic energy issues such as security of supply or policies to move towards low carbon energy sources while strengthening the ongoing scientific collaboration on energy technologies" (European Commission 2009). It launched Working Groups on Energy Policies, Global Energy Security and Global Markets, and Energy Technologies Research Cooperation (ibid.).

In the early 2010s, the Council discussed issues such as the diversification of the European gas supply via the Southern Gas Corridor (which the US supported), and served as a platform to review and strengthen scientific and regulatory collaboration in the energy domain (European Commission 2010; 2011; 2012). At this point, the prospect of transatlantic gas trade was not yet an object of serious discussion. Instead, the focus was on a potential replication of the American shale revolution in Europe (Bocse 2020). The 2012 Joint Statement of the Council for instance "recognised the expansion of shale gas and shale oil production in the United States" and "acknowledged the continued importance of exchanging information on best practices and regulatory requirements" in this respect (European Commission 2012).

Indeed, observing the spectacular upsurge in American unconventional gas and oil production, the question rose whether a "European shale revolution" was a possible solution to the EU's energy security woes. After all, shale formations containing natural gas were not unique to the US; they could be found across the globe. Studies indicated the presence of sizeable reserves of shale gas in Europe (German Federal Institute for Geosciences and Natural Resources 2013; US Energy Information Administration 2013). With the blessing and support of the US Department of State's

Bureau of Energy Resources, oil majors Chevron and ExxonMobil and other American companies commenced exploratory drilling in Poland, Germany and other EU member states (Bocse 2020). At the same time, EU and US officials engaged in frequent talks on regulatory matters, as the EU was considering the development of new legislation in the area of shale gas extraction/fracking (ibid.).

However, the European shale revolution failed to materialise. A combination of factors – among others, mineral rights held by the state rather than the landowner, shale formations with a less favourable geology, a higher population density, the greater importance attached to environmental issues, public concern, more rigid market structures – hampered attempts to emulate the US shale boom in Europe (Bocse 2020; McGowan 2014; Van de Graaf et al. 2017).

In the context of a further deterioration of EU-Russia relations following the 2014 Ukraine crisis, the possibility of transatlantic gas trade then became the main focus of EU-US energy cooperation. This is reflected in the April 2014 and December 2014 Joint Statements of the EU-US Energy Council, which both "welcomed the prospect of US LNG exports in the future since additional supplies will benefit Europe and other strategic partners" (European Commission 2014a; 2014b).

An important obstacle to the establishment of transatlantic gas flows was however the American licensing regime for natural gas exports. Under the Natural Gas Act, gas exports to third countries require the authorisation of the US Department of Energy, which has to determine whether these are consistent with the public interest. Owing to scepticism towards import reliance, uncertainty regarding the ramifications of permitting exports and the long-pursued objective of US "energy independence", there existed a degree of reluctance on the American side to reform this system, as well as to grant licences for the export of LNG to Europe (Conley et al. 2016).

After persistent lobbying efforts by both the Commission and individual member states, the Department of Energy started approving export licences, in particular after the Ukraine crisis in 2014 (Bocse 2020). However, it would still take more than two years for the first LNG vessel to arrive in Europe, in April 2016 (European Commission 2022b).

The EU pinned its hopes on the Transatlantic Trade and Investment Partnership (TTIP), the free trade agreement that was under negotiation between the EU and the US since 2013, as a way to remove this tedious process of regulatory authorisation. Namely, pursuant to the aforementioned Natural Gas Act, exports to third countries with which the US has a free trade agreement are to be deemed automatically consistent with the public interest and require immediate approval by the Department of Energy (see Natali et al. 2015). However, TTIP negotiations proceeded slowly under the Obama administration and were put in the colloquial freezer under the Trump administration.

Nevertheless, the Trump administration hardly proved an impediment to the further development of the transatlantic gas trade. In fact, the very opposite was true. While EU-US relations were arguably not in their best shape under Trump's presidency, energy emerged as one of the very few areas where a high degree of mutual understanding was found across the Atlantic. The previous American skittishness was replaced by a strong ambition to project the newfound natural wealth of the shale revolution beyond US borders, as President Trump called for not only American energy independence, but also "American energy dominance" across the globe (Trump 2017). This shift in policy could be attributed to American commercial interests, but could equally be seen in light of the historical commitment of the US to the diversification and security of the EU's energy supply (cf. Bocse 2020).

Particularly a visit by Commission President Juncker to the White House in July 2018 appeared important for lifting off the transatlantic gas trade. In a Joint Statement, President Juncker and President Trump agreed to strengthen their strategic cooperation with respect to energy and increase the export of American LNG to the EU (European Commission 2018a). A rapid expansion of transatlantic gas flows ensued. While the total amount of US LNG imported by the EU between April 2016 and July 2018 equalled a mere 2.8 billion cubic metres (bcm), by early 2022, this had increased to a total of 60 bcm (European Commission 2018b; 2022b).

This seemingly spectacular growth of EU-US LNG trade amounted to relatively little in terms of diversification of the European gas supply, as the volumes at hand were still negligible when compared to the total amount of gas imported by the EU per year (in 2021, this amounted to 337.5 bcm [Directorate-General for Energy 2021]). However, the US contributed to EU diversification in other ways as well. Infrastructure projects capable of reducing the import reliance on Russia could count on Washington's diplomatic backing. The Southern Gas Corridor (SGC), the EU's initiative to bring gas from the Caspian region to Europe, was implemented with the support of both the Obama and Trump administrations. US officials for instance took part in meetings of the SGC Advisory Council, instituted in 2015 as a venue to improve the coordination between different stakeholders and to accelerate the SGC's construction (Prontera 2019, p. 159).

In line with a long tradition (cf. the Reagan administration's opposition to Yamal), the US also opposed and attempted to obstruct pipeline projects capable of further entrenching the EU's dependence on Russia, notably the notorious Nord Stream 2 project.[1] Announced in 2015 by President Putin, this pipeline would be able to bring 55 bcm of Russian gas to Europe via the Baltic Sea per year, and make Gazprom significantly less reliant on the traditional transit routes via Central and Eastern Europe. Together with Ukraine and Eastern European member states, the US heavily objected to Nord Stream 2. In 2017, the US Senate then passed the so-called Countering America's Adversaries Through Sanctions Act (CAATSA), which would allow for the imposition of sanctions against the companies involved in the construction of Nord Stream 2.

This was – in line with another long tradition – strongly condemned in Western Europe. Germany and Austria, soon thereafter joined by France and the Commission, accused the US of meddling in European affairs, and of attempting to undermine Nord Stream 2 in order to open up the European gas market for American LNG (Schmidt-Felzmann 2020). However, CAATSA authorised but did not require the imposition of sanctions on Nord Stream 2, and implementation guidelines by the US State Department later excluded the project from sanctions under the bill.

As such, construction of Nord Stream 2 went ahead and the pipeline was expected to become operational by mid-2020. This would change with the adoption of a new bill by the US Congress in late 2019, the Protecting Europe's Energy Security Act (PEESA), which effectively imposed sanctions on companies involved in pipe-laying activities for Nord Stream 2. This suspended pipe-laying for 12 months, but was not successful in halting Nord Stream 2 completely. In February 2021, construction resumed and was eventually completed in September of that year (Reuters 2021).

Certification by the German energy regulator, the Bundesnetzagentur, was still required before Nord Stream 2 could enter operation. In October 2021, the German Ministry for Economic Affairs issued a binding opinion stating that the pipeline did not threaten the security of supply of Germany or the EU, a pre-condition for certification by the Bundesnetzagentur (German Federal Ministry for Economic Affairs and Energy 2021). On February 22, 2022, German Chancellor ordered the withdrawal of this opinion and as such suspended the certification process of Nord Stream 2 (Reuters 2022a). With Russia's invasion of Ukraine a mere two days later, there is very little chance that this will ever change.

The war and the securitisation of EU energy policy

The 2009 gas crisis and the 2014 Ukraine crisis delivered significant blows to the EU's perception of Russia as a reliable energy supplier. Nevertheless, it is worth noting that the share of Russian gas in total EU gas imports rose from 30.5% in 2010 to 38% in 2020 (Eurostat 2022). While the dependence on Russia became understood in security terms, it ultimately remained perceived and treated as something governable and manageable. The European Energy Security Strategy launched in the aftermath of the Ukraine crisis for instance talked about how the reliance on imports made the EU "vulnerable to external energy shocks" (European Commission 2014c, p. 2). This required "a hard-headed strategy for energy security, which promotes resilience to these shocks and disruptions to energy supplies in the short term and reduced dependency on particular fuels, energy suppliers and routes in the long-term" (ibid.).

The grammar of the Energy Security Strategy closely aligns with a logic of riskification/risk security, which Corry (2012, p. 248) describes as the construction of an issue as "a long-term problem that requires governance, transparency, precautionary measures and increased cooperation", which tends to result in "programmes for permanent changes aimed at reducing vulnerability and boosting governance-capacity of the valued referent object itself".[2]

Arguably, the war in Ukraine has shifted European energy discourse and policy beyond riskification, and introduced the logic of existential threat. Russian energy imports are frequently portrayed as weapons and direct causes of harm to European/Ukrainian security. The REPowerEU Plan of May 2022 argues how "high amounts paid for Russia's fossil fuels are helping Russia sustain its war against Ukraine" (European Commission 2022c, p. 1), and stipulates that Russia uses its energy exports to Europe "as an economic and political weapon" (ibid. p. 20). As such, the dependence on Russian gas, coal and oil needs to be phased out "as soon as possible", as affirmed by EU heads of state in the Versailles Declaration. This is not about reducing the EU's vulnerability to supply disruptions, but about survival, as evidenced by Commission President von der Leyen during the State of the European Union in September 2022:

> This is not only a war unleashed by Russia against Ukraine. This is a war on our energy, a war on our economy, a war on our values and a war on our future.

In other words, Russia's war in Ukraine has instigated a process of securitisation in European energy policy; the EU's energy dependency on Russia is not anymore understood as a risk to be mitigated via precautionary measures, but as an existential threat to be eliminated via "exceptional measures [...] aiming for survival" (Corry 2012, p. 249).

Whereas the riskification process of the 2010s prompted changes *within* the existing market-oriented policy paradigm, leading to what Herranz-Surrallés (2018) called the "Geopolitically embedded Market-Liberal Frame" in the context of Euro-Mediterranean energy relations following the Arab Spring, this securitisation process is now causing a wholesale shift *of* this geopolitically embedded market-liberal frame/policy paradigm.

Member states have agreed to an unprecedented supranational deployment of hard economic power in the energy sphere, first with the import ban on Russian coal as part of the fifth sanction package against Russia in April 2022 and later with the embargo on imports of Russian seaborne crude and petroleum products as part of the sixth sanction package in June 2022 (European Commission 2022d; 2022e).

Other measures/debates similarly indicate the EU's move beyond the market-liberal policy paradigm. Amid soaring energy prices, member states have called for far-reaching intervention in European electricity and natural gas markets to protect end consumers (e.g. Council of the European Union 2022). Whereas it initially pushed back against these calls, the Commission ultimately conceded with Commission President von der Leyen arguing in June that the current electricity market design was in need of reform (Euractiv 2022). Later, in September 2022, the Commission advanced different proposals for "an emergency intervention in Europe's energy markets to tackle recent dramatic price rises", including a temporary revenue cap on non-gas electricity producers and a temporary "solidarity contribution" on windfalls profits in the fossil fuel industry (European Commission 2022f).

The Commission has advocated for a departure from market-based governance in other respects as well, for instance with its proposals for a joint purchasing mechanism for natural gas. Such a mechanism is envisaged by the Commission as a way to support the purchase of gas from third countries by pooling the gas demand of member states and "making optimal use of the collective political and market weight of the EU" (European Commission 2022g). In less euphemistic terms, the Commission proposes the establishment of a buying cartel in order to distort market competition and strengthen the EU's bargaining position vis-a-vis external suppliers. Considering the Commission's traditional pro-market orientation, this represents a highly significant shift, likely with large repercussions for the future direction of energy governance in the EU.

Outlook for transatlantic energy relations

The securitisation process and accompanying paradigm shift in EU energy policy described in the previous section have radically altered the position of LNG in the European energy mix. In its 2016 Communication on an EU strategy for LNG and gas storage, the Commission labelled LNG as a "major opportunity for the EU, particularly when it comes to gas security and resilience", which could make "a major contribution" to diversifying the supply of member states that were "heavily dependent on a single supplier, and hence vulnerable to supply interruptions" (European Commission 2016, p. 2). In other words, LNG was seen as something that could help to mitigate the risk posed by EU import dependency and increase the resilience of the European gas system.

The war in Ukraine has now transformed LNG into a central component in the EU's strategy to end the reliance on Russian fossil fuels. Under the REPowerEU Plan proposed by the Commission in May 2022, it has to replace 50 bcm or almost one-third of the 155 bcm of natural gas that the EU imported from Russia in 2021. The import of additional LNG is thus no longer an opportunity or optional precaution, but a necessary emergency measure to eliminate an existential threat.

As such, a new security logic underpins the transatlantic gas trade, set to significantly bolster EU-US energy cooperation. This is already illustrated by the Joint Statement issued by the Commission and the US in March 2022, where both parties affirmed their commitment to "the objective of addressing the energy security emergency – to ensure energy supply for the EU and Ukraine" (European Commission 2022h). Concretely, the US pledged to "work with international partners" to supply an additional 15 bcm of LNG to the EU in the course of 2022, and to maintain "an enabling regulatory environment with procedures to review and expeditiously act upon applications to permit any additional export LNG capacities" (ibid.). The Commission, on the other hand, would "work with EU Member States toward ensuring stable demand for additional U.S. LNG until at least 2030 of approximately 50 bcm/annum" (ibid.).

The deal was met with scepticism, as American LNG export facilities were operating near full capacity and much of the global LNG supply is already locked into long-term contracts. However, in the first six months of 2022, the US already exported 39 bcm of LNG to the EU, compared to a total of 34 bcm for all of 2021 (Reuters 2022b). US LNG exports are now likely to significantly exceed the target of 15 bcm agreed in March. This should be attributed principally to surging European gas prices (Financial Times 2022), but is nonetheless illustrative of the current "securitisation" of the EU-US gas trade.

The question is now whether the resultant expansion of transatlantic gas flows will just help the EU to phase-out Russian gas, or will also entrench the dependence on fossil fuels across the Atlantic. The March Joint Statement may reaffirm the transatlantic commitment to climate objectives and state that both parties "will undertake efforts to reduce the greenhouse gas intensity of all new LNG infrastructure and associated pipelines" (European Commission 2022h), these pledges risk being overshadowed by short-term security of supply considerations. This is a predictable consequence of the introduction of a logic of existential threat; when reducing the dependence on Russia is understood in existential terms, environmental concerns may fade into insignificance.

The May 2022 Joint Statement by the Trade and Technology Council (TTC) shows how transatlantic energy relations can go beyond gas. The envisaged collaboration on green tech and on solar and rare earth supply chains can help to accelerate the clean energy transition on both sides of the Atlantic, while simultaneously ensuring that this does not come with new external dependencies and vulnerabilities. As the European energy crisis deepens, it will be crucial for both transatlantic partners to not lose sight of these topics paramount to a secure, affordable and sustainable energy future.

Notes

* Simon Dekeyrel is a policy analyst at the European Policy Centre in Brussels. Any views, thoughts, and opinions expressed in this chapter solely belong to the author and do not reflect the views, opinions, policies, or position of the European Policy Centre.

1 The European Commission also undertook attempts to undermine Nord Stream 2. Specifically, it attempted to stymie the project through a selective and strategic application of the regulatory tools at its disposal (see de Jong and Van de Graaf 2021).

2 In securitisation theory, the "referent object" refers to that which is threatened. In the case of the European Energy Security Strategy, this would be the energy security of the EU.

References

Bocse, A. M., 2020. From the United States with shale gas: Ukraine, energy securitization, and the reshaping of transatlantic energy relations. *Energy Research & Social Science*, 69, 1–12.

Conley, H., Ladislaw, S., and Hudson, A., 2016. The US-EU energy relationship. *In*: J. M. Godzimirski, ed. *EU Leadership in Energy and Environmental Governance: Global and Local Challenges and Responses*. London: Palgrave Macmillan, 159–180.

Corry, O., 2012. Securitisation and 'Riskification': Second-order security and the politics of climate change. *Millennium: Journal of International Studies*, 40 (2), 235–258.

Council of the European Union, 2022. *Extraordinary transport, telecommunications and Energy Council (Energy), 9 September 2022* [online]. Available from: https://www.consilium.europa.eu/en/meetings/tte/2022/09/09/ [Accessed 15 September 2022].

Dannreuther, R., 2015. Energy security and shifting modes of governance. *International Politics*, 52 (4), 466-483.

de Jong, M. and Van de Graaf, T., 2021. Lost in regulation: Nord Stream 2 and the limits of the European Commission's geo-economic power. *Journal of European Integration*, 43 (4), 495–510.

Directorate-General for Energy, 2021. *Quarterly report on European gas markets. Fourth Quarter of 2021*. Available from: https://energy.ec.europa.eu/system/files/2022-04/Quarterly%20report%20on%20European%20gas%20markets_Q4%202021.pdf [Accessed 15 September 2022].

Euractiv, 2022. *EU chief announces electricity market overhaul amid 'skyrocketing' prices* [online]. Available from: https://www.euractiv.com/section/electricity/news/eu-chief-announces-electricity-market-overhaul-amid-skyrocketing-prices/ [Accessed 15 September 2022].

European Commission, 2000. Towards a European strategy for the security of energy supply. COM(2000) 769 final.

European Commission, 2009. *New EU-US Energy Council to boost transatlantic energy cooperation* [online]. Available from: https://ec.europa.eu/commission/presscorner/detail/en/IP_09_1674 [Accessed 15 September 2022].

European Commission, 2010. *EU-US Energy Council. Press Statement* [online]. Available from: https://energy.ec.europa.eu/system/files/2015-08/2010.11.19%25202nd%2520Press%2520statement%2520final_0.pdf [Accessed 15 September 2022].

European Commission, 2011. *Joint Press Statement. The EU-U.S. Energy Council* [online]. Available from: https://energy.ec.europa.eu/system/files/2015-08/2011.11.28%25203rd%2520Press%2520statement%2520final_0.pdf [Accessed 15 September 2022].

European Commission, 2012. *The EU-U.S. Energy Council. Joint Press Statement* [online]. Available from: https://energy.ec.europa.eu/system/files/2015-08/2012.12.05%25204th%2520Press%2520statement%2520final_0.pdf [Accessed 15 September 2022].

European Commission, 2014a. *EU-US Energy Council – Joint Press Statement* [online]. Available from: https://energy.ec.europa.eu/system/files/2015-08/2014.04.02%25205th%2520Press%2520statement%2520final_0.pdf [Accessed 15 September 2022].

European Commission, 2014b. *Joint Statement EU-US Energy Council* [online]. Available from: https://energy.ec.europa.eu/system/files/2015-08/2014.12.03%25206th%2520Press%2520statement%2520final_0.pdf [Accessed 15 September 2022].

European Commission, 2014c. European Energy Security Strategy. COM(2014) 330 final.

European Commission, 2016. An EU strategy for liquefied natural gas and gas storage. COM (2016) 49 final.

European Commission, 2018a. Joint U.S.-EU Statement following President Juncker's visit to the White House. STATEMENT/18/4687.

European Commission, 2018b. EU-U.S. Joint Statement of 25 July: European Union imports of U.S. Liquefied Natural Gas (LNG) are on the rise. IP/18/4920.

European Commission, 2022a. REPowerEU: Joint European Action for more affordable, secure and sustainable energy. COM(2022) 108 final.

European Commission, 2022b. *EU-US LNG Trade: US liquefied natural gas (LNG) has the potential to help match EU gas needs* [online]. Available from: https://energy.ec.europa.eu/system/files/2022-02/EU-US_LNG_2022_2.pdf [Accessed 15 September 2022].

European Commission, 2022c. REPowerEU Plan. COM(2022) 230 final.

European Commission, 2022d. Ukraine: EU agrees fifth package of restrictive measures against Russia. IP/22/2332.

European Commission, 2022e. Russia's war on Ukraine: EU adopts sixth package of sanctions against Russia. IP/22/2802.

European Commission, 2022f. Energy prices: Commission proposes emergency market intervention to reduce bills for Europeans. IP/22/5489.

European Commission, 2022g. Energy Security: Commission hosts first meeting of EU Energy Purchase Platform to secure supply of gas, LNG and hydrogen. IP/22/2387.

European Commission, 2022h. *Joint Statement between the European Commission and the United States on European Energy Security* [online]. Available from: https://ec.europa.eu/commission/presscorner/detail/en/statement_22_2041 [Accessed 15 September 2022].

European Council, 2022. *Informal meeting of the Heads of State or Government. Versailles Declaration* [online]. Available from: https://www.consilium.europa.eu/media/54773/20220311-versailles-declaration-en.pdf [Accessed 15 September 2022].

Eurostat, 2022. *Energy production and imports* [online]. Available from: https://ec.europa.eu/eurostat/statistics-explained/index.php?title=Energy_production_and_imports#Production_of_primary_energy_decreased_between_2010_and_2020 [Accessed 15 September 2022].

Financial Times, 2022. *Europe and Asia intensify battle to secure gas supplies* [online]. Available from: https://www.ft.com/content/93c6570b-10f9-46cf-8310-2caa319c00a3 [Accessed 15 September 2022].

German Federal Institute for Geosciences and Natural Resources, 2013. *Energy Study 2013: Reserves, resources and availability of energy resources* [online]. Available from: https://www.bgr.bund.de/EN/Themen/Energie/Downloads/energiestudie_2013_en.pdf;jsessionid=E0692781655803C3CEB93DFA39679AAB.1_cid321?__blob=publicationFile&v=2 [Accessed 15 September 2022].

German Federal Ministry for Economic Affairs and Energy, 2021. *Bundeswirtschaftsministerium übermittelt Versorgungssicherheitsanalyse im Zertifizierungsverfahren Nord Stream 2 an Bundesnetzagentur* [online]. Available from: https://www.bmwk.de/Redaktion/DE/Pressemitteilungen/2021/10/20211026-bmwi-uebermittelt-versorgungssicherheitsanalyse-im-zertifizierungsverfahren-nord-stream-2-an-bundesnetzagentur.html [Accessed 15 September 2022].

Herranz-Surrallés, A., 2018. Thinking energy outside the *frame*? Reframing and misframing in Euro-Mediterranean energy relations. *Mediterranean Politics*, 23 (1), 122–141.

Högselius, P., 2013. *Red gas: Russia and the origins of European energy dependence*. London: Palgrave Macmillan.

Maltby, T., 2013. European Union energy policy integration: A case of European Commission policy entrepreneurship and increasing supranationalism. *Energy Policy*, 55, 435–455.

McGowan, F., 2014. Regulating innovation: European responses to shale gas development. *Environmental Politics*, 23 (1), 41–58.

Natali, P., Egenhofer, C., and Molnar, G., 2015. TTIP and Energy. *In*: D. S. Hamilton and J. Pelkmans, eds. *Rule-Makers or Rule-Takers? Exploring the Transatlantic Trade and Investment Partnership*. London: Rowman & Littlefield International, 479–504.

Natorski, M. and Herranz-Surrallés, A., 2008. Securitizing moves to nowhere? The framing of the European Union's energy policy. *Journal of Contemporary European Research*, 4 (2), 70–89.

Noël, P., 2010. *Ensuring success for the EU Regulation on gas supply security*. Cambridge: Electricity Policy Research Group, University of Cambridge.

Perle, R., 1981. *Statement submitted by Richard Perle, Assistant Secretary for International Security Policy, Department of Defense, to the Committee on Banking, Housing, and Urban Affairs*. United States Senate, Washington, DC. 12 November.

Perović, J., 2017. The Soviet Union's Rise as an International Energy Power: A Short History. In: J. Perović, ed. *Cold War Energy: A Transnational History of Soviet Oil and Gas*. London: Palgrave Macmillan, 1–43.

Pirani, S., Stern, J., and Yafimava, K., 2009. *The Russo-Ukrainian gas dispute of January 2009: A comprehensive assessment*. Oxford: Oxford Institute for Energy Studies.

Prontera, A., 2019. *Beyond the EU Regulatory State: Energy Security and the Eurasian Gas Market*. London: ECPR Press.

Reuters, 2021. *Russia completes Nord Stream 2 construction, gas flows yet to start* [online]. Available from: https://www.reuters.com/business/energy/russias-gazprom-says-it-has-completed-nord-stream-2-construction-2021-09-10/ [Accessed 15 September 2022].

Reuters, 2022a. *Germany freezes Nord Stream 2 gas project as Ukraine crisis deepens* [online]. Available from: https://www.reuters.com/business/energy/germanys-scholz-halts-nord-stream-2-certification-2022-02-22/ [Accessed 15 September 2022].

Reuters, 2022b. *Analysis: U.S. LNG exports to Europe on track to surpass Biden promise* [online]. Available from: https://www.reuters.com/business/energy/us-lng-exports-europe-track-surpass-biden-promise-2022-07-26/ [Accessed 15 September 2022].

Schmidt-Felzmann, A., 2020. Gazprom's Nord Stream 2 and diffuse authority in the EU: managing authority challenges regarding Russian gas supplies through the Baltic Sea. *Journal of European Integration*, 42 (1), 129–145.

Stern, J., 2006. *The Russian-Ukrainian gas crisis of January 2006*. Oxford: Oxford Institute for Energy Studies.

The White House, 2006. *U.S.-EU Summit Declaration: Promoting Peace, Human Rights and Democracy Worldwide* [online]. Available from: https://georgewbush-whitehouse.archives.gov/news/releases/2006/06/20060621-2.html [Accessed 15 September 2022].

Trump, D., 2017. *Remarks by President Trump at the Unleashing American Energy Event* [online]. Available from: https://trumpwhitehouse.archives.gov/briefings-statements/remarks-president-trump-unleashing-american-energy-event/ [Accessed 15 September 2022].

US Energy Information Administration, 2013. *Technically recoverable shale oil and shale gas resources: An assessment of 137 shale formations in 41 countries outside the United States* [online].

Available from: https://www.eia.gov/analysis/studies/worldshalegas/archive/2013/pdf/fullreport_2013.pdf [Accessed 15 September 2022].
US Energy Information Administration, 2019. *The U.S. leads global petroleum and natural gas production with record growth in 2018* [online]. Available from: https://www.eia.gov/todayinenergy/detail.php?id=40973 [Accessed 15 September 2022].
US Energy Information Administration, 2022. *U.S. energy facts explained –Imports & Exports* [online]. Available from: https://www.eia.gov/energyexplained/us-energy-facts/imports-and-exports.php [Accessed 15 September 2022].
Van de Graaf, T., Haesebrouck, T. and Debaere, P., 2017. Fractured politics? The comparative regulation of shale gas in Europe. *Journal of European Public Policy*, 25 (9), 1276–1293.

13

TRANSATLANTIC TRADE RELATIONS

Domestic Obstacles and Strategic Opportunities

L. Johan Eliasson

EAST STROUDSBURG UNIVERSITY, PA

European nations and the United States (US) were instrumental in erecting in the post–World War II international rules-based trading system and multilateral trade agreements. Today the European Union (EU) and the US have the deepest, most integrated trade and investment relationship in the world.[1] They share similar values and have many common interests in and concerns about rules-based trade, even if there are some differences in their views on how the international trading system should evolve.[2] The two allies also have a long history of clashing over regulatory and political differences on trade, while simultaneously promoting transatlantic commercial exchange and integration (e.g. Dür 2010; Farrell and Newman 2019; Pelkmans and de Brito 2015). The creation of a 'transatlantic market place' has occasionally been stated as a goal, though a comprehensive trade agreement has proven elusive (Eliasson and Garcia-Duran 2019; Young 2017). However, in a world increasingly divided between illiberal/authoritarian and democratic systems, where economic interdependence can be (and is) weaponized, the transatlantic partners recognize the need for renewed, close cooperation (e.g. European Commission 2020; USTR 2022).

This chapter discusses areas where transatlantic cooperation and coordination can strengthen not only bilateral ties, but serve to strengthen the international trading system. It starts by presenting the domestic debates influencing trade policy and strategies in the US and the EU. It thereafter focuses on three specific issue-areas, namely labour rights, trade defence instruments, and reforming the World Trade Organization. These are also discussed within Working Group 10 of Trade and Technology Council (TTC). The latter was erected in 2021 as the hub for transatlantic for high-level, sustained discussions aimed at coordinating and cooperating on issues affecting emerging and critical technologies and trade. The argument in this chapter is twofold, (a) that domestic (US) and national level (EU) political

 DOI: 10.4324/9781003283911-16

developments matter for transatlantic trade cooperation, and (b) that the EU – notwithstanding remaining differences – has moved closer to America's position on many issues. This helps facilitate common transatlantic positions vis-a-vis challengers and rivals, and allows the transatlantic partners to present common positions in international organizations and other fora. The third section concludes.

Domestic debates and trade policies

Domestic politics affects all aspects of foreign policy, including trade, and the second decade of the twenty-first century brought changes on both sides of the Atlantic.

The United States

The history of US commerce is one of domestic contestation and politicization of trade and trade agreements (Johnson 2018). Tariffs were the main source of federal revenue until 1913, and remained the object of political contestation and bargaining thereafter, often in relations with Europe. After a brief lull in the mid-2000s, globalization and trade re-emerged as contentious politics domestically during the Obama administration. When entering office in 2009, labour unions opposed ratification of three free trade agreements (FTAs) negotiated by the G. W. Bush administration with small Latin American countries. Only after several years' delay and partial renegotiations to strengthen labour provisions were they finally passed – with Republican support. However, ratification of the larger Transpacific Partnership agreement (TPP), which the Obama administration negotiated, crashed into a wall of labour union and Congressional opposition after the biggest labour unions engaged in their largest ever anti-trade campaign. Republicans, encouraged by a wave of support from Caucasian, blue-collar workers who believed then candidate Trump's argument that others were cheating Americans, and that globalization was fleecing the US, refused to help President Obama pass TPP.

Trump's protectionist rhetoric appealed to large swaths of the rural population and older Caucasians concerned about 'the American way of life'. Arguments that others were taking advantage of America found a receptive domestic audience, helping Trump win some Democratic strongholds, including districts with large sections of unionized labour (Morgans 2018; Mutz 2018). Backed by public opinion and unions, with the argument that trade deficits are bad and others cheat, President Trump then formally withdrew from the TPP and the Paris Accord, was uninterested in continuing negotiations on the Transatlantic Trade and Investment Partnership (TTIP), started tariff wars with China, and imposed tariffs on steel and aluminium from friends and foes alike; threatened to reset US tariffs from its low average bounded rate, imposed export bans on semiconductors, refused reappointments or renewals of any World Trade Organization (WTO) appellate body (AB) member, and preferred a return to a power-based GATT-system. While China was the main target, Trump also referred to Europe as a 'foe' and 'threat', that was 'taking advantage' of the US (BBC 2018). After entering office in 2021, the Biden administration reached out to traditional allies, embraced dialog in international organizations, and employed a rhetoric far more conciliatory than that of his predecessor; however, policy changed little. He kept the tariffs on Chinese imports, remained aloof on WTO reforms, strengthened 'Buy American' provisions in federal contracts, ordered a reduction in waivers to such provisions and created a director of Made in America.[3]

Globalization and free trade was supposed to make Americans better off while expanding democracy, but many Americans now believe that others have taken advantage of the US (Mutz 2021). There is widespread political scepticism about the feasibility, and even usefulness, of a rules-based trading system, underpinned by complicated cross-party suspicion about globalization, international trade, and, in particular, trade agreements (Johnson 2018; Mutz 2021) This bi-partisan grassroots scepticism of trade agreements and globalization has been reinforced from the top. Pundits and politicians across political parties, including Presidents Obama, Trump, and Biden, have long promoted the idea that as long as the playing field is levelled Americans can beat anyone, leaving 'fair trade' to mean 'America wins while others lose' (Mutz 2021; Reinsch 2022). This facilitates narratives of blaming others, 'they produce' and 'take our jobs', and 'imports bad – exports good', all of which in turn resonate with labour unions, manual labourers, and far-right supporters alike (Lovely 2022; Mutz 2021).

Democrats (whose leadership still relies heavily on the anti-trade, labour movement to get elected) largely trust Biden to use trade policy to protect and promote labour union interests. The educated, urban elite ('progressive cosmopolitans') who believe in labour rights, combatting climate change, and liberal trade policies, tend to vote Democrat, but are not very active on trade policy and constitute the minority of the US population. Republicans (voters and officials) do not trust that Biden will defend and promote American interests, and have become fond of laws subsidizing and protecting American businesses. Congress has a rapidly shrinking plurality of pro-trade Republicans, and even fewer such Democrats; politicians in both parties frequently tout managed trade and mercantilist policies (Bacchus 2022; Cass 2022).

US trade policy has thus taken a turn towards economic nationalism, which stresses the primacy of the state, national security interests, and the importance of military power to back economic interests. There is cross-party support for 'America first' policies and for subsidizing and protecting American businesses and jobs (Bade 2021; Posen 2021; Younis 2021). The focus is on relative rather than absolute economic gains, where the state plays an active economic role (ranging from domestic economic interventions to external protectionism). While Russia's invasion of Ukraine – and China's tacit support – certainly amplified the trade-security nexus (e.g. restrictions on dual-use exports), there is broad-based domestic support for employing offensive, proactive trade tools, including tariffs, at times with little consideration for their effects on economic growth, bilateral trade ties, or multilateralism (Bacchus 2022; Bown and Russ 2021). In short, 'polite protectionism' reigns (Bacchus 2022).

European Union

Trade policy has been the prerogative of the European Commission since the creation of the EU. Free internal trade was a driving force in EU integration, and it helped strengthen public acceptance of the EU project. This allowed the EU to continuously pursue a liberalizing trade agenda (Orbie and De Ville 2020), albeit one balanced with 'measures designed to cushion the domestic economy from external disruptions' (Ruggie 1982: 405) in order to ensure a domestic margin of manoeuvre to preserve political and social stability, what Ruggie (1982) coined 'embedded liberalism'. However, protests against a Multilateral Investment Agreement (1997), and a new round of multilateral trade negotiations at the World Trade Organization (WTO) in 1999, led the European Commission to explicate that trade policy was aimed at 'managing globalization' (European Parliament 1999). Thereafter a 'permissive condition', where trade was accepted, supported and largely unchallenged by the public lasted until TTIP negotiations began in 2013.

TTIP was the EU's first trade negotiation with an economic equal, and it evoked and hardened differences across the EU. Northern European countries have traditionally favoured trade, globalization and increased market access, while the opposite has dominated western continental Europe and southern states, where combative relations between unions and employers dominate, leaving them more sceptical of trade and globalization. East and central European publics have largely supported liberalizing trade policies since joining the EU, with very few civil society organizations (CSOs) or labour unions speaking up against globalization, trade or trade agreements. CSOs across Germany, Austria, the United Kingdom, Belgium and France, along with many unions, nonetheless led EU-wide challenges to TTIP, evoking deep-rooted continental European ideas about 'wild west' American capitalism and European superiority (e.g. on food and health) alongside fears of losing the status quo between free trade and social market regulations (Bauer 2016; Eliasson and Garcia-Duran 2019). Protests, social media campaigns, and declining public support permeated several European governments' positions over the following years, politicizing EU trade policies and influencing strategy. CSOs' protests ultimately led to the demise of TTIP, while helping shape the European Commission's trade strategy, which evolved from stressing trade liberalization, to emphasizing sustainability, consumer protection, labour rights and resilience (Eliasson and Garcia-Duran 2018; 2019).

Between 2019 and 2022 EU public opinion grew very sceptical of China's international intentions, and the EU began increasing its own capabilities to defend fair trade, while also promoting a return to a rules-based liberal international trading order (European Commission 2021a). The EU's 2021 trade strategy represents a new balance between fair trade and geopolitics; between labour and sustainability, and trade as a foreign policy tool (realist). Recognizing several threats to the international trading system, the EU must now be able to act independently (of WTO rulings and allies) when necessary (European Commission 2021a). In sum, EU trade policy is a mix of managed globalization and realism, where the public expects the EU to support multilateralism and international norms where possible, but accepts unilateralism if done to defend fair trade.

Domestic support for transatlantic relations is important (Riddervold and Newsome 2022). European public opinion of the US has a greater impact on policy than vice versa. There is a sharp partisan divide in the US, where conservative

Republicans are less interested in specific areas of cooperation where the US may have to compromise (cf. Brooks 2022). However, and notwithstanding the protectionist turn in the US and TTIP's failure, public support for transatlantic economic cooperation *writ large* has remained fairly positive on both sides of the Atlantic (German Marshall Fund 2021; Pew 2013). There is domestic support on both sides for general transatlantic economic cooperation, and a tougher approach towards China on climate, human rights, cyber and territorial expansion (Ibid 2021). Thus, cooperation and coordination in certain areas are likely to enjoy public backing.

Opportunities for coordination and cooperation

Labour rights

The 2021 EU trade strategy and the 2022 'US Trade Policy Agenda' both emphasize the need to address domestic discontent with globalization and job dislocation, while promoting high labour standards abroad. When launching the TTC both parties also pledged 'to protect workers and labour rights, and combat forced and child labour' as part of addressing common trade challenges (White House 2021a). With increasingly complementary developments, and notwithstanding different domestic motivations, the end goals of higher labour standards overlap. The TTC can serve as a forum for a coordinated transatlantic approach that can then be carried forward through bilateral agreements and joint initiatives in multilateral settings. When the TTC Working group 10 held stakeholder meetings in 2021–22, there were calls for harmonization of labour policies/standards in line with international standards (e.g. International Labour Organization Conventions), and enforcement policies, referring to the Rapid Reaction Mechanism (RRM) for labour petitions in the US-Mexico-Canada agreement (USMCA) as an example both could employ.

The US has a better track record of agreements with enforceable labour provisions that largely comply with International Labour Organization (ILO) standards, for example the Cambodia Textile Agreement (Wells 2007) and the USMCA, despite the US not ratifying all the ILO conventions. For the US, the purpose of labour provisions is primarily to prevent a lack of labour standards in exporting countries from undermining (outcompeting) domestic manufacturing. For the EU, it is a matter of promoting the social standards prevailing inside the EU and upholding its commitment to international norms. Yet, the EU has few agreements with enforceable labour standards, and has occasionally been accused of being unwilling to reduce or cut market access to countries with labour violations (Vogt 2015), often for fear of worsening the situation for workers. Nonetheless, working through its bilateral agreements with Vietnam, Georgia and South Korea, and supported by the ILO, the EU convinced all three to adopt new labour codes in 2020 and 2021; Korea also ratified three ILO conventions in 2021 (European Commission 2021d). These represent the first instances ever of the EU seeking consultations with a partner for failing to adopt or enforce a labour standard.

In February 2022, the Commission presented a Directive on Corporate Sustainability and Due Diligence that includes sustainability and labour rights provisions in supply chains. The EU's proposal is extensive in its aspiration, yet vague, with no American equivalence (European Commission 2022). It is a part of the EU's attempts to address sustainability and human rights concerns within trade, and because it focuses on large firms (many of which are American), this may cause disagreements with the US. However, there is growing support in the US Congress (and in the general public) for regulating corporations' responsibility in supply chains.

The May 2022 TTC also resulted in a new EU-US 'Trade and Labour Dialogue' with representatives from labour unions, industry and government officials focused on addressing worker-rights issues, and establishing an early alert mechanism for shared concerns dealing with third-countries. Such discussions would be further strengthened if the TTC directly engaged the US Congress and the European Parliament. Both legislatures debate, develop and vote on legislation in key areas discussed in the TTC, so inviting the existing Transatlantic Legislators' Dialogue to select TTC meetings would enhance transparency and strengthen legislators' mutual understanding of issues.

Trade defences

Both transatlantic partners recognize the need for strong trade defences against 'non-market distortive policies and practices that pose particular challenges for U.S. and EU workers and businesses' (White House 2021a). The pandemic, changing geo-political concerns and domestic disgruntlement led both the US and the EU to reconsider supply chain resilience and import dependence in select sectors; there is renewed appetite for industrial policies, including subsidies, notwithstanding separate efforts to counter certain state subsidies in other countries (Tai 2022). Coordination across the Atlantic could thus strengthen the case for rules-based trade.

The US aims to ensure its trade defence tools are 'fit for today's economy' (Tai 2022). This includes new export controls and stricter investment screening. In 2018, Washington reformed the law on the authorization of foreign investments (the Foreign Investment Risk Review Modernization Act – FIRRMA), thus strengthening control over investments in American companies considered strategic, especially in new technologies; the law is part of the legal framework of the Committee on Foreign Investments in the US (CFIUS). There are comparable developments in Europe. While the EU retains its traditional emphasis on multilateralism and 'peace through trade' diplomacy, EU Trade Commissioner Dombrovskis has acknowledged that 'trade is increasingly being weaponized and the EU and its member states are becoming targets of economic intimidation' (Moens 2022). Thus, in response to America's and China's geopolitical focus in trade policy (including its trade wars), the EU has adopted or proposed six new trade defence instruments in 2019–2022: a foreign investment screening mechanism (FIRRMA was an inspiration), foreign subsidies regulation, anti-coercion instrument, international procurement instrument, carbon border adjustment mechanism, and a corporate due diligence regulation.

The EU's anti-coercion regulation in particular presents another opportunity to strengthen both Europe's and the transatlantic partners' efforts at upholding global rules of trade. The regulation (final approval expected by late 2023) is an 'instrument to deter and counteract economic coercion by third countries in order to safeguard its rights and interests and those of its Member States … therefore the instrument would be most successful if there is no need to use it' (European Commission 2021c: 1,10).[4] This fills a gap in the EU that is covered in the US by the broad-ranging section 301 of the Trade Act of 1974, which 'gives the USTR, at the direction of the President, broad authority to respond to unfair trade practices [that are] unreasonable or discriminatory and burdens or restricts United States commerce' (Manuk 2022). The compatibility of EU and US legislation will increase their respective deterrence value, as they enable more coordinated and comparable transatlantic responses to third-party discriminatory practices. Furthermore, if third parties are convinced that the EU and US are willing to use coercive trade defence tools, then returning to WTO rules may appear more attractive.

The COVID-19 pandemic (with shipping delays, lockdowns and increased weaponization of trade) also served as a wakeup call for supply chain dependencies. Both sides now emphasize resiliency (e.g. diversifying sourcing of critical products) and working with allies. Both also proposed new industrial subsidies, with each allocating roughly $/€ 50 bn for state-backed investments and subsidies to expand and upscale semi-conductor manufacturing in the US and Europe. Recognizing the mutual challenge, the two also agreed in May 2022 'to avoid subsidy races by advancing common goals for incentives granted in respective territories and an exchange of information regarding such incentives on a reciprocal basis', and to limit subsidies to what is 'necessary, appropriate and proportionate for public policy objectives' (White House 2022b: 5,14).

There is great value in coordination through the TTC because of how the debates on industrial policy differ on the two continents. While both focus on the reorientation of industry investments away from China, Russia and similar authoritarian regimes, the debate in the US centres around targeted assistance, re-shoring and 'friend-shoring' (agreements with reliable partners), and 'Buy America' provisions (USTR 2022:7; White House 2022a), reflecting domestic concerns about jobs. The Inflation Reduction Act of 2022 includes extensive incentives to 're-shore' and 'friend-shore' production, giving preferential tax treatment and subsidies to manufacturing electric vehicle (EV) components inside the US, and in countries with whom the US has FTAs. The EU insists that domestic content requirements violate WTO rules, and will challenge these provisions, initially through TTC working groups, and if that fails, through the WTO.[5] The EU has rules on state aid, and both the Commission and the European Parliament have made clear that supply chain disruptions and Russia's war in Ukraine are reasons to accelerate, complete, and ratify new FTAs – Europe's version of 'friendshoring', but without discriminating against friendly partners (read the US).

The TTC facilitated rapid transatlantic coordination on sanctions and export controls in the wake of Russia's invasion of Ukraine in February 2022 (Inside US Trade 2022). Continued coordination on supply chains and export controls (beyond arms and dual-use products and against other regions and countries) would signal to both domestic groups and international partners and competitors that shared values can translate into specific policies. For example, if 'necessary, appropriate and proportionate' subsidies can be specified bilaterally, it can prevent transatlantic clashes, serve as a model for others (e.g., the Regional Comprehensive Economic Partnership has no such regulations) and as a baseline for reforms at the WTO. As the Commission likes to emphasize, 'while we are still the most influential regulators, both the EU and the US face increasing standard competition from third country actors. Where both sides agree, the world usually follows' (European Commission 2020: 6).

However, the transatlantic partners have not always led by example. In 2018, President Trump imposed tariffs of 25% and 10%, respectively, on all imported steel and aluminium (irrespective of source), citing threats to national security under a 1962 national Security Act ('section 232'). The EU retaliated with billions of Euros of tariffs on select US goods from primarily Republican states. When Biden eased trade frictions with Europe in October 2021, it was done through a bilateral agreement with tariff-rate quotas – a managed trade deal disregarding WTO rules.[6] In continued concessions to domestic American producers and their Congressional representatives in swing districts that often determine national elections, the rules-of-origin were also altered. Ostensibly done to prevent excess Chinese steel from entering the US after being 'substantially transformed' in Europe (e.g. Chinese metal slabs turned into stainless steel), the new rules requiring steel to be 'melted and poured' in Europe will limit European exports, especially of certain stainless steel.[7] The agreement also posits transatlantic negotiations on a larger 'arrangement' (not agreement) to reduce emissions and global overcapacity in steel and aluminium production, but as of late 2022 there were no details on how this would be achieved. Any agreed provisions would have to build on and complement domestic measures, such as subsidies for industrial decarbonization (the 2021 Infrastructure Investment and Jobs Act in the US) and the EU's revised Emissions Trading Scheme and Carbon Border Adjustment Mechanism. The EU agreeing to provisions it previously deemed unacceptable also signals recognition of the new reality of a more mercantilist US, where the 'arrangement' was hailed by Republicans and Democrats as 'saving American jobs' (Bown 2021).[8]

In another example, regarding domestically popular subsidies to their respective airline industries, it took the EU and US 16 years and two WTO AB decisions (one against each side) before agreeing to tariff suspensions (not elimination) while negotiating a mutually agreeable permanent solution by 2027 (European Commission 2021b). Neither side wanted, nor could ill-afford, a continued battle over airline subsidies. The domestic political costs of radically changing practices were too high, but so were the costs of allowing tariff relations to remain in place. Thus, both sides accepted a bilateral agreement which violates the very rules they seek to uphold; not a strong basis on which to propose WTO reforms.

WTO reform

Every major development in the WTO has begun with the transatlantic partners first reaching an understanding, thus 'setting the parameters for the rest of the bargains' (Hoekman et al. 2021: 28). Both parties now resolve to stand together to protect our businesses and workers from unfair trade practices, in particular those posed by non-market economies that are undermining the world trading system. … We intend to seek to update the WTO rulebook with more effective disciplines on industrial subsidies, unfair behaviour of state-owned enterprises, and other trade and market distorting practices.

(*White House 2021b*)

A common transatlantic approach provides great leverage vis-a-vis third countries. However, there are longstanding transatlantic differences to resolve, with consequences for the WTO and the world trading system.

Both agree that China's accession agreement to the WTO was inadequate in addressing state subsidies (Bown 2019: 25, ftn. 80). The US, with few state-owned enterprises (SOEs) or enterprises with state investments, wants to force changes in China's SOEs (cf. Tai 2022). Under Trump, the US classified all Chinese SOEs as subsidizing bodies, capable of assisting other firms, thus allowing for the imposition of countervailing duties on their products. The US House and Senate passed separate competition bills in 2020 and 2021, each with trade sections requiring changes to all aspects of financial, trade and investment relations with China. Though the sections proved irreconcilable, they manifest a deep and widespread hostility to China. Members of both parties have also vowed to re-attempt passage. While critical of China, the EU argues that it is not state ownership per se, but only unfair and illegal subsidies that should be addressed.

There is broad-based domestic American scepticism about the WTO in general, and the US has longstanding concerns with AB rulings on safeguards and 'zeroing' (America's peculiar way of calculating anti-dumping duties by counting products whose values exceed costs in the US as 'zero', rather than balancing those against products within the same sector that are dumped). Both the Bush and Obama administrations showed their dissatisfaction with the WTO AB decisions (considered too judicial, too expansive in scope, and insufficiently deferential to domestic investigations) by refusing to support reappointment of the American members of the AB in both 2007 and 2011; in 2016, the Obama administration blocked other reappointments, while President Trump blocked both reappointments and new members, bringing the WTO's AB to a standstill in December 2020. America's objections have thus been consistent across administrations, and are supported by industry domestically.[9]

The EU shares some American concerns about process, such as ensuring that arbitrators only rule on the issue at hand, that previous cases are not seen as precedents, and that all rulings are made within stipulated time frames (European Commission 2021a: Annex). However, the EU strongly believes you need the WTO's AB, 'in a geopolitical world … [you] … can't have a rules-based system without a functioning dispute system' (Garcia-Bercero 2022a). To this effect, in 2020, the EU led 17 WTO members in setting up an interim arrangement for appeals, the Multi-Party Interim Appeal Arbitration Arrangement (MPIA). While technically an arbitration procedure under Article 25, where the parties only need to notify the WTO DSB of their intention to arbitrate, the signatories agreed to abide by MPIA panel decisions (WTO 2020). The US has shown no interest in joining.

The MPIA is a temporary arrangement, and long-term solutions are needed. Jennifer Hillman (2019), a previous AB member, presented a three-pronged solution focused on the 'Walker principles' (set forth by New Zealand's WTO ambassador). This entails a strict reading of the AB's remit (including the time it takes to issue decisions), a more deferential standard of review for antidumping investigations, limiting the scope of decisions to only the narrow band of issues raised by plaintiffs in order to avoid prescriptive or advisory rulings, and taking 'previous AB or panel reports into account only to the extent they are relevant and not as precedent' (Hillman 2019). These would appear to address longstanding American concerns, and are compatible with the EU's position (European Commission 2021a: Annex), but have been unpersuasive on the Trump and Biden administrations (Lester 2020).

The US wants more changes to both process (a more flexible, less judicial, and institutionalized body) and substance (such as zeroing and transparency notifications) but has remained vague on details, leaving others to complain about 'no engagement', 'no discussion whatsoever' (Aarup 2021). The EU in turn acknowledges that there cannot be just one large procedural and substantive WTO reform (Garcia-Bercero 2022b), but that incrementalism will reign. To break the impasse, and build on transatlantic coordination, Reinsch and Caporal (2021: 20ff) propose a compact of developed democracies willing to abide by general principles of the rule-of-law and transparent market-based economic principles as a supplement to the WTO, and a reference point for future reforms of the latter.

The 2022 WTO Ministerial meeting agreed only to attempt a resolution to the dispute settlement system by 2024. All discussions about reconstituting the WTO's dispute settlement system raises serious questions about what type of institutionalized, rules-based multilateral trading system the US can support, and on what the transatlantic partners can agree. The US remains more comfortable with power politics and the weaponization of trade than does the EU. The EU would support more transparency and flexibility, but details of what the US would (or could) accept at the WTO remains unclear, not least because of Congressional scepticism. Any proposal that can be perceived as 'weak' on China, while rejecting 'zeroing', will face insurmountable objections in the US House and Senate, where scepticism of multilateral institutions is widespread and runs deep. However, this could be overcome if the transatlantic partners can agree on definitions of digital services and SOEs, the parameters for permissible subsidies (the EU and US are now subsidising chips production), and an incremental and narrow resurrection of the AB. This may also be sufficient to attract other key players, including China, India, South Africa and other third parties (Hoekman et al. 2021).

Conclusion

This chapter has discussed how transatlantic cooperation and coordination is possible on labour policy, trade defence instruments and WTO reforms. It highlighted domestic developments, especially in the US, where trade scepticism, fear of job losses, outsourcing, the rise of China, perceptions of unfair trade and protectionist preferences and policies permeate large sections of the population and elected officials across the political spectrum. The target is primarily China, but these developments affect relations with all partners, including the EU. European public opinion and policy makers also expect trade policy to defend labour and sustainability, but prefer multilateralism, and have only lately accepted that the EU may have to act alone. The Commission has also developed instruments to employ a strategic use of trade, balancing normative goals with material interests.

Cooperation on promoting enforceable labour rights appears likely, with similar legislative developments across the Atlantic – notwithstanding different domestic motivations. On trade defence instruments, the EU has begun catching up to America's tool kit, thus enabling coordination against third parties (read China). The US administration and Congress also view the TTC as an avenue of transatlantic balancing against China; a description the EU rejects, even though most of the discussions in at least seven of the ten working groups deal with issues and developments directly or indirectly addressing Chinese policies. However, on WTO reform the transatlantic partners' ability to address common concerns must start with reconciling bilateral differences. The US and the EU must – at minimum – agree to treat each other as trusted partners whose products are not a threat to national security, and to not weaponize trade against one another. Language to this effect was inserted by the EU in the May 2022 TTC draft conclusions, before the US insisted on its removal. Differing domestic preferences on multilateralism, and an EU far less comfortable with power politics than the US, may continue to hinder coordination on significant WTO reforms for the foreseeable future.

Acknowledgment

This work was supported by the Spanish Ministry for Science and Innovation under Grant PID2020-116443GB-I00, "The Emergence of European Sovereignty in a World of Systemic Rivalry: Strategic Autonomy and Permissive Consensus", EUSOV.

Notes

1 See https://policy.trade.ec.europa.eu/eu-trade-relationships-country-and-region/countries-and-regions/united-states_en for latest figures.
2 This chapter focuses on EU-US relations, while recognizing that Canadian, Mexican and British interests are important to transatlantic relations.
3 These restrictions on public contracts affect allies, especially European firms, since firms from non-market economies are already prevented from bidding.
4 Find legislative updates here: https://www.europarl.europa.eu/thinktank/en/document/EPRS_BRI(2022)729299
5 Japan and South Korea also assert that the EV content requirements violate WTO rules.
6 Unlike the deals the US agreed with South Korea and Brazil, European firms can export steel above the set quotas, and US importers retain exemptions for numerous classifications of steel not produced domestically, thus potentially providing EU firms market access at levels equal to those achieved in 2018.
7 Separately, the administration also refused to remove EU steel and aluminium from its list of imports threatening national security.

8 The EU also imposed several anti-dumping duties on Chinese (and Indonesian and Indian), steel and aluminium products, but has no TRQ agreements. The EU has rejected other WTO rulings, for example on refusing importation of American beef. 'DISPUTE DS26 European Communities – Measures Concerning Meat and Meat Products (Hormones)' World Trade Organization, Appellate Body ruling (November 2011).

9 In a small show of good faith, the US adopted a 2021 panel ruling that it had imposed illegal anti-subsidy duties on Spanish olives, rather than appealing to the defunct AB.

References

Aarup, S. 2021. 'All talk and no walk': America ain't back at the WTO, Politico, 23 November.

Bade, G., 2021. Lay out the strategy': Corporate America grows impatient on Biden's China trade review. *Politico*, [online] Available from: https://www.politico.com/news/2021/08/16/corporate-america-biden-china-trade-504889 [Accessed 5 February 2022].

Bacchus, J., 2022. Biden and Trade at One Year: The Reign of Polite Protectionism. CATO Policy Analysis 926.

Bauer, M., 2016. *Manufacturing Discontent: The Rise to Power of Anti-TTIP Groups*. Brussels: European Centre for International Political Economy. [online] Available from: http://ecipe.org/publications/manufacturing-discontent-the-rise-to-power-of-anti-ttip-groups/ [Accessed 4 May 2019].

BBC, 2018. Donald Trump: European Union is a foe on trade. [online] Available from: https://www.bbc.com/news/world-us-canada-44837311 [Accessed 2 July 2022].

Bown, C., 2019. The 2018 trade war and the end of dispute settlement as we knew it. In: M. Crowley (ed.), *Trade War: The Clash of Economic Systems Threatening Global Prosperity*. Brussels: CEPR Press, pp. 21–32.

Bown, C., 2021. The false allure of managed trade. *Wall Street Journal*, [online] Available from: https://www.wsj.com/articles/the-false-allure-of-managed-trade-11639666704 [Accessed 19 March 2022].

Bown, C. and Russ, K., 2021. Biden and Europe remove Trump's steel and aluminum tariffs, but it's not free trade. *PIIE*, 11 November, Available from: https://www.piie.com/blogs/trade-and-investment-policy-watch/biden-and-europe-remove-trumps-steel-and-aluminum-tariffs [Accessed 19 March 2022].

Brooks, S., 2022. Public and elite opinion relating to the EU-US relationship, in D. Abelson and S. Brooks (eds.), *Transatlantic Relations, Challenges and Resilience*, Various: Routledge, pp. 223–238.

Cass, O., 2022. Republicans are shifting on free markets and China. *Financial Times*, p. 19. 21 March.

Dür, A., 2010. *Protection for Exporters. Power and Discrimination in Transatlantic Trade Relations 1930-2010*. Ithaca: Cornell University Press.

Eliasson, L.J. and Garcia-Duran, P., 2018. TTIP Negotiations: Interest groups, anti-TTIP civil society campaigns and public opinion. *Journal of Transatlantic Studies*, 16 (2): 101–116.

Eliasson, L.J. and Garcia-Duran, P., 2019. *Civil Society, Rhetoric of Resistance, and Transatlantic Trade*. Cham and New York: Palgrave.

European Commission, 2020. Joint communication to the European Parliament, The European council, and the council. A new EU-US agenda for global change, Brussels, JOIN (2020) 22 final.

European Commission, 2021a. Trade policy review – An Open, Sustainable and Assertive Trade Policy, COM (2021) 66 final.

European Commission, 2021b. Understanding on a cooperative framework for Large Civil Aircraft. Available from: https://trade.ec.europa.eu/doclib/docs/2021/june/tradoc_159645.pdf [Accessed 2 July 2022].

European Commission, 2021c. Proposal for a Regulation of the European Parliament and of the Council on the protection of the Union and its Member States, COM (2021) 775, final.
European Commission, 2021d. Report from the Commission to the European Parliament, the Council, The European Economic and Social Committee, and the committee of the Regions on the Implementation and Enforcement of EU Trade Agreements, COM (2021) 654, final.
European Commission, 2022. Effectively Banning Products Produced, Extracted or Harvested with Forced Labour, COM (2022)3862254, Published Initiatives.
European Parliament, 1999. Hearing of M. Pascal Lamy. 2 September. Available from: https://www.europarl.europa.eu/press/sdp/newsrp/en/1999/n990902.htm [Accessed 2 July 2022].
Farrell, H. and Newman, A., 2019. *Of Privacy and Power The Transatlantic Struggle over Freedom and Security*. Princeton: Princeton University Press.
Garcia-Bercero, I., 2022a. Keynote Speech. *Between Interests and Values: The Future of EU Trade Policy*. University of Amsterdam, 13 May.
Garcia-Bercero, I., 2022b. *Transatlantic Perspectives on WTO Reform: Challenges and Opportunities for MC12*. Globe Webinar, Leuven University, 2 June.
German Marshall Fund, 2021. Transatlantic trends 2021. [online] Available from: https://www.gmfus.org/news/transatlantic-trends-2021 [Accessed 9 June 2022].
GSA Administration, 2022. *Federal Acquisition Regulation: Amendments to the FAR Buy American Act Requirements*. Washington DC: Federal Register, 87 FR 12780.
Hillman, J., 2019. *A Reset of the World Trade Organization's Appellate Body*. New York: Council On Foreign Relations. [Online] Available from: https://www.cfr.org/report/reset-world-trade-organizations-appellate-body#:~:text=The%20Trump%20administration%20has%20destroyed,get%20it%20back%20on%20track [Accessed 7 June 2021].
Hoekman, B., Xinquan, T., and Wolfe, R., 2021. *Rebooting Multilateral Trade Cooperation: Perspectives from China and Europe major powers*. Brussels: CEPR Press.
Inside US Trade, 2022. EU ambassador: Trade and Technology Council aided joint response to Russia. 14 March.
Johnson, D.C., 2018. *The Wealth of a Nation*. Oxford: Oxford University Press.
Lester, S., 2020. *Can Interim Appeal Arbitration Preserve the WTO Dispute System?*. [online] CATO, Available from: https://www.cato.org/free-trade-bulletin/can-interim-appeal-arbitration-preserve-wto-dispute-system#trump-administrations-destruction [Accessed 8 July 2022].
Lovely, M., 2022. Sanctions, Russia's war, and the future of trade. *Trade Winds Webinar*, PIIE, 20 April.
Manuk, I., 2022. *Court Ruling Questions Tariff Process, But Procedural Flaws Remain in Place.* [online] Council on Foreign Relations, Available from: https://www.cfr.org/blog/court-ruling-questions-tariff-process-procedural-flaws-remain-place?utm_medium=social_share&utm_source=tw [Accessed 7 June 2022].
Moens, B., 2022. Free traders fear EU risks going over to the dark side with new superpower. *Politico*. [online] 9 February. Available from: https://www.politico.eu/article/free-traders-fear-eu-dark-side-new-superpower/ [Accessed 6 June 2022].
Morgan, S. L., 2018. Status Threat, Material Interests, and the 2016 Presidential Vote. *Socius: Sociological Research for a Dynamic World*. [online] 4 Available from: 10.1177/2378023118788217 [Accessed 8 June 2022].
Mutz, D., 2018. Status threat, not economic hardship, explains the 2016 presidential vote. *PNAS*, 115(19). [online] Available at from: 10.1073/pnas.1718155115 [Accessed 8 June 2022].
Mutz, D., 2021. *Winners and Losers: The Psychology of Foreign Trade*. Princeton: Princeton University Press.
Orbie, J. & De Ville, F. 2020. Impact of the COVID-19 Crisis on EU Trade Policy: Our Five Cents to the Debate, United Nations University Institute of Comparative Regional Integration Studies.

Pelkmans, J. and de Brito, C., 2015. *Transatlantic MRAs: Lessons for TTIP?* Centre for European Policy Studies, Special Report no. 101.

Pew Research Center, 2013. The Public Supports a Transatlantic Trade Pact – For Now. *Pew Research Center Global Attitudes & Trends.* Washington DC. 19 February. Available from: http://www.pewglobal.org/2013/02/19/the-public-supports-a-transatlantic-trade-pact-for-now-2/ [Accessed 8 June 2022].

Posen, A. 2021. The price of nostalgia. America's self-defeating economic retreat. *Foreign Affairs* 100(3): 28-48.

Reinsch, W., 2022. Trade Guys. [podcast] 20 April. Available from: https://www.csis.org/podcasts/trade-guys [Accessed 8 May 2022].

Reinsch, W. and Caporal, J., 2021. Toward a New Global Trade Framework. CSIS. [online] Available from: https://csis-website-prod.s3.amazonaws.com/s3fs-public/publication/210202_Trade_Commission_Toward_New_Global_Trade_Framework.pdf [Accessed 18 June 2022].

Riddervold, M. and Newsome, A. 2022. Introduction: Out with the old in with the new? Explaining changing EU-US Relations. *Politics and Governance*, 10(2): 128–133.

Ruggie, J., 1982. International regimes, transactions, and change: Embedded liberalism in the postwar economic order. *International Organization*, 36(2): 379–415.

Tai, K., 2022. Testimony of Ambassador Katherine Tai before the Senate Finance Committee hearing on the President's 2022 Trade Policy Agenda. 31 March.

United States Trade Representative, 2022. The 2022 Trade Policy Agenda and 2021 Annual Report of the President of the United States on the Trade Agreements Program. March.

Vogt, J. S., 2015. The evolution of labor rights and trade – A transatlantic comparison and lessons for the transatlantic trade and investment partnership. *Journal of International Economic Law*, 18 (4): 827–860.

Wells, D., 2007. Best practice' in the regulation of international labor standards: Lessons of the U.S.-Cambodia Textile Agreement. *Comparative Labor Law and Policy Journal*, 27 (3): 357–376.

White House, 2021a. EU-US trade and technology council, inaugural joint statement, 29 September.

White House, 2021b. U.S.-EU summit statement, 15 June.

White House, 2022a. Executive order on America's Supply Chains; A Year of action and progress. Report, February.

White House, 2022b. U.S.-EU joint statement of the trade and technology council, 16 May.

World Trade Organisation, 2020. Multi-party interim appeal arbitration arrangement pursuant to Article 25 of the DSU, addendum to statement on a mechanism for developing, documenting and sharing practices and procedures in the conduct of WTO Disputes, JOB/DSB/1/Add.12, 30 April.

Young, A., 2017. *The New Politics of Trade Lessons from TTIP.* Newcastle: Agenda Publishing.

Younis, M., 2021. Sharply Fewer in U.S. View Foreign Trade as Opportunity. *Gallup News*, [online] 31 March. Available from: https://news.gallup.com/poll/342419/sharply-fewer-view-foreign-trade-opportunity.aspx

14

TAKING BACK CONTROL

The Political Economy of Investment Screening in the US and EU

Michelle Egan

AMERICAN UNIVERSITY, WASHINGTON DC, USA

Introduction

When Democratic Senator Sherrod Brown complained that 'foreign investments should lead to good-paying jobs in Chillicothe and Chardon – not huge payouts for the Chinese government', he was seeking to expand foreign investment screening beyond its national security focus to include the impact on American jobs and growth. While seeking bipartisan support for the proposed Foreign Investment Review Act, such comments reflect a broader global trend in which investment screening mechanisms have proliferated over the past decade. While foreign direct investment (FDI) was once an indicator of economic openness and a driver of economic integration, states have more recently sought greater control over the entry of FDI into specific sensitive sectors in their domestic economies (OECD 2021). The rise of state-owned enterprises and sovereign wealth funds has led to increased pressure to regulate the effects of financial 'market entry' through greater scrutiny of the origin and scope of such investment and the economic and national security implications of foreign ownership (Cuervo-Cazurra, Grosman, and Mengginson 2022). While some of this is tied to efforts at promoting reshoring, reducing dependence on global supply chains, and fostering domestic employment, there has also been a concern about the impact of foreign investment on technology transfer, given the growth of international production and the diffusion of new technologies, production methods and technical skills beyond domestic borders.

On both sides of the Atlantic, the US and EU are ramping up investment screening efforts as they adjust to this changing economic and security environment and to rising economic competition. The EU and US have adopted new and enhanced screening mechanisms to address foreign investment transactions, reflecting a trend in the global political economy that widens the scope regulatory scrutiny beyond national security provisions (Gertz 2021). Such FDI tends to be either cross-border mergers and

DOI: 10.4324/9781003283911-17

acquisitions, where the investor acquires companies and assets leading to the transfer of ownership, or greenfield investment, where the investor creates new subsidiaries from scratch, building its operations in a different host which is the more expensive foreign investment strategy as it relies on resources and capabilities of the country of origin. Much FDI is dependent on the ease of doing business, including existing infrastructure and legal and regulatory frameworks that influence investor preferences (Chaisse and Burnay 2022; Olivieri 2021). This led the US and EU to be the site of significant inward investment due to their favorable business climate. What is striking is the size of US-EU FDI flows in the global economy even taking covid into account, the business environment is one of deep connections. FDI into the US surged between 2020 and 2021 mainly reflecting a 378.4 billion increase from Europe which invested 3,186 billion into the US in 2021. This dwarfed investment from Latin America (239 billion) and Asia-Pacific (971 billion) (BEA 2021). For Europe, FDI declined in 2020, with a significant drop in Chinese FDI in the EU-27 and the US to EUR 6.5 billion in 2020, while overall FDI into the EU was €8,589 billion at the end of 2020.

Yet as new and tightened investment screening mechanisms emerge, much of the existing literature is in international investment law, focusing on international arbitration (Chaisse and Burnay 2022), whereas the more recent international political economy (IPE) literature on investment screening has focused on the increased securitization of investment (Bauerle Danzmann 2021), the institutional development of investment screening mechanisms (Chan and Meunier 2021; Olivieri 2019/2020) and the surge of restrictions on investment driven by the geopolitical pressures stemming from increased global power competition (Defraigne 2017; Le Corre and Sepulchre 2016). The purpose of this chapter is to build on the IPE literature to analyze the institutional development and current structure of investment regimes in the US and EU, the ways in which these regimes respond to global economic crises, and the ability of these regimes to foster transatlantic cooperation in the context of rising global and strategic competition. To do so, this chapter proceeds as follows. It first provides a brief history of US and European investment regimes and highlights the sectoral and geographic scope of FDI in the US and EU. It then compares investment policy responses to the eurozone crisis and the COVID-19 pandemic, both of which affected global FDI flows. The fourth section of this chapter examines whether, given the different origins and institutional structures of their respective investment regimes, there is an opportunity for the US and EU to further align investment policies in order to, first, address their common interests of promoting health and safety objectives, human rights, and environmental protection (Esplugues Mota 2018:10; Executive Order 11858 1975), and second, to balance China's increasingly prominent role as a global investor with these interests and with the broader economic and strategic concerns prompted by China's growth.

While there exists no international investment framework that addresses the relationship between FDI and national security issues, both the US and the EU have developed investment policy strategies that expand their right to regulate FDI based on its potential impact on national security, public health, intellectual property, and supply chain diversification and resilience. These new offensive strategies contrast with previously defensive investment policy strategies whereby states were forced to respond to foreign investors who possessed broad investment rights, including the right to pursue arbitration. This chapter therefore contributes to scholarship on FDI that examines the shift from *ex post* protection of investments to *ex ante* scrutiny of foreign investment.

History and development of screening mechanisms

The United States

The Committee on Foreign Investment in the United States (CFIUS) is one of the oldest and most active national-level bodies that screen foreign investment. Established in 1975 by executive order, it operated in 'relative obscurity' for several decades (CRS 2020).[1] CFIUS is an interagency committee comprising fifteen departments and agencies that are authorized to review transactions. Under the 2007 Foreign Investment and National Security Act (FINSA) and the 2017 Foreign Investment Risk Review Modernization Act (FIRRMA), the scope, mandate, and obligations of the Committee have broadened significantly, especially regarding its authority to approve or reject certain FDI transactions.[2]

CFIUS was relatively inactive with few meetings in the first five years of its operations, and in most cases, filing with CFIUS was voluntary, so it was considered a legal provision to avoid subsequent problems of potential disinvestment. It targeted OPEC members due to concerns about investment in US portfolio assets (CRS 2020). It garnered political attention again with increased scrutiny in the 1980s by investigating several foreign investment transactions particularly by Japanese firms including the proposed sale of Fairchild Semiconductor to Fujitsu. This led to legislative action with the Exon-Florio amendment to the Defense Production Act, which specified the basic review process of foreign investments where there were national security concerns.[3] The statute and current revisions provided the President with the authority to block proposed or pending foreign mergers, acquisitions, or takeovers on national security grounds. The President delegated the administration of the Exon-Florio provision to CFIUS, which broadened their role in US investment policy with recommendations to approve or block a proposed transaction (CRS 2020). The pressure for increased scrutiny was amplified by concerns about the takeover of US ports by Dubai Ports World – a Dubai state-controlled enterprise – to acquire six US ports in 2006 that led to the prospect that an approved transaction could be revisited when previously voluntary compliance had been based on any approval being exempt from any future reviews or actions.

FINSA expanded agency membership along with designating a lead agency to review the transaction and determine the scope of national security concerns by allowing U.S. regulators to weigh the risks of investment by state-controlled entities (Rose 2015). FINSA provided for executive agency accountability to Congress, as well as link matters of trade and security, while also seeking to provide more predictability for firms given that there was no statute of limitations on its oversight and scrutiny (Rose 2015). In 2018, the Foreign Investment Risk Review Modernization Act (FIRRMA) passed with almost unanimous agreement to broaden those transactions subject to review by CFIUS to include real estate and critical infrastructure. It further 'allows CFIUS to discriminate among foreign investors by country of origin', ostensibly to appease bipartisan concerns over China's increased investment the US technology sector (CRS 2020: 15–16). Under the Act, any 'non-controlling' foreign investments in critical technologies or infrastructures or in businesses that collect personal data from U.S. citizens are also subject to review (CRS 2020: 16). FIRRMA has recently expanded further to include new objectives such as sustainability (Olivieri 2021). The broadening of scrutiny under FIRRMA led CFIUS to recommend to President Trump to block the acquisition of *Lattice Semiconductor* by a U.S. American company that was viewed as under the control of the Chinese government (see Olivieri 2021: 78). However, CFIUS is increasingly identifying and investigating non-notified transactions with 117 transactions subject to further consideration based on referrals from other agencies, commercial databases, firm complaints, and congressional requests in 2020 alone (Wang 2021).

In 2021, under the Biden Administration, there were 272 notices, only 10% had some mitigation measures and no presidential actions were taken on any transaction. However, there has been a sharp rise in non-notified transactions that CFIUS has proactively identified for further review.

European Union

The United States is not the only country to have established a foreign direct investment screening mechanism for security purposes. Europe has also expressed concerns about FDI which reflects a shift from a more defensive trade policy that often-addressed European economic competitiveness in relation to its trade and investment partners. In 1968 Jean Jacques Servan-Screiber in *The American Challenge* compared the US' seemingly unassailable economic lead in terms of technology and investment with Europe's lack of competitiveness and productivity. Though attention shifted to the influx of Japanese investment in the 1970s and 1980s which increased in the financial and manufacturing sector,[4] Japanese FDI activity accelerated in part due to the Single European Market. In the 1980s, despite various barriers to limit Japanese imports and the imposition of voluntary export restraints, Europe maintained a trade imbalance with Japan that mirrored an imbalance in FDI. Japanese FDI in Europe was ten times greater than European FDI in Japan. This has shifted again as Phillipe le Corre and Alain Sepulchre in *China's Offensive in Europe* expressed concern about the advancement of Chinese investment through state-owned enterprises, which has led to the acquisition of infrastructure, manufacturing and technology firms in Europe and generated new concerns against a different foreign competitor (Le Corre and Sepulchre 2016). In response, the European Union has opted for greater scrutiny with European Commission Executive Vice President Valdis Dombrovskis stating that 'the EU is and will remain open to foreign investment. But this openness is not unconditional' (EC 2021a).

While investment screening in the EU remains the prerogative of individual member states with no European provision to suspend domestic FDI, the EU-wide adoption of Regulation 452/2019, which became operational in October 2020, provides a minimum standard for those states that have had or plan to adopt investment screening mechanisms (EC 2021b; see table below).[5] It further allows all EU member states and the European Commission to scrutinize potential FDI transactions in any other member state, regardless of whether the latter state has a screening framework in place (EC 2021c: 12–13). Given the institutional structure of the EU, member states responded to the proposed legislation based on their individual interests. Regarding Chinese FDI, Germany expressed concerned about public security, given a spate of investment in its technology sector, while the Bulgarian response was more muted given that Chinese investment there focused on low-risk real estate transactions. While the Regulation does not in itself require EU states to introduce investment-screening mechanisms, the proposed FDI screening proposals were endorsed by Germany, France, and Italy, which had all experienced a surge in Chinese FDI (Chan and Meunier 2021). They were opposed by Greece and Portugal, in part due to their dependence on Chinese investment during the euro crisis, even though they rank behind many other European countries for Chinese FDI (Chan and Meunier 2021). Malta, Cyprus, Ireland, and Luxembourg which have served as intermediaries for FDI or offered low corporate tax rates and other benefits were concerned that any screening mechanism would impact their attractiveness for FDI (Chan and Meunier 2021; Meunier 2019).

The legislation provides for cooperation between member states, and between national entities and the European Commission, which is assigned a complimentary role to national screening mechanisms to assess potential risks and provide evaluations for member states (Olivieri 2021: 102). The Commission's role does not supplant that of national screening mechanisms in place but rather provides a supporting role as well as provide other member states who feel that their national security or public order may be affected by a FDI in another member state to give due consideration to expressed concerns. So far, in its first annual report under the new legislation, in 2020, seven Member States reviewed 1,793 investment dossiers, with out of which 359 foreign investments undergoing formal screening. Of those 359 screened transactions, only 2% were blocked and 12% were authorized with conditions (EC 2021b). Despite a low number of screened cases, and some states without a national investment regime, there are concerns about the extra layer of notification under the regulation, and the extent to which other member states are impacted by specific transactions. Even then, concerns remain about the judicial reviewability of blocking decisions by the member state executive or screening bodies given that most are cleared at national level as broad discretionary powers can have political consequences as precedent is still scarce.

Although the US and EU share many regulatory objectives in investment screening, they have structured their regulatory oversight differently. While the United States, through its Committee on Foreign Investment in the United States (CFIUS), presents the most comprehensive screening program, the EU did not follow the US model in terms of institutional structure – despite relying heavily on US expertise and knowledge – through information sharing and parliamentary testimony about the design and operation of the American investment regime. Consequently, the US approach is built around horizontal interagency cooperation, while the EU model is one of decentralized enforcement with the establishment of national screening and notification to the European level.

While there are some commonalities as most investment mechanisms regimes apply to defense industries, critical infrastructure, information technology, data, and strategic industries, as well as new and emerging technologies coupled with trigger mechanisms to review investment screening, the degree of power and oversight between the EU and US varies (Evenett 2021). In the US, CFIUS can conditionally block a foreign investment and has also engaged in post-review processes. In the EU, the new legislation does not enable the European Commission to screen and block investment coming into its member states. This difference is reflected in the Lisbon Treaty which formally shifts FDI competences to the EU level, but as member states were reluctant to transfer competences, some key decisions on investment were retained by member states.

FDI governance and restricting investment during crises

Crises such as the eurozone crisis and the COVID-19 pandemic have created fears that foreign investors – notably Chinese investors – will engage in distressed asset purchases, taking advantage of depressed equity values to go on a spending spree.[6] While the financial crisis in 2008–2009 was about alleviating debt leading to the sale of specific assets, the pandemic has led to more restrictive investment practices that are tied to maintaining the resilience of global supply chains. This raises a key question as to why governments are choosing a different path in the face of the deep economic disruption during the pandemic as distinct from the earlier financial crisis.

During the eurozone crisis, there were significant pressures on governments due to the imposition of austerity measures in Greece which then spread to Ireland, Portugal, Italy, and Hungary. The high-profile cases of Chinese companies Costco Shipping Ports and China Merchant Port Holdings buying Piraeus in Greece along with concerns about the prospect of a significant Chinese presence in Europe (Le Corre 2018). While Chinese investment was heavily concentrated in three countries – UK, Germany, and France – it has increased in Southern Europe in the aftermath of the financial crisis, and then expanded to Central and Eastern Europe as part of the BRI (Hanemann et al. 2021; Meunier 2019). Such investment covers all sectors with no discernable pattern as China has sought to diversify risk (Johnson 2018; Meunier 2019).

Despite a few exceptions, there is not much attention given to the European policy response prior to the introduction of the investment screening legislation. There was concern about national investment practices that were in breach of EU obligations on the right of establishment and free movement of capital due to their provisions of 'golden shares' by the government to protect privatized assets. Previously, the European Commission had sought to distinguish between discriminatory and non-discriminatory measures on investment and expressed concerns that national laws that sought to protect strategic and financially vulnerable assets against foreign takeovers inhibited investment. After CJEU legal judgments against such practices (Olivieri 2021), the European Commission focused on their effects on the internal market rather than on overseas investors. Hence, the Commission pushed a more liberalization approach so that Chinese foreign direct investment exploded in the wake of the financial crisis from 2008 to 2016 to 37.3 billion euros without much European oversight (Deni and Schatzer 2020).[7] However, European attitudes toward China have hardened significantly since the eurozone crisis being labelled a 'systemic rival' in 2019. This is driven by Chinese investment that has been criticized for its predatory efforts to undercut rivals as well as concerns about forced technology transfers (Deni and Schatzer 2020).

While many governments aggressively courted new investments in the wake of the financial crisis, the pandemic has led to a reevaluation of direct investment with a focus on ensuring domestic supplies with changes enacted to investment screening for health services and medical goods (Gertz 2021). While not traditionally strategic, these sectors have become so during the pandemic, and the protection of healthcare industries due to concerns about supply chains has gained traction (Bauerle Danzman and Meunier 2021). According to the Organisation for Economic Co-operation and Development (OECD), the current tightening of controls over inward investment in response to the severe economic disruption differs from the financial crisis even though company valuations have also plunged amid economic uncertainty (OECD 2020). The United States' dependency on foreign supply chains for personal protective equipment and pharmaceuticals has become of increased concern for regulators involved in investment screening. While increased political pressures have generated attention toward domestic investment into the United States, investment can be used as a foreign policy tool so that legal restrictions on outward investment through executive order can also halt any economic activity in sectors of foreign governments.[8]

The European Commission issued guidelines that explicitly stated that member states are empowered to address vulnerabilities and impose measures to protect their national interests. The Commission emphasized that the 'current health crisis [should] not result in a sell-off of Europe's business and industrial actors' (EC 2020: 1). In response, Germany, Italy, Austria, and Spain have introduced or amended legislation that further tighten rules on inward FDI control in 2020 and 2021 (EC 2021b). The rationale for FDI restrictions have widened in scope during the pandemic as national government powers have expanded to include new sectors such as biotechnology and therapeutics and other critical technologies. Yet there are continued problems due to the lack of harmonization of screening rules across Europe. But unlike the previous financial crisis, there has been a concerted recognition of the need to address the risk of a fire sale in the immediate aftermath of the pandemic. The European Commission has offset some of the necessary investment needed to support a recovery by a massive program of financing through loans and grants known as Next Gen. Yet the pandemic has also illustrated the extent to which investment screening is evolving to a more regulatory tool that reflects a shift away from globalization toward exercising more sovereign oversight over the economy (OECD 2020; Kowalski 2020: 141).

Transatlantic cooperation on investment screening

As a global rise in protectionist FDI continues across different sectors along with the lowering of thresholds for investment that require prior approval, Europe and the

United States are at the forefront of efforts at regulating the global economy on a topic that has not been emphasized in transatlantic relations. While transatlantic attention has focused principally on investment screening mechanisms toward China due to security and competition concerns, the weaponization of investment in Russia due to threats of expropriation of foreign assets and currency holdings through nationalization threats shifts attention back to investment treaties and arbitration. Even if circumstances change politically, Russian action invites legal claims through international investment agreements and discourages future investment whereas Chinese investment has generated divisions in Europe as well as a Global Gateway fund to compete with China's Belt and Road Initiative (BRI). Cooperation between the US and EU is critical to stave off risky foreign direct investments and economic distortions. Due to the absence of international rules on investment screening, they could work together to avoid 'forum shopping' among foreign investors and share information especially given that FIRMMA in the US provides an opportunity to provide preferential status for those with reliable screening mechanisms.

Despite heightened tensions and trade frictions driven by domestic protectionist measures as well as concerns about the viability of the multilateral trading system, there are new opportunities for the US and EU to coordinate on key global technology, economic, and trade issues through the newly launched Transatlantic Trade and Technology Council (TTC). The TTC began in November 2020 as a diplomatic forum to deal with increased geoeconomics concerns rather than a broader trade deal that focuses on regulatory cooperation. It has created new mechanisms to put key issues on the agenda (EC 2021a; USTR n.d.). While TTC has been preceded by prior efforts at transatlantic cooperation, including the 1995 New Transatlantic Agenda (NTA), which was followed by the 1998 Transatlantic Economic Partnership (TEP), the 2007 Transatlantic Economic Council (TEC), and most recently, the Transatlantic Trade and Investment Partnership (TTIP), the goal of trade and investment cooperation has a much clearer strategic intent. Europeans and Americans want to set global standards in high technology sectors while also ensuring that they protect their national security and industrial interests against pressures from non-market economies (Leonard and Shapiro 2020).

Of the ten working groups, the TTC has a specific working group on investment screening that brings together different agencies on both sides of the Atlantic. As noted earlier, investment screening mechanisms have become more salient reflecting increased concerns in the US that great power rivals such as China and Russia are weaponizing rising levels of economic interdependence potentially redefining international norms (Bauerle Danzmann 2021). Europe has shifted its perspective, developing more trade strategies to deal with the array of challenges presented by China. Europe also faces the weaponization of gas supplies, and both the US and EU agree on the need for energy diversification. European states are heavily dependent on Russian gas as they move away from coal and fossil fuels. That said, US oil and gas exports to Europe could be increased, coupled with greater attention toward investment in transatlantic energy and infrastructure through clean technology and renewables would diminish dependence on Russia. Coordination on investment screening would also be beneficial in new energy technologies and data protection not just focusing on foreign acquisitions to reflect changing issues in energy security (Rajavuori and Huhta 2020). This would also complement efforts at investment screening toward China given the need to address economic coercion through export restrictions, forced technology transfer and other measures that has expedited the need for transatlantic cooperation. The US and EU need to compete more effectively with China's BRI, as well as develop a consistency in responses to Chinese FDI. This might include their respective Build Back Better and Connectivity Strategy as well as their long tradition of technical assistance and support for standards infrastructure in third countries to counter China's influence. This means focusing on the broader bilateral economic and technology relationship as this underpins much of the concerns about long-term competition with China due to the shift in FDI to critical technologies, infrastructure, and non-controlling investments through venture capital and other financial instruments (Meunier 2019).

As European views of China have deteriorated because of targeted sanctions and human rights concerns, it has provided an opportunity for greater transatlantic cooperation and coordination which has been missing in recent years. Europe has noted that China is a 'systemic rival' seeking to address some of their market access challenges through a Comprehensive Agreement on Investment (CAI). The lack of coordination with the US generated significant pushback from the incoming Biden Administration (Chaisse and Burnay 2022). While the CAI is now on hold (or dead), China has targeted European supply chains, and in doing so has challenged the integrity of the single market. As a result, Europe is strengthening its trade defense measures with anti-coercion measures as well as restrictions on foreign subsidies in the single market. The TTC represents an opportunity for the US and EU to foster policy coordination on investment practices, and leverage this to address a list of shared economic concerns about China. They could assess the diversity of investment structures as well as the screening processes to build mutual trust and reciprocal information after a period in which tensions were exacerbated as the US had unilaterally negotiated a Phase One trade deal with China, and the EU had announced an EU-China investment deal (Gewirtz et al. 2021). In doing so, however, the US and the EU need to maintain realistic expectations as the controversy, and even resistance, to Chinese FDI is not held by all European states.

In fact, despite a slump in FDI in Europe, Poland became one of the most significant recipients of Chinese FDI though strict Chinese capital controls on outbound investment also account for the reduced flows of foreign direct investment toward Europe (Defraigne 2017). Pandemic disruptions and political tensions have played a role in the new investment climate especially as economic sanctions toward Russia underscore the potential of secondary sanctions on Chinese investment in Russia. As Rhodium group reported, 'Supply chain safety rules, next generation antitrust policies, and new initiatives to protect personal data could all have a profound effect on Chinese companies and investors' in the US (Hanemann et al. 2021). Such actions by the Biden Administration may lead to more coordinated action with Europe given that both economies are searching for the right balance between efficiency and resilience. They should capitalize on transatlantic cooperation through cross-border financing on infrastructure, green technology, and connectivity, to enhance the competitiveness of their companies, and push for investment practices with higher standards given their market leverage.

The TTC might consider a wider and perhaps agreed upon definitions for 'critical' infrastructures, technologies, factors of production, and information, in the research, telecommunications, information technology, finance, and health sector. This would require transatlantic coordination as well as engagement with national screening mechanisms. Cooperating on investment screening in the TTC may need to consider the ways in which the US and EU justify the increasing protection of national interests, and how they define 'national security' as well as other interests such as 'essential security' or 'public policy'. However, there are stumbling blocks to greater cooperation as EU member states are responsible for review of investment along national security lines with the European Commission serving as a coordination and monitoring body. The US and EU could review the risks of global business strategies built around China and Russia. The current Biden executive order prohibiting new investment in Russia – covering any entity under US law – including foreign firms – differs from the European Union which has also opted for export controls on specific goods and technologies and sanctions. While Europe initially opted for select investment prohibitions in several sectors, it has expanded investment restrictions so there could be room for further cooperation on co-ordinated legal guidelines for future investment restrictions (Bauerle Danzmann Drezner 2021; White House 2022).

The transatlantic partners need to figure out the modalities as to how they will cooperate to ensure that the TTC generates tangible outcomes. While the focus of prior transatlantic efforts was regulatory alignment, there is a different emphasis on resilience and security due to the increased importance of global supply chains. As the US and EU focus on the origin and target of foreign investment and the control exerted by governments of third countries, the transatlantic partnership would benefit from coordinating strategic exemptions and carveouts. Yet such a focus on national security neglects the competition concerns due to the erosion of a 'level playing field' because of FDI driven by state-owned enterprises (Kowalski 2020: 138). This may raise the prospect of closer coordination on types of remedies that might resolve issues – by fostering transparency and openness – to address potential issues before they arise.

However, there are constraints on their cooperation within TTC due to their different implementation strategies, as well as their own domestic economic priorities. The United States is also considering outward investment in terms of risk factors while the European Union is looking at the effects of inward investment on the single market. If the US and EU want to create a 'level playing field', then investment screening needs to get the same level of attention as industrial subsidies, export controls, and technology platforms. While legally, this may entail greater procedural certainty as well as mitigation measures due to potential breaches of a contract given the ambiguity of national security provisions, the pursuit of return on investments and technological acquisition of high value assets can reduce competition, impact international supply chains, and hence create negative externalities if there is concentration across key sectors.

There is a significant opportunity for strong coordination and learning that could generate a 'Washington effect' in Europe. Cooperation has been enhanced as CFIUS has helped build capacity and training for those with nascent investment screening regimes in Europe, and even bolstered and supported those with existing investment regimes such as Germany, by pushing them to increase scope and enforcement capacity in technology screening for national security reasons.

The TTC is an important political sign that the US and EU want to cooperate on key issues but will need to adapt to the surge of economic sanctions and export controls to consider measures to review current investments in a more coordinated manner. As European and American companies have pulled out of Russian operations and investments, there needs to be attention to the linkages between sanctions, export controls, supply chains, and investment screening to deal with the changing geo-political environment. With sanctions against Russia and trade tensions with China there has been a shift in trade orthodoxy from efficiency to resilience in supply chains. The EU has focused on technological sovereignty but in the context of TTC and transatlantic relations, they might consider how to relocate supply chains within regional trading blocs of politically allied countries to shore up supply chains and safeguard access to key goods such as chips and electronics. At the second TTC summit in May 2022, the EU and US focused on policy coordination across their industrial base as a key component in their transatlantic economic strategy. However, investment screening has not garnered the same attention as other issues. The goal is not about setting global rules in investment screening but rather part of a complex work program to coordinate policies that needs to deliver results in real time.

Conclusion

Investment screening has shifted from being a tool for developing countries to restrict investment to one that has fostered increased scrutiny among states that have traditionally high degree of openness to foreign direct investment. While transatlantic cooperation on investment screening has recently emerged to amplify their respective security and health concerns over the technological and strategic implications of specific foreign investments, it is a part of a larger trend of closer FDI scrutiny as more jurisdictions adopt such screening regimes or strengthen practices currently in place (see Table 14.1). Increased government intervention has created additional political and regulatory concerns that may provide a deterrent to specific investment practices, there are a variety of views about the acceptability of public and private investment in the transatlantic space.

Much of the legal and political attention has focused on inward investment to meet certain public policy objectives, but there is also a corresponding need for the transatlantic relationship to focus on coordination on common rules of outward investment. As the US moves forward with legislative proposals on outbound investment as well, the EU should pay attention to these developments given the geopolitical impact of transfer of potentially sensitive technologies, the outsourcing of critical production, and intersection of global supply chains (Hanemann et al. 2022).

Table 14.1 National Investment Screening Mechanisms among EU Member States

EU Member State	*Year of Adoption*	*Minimum Threshold (current)*	*Notes*
Austria	2011	10%	Superseded by Investment Control Act (2020)
Belgium	*2022 (pending)*	10%	Effective January 2023 after the governments of Belgium's nine federated entities have, after lengthy negotiations, agreed on the text of a cooperation agreement
Bulgaria	*No national legislation adopted or pending*	*N/A*	
Croatia	No national legislation adopted; Initiated legislative and consultative process	*N/A*	
Cyprus	*No national legislation adopted or pending*	*N/A*	
Czech Republic	2021	10%	Effective May 2022
Denmark	2021	10%	Effective June 2021
Estonia	2023	*N/A*	Effective September 2023 Foreign Investment Reliability Assessment Act
Finland	2012	10%	Amended in 2020
France	1966	10% (temporary; lowered from 25%)	Latest amendment in 2021
Germany	2004	10%	Latest amendment in 2020
Greece	*No national legislation adopted*	*N/A*	*Draft legislation pending*
Hungary	2018	10%	Added insurance sector

(Continued)

Table 14.1 (Continued)

EU Member State	*Year of Adoption*	*Minimum Threshold (current)*	*Notes*
Ireland	Pending Legislative adoption	*N/A*	Draft legislation pending (Screening of Third Country Transactions Bill) under consideration by Committee on Enterprise, Trade and Employment January 2023
Italy	2012	10%	
Latvia	*2017*	10%	Amended in Feb. 2021
Lithuania	2018	10%	Amended in June 2020
Luxembourg	Draft legislative consultative process	*N/A*	*Draft legislation pending as of 2022*
Malta	2020	10%	
Netherlands	Sector-specific legislation from various years 2022	*N/A*	Comprehensive Investment Screening Bill passed Senate in June 2022 and in force 2023. currently determined in separate pieces of legislation related to telecommunications, energy production and energy transportation
Poland	2015	20%	
Portugal	2014	None; investigations initiated by government based on subjective criteria	Governmental working group established to amend legislation
Romania	2012 Amended 2022	None; review process not public but initiated based on foreign control of entities in certain sectors	New regime 2022 (FDI Ordinance)

Slovakia	2021	None; legislation broadly covers any foreign control over critical infrastructure; expanded in 2022	New regime March 2023
Slovenia	2020	10%	
Spain	1993	10%	Amended in 1999, 2003, 2010, 2013, 2014, 2020
Sweden	Consultation 2021	*N/A*	Expected 2023

All but two EU Member States (Bulgaria and Cyprus) now have screening mechanisms in place or are in the process of establishing them. Others have adopted new mechanism, amended existing legislation or initiative consultative process or legislative measure to adopt new mechanism.

Original table compiled with data from: Di Falco 2022, Deloitte Legal 2021, European Commission 2021a, van den Berg and Immerzeel 2021, Prompers and Smit 2021, OECD 2021, UNCTAD 2021, White & Case 2021, Van Bael & Bellis 2020.

Investment screening is one instrument of a larger political and economic toolbox to defend EU, US, and potentially transatlantic interests. This is driven by concerns about the growing assertiveness and coerciveness of trade practices, the authoritarian political climate, and the move away from market reforms that has given a sense of urgency toward transatlantic cooperation. China's integration in the world economy has created frictions due in part to the significant trade imbalances as well as the lack of enforcement of obligations at the WTO level to amend their trade regime.[9] As Europe and the United States focus on building strategic sovereignty in this area, the rise of foreign state investment has received less attention in the political economy literature suggesting that scholarship focus on evaluating the commercial successes or failures of such transnational investment flows on local economic growth and the geographic and sectoral impact of these flows of capital on domestic competitors. Given the emphasis on increasing domestic capacity through subsidizing their industrial base with increased domestic or regional investment funds in the US and EU, this has implications for strategies toward FDI and the relationship between domestic investment and foreign capital.

While there are shared concerns in which the TTC is a step toward rebuilding mutual trust and economic cooperation, the two sides need to generate tangible outcomes. This might include exchanges of information on screening of specific investments with the right of either side to provide input into the deliberations. Such cooperation could provide important lessons for those new investment screening bodies Europe, particularly at the national level. This might be modeled on the level of cooperation that has evolved in transatlantic competition policy (Damro and Guay 2016). There might also be discussion of threshold levels for review as well as common understandings of state-owned enterprises and other legal concepts. Such coordination might lead to an appeal process by domestic firms adversely affected by firms that receive unfair subsidies. While inward investment is linked to the new regulation on the distortive effects of foreign subsidies in the internal market that allowed foreign subsidies to escape scrutiny, it would be harder to foster greater transatlantic accord if foreign undertakings in the United States were also subject to increased scrutiny over subsidies as the US does not have the same state aid provisions in their domestic market. It might also be important for transatlantic cooperation in investment screening to be able to voice concerns ex ante before an acquisition was made as well as determine some common rules for ex post evaluation if needed. And as the US and EU cooperate on inward investment screening, they might want to avoid regulatory divergence on outward investment rules to prevent capital markets from supplying investment in key sectors that may lead to strategic vulnerabilities if supply chains are disrupted. They should also be promoting their strategic values as trade has evolved beyond efficiency concerns to also focus on sustainability, health, and labor rights, so that their investment screening should also consider whether investment has detrimental domestic impacts on specific communities and whether that investment is tied to companies that do not protect labor or environmental rights in their supply chains. Investment screening has focused primarily on strategic security implications but needs to consider the offensive as well as defensive means to address foreign investment with significant national security related vulnerabilities as well as the effects on domestic market competition if investment leads to concentration of key supplies by foreign owned companies. As there is an increased focus on values-based trade, the US and EU can also leverage other goals such as sustainability and worker rights by linking them to investment decisions as well. Yet this will likely be overshadowed by a balance between national security and openness and how to accommodate non-market economies in the global economy.

Notes

1 For a general overview of CFIUS, see CRS 2020.
2 https://www.congress.gov/bill/115th-congress/house-bill/5841/text; https://www.congress.gov/110/plaws/publ49/PLAW-110publ49.pdf
3 The Exon-Florio amendment was enacted through the passage of the Omnibus Trade and Competitiveness Act of 1988.
4 Despite increased European concerns, Japanese FDI has a long history in Europe. See Mason (1992).
5 At present, eighteen EU member states have adopted national legislation enacting screening mechanisms (EU 2021: 11). Of these, twelve states-imposed screening mechanisms prior to 2020. and five have draft legislation pending.
6 Meunier (2019) states that China did not get many economic bargains. According to the World Bank, net inflows into the EU dropped precipitously after 2007, which is when they were at peak so while Chinese investment increased, overall FDI into Europe fell.
7 Meunier (2019) confirms the surge in FDI.
8 Using IAPPA the Biden Administration applied this EO to US investments in any sector of the Russian economy.
9 Steve Charnovitz has pointed out the US has not made use of WTO mechanisms against China.

References

Bauerle Danzmann, S. (2021) 'Investment screening in the shadow of weaponized interdependence', in D.W. Drezner, H. Farrell, and A.L. Newman (eds.), *The Uses and Abuses of Weaponized Interdependence*, Washington, DC: Brookings, pp. 257–272.
Bauerle Danzman, S. and Meunier, S. (2021). The Big Screen: Mapping the Diffusion of Foreign Investment Screening Mechanisms. Working Paper, SSRN. September 2021.
Chaisse, J. and Burnay, M. (2022) Introduction – CAI's Contribution to International Investment Law: European, Chinese, and Global Perspectives, *The Journal of World Investment & Trade*, 23(4), 497–520, 10.1163/22119000-12340258
Chan, Z.T. and Meunier, S. (2021) 'Behind the screen: Understanding national support for a foreign investment screening mechanism in the European Union', *Review of International Organizations*, 17: 1–29, 10.1007/s11558-021-09436-y.
Congressional Research Service [CRS] (2020) 'The Committee on Foreign Investment in the United States', available at crsreports.congress.gov/product/pdf/RL/RL33388 (accessed 2 September 2022).
Cuervo-Cazurra, A., Grosman, A., and Megginson, W.L. (2022) 'A review of the internationalization of state-owned firms and sovereign wealth funds: Governments' nonbusiness objectives and discreet power', *Journal of International Business Studies*, May: 1–29, 10.1057/s41267-022-00522-w.
Damro, C. and Guay, T.R. (2016) *European Competition Policy and Globalization*, New York: Palgrave Macmillan.

Defraigne, J.C. (2017) 'Chinese outward direct investments in Europe and the control of the global value chain', *Asia Europe Journal*, 15: 213–228, 10.1007/s10308-017-0476-3.
Deni, J.R. and Shatzer, J. (2020) 'China's economic statecraft in Europe during the pandemic', *War on the Rocks*, 16 October, available at www.warontherocks.com/2020/10/chinas-economic-statecraft-in-europe-during-the-pandemic (accessed 2 September 2022).
Deloitte Legal (2021) 'Foreign direct investment in Central Europe' available at www2.deloitte.com/content/dam/Deloitte/ce/Documents/legal/ce-foreign-direct-invest ment-in-central-europe-1.pdf (accessed 2 September 2022).
Di Falco, C. (2022) 'Italy: Global rules on foreign direct investment', *Norton Rose Fulbright*, available at www.nortonrosefulbright.com/en/knowledge/publications/503220b7/italy (accessed 2 September 2022).
Esplugues Mota, C. (2018) 'A more targeted approach to foreign direct investment: The establishment of screening systems on national security grounds', *Brazilian Journal of International Law*, 15(2): 440–466, 10.5102/rdi.v15i2.5365.
European Commission (2020) 'EU foreign investment screening becomes fully operational' [press release], 9 October, available at www.ec.europa.eu/commission/presscorner/api/files/document/print/en/ip_20_1867/IP_20_1867_EN.pdf (accessed 2 September 2022).
European Commission [EC] (2021a) 'EU-US trade and technology council: Commission launches consultation platform for stakeholder's involvement to shape transatlantic cooperation' [press release], 18 October, available at https://ec.europa.eu/commission/presscorner/detail/en/IP_21_5308 (accessed2 September 2022).
European Commission (2021b) 'First Annual Report on the Screening of Foreign Direct Investments into the Union', 23 November, available at www.trade.ec.europa.eu/doclib/dos/2021/November/tradoc_159935.pdf (accessed 2 September 2022).
European Commission (2021c) 'Frequently asked questions on Regulation (EU) 2019/452 establishing a framework for the screening of foreign direct investments into the Union', 22 June, available at https://trade.ec.europa.eu/doclib/docs/2019/june/tradoc_157945.pdf 2 September 2022).
Evenett, S.J. (2021) 'What caused the resurgence in FDI screening?' SUERF Policy Note, Issue No. 240, available at www.suerf.org/docx/f_942daac277daced487d09ddcbe753d73_24933_suerf.pdf (accessed 2 September 2022).
Executive Order 11858 (7 May 1975) 'Foreign investment in the United States', 40 FR 20263, 3 CFR, 1971-1975 Comp., p. 990, available at www.archives.gov/federal-register/codification/executive-order/11858.html (accessed 2 September 2022).
Gertz, G. (2021) 'Investment screening before, during, and after COVID-19' *Global Perspectives*, 2(1): 24538, 10.1525/gp.2021.24538.
Gewirtz, P. et al. (2021) 'A roadmap for U.S.-Europe cooperation on China', Paul Tsai China Center, Yale Law School, available at https://law.yale.edu/sites/default/files/area/center/china/document/roadmap_for_us-eu_cooperation_on_china.pdf (accessed 2 September 2022).
Hanemann, T. et al. (2021) 'Two-way street—US-China investment trends—2021 update', Rhodium Group, available at www.rhg.com/research/twowaystreet-2021 (accessed 2 September 2022).
Hanemann, T. et al. (2022) 'Two-way street—An outbound investment screening regime for the United States?', Rhodium Group, available at www.rhg.com/research/tws-outbound (accessed 2 September 2022).
Johnson, K. (2018) 'Why is China buying up Europe's ports?', *Foreign Policy*, 2 February, available at foreignpolicy.com/2018/02/02/why-is-china-buying-up-europes-ports/ (accessed 2 September 2022).
Kowalski, P (2020) 'Will the post-COVID world be less open to foreign direct investment?', in R. Baldwin and S. Evenett (eds.), *COVID-19 and Trade Policy: Why Turning Inward Won't Work*, London: CEPR Press, pp. 131–149, available at www.cepr.org/sites/default/files/publication-files/60044-covid_19_and_trade_policy_why_turning_inward_won_t_work.pdf (accessed 2 September 2022).

Le Corre, P. (2018) 'Chinese investments in European countries: Experiences and lessons for the "Belt and Road" initiative', in M. Mayer (ed.), *Rethinking the Silk Road: China's Belt and Road Initiative and Emerging Eurasian Relations*, New York: Palgrave Macmillan, pp. 161–176, 10.1007/978-981-10-5915-5.

Le Corre, P. and Sepulchre, A. (2016) *China's Offensive in Europe*, Washington, DC: Brookings.

Leonard, M. and Shapiro, J. (2020) 'Sovereign Europe, dangerous world: Five agendas to protect Europe's capacity to act', European Council on Foreign Relations, available at ecfr.eu/publication/sovereign-europe-dangerous-world-five-agendas-to-protect-europes-capacity-to-act/ (accessed 2 September 2022).

Mason, M. (1992) 'The origins and evolution of Japanese direct investment in Europe', *Business History Review*, 66(3): 435–474.

Meunier, S. (2019) 'Chinese direct investment in Europe: Economic opportunities and political challenges', in K. Zeng (ed.), *Handbook on the International Political Economy of China*, Northampton, MA: Edward Elgar, pp. 98–112.

Office of the United States Trade Representative [USTR] (n.d.) 'U.S.-E.U. Trade and Technology Council (TTC)' Washington, DC, available at ustr.gov/useuttc (accessed 2 September 2022).

Olivieri, B. (2019/2020) 'Safeguarding national security interests: An overview of global screening procedures on foreign direct investment' [master's thesis], Tesi di Laurea in Dirittointernazionale , Luiss Guido Carli, relatore PietroPustorin.

Organization for Economic Cooperation and Development [OECD] (2020) 'Investment screening in times of COVID-19 and beyond', Paris 7 July, available at www.oecd.org/coronavirus/policy-responses/investment-screening-in-times-of-covid-19-and-beyond-aa60af47/ (accessed 2 September 2022).

Organization for Economic Cooperation and Development (2021) *Freedom of Investment Process: Investment Policy Developments in 62 Economies Between 16 October 2020 and 15 October 2021*, available at www.oecd.org/investment/investment-policy/Investment-policy-monitoring-October-2021-ENG.pdf (accessed 2 September 2022).

Prompers, L. and Smit, G. (2021) 'New Dutch FI regime on the horizon—What you need to know', Linklaters, available at www.linklaters.com/en-us/insights/blogs/foreigninvestmentlinks/2021/september/new-dutch-fi-regime-on-the-horizon—what-you-need-to-know (accessed 2 Setpember 2022).

Rajavuori, M. and Huhta, K. (2020) 'Investment screening: Implications for the energy sector and energy security', *Energy Policy* 144: 111646, 10.1016/j.enpol.2020.111646.

Rose, P. (2015) 'The Foreign Investment and National Security Act of 2007: An assessment of its impact on sovereign wealth funds and state-owned enterprises' in *Research Handbook on Sovereign Wealth Funds and International Investment Law*, Edward Elgar Publishing, Ohio State Public Law Working Paper No. 231, 10.2139/ssrn.2387562.

United Nations Conference on Trade and Development (2021) 'Temporary measure to lower the control threshold triggering the FDI screening regime extended for another year', Investment Policy Monitor, available at investmentpolicy.unctad.org/investment-policy-monitor/measures/3790/france-temporary-measure-to-lower-the-control-threshold-triggering-the-fdi-screening-regime-extended-for-another-year-(accessed 2 September 2022).

US Bureau of Economic Analysis [BEA] (2021), 'Direct Investment Positions, 2020-2021', available at www.bea.gov/data/intl-trade-investment/direct-investment-country-and-industry (accessed 2 September 2022).

Van Bael & Bellis (2020) 'Foreign direct investment: Romania', available at www.vbb.com/insights/FDI/Romania (accessed 2 September 2022).

van den Berg, P. and Immerzeel, M. (2021) 'The foreign investment regulation review: Netherlands', *The Law Reviews*, 17 October, available at thelawreviews.co.uk/title/the-foreign-investment-regulation-review/netherlands (accessed 2 September 2022).

Wang, B. (2021) 'CFIUS ramps up oversight of China deals in the US', *The Diplomat*, 14 September, available at thediplomat.com/2021/09/cfius-ramps-up-oversight-of-china-deals-in-the-us/ (accessed 2 September 2022).

White & Case (2021) 'Foreign direct investment reviews 2021: Romania', available at www.whitecase.com/insight-our-thinking/foreign-direct-investment-reviews-2021-romania (accessed 2 September 2022).

White House (2022) 'Fact Sheet: United States, European Union, and G7 to announce further economic costs on Russia', 11 March, available at www.whitehouse.gov/briefing-room/statements-releases/2022/03/11/fact-sheet-united-states-european-union-and-g7-to-announce-further-economic-costs-on-russia/ (accessed 2 September 2022).

SECTION III

Norm Promotion Practices of the EU and US in the Digital Age

15

THE FUTURE OF THE EU-US PRIVACY SHIELD

Elaine Fahey and Fabien Terpan

CITY LAW SCHOOL, CITY, UNIVERSITY OF LONDON AND CESICE (CENTRE D'ÉTUDES DE LA SÉCURITÉ INTERNATIONALE ET DES COOPÉRATIONS EUROPÉENNES), SCIENCES PO, GRENOBLE

Introduction

Many landmarks in the history of EU-US relations date to the Transatlantic Declaration of 1990, expanded through the New Transatlantic Agenda (NTA) in 1995 (Pollack 2005, p. 900), have been in soft law instruments. Traditionally, political science accounts have contended that EU-US relations are law-light institution-light (Pollack 2005, p. 916; Fahey 2014, p. 370). To a degree, despite immense amounts of engagement, activities and cooperation, there are limited legal outcomes as a matter of international law for several decades of cooperation, before and after the NTA. There are eight data transfer agreements, not all international agreements, some hybrid regimes, comprising an array of legal bases (Christakis and Terpan 2021). There are also many conclusions that EU-US relations have been plagued by overly complex or inadequate governance, institutions, legal agreements or enforcement (Petersmann 2015; Pollack and Shaffer 2009). Soft law and its complex enforceability, construction and classification is a thorny one. EU-US relations have contributed to many of these challenges through an evolving variety of increasingly complex, novel or simply hybrid transatlantic instruments (Shaffer 2002).

Data transfer between the European Union (EU) and the United States (US) is an important issue, given the extent of transatlantic business relationship. However, the degree of data protection and privacy afforded by the EU and the US is quite different, with EU law being far more protective than US law. This does not mean that data transfer is impossible, but at least from a European perspective, it means that a solution needs to be found in order to make data transfer compatible with EU law. From a US perspective, this can be seen as an EU requirement of approximation to European law, which is, of course, highly problematic for both legal and political reasons.

The European Commission and the US administration negotiated two different arrangements aimed to protect the fundamental rights of EU citizens whose personal data is transferred to the United States for commercial purposes, and thus facilitating

DOI: 10.4324/9781003283911-19

data flows across the Atlantic. The main purpose of these arrangements was to allow the free transfer of data to US companies, provided that the latter had received a proper certification. Both arrangements were enshrined in EU law by an 'adequacy decision' adopted by the European Commission on the basis of the EU legislation on data protection, a form of complex hybrid governance.[1]

The first arrangement, called Safe Harbour, was endorsed by the European Commission in a Decision of 26 July 2000.[2] In the Case of *Schrems v. European Data Commissioner* (C-362/14)[3] (hereafter Schrems I), the Court of Justice of the European Union (CJEU) issued a preliminary ruling declaring the adequacy decision invalid. This decision forced the EU and the US to negotiate urgently a new framework capable of securing transfer of data from Europe to the US, the so-called Privacy Shield, which came into force in July 2016, based on a Commission new adequacy decision of 12 July 2016.[4] The new framework was supposed to address the issues raised by the Court of justice. This was immediately followed by judicial actions against the Privacy Shield, in the form of actions for annulment brought before the General Court of the CJEU (T-670/16 and T-738/16) and preliminary references.[5] This judicial phase culminated in a recent CJEU judgment (C-311/18)[6] (hereafter Schrems II) invalidating it.

In a previous article we argued that the invalidation of the EU-US arrangements by the CJEU can be explained by a lack of institutionalisation, the latter being defined as "the process by which an organisation becomes increasingly subject to rules, procedures and stable practices" (Fahey and Terpan 2021). Our main argument was that because institutionalisation through EU-US arrangements is weak or informal, negative judicialisation (invalidation of the Safe Harbour and the Privacy Shield) is more likely, with courts and tribunals of the most protective legal order – in the end the CJEU – are prone to make their own rules prevail.

In the present article, we go one step further by focusing on the very nature of the rules established between the EU and the US, in order to discuss the degree of normativity that is required to make the arrangement stable and protected from another invalidation by the CJEU. Based on previous research on soft and hard law (Terpan 2015; See also: Saurugger and Terpan 2021), we argue that norms can be situated on a continuum, from non-legal norms to proper hard law, with in-between an array of different kinds of soft norms. While this idea of a continuum goes against a clear-cut classification in the three categories – non-legal norms, soft law and hard law – it remains useful to situate those norms on the continuum in order to explain, at least partially, their efficiency, or lack thereof.

The identification of soft law is based on two main criteria, obligation and enforcement. Obligation relates either to the act intself -the *instrumentum*- or to the content of the act -the *negotium*. A legally binding act such as a Treaty is considered hard, whereas a non-legally binding act such as a memorandum of understanding or a common declaration between two parties is at most soft law. When looking within the act, two kinds of provisions can be distinguished, those who contain proper commitments and those who are written in a way that soften their content. The second criteria, enforcement, makes the evaluation even more complex. Indeed, the soft-hard continuum also depends on the way the obligation – soft or hard – is enforced. Enforcement, here, is defined in a broad manner, going from soft forms (monitoring, peer review) to harder ones (judicial control).

In the context of this chapter, we assume that the stability of the EU-US data transfer arrangement is dependent on its legal characteristics. The stronger the commitments and the enforcement mechanism, the lower the probability that the arrangement is invalidated. Drawing on this, we discuss whether a hardening of the common rules and mechanisms could help to frame and stabilise the transfer of data between the European Union and the United States. For this, we will come back to the Safe Harbour and the Privacy Shield, in a first section, to get a clear view of why these arrangements were deemed inadequate. A second section will explain the situation created by the ruling in Schrems II while a third one will explore the possible evolutions of the data transfer regime, considering the on-going discussions between EU and US authorities, and the perspective of stronger commitments and mechanisms. Finally, a fourth section will study the current debate over US state and federal privacy law, as it could affect the EU-US relationship.

Why previous regimes were not seen as 'essentially equivalent' to EU data protection law: the safe harbour and Privacy Shield agreements fragilities

The Safe Harbour was an EU-US arrangement setting up a series of principles and rules endorsed by US authorities. On the basis of the General Data Protection Regulation (GDPR), it was considered 'essentially equivalent' to EU data protection law by the European Commission in its adequacy decision of 26 July 2000. The essence of the Safe Harbour was to require US companies to treat the data of EU citizens as if the data were physically in Europe, operating through a voluntary self-certification system with public enforcement conducted by the US Federal Trade Commission.

The Safe Harbour Agreement was understood at the time of its adoption to amount to a new form of mutual recognition or new form of global engagement through complex governance (Shaffer 2002) and capable of being understood in a variety of ways. Shaffer famously summed up the Agreement as being understood to be anything from the EU's exercise of coercive market power in an extraterritorial fashion in an attempt to leverage up privacy standards within the United States, a capitulation by EC bureaucrats to U.S. trading concerns through a weak agreement filled with loopholes or a compromise through new institutional development pursuant to which free transatlantic information flows could be preserved while satisfying legitimate European concerns (Shaffer 2002).

The Safe Harbour Agreement was poorly institutionalised, and suffered legal weaknesses that led to its inevitable invalidation by the CJEU (negative judicialisation). This can be further explained by the (soft law) nature and structure of the relationship (Kuner 2017). The only binding and enforceable element in the Safe Harbour was the adequacy decision made by the European Commission on 26 July 2000.[7] Apart from this, the Safe Harbour was made of a series of soft law documents whereby US authorities gave assurances to the EU and to which the adequacy decision referred. Negative judicialisation has then triggered the adoption of the Privacy Shield, which was presented as a strengthened and more institutionalised version of the Safe Harbour but which was in reality mostly weakly institutionalised masked by new terminology, some enhanced governance but little else.

The Privacy Shield: still a soft law arrangement

The soft dimension of the Privacy Shield is obvious when looking at the content of the arrangement.

First, the Privacy Shield replicates the structure of the Safe Harbour, with one legally binding decision of the Commission referring to a series of informal letters addressed by US authorities to the European Union. No real legal guarantees are provided in these letters. The Privacy Shield is not an external agreement based on Article 218 TFEU including mutual commitments. Thus, the first criterion of soft law (lack of obligation) is clearly met in all documents pertaining to the Privacy Shield, with the exception of the Commission's adequacy decision.

Secondly, a strengthened monitoring of the framework has been established by the 2016 adequacy decision of the Commission, with annual joint reviews by EU and US authorities to monitor the correct application of the arrangement discussed next, and a public report to be submitted by the Commission to the European Parliament and the Council. The first review took place in Washington, DC on 18 and 19 September 2017, the second on 18 and 19 October 2018 in Brussels and the third in Washington on 12 and 13 September 2019. This review process was established in order to address the issue raised by the Court in Schrems I about the weaknesses of the assessment made by the EU Commission. Indeed, under the Safe Harbour, the Commission did not directly and continuously assess the adequacy of US rules but mostly relied on self-assessment by US authorities. In contrast to this, the annual reviews under the Privacy Shield have led to the adoption of three reports, published by the Commission in 2017, 2018 and 2019:[8] the Commission was not fully dependent on declarations made by US authorities when itself evaluating the framework. However, although the review process is an improvement, this does not change the fact that the adequacy in itself mainly depends on evolutions in US law and practices. The Commission cannot go beyond recommendations to US authorities and is dependent on the latter's willingness to respond to these demands.

Thirdly, the guarantees provided by US law were supposed to be stronger on both commercial and surveillance aspects of the Privacy Shield; in fact, the hardening of soft law was rather limited, or even fake.

The ostensibly 'light-touch' enforcement practices of the Federal Trade Commission indicated only limited formalisation of the guarantees. Commercial providers were not subject to meaningful infrastructures.[9] As to surveillance, the embryonic role of the now permanent Ombudsman and newly constituted PCLOB indicated further layers of oversight and accountability being put in place – slowly but surely, and in embryonic form. However, the Ombudsman mechanism did not provide for the necessary limitations and safeguards with regard to the interferences authorised by the U.S. legislation[10] and did not ensure effective judicial protection against such interferences. There was no real improvement in terms of effective administrative and judicial redress for the data subjects whose personal data are being transferred.

In the end, both the monitoring of the Privacy Shield and the guarantees offered by US authorities can be seen as a very soft enforcement mechanism (our second criteria), confirming the soft law nature of the arrangement. The only hard law component – the adequacy decision – is thus weakened by the softness of the arrangement and of the US guarantees, a situation which inevitably led to negative judicialisation.

The Privacy shield: subject to negative judicialisation

The CJEU, in the Case of *Schrems* II, held that the Commission's finding that US law was of an adequate level of protection essentially equivalent to EU law under the GDPR read in light of the Charter, was called into question by section 702 FISA and E.O. 12333 because they authorised surveillance programmes such as PRISM and UPSTREAM. FISA did not indicate limitations on powers and E.O. did not confer enforceable rights on EU citizens against the US authorities. This violated the principle of proportionality because surveillance programmes could not be regarded as limited to what was strictly necessary. Moreover, Ombudsman could not remedy deficiencies which the Commission had found (e.g. lack of a redress mechanism) as to the transfers impugning findings as to adequacy with respect to essential equivalence as guaranteed by Article 47 of the Charter.

The decision was not just exclusively about US surveillance laws but was also about the fragile nature of the Privacy Shield architecture. The lack of a robust institutional framework here overall was of salience to the CJEU as well as from the lack of truly legal guarantees provided by US authorities.

Since the European Charter of Fundamental Rights has become binding and the GDPR entered into force, the CJEU acquired solid legal grounds to exert a judicial control over the Privacy Shield. Therefore, it was unlikely that a limited hardening of the EU-US framework could prevent negative judicialisation. This was confirmed by the CJEU landmark ruling in the Case of *Schrems* II.

Post-*Schrems* II: a period of high uncertainties

No legal vacuum but a legal mess

The Court's ruling in *Schrems* II has opened a new period of uncertainties (Christakis 2020a). Once again, the EU-US relationship has been destabilised, with important consequences for business transatlantic relations. Total 5,300 companies, which used to rely on the Privacy Shield, need to find other ways to transfer data from Europe to the US, while the flow of data underpins 900 billion euros in cross-border commerce every year. The issues raised by *Schrems* II are even more significant that no grace period has been allowed for Privacy Shield transfers, contrary to what had been decided after *Schrems* II (EDPB 2020a). At the very least, EU Data Protection Authorities could slow-roll enforcement, giving companies time to figure out how to respond, as they did when Safe Harbor was invalidated (Daskal 2020). But companies cannot rely on the existing framework until a new arrangement is adopted.

As the CJEU made clear in *Schrems* II, the invalidation did not create a legal vacuum and the absence of an adequacy decision is clearly foreseen by article 49 GDPR.[11] However, this article is supposed to cover a limited number of specific situations. A transfer is possible under Article 49 under specific conditions such as:

- the data subject has explicitly consented to the proposed transfer, after having been informed of the possible risks of such transfers for the data subject due to the absence of an adequacy decision and appropriate safeguards;
- the transfer is necessary for important reasons of public interest;
- the transfer is necessary in order to protect the vital interests of the data subject or of other persons, where the data subject is physically or legally incapable of giving consent.

Obviously, Article 49 is not supposed to replace a general arrangement between the EU and a third state, which the EDPB had made it clear (2018). The remaining options are to be found in Articles 46 and 47 of the GDPR.

In the absence of an adequacy decision

> a controller or processor may transfer personal data to a third country or an international organisation only if the controller or processor has provided appropriate safeguards, and on condition that enforceable data subject rights and effective legal remedies for data subjects are available. (Art. 46-1 GDPR)

These appropriate safeguards, according to Art. 46-2 GDPR, may be provided for by:

- a legally binding and enforceable instrument between public authorities or bodies;
- binding corporate rules in accordance with Article 47;
- standard data protection clauses adopted by the Commission in accordance with the examination procedure referred to in Article 93(2);
- standard data protection clauses adopted by a supervisory authority and approved by the Commission pursuant to the examination procedure referred to in Article 93(2);
- an approved code of conduct pursuant to Article 40 together with binding and enforceable commitments of the controller or processor in the third country to apply the appropriate safeguards, including as regards data subjects' rights; or
- an approved certification mechanism pursuant to Article 42 together with binding and enforceable commitments of the controller or processor in the third country to apply the appropriate safeguards, including as regards data subjects' rights.

Among the list of safeguards, two main options are more likely to be used: standard contractual clauses and binding corporate rules (see also article 47 GDPR).[12] In our views, both options pose serious challenges.

Standard contractual clauses and binding corporate rules

Data transfers from the EU to other countries, including the US, can be based on contractual clauses ensuring appropriate data protection safeguards. This includes model contract clauses, the so-called standard contractual clauses (SCCs), that have been 'pre-approved' by the European Commission. The last version of the SCCs has been approved by the Commission on 4 June 2021 (European Commission 2021a).

The Court in *Schrems* II has clearly indicated that the SCCs remain valid provided that these maintain, in practice, a level of protection that is essentially equivalent to the one guaranteed by the GDPR in light of the EU Charter. This responsibility falls primarily to the exporter, who need to "verify whether the law of the third country of destination ensures adequate protection under EU law" (Para 134) and "whether the level of protection required by EU law is respected in the third country concerned" (Para 142). The Court adds that the adequacy assessment by private companies is placed under the control of DPAs, who have the power to terminate the transfer (Para 146), a power that does not seem so easy to exert. If DPAs disagree on the adequacy of foreign law to EU law, then it is the EDPB, and not the Commission, who is charged of solving the problem (Para 147). This confirms a tendency towards agencification that can be observed in other areas of EU law. To provide guidance on how to assess the adequacy of foreign law, the EDPD has issued a "Recommendation on the European Essential Guarantees for surveillance measures" (2020c), which should not make data transfer easier given the extent of what is required (Christakis 2020b; 2020c; 2020d). Overall, all this process is obviously time consuming and supposes that different actors, private companies and public agencies, should make a difficult assessment of foreign law.

Whatever we think about the workability of this complex system of adequacy assessment, the problem is that the CJEU, in *Schrems* II, has just said that the US level of protection is not essentially equivalent to EU law. How could SCCs be considered as 'essentially equivalent' in a context where the Privacy Shield was invalidated and US law has not been genuinely transformed? Two main answers are possible. If all types of data are potentially subject to the US surveillance programmes under US Foreign Intelligence Surveillance Act Section 702, Executive Order 12333 and Presidential Policy Directive 28, then transferring data on the basis of SCCs is not legal. If, on the contrary, those programmes are limited to communication service providers and do not concern the data transferred by other types of companies, then SCCs would be an option for the latter but not for the former.

In *Schrems* II, the CJEU mentions the possibility for the controller or processor to provide 'additional safeguards' to those offered by the SCC (Para 134). This has given rise to much scepticism? Even the EDPB at first did not seem to know what exactly these measures could be,[13] before finally adopting a recommendation aimed at clarifying the notion (2020b).

Discussing the possible legal or technical nature of these measures, Christakis argues:

> If one considers, for instance, that one of the main concerns of the Court was that the US system of surveillance does not offer effective judicial

> remedies to EU citizens, it is hard to imagine how any 'additional safeguards' introduced by the data controller could change this. (2020a)

Given the uncertainties of the SCCs, would the Binding Corporate Rules (BCR) (Bender and Ponemon 2006; Proust and Emmanuelle 2011; Moerel 2012) be the optimal solution to legally transfer data from Europe to the US? Article 47(1) GDPR says:

> The competent supervisory authority shall approve binding corporate rules in accordance with the consistency mechanism set out in Article 63, provided that they: are legally binding and apply to and are enforced by every member concerned of the group of undertakings, or group of enterprises engaged in a joint economic activity, including their employees; expressly confer enforceable rights on data subjects with regard to the processing of their personal data.

A list of what the BCRs should at least specify is laid down in Article 47(2).

BCRs brings legal certainty as it is approved a priori by the competent supervisory authority. However, companies might not have the necessary means to engage in the costly and time-consuming establishment of BCRs. And, in the end, BCRs are facing the same problem as SCCs: they could prove useless in a context where the US law still does not meet the European standards.

The *Schrems* II ruling may not have created a legal vacuum, but it certainly has led to a legal mess, with an even weaker legal framework than before, as the system of certification provided by the Privacy Shield is no longer applicable, and a still high risk of negative judicialisation. Negative judicialisation could become even more fragmented, due the diversity of data transfer mechanisms and the uncertainties that was created. Based on its detailed assessment of *Schrems* II, the EDPB has been trying to provide further clarification for stakeholders and guidance on the use of instruments for the transfer of personal data to third countries pursuant to the judgment. But the capacity of the EDPB to bring more coherence and certainty to the system is questionable and its contribution in terms of adequacy assessment could probably be challenged before the CJEU under Article 263 TFEU. This is why the negotiation of third arrangement – Privacy Shield 2.0 – has finally been put on agenda by EU and US authorities.

Towards Privacy Shield 2.0: what could it include, and will it be enough?

Political changeover in the US has brought to power a new administration, more concerned with strengthening the transatlantic relationship than the previous one, and more engaged with data arrangements at international level.

The current US Trade Representative has made it clear that trade agreements are from a previous century and not in line with the Biden administration philosophy that soft law framework agreements constitute the future of international economic law. For instance, the Indo Pacific Economic Partnership (IPEF) of which the US is party to amongst others in the Indo Pacific region has many outlined objectives on data flows and data localisation and the digital economy across borders using soft law as its main framing device.

The agreement perceived by many to be the most contemporary and cutting-edge digital governance trade agreement is also a soft law non-binding partnership, the 2020 Digital Economy Partnership Agreement (DEPA) between Chile, New Zealand and Singapore 2020.[14] It is not formulated as a trade agreement but rather intended to address the broader issues of the digital economy through a soft law agreement. Its breadth and flexibility are significant in so far as it purported to traverse a range of contemporary challenges issues, such as those in the areas of artificial intelligence (AI) and digital inclusion.

DEPA's 'soft' approach to rulemaking and norm-setting is alleged to have been effective in an Asian context, ie Asia-Pacific Economic Cooperation (APEC) forum (including on digital governance) and worthy of replication. To enable shaping rules and norms in this critical area has in this context appears more significant and efficient to lengthy trade agreement negotiations (Goodman 2021). Yet such a framework contrasts considerably with the very different type of debate taking place across the Atlantic in the context of the post–Privacy Shield negotiations, reaching an agreement on the transatlantic privacy framework which includes a binding transatlantic court, to deal with the complex question of high standards and international data flows.

We know that the CJEU did not take a principled position against surveillance, but rather required safeguards and remedies, which leaves room for negotiation. What we do not know, however, is the exact mechanism and practice which could, for sure, avoid a new invalidation.

A Transatlantic Trade and Technology Council, as proposed by the EU in late 2020 and already in place by Autumn 2021, could provide an important bedrock from which important data privacy agreements evolve (European Commission 2021b; Bown and Malmström 2021). The EU-US Joint Agenda for Global Change included a Transatlantic Trade and Technology Council, putatively developing a loose institutionalisation of key global challenges currently not well covered by, for example, the WTO, including data transfers. It is difficult to determine precisely what level of institutionalisation is needed bilaterally, never mind bilaterally. The Council is a soft governance entity, derived from a non-binding agreement. It is a formula that the EU increasingly uses, for example, with India, where a new EU-India Trade and Technology Council was similarly established as a soft law arrangement in the absence of an international law agreement framework pursuant to Article 218 TFEU (European Commission 2022b). Thus, although relating more broadly to digital governance, it is a notable trend in the era of digitisation.

In March 2022, Ursula Von der Leyen and Joe Biden has announced that the EU and the US had reached an agreement in principle for a new Trans-Atlantic Data Privacy Framework on the basis of which data will be able to flow freely and safely between the EU and participating U.S. companies. It is a remarkable development which seems to elevate the plan of institutions in the protection of rights of citizens and businesses.

This agreement will contain "a new set of rules and binding safeguards to limit access to data by U.S. intelligence authorities to what is necessary and proportionate to protect national security" (European Commission 2022a). In this context, "US intelligence agencies will adopt procedures to ensure effective oversight of new privacy and civil liberties standards" (European Commission 2022a). The agreement also includes "a new two-tier redress system to investigate and resolve complaints of Europeans on access of data by U.S. Intelligence authorities, which includes a Data Protection Review Court" (European Commission 2022a). The White House has made it clear in a Briefing released on 25 March 2022 that

> the United States has made unprecedented commitments to: Strengthen the privacy and civil liberties safeguards governing U.S. signals intelligence activities; Establish a new redress mechanism with independent and binding authority; and Enhance its existing rigorous and layered oversight of signals intelligence activities. (2022)

The White House also stresses out that, under the New Framework, signals intelligence collection may be undertaken "only where necessary to advance legitimate national security objectives, and must not disproportionately impact the protection of individual privacy and civil liberties" (2022). EU individuals may seek redress from a new multi-layer redress mechanism "that includes an independent Data Protection Review Court that would consist of individuals chosen from outside the U.S. Government who would have full authority to adjudicate claims and direct remedial measures as needed" (The White House 2022). Regarding commercial aspects, the mechanism will continue to rely on the requirement for companies to self-certify their adherence to the Principles through the U.S. Department of Commerce, but there will be strong obligations for companies processing data transferred from the EU. In addition, the agreement should foresee Specific monitoring and review mechanisms.

It might not be easy to precisely evaluate the nature of the proposed and published mechanisms, but the new set of rules are clearly presented as being more binding and accompanied with stronger enforcement, resulting in a hardening of the EU-US data protection framework. We know for sure that soft arrangements, based on merely declaratory and loose commitments, entail a strong risk of negative judicialisation in all areas where judicial scrutiny is possible. We also know that US cannot fully align with EU law. But the idea was to include U.S. commitments in an Executive Order that will form the basis of a draft adequacy decision by the Commission to put in place the new Trans-Atlantic Data Privacy Framework. Accordingly, on 7 October 2022, President Biden signed Executive Order 'enhancing safeguards for United States signals intelligence activities,' which along with Regulations issued by the Attorney General implemented into US law the agreement in principle announced in March 2022. It purported to issue new binding safeguards to address all issues raised by the CJEU, in particular allegedly binding safeguards, a first instance Civil Liberties Protection Officer and Data Protection Review Court, as a means to procure an adequacy decision. It should be welcome by the European Commission, who was at pains to indicate that standard contractual clauses still were possible for businesses to use, although the breadth and depth of the hardening of soft law here remains problematic.

At the time of writing, doctrinal analyses try to figure out how the new US measures could meet the requirements of *Schrems* II. Christakis, Propp and Swire, in particular, have discussed the sensitive issue of the Redress mechanism (2022a; 2022b). But it will only be possible to more accurately assess the Privacy Shield 2.0 and its adequacy to European standards once it has been transformed into legal documents, before the CJEU is eventually called upon to do so. A significant legalisation of soft law governance may yet occur and align further with the CJEU vision.

Could the transatlantic privacy relationship be facilitated by US domestic changes?

Apart from a strengthened EU-US framework, the relationship between the EU and the US could be facilitated by an evolution of US data protection laws. Several US states have recently adopted the GDPR de facto if not de jure, demonstrating the force of EU rules and values, which may generate further instititutionalisation pressures outside of the EU (Frankenreiter 2021; Fahey 2022).

Currently, three states in the US have three different comprehensive consumer privacy laws: California (CCPA and its amendment, CPRA), Virginia (VCDPA) and Colorado (ColoPA). Since 2019, a bipartisan data privacy agreement in the US has been faltering between Democrats and Republicans on two key issues. Firstly, whether a federal bill should preempt state privacy laws, and secondly, whether it should create a private right to action allowing individuals, not just the government, to sue companies for violations. Members of the U.S. Congress appear to be likely to realise the finalisation of comprehensive federal privacy legislation in 2022. On July 20, 2022, the House Committee on Commerce & Energy (House Committee) published an amended version of the American Data Privacy and Protection Act (ADPPA) (H.R. 8152) (Kern 2022; Kerry 2022; Linn 2017). The ADPAA will reshape web use and overhaul data laws beyond the U.S in how business and organisation can handle customer and user information. It is one of the most significant regulations overseeing data-collection practices in the United States. It is first Act of its ilk and is projected to provide thorough, comprehensive data privacy measures in the US. One of the most distinctive features of the new bill is its focus upon data minimisation. This principle holds that the data controller shall limit the collection of personal information to only what is relevant and necessary to achieve the ascertained purpose.

A notable caveat is that the list of permitted purposes spelled out in the bill includes targeted advertising, which is the economic driver of most surveillance to begin with. If the bill in its current form becomes law, it would be insufficient in preventing target advertising which is contrary to what data privacy advocates have been advocating. However, it imposes much tougher restrictions on targeted advertising than any legislation in the U.S. and perhaps the world and would prohibit targeting ads to minors and targeting ads based on 'sensitive data,' for example, medical information, precise geolocation and private communications – as well as 'information identifying an individual's online activities over time and across third-party websites or online services.' To the extent that the new bill would still allow targeted advertising, it would require companies to give users the right to opt out. It would confer upon the Federal Trade Commission (FTC) powers to create a standard for a universal opt-out that businesses would have to comply with, meaning users could decline all targeted advertising in one click. In addition to the ADPAA's take on data-minimisation, the new bill contains provisions that data privacy experts have long called for, including transparency standards, anti-discrimination rules, increased oversight for data brokers, and new cybersecurity requirements.

Since the House Committee has introduced the ADPPA bill, it is said to be notable that the tech industry has not expressed significant dissent as to the bill possibly indicative of the bill's weaknesses. The bill gives the FTC new authority to issue rules and enforce them, but it does not direct any new resources to the agency raising concerns as to an enforcement deficit. The ADPPA appears to align well with consensus emerging on many fronts – bipartisanship and among advocacy organisations, a consensus that boded well in theory at least for the bill if or when the full House votes on it.

Conclusion

The invalidation of the Privacy Shield has shown how serious the CJEU was with regard to the protection of EU citizens' data. It may not have created a legal vacuum with the GDPR offering different alternative possibilities including standard contractual clauses and binding corporate rules. But it certainly has opened a phase of uncertainties and legal complexity which is not favourable to a smooth and continuous flow of data across the Atlantic.

In this chapter, we used the notion of soft law, defined as an act comprising a soft dimension with regard to either the obligation or the enforcement mechanism. We argued that the Adequacy Decision of the Commission – a hard law act – suffers from a major weakness derived from the softness of the guarantees provided by the US government.

Could these guarantees be sufficiently strengthened/hardened to avoid any possible invalidation by the CJEU in the future? The EU-US relationship has further developed since the election of Joe Biden as President, including in the area of data privacy. A Transatlantic Trade and Technology Council has been created and an agreement in principle has been found in March 2022 for a new Trans-Atlantic Data Privacy Framework. It is too soon to precisely evaluate the new set of rules included in the Framework, but the trend is clearly towards more binding rules and stronger enforcement, which can be seen as a move towards hard law.

Besides, apart from the hardening of EU-US arrangements, the strengthening of US domestic rules on data protection could also contribute to the securing of transatlantic data flows. While several US states have brought their own legislation closer to GDPR standards, it remains to be seen whether such an evolution could occur at federal level. The deepening and widening of legal cooperation beyond soft law thus appears to be a salient metric of the transatlantic partnership – for now at least, given that it constitutes one of the world's most complex global governance, economic and legal structures.

Notes

1 The adequacy decisions on the Safe Harbour and the Privacy Shield were based on Art. 25 of the Directive 95/46/EC of the European Parliament and of the Council of 24 October 1995 on the protection of individuals with regard to the processing of personal data and on the free movement of such data; Article 25 of the Directive provided that Member States would prohibit all data transfers to a third country if the Commission did not find that they ensured an adequate level of protection.

2 Commission Decision of July 26, 2000 pursuant to Directive 95/46/EC of the European Parliament and of the Council on the Adequacy of the Protection Provided by the Safe Harbour Privacy Principles and Related Frequently Asked Questions Issued by the US Department of Commerce, 2000/520/EC, O.J.(L 215) 7.

3 Case C-362/14, Maximillian Schrems v. Data Protection Commissioner, ECLI:EU:C:2015:650.

4 Commission Implementing Decision (EU) 2016/1250 of July 12, 2016 pursuant to Directive 95/46/EC of the European Parliament and of the Council on the Adequacy of the Protection Provided by the EU-U.S. Privacy Shield (notified under document C) (2016) 4176) 2016 O.J. (L 207) 1.

5 Case T-670/16 - Digital Rights Ireland v. Commission; Case T-738/16 La Quadrature du Net and Others v. Commission.

6 Case C-311/18, Data Protection Commissioner v. Facebook Ireland Limited, Maximillian Schrems, ECLI:EU:C:2019:1145.

7 Commission Decision of July 26, 2000, *op. cit.*

8 European Commission. *Report From the Commission to the European Parliament and the Council on the first annual review of the functioning of the EU–U.S. Privacy Shield.* SWD (2017) 344 final; European Commission. *Report From the Commission to the European Parliament and the Council on the second annual review of the functioning of the EU–U.S. Privacy Shield.* SWD (2018) 497 final; European Commission. *Report From the Commission to the European Parliament and the Council on the third annual review of the functioning of the EU–U.S. Privacy Shield.* SWD (2019) 390 final; See also European Commission. *EU-US data transfers* [online]. https://ec.europa.eu/info/law/law-topic/data-protection/international-dimension-data-protection/eu-us-data-transfers_en. [Accessed 30 September 2022]. These reports are based on the discussions held during the annual review but are also informed by a study commissioned by the Commission, which takes into consideration publicly available material, such as: court decisions; implementing rules and procedures of relevant U.S. authorities; annual reports from independent recourse mechanisms; transparency reports issued by Privacy Shield-certified companies through their respective trade associations; reports and studies from NGOs active in the field of fundamental rights and in particular digital rights and privacy; press articles and other media reports. In addition to the collection of written input, and prior to the annual reviews, the Commission had meetings with industry and business associations and with non-governmental organisations.

9 As far as the commercial dimension was concerned, they included stricter obligations on certified companies receiving personal data from the EU, regarding limitations on how long a company may retain personal data (data retention principle) or the conditions under which data can be shared with third parties outside the framework (accountability for onward transfers principle). Citizens rights are intended to be better protected through information rights, enforceable at national level. DPAs acquired much more significance, whereas US enforcement rested largely with the FTC and appears to strike an imbalance overall through divergent and disparate institutionalisation and enforcement. The DoC provided more regular and rigorous monitoring and EU citizens had enlarged possibilities to obtain redress.

10 Annex VI to the Privacy Shield Decision contained a letter from the Office of the Director of National Intelligence to the United States Department of Commerce (DoC) and to the

International Trade Administration from 21 June 2016, in which it is stated that PPD 28 allowed for 'bulk' collection of a relatively large volume of signals intelligence information or data under circumstances where the Intelligence Community cannot use an identifier associated with a specific target to focus the collection. Similarly, other NSA's activities and surveillance programmes can be based on Executive Order 12333 (E.O. 12333).

11 It noted in para. 15: "Where a transfer could not be based on a provision in Article 45 or 46, including the provisions on binding corporate rules, and none of the derogations for a specific situation referred to in the first subparagraph of this paragraph is applicable, a transfer to a third country or an international organisation may take place only if the transfer is not repetitive, concerns only a limited number of data subjects, is necessary for the purposes of compelling legitimate interests pursued by the controller which are not overridden by the interests or rights and freedoms of the data subject, and the controller has assessed all the circumstances surrounding the data transfer and has on the basis of that assessment provided suitable safeguards with regard to the protection of personal data. The controller shall inform the supervisory authority of the transfer. The controller shall, in addition to providing the information referred to in Articles 13 and 14, inform the data subject of the transfer and on the compelling legitimate interests pursued." See also para. 202.

12 Kuner argues though that codes of conduct and certification "seem worthy of investigation as potentially a new way forward." See Kuner 2020.

13 "The EDPB to is looking further into what these additional measures could consist of," said Andrea Jelinek, Chair of the EDPB, in her Statement on the Court of Justice of the European Union Judgment in Case C-311/18 - Data Protection Commissioner v Facebook Ireland and Maximillian Schrems, 17 July 2020.

14 For details and the text of the DEPA, see: https://www.mfat.govt.nz/en/trade/free-trade-agreements/free-trade-agreements-in-force/digital-economy-partnership-agreement-depa/depa-text-and-resources/ [Accessed 30 September 2022]. See also Burri 2021; Aaronson 2021.

References

Aaronson, S. 2021. The One Trade Agreement Biden Should Sign Up for Now [online]. 8 March. *Barron's*. https://www.barrons.com/articles/the-one-trade-agreement-biden-should-sign-up-for-now-51614607309 [Accessed 30 September 2022].

Bender, D. and Ponemon, L. 2006. Binding Corporate Rules for Cross-border Data Transfer. *Rutgers Journal of Law & Urban Policy*, 3(2), 154–171.

Bown, C. P. and Malmström, C. 2021. What is the Transatlantic Trade and Technology Council [online]. 24 September. *PIIE*. https://www.piie.com/blogs/trade-and-investment-policy-watch/what-us-eu-trade-and-technology-council-five-things-you-need [Accessed 30 September 2022].

Burri, M. 2021. Towards a New Treaty on Digital Trade. *Journal of World Trade*, 55(1), 77–100.

Christakis, T. 2020a After Schrems II: Uncertainties on the Legal Basis for Data Transfers and Constitutional Implications for Europe [online]. 21 July. *European Law Blog*. https://europeanlawblog.eu/2020/07/21/after-schrems-ii-uncertainties-on-the-legal-basis-for-data-transfers-and-constitutional-implications-for-europe/ [Accessed 30 September 2022].

Christakis, T. 2020b. "Schrems III"? First Thoughts on the EDPB post-Schrems II Recommendations on International Data Transfers (Part 1) [online]. 13 November. *European Law Blog*. https://europeanlawblog.eu/2020/11/13/schrems-iii-first-thoughts-on-the-edpb-post-schrems-ii-recommendations-on-international-data-transfers-part-1/ [Accessed 30 September 2022].

Christakis, T. 2020c. "Schrems III"? First Thoughts on the EDPB post-Schrems II Recommendations on International Data Transfers (Part 2) [online]. 16 November.

European Law Blog. https://europeanlawblog.eu/2020/11/16/schrems-iii-first-thoughts-on-the-edpb-post-schrems-ii-recommendations-on-international-data-transfers-part-2/ [Accessed 30 September 2022].

Christakis, T. 2020d. "Schrems III"? First Thoughts on the EDPB post-Schrems II Recommendations on International Data Transfers (Part 3) [online]. 17 November. *European Law Blog*. https://europeanlawblog.eu/2020/11/17/schrems-iii-first-thoughts-on-the-edpb-post-schrems-ii-recommendations-on-international-data-transfers-part-3/ [Accessed 30 September 2022].

Christakis, T. and Terpan, F. 2021. EU-US Negotiations on Law Enforcement Access to Data: Divergences, Challenges and EU Law Procedures and Options. *International Data Privacy Law*, 11(2), 81–106.

Christakis, T., Propp, K., and Swire, P. 2022a. EU/US Adequacy Negotiations and the Redress Challenge: Whether a New U.S. Statute is Necessary to Produce an "Essentially Equivalent" Solution [online]. 31 January. *European Law Blog*. https://europeanlawblog.eu/2022/01/31/eu-us-adequacy-negotiations-and-the-redress-challenge-whether-a-new-u-s-statute-is-necessary-to-produce-an-essentially-equivalent-solution/ [Accessed 30 September 2022].

Christakis, T., Propp, K., and Swire, P. 2022b. EU/US Adequacy Negotiations and the Redress Challenge: How to Create an Independent Authority with Effective Remedy Powers [online]. 16 February. *European Law Blog*. https://europeanlawblog.eu/2022/02/16/eu-us-adequacy-negotiations-and-the-redress-challenge-how-to-create-an-independent-authority-with-effective-remedy-powers/ [Accessed 30 September 2022].

Daskal, J. 2020. What Comes Next: The Aftermath of European Court's Blow to Transatlantic Data Transfers [online]. 17 July. *Just Security*. https://www.justsecurity.org/71485/what-comes-next-the-aftermath-of-european-courts-blow-to-transatlantic-data-transfers/ [Accessed 30 September 2022].

European Commission. 2021a. *European Commission Adopts New Tools for Safe Exchanges of Personal Data* [online]. Press release, 4 June. https://ec.europa.eu/commission/presscorner/detail/en/ip_21_2847 [Accessed 30 September 2022].

European Commission. 2021b. EU-US Trade and Technology Council Inaugural Joint Statement (Pittsburg Statement) [online]. Press Release. 29 September. https://ec.europa.eu/commission/presscorner/detail/en/STATEMENT_21_4951 [Accessed 30 September 2022].

European Commission. 2022a. *Trans-Atlantic Data Privacy Framework*. March. https://ec.europa.eu/commission/presscorner/detail/en/FS_22_2100 [Accessed 30 September 2022].

European Commission. 2022b. EU-India: Joint press release on launching the Trade and Technology Council [online]. Press Release. 25 April. https://ec.europa.eu/commission/presscorner/detail/en/IP_22_2643 [Accessed 30 September 2022].

European Data Protection Board (EDPB). 2018. *Guidelines 2/2018 on Derogations of Article 49 under Regulation 2016/679 Adopted on 25 May 2018*.

European Data Protection Board (EDPB). 2020a. European Data Protection Board Publishes FAQ Document on CJEU Judgment C-311/18 (Schrems II) [online]. https://edpb.europa.eu/news/news/2020/european-data-protection-board-publishes-faq-document-cjeu-judgment-c-31118-schrems_en [Accessed 30 September 2022].

European Data Protection Board (EDPB). 2020b. *Recommendations 01/2020 on Measures that Supplement Transfer Tools to Ensure Compliance with the EU Level of Protection of Personal Data*. https://edpb.europa.eu/our-work-tools/documents/public-consultations/2020/recommendations-012020-measures-supplement_en [Accessed 30 September 2022]

European Data Protection Board (EDPB). 2020c. *Recommendations 02/2020 on the European Essential Guarantees for Surveillance Measures*. https://edpb.europa.eu/our-work-tools/our-documents/recommendations/recommendations-022020-european-essential-guarantees_en [Accessed 30 September 2022].

Fahey E. 2022. *The EU as a Global Digital Actor*. Hart Oxford: Hart.

Fahey, E. 2014. On The Use of Law in Transatlantic Relations: Legal Dialogues Between the EU and US. *European Law Journal*, 20(3), 368–384.
Fahey, E. and Terpan, F. 2021. Torn Between Institutionalisation & Judicialisation: The Demise of the EU-US Privacy Shield. *Indiana Journal of Global Legal Studies*, 28, 205–244.
Frankenreiter, J. 2021. The Missing 'California Effect' in Data Privacy Law. Washington University in St. Louis Legal Studies Research Paper No. 21-07-01.
Goodman, M. 2021. DEPA and the Path Back to TPP [online]. 15 July. *CSIS*. https://www.csis.org/analysis/depa-and-path-back-tpp [Accessed 30 September 2022].
Kern, R. 2022. Bipartisan Draft Bill Breaks Stalemate on Federal Data Privacy Negotiations. 3 June. *Politico*. https://www.politico.com/news/2022/06/03/bipartisan-draft-bill-breaks-stalemate-on-federal-privacy-bill-negotiations-00037092 [Accessed 30 September 2022].
Kerry, C. 2022. The FTC Ups the Ante for Federal Privacy Legislation. 26 August. *Lawfare Blog*. https://www.lawfareblog.com/ftc-ups-ante-federal-privacy-legislation [Accessed 30 September 2022].
Kuner, C. 2017. Reality and Illusion in EU Data Transfer Regulation Post Schrems. *German Law Journal*, 18(4), 881–918.
Kuner, C. 2020. The Schrems II judgment of the Court of Justice and the Future of Data Transfer Regulation [online]. 17 July. *European Law Blog*. https://europeanlawblog.eu/2020/07/17/the-schrems-ii-judgment-of-the-court-of-justice-and-the-future-of-data-transfer-regulation/ [Accessed 30 September 2022].
Linn, E. 2017. A Look into the Data Privacy Crystal Ball: A Survey of Possible Outcomes for the EU-U.S. Privacy Shield Agreement. *Vanderbilt Law Review*, 50, 1311–1358.
Moerel, L. 2012. *Binding Corporate Rules: Corporate Self-Regulation of Global Data Transfers*. Oxford: Oxford University Press.
Petersmann, E.-U. 2015. 'Transformative Transatlantic Free Trade Agreements without Rights and Remedies of Citizens?. *Journal of International Economic Law*, 18, 579–607.
Pollack, M. 2005. The New Transatlantic Agenda at Ten: Reflections in an experiment in International Governance. *Journal of Common Market Studies*, 43, 899–919.
Pollack, M. and Shaffer, G. 2009. *When Cooperation Fails: The International Law and Politics of Genetically Modified Foods*. Oxford: Oxford University Press.
Proust, O. and Emmanuelle, E. 2011. Les Binding Corporate Rules: une solution globale pour les transferts internationaux. *Lamy droit de l'immatériel*, 74, 97–102.
Saurugger, S. and Terpan, F. 2021. Normative Transformations in the European Union: on Soft and Hard Law. *West European Politics*, 44(1), 1–20.
Shaffer, G. 2002. Managing U.S.-EU Trade Relations Through Mutual Recognition and Safe Harbor Agreements: 'New' and 'Global' Approaches to Transatlantic Economic Governance?. *Columbia Journal of European Law*, 9, 29–77.
Terpan, F. 2015. Soft Law in the European Union - The Changing Nature of EU Law. *European Law Journal*, 21(1), 68–96.
The White House. 2022. *Fact Sheet: United States and European Commission Announce Trans-Atlantic Data Privacy Framework*. 25 March. https://www.whitehouse.gov/briefing-room/statements-releases/2022/03/25/fact-sheet-united-states-and-european-commission-announce-trans-atlantic-data-privacy-framework/ [Accessed 30 September 2022].

16

THE EU AND US TRANSATLANTIC AGENDAS ON TAXATION

Maria Kendrick

SENIOR LECTURER IN LAW IN THE CITY LAW SCHOOL AT CITY, UNIVERSITY OF LONDON, FELLOW OF THE CENTRE OF EUROPEAN LAW AT KING'S COLLEGE LONDON AND MEMBER OF THE INSTITUTE FOR THE STUDY OF EUROPEAN LAW

Introduction

Modern attempts to reach international consensus on how to transform the international tax system in order to grapple with the global imperative of digitalisation appear to have made progress. This is in contrast to historical efforts to re-evaluate and alter norms of taxation, which revolved around concepts of physical brick-and-mortar presence and residence. The impetus for such apparent breakthroughs can be linked to the traditional rationale of revenue raising. The need to raise tax revenue to fund public spending has been around since time immemorial; however, the modern mix of digitalisation and globalisation of the economy has created a new focus on tax avoidance and good governance in the area of taxation, and essentially 'fair' taxation (OECD 2013). This has been spurred on, especially at the EU level, by the need to generate its own resources, specifically in order to 'support' the COVID-19 recovery. In the US, changes in the administration have brought with them significant differences in viewpoints as to the role of the American State and the position of corporations, especially home-grown American multinational enterprises (MNEs), as part of the economy. However, the EU and US home-grown agendas on taxation do not operate in a domestic or regional vacuum. In order to achieve successful implementation of their own local agendas on taxation, they need to dominate the transatlantic space. Control over norm promotion practices in international taxation is essential for the system to work in their favour, and for the money to come their way. Or more importantly, for tax revenue not to go in the other direction.

This contribution will consider both EU and US transatlantic agendas on 'fair' corporate taxation in a digitalised economy. What will become apparent is that both the EU and the US are trying to ensure that their own transatlantic agendas on taxation become the basis of the new norms of the digital age. We will see the position of the

DOI: 10.4324/9781003283911-20

EU in wanting to occupy, and indeed dominate, the transatlantic space and agenda on digitalisation and tax to further EU integration and an idea of European sovereignty. The US is seeking to ensure that changes in its own tax system do not become disincentives, to American MNEs especially, paying tax at home because they differ too significantly from international norms. Both the EU and US transatlantic agendas on taxation therefore demonstrate a desire to harmonise corporate tax to make it 'fair' in order to facilitate new norm promotion practices in the digital age, but according to their own agendas. The recent progress in reaching consensus on reforming the international tax system in the face of digitalisation of the economy can be attributed to changes in the US Administration and its views on corporate tax. A renewed focus in the Organisation for Economic Co-operation and Development (OECD)/G20 on the BEPS Inclusive Framework would arguably not have been possible if it was not for American proposals with significant political impetus behind them. The EU, however, wishes to 'be among the first to implement the recent historic global tax reform agreement' and has already published a proposal for a Directive implementing Pillar Two on the OECD Inclusive Framework. However, this proposal differs from what the US envisaged, in order for the EU to comply with the principles of its own internal market, and has therefore been formulated in its own image. Which agenda will come to dominate the transatlantic space, and whether harmonisation according to either agenda can be achieved, is still an evolving issue.

What is crystalising though are efforts on the part of both the EU and the US to attempt to use 'fairness' to guide norm promotion practices in the digital age according to their own transatlantic tax agenda. This is problematic because norms of tax fairness theory are an uncomfortable fit with both agendas, which are in actuality premised on successful implementation of their own local priorities on taxation in the transatlantic space to ensure domination and control. This submission will consider if 'fairness' is being used as an undefined and vacuous concept transformed into a mantra used to justify the global tax harmonisation agendas of both the EU and the US. This submission will consider if proposals on fair taxation in the digital economy are not just being used as a proxy to justify the harmonisation of direct taxation of the digital economy and ultimately uniform standard setting of global tax based on particular, even unilateral, norm promotion practices of the EU and US in the Digital Age.

The meaning of 'Fairness' in taxation

The meaning of 'fairness' in taxation is not as simple or as uncontroversial as one may assume, or hope. Fairness is a 'slippery' (Bizioli 2019) concept, usually equated with ideas of equality or equity. The meaning of equity and equality are also not universally agreed upon in the context of taxation, with two principles said to form their basis; the ability to pay and the benefit principle. For Kaufman, both the benefit principle and the ability to pay principle are norms of tax fairness, although competing norms (Kaufman 1998). According to Dodge, tax fairness is a norm in itself (Dodge 2005).

A 'fair' tax is considered one that is levied in accordance with the taxpayer's ability to pay, based on the level of financial resources they have available to them.

Sometimes referred to as 'equity', there are further categorisations into Horizontal Equity, meaning that where two persons have the same ability to pay they should bear the same tax burden, and Vertical Equity, meaning that where one taxpayer has a greater ability to pay than the other they should bear a higher tax burden (Oats 2021). The latter is usually a justification for applying a progressive tax rate, being a tax rate which increases as the tax base increases. However, ability to pay is not an uncontentious ground on which to levy taxation, because the question of what financial resources should be taken into account can be problematic. An alternative perspective and interpretation of this norm is based on the principle of solidarity, being a citizen's contribution to the common good (Schön 2009).

Another way of defining the meaning of 'fairness' in taxation is the benefit principle. This norm is linked to the social contract theory espoused in the tax context by many writers, including Hobbes, Smith, Friedman and Hayek ("Büttner, Thiemann (2017); Devereux, Vella (2017); Farrar et al., (2020); Friedman (1962); Halehehner et al., (2019); Hayek (1960); Hobbes (1909); Smith, Cannan (2003)", where individuals contribute to support the state and government to the extent to which they receive peace, defence and protection. More modern interpretations suggest that taxes should be levied in accordance with the amount of usage, or 'benefit' a taxpayer receives from the provision of state or government services. This meaning of fairness is problematic for reasons such as quantification and measurability. Another interpretation of this principle is a tax on the ability to do business. In essence, states and governments facilitate the provision of a functioning market in which businesses can operate (Dodge 2005).

The benefit principle and ability to pay principle are considered as competing, basically because the ability to pay principle focuses on the economic wealth (or lack of) of the taxpayer, whereas with the benefit principle, the focus is on the level of service provision by the state. By their very nature, welfare systems are theoretically designed to provide those with the least ability to pay with the greatest service provision. Economic equality is also interpreted as applying among states, being a question of economic justice between states regarding the distribution of the authority to tax and therefore revenue from taxation (Debelva 2018). This perspective is prominent at an international level. This is evident from the rhetoric surrounding the reforms dubbed 'Pillar One' agreed as part of the OECD/G20 Inclusive Framework on Base Erosion and Profit Shifting, although the delays to the design and implementation of this proposal are displaying the difficulties with the realisation of substantive legal support for the political narrative.

Both the EU and the US emphasise not only the need for change but how changes to taxation should occur, and importantly how changes should occur in accordance with their ideas and proposals, are in order to create a 'fairer' tax system. Which concept of 'fairness' have the EU and US stated they support? There is criticism on how norm promotion practices have been adopted by both the EU and the US. Confusion abounds. Not only confusion but also other motives or issues are apparent, as Bizioli suggests,

The reference to tax fairness contained in the official documents of the international organisations [the EU and the OECD] is, therefore, an exercise of rhetoric (or, in other words, rather pleonastic) since it purports the need to re-establish the tax equality in a changed (and changing) economic world. However, the same documents do not contain any attempt or show any effort to assess the fundamental criteria according to which the tax burdens should be (equally) distributed among the taxpayers. Any reference to the 'value' created through the digital businesses is, in fact, a reference to an empty concept that is not defined either by the international documents or by the OECD Member States tax jurisdictions. (Bizioli 2019, p.61)[1]

Contrast this opinion with the EU Commission Expert Group on Taxation of the Digital Economy (European Commission 2014), which focuses on equality according to distribution between states on the basis that the EU will leave the other issues of fairness between individuals to the national tax systems.However, it makes a lot about fairness being needed to support national tax systems and much of what the EU is attempting to do with tax has a significant impact on the workings of national tax systems.

Devereux *et al.* (2021) consider fairness between countries as being an alternative approach. The idea of essentially equality of tax law between states has been propounded by Vogel (1988a; 1988b; 1988c) from the perspective of which country should have the right to tax and collect tax revenue. The basis of this approach is that the country in which economic activity is taking place should receive some of the revenue from taxing profit made by businesses through the use of publicly provided goods and services within that country's jurisdiction. This reflects the point of view that jurisdiction to tax and allocation of taxing rights should reflect the locations within which economic activity takes place. Devereux *et al.* (2021) however argue that this does not necessarily justify a tax on business profit as opposed to a fee for the use of goods and services and what is an equitable basis of the allocation of taxing rights between countries is debatable. On the basis of fairness, should taxing rights be claimed more by the country of residence of the shareholders [reflecting Devereux et all opinion that the focus really should be on the individual who pays the tax, or incidence, rather on the business], the country where production takes place, or the country in which the final good is consumed? There does not seem to be any clear basis to answer this question. There is no 'scientific' method to identify the 'right' allocation of taxes between countries (Devereux *et al.* 2021 p.39).

With all the debate and difficulty defining and rationalising these competing concepts of 'fairness' why do we therefore see the EU and the US so fervently utilising the rhetoric of 'fairness' to justify what are arguably very substantial reforms to taxation devised in response to digitalisation? There is not much indication given in the language used, which tends to be tautologous, citing digitalisation of the economy as the reason why a 'fair' tax system needs to be created to ensure MNEs pay their 'fair' share. As Devereux *et al.* identify, 'Ultimately, these notions of fairness are almost impossible to operationalize in designing a business-level tax on profit' (Devereux *et al.* 2021 p.40).

As Bizioli suggests (Bizioli 2019), there is no explicit choice between these competing principles and priorities, instead there seems to be vacuous tautologous rhetoric, so what is the real motivation?

'Fairness' as an uncomfortable fit with both EU and US agendas on taxation?

The benefit principle, the ability to pay principle and the equality between States principle, can be said to be norms of tax fairness theory. The agendas of both the EU and the US, especially as they are seen as demonstrated in international fora, such as the OECD in the recent BEPS Inclusive Framework political negotiations and proposals, which respond to the digitalisation of the economy, can be tested against these norms to demonstrate that they are an uncomfortable fit with these norms of 'fairness'. What has been achieved in the international sphere will be considered briefly first, before moving on to consider the specific regional agendas of both players in the transatlantic sphere.

The OECD BEPS Inclusive Framework is intended to respond to the digitalisation of the economy, particularly as digitalisation supposedly facilitates tax avoidance by digital MNEs. The proposals in the form of the two pillar solution apply to large MNEs which have a significant turnover, as indicated by the thresholds above which the proposals will apply. For Pillar One, the in-scope companies are the MNEs with global turnover above 20 billion euros, and for Pillar Two, the GloBE rules will apply to MNEs that meet the 750 million euros threshold. Are the thresholds linked to ability to pay? Surely such threshold setting is not done at such a high level on the basis that businesses trading below such thresholds do not have the ability to pay? Perhaps the benefit principle would suggest that this high a threshold should be set, but then again the services provided by states and market conditions which they facilitate would be equally beneficial to even moderately smaller businesses. Equality between states is also not the most likely fairness norm to apply, as it has been well observed that MNEs of such size to be caught by the thresholds trade less in developing than developed countries. Instead, it is clear that there are a few particular companies, especially American companies, which are the subject, or target of these proposals, demonstrating the uncomfortable fit with both the EU and US agendas and 'fairness' as a justification, even when one looks at one aspect, such as threshold values. This is also true when one considers the final incidence of the tax which will likely fall on the individuals, either consumers or employees, who will likely be worse off as a result of taxes being levied on business profit, as this has an effect on the prices of the goods and services that it sells, and the prices of the inputs that it uses, including wages paid to its employees. As a result, as prices adjust, the tax can be passed onto consumers in the form of higher prices, employees in the form of lower wage, or other suppliers in the form of lower prices paid for inputs (Devereux *et al.* 2021).

As will be discussed briefly further, unilateral digital services taxes (DSTs) which form(ed) part of the EU agenda, as its digital levy, are not compatible with the US agenda, particularly where they are considered to target US companies (Mason and Parada 2020). As not in keeping with the US agenda, they are not said to promote 'fairness'; however, do not unilateral DSTs better align with the benefit principle because they are closer to the jurisdiction, that is, nation state or government from which they derive their benefit? Or could it perhaps be said that for a nation state to devise its own DST, as many have done, that befits its own specific tax system that better reflects the differences between states? Whatever one's opinion on these questions, they demonstrate that 'fairness' is not at the heart of the agendas of the EU and US because of the uncomfortable fit the concept has with the policies of both parties. They each utilise the rhetorical term 'fairness' to further their own agendas, to which this submission will now turn.

The EU agenda

The EU has a tax harmonisation agenda (European Commission 2017; Kendrick 2021) and extensive digital agenda, in some respects, the two overlap (European Commission 2014). However, although there is much reference to 'fairness' in support of the Commission and EU proposed action on taxation, there is little definition given beyond superficial reference to distributional priorities. As well as the lack of detailed definitional reference to the concept of 'fairness' the EU seeks to employ and support, there have been various policy changes which all purport to be based on providing a fair and efficient tax system, despite some policies in particular being based on distinct differences in the tax base and tax rate. A brief summary of the EU's agenda now follows, through which the flux of proposals will become apparent. What this actually demonstrates is that the EU is really attempting to harmonise taxation, and influence transatlantic policy in its own image by doing so. This will be expressed in the penultimate part of this chapter.

Four of the EU's most recent corporate taxation initiatives are: the Common Consolidated Corporate Tax Base (CCCTB); the Common Corporate Tax Base (CCTB) (European Parliament 2018); both of which have now been abandoned in preference of Business in Europe: Framework for Income Taxation (BEFIT) (European Commission 2021); and the digital levy, which has been proposed, then postponed, then potentially held in reserve should the current OECD proposals not prove forthcoming (Kendrick 2021; 2022). There is some but not much detailed reference to definitional concepts of 'fairness' to support the rhetoric used by the European Commission (European Commission 2018). The significance and the number of changes themselves, however, do call into question the sincerity of the commitment of the EU to achieving fairness. The digital levy is a case in point. Initially, full harmonisation of corporate tax was proposed in the CCCTB, and whilst the consolidation aspect of the proposal proved too progressive from a state sovereignty perspective, the reduced more palatable CCTB was suggested with harmonisation as the goal (Kendrick 2021). With a lack of support from Member States translating into an inability to surmount the unanimous voting threshold required by the legal basis in the Treaty (Article 115 TFEU), a digital levy, also known as digital services tax, was proposed as an interim option (Kendrick 2021). It was the potential clash of this unilateral measure by the EU, seen from the perspective of the OECD global coordination efforts, which led a fervent United States to seek an end, potentially permanently, to this proposal. The OECD Inclusive Framework political agreement of 8 October 20221 confirmed the US agenda on unilateral digital taxes thus:

The Multilateral Convention (MLC) will require all parties to remove all Digital Services Taxes and other relevant similar measures with respect to all companies, and to commit not to introduce such measures in the future. No newly enacted Digital Services Taxes or other relevant similar measures will be imposed on any company from 8 October 2021 and until the earlier of 31 December 2023 or the coming into force of the MLC. The modality for the removal of existing Digital Services Taxes and other relevant similar measures will be appropriately coordinated. The IF notes reports from some members that transitional arrangements are being discussed expeditiously (OECD 2021).

The EU's position is that it intends for the Inclusive Framework to be implemented in EU law but with a different strategy adopted for Pillar One and Pillar Two. The EU Commission has put forward a proposal for a Directive implementing Pillar Two into EU law (European Commission 2021b). The Directive largely tracks the OECD agreement, while adding domestic application to comply with EU anti-discrimination requirements. In essence, it includes purely domestic groups, not just cross border international companies, to ensure that the new 15% minimum effective tax rate for large companies will be applied in a way that is fully compatible with EU law. Estonia has expressed concerns about the domestic application of the proposed EU version of the Pillar Two rules, 'mandatory implementation that might impact not only the multinational companies but also internal … that was not part of the deal in the OECD'. Not to be deterred completely by the US seeking to assert its own agenda for norm promotion through political pressure to drop its digital levy proposal, the EU has suggested that it wishes to be the first to implement the Pillars, in compliance with EU law, presumably to show the way. However, this has not proved to be as easy as hoped, to the extent that there have been calls for the resurrection of the digital levy if progress is stalled (European Parliament 2022; Tax Notes 2022). This demonstrates that the EU is determined to have its own agenda on taxation and to utilise it to influence norm practices, with digitalisation being the spur.

The fluctuation and changes in proposals demonstrate that if it was one of the conceptions of fairness discussed earlier which really was the driving force then there would be consistency and potentially a static approach adopted by the EU. Instead, we see manoeuvrability to appease Member States and the US agenda, which dislikes unilateral digital taxes, as displayed at the OECD level and then the potential for change again back to the digital levy proposal if, despite the wishes of the US, the EU cannot implement its own design of the two Pillars through Directives compatible with EU Law.

The US agenda

Having pushed at the OECD level for the two-pillar solution to addressing the tax challenges arising from the digitalisation of the economy, the US has had issues of its own implementing the substance of the proposals. The difficulty arose from problems with obtaining approval in Congress to the economic reforms suggested by the Biden Administration, which were significantly wider than just corporate tax reform. There has recently been progress on these wider economic reforms, in the form of the Inflation Reduction Act (IRA 2022), and these extend to corporate taxation. However, the provisions of the IRA are certainly not a reproduction of the two pillars proposed at the OECD level. The taxation element of the IRA contained in SEC. 10101 of the IRA comprises a Corporate Alternative Minimum Tax (AMT) also known as the book minimum tax. The only form of consensus which it seems to have stimulated is on the interpretation that it is *a* proposal on corporate tax but not the same as *the* proposal which has come from the OECD. Divergence between the US and the OECD appear to centre, broadly speaking, on two main areas. First, whilst both appear to provide for an effective tax rate of 15%, the AMT assesses a company's worldwide income and average tax rate, whereas Pillar Two seeks to inhibit that practice by taxing firms on a country by country basis. The AMT is therefore arguably more akin to the GILTI US regime than it is to Pillar Two. Second, the IRA allows for exemptions on tax credits and capital investments, where the OECD agreement would likely not.

The concept of 'fair' taxation has not been absent from the US agenda, seen in collaboration within, or domination of the OECD, even to the extent that it acted arguably as the impetus behind recent progress on an international agreement at the OECD, but it is certainly fairness as a convenient tool to promote what is beneficial to the US in terms of raising, and domesticating, tax revenue from MNEs.

Whilst it is rather early days to properly assess the implementation of the IRA and its implications for the norm promotion practices of the US in the digital age, it is fair to say that it is becoming apparent that in tax norm promotion as with other areas of trade, there is an America first focus and agenda. There is therefore the potential for the beginning of a research agenda to follow the extent to which the US is able to influence the development of global taxation and crucially the extent to which it is successful in keeping and repatriating the tax revenue, which is the underlying rationale of the IRA. It is also notable in the wider context of EU and US transatlantic relations that the dialogue between them has a distinct focus on digitalisation, extending, for example, to big tech, but that this has inevitable natural consequences for taxation. The main recent example of this dialogue – or exertion of pressure – is on DSTs, as briefly outlined earlier in relation to the EU's proposed digital levy. There is scope to develop further a research agenda on how both the EU and the US use what appear to be neutral fora, such as the OECD (Geringer 2022), to push their agendas by using 'neutral' terminology and rhetoric, such as 'fairness' to try and hide norm promotion practices in line with their own agendas.

'Fairness' as a proxy for harmonisation?

The rhetorical resort to 'fairness' can be seen as a narrative smokescreen behind which the EU and US promulgate their agendas, utilising the undefined concept to hide self-interest as altruism (de la Feria 2022) or as a form of policy legitimation (Halliday 2010). What are their ultimate agendas? In the context of digitalisation, resort to 'fairness' masks attempts to harmonise global taxation on the basis of their specific agendas. The EU and US home-grown agendas on taxation do not operate in a domestic or regional vacuum. In order to achieve successful implementation of their own local agendas on taxation, they need to dominate the transatlantic space. Control over norm promotion practices in international taxation is essential for the system to work in their favour, and for the money to come their way. Or more importantly, for tax revenue not to go in the other direction. In other words, the norms they are promoting are not those of fairness but of harmonisation. 'Fairness' is therefore a proxy for harmonisation.

The brief discussion earlier outlines how uncomfortable the fit is with both EU and US agendas and the concept of 'fairness' in either principled guise of the ability to pay principle, the benefit principle or equality between states, but there is also evidence that the subtext of 'fairness' is harmonisation. Just recently, the EU's harmonisation agenda in direct taxation, for which there is no explicit legal basis, and therefore competence, in the Treaty, was confirmed at the ECOFIN meeting by all Member States with representatives in attendance (ECOFIN 2022). The EU proposal for a Directive on Pillar Two already differs from what was agreed with the US in the OECD because of the clear priority to further the EU internal market, the basis on which indirect tax is harmonised, rather than pursue international standards of 'fairness' in taxation. The EU wishes to 'be among the first to implement the recent historic global tax reform agreement' although proposals are easier to suggest than implementation is to achieve (M. Kendrick 2022). The US has proceeded to devise a different tax to that agreed at the OECD level in its AMT, although arguably trying to achieve the same ultimate aim which is to repatriate American tax revenue from large digital businesses to its own Treasury. This in turn will likely, so the US will hope, promote international tax norms in its own image.

Conclusion

The EU and US home-grown agendas on taxation do not operate in a domestic or regional vacuum. In order to achieve successful implementation of their own local agendas on taxation, they need to dominate the transatlantic space. Control over norm promotion practices in international taxation is essential for the system to work in their favour, and for the money to come their way. Or more importantly, for tax revenue not to go in the other direction.

This contribution considered both the EU and US transatlantic agendas on 'fair' corporate taxation in a digitalised economy. What became apparent is that both the EU and the US are trying to ensure that their own transatlantic agendas on taxation become the basis of the new norms of the digital age. The EU wants to occupy, and indeed dominate, the transatlantic space and agenda on digitalisation and tax to further EU integration through harmonisation in tax. The US is seeking to ensure that changes in its own tax system do not become disincentives, to American MNEs especially, paying tax at home because they differ too significantly from international norms, and so it is rather altering international norms and then adjusting its own US tax law to fit, and arguably influence, how international tax law progresses.

Both the EU and US transatlantic agendas on taxation therefore demonstrate a desire to harmonise corporate tax to make it 'fair' in order to facilitate new norm promotion practices in the digital age, but according to their own agendas.

Note

1 The documents referred to in this passage are: European Commission COM (2017) 547 Final 'Communication from the Commission to the European Parliament and the Council: A Fair and Efficient Tax System in the European Union for the Digital Single Market'; Commission, 'Proposal for a Council Directive on the Common System of a Digital Services Tax on Revenues Resulting from the Provision of Certain Digital Services' COM (2018) 148 Final; OECD/G20 Base Erosion and Profit Shifting Project, (2018). 'Tax Challenges Arising from Digitalisation - Interim Report 2018'.

References

Bizioli, G., (2019). 'Fairness of the Taxation of the Digital Economy: Challenges and Proposals for Reform', In: Haslehner, W., Kofler, G., Pantazatou K., and Rust A., (eds.), *Tax and the Digital Economy*. Wolters Kluwer 49–65.

Büttner, T. and Thiemann, M., (2017). 'Breaking Regime Stability? The Politicization of Expertise in the OECD/G20 Process on BEPS and the Potential Transformation of International Taxation', *Accounting, Economics and Law* 7: 1.

De law Feria, R., (2022). 'The Perceived (Un)Fairness of the Global Minimum Corporate Tax Rate', In W. Haslehner et al. (eds), *The Pillar 2 Global Minimum Tax*. Edward Elgar, forthcoming.

Debelva, F., (2018). 'Fairness and International Taxation: Star-Crossed Lovers?', *World Tax Journal* 10: 563–583.

Devereux, M. P., and Vella, J., (2017). 'Implications of Digitalisation for International Corporate Tax Reform', In Gupta, S., Keen, M., Shah, A., and Verdier, G., (eds.), *Digital Revolutions in Public Finance*. Washington DC: International Monetary Fund 91–112.

Devereux, M. P., Auerbach, A. J., Keen, M., Oosterhuis, P., Schön, W., and Vella, J., (2021). *Taxing Profit in a Global Economy*. Oxford: Oxford University Press.

Dodge, J., (2005). 'Theories of Tax Justice: Ruminations on Benefit, Partnership, and Ability-to-Pay Principles', *Tax Law Review* 58: 399–462.

ECOFIN (2022). Czech Presidency of the Council of the European Union, Informal Meeting of Economic and Financial Affairs Ministers and Central Bank Governors, September 2022, https://czech-presidency.consilium.europa.eu/en/news/informal-meeting-of-economic-and-financial-affairs-ministers-and-central-bank-governors/ [accessed 13 September 2022].

European Commission (2014). 'Expert Group on Taxation of the Digital Economy', https://taxation-customs.ec.europa.eu/expert-group-taxation-digital-economy_en [accessed 12 September 2022].

European Commission (2014). Report of the Expert Group on Taxation of the Digital Economy, https://taxation-customs.ec.europa.eu/system/files/2016-09/report_digital_economy.pdf [accessed 12 September 2022].

European Commission COM (2017). 547 Final 'Communication from the Commission to the European Parliament and the Council: A Fair and Efficient Tax System in the European Union for the Digital Single Market'.

European Commission (2018). Questions and Answers on a Fair and efficient Tax System in the EU for the Digital Single Market, Brussels. Available from: https://ec.europa.eu/commission/presscorner/detail/en/MEMO_18_2141 [accessed 29 April 2022].

European Commission COM (2021). 251 Final, 'Communication From the Commission to the European Parliament and the Council: Business Taxation in the 21st Century', Brussels, https://ec.europa.eu/taxation_customs/system/files/2021-05/communication_on_business_taxation_for_the_21st_century.pdf [accessed 31 August 2021].

European Commission (2021b). COM(2021) 823 final 'Proposal for a Council Directive on ensuring a global minimum level of taxation for multinational groups in the Union'.

European Parliament (2018). Press Release 'New EU corporate tax plan, embracing "digital presence", approved in committee', https://www.europarl.europa.eu/news/en/press-room/20180219IPR98113/new-eu-corporate-tax-plan-embracing-digital-presence-approved-in-committee [accessed 12 September 2022].

European Parliament (2022). Draft Opinion on the proposal for a Council decision amending Decision (EU, Euratom) 2020/2053 on the system of own resources of the European Union (COM(2021)0570–C9-0034/2022-2021/0430(CNS)), https://www.europarl.europa.eu/doceo/document/ECON-PA-734455_EN.pdf [accessed 12 September 2022].

Farrar, J. et al., (2020). 'Tax Fairness: Conceptual Foundations and Empirical Measurement', *Journal of Business Ethics* 162: 487–503.

Friedman, M., (1962). *Capitalism and Freedom*. Chicago: University of Chicago Press.

Geringer, S., (2022). 'Implications of the OECD MTC Commentary's Dynamic Interpretation in ECJ Case Law: The OECD as EU Legislator?', In Hultqvist A. and Lindholm. J. (eds) *The Power to Tax in Europe*. Oxford: Hart Publishing, Forthcoming.

Halehehner, W., Kofler, G., Pantazatou, K., and Rust, A., (2019). *Tax and the Digital Economy: Challenges and Proposals for Reform*. Wolters Kluwer.

Halliday, T., et al., (2010). 'Rhetorical Legitimation: Global Scripts as Strategic Devises of International Organizations', *Socio-Economic Review* 8: 77–112.

Hayek, F. A., (1960). *The Constitution of Liberty*. Chicago: University of Chicago Press.

Hobbes, T., (1909). *Leviathan, reprinted from the edition of 1651*. Oxford: Clarendon Press.

Inflation Reduction Act of 2022 (2022). H.R. 5376, text available at https://www.taxnotes.com/research/federal/legislative-documents/public-laws-and-legislative-history/inflation-reduction-act-of-2022-%28p.l.-117-169%29/7dybc [accessed 12 September 2022].

Kaufman, N., (1998). 'Fairness and the Taxation of International Income', *Law and Policy in International Business* 29: 145–203.

Kendrick, M., (2021). 'The Future of Differentiated Integration: The Tax Microcosm', *Journal of International and Comparative Law* 7 (2): 371–387.

Kendrick, M., (2022). 'The Legal (Im)possibilities of the EU Implementing the OECD/G20 Inclusive Framework on Base Erosion and Profit Shifting', *Global Trade and Customs Journal* 17 (1): 19–24

Mason, R. and Parada, L., (2020). 'The Legality of Digital Taxes in Europe', *Virginia Public Law and Legal Theory* Research Paper No. 2020-50.

Oats, L., (2021). *Principles of International taxation*. 8th ed. London: Bloomsbury Professional Tax.

OECD BEPS Action Plan on Base Erosion and Profit Shifting, (2013). Available from: https://www.oecd.org/ctp/BEPSActionPlan.pdf [Accessed 17 April 2022].

OECD/G20 Base Erosion and Profit Shifting Project, (2021). 'Statement on a Two-Pillar Solution to Address the Tax Challenges Arising From the Digitalisation of the Economy' 8 October 2021, https://www.oecd.org/tax/beps/statement-on-a-two-pillar-solution-to-address-the-tax-challenges-arising-from-the-digitalisation-of-the-economy-october-2021.pdf [accessed 10 October 2021].

Schön, W., (2009). 'International Tax Coordination for a Second-Best World (Part I)', *World Tax Journal* 1: 67–114.

Smith, A. and Cannan, E., (2003). *The Wealth of Nations*. 8th ed. New York: Bantam Classic.

Tax Notes (2022). 'EU Lawmakers Push for Digital Levy Proposal for End of 2025', https://www.taxnotes.com/tax-notes-today-global/digital-economy/eu-lawmakers-push-digital-levy-proposal-end-2025/2022/08/30/7f1fq [accessed 12 September 2022].

Vogel, K., (1988a). 'Worldwide vs. Source Taxation of Income – A Review and Re-Evaluation of Arguments (Part I)', *Intertax* 8-9: 216–229.

Vogel, K., (1988b). 'Worldwide vs. Source Taxation of Income – A Review and Re-Evaluation of Arguments (Part II)', *Intertax* 10: 310–320.

Vogel, K., (1988c). 'Worldwide vs. Source Taxation of Income – A Review and Re-Evaluation of Arguments (Part III)', *Intertax* 11: 393–402.

17

THE "BENEFICIAL DIVERGENCE" IN THE TRANSATLANTIC APPROACH TO COMPETITION LAW ENFORCEMENT TOWARDS PLATFORM AND ECOSYSTEM COMPETITION

Giulio Kowalski

Introduction

This chapter explores the concept of 'beneficial divergence' between EU and US antitrust enforcement against digital platforms and ecosystems. By analysing recent antitrust cases against Google in both regions, the chapter shows that US enforcers seem to adopt a more 'holistic' approach to antitrust enforcement, paying particular attention to the inner workings of digital firms than the European Commission ('EC'), including their business and operating models. This approach would better capture the mechanics of harm caused by anticompetitive practices, potentially providing useful indications for effective remedial intervention under competition law. In this regard, the chapter draws on strategic management namely the process of developing and executing a company's strategy to achieve long-term goals. One of the critical components of strategic management is analysing and optimizing a company's business and operating model to ensure the achievement of its business objectives (Lynch, 2018; Wheelen and Hunger (2017)). The chapter argues that insights from strategic management provide crucial knowledge about the (anticompetitive) behaviour of digital firms to inform competition enforcement. The beneficial divergence presents an opportunity for competition authorities to develop

 DOI: 10.1201/9781003143642-21

and share best practices based on such insights and adapt antitrust towards welfare-enhancing digital markets.

Platforms and ecosystems: distinguishing different business structures

Most strategy literature considers that ecosystems are often based on platforms, which enable the connections between ecosystem actors and possibly end users. Platforms and ecosystems are not the same, though, and should not be conflated (Jacobides and Lianos, 2021). A platform may be defined as a new business model, a new social technology, a new infrastructural formation, or all three at once (Jacobides and Lianos, 2021). Platforms provide the foundation for the web of interactions that define ecosystems; if platforms are about technologies, ecosystems are about interorganisational relations (Jacobides et al., 2020). Ecosystems, which often draw on platforms, arise not from centralised control but from the interactions between the components of a correlated system (Jacobides and Lianos, 2021). Ecosystems refer to multi-actor groups of collaborating complementors (i.e., 'theory of the firm' alternatives to vertical integration or supply-chain arrangements) and multiproduct bundles offered to customers (i.e., horizontally or diagonally connected goods and services that are 'packaged' together), focused on customer ease - and lock-in (Jacobides et al., 2021).

Platforms

The platform business model is the primary business model of the digital economy (Cusumano et al., 2019). Important to note in passing that the platform business model is so prevalent in the present economy since internet and digital technologies have dramatically reduced the number of transaction costs thereby facilitating a wide array of interactions which the platform as an intermediate facilitates (Belleflamme & Peitz, 2021). This final observation highlights the key defining element of the platform: the facilitation of interaction between different groups of users. Relevant legal, business and economic literature seems to have based the definition of platform on that concept and that of network effects (e.g., Belleflamme & Peitz, 2021; O'Donoghue & Padilla, 2020; Cusumano et al., 2019; Parker et al., 2017). In particular, this research adopts the definition put forward by Belleflamme & Peitz (2021) referring to a platform as an entity that brings together economic agents and actively manages network effects between them.

Even though it is not possible to illustrate all the key concepts relating to platforms and ecosystem and the way they compete, the two fundamental building blocks of the definition of platform are dealt with in turn.

The first crucial characteristic of platforms is their role as intermediaries.[1] Platform-intermediation consists in particular of a set of users, individuals or firms, whose interactions are subject to network effects, along with one or more intermediaries (i.e., platforms) who facilitate such users' interactions (O'Donoghue & Padilla, 2020).[2] Basically, Intermediation means providing access (Bourreau, 2020) to a set of users (e.g., consumers) to another (e.g., advertisers). In other words, intermediation is akin to the gatekeeping function: digital platforms provide gateways for a large number of (business) users to reach other (end) users everywhere in different markets (Regulation (EU) 2022/1925, 'DMA'). Users interact through the platform directly (e.g., buyers and sellers using the Amazon marketplace) or indirectly (e.g., advertisers using targeted advertising services provided by Google). Typically platforms are 'multisided' meaning that they intermediate between more than one group of customers on their different 'sides'.[3] In other words, multisidedness means that platforms bring two or more different types of economic agents together and facilitate interactions between them by reducing transaction and search costs for such agents (e.g., internet users and advertisers) (Evans & Schmalensee, 2013).

The second critical feature of platforms is network effects. It is worth highlighting that by interacting on the platform, customers form a network. This in particular means that the utility for platforms' customers is not only, and sometimes not even primarily, derived from the platform's product or service; on the contrary, customers will derive their utility from the increased adoption of that product or service by other users (Belleflamme & Peitz, 2021). Such an increase in adoption will allow further valuable interactions, therefore attracting more users which in turn will create more value and attract further users. The cycle repeats itself resulting in a 'positive feedback loop' (OECD, 2015).[4] Where platforms allow users to interact with other users (i) from the same group, they generate within-group network effects (e.g., one-sided platform)[5]; (ii) from a different group (e.g., two/multisided platforms exhibiting cross-group network effects)[6]. For instance, Google, as well illustrated by the DoJ, allows interaction between users searching for information on one side of the market, and vendors or advertisers who have services or products to sell on the other side of the market (U.S. v. Google, 2020).

Ecosystems

Beyond platforms, competition in the digital economy is also increasingly a competition between ecosystems (Crémer et al., 2019). Platforms can develop into multi-actor or multi-product ecosystems (Jenny, 2021). In fact, ecosystems are based on and have evolved around a central, multisided platform (Jacobides & Lianos, 2021; Bourreau, 2020; Reeves et al., 2019) known as the 'orchestrator'. The orchestrator sets the rules of engagement and is in charge of governance (Jacobides & Lianos, 2021). More specifically, platforms are the technologically-based solutions that allow multiple actors to interact, while ecosystems are groups of connected products or services and the players that collaborate to produce them (Jacobides, 2022). Put simply, platforms are made of technology, while ecosystems are made of products, people and organisations.

In light of the above, business ecosystems can be generally defined as networks of business entities that work together to create and capture value (Petit & Teece 2020; Jacobides et al., 2018). Indeed, an ecosystem typically relies on technological leadership of one or more firms that provide a 'platform' around which other system members called 'complementors' (i.e., supply chain actors providing inputs and complementary goods) align their investments and strategies (Jenny, 2021; Petit & Teece, 2020; Jacobides et al., 2018). For ecosystems to thrive, the role of complementors is crucial. Complementors, which are supply chain actors providing inputs and complementary goods, are an essential part of ecosystems and align their investments and strategies around the platform to create, deliver and capture value (Jenny, 2021; Petit & Teece, 2020; Jacobides et al., 2018; Zhu, & Liu (2018). While the platform's core technology, products or services are important, the real value addition stems from interaction with and amongst complementors (Petit & Teece, 2020). Ecosystems can be classified as multiactor or multiproduct. Multiactor ecosystems refer to independent actors collaborating through complementary activities to provide a collectively produced product or service. In contrast, multiproduct ecosystems offer a collection of complementary goods and services bundled together and aim to lock-in customers by making it difficult to consume elsewhere (Jacobides and Lianos, 2021). Big Tech firms use both approaches, with the Apple ecosystem being an example of both multiactor and multiproduct ecosystems (Jacobides et al., 2020): an offer of multiple products (i.e., iOS, iPhone, iPad, MacBook, Apple TV, etc.) is combined with a multitude of app developers (i.e., the actors/complementors) who abide by iOS rules in exchange for the right to sell through this ecosystem (Jacobides, 2022; Jacobides et al., 2020). While there are links between these two types of ecosystems, each ecosystem's drivers and logic remain distinct. The development of a profitable multiproduct ecosystem focuses on the overall value proposition of the product bundle to achieve customer lock-in, while engaging in a multiactor ecosystem involves determining a firm's boundaries and partnership arrangements (Jacobides, 2022). The reciprocal interaction among heterogeneous ecosystem members (also called 'co-evolution') should lead to 'generativity', meaning new output structures or behaviours. (Jacobides and Lianos, 2021; Petit & Teece, 2020; Moore, 2006; Wareham et al., 2014). Co-evolution can create entirely new services and industries. This is what happened when interactions with merchants led Amazon to develop Amazon Web Services ('AWS'), now Amazon's main moneymaking segment. Initially designed as a set of APIs, AWS incrementally morphed into a complete infrastructure, computing, storage and database service for developers (Petit & Teece, 2020).

Platform and ecosystem as the dominant business model in the digital economy

In the following, the inquiry delves deeper into the internal operations of digital firms by analysing their business and operating models through the lens of strategic management. This exploration aims to uncover the 'black box' (Colomo, 2021) of these firms and develop functional guiding principles to improve competition enforcement against platforms' and ecosystems' anti-competitive practices. As it will be seen in the Google case studies below, the US would seem more prone to incorporating insights concerning the internal functioning of digital firms in the enforcement activity against platforms than the EU, resulting in a 'beneficial divergence' between their approaches. However, before diving into the core elements of any digital business and operating model, it is necessary to first understand the concept of "digital", broken down into *digitisation* and *digitalisation* and how these processes are transforming the economy (Iansiti and Lakhani, 2020). While "digitisation" refers to the conversion of data from analog to digital form, "digitalisation" identifies the application of digitisation to organisational and social processes such as the economy (Bukht & Heeks, 2018; UNCTAD, 2019), related connectivity of digital assets and digitalisation supports an economy-wide redesign of value creation, delivery and capture processes (Gawer, 2022; Autio et al., 2018). In a nutshell, digitisation allows a redesign of the business and operating model of firms allowing digital platforms and ecosystems to thrive as the most adopted business model in the digital economy.

The "digital" element of the economy: digitisation and the digital economy

There is not a single definition for 'digital economy' and since first coined in the mid-1990s (typically the origin of the term is referred to Tapscott, 1996), such definition has evolved over several decades, reflecting the rapidly changing nature of technology and its use by enterprises and consumers (e.g., Tapscott, 1996; Brynjolfsson and Kahin, 2000; Bukht and Heeks, 2018; Barefoot et al., 2018; IMF, 2020; UNCTAD, 2019; OECD, 2020).

An attempt at a definition was recently made by the OECD that defined the digital economy as all economic activity reliant on (i.e. only exists thanks to), or significantly enhanced by (i.e. existed before but is improved by) the use of digital inputs, including digital technologies, digital infrastructure, digital services and data (OECD, 2020). The very comprehensive definition emphasises that the key factor in the digital economy is technological sophistication (Knichrehm et al, 2016; Akman, 2022), more precisely, digitisation and digitalisation. In other words, based on the OECD definition, the digital economy would stem from the adoption of digital technologies in economic activity that have supported the *digitisation* of inputs and *digitalisation* of economic processes.

It is worth pointing out the reasons why the process of digitisation (and the consequent digitalisation of the economy) is such a disruptive factor that has been transforming the economy as follows. In sum, When an activity is digitised (e.g., converting a photograph into pixels), profound changes take place. This is particularly true for four reasons.

First, a digital representation of a physical element (such as a traditional picture turned into a digital one made of pixels) is infinitely 'scalable'. This means that it is now possible to easily and perfectly replicate and transmit it at virtually zero marginal cost to a near-infinite number of recipients, anywhere in the world (Iansiti & Lakhani, 2020).

Second, digitising an activity makes it easily connectable, also at zero marginal cost, to limitless other, complementary activities, dramatically increasing the scope of such activity (Iansiti & Lakhani, 2020). This is also thanks to the modular architecture of digital firms. The effect of such a reduction in friction has made it possible to identify and exploit complementarities across users, machines and sectors through the use of data, software and networks (Gawer, 2022). The significance of connectivity is key for the illustration of platforms' business model. As Gawer (2022) illustrates, connectivity allows data to be shared linking objects, individuals and organisations who consume as well as generate data. Also, digital technologies are based on reprogrammable functionality, repurposable digital devices, fungible software, data analytics technologies and installed user-base data that can allow expansion in multiple markets (Gawer, 2022). In particular, complementarities between the processes of data generation, connectivity and aggregation help reduce transaction costs over time, which impacts firm boundaries and the architecture of the value chain (Gawer, 2022). Finally, digitalisation also creates economic forces that facilitate firms' expansion of scope. Digitalisation makes market entry easier, as firms that can capture and aggregate data from various sectors can unearth and exploit new kinds of synergies. Such data-driven market entry results in the expansion of the scope of digital platform firms.

Third, such digital activity can embed processing instructions, AI algorithms that shape behaviour and enable a variety of possible paths and responses. These technologies (particularly machine learning algorithms) can learn as it processes data (i.e., Machine Learning), continuously training and improving the algorithms that are embedded in it (Iansiti & Lakhani, 2020). The digital representation of human activity can thus learn and improve itself in ways that analogue processes cannot (Iansiti and Lakhani, 2020).

Fourth, Internet and digital technologies have reduced the number of transaction costs and enabled individuals to interact with minimal friction (Belleflamme and Peitz, 2021; Gawer, 2022).

"Digital" business and operating models

The impact of digitisation on the economy has disrupted the business and operating models of platforms and ecosystems. This includes the use of advanced machine learning techniques and modular architecture in creating, capturing, and delivering value. While these digital models share similarities, platforms and ecosystems create unique strategies and operations based on these similarities. Digital business models that share these common traits can generate revenue differently, such as through advertising (e.g., Google) or selling devices (e.g., Apple) or both (Etro, 2020).

The aim of the following analysis is, however, to identify the key shared characteristics of digital business and operating models that make them so effective in creating, capturing, and delivering value.

Digital business model

The value of a firm is shaped by two concepts. The first one is the business model. A business model can be defined, as the core strategy or set of strategies that a firm pursues to monetise its assets (Colomo, 2021). More generally, the business model is the way in which the firm promises to create and capture value for its customers. The business model thus encompasses the strategy of the firm: how it seeks to differentiate itself from competitors by providing and monetising its unique set of goods or services (Iansiti & Lakhani, 2020).[7]

The reliance of a digital company on modular architecture and (connectable)[8] digital technologies allows the latter to adopt a specific business strategy based on exploiting digital connections through powerful software infrastructure and connecting different networks, markets and, crucially, industries (Iansiti & Lakhani, 2020). Thus, the real competitive advantage for digital firms comes from their ability to leverage digital connections (i.e., connect) among different industries and business networks. In other words, the competitive advantage is moving towards the business organisations that are central in connecting businesses, aggregating data flowing between them and extracting value through powerful analytics and AI (Iansiti & Lakhani, 2020).

Google, Facebook, Alibaba Tencent and all the other digital conglomerates are accumulating data and building the software infrastructure as well as the analytics and AI necessary to create, sustain and grow a competitive advantage in the form of synergies between (traditionally siloed) industries and markets (Iansiti & Lakhani, 2020). Most importantly from a competition point of view, as firms link to each other and different networks also aggregate various data flows, they accumulate both network and learning effects that might turn (and have turned) into barriers to entry in the relevant market. For instance, Google's dominant position in the online search market is protected by powerful network effects, which benefit its search engine directly and indirectly. Direct network effects stem from more people using the search engine, leading to more accurate and relevant search results, while indirect network effects arise from more users attracting more advertisers and generating revenue growth. Competitors face the challenges of high costs and complexity in building a search engine with comparable scale and accuracy, making it difficult to challenge Google's dominance in the market.[9]

Digital operating model

The second essential function of the value for undertakings is the firm's operating model. This concept encompasses the systems, processes and capabilities that enable the delivery of the goods and services (i.e., the value) to the firm's customers (Iansiti & Lakhani, 2020). The overarching objective of an operating model is to deliver value at scale, achieve sufficient scope and respond to changes by engaging in sufficient learning (Iansiti & Lakhani, 2020). Indeed there are three main challenges in corporate governance: generating and driving economies of scale and scope as well as developing the operating capability to improve and innovate (i.e., learning) (Teece et al., 1997). While scale[10] and scope[11] are quite well-understood concepts, it is maybe worth defining the concept of 'learning'. The learning function of a business' operating model consists essentially of the company's ability to drive continuous improvement, increase operating performance over time and develop new products and services (Iansiti & Lakhani, 2020).

Digital technologies have heavily transformed how firms deliver value to their customers. Traditionally, the expansion of the scale, scope or learning function of a firm would increase the complexity of the organisation and makes managing it more challenging (Iansiti & Lakhani, 2020). Ultimately, increased scale (e.g., large user base), broadened scope (e.g., wider product offer) or boost in innovation (e.g., higher R&D expenditure) would lead any managerial process to stop working well (Iansiti & Lakhani, 2020). This is precisely where a digital firm differs from traditional firms (Iansiti and Lakhani 2020).

For instance, in the retail industry, product suggestions have traditionally been made by employees in stores, which is constrained by factors such as limited staffing and time-consuming training processes. In contrast, Amazon's algorithms process vast amounts of data on consumer purchasing patterns and preferences, generating personalized product suggestions that improve over time as more data is ingested. This generative process is made possible by the AI Factory model, which allows for faster learning and adaptation through increased scale and diversity of products and customers (Iansiti and Lakhani 2020).

Strategy, operations and competition

In light of the foregoing, **a** close link between the inner-functioning of the platforms and ecosystems and the way in which they compete may be established. Indeed, digital companies have a strong strategic incentive to leverage the connectivity allowed for by the digital technologies and modular software infrastructure making up their operating model (i.e., the 'AI Factory'). Therefore, it would seem logical for a platform to leverage such advantages and particularly the data coming from their ever-expanding networks to thrive in the marketplace. Moreover, it is also worth noting that the leveraging 'attitude' does not only serve the profit-maximisation goal of the platform but creates a significant amount of value for the different groups of customers that the platform intermediate.[12] Nonetheless, there have been cases where the expansion of digital platforms in a neighbouring market has configured, for instance, an anticompetitive exclusion of rivals (e.g., anticompetitive tying; see the analysis of EC, 2018 below) or the elimination of an (at the time) smaller competitor with a high future potential to become a significant competitive threat for the digital incumbent (so-called 'killer acquisitions').[13] In the analysis below, the chapter considers some of these cases and highlights the strict link between the business (i.e. strategy) and operating model (i.e. operations) on one side and digital platforms' and ecosystems' market behaviour on the other.

Emerging issues in platform competition: the 'beneficial divergence' between the EU and US case law

All the foregoing emphasises the fundamental characteristics that allow digital platforms to thrive in digital markets, with particular reference to the operating model and the overall strategy of such economic agents. However, such features are also relevant in the competition analysis since they could create incentives for digital firms to distort competition. For instance, the intensive data accumulation and analysis required for the functioning of the AI Factory can definitely generate product improvement and a positive feedback loop where the platform value increases as more users join and as more complementary products and services become available. However, this risks raising entry barriers (particularly i.e., switching costs for consumers and network effects) into a specific market, with (even efficient) competitors unable to overcome them and consumers 'locked in' the incumbent's platform or ecosystem. In short, the incentives created by the strategy and operations of digital firms are strictly linked to the (anticompetitive) market behaviour of platforms and ecosystems.

In the following, the chapter highlights how US competition enforcers seem to pay more attention to such link than the EC. In particular, the case studies analysed below would show that by considering the proper functioning of digital platforms and ecosystems (in particular business and operating models) in the competitive analysis US enforcers would better describe the mechanics of harms produced by digital companies and perhaps provide useful cues on the appropriate remedy design. In this sense, US agencies appear to carry out a more 'holistic' competition analysis that the EU Commission. This is particularly true in ongoing cases in the US against Google: the one filed by the DoJ (U.S. v. Google, 2023) which is similar in focus to the European Commission's Android decision (EC, 2018), and the one led by the State of Texas (Texas v Google, 2021) which focuses on advertising markets in a manner similar to the European Commission's AdSense decision (EC, 2019; Monti, 2022).

The more holistic US approach in regulating digital platforms would be particularly apparent since the US would give more prominence than the EU to specific features characterising the platforms' and ecosystems' business and operating model namely (according to the particularly effective three-pronged analytical framework put forward by Monti, 2022) (i) the multi-market analysis of the effects; (ii) the role of dynamic com-petition (i.e., competition on innovation) in EU and US competition analysis and (iii) the interrelation between data protection and competition.

This divergence between the EU and US models briefly illustrated above can be described as a 'beneficial divergence' between the two systems. In particular, the 'beneficial divergence' may be an opportunity for cross-fertilisation and best-practice sharing for intervention in digital markets between EU and US competition enforcers, in the appropriate fora.[14] The following analysis elaborates upon such divergence to show that, if backlit, the US antitrust analysis mirrors the functioning of a digital platform, and particularly its business and operating model.

Google's Ad-based business model

To better comprehend the subsequent analysis, it is crucial to first explain in simple terms how Google generates profits. Google's primary revenue stream comes from digital advertising. This implies that Google offers, for instance, its core service, which is search, for free. Once a substantial number of users are attracted, Google capitalises on the data collected from these users and provides targeted advertising services on the other side of the platform (Geradin & Katsifis, 2019). In this business model, data play a pivotal role. By comprehending the preferences and requirements of specific consumers at any given moment, advertisements can be specifically targeted to individuals who are deemed most likely to make a purchase (CMA, 2019). By developing an ecosystem of complementary products and services around its core service, Google has accumulated even more extensive data (CMA, 2019). This results in greater advertising revenues, enabling Google to invest at a greater rate than its rivals, which in turn creates a feedback loop (i.e., network effects) that further cements Google's powerful market position (CMA, 2019).

Multi-market analysis of effects

Both the EC and the DoJ have challenged a number of Google's anticompetitive behaviours that have allowed Google to cement its position in the online search market and online advertising markets (U.S. v. Google, 2020; EC, 2018). In particular, Google's illegal conduct consisted of, first, tying practices. Indeed, Google imposed preinstallation agreements on device manufacturers whereby key apps for consumers (e.g., the Play Store) could only be obtained subject to the pre-installation of the Google Search app and browser app (Chrome) in Android devices. Furthermore, Google also made payments (i.e., revenue-share agreements) to certain large device manufacturers and mobile network operators on condition that they exclusively pre-installed the Google Search app on their Android devices. Third, Google prevented manufacturers wishing to pre-install Google apps from selling smart mobile devices running on alternative versions of Android that were not approved by Google (so called "Android Forks") (U.S. v. Google, 2020; EC, 2018; Monti & Feases, 2021).

Overall, Google's exclusionary agreements denied rivals (e.g., browsers and online search engines) access to the most important distribution channels. The EU and US agencies agree that anticompetitive effects consisted in the reduction of the quality of general search services (including dimensions such as privacy, data protection, and use of consumer data), lessening choice in general search services, and impeded innovation. However, the DoJ goes a step further by emphasising that Google's exclusionary conduct also substantially forecloses competition in the search advertising and general search text advertising markets, harming advertisers (Monti, 2022; U.S. v. Google, 2020).

While the competition agencies agree that Google's conduct occurs in the market for general search, they carry out a divergent market definition with only one overlapping market. The EC defines markets in the (i) licensing of smartphones for operating systems, (ii) app stores, (iii) general search and (iv) non-OS-specific web browsers. The United States focuses instead on (i) general search, (ii) search advertising and (ii) general search text advertising (U.S. v. Google, 2020; EC, 2018). Clearly, the only overlapping market in the two analyses is the market for general search engines What it is important to note here is that the DoJ's focus on the online advertising market signals a 'more holistic' approach which pays closer attention to the dynamics of competition in multi-sided markets (Monti, 2022). This difference leads the DoJ to design its case in a manner which is quite different from that of the Commission even if the conduct under consideration is similar. Thus, while the EC places the focus on Google's tying practices and tests them against the standards set for tying by the EU case law, the DOJ emphasises on the two ways by which Google's practices foreclose access to competitors in general search: first, competing search engines are denied access at scale on devices running Android due to, for example, antiforking clauses imposed on manufacturers revenue sharing agreements provided Google search is the default search engine and the deal with Apple that made entry of a competing search engine on the Apple ecosystem impossible. Second, as a result, competing search engines are denied the capacity to raise revenue via advertising because they cannot grow to such an extent to provide an attractive prospect for advertisers (Monti, 2022; Monti & Feases, 2021; U.S. v. Google, 2020; EC, 2018).

In practice the DoJ analysis links the exclusionary conduct on the general search market with the lack of access to the revenue in the advertising market, claiming that the monopolisation of the search and advertising markets are closely interconnected (Monti, 2022). This approach allows the DOJ to explore competitive harm more holistically: indeed the DoJ examines the competitive harm on both sides of the market, the consumer side and the advertising side (Monti, 2022).[15]

Not only does the DoJ approach seem more effective to provide a 'full picture' of competitive harm, it appears to be also warranted by the platform business models described above. Indeed, the competitive analysis in U.S. v. Google, (2020) clearly takes into account two essential elements of numerous digital platforms to devise its theory of harm: the intermediation function and multisideness. On the contrary, concerns about the impact of platforms on advertising were not central in the European Google Android case where the EC looked only at the harm on the consumer side (Monti, 2022). Indeed, the EC did not define a market for digital advertising in its Android case. However, it considered harm in the advertising market in the Google Adsense case (EC, 2019; Monti, 2022).

Most importantly, the DoJ understood that the real competitive advantage for Google came from its ability to connect the different markets it is active in (general search, search advertising and general search text advertising) and monetise the data and audience (i.e., the scale) 'flowing' from the search market by selling advertising. Data coming from the search market are also used to continuously improve Google's algorithms to best respond to user queries in terms of results and ads and generate profits as a result (U.S. v. Google, 2020).

Limiting innovation: 'Next Generation' digital markets

As it was specified above, the conduct levelled against Google by the DoJ and the EC is exclusionary. However, as Monti (2022) notices, while the EC makes some reference to the impact that the conduct may have on innovation, the DOJ's appraisal is more precise on the likely future effects. The EC's decision (EC, 2018) includes a detailed analysis of past innovation - particularly Android forks such as Amazon's Fire OS - quashed by antifragmentation agreements as evidence that Google's conduct can well hinder innovation (EC, 2018). However, the EC does not assess the future impact of Google's conduct. In this regard, the EC merely argued that Google's exclusionary behaviours (the revenue share payments and the tying of the Play Store with Chrome and the Google search app in particular) deter innovation because they prevent the development of competitors (EC, 2018).

Conversely the DOJ's appraisal is more precise on the likely future effects (Monti & Feases, 2021). In particular, the DoJ claims that Google's exclusive dealing is aimed at controlling (not only present but also emerging) channels for search distribution such as smart watches, smart speakers, smart TVs and connected automobiles (DoJ V Google, 2020). For instance, the DoJ mentions the licensing agreements between Google and 'smart watch manufacturers' providing for a free licence of Google's 'free' smart watch operating system (Wear OS) conditioned upon the prohibition on preinstallation manufacturers from preinstalling any third-party software (e.g., rival search services) (DoJ V Google, 2020). The defendant's strategy, according to the DOJ, is clear: by conquering new distribution channels for its search engine Google will try to keep its solid position in the market for search services as these evolve (Monti and Feases, 2021).

The particular attention devoted by the DoJ to the expected expansion of Google's practices to nascent distribution channels is important because it highlights the consideration of the DoJ for the real competitive advantage of the platform business model: the strategic leveraging (e.g., tying) of digital connections among different industries and business networks granted by the adoption by of a modular architecture and digital technologies based on AI and more specifically machine learning (Iansiti and Lakhani, 2020). Most importantly from a competition point of view, as firms link to each other and different networks also aggregate various data flows, they accumulate both network and learning effects (Iansiti & Lakhani, 2020). The DoJ attentive scrutiny of future effects of Google's conduct is very important, again, because it would allow a more holistic and complete analysis of the competitive harm caused by Google's conduct. Furthermore, such an analysis would provide the DoJ with a base to adopt forward-looking remedies like - in the US *Microsoft* case - that would attempt to protect competition not only in the short, but also in the long run (New York v. Microsoft, 2002; States v. Microsoft Corp, 2002). This may clearly influence the design of remedies in EU competition enforcement too.

The interrelation between competition and privacy

A third element of divergence between the DoJ and the EC approach to digital platform and ecosystem competition is the consideration of the interrelation between privacy and competition law.

This is particularly the case of the case brought by Texas against alleged Google's monopolisation of and anticompetitive agreements to distort competition on the 'ad tech stack', namely the digital advertising value chain (Geradin & Katsifis, 2019). The case is particularly concerned with the open display advertising market. In the open display market, a wide range of publishers (e.g., online newspapers) sell their inventory to a wide range of advertisers through a complex chain of intermediaries that run auctions on behalf of the publishers and advertisers (CMA, 2019).

Open display advertising is heavily reliant on internet users' personal information (e.g., browsing history and location). Such information is used primarily to compile profiles about individual users that reflect their likely interests and, based on these, target advertising to such users (CMA, 2019). Therefore consumers' data is essential to provide (and improve)[16] target advertising services. Google owns the largest intermediaries at each level of the value chain (U.S. v. Google, 2023; Texas v Google, 2021; EC, 2017; CMA, 2019) and its entire business model is to collect comprehensive data about every user in the service of brokering targeted ad sales between publishers and advertisers (Texas v Google, 2021).

In this regard, it is important to emphasise how the US cases considered Google's use of data protection as an anticompetitive behaviour. First, in Texas' complaint, it is alleged that Google would have used privacy concerns to gain a competitive edge over competitors. As a publisher ad server and ad exchange (i.e., two different digital advertising intermediaries), Google supports publishers to sell their online inventories (i.e., advertising spaces such as a banner-style advert on a newspaper website) by collecting bids from advertisers and allowing real-time auctions and deciding what ad to serve on the publishers' inventory based on the bids received (CMA, 2019). In particular, Google collects all the information about the publisher's website visitors in a unique ID. Competing publisher ad servers and ad exchanges need to know such information to set a competitive price for those inventories (and estimated impressions) and sell it to an advertiser willing to pay that price (U.S. v. Google, 2023; Texas v Google, 2021). In particular, when exchanges cannot identify users in auctions (e.g., through cookies), the prices of impressions on exchanges can fall by about 50 percent, according to one Google study (Texas v Google, 2021). Based on this, the Texas' complaint claims that the 'privacy concerns' alleged by Google to justify the restriction of publishers' ability to access and share the user IDs are just 'an excuse to advantage itself over its competitors'. Indeed, Google was not impacted by the constraint and is able to freely use that very same information to offer intermediary services that can ensure a competitive price to publishers (Texas v Google, 2021).

Second, privacy was also a DoJ's relevant argument against Google's monopoly in search and search advertising. In particular, the DoJ linked consumer choice, quality and the degree of data protection. The DoJ argued that If Google's services became the only choice for users, this would lower the degree of privacy and data protection since users would be required to accept the terms imposed by their only choice of search engine. Conversely, had there been competition, users would have been able to choose a search engine on the basis of which one better matched the value they place on privacy. And had there been the opportunity to compete, new entrants would likely have introduced different products (Monti & Feases, 2021; U.S. v. Google, 2020).

The focus on the interlace between data protection and competition is important because it sheds further light on the anticompetitive effects of Google's conduct and the risks for consumer welfare (Monti, 2022). On the contrary, the EC's approach to such interface would be more 'conservative' (Monti, 2022), at least in abuse of dominance cases. For instance, the EC only mentioned data protection in Google Android to illustrate Google's business model (Monti, 2022; Google Android, 2018) whereas any reference to interface between data protection and competition is absent from the competitive analysis in both Google Shopping (EC, 2017) and Google Adsense (EC, 2017). Conversely, under EU merger control, the role and importance of data and privacy in the competitive assessment would seem to be increasing, perhaps due to the considerable number of data-driven acquisitions in digital markets occurred in the last 10 years (Wasastjerna, 2019). In light of the foregoing, it is important to note that the EC has recently launched an investigation against Google declaring that will take into account the need to protect user personal information, since 'Competition law and data protection laws must work hand in hand to ensure that display advertising markets operate on a level playing field in which all market participants protect user personal data in the same manner'. Whether this claim means that the EC is actually adopting a more holistic approach to competition law remains to be seen. In conclusion, it can be argued that the US cases (Texas v Google, 2021 and DoJ v Google 2020) have clearly shown how a better understanding of data management (and governance) by platforms may in turn lead to a surface concealed anticompetitive conduct derived primarily by the mechanics of the platform (digital) business and operating model.

Conclusions

The analysis above intended to highlight a beneficial divergence in transatlantic competition enforcement in the digital sphere. In particular, US enforcers to consider more the insights coming from the analysis of platforms' and ecosystems' business and operating model than the EC. The analysis of the case law above signalled how this aspect might be crucial for a deeper understanding of new mechanics of competitive harm in the digital age and, in turn, the design of more effective remedies and legal tests. This chapter is not intended to criticise the EC's approaches to regulating digital firms, considering the various factors that contributed to the EC's approach. Notably, Monti (2022) emphasises how in 2020 the US enforcers may have had a more insightful understanding of digital markets than the EC in 2010, 2013, and 2016 (EC, 2017; EC, 2018; EC, 2019). Moreover, the chapter would intend to be a call for an interdisciplinary approach to competition law and particularly for crossfertilisation between (but not limited to) the field of strategic management and competition law. Irrespective of what the reasons for the different approaches between the EU and the US might be, it is important to highlight how the 'beneficial divergence' might be used as an analytical blueprint by the EC to consider a potential cross-fertilisation between systems. This in particular to further adapt competition enforcement approaches to digital business and operating models, as called for in different high profile reports on competition law in the digital age (EC, 2019; Furman et al., 2019; Stigler Centre, 2019) and as Europe has already started doing.[i]

i See for instance the initiatives of the ec concerning market definition (Review of the Commission Notice on the definition of relevant market for the purposes of Community competition law. (2022). URL: https://competition-policy.ec.europa.eu/public-consultations/2022-market-definition-notice_en [Accessed April 27, 2023]) and Commission of the European Communities. (2023). Amendments to the Communication from the Commission – Guidance on the Commission's enforcement priorities in applying Article 82 of the EC Treaty to abusive exclusionary conduct by dominant undertakings (Text with EEA relevance). Retrieved from https://eur-lex.europa.eu/legal-content/EN/TXT/?uri=uriserv%3AOJ.C_.2023.116.01.0001.01.ENG&toc=OJ%3AC%3A2023%3A116%3ATOC

Notes

1 On the intermediation function of platforms see e.g., Armstrong, M., 2006; Hagiu & Wright 2015; Bundeskartellamt, 2016; ACCC, 2019; Rysman, M., 2009.

2 For *example search engines allow interaction between users searching for information – on one side of the market – and vendor or advertisers who have services or products to sell – on the other side of the market (*O'Donoghue & Padilla, 2020*, 1059). This is true, however, also for one-sided platform where the firm intermediate between user of the platform and let them interact through the platform itself (e.g., WhatsApp before being acquired by Facebook).*

3 For instance, in the case of search engine, users of the search engine service and advertiser on the other side.

4 For example, the more people use services such as Google Search, or recommendation engines such as that provided by Amazon, or navigation systems such as that provided by TomTom, the more accurate the services become in delivering requested sites and products and providing traffic information which in turn attract more users. And the virtuous cycle repeats itself.

5 E.g. an electronic communication service such as WhatsApp before being acquired by Facebook.

6 E.g., Platforms such as Facebook and Amazon.

7 Pipeline firm is a synonym for traditional firm, namely a firm that designs, manufactures and sell a product or service while a user purchases it. Because of its simple, single-track shape, we may also describe a pipeline business as a linear value chain. See Parker et al., 2017, 6.

8 As it was explained above, the main characteristic of digitised activities is that they allow connectivity between complementary products and services.

9 Learning effect refers to the increase in value captured by the firm with the increase of the amount of data flowing through the firm's network. See Iansiti & Lakhani, 2020, 128.

10 The ability of a company to grow and expand its operations without a significant increase in costs or decrease in efficiency.

11 The range of activities a company performs as well as products and services it offers to its customers.

12 This is particularly true with regard, for example, to social media, where the benefit perceived by consumers is clearly visible in an upward trend in the daily social media consumption worldwide. See 'Daily time spent on social networking by internet users worldwide from 2012 to 2020' <https://www.statista.com/statistics/433871/daily-social-media-usage-worldwide/> accessed 5 December 2021.

13 For instance, the *Google Android* and *Google Shopping* cases brought against the online search big tech by the EC under Article 102 TFEU or the *Facebook/Whatsapp* merger.

14 For instance the EU-US Joint Technology Competition Policy Dialogue. See EU-U.S. Joint Technology Competition Policy Dialogue Inaugural Joint Statement of December 7th 2021. Available at https://ec.europa.eu/commission/presscorner/detail/en/IP_21_6671 (Accessed 10 September 2022).

15 Indeed, the EC did not even define a market for digital advertising in its Android case. However, it considered harm in the advertising market in the *Google Adsense* case (EC, 2019).

16 Transaction between publishers and advertisers are automated through technologies using algorithms able to improve and learn from the data processed. See e.g., CMA, 2019 and Texas v Google, 2020.

References

ACCC. (2019). Digital Platforms Inquiry - Final Report. Retrieved from https://www.accc.gov.au/focus-areas/inquiries/digital-platforms-inquiry/final-report

Akman, P. (2022). Regulating Competition in Digital Platform Markets: A Critical Assessment of the Framework and Approach of the EU Digital Markets Act. *European Law Review*, 47, 85.

Armstrong, M. (2006). Competition in two-sided markets. *The RAND Journal of Economics*, 37(3), 668–691. Available at: 10.1111/j.1756-2171.2006.tb00037.x.

Autio, E., Nambisan, S., Thomas, L.D.W., & Wright, M. (2018). Digital affordances, spatial affordances, and the genesis of entrepreneurial ecosystems. *Strategic Entrepreneurship Journal*, 12(1), 72–95. 10.1002/sej.1266.

Belleflamme, P., & Peitz, M. (2021). *The Economics of Platforms*. Cambridge: CUP.

Barefoot, K., Curtis, D., Jolliff, W., Nicholson, J.R., & Omohundro, R. (2018). Defining and Measuring the Digital Economy. *Bureau of Economic Analysis (BEA) working paper*. Available at: https://www.bea.gov/system/files/papers/WP2018-4.pdf

Bourreau, M. (2020). Some Economics of Digital Ecosystems – Note by Marc Bourreau. *Hearing on Competition Economics of Digital Ecosystems, European Parliament*, 3 December 2020.

Bourreau, M., & de Streel, A. (2019). Digital conglomerates and EU competition policy. Telecom ParisTech, CERRE; University of Namur, CRIDS/NADI, CERRE.

Brynjolfsson, E., & Kahin, B. eds. (2000). *Understanding the digital economy: data, tools, and research*. MIT Press.

Bukht, R., & Heeks, R. (2018). Defining, conceptualising and measuring the Digital Economy. *International Organisations Research Journal*, 13(2), 143–172.

Bundeskartellamt (2016). Market power of platforms and networks: Preliminary findings and proposals for a sector-specific competition law (Report No. 5/2016). *Bundeskartellamt*. https://www.bundeskartellamt.de/SharedDocs/Publikation/EN/Berichte/Sektorspezifisch/Plattformmacht_EN.pdf?__blob=publicationFile&v=6

Colomo, P.I. (2021). Product design and business models in EU antitrust law. London School of Economics - Law Department Working Paper. <https://papers.ssrn.com/sol3/papers.cfm?abstract_id=3925396> accessed 4 December 2021, 3.

Competition and Market Authority (2019). Online platforms and digital advertising. rep. Available at https://www.gov.uk/cma-cases/online-platforms-and-digital-advertising-market-study

Crémer, J., Schweitzer, H., & Montjoye, Y. A. de. (2019). Competition policy for the digital era. *European Commission - Directorate General for Competition*. Available at: https://ec.europa.eu/info/publications/competition-policy-digital-era_en

Cusumano, M.A., Gawer, A., & Yoffie, D.B. (2019). *The business of platforms: Strategy in the age of Digital Competition, Innovation, and power*. New York, NY: Harper Business, an imprint of HarperCollinsPublishers.

EC (2017). Case AT.39740, Google Shopping.

EC (2018). Case AT.40099, Google Android.

EC (2019). Case AT.40411, Google Search (AdSense).

Etro, F. (2021). Device-funded vs ad-funded platforms. *International Journal of Industrial Organization*, 75, 102711. doi:10.1016/j.ijindorg.2021.102711.

Evans, D.S., & Schmalensee, R. (2013). *The Antitrust Analysis of Multisided Platform Businesses*, Working Paper 18783, National Bureau of Economic Research. Available at: https://www.nber.org/papers/w18783 (Accessed: March 7, 2023).

Furman, J., & Others (2019). Unlocking digital competition: Report of the Digital Competition Expert Panel. Retrieved from https://www.gov.uk/government/publications/unlocking-digital-competition-report-of-the-digital-competition-expert-panel

Gawer, A. (2022). Digital platforms and ecosystems: remarks on the dominant organizational forms of the digital age. *Innovation*, 24(1), 110–124.

General Court of the European Union (GC) (2022). T-604/18 | Google and Alphabet v Commission (Google Android).

Geradin, D., & Katsifis, D. (2019). An EU competition law analysis of online display advertising in the programmatic age. *European Competition Journal*, 15(1), 55–96. Available at: 10.1080/17441056.2019.1574440.

Hagiu, A., & Wright, J. (2015). Multi-sided platforms. *International Journal of Industrial Organization*, 43, 162–174. Available at: 10.1016/j.ijindorg.2015.03.003.

International Monetary Fund ('IMF'). (2018). Measuring the Digital Economy. *IMF Policy Paper.* Available at: https://www.imf.org/en/Publications/Policy-Papers/Issues/2018/04/03/022818-measuring-the-digital-economy

Jacobides, M.G., Cennamo, C., & Gawer, A. (2021). Distinguishing between platforms and ecosystems: complementarities, value creation and coordination mechanisms. *Working paper, under review.* https://www.jacobides.com/ongoing-projects

Jacobides, M.G., Cennamo, C., & Gawer, A. (2020). Distinguishing between platforms and ecosystems: Complementarities, value creation, and coordination mechanisms.

Jacobides, M., Bruncko, M., & Langen, R. (2021). Regulating big tech in Europe, Evolution. *Evolution.* Available at: https://www.evolutionltd.net/post/regulating-big-tech-in-europe (Accessed: March 7, 2023).

Jacobides, M.G. (2022). How to compete when Industries Digitize and collide: An Ecosystem Development Framework. Available at: https://journals.sagepub.com/doi/10.1177/00081256221083352 (Accessed: March 13, 2023).

Jacobides, M.G., & Lianos, I. (2021). Ecosystems and competition law in theory and practice. *Industrial and Corporate Change*, 30(6), 1199–1229.

Jacobides, M.G., Cennamo, C., & Gawer, A. (2018) Towards a theory of ecosystems. *Strategic Management Journal*, 39(8), 2255–2276. Available at: 10.1002/smj.2904.

Knickrehm, M., Berthon, B., & Daugherty, P. (2016). Digital Disruption: The Growth Multiplier. Available at: https://www.accenture.com/_acnmedia/PDF-3/Accenture-Strategy-Digital-Disruption-Growth-Multiplier.pdf&usg=AOvVaw1vedaSYQT_HpyYePcjVEB_ [Accessed 9 May 2023].

Lynch, R. (2018). *Strategic management*. Pearson. (Lynch, 2018).

Monti, G., & Feases, A.R. (2021). The case against google: Has the U.S. Department of Justice become European? *Antitrust Journal*, 35(2).

Moore, J.F. (1993). Predators and prey: a new ecology of competition. *Harvard Business Review*, 71(3), 75–86.

Moore, J.F. (2006). Business ecosystems and the view from the firm. *The Antitrust Bulletin*, 51(1), 31–75.

O'Donoghue, R., & Padilla, J. (2020). *The Law and Economics of Article 102 TFEU*. London: Bloomsbury Publishing.

OECD (2020). A Roadmap Toward A Common Framework For Measuring The Digital Economy. accessed 11 October 2021, https://www.oecd.org/sti/roadmap-toward-a-common-framework-for-measuring-the-digital-economy.pdf, p. 34.

OECD. (2019). A Roadmap Toward A Common Framework For Measuring The Digital Economy. OECD Digital Economy Papers, No. 278. Available at: https://www.oecd-ilibrary.org/science-and-technology/a-roadmap-toward-a-common-framework-for-measuring-the-digital-economy_25a9f056-en

OECD. (2015). *Data-Driven Innovation: Big Data for Growth and Well-Being.* OECD Publishing.

Petit, N., & Teece, D.J. (2020). Taking ecosystems competition seriously in the Digital Economy: A (preliminary) Dynamic Competition/Capabilities Perspective. *SSRN Electronic Journal [Preprint].* Available at: 10.2139/ssrn.3745453.

Reeves, M., Lotan, H., Legrand, J., & Jacobides, M.G. (2019). How business ecosystems rise (and often fall). *Sloan Management Review.*

Regulation (EU). 2022/1925 of the European Parliament and of the Council of 6 April 2022 on contestable and fair markets in the digital sector and amending Directives 2002/21/EC and 2011/83/EU and Regulation (EU) No 531/2012.

Rysman, M. (2009). The economics of two-sided markets. *Journal of Economic Perspectives*, 23(3), 125–143. Available at: 10.1257/jep.23.3.125.

Stigler Centre. (2019). Stigler Committee on Digital Platforms: Final report. Retrieved from https://www.law.uchicago.edu/files/stigler-committee-report-on-digital-platforms.pdf
Tapscott, D. (1996). *The Digital Economy: Promise and Peril In The Age of Networked Intelligence.* McGraw-Hill Education.
Teece, D.J., Pisano, G., & Shuen, A. (1997). Dynamic capabilities and strategic management. *Strategic management journal*, 18(7), 509–533.
Teece, D.J., Pisano, G., & Shuen, A. (1997). Dynamic Capabilities and Strategic Management. *Strategic Management Journal*, 18.
Texas v Google, filed (Mar. 15, 2021).
U.S. v Google, filed (October 20, 2020).
U.S. v Google, filed (Tuesday, January 24, 2023).
United Nations Conference on Trade and Development ("UNCTAD"). (2019). Digital Economy Report 2019: Value Creation and Capture: Implications for Developing Countries. *UNCTAD*. Available at: https://unctad.org/system/files/official-document/der2019_en.pdf
United States v. Microsoft Corp., No. 98 1232 (D.D.C. Nov. 12, 2002).
Wasastjerna, M.C. (2019). The implications of Big Data and privacy on competition analysis in merger control and the controversial competition-data protection interface. *European Business Law Review*, 30(3), 337–365.
Wheelen, T.L., & Hunger, J.D. (2017). Strategic management and business policy: Globalization, innovation and sustainability. *Pearson*. (Wheelen & Hunger, 2017).
Zhu, F., & Liu, Q. (2018). Competing with complementors: An empirical look at Amazon.com. *Strategic Management Journal*, 39(10), 2618–2642. Available at: 10.1002/smj.2932.

18

WHO OCCUPIES THE TRANSATLANTIC DATA PRIVACY SPACE? ASSESSING THE EVOLVING DYNAMICS, UNDERLYING REASONS AND THE WAY FORWARD

Maria Tzanou

SCHOOL OF LAW, UNIVERSITY OF SHEFFIELD, UK

Introduction

The decades-long history of transatlantic data privacy relations has been described as fraught with 'disagreements', 'wars' and 'battles' (Tzanou 2015), immortalised by 'headline' moments such as the CJEU's invalidation of Safe Harbour in 2015[1] and of Privacy Shield in 2020.[2] The debate and legal research in the area predominantly focus on these tensions and miss out on advancing a broader discussion regarding the underlying rationale of these potential disagreements that goes beyond oversimplified explanations of privacy vs. security or the alleged differences between the 'two western cultures of privacy' (Whitman 2003). Such broader discussion is important because it strives to move beyond the identification of current weaknesses and shortcomings in transatlantic data privacy relations towards a meaningful exploration of potential ways to bridging these differences.

This chapter argues that the EU-US data privacy relations are complex, multifaced, constantly evolving and rooted on a combination of different underlying reasons some of which are unrelated to the transatlantic space. In this vein, the chapter makes three distinct contributions to the debate regarding EU-US data privacy relations: First, it explores the evolving dynamics of the EU-US data privacy relations by focusing on their different layers of complexity. Second, it examines the potential justifications of these troubled relations and,

 DOI: 10.4324/9781003283911-22

third, it offers some suggestions regarding the potential ways forward in light of recent developments.

Multifaceted, complex and evolving dynamics

The present section explores overall trends and patterns in the EU-US data privacy relations and their development over time. The focus is on the 'big picture', providing a broad-brush discussion of the complexities of the EU-US data privacy dynamics.

Institutions and Procedures: The multiplicity of institutional actors involved makes the EU-US divide particularly complex. The trend to be noted here is a move from a commercial to a security/surveillance approach to data protection which can be observed both in the US and the EU context -insofar as its relations with the US are concerned (Zalnieriute 2022). For instance, transatlantic data privacy policy negotiations initially fell under the remit of the US Department of Commerce and the European Commission's DG Internal Market. After 9/11, they progressively moved in the US to the Department of Homeland Security and the US Department of Justice with the involvement of actors such as the Director of National Intelligence (Tzanou 2018). In the EU, the DG Justice and Home Affairs has been responsible for such negotiations since 2005. This shift in the main negotiating institutions on both sides of the Atlantic demonstrates that both sides perceive their relations in this area as based on a data sharing model with security interests at its core (Zalnieriute 2022).

Procedures matter in EU-US relations and they have influenced the dynamics of transatlantic data transfers. The EU's institutional involvement in transatlantic data transfers has expanded over time, moving from a more centralised, executive approach (with the Commission and the Council at its heart) to a more fragmented one that includes additional levels of institutional scrutiny and control, both at the horizontal and the vertical level. At the horizontal level, the entry into force of the Lisbon Treaty has democratised the EU's procedures for adopting international agreements, by bringing a further institutional actor at the forefront: the European Parliament (Tzanou 2018). As a result, the EU has experienced significant inter-institutional cleavages regarding its data privacy position towards the US which saw many of the EU-US agreements being opposed to and eventually challenged before the CJEU by institutions such as the European Parliament.

A further movement towards the *decentralisation* of institutions in the field of data privacy has taken place at the vertical level (between the EU and its Member States). More particularly, following *Schrems I*, DPAs at the Member State level have been given additional powers to block international transfers -if deemed not essentially equivalent. Such a power includes the autonomy of DPAs to explicitly go against an opposing Commission adequacy decision. Furthermore, national courts have an 'obligation' to refer to the CJEU a preliminary question about the validity of the adequacy decision under Article 267 TFEU[3] in cases where they consider potential infringements of data subjects rights.

While these moves demonstrate the expanding force of EU data protection law, it should not go unnoticed that data privacy has throughout the years being considered a commercial/consumer law issue – internally – in the US, with big tech companies pushing strongly for self-regulatory models rather than other forms of regulation (Zalnieriute 2022). The US Federal Trade Commission (FTC) is the main venue of enforcement for data privacy matters in the US and while it has rendered some seminal decisions, imposing significant fines to companies such as Facebook (now Meta), the 'FTC- model' (Zalnieriute 2022) is revealing of the US approach to data privacy: this is not a fundamental rights concern; rather, it is viewed primarily as a trade issue internally and a security matter externally.

Actors: Informal actors are often overlooked in this context, but have played an important role in the EU-US data privacy relations. These involve, first of all, private commercial companies that have been at the centre of the EU-US data privacy disagreements with important commercial interests in the area. For instance, Facebook has been a party involved in a significant amount of litigation before EU courts, with both the *Schrems I* and *Schrems II* judgements being rendered in a dispute involving Facebook. Moreover, private parties from the US have engaged in extensive lobbying on data protection matters that has not been viewed very positively in Europe (Rossi 2018, p. 101). Remarkably, following the *Schrems II* judgement, private companies, such as Facebook, have been assigned by the CJEU a de facto normative role in transatlantic data transfers: they are now required to assess the legality of third countries' regimes in the context of Standard Contractual Clauses (SCCs) and ascertain that these 'do not go beyond what is necessary to safeguard national security'.[4]

At the European side, privacy advocates have had a significant involvement in EU-US data privacy relations, with one individual, Max Schrems, initiating and engraving his name on the most important challenges concerning transatlantic data transfers decided by the CJEU. The power imbalance between the different actors involved on the two sides of the Atlantic should not go unnoticed: it is certainly revealing of the divergent interests at stake and the clashes that arise thereof.

Rules: The transatlantic privacy space is an example of weak *institutionalisation* (Tzanou 2018; Fahey and Terpan 2021). It is built around multiple, fragmented, asymmetric rules that – often – lack legal clarity and legal certainty. Many of these rules have been negotiated and re-negotiated several times (Tzanou 2018). Four PNR and three TFTP agreements have been adopted between the EU and the US, and Privacy Shield, which replaced the invalidated Safe Harbour, has also been annulled. A closer look at the structure of these agreements shows that the rules contained therein are uncertain and inconsistent. They are often included in various, scattered legal texts, letters, attachments, representations and assurances exchanged between the EU and the US that hardly resemble a typical international law agreement; instead they are reminiscent more of soft law provisions (Tzanou 2018).

Moreover, many of the rules established in the transatlantic data privacy space display an asymmetry of data flows or a certain form of unilateralism as they primarily concern the transfer of data from Europe to the US. Finally and more importantly, a closer examination of the transatlantic data privacy agreements reveals numerous problems from the point of view of fundamental rights (Tzanou 2018).

This weak institutionalisation has brought forward strong *judicialisation* (Fahey and Terpan 2021): on the EU side, the CJEU has been asked to step in and fix the arising substantive issues. This has not always been done cautiously by the Court. For instance, the CJEU's fundamental rights analysis in *Schrems I* centred on the 'essence' of EU fundamental rights, failed to pay due account to the complexities of the transatlantic context and made the Court's judgment susceptible to valid criticisms from the other side of the Atlantic while at the same time undermining the normative value – and the actual scope – of the essence of EU fundamental rights (Tzanou 2020). The increasing role that the CJEU occupies in the transatlantic data protection space has also produced unexpected consequences that often arise despite the intentions of the Court: as seen above, a *fragmentation* of the institutional and private actors involved in transatlantic data privacy relations and an increased *privatisation* of oversight and review mechanisms.

The CJEU's involvement in the transatlantic space has also established a further normative trend of *constitutionalising* transatlantic data transfers. Initially in *Schrems I*, the constitutionalisation of international data transfers was based on red lines. It should be recalled that in its application of Article 52(1) EUCFR,[5] the Court found that the essence of the fundamental right to privacy (Article 7 EUCFR) was breached because the US mass online surveillance programmes gave access on a generalised basis not only to communications metadata but to the actual content of electronic communications;[6] and the essence of the right to effective judicial protection (Article 47 EUCFR) was compromised because the US legislation did not provide EU persons with sufficient guarantees and effective legal remedies to exercise their data access, rectification and erasure rights.[7]

Subsequently, in *Schrems II* – as well as in further cases concerning Member States' national security measures – the CJEU moved towards an approach of *proceduralisation* of surveillance (Tzanou and Karyda 2022; Tzanou 2022). Foreign surveillance measures are no longer prohibited but they are proscribed by several conditions and safeguards. In particular, the CJEU constructed in *Schrems II* a four-prong fundamental rights test applicable to the merits of the examination of foreign surveillance programmes. This requires that limitations to fundamental rights (i) must be provided for by law; (iii) their legal basis must itself define the scope of the limitation on the exercise of the right concerned; (iii) to satisfy the requirement of proportionality, the legislation in question must lay down 'clear and precise rules governing the scope and application' of the relevant measures and impose 'minimum safeguards, so that the persons whose data has been transferred have sufficient guarantees to protect effectively their personal data against the risk of abuse'; and, (iv) the third country must provide 'effective and enforceable data subject rights' for persons whose personal data is transferred.

The CJEU's four-prong test developed in *Schrems II* not only revealed a progressive abandonment of its initial prohibitive approach to surveillance in favour of a more permissive and proceduralised one, but it also demonstrated the Court's willingness to flesh out an amended fundamental rights test to assess the merits of external surveillance (Tzanou 2020, pp. 113–114). This new test applicable to external relations has focused on 'minimum safeguards' so that the persons whose data has been transferred to third countries have some enforceable rights and sufficient protection 'against the risk of abuse', and, therefore, differs from the way the Court has applied the analytical framework of Article 52(1) EUCFR in the context of internal surveillance cases (Tzanou 2020, pp. 113-114). That being said, the US measures were still found in *Schrems II* as failing fundamental rights' standards, despite the Court's attempt to be more flexible in its approach to the transatlantic context.

Looking ahead, it remains to be seen how the CJEU's flexible approach will be interpreted by political institutions on both sides of the Atlantic. Interestingly, the 'in principle data transfer' agreement between the EU and the US-which aims to replace the invalidated Privacy Shield – announced on 25 March 2022[8] indicates that the US administration is willing to focus on two elements: (i) ensure that data processing in the context of signal intelligence activities is *proportionate*; and (ii) provide for *redress mechanisms*.[9] This focus seems to reflect the CJEU's new approach towards 'minimum standards' proceduralisation in the external context, although it remains an issue how it could be attained in practice to satisfy the Court.

The aforementioned analysis revealed a number of different trends that have developed over the years in the EU-US data privacy context: the *commercialisation* of data protection issues; the progressive *securitisation* of data transfers; weak *institutionalisation* of the transatlantic space; *fragmentation* of the institutions and procedures involved at the EU side; overall *privatisation* of many aspects of the transatlantic relations, including the provision by private companies of 'compelled assistance' to US authorities to access data, lobbying to EU institutions, significant litigation and more recently the outsourcing to private parties of the oversight and review mechanisms of EU data protection standards; increased *judicialisation*, evident from the involvement of the CJEU on transatlantic matters; *agencification* of the handling of EU's external data privacy relations through the involvement of DPAs; and, finally a progressive move from *constitutionalisation* to *proceduralisation* of surveillance measures. These trends overlap but often conflict with each other creating further complications and tensions in the transatlantic context.

The reasons underpinning the EU-US 'troubled' data protection relations

The legal issues

Several specific legal issues have arisen over the years in the context of the different EU-US data transfer frameworks. Regarding adequacy findings, as discussed earlier, the CJEU developed in *Schrems II* a four-prong test of 'minimum requirements'. The European Data Protection Board (EDPB) further clarified the four 'core elements' that are to be found in a third country when assessing the interference, entailed by a third country surveillance measures, with the rights to privacy and data protection (EDPB, 2020). These so-called 'Essential Guarantees' are: (i) rule of law- processing should be based on clear, precise and accessible rules; (ii) necessity and proportionality with regard to the legitimate objectives pursued; (iii) existence of an independent oversight mechanism; and (iv) effective remedies available to the individual (EDPB 2020). The EDPB noted that the Essential Guarantees

> should not be assessed independently, as they are closely interlinked, but on an overall basis, reviewing the relevant legislation in relation to surveillance measures, the minimum level of safeguards for the protection of the rights of the data subjects and the remedies provided under the national law of the third country. (EDPB 2020, para 48)

All the four Essential Guarantees contain – still – unresolved legal issues for the attainment of a robust US adequacy finding that will withstand the CJEU's scrutiny. Insofar as the rule of law Essential Guarantee, is concerned, the Court clarified when considering Presidential Policy Directive 28 (PPD-28)[10] – an instrument that sets out key privacy protections in signals intelligence activities – that the assessment of the applicable third country law should focus on whether it can be invoked and relied on by individuals before a court, which requires granting data subjects actionable rights.[11]

Regarding the Guarantee of necessity and proportionality, the CJEU requires that the foreign legislation must 'indicate in what circumstances and under which conditions a measure providing for the processing of such data may be adopted, thereby ensuring that the interference is limited to what is strictly necessary. The need for such safeguards is all the greater where personal data is subject to automated processing'.[12]

The Ombudsperson under Privacy Shield did not meet the standards of an independent oversight mechanism as the Ombudsperson was appointed by the Secretary of State, was an integral part of the US State Department[13] and there was no indication that the Ombudsperson had the power to adopt binding decisions on intelligence services as well as no mention of any legal safeguards that would accompany the political commitment on which data subjects could rely.[14]

Finally, the lack of effective redress was an issue affecting the essence of the fundamental right to effective judicial protection under Article 47 EUCFR[15] and in *Schrems II* the Court reiterated that 'data subjects must have the possibility of bringing legal action before an independent and impartial court in order to have access to their personal data, or to obtain the rectification or erasure of such data'.[16]

The aforementioned outstanding legal issues reveal the underlying and over-arching legal tension between the EU and the US: *extraterritorial US surveillance* vs. *extraterritorial application of EU data privacy rights* (Tzanou 2020, p. 115). The US extraterritorial surveillance is designed to target non-US persons and is founded on the basis of historic concepts that consider US citizenship, residence or the presence of an individual on US soil as 'criteria of categorical normative relevance with regard to the enjoyment of the right to privacy' (Milanovic 2015, p. 89). Indeed, – as I have argued elsewhere – US surveillance programmes are 'inherently discriminatory on grounds of nationality' (Tzanou 2017a, p. 556). At the same time, personal data can be transferred to a third country pursuant to Article 45(1) GDPR where the Commission has decided that this ensures an adequate level of protection. The

Court has clarified that the validity of Commission adequacy decisions should be ascertained on the basis of its compliance with the GDPR 'read in the light of the Charter'.[17] It has also established that the GDPR applies to

> the transfer of personal data for commercial purposes by an economic operator established in a Member State to another economic operator established in a third country, irrespective of whether, at the time of that transfer or thereafter, that data is liable to be processed by the authorities of the third country in question for the purposes of public security, defence and State security.[18]

The political issues

It has been argued that 'many legal disputes concerning data transfers are essentially political arguments in disguise' (Kuner 2017, p. 881). Transatlantic data privacy relations are an example of such political disagreements. These are often described as 'cultural differences' between the two sides following James Whitman's (2003) popular account. Beyond this socio-cultural 'values' explanation of the EU-US arguments concerns several other political influences both at the macro and the micro levels.

At the macro level, the opposing legal claims for extraterritoriality identified above can be seen through a political lens as well: On the one hand, the US would like the EU to enable unfettered flows of personal data internationally for purposes of economic growth and to allow the access of US authorities to data held by commercial entities for national security purposes. On the other hand, the EU would like the US to converge its data protection and fundamental rights standards with the EU's as much as possible with the ambitious goal to 'ensure that when companies active in the European market are called on the basis of a legitimate request to share data for law enforcement purposes, they can do so without facing conflicts of law and in full respect of EU fundamental rights' (Commission 2020, p. 13).

At the micro-level, political factors have significantly influenced transatlantic privacy relations. The secrecy surrounding several US programmes accessing EU originating data that had been brought into light only following media revelations has caused a gradual erosion of trust, particularly from the EU side. The US Terrorist Finance Tracking Programme (TFTP) commenced in 2001, but was only revealed to European through US newspaper articles in 2006 (Tzanou 2017b). The revelations by Edward Snowden in 2013 (Greenwald and MacAskill 2013; Gellman and Poitras 2013) that the US had been operating secret mass electronic surveillance programmes that grant it access to Internet data, such as email, chat, videos, photos and file transfers held by leading Internet companies, including Facebook, Google, Microsoft, Yahoo, Skype, Apple and YouTube, led to a widespread public outcry in Europe and an almost complete breakdown of trust (Wright and Reinhard Kreissl 2013; Rossi 2018). As the European Parliament pointed out,

> Trust has been profoundly shaken: trust between the two transatlantic partners, trust between citizens and their governments, trust in the functioning of democratic institutions on both sides of the Atlantic, trust in the respect of the rule of law, and trust in the security of IT services and communication (European Parliament 2014).

Furthermore, the arising disagreements reflect the political interests of different administrations over time. In an attempt to repair US relationships with the EU – and internationally – after the Snowden revelations, President Obama made, in 2014 – what has been called – 'an unprecedented speech' and issued PPD-28 which aimed to extend to foreign nationals some privacy protections in the context of signals intelligence. President Obama's speech (2014) was considered 'unprecedented' (Machtiger 2021) because it was the first time ever a US President was speaking publicly about signals intelligence and announcing changes to this. A change in US administration some years later, was marked by President Trump signing in 2017 the 'Enhancing Public Safety' executive order which provided that 'agencies shall, to the extent consistent with applicable law, ensure that their privacy policies exclude persons who are not United States citizens or lawful permanent residents from the protections of the Privacy Act regarding personally identifiable information'.[19] A further change to the US administration under President Joe Biden has seen the US and the EU Commission announcing on 25 March 2022 that they have committed to a new Trans-Atlantic Data Privacy Framework, which 'will foster trans-Atlantic data flows' and 'address the concerns' raised by the CJEU in *Schrems II*.[20] In a Joint Statement between the US and the Commission, it was emphasised that 'this deal in principle reflects the strength of the enduring US-EU relationship, as we continue to deepen our partnership based on our shared democratic values'.[21]

Political questions in the context of transatlantic relations are raised by private parties as well. The extensive and aggressive US lobbying on data protection matters has produced resentment on the EU side. For instance, during the negotiation of the GDPR, an American commentator observed that the American companies' lobby in Europe was a 'very intense' attempt to 'weaken' European privacy rules (Dembosky 2013). Similarly, the US's side is often angered by – what is perceived – as EU's pressure on data privacy matters. For example, the CJEU's *Schrems II* judgement was considered by an American commentator as 'gobsmacking in its mix of judicial imperialism and Eurocentric hypocrisy', further noting that 'it is astonishing that a European court would assume it has authority to kill or cripple critical American intelligence programs by raising the threat of massive sanctions on American companies' (Baker 2020).

It seems, thus, that transatlantic privacy relations tend to go around in circles as they are rooted on various political factors across both sides of the Atlantic. Ultimately, as Kuner has correctly observed, 'the problem is not that there is political disagreement about how to regulate international data transfers, but that the EU and the US often seem unwilling to consider positions that go beyond the underlying assumptions of their own systems' (Kuner 2017, p. 917).

Concluding remarks: the way forward for transatlantic relations

The transatlantic data privacy conflict is complex, multi-faced and influenced by constantly evolving legal and political dynamics. Over the years different approaches have been followed to resolve this. On the EU side, this has been attempted through democratisation of foreign relations with the involvement of the European Parliament, increased judicialisation and agencification. On the US side, the securitisation of data transfers has been pursued through 'aggressive' attempts to assert its regulatory vision in the transatlantic context (Kuner 2017).

What is the way forward for transatlantic data transfers then? Will they be trapped between weak institutionalisation and strong judicialisation and, thus, doomed forever? What is clear is that a solution that addresses all the aforementioned identified issues is not possible. Indeed, many of these have nothing to do with data transfers or fundamental rights as such, but depend on completely different political interests and priorities.

While the politics of the EU-US data privacy disputes are difficult to resolve, I argue that the law has still a role to play in this regard. Lines of communication and compatibility between different regulatory systems can and *should* be found though the law (Kuner 2017). Indeed, the different transatlantic data privacy legal disputes over the years, have made clear the issues that the two sides need to address in order to find common approaches that allow for data flows while respecting fundamental rights. The CJEU's bold move to establish another test for the assessment of fundamental rights in the external context in *Schrems II* is a useful step forward towards a more conciliatory approach. A 'minimum standards' approach to ascertain external interference with data privacy rights appears to be a more effective method of regulating international data transfers that reflects a 'reasonable degree of pragmatism in order to allow interaction with other parts of the world'.[22]

At the same time, the US side should commit to implement some meaningful, material legislative changes to ensure the necessity and proportionality of its surveillance practices affecting non-US persons and provide for effective judicial redress rights to foreign nationals. In the absence of these legislative changes, any EU-US agreement would fall (again) prey of political hopes missing the opportunity to address legal realities (Kuner 2017). The lessons learnt from the transatlantic data privacy saga are there for the EU and the US administrations who should finally make a serious commitment to break the trend of data transfer agreements, whose mere purpose is to 'buy another couple of years' (noyb and European Center for Digital Rights 2022).[23] Only a real commitment based on mutual trust, conciliation and substantive legislative change might sustain an EU-US data transfer framework over political influences and judicial intervention over time.

Notes

1 Case C-362/14 *Maximillian Schrems v Data Protection Commissioner* (*Schrems I*), ECLI:EU:C:2015:650.

2 Case C-311/18 *Data Protection Commissioner v Facebook Ireland Limited and Maximillian Schrems* (*Schrems II*) ECLI:EU:C:2020:559.

3 For a critical perspective on this see Claes Granmar (2022).
4 *Schrems* II (n 3), para 149.
5 Article 52(1) EUCFR provides: 'Any limitation on the exercise of the rights and freedoms recognised by this Charter must be provided for by law and respect the essence of those rights and freedoms. Subject to the principle of proportionality, limitations may be made only if they are necessary and genuinely meet objectives of general interest recognised by the Union or the need to protect the rights and freedoms of others'.
6 *Schrems I* (n 2), para 94.
7 Ibid, para 95.
8 European Commission and United States Joint Statement on Trans-Atlantic Data Privacy Framework, Press release, 25 March 2022, Brussels https://ec.europa.eu/commission/presscorner/detail/en/ip_22_2087.
9 Emphasis added.
10 Presidential Policy Directive/ PPD-28 Signals Intelligence Activities, 17 January 2014.
11 *Schrems II* (n 3), para 181.
12 Ibid, para 180.
13 Ibid, para 195.
14 Ibid, para 196.
15 Schrems I (n 2), para 95.
16 *Schrems II* (n 3), para 194.
17 *Schrems II* (n 3), para 161.
18 Ibid, para 89.
19 Executive Order: Enhancing Public Safety in the Interior of the United States, January 25, 2017, <https://www.whitehouse.gov/the-press-office/2017/01/25/presidential-executive-order-enhancing-public-safety-interior-united>, Section 14.
20 Press Release, European Commission and United States Joint Statement on Trans-Atlantic Data Privacy Framework, 25 March 2022, https://ec.europa.eu/commission/presscorner/detail/en/ip_22_2087
21 The White House- Briefing Room, FACT SHEET: United States and European Commission Announce Trans-Atlantic Data Privacy Framework, 25 March 2022, https://www.whitehouse.gov/briefing-room/statements-releases/2022/03/25/fact-sheet-united-states-and-european-commission-announce-trans-atlantic-data-privacy-framework/
22 Opinion of AG Saugmandsgaard Øe in Case C-311/18 *Data Protection Commissioner v Facebook Ireland Limited, Maximillian Schrems*, delivered on 19 December 2019, ECLI:EU:C:2019: 1145, para 7.
23 noyb – European Center for Digital Rights, 'Open Letter -Announcement of a New EU-US Personal Data Transfer Framework', 23 May 2022 https://noyb.eu/en/open-letter-future-eu-us-data-transfers

References

Baker, 'How Can the U.S. Respond to Schrems II?' *Lawfare*, 21 July 2020 www.lawfareblog.com/how-can-us-respond-schrems-ii.

Communication From the Commission to the European Parliament and the Council, ' Data protection as a pillar of citizens' empowerment and the EU' s approach to the digital transition – two years of application of the General Data Protection Regulation', Brussels, 24 June 2020, COM(2020) 264.

European Parliament resolution of 12 March 2014 on the US NSA surveillance programme, surveillance bodies in various Member States and their impact on EU citizens' fundamental rights and on transatlantic cooperation in Justice and Home Affairs (2013/2188(INI)), P7_TA(2014)0230.

Fahey and Terpan, 'Torn between Institutionalisation & Judicialisation: The Demise of the EU-US Privacy Shield' *Ind J Global Legal Stud* (2021) 28 205.

Dembosky, 'Facebook Spending on Lobbying Soars'. Financial Times, online edition, 24.

EDPB, 2020. Recommendations 02/2020 on the European Essential Guarantees for surveillance measures, Adopted on 10 November 2020.

Gellman and Poitras, 'U.S., British intelligence mining data from nine U.S. Internet companies in broad secret program', The Washington Post, 7 June 2013.

Granmar, 'Ex-ante measures regarding data transfers and ex-post enforcement of rights' European Law Blog, 8 July 2022, https://europeanlawblog.eu/2022/07/08/ex-ante-measures-regarding-data-transfers-and-ex-post-enforcement-of-rights/.

Greenwald and MacAskill, 'NSA Prism program taps in to user data of Apple, Google and others', *Guardian*, 7 June 2013.

January 2013, https://www.ft.com/content/cfaf0c78-65b2-11e2-a17b-00144feab49a

Kuner, 'Reality and Illusion in EU data transfer regulation post-Schrems' *German Law Journal* (2017) 18(4) 881.

Machtiger, 'Fixing PPD-28: Implementation Issues and Proposed Revisions for Privacy Protections in Signals Intelligence' *NYU Journal of Legislation & Public Policy* (2021) 23 277. Available at SSRN: https://ssrn.com/abstract=3853240.

Milanovic, 'Human Rights Treaties and Foreign Surveillance: Privacy in the Digital Age' *Harvard International Law Journal* (2015) 56 81, 89.

noyb – European Center for Digital Rights, 'Open Letter -Announcement of a New EU-US Personal Data Transfer Framework', 23 May 2022, https://noyb.eu/en/open-letter-future-eu-us-data-transfers

Obama, President, Remarks by the President on Review of Signals Intelligence (Jan. 17, 2014), https://obamawhitehouse.archives.gov/the-press-office/2014/01/17/remarks-president-review-signals-intelligence.

Rossi, 'How the Snowden Revelations Saved the EU General Data Protection Regulation' *The International Spectator* (2018) 53(4) 95, 101.

Tzanou and Spyridoula Karyda, 'Privacy International and Quadrature du Net: One Step Forward Two Steps Back in the Data Retention Saga?' *European Public Law* (2022) 28(1) 123.

Tzanou, 'European Union Regulation of Transatlantic Data Transfers and Online Surveillance' *Human Rights Law Review* (2017a) 17 (3) 545, 556.

Tzanou, 'Public Surveillance before the European Courts: Progressive legitimisation or a shift towards a more pragmatic approach?' VerfBlog, 2022/4/06, https://verfassungsblog.de/os6-courts-surveillance/.

Tzanou, 'Schrems I and Schrems II: Assessing the Case for the Extraterritoriality of EU Fundamental Rights' in Federico Fabbrini et al. (eds.) *Data Protection Beyond Borders Transatlantic Perspectives on Extraterritoriality and Sovereignty* (Hart Publishing, 2020) 99.

Tzanou, 'The EU-US Data Privacy and Counterterrorism Agreements: What Lessons for Transatlantic Institutionalisation?' in Elaine Fahey (eds.), *Institutionalisation of EU-US Relations: Multidisciplinary Perspectives on Transatlantic Trade and Data Privacy* (Springer, 2018), 55.

Tzanou, 'The war against terror and transatlantic information sharing: spillovers of privacy or spillovers of security?' *Utrecht J Int Eur Law* (2015) 31(80) 87.

Tzanou, *The Fundamental Right to Data Protection: Normative Value in the Context of Counter-Terrorism Surveillance* (Hart Publishing, 2017b).

Whitman, 'The Two Western Cultures of Privacy: Dignity Versus Liberty', *Yale Law Journal* (2003) 113 1151.

Wright and Kreissl, 'European responses to the Snowden revelations: A discussion paper' December 2013.

Zalnieriute, 'Data Transfers After *Schrems II*: The EU-US disagreements over data privacy and national security', *Vanderbilt Journal of Transnational Law* (2022) 55 (1) 38.

SECTION IV

The Political and Economic Character of Transatlantic Relations

19

THE TRANSATLANTIC REGULATORY RELATIONSHIP

Limited Conflict, Less Competition and a New Approach to Cooperation

Alasdair R. Young

THE SAM NUNN SCHOOL OF INTERNATIONAL AFFAIRS, GEORGIA INSTITUTE OF TECHNOLOGY

The European Union and the United States are considered the world's two regulatory great powers (Sapir 2007: 12; Drezner 2007: 35–6). As they both have relatively open economies and their economic relationship is very complex (see Eliasson this volume), regulatory differences are the primary grit in the transatlantic economy. These differences sometimes result in high-profile trade disputes and contribute to perceptions of regulatory competition. Regulatory differences have also prompted extensive efforts to mitigate their adverse economic effects through cooperation. This chapter surveys transatlantic regulatory conflict, competition and cooperation.

It advances four complementary arguments. First, transatlantic regulatory conflicts are the exception rather than the rule, although regulatory differences are a persistent source of trade friction. Second, transatlantic regulatory competition is extremely rare and largely inadvertent. Third, transatlantic regulatory cooperation has struggled to address differences rooted in very different domestic political contexts. Fourth, a new, more fruitful, approach to transatlantic regulatory cooperation may be emerging in which there is less emphasis on resolving relatively small differences between specific rules and much more attention to what the EU and US have in common in terms of shared regulatory objectives. That development has been spurred by increased concern about China's efforts to shape the global regulation of new technologies.

This chapter begins by explaining the origins of transatlantic regulatory differences. It then turns to the consequences of those differences and the bilateral efforts to address them. It then pivots to consider the extent to which the EU and US

DOI: 10.4324/9781003283911-24

engage in regulatory competition with each other. It then identifies indications of a new approach to transatlantic regulatory cooperation that focuses on shared values rather than technical differences. The chapter concludes by taking stock of the state of the transatlantic regulatory relationship.

The (inadvertent) origins of limited regulatory conflict

The EU and the US are often depicted as having fundamentally different approaches to regulation (Bradford 2020: 39 and see Petersmann this volume; for reviews see Young 2009: 668–669; Wiener 2011a: 7–23; Vogel 2012: 24–34). Informed by this perception of fundamental differences and by a number of high-profile transatlantic disputes, the transatlantic regulatory relationship is frequently depicted as highly conflictual, even amounting to "system friction" (for a review see Young 2009: 670). Neither of these conventional wisdoms, however, is accurate.

First, transatlantic regulatory differences do not stem from fundamental differences. Rather, each jurisdiction's regulatory choices are highly contingent. Enduring differences – such as tolerances for risk in general and attitudes toward government intervention – cannot explain variation in the relative stringency of regulations across issues or over time or within jurisdictions. While the EU has more stringent regulations on some issues – such as genetically modified crops, chemicals, and climate change – the US has more stringent rules on others – such as choking hazards in food and particulate matter in air pollution (Wiener and Almanno 2015: 104). In addition, the US tended to regulate more aggressively than the EU to protect the environment and consumers until about 1990 after which the positions reversed (Vogel 2012: 24–34). Further, some EU member state governments, such as Poland's, are much less enthusiastic about addressing environmental problems, including climate change than others, such a Germany's. In the US, California has adopted regulations on animal welfare, the environment, and privacy that are closer to EU rules than to US laws. Moreover, Democratic administrations tend to have policy preferences much closer to European preferences on a range of regulatory issues, most notably the environment, than do Republican ones. Relative regulatory stringency is far more variable than assumed systemic differences would suggest.

Rather, transatlantic regulatory differences are shaped by different legal traditions, different problems that need to be addressed, different regulatory priorities, and different constellations of domestic political actors (Wiener and Almanno 2015: 103). Which problems are understood to require action can be influenced by public perceptions of risk, which in turn are affected by events, such as high-profile regulatory failures (Vogel 2012: 291; Wiener 2011b: 540). These factors help to explain differences in transatlantic regulations but which jurisdiction's rules are more stringent is highly contingent.

Second, while there are undoubtably differences in what, how and how stringently the EU and the US regulate different products and services, those differences are small when compared to range of regulations adopted (and not) around the world (Wiener 2011a: 6; Wiener and Almanno 2015: 114). A focus on what is different can mask what the EU and US have in common in terms of shared policy objectives.

Third, and echoing the need to avoid focusing only on problems, the transatlantic regulatory relationship is not nearly as fraught as is commonly assumed. The perception of regulatory conflict is heavily informed by the US's complaints before the World Trade Organization (WTO) against the EU's ban on hormone-treated beef and its moratorium on the approval of genetically modified crops. The US won both complaints and imposed tariffs in an effort to force the EU to lift its ban on hormone-treated beef. In the end, the EU changed the form but not the substance of its ban and a dissatisfied US eventually settled for compensation in the form of a quota for hormone-free beef (Young 2021: 76–80). The EU lifted its moratorium on the approval of genetically modified varieties for sale, but the approval process remains too slow for American liking and approvals for cultivation remain stalled and member states can still ban EU-approved varieties (Young 2021: 120–127). The US, however, has not pursued the dispute. Both issues still rankle US farmers although the political heat has gone out of them.

These trade disputes, however, are very much the exception, not the rule. In fact, they are two of only four transatlantic regulatory disputes in more than 27 years of the WTO's existence (through at least mid-2022). Neither of the other two – a US complaint against the EU's ban on the use of anti-microbial treatments for chicken and an EU complaint against a US ban on poultry imports on unspecified safety grounds – were pursued. Trade disputes thus arose concerning a minute proportion of the regulations that the EU and the US have adopted. Even broadening the lens of a what constitutes a trade dispute considerably to include policies identified as barriers by the other side does not dramatically change the picture. During 1995–2007 (the first 13 years of the WTO), the US Trade Representative identified only 28 of the 676 regulations that the EU notified to the WTO as trade barriers (just over 4%), while the EU griped about only 33 of the 2,275 regulations the US notified during the same period (just over 1%) (Young 2009: 674). The transatlantic regulatory relationship, therefore, is much more peaceful than a focus on the high-profile dispute suggests.

The trials and tribulations of transatlantic regulatory cooperation

That regulatory disputes are rare, however, does not mean that regulatory differences do not matter. Because all goods and services must comply with the rules of the jurisdiction in which they are sold, firms operating in the large, interpenetrated transatlantic economy have to comply with different sets of rules. In some instances, the firm can choose to comply with the more stringent rule and sell in both markets. In other instances, however, the US and EU requirements are incompatible or even contradictory, such as with automobile safety regulations (see Commission 2016: Annexes 1 and 3–7). Service providers operating in both markets may be subject to supervision by two sets of regulators with different performance requirements. Some firms – including airlines and technology platforms – have at times found themselves caught between having to comply with demands for information from US security services and EU requirements to protect their customers' privacy. Such "rule overlap," while rare, presents profound problems for those companies operating in the transatlantic economy (Farrell and Newman 2016).

In addition to the costs of complying with foreign rules there are also costs associated with demonstrating that one's product complies with those rules, including testing and certification costs (Chase and Pelkmans 2015: 30). Such costs particularly deter small- and medium-sized enterprises (and even not such small firms) from exporting as they do not have the volume of exports that would make incurring these costs worthwhile (Chase and Pelkmans 2015: 30; Workman 2014: iv). Regulatory differences, even minor ones, therefore, can impede trade.

Approaches to international regulatory cooperation

The US and EU have consequently invested considerable effort in trying to mitigate the adverse consequences of different regulatory requirements for their firms. In the absence of a bilateral trade agreement, the transatlantic economic relationship is governed by WTO rules. As noted earlier, the US and EU have on (rare) occasion sought to address regulatory barriers through WTO complaints, but even rulings favorable to the complainant did little to improve the situation on the ground. Moreover, WTO rules have little purchase on the regulation of services, so much of the value of the transatlantic economy falls outside the reach of multilateral dispute settlement.

Spurred by persistent friction stemming from regulatory differences and recognizing that the WTO was ill-suited to addressing them, the EU and US constructed a series of frameworks for regulatory cooperation. Transatlantic regulatory cooperation began with the Transatlantic Declaration in 1990 and accelerated after the New Transatlantic Agenda (NTA) in 1995 and the Transatlantic Economic Partnership (TEP) in 1998. These efforts created a web of new bilateral channels for political and policy dialogue. They extended from bilateral summits at the highest political levels to an NTA Task Force at the operational level of policy-specialist officials. In 2007, the EU and US, in an effort to give greater political impetus to regulatory cooperation, created the Transatlantic Economic Council (TEC). The unsuccessful Transatlantic Trade and Investment Partnership (TTIP) negotiations (2013–16) were the most recent and most ambitious attempt to address transatlantic regulatory differences (see Eliasson this volume). International regulatory cooperation, however, is very difficult and these transatlantic efforts have produced limited results.

Because the adverse trade effects of domestic regulations are usually side-effects of realizing other policy objectives, they, unlike tariffs, cannot simply be traded away. Regulatory cooperation, therefore, focuses on how to liberalize trade while still achieving the underlying public policy objectives (OECD 2013: 15). There is a tendency in the literature on international regulatory cooperation to assume that the means to square this circle is through harmonization – the adoption of a common rule by both parties (Koenig-Archibugi 2010: 416; Winslett 2019: 101). Adopting a common rule, however, entails adjustment costs – regulators need to change their rules and producers must adapt their products to new requirements (Büthe and Mattli 2011: 12; Drezner 2007: 45–7; Krasner 1991: 336; Winslett 2019). If the common rule is the same as that of one of the partners, there are also distributional implications, as one party benefits from greater market access at no cost, while the other bears all of the costs in exchange for the benefit of a larger market. These adjustment costs and distributional implications mean that regulatory harmonization is very difficult to agree and it is rarely pursued (OECD 2013).

Harmonization, however, is only one form of regulatory cooperation (OECD 2013: 22). Parties can mitigate the adverse trade effects of their rules by accepting that the other's rule as it stands is equivalent in effect to its own. Mutual acceptance of equivalence avoids the adjustment costs of harmonization but is often viewed as deregulatory by civil society organizations that doubt whether the parties' rules really are equivalent in effect and expect firms of both parties to comply with which ever requirement is less demanding. Regulators may also not be persuaded that the other's rule really is equivalent in effect or, if it is, that the rule is enforced effectively. Regulatory coordination can also include aligning data and testing requirements and accepting the other party's certifications of conformity. These steps can lower the costs firms incur for complying with different rules. Most international regulatory cooperation, therefore, is not nearly as ambitious as the pursuit of harmonization.

The experience of transatlantic regulatory cooperation

In line with wider international experience, the US and EU have never seriously attempted regulatory harmonization, although US agricultural interests have pushed for the EU to align its food safety rules with those of the US. There has been greater, although still limited, transatlantic interest in agreeing common rules where neither has yet regulated. In this instance, there are no adjustment costs, although both parties still have to implement any agreement through their respective domestic processes. These efforts have not borne much fruit, with electric vehicle standards, agreed within the World Forum for Harmonization of Vehicle Regulations, being the most significant example.

Rather, the most ambitious transatlantic efforts at regulatory cooperation have focused on establishing the equivalence of the two jurisdictions' rules. Under the 1999 Veterinary Equivalence Agreement (VEA), EU and US regulators agreed on a product-by-product basis, which of the exporter's rules achieved the importing party's level of sanitary protection. Many more EU measures were accepted as equivalent by the US than the other way around (McNulty 2005: 6). In 2004, the US and EU established the equivalence of their maritime equipment regulations (Commission 2013: 5). This agreement was made possible by prior alignment of rules through the International Maritime Organization. In 2011 the EU and US concluded the Agreement on Cooperation in the Regulation of Civil Aviation Safety, which requires acceptance, in most cases, of findings of compliance and approvals made by the other party and agreement that the other party's standards are "sufficiently compatible to permit reciprocal acceptance of approvals and findings of compliance with agreed upon standards" (Eisner 2016: 34). The US's Federal Aviation Administration only gradually accepted that the authorities in all EU member states could be relied upon to make correct determinations. Trust had to be established. Efforts to establish the equivalence of US and EU automobile regulations during the TTIP negotiations foundered because analysis revealed that the two sets of regulations, while largely equivalent in effect, had important areas of difference (Young 2017). Equivalence, therefore, rests on both the regulators establishing that the rules are actually equivalent in effect and both sets of regulators trusting their counterparts to effectively enforce those rules.

The US and EU officials have also established equivalence to mitigate the adverse effects of their financial regulations for the other's firms (Peterson et al. 2005: 31). For instance, the US Securities and Exchange Commission (SEC) modified how it regulated financial conglomerates, large financial services groups engaged in both banking or investment and insurance, such that the Commission was willing to consider it equivalent to the EU's 2002 Financial Conglomerates Directive (Bach and Newman 2007: 838; Posner 2009: 673). This meant that their activities in Europe could be regulated by the US rather than being supervised by European regulators. In 2007, the SEC deemed European accounting standards acceptable for European firms seeking to list on American stock exchanges, rather than require them to use US accounting standards (the EU already accepted US standards) (Pollack and Shaffer 2009: 99; Posner 2009: 672). These efforts eased the implications of regulatory differences for financial firms operating across the Atlantic.

EU and US officials have sought unsuccessfully to find a similar framework to overcome the implications of rule clash for the transfer of personal data (see Fahey and Terpan this volume). Under successive EU laws – the 1995 Privacy Directive and the 2016 General Data Protection Regulation (GDPR) – the transfer of personal data from the EU is restricted to jurisdictions whose laws provide equivalent protections or require firms to take bespoke steps. The EU and US have sought to agree a framework that provides protections equivalent in effect to the EU's that US companies can choose to comply with and thus benefit from unimpeded data flows. The 2000 Safe Harbour Agreement and the 2016 Privacy Shield, however, were both struck down by the European Court of Justice for not actually being equivalent in effect particularly because they did not provide sufficient protections for European citizens, given the ability of the US government to require private firms to turnover personal data on national security grounds. In March 2022 the US and EU announced a political agreement on a replacement for the Privacy Shield, but it remains to be seen whether its provisions are sufficiently equivalent to EU requirements to survive a legal challenge.

The US and EU have also sought to reduce the costs associated with complying with their different rules. Toward that end, in 1998, the US and EU concluded six sectoral mutual recognition agreements (MRAs). Under these agreements, the EU agreed to accept American certification bodies' determinations that American products comply with EU rules and vice versa. Despite their limited objectives, only three MRAs – those covering telecommunications equipment, electromagnetic compatibility of equipment and appliances and recreational craft – became operational. The MRAs were so difficult to implement because the US and EU have very different systems for certifying products (Egan and Nicola 2022). In 2017, however, the European Medicines Agency and the US Food and Drug Administration concluded an agreement that enables them to accept the other's inspections of medicine manufacturing facilities' compliance with good manufacturing processes (GMP).

The regulators saw this agreement as a way to free-up resources that can be re-deployed where the need is greater (FDA 2017). This agreement was easier to implement than other MRAs as government agencies are responsible for certification in both jurisdictions. As with aviation safety, however, it took some time for the US regulator to accept that the regulators of all of the EU's member states could be trusted with the task.

Top-down efforts at regulatory cooperation such as under the New Transatlantic Agenda and in the TTIP negotiations have been largely unsuccessful. This is not because of the inability of the US and the EU to agree common rules, for they have not tried. Rather the challenge has been persuading regulators (and courts) on both sides that the regulations really are equivalent in effect, especially in terms of their implementation and enforcement. Nonetheless, there have been some notable successes when regulators have seen the benefits of cooperation and taken the lead, as they did with respect to pharmaceutical factory inspections and aviation safety.

The US-EU Trade and Technology Council (TTC), which was launched in 2021, is the latest top-down attempt to advance transatlantic regulatory cooperation, although such cooperation is not the main focus of the TTC (see Eliasson this volume). Moreover, the TTC is explicitly forward looking and is not intended to address existing regulatory differences (Dombrovskis 2021; Hamilton 2022), which have been the main focus of transatlantic regulatory cooperation to date. Rather, the focus is on greater transatlantic cooperation in responding to the challenge posed by China's technological rise (see below).

Great power (regulatory) competition

Given their status as regulatory great powers and their regulatory differences, the EU and the US are often perceived to be engaged in regulatory competition around the world. This is a rather one-sided competition with the EU much more actively engaged than the US. Bradford (2012: 5) claims that the EU is "the predominant regulator of global commerce" (see also Barker 2020; Bradford 2020: 101 and 167). The impression of the EU's regulatory influence is echoed in the press, with, for example, The *New York Times* (19 October 2013: A1) calling the EU a "regulatory superpower" (see also the *Wall Street Journal*, 23 April 2002 and 26 October 2007; Kang 2022).

Transatlantic regulatory competition: from inadvertent to non-existent

The most common form of transatlantic regulatory competition is inadvertent and driven by market forces. Anu Bradford (2012; 2020) has coined the term the "Brussels effect" to capture the influence of EU rules beyond its borders. The "Brussels effect" describes how companies modify their products or services to comply with EU's stringent rules and sell them around the world. The logic underpinning the Brussels effect is that the EU's market is too valuable for foreign firms to ignore. It also tends (at least in certain domains) to adopt the world's most stringent standards, which it is able to enforce effectively. Having gone to the trouble of developing a product or service to comply with the EU's requirements, companies sell the same product or service worldwide as it will exceed the requirements of jurisdictions with less stringent rules. A crucial specification associated with the Brussels effect is how feasible or costly it is for a company to differentiate a product or service for different jurisdictions, what Bradford (2020: xv) calls "divisibility." If the product or service is not divisible, then a company will have a particularly strong incentive to meet the EU's requirements irrespective of where it plans to sell its product or service.

A more profound form of regulatory influence is when governments align their rules with the EU's (Young 2015a). This process, known as "trading up" (Vogel 1995) or the "de jure Brussels effect" (Bradford 2020), depends on the domestic politics of the other jurisdiction. Whether rule alignment occurs depends on the incentives for the externally oriented firms to lobby for change in their home market (the incompatibility of home and EU requirements; the domestic competitive advantage they might gain from a rule change); the presence of other actors that favor the rule change for other reasons; the strength of opposition to the rule changes; and how difficult it is to adopt change (the number of veto players). Although other countries and some US states, most notably California, have adopted EU-style rules, the US as a whole has largely been immune to the de jure Brussels effect (Vogel 2012: 283). This form of regulatory competition is passive and is driven by market forces.

Data privacy, particularly the EU's GDPR, is a commonly cited example of the Brussels effect (see Bradford 2020: 142; Burwell and Propp 2020: 2; Garcia Bercero and Nicolaidis 2021: 12). Firms around the world have clearly adapted their privacy practices to comply with the EU's requirements. Many governments have also aligned their privacy rules with EU requirements, but here the process is not that purely of market-based competition. Rather, the Commission actively vets governments' privacy rules to see if they provide equivalent protection to the EU's, what Jarlebring (2022: 539), calls "regime vetting." Regime vetting creates an extra incentive for domestic rule change, but it is rare. It is also intended to ensure the effectiveness of EU protections (to prevent data "leakage") rather than as a form of regulatory imperialism.

By contrast, the Commission (1996: 4; 2006: 5; 2015; 2021: 16) has long expressed rhetorical commitment to exporting EU rules through trade agreements. Getting trade partners to adopt EU regulations would both eliminate regulatory obstacles to European exports and create new barriers to the imports from jurisdictions that do not follow EU rules. It would thus give EU firms a considerable competitive advantage. This is what the Trump Administration had in mind when it expressed its desire to stop the EU from exporting its food safety regulations (USTR 2019: 2). Reflecting Commission rhetoric, many scholars depict the EU as exporting its rules and thus engaging actively in regulatory competition (Piermartini and Budetta 2009: 291; Stoler 2011: 217; Melo Araujo 2016: 25; Meissner 2018: 43). Despite the Commission's rhetoric, however, the EU has not actually actively sought to export its rules except through its association agreements and accession processes (Woolcock 2007; Young 2015b; 2022). The closest the EU comes to exporting its rules in its conventional trade agreements is to encourage its partners to accept the equivalence of United Nations Economic Commission for Europe (UNECE) automobile safety standards (Young 2022). Moreover, accepting the equivalence of UNECE standards does not preclude the EU's partners from accepting another jurisdiction's (i.e., the US) rules as also equivalent. Thus, there is a considerable gap between the rhetoric and the reality of EU rule export. Moreover, the US does not actively export its own regulations (Young 2022). Trade agreements, therefore, are not instruments of transatlantic regulatory cooperation.

That said, both the US and the EU have long sought to induce their trade partners to improve their labor and environmental protections (Postnikov 2019). The EU seeks to promote the ratification and implementation of multilateral environmental agreements and core labor standards through its GSP+ system of trade preferences and through establishing dialogues under the sustainable development chapters of its trade agreements. The US tries to export its domestic standards in trade agreements that have sanctioning mechanisms. While there are important differences in which standards the EU and US promote and how they promote them, their objectives – strengthening labor and environmental protections in their trade partners – are compatible and potentially complementary, so there is no transatlantic regulatory competition in this regard.

The Commission's 2021 trade policy review (Commission 2021: 13) suggested a more general shift toward seeking to export EU rules through unilateral trade measures. These efforts are particularly associated with promoting sustainability and include measures such as proposals for a carbon border adjustment mechanism (CBAM), to discourage deforestation, and to exclude forced labor from EU value chains. Such efforts are also consistent with US objectives – if the EU succeeds the US also benefits – and so do not represent regulatory competition, although the EU's CBAM is a potential source of transatlantic tension if US efforts to address climate change are not considered sufficient and US exports face new levies as a result. Active transatlantic regulatory competition, therefore, is not a thing.

A new approach to transatlantic regulatory cooperation in competition with China

While depictions of transatlantic regulatory competition are overblown, there is brewing regulatory competition between the EU and the US on one side and China on the other. Policymakers on both sides of the Atlantic have expressed concern about China's efforts to overcome the West's technological advantage (Commission 2021: 14; NIC 2021: 54). In this context, the US government (USCE&SRC 2020: 5) and the European Commission (2022) are alarmed by China's efforts to secure important leadership positions in the key international standard setting bodies and to increase dramatically its participation in those bodies' committees.

Setting international standards is seen as giving a jurisdiction's firms a competitive advantage as all other firms have incentives to use that standard (Commission 2021: 16; EPSC 2019: 7; Sinkkonen and Sinkkonen 2021: 47). Standard setting is also viewed as a way of shaping technologies in ways that help to protect a jurisdiction's interests and values, such as protecting privacy or curbing security threats (EPSC 2019: 7; Seaman 2020: 15; USCE&SRC 2020: 105). Thus, shaping international standards is politically important.

In response to China's activities, the U.S.-China Economic and Security Review Commission (2020: 23) recommended that Congress take steps to improve the effectiveness of the US in international standard setting. The EU's 2022 standard strategy calls for better coordination within the EU and closer cooperation with like-minded countries, including the US, to offset China's more "assertive" approach (Commission 2022: 6). In May 2022, under the auspices of the TTC the EU and US launched the Strategic Standardisation Information mechanism "to encourage engagement in new standardisation opportunities and explore taking coordinated action if standardisation activities pose a challenge to EU- U.S. strategic interests and values" (U.S.-EU 2022: 8).

In addition, as part of their ceasefire over the US's Section 232 tariffs on steel and aluminum the US and EU agreed to work with "like-minded" governments on a Global Arrangement on Sustainable Steel and Aluminum." Part of that objective is to agree a standard for low-carbon-intensity steel and aluminum (Fefer 2021). The intention to exclude steel and aluminum imports from nonparticipants that do not meet that standard or do not meet market-oriented conditions or that contribute to excess capacity. Thus, the US and EU are seeking to cooperate on standard setting as part of responding to what they see as the distorting effects of Chinese over capacity in aluminum and steel.

Thus, while EU-US regulatory competition is rare and inadvertent when it does occur, the EU and US are cooperating actively to confront what they perceive as China's challenge.

Conclusion

The transatlantic regulatory relationship is not nearly as politically fraught as is commonly thought. High-profile regulatory disputes are very much the exception. While regulatory differences do create trade frictions, the two sides recognize that regulatory differences have their origins in different domestic politics, which means that they are difficult to change and to a considerable extent the two side accept that differences will persist. That is why WTO regulatory disputes have been so rare and why the EU and US have not pursued regulatory harmonization. Rather, they have sought to mitigate the adverse trade effects of regulatory differences. These efforts have been most successful when regulators have seen the benefits of cooperation (primarily in terms of burden sharing) and are persuaded that their rules or processes are equivalent in effect and appropriately implemented.

In addition, despite some concerns, the US and EU do not actively engage in regulatory competition with each other. What competition there is is largely inadvertent and the product of market forces. The EU and US are, however, gearing up to cooperate to resist China's efforts to shape global rules. This shift entails focusing less on the technical differences between them and emphasizing their common regulatory objectives.

Acknowledgments

I am grateful to the Neal Family Endowment, a GT CIBER Research Associate Award, the Sam Nunn School of International Affairs and a Jean Monnet Center of Excellence grant (Erasmus+ Agreement 20498-EPP-1-2020-1-US-EPPJMO-CoE) for financial support. All views are my own and are in no way endorsed by the European Commission. Sydney Blakeney, Emmett Miskell and Vignesh Sreedhar provided excellent research assistance. I would also like to thank Elaine Fahey and an anonymous referee for comments on an earlier version of this chapter. All shortcomings remain my own.

References

Bach, D. and Newman, A. L. (2007), "The European Regulatory State and Global Public Policy: Micro-Institutions, Macro-Influence," *Journal of European Public Policy*, 14/6, 827–846.

Barker, T. (2020), "Europe Can't Win the Tech War It Just Started," *Foreign Policy*, 16 January.

Bradford, A. (2012), "The Brussels Effect," *Northwestern University Law Review*, 107/1, 1–68.

Bradford, A. (2020), *The Brussels Effect: How the European Union Rules the World*, Oxford University Press.

Burwell, F. G. and Propp, K. (2020), "The European Union and the Search for Digital Sovereignty: Building "Fortress Europe" or Preparing for a New World?" Atlantic Council Future Europe Initiative Issue Brief, June.

Büthe, T. and Mattli, W. (2011), *The New Global Rulers: The Privatization of Regulation in the World Economy*, Princeton University Press.

Chase, P. and Pelkmans, J. (2015), "This Time It's Different: Turbo-Charging Regulatory Cooperation," in D.S. Hamilton and J. Pelkmans (eds), *Rule-Makers or Rule-Takers? Exploring the Transatlantic Trade and Investment Partnership*, London: Rowman and Littlefield International, 17–60.

Commission (1996), "The Global Challenge of International Trade: A Market Access Strategy for the European Union," COM(96) 53 final, 14 February.

Commission (2006), "Global Europe: Competing in the World," COM (2006) 567 final, 4 October.

Commission (2013), "Initial Position Paper: Technical Barriers to Trade," 20 June. (leaked version)

Commission (2015), "Trade for All: Towards a more responsible trade and investment policy," COM(2015) 497 final, 14 October.

Commission (2016), "TTIP-Car Safety Analysis in the EU and US in Relation to US and EU Regulatory Standards on Crash Testing," Grow.ddg1.c.dir(2016)3880469, 12 July.

Commission (2021), "Trade Policy Review – An Open, Sustainable and Assertive Trade Policy," COM(2021) 66 final, 18 February.

Commission (2022), "An EU Strategy on Standardisation Setting global standards in support of a resilient, green and digital EU single market," COM(2022) 31 final, 2 February).

Dombrovskis, V. (2021), *A Conversation with European Commission Executive Vice President Valdis Dombrovskis*, University of Pittsburgh, 30 September.

Drezner, D. W. (2007), *All Politics is Global: Explaining International Regulatory Regimes*, Princeton University Press.

Egan, M. and Nicola, F. (2022), "The Regulatory Disconnect in Transatlantic Trade," paper to the European Union Studies Association Conference, Miami, FL, 19–21 May.

Eisner, N. (2016), "Facilitating Earlier Information Sharing and Cooperation between the US Department of Transportation and the EU," in D.R. Pérez and S. E. Dudley (eds), *US-EU Regulatory Cooperation: Lessons and Opportunities*, George Washington University Regulatory Studies Center, April, 12–49.

EPSC [European Political Strategy Centre] (2019), "Rethinking Strategic Autonomy in the Digital Age" EPSC Strategic Notes Issue 30, European Commission, July.

Farrell, H. and Newman, A. (2016), "The New Interdependence Approach: Theoretical Development and Empirical Demonstration," *Review of International Political Economy*, 23/5, 713–736.

FDA [Food and Drug Administration] (2017), "Mutual Recognition Promises New Framework for Pharmaceutical Inspections for United States and European Union," FDA News Release, 2 March.

Fefer, R. F. (2021), "What's in the New U.S.-EU Steel and Aluminum Deal?" Insight IN11799, Congressional Research Service.

Garcia Bercero, I. and Nicolaidis, K. (2021), "The Power Surplus: Brussels Calling, Legal Empathy and the Trade-Regulation Nexus," CEPS Policy Insight PI2021-05, March.

Hamilton, D. (2022), "Remarks to the U.S.-EU Trade and Technology Council U.S. Stakeholder Roundtable," 19 April.

Jarlebring, J. (2022), "Regime Vetting': A Technique to Exercise EU Market Power," *Journal of European Public Policy*, 29/4: 530–549.

Koenig-Archibugi, M. (2010), "Global Regulation," in R. Baldwin, M. Cave, and D. Lodge (eds), *The Oxford Handbook of Regulation*, Oxford: Oxford University Press, 406–433.

Krasner, S. D. (1991), "Global Communications and National Power: Life on the Pareto Frontier," *World Politics*, 43/3, 336–366.

McNulty, K. (2005), "The US–EU Veterinary Equivalence Agreement: Content and Comparison," *GAIN Report E35219*, 24 October, Washington DC: USDA Foreign Agricultural Service.

Meissner, K. L. (2018), *Commercial Realism and EU Trade Policy: Competing for Economic Power in Asia and the Americas*, London: Routledge.

Melo Araujo, B. A. (2016), *The EU Deep Trade Agenda: Law and Policy*, Oxford University Press.

NIC (2021), *Global Trends 2040: A More Contested World*, Washington, DC: National Intelligence Council, March.

OECD (2013), *International Regulatory Co-operation: Addressing Global Challenges*, Organization for Economic Cooperation and Development.

Peterson, J., Bruwell, F., Epstein, R., Pollack, M. A., Quinlan, J., Wallace, H., Young, A. R., and Deloitte Brussels. (2005), "Review of the Framework for Relations between the European Union and the United States: An Independent Study," *Tender Official Journal*, 2004/S 83–070340.

Piermartini, R. and Budetta, M. (2009), "A Mapping of Regional Rules on Technical Barriers to Trade," in A. Estevadeordal, K. Suominen, and R. Teh (eds), *Regional Rules in the Global Trading System*, Cambridge University Press, 250–315.

Pollack, M. A. and Shaffer, G. (2009), *When Cooperation Fails: The International Law and Politics of Genetically Modified Foods*, Oxford: Oxford University Press.

Posner, E. (2009), "Making Rules for Global Finance: Transatlantic Regulatory Cooperation at the Turn of the Millennium," *International Organization*, 63/4, 665–699.

Postnikov, E. (2019), "Unravelling the Puzzle of Social Standards' Design in EU and US Trade Agreements," *New Political Economy*, 24/2: 181–196.

Sapir, A. (2007), "Europe and the Global Economy," in A. Sapir (ed), *Fragmented Power: Europe and the Global Economy*, Brussels: Bruegel, 1–20.

Seaman, J. (2020), "China and the New Geopolitics of Technical Standardization" Notes de l'Ifri (Paris: Ifri), January.

Stoler, A. L. (2011). "TBT and SPS Measures in Practice," in J.-P. Chauffour and J.-C. Maur (eds), *Preferential Trade Agreement Policies for Development: A Handbook*. Washington, DC: The World Bank. 217–234.

Sinkkonen, E. and Sinkkonen, V. (2021). "A Multi-Dimensional View of US-China Great-Power Competition," in N. Helwig (ed.), *Strategic Autonomy and the Transformation of the EU: New Agendas for Security, Diplomacy, Trade and Technology, FIIA Report 67*. Helsinki: Finnish Institute of International Affairs.

USCE&SRC (2020), "2020 Report to Congress of the U.S.-China Economic and Security Review Commission" December.

US-EU (2022), "U.S.-EU Joint Statement of the Trade and Technology Council," Paris, 16 May. https://www.whitehouse.gov/wp-content/uploads/2022/05/TTC-US-text-Final-May-14.pdf.

USTR [United States Trade Representative] (2019), *United States-European Union Negotiations; Summary of Specific Negotiating Objectives*, Washington DC: USTR, January.

Vogel, D. (1995), *Trading Up: Consumer and Environmental Regulation in a Global Economy*, Harvard University Press.

Vogel, D. (2012), *The Politics of Precaution: Regulating Health, Safety and Environmental Risks in Europe and the United States*, Princeton University Press.

Wiener, J. B. (2011a), "The Rhetoric of Precaution," in J.B. Wiener, M. D. Rogers, J.K. Hammitt, and P.H. Sand (eds), *The Reality of Precaution: Comparing Risk Regulation in the United States and Europe*, Washington, DC: RFF Press, 3-??.

Wiener, J. B. (2011b), "The Real Pattern of Precaution," in J.B. Wiener, M. D. Rogers, J.K. Hammitt, and P.H. Sand (eds), *The Reality of Precaution: Comparing Risk Regulation in the United States and Europe*, Washington, DC: RFF Press, 519–565.

Wiener, J.B. and Almanno, A. (2015), "The Future of International Regulatory Cooperation: TTIP as a Learning Process Toward a Global Regulatory Laboratory," *Law and Contemporary Problems*, 78/1: 103–136.

Winslett, G. (2019), "Choosing Among Options for Regulatory Cooperation," *Global Governance*, 25/1, 100–122.

Woolcock, S. (2007), "European Union Policy Towards Free Trade Agreements," *ECIPE Working Paper 3/2007*, Brussels: European Centre for International Political Economy.

Workman, G. (2014), *The Transatlantic Trade and Investment Partnership: Big Opportunities for Small Business*, Washington, DC: Atlantic Council, November.

Young, A.R. (2009), "Confounding Conventional Wisdom: Political not Principled Differences in the Transatlantic Regulatory Relationship," *British Journal of Politics and International Relations*, 11/4: 666–689.

Young, A.R. (2015a). "Europe's Influence on Foreign Rules: Conditions, Context and Comparison," *Journal of European Public Policy*, 22(9): 1233-1252.

Young, A.R. (2015b), "Liberalizing Trade, Not Exporting Rules: The Limits to Regulatory Coordination in the EU's "New Generation" Preferential Trade Agreements," *Journal of European Public Policy* 22/9: 1253–1275.

Young, A.R. (2017), *The New Politics of Trade: Lessons from TTIP*, Agenda Publishing.

Young, A.R. (2021), *Supplying Compliance with Trade Rules: Explaining the EU's Responses to Adverse WTO Rulings*, Oxford University Press

Young, A.R. (2022), "Product Regulations: You Can Drive My Car, Otherwise Let it Be" in J. Adriaensen and E. Postnikov (eds), *The Geo-Economic Turn in Trade Policy? EU Trade Agreements in the Asia-Pacific*, Palgrave Macmillan, 149–173.

20

BILATERAL, TRILATERAL OR – QUADRILATERAL? THE UK-US TRADE RELATIONS IN A GLOBAL CONTEXT

Peter Holmes[1] *and Minako Morita-Jaeger*[2]

[1]FELLOW UK TRADE POLICY OBSERVATORY, UNIVERSITY OF SUSSEX
[2]SENIOR RESEARCH FELLOW IN INTERNATIONAL TRADE, UNIVERSITY OF SUSSEX BUSINESS SCHOOL AND POLICY RESEARCH FELLOW, UK TRADE POLICY OBSERVATORY, UNIVERSITY OF SUSSEX

Introduction*

One of the UK's ambitions in leaving the EU was having its own trade policy and striking a trade deal with the US. However, the UK-US bilateral economic relationship is not just a bilateral affair, but it depends on the whole EU-UK-US trilateral relationship. Furthermore, the bilateral relation is likely to be closely related to the Indo-Pacific. This chapter sheds light on the UK-US trade relations after the UK left the EU and tries to identify the key features in a global context.

We address the following three questions: (i) What are economic and political factors that have shaped and will shape UK's position on the UK-US bilateral trade relationship? (ii) What are international factors that impact the UK-US trade relations in a global strategic context? and (iii) How could the UK-US bilateral trade relationship evolve? We construct the chapter as follows. We first look at the economic facts by analysing UK-US trade and investment relations. Then we examine economic and political factors that shape the UK's government aims in promoting the UK-US bilateral trade relationship from pre-Brexit to post-Brexit since domestic politics plays an important part in analysing foreign policy. Third, we explore key factors that affect the relationship in the international context. Finally, we provide some reflections on how the UK-US bilateral trade relationship could evolve.

We try to avoid assuming that the political landscape will necessarily always remain as it is at the time of writing (mid 2022). We cannot predict the future but will try to highlight the questions that researchers need to explore to see what scenarios might result from the forces that have driven the UK-US trade relations to where it is.

DOI: 10.4324/9781003283911-25

UK-US trade and investment relations

UK-US trade and investment relations clearly show that we cannot overlook the EU's economic presence. For the UK, the US is its largest partner as a single country, but the EU is its predominant partner in terms of both goods and services trade. The EU dominates almost half of the UK's trade (Figure 20.1). The share of UK's exports to the EU (42%) is double that of the US (21%). And the share of UK imports from the EU (51%) is more than four times larger than the share of imports from the US (12%). Although UK-EU trade decreased after the UK left the EU in January 2021, the EU will remain as the largest trade partner for the UK in the foreseeable future. For the US, the EU is its largest trade partner whereas the UK ranks as 10th. The share of US exports to the EU (18%) is three times larger than the share of the UK (6%). The share of US imports from the EU is almost five times larger than the share of the UK (4%) (Figure 20.2).[1]

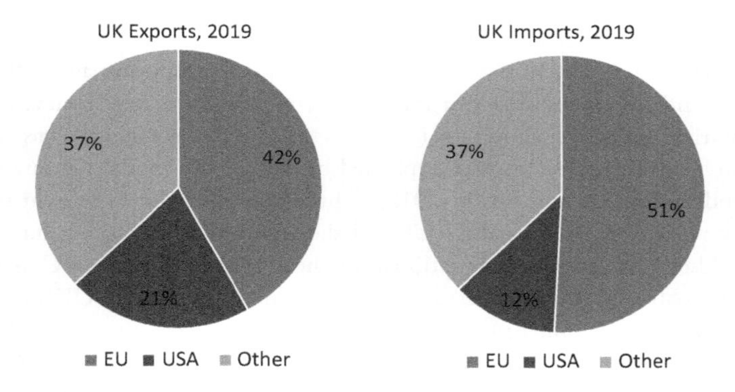

Figure 20.1 UK's exports and imports with the EU, the US and rest of the world

Source: ONS Pink Book 2021.

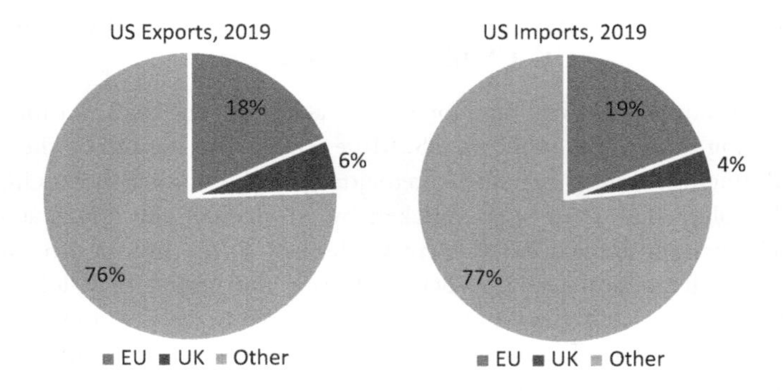

Figure 20.2 US trade with the EU, UK and the rest of the world

Source: BEA, International Trade in Goods and Services | U.S. Bureau of Economic Analysis (BEA) (accessed in May 2022).

Also, the EU shows a strong presence in the UK and the US's global value chain activities in goods and services. For the UK, its largest supply chain partner is the EU while the role of the US is very limited. The foreign value-added share of UK final demand (2018) accounted for 23.8%, of which 11.4% originated in the EU and 3.1% in the US (Figure 20.3). For the US, the EU, China, Canada and Mexico are its major supply chain partners and its relationship with the UK is negligible. The foreign value-added share of US final demand (2018) accounted for 12.2%, of which 2.5% originated in the EU, 2.2% in China, 1.1% in Canada, 1.0% in Mexico. The UK's share was only 0.5% (Figure 20.4).

Comparing the volumes of goods trade, services trade and Foreign Direct Investment (FDI), the presence of the EU overwhelms the UK-US relations in goods, services and investment (Figure 20.4 and 20.5). Services trade and investment are relatively more important in UK-US economic relations than goods trade. Especially for the UK, a gap between services exports to the US and ones to the EU is not so big (Figure 20.6).

The above demonstrates that UK and US trade reflects the gravity theory in international trade, namely that bilateral trade exports proportionally reflect economic size and are inversely proportional to geographic distance (Chaney, 2018). In fact, empirical evidence shows that services trade where the UK has a strong comparative advantage is also well explained by the gravity model Kimura and Lee (2006) and Springford and Lowe (2018). This means that the US could not economically replace the EU after the UK left the EU, unless something fundamental changes. Also, it is economically rational for the US to look at the EU as its main strategic transatlantic partner due to its strong economic ties. The UK's bargaining power is limited in comparison with the EU. Lastly, given the relatively strong relationship in services and investment between the UK and the US, market access and rules on services and investment would be critical if the two countries negotiate a trade deal. In short, EU-UK-US trilateral dimension is a strong economic fact that impacts the UK-US trade relationships.

Factors that shape UK government's position of promoting the UK-US bilateral trade deal

This section addresses our first question on the factors shaping the UK's motivations in its evolving relationship with the US. More starkly than used to be the case, we have to distinguish motives vs interests in the traditional economic sense. UK politics and trade policy after 2016 was overtaken by an ideologically driven strategy of Brexit (Holmes and Rollo, 2020). Here we look at (i) the historical background, (ii) the national political ideology behind Brexit, the notion of 'Global Britain' (a domestic factor), and (iii) how the UK's ambitions were seemingly but not durably endorsed by the Trump Administration (an external factor). In this section, we focus very much on the UK side of the equation. First because the bilateral relation is by definition specific to the UK; and where US-UK relations differ from general Transatlantic relations is not largely due to demands from the British side. Second, the pressures for change have been greatest on the UK side.

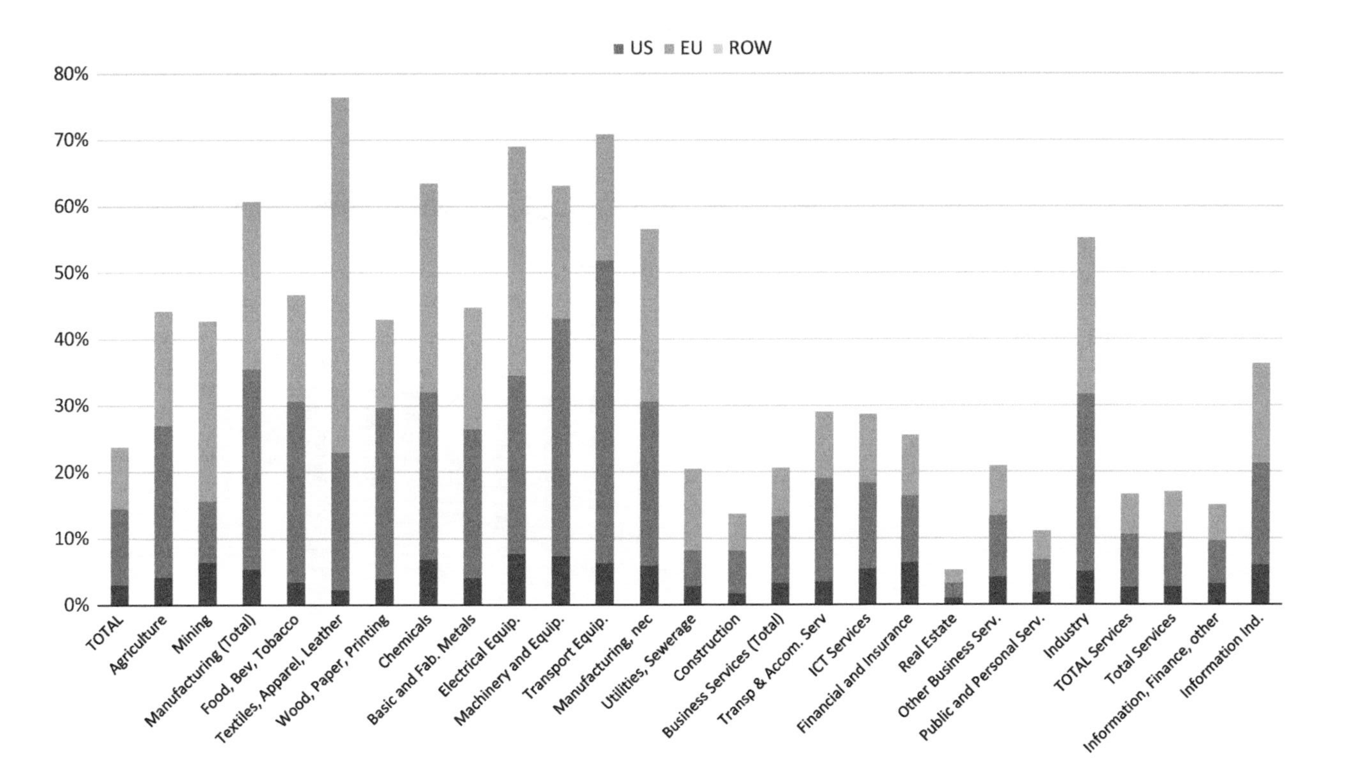

Figure 20.3 Origin of value added in UK final demand, % of total value added in final demand, 2018

Source: OECD Trade in Value Added (TIVA) database.

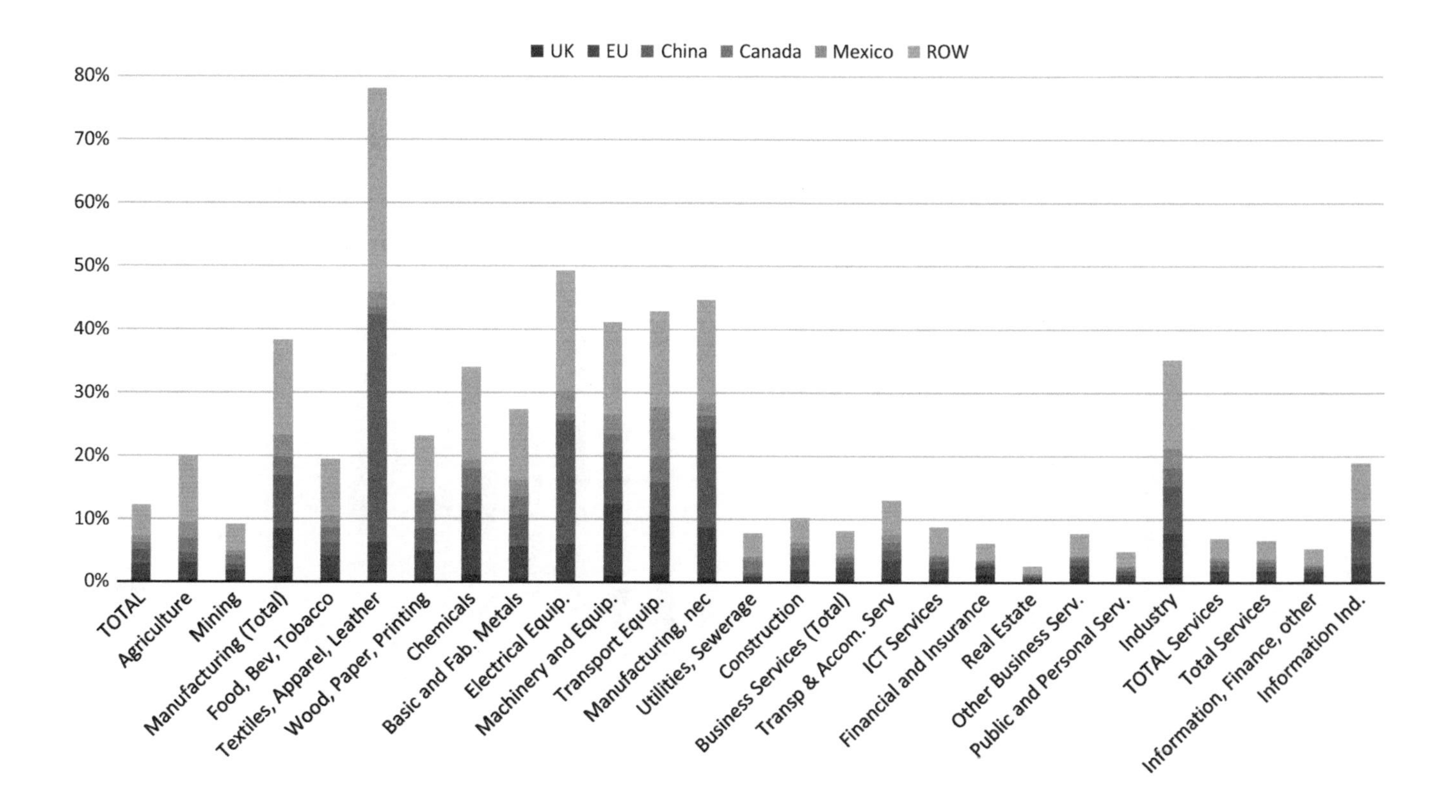

Figure 20.4 Origin of value added in US final demand, % of total value added in final demand, 2018

Source: OECD Trade in Value Added (TIVA) database.

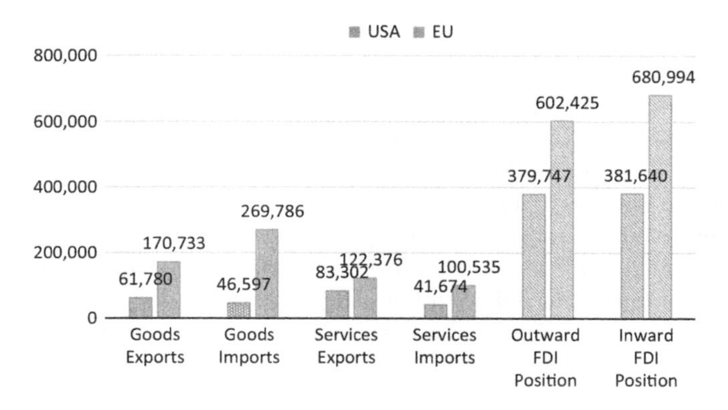

Figure 20.5 UK-Reported trade and FDI position with the US and the EU (£ million), 2019

Source: ONS Pink Book 2021 and ONS Dataset of FDI involving UK companies (directional).

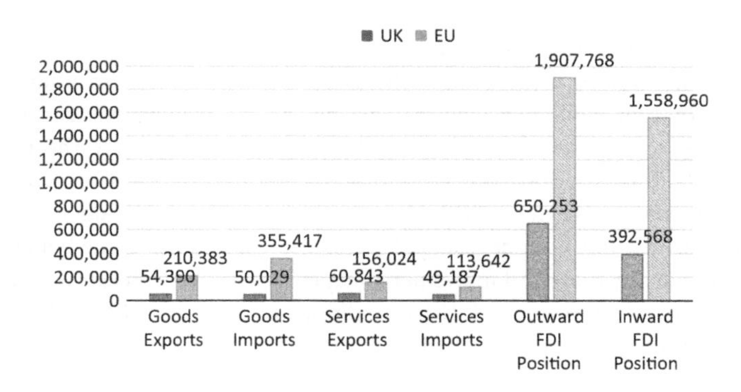

Figure 20.6 US-Reported trade and FDI position with the UK and the EU (£ million), 2019

Source: BEA, International Trade in Goods and Services | U.S. Bureau of Economic Analysis (BEA) (accessed in May 2022). The data in USD was converted into GBP.

Historical background

The UK and the US were clearly rivals in the 19th century but there has been a perception of an indissoluble bond since the US entry into World War 1 and above all World War 2. In fact, outside the military sphere the strength of the relationship has varied over time. Lend-lease and Marshall Aid were of vital economic importance, but the UK also suffered from US isolationism in the 1930s, and post 1945, the US was as keen to keep UK imperial ambitions in check as it was to have the UK as an ally (Thorne, 1978). Successive UK governments have referred to the 'Special Relationship' but the significance of this term has been questioned by some historians (Reynolds, 1988). The US Embassy website in 2022 has a page on the anniversary of the 'Special Relationship',[2] but it refers to Churchill's 1946 speech rather than recognising the existence of a special relationship as such.

British foreign policy above all in the military domain was heavily focussed on preserving this relationship but politicians were always aware that the economic side was less intense. British Policy was always to see relations with the US and the European Economic Community (EEC), later the EU, as complementary. US multinational corporations (MNCs) came to the UK as a supply base for the EEC. In the 1950s, the UK sought unsuccessfully to promote a vision of close trade relations with Europe while resisting political integration. De Gaulle notoriously refused UK membership of the EEC in the 1960s seeing the UK as a US Trojan Horse. In many ways, he was right. The UK political class did embrace the European *Economic* Community from the 1970s, whilst trying to stay as close as possible to the US. UK governments frequently sided with the US on certain global trade policy issues. The UK was clearly sympathetic to US desires for agricultural trade liberalisation and to some aspects of US regulatory policies. But having made its case within the European system, the UK was generally a loyal supporter of the EEC and eventually EU position. UK influence in the trade directorate in Brussels was very significant. UK Commissioners were attracted to this portfolio, and the UK government was seen as an ally by those in the Commission who sought to pull the EU position in a more liberal direction. In a private discussion with one of the authors in the 1990s, a senior UK trade official observed that the UK would never seek to undermine the EU position on points where it disagreed because of the overall advantage to the UK of maintaining the consensus on the broader range of issues where the UK's view had prevailed. This anecdotal observation was supported by the Cameron government's Competences Review (HM Government, 2014) which suggested the UK gained from its role in EU trade policy. Reviewing what it saw as the benefits of EU trade agreements the trade and investment chapter argued that 'Because of these sorts of impacts on the economy, the UK has traditionally been one of the EU's strongest advocates of trade and investment liberalisation through international agreements' (HM Government, 2014). Overall, the authors of the Competences Review felt that the advantage of being able to influence the EU as a whole was broadly considered to be more of an advantage than the ability to unilaterally adopt its own (perhaps US style) policies (Holmes and Rollo 2020). The UK considered that its successful promotion of a deregulatory and privatisation agenda within the EU combined with opt outs in many areas (e.g. Schengen, EMU etc) gave it the best of both worlds. Our argument here is not so much that this analysis was true but that it almost certainly represented the consensus overall assessment of the main economic actors and policy makers.

The Global Britain rhetoric and the US

The Brexit agenda did not emerge from a perception of economic interests aligned to the US rather than the EU (Holmes and Rollo, 2020). This came afterwards. External trade policy was not as prominent in the Referendum campaign as it later became. Brexit was driven by a created perception of UK domestic policies, including immigration having been driven by a cosmopolitan Europhile elite. The 'levelling up agenda' has no relationship with the US. The 'Global Britain' rhetoric was paradoxically built around the idea that deep free trade arrangements were beneficial (apart from the one with the EU). The pro-Brexit campaign was based on two contradictory elements: a nationalist anti-globalisation sovereigntist thread and a pro-free trade project which was initially embraced by the Johnson government between mid-2019 and COVID-19.[3]

The Johnson government promised a commitment to 'Global Britain'[4] inspired by the free trade rhetoric which Johnson proclaimed in his Feb 3 2020 speech.[5] The rest of the world was going to follow Britain in opening up to globe free trade. This came just as the COVID crisis was starting. Together with the Ukraine war this has been a driving force in the opposite direction. Whether 'Global Britain' was inspired by genuine free trade ideology or a nostalgia for a world in which the UK led a hegemonic 'Anglosphere' (Mycock and Wellings, 2017) was not clear, but what did become clear was that while globalisation has not been totally reversed, its nature has changed (Baldwin 2022). Debates about re-shoring and 'friendshoring' make it clear that there is no 19th-Century free trade era to return to. At the same time the Integrated Review in 2021 (HM Government, 2021), which had nine references to the US and four to the EU, stressed the UK commitment to a Multilateral System. It called for both action against countries abusing IPR and subsidies, (without mentioning China) and for restoration of the WTO Dispute Settlement system, the main aims of the EU and the US. It also embraced environmental goals.

The Trump administration appeared to offer a flagship project to reflect a new ordering of relations. A trade deal with the US would replace that with the EU. Economically this was highly problematic as we suggest earlier, but there were also deep political differences between the two populist governments (Schuyler and Raymond, 2017). Trump's crudely mercantilist trade policy was far removed from the ostensibly free trade regime of Johnson and as a result the UK was forced to claim that it had always intended to align itself with the CPTPP post Brexit.

Both Johnson and Truss started with an inclination to adopt a regulatory model close to that of the (Southern) US. However economic interests held in check until recently are beginning to emerge since Sunak has been in power. Industry is stressing the primacy of regional value chains and as we noted above services are also best delivered to nearby markets.

The departure of Trump has highlighted the fundamental differences between the US and the UK. As we noted, the UK Brexit camp had two contradictory aims, ultra-liberalism and ultra-nationalism. Both were actually irreconcilable with Trump's goals. Now the Biden administration has committed itself to a 'worker focussed' trade policy, pushing for 'reshoring' of high skill jobs. It is not clear how the UK can fit into this vision. But the US sees the EU as a strong potential[6] partner and has resisted UK attempts to be admitted to the EU-US Trade and Technology Council.

A key unknown is of course the future of the UK political situation. Rishi Sunak replaced Liz Truss as PM but an election is due in 2024. The March 2022 UK-US joint statement[7] stresses common commitments to such themes as to 'Support the protection of labor rights and the environment, with one another and our other trading partners'. The policy pronouncements of Ms Truss as a candidate suggest her inclinations are in a different direction. A particular issue is the Northern Ireland situation. If the "Windsor Framework" succeeds it is likely to smoothe relations with both the EU and the US. Speculation at this stage cannot get us very far, but we must recognise that if economic forces or other forms of 'realism' come as drivers of policy, the likely choices become more predictable. After 2024 a less anti-EU government, even a pro EU coalition, may come to power, willing to renegotiate the TCA and align to EU norms. This would be a return to economic realism and would make the course of events more likely to return to past trends, with the UK seeking closer alignment with the EU alongside a political alliance with the US, highlighting the point that the choice between partnership with the US and the EU is a false dichotomy.

Concerns on regulatory standards

Since trade in goods between the two countries are mostly subject to zero or very low tariffs except for some products (e.g. cars, chemicals and agricultural products), non-tariff issues would become the core issues if the UK and US negotiated on trade issues.

Regulatory divergence between the UK and the US will be the most difficult challenge. Although both the EU and the US have high-quality regulatory regimes, they take different regulatory approaches reflecting political, economic, institutional and different societal values (Garcia Bercero et al., 2018). Young[8] argues that US-EU divergences are rarely designed to restrict trade but reflect a mix of domestic political forces, broad social preferences, focussed lobbyists and regulators' own wishes. This also applies to UK-US divergences: a wish on the part of UK trade negotiators to align with the US will run up against internal factors.

After leaving the EU, the UK basically maintained EU regulations, although the Johnson government aimed to make the UK more like the US (Smith et al., 2021). British stakeholders do not support divergence from the EU regulations (Henig, 2018). To what extent the UK will actually divert from EU's regulations for the sake of regulatory autonomy depends on the future domestic political landscape. Industry very much wants the UK to remain part of the European standards ecosystem and moves to abandon this linkage have been slow to materialise.[9]

The Transatlantic Trade and Investment Partnership (TTIP) negotiations revealed that civil society in Europe was concerned that regulatory cooperation with the US may result in lowering regulatory standards (van Loon 2018). UK public opinion has, since the days of TTIP, been alarmed by the idea of reducing food safety standards and moves that might be seen as further privatising the National Health Service (NHS). In the case of food standards, the EU/UK takes stricter regulations on agriculture and foods (e.g. pesticide use, food additives and GM crops) than the US does. Under its trade policy framework, sanitary and phytosanitary standards (SPS) that deal with food safety and animal and plant health, the UK takes the EU's precautionary principle while the US takes the 'science-based' approach in justifying regulations. For a UK-US trade deal, the US clearly expected the UK to implement SPS measures based on science to open the

UK's agricultural market (USTR 2019). The British public expressed strong concerns that the UK-US trade deal might threaten UK's food standards and animal welfare during the pre-negotiation consultations (Department for International Trade, 2020).

As for the NHS, the US negotiating objectives aimed to secure 'full market access for U.S. products' including pharmaceutical products (USTR, 2019). Facing strong public concerns that NHS might not be excluded from negotiation deal with the US and the deal may harm NHS (Clift, 2019), the then UK government stated that protecting the UK's right to regulate in the public interest and public services, including the NHS, is of the utmost important (Department for International Trade, 2020). After COVID-19, the popularity of the UK health delivery system is greater than ever. Thus, the NHS is an almost untouchable area for the UK government for any future trade deal, especially with the US.

An important issue is differences in data governance. After the UK left the EU, the UK concluded a comprehensive digital chapter in its bilateral free trade agreements (FTAs) with Australia, Japan and New Zealand and Digital Economy Agreement with Singapore between 2021 and 2022. The UK's policy shift shows a clear departure from the EU style data governance, which regards human rights as a fundamental right in its data governance, towards the Asia-Pacific style market and innovation focused data governance (Morita-Jaeger, 2021). At the domestic level, the UK government is trying to harness regulatory sovereignty from the EU and is undertaking UK Data Reforms that aims to simplify the UK GDPR that succeeded the EU GDPR, 2018 (at the time of September 2022).

The British public has a strong opinion that the UK's future trade deals should not reduce the level of data and digital protection (Which?, 2021). Also, the main business concern of the UK Data Reforms is that the UK's new data privacy regimes may endanger the EU's data adequacy decision (Brown, 2022). In the context of the UK-US trade relations, maintaining high level data privacy protection would be the key issue.[10]

In addition, different standardisation systems and US federalism in government procurement and services regulation could cause domestic constraints on the UK side. Even in 2018, US commentators were sceptical about the chances of a full FTA ever being signed (Balls et al., 2018).

International factors that constrain or impact the UK-US trade relations

The Bilateral dimension

Whereas a strong political motive to build the post-Brexit UK-US trade relations exists on the UK side, there are strong political constraints on the US side. As history shows, ideas and institutional constraints on the US side (Goldstein, 1988) are influential factors on UK-US trade relations. Although the Trump administration endorsed the idea of Brexit hardliners at the Conservative party to sell the UK-US FTA as the top priority of an independent trade policy, the Biden administration

(2021–) took a very different position on UK-US relationships. First, the US's ideological approach is quite different from the UK. As we have discussed, the Biden administration prioritises the domestic agenda and its worker-centred trade policy focuses on promoting 'fair competition', addressing the relation between forced labour and supply chains and non-market economies all of which strongly reflect geostrategic competition with China.[11] Second, the US is interested in addressing this trade agenda with its allies but not in promoting global trade through FTAs as it did when it led the TTP negotiations and promoted TTIP during the Obama administration in the early 2010. The US considers an FTA to be 'a very 20th century tool' and has no strategic intentions to use an FTA as a policy framework to promote UK-US trade relations.[12] Third, there are institutional problems. Trade Policy Authority (TPA) constitutes an institutional constraint to the US government negotiating new trade agreements on behalf of Congress (Sracic, 2021). Even if there is a political will, the Biden Administration cannot easily negotiate new trade agreements as TPA has expired.

Although the UK and the US commenced a series of bilateral trade talks to deepen its trade and investment ties called the UK-US Dialogue on the Future of Atlantic Trade from March 2022, the framework can be seen as a weak imitation of the EU-US Trade and Technology Council that is the reinvented EU-US trans-atlantic dialogue with more specific focuses on digital technologies. Indeed, the soft policy dialogues which the Biden administration can offer cannot be a precursor of a UK-US FTA, which requires market access negotiations. While the UK government publicly sells the bilateral dialogue as a £200 bn boost to trade,[13] the US simply intends to make use of the dialogue to collectively discuss the Biden Administration's worker-centred trade policy agenda with China in mind. The selected topics for discussion, such as small and medium-sized enterprises (SMEs), harnessing benefits of digital trade for wider stakeholders, levelling up for opportunities and gender equality, resilient supply chains, food security and environment, strongly reflect the US's interest rather than the UK's interest in market opportunities in the US.[14]

The absence of the UK-US FTA negotiations brought the UK a new idea of pursuing the state-level trade pacts, starting from Indiana and North Carolina in 2022. At a first glance, the state-level trade deals look promising since the US federal system and different regulatory frameworks across states constitute de-facto trade barriers for foreign business providers, especially in financial services (Berge and Bigart, 2020). However, the economic value of state-level mini deals looks very thin. US states have been very reluctant to open their public procurement. They are simply Memoranda of Understanding, which do not create any legal obligation and they cannot address any of the big issues that lie in federal jurisdiction.[15]

The Trilateral dimension

The critical point of the UK-US relation is that the UK's relation with the EU strongly affects the US position. President Biden, an Irish-American, has deep concerns over Irish policy, that is maintaining the Good Friday Peace Agreement. The US government, including the US Trade Representative Katherine Tai, repeatedly warned that any actions to undermine the Northern Ireland Protocol could hurt US-UK trade relations.[16]

Reacting to then Prime Minister Johnson's intention to unilaterally invoke Article 16 of the Northern Ireland Protocol in April 2022, the US government asked the UK (and the EU) to take a cooperative approach.[17] The Johnson government's antagonistic approach over the UK-EU Trade and Cooperation Agreement and the Northern Ireland Protocol diminished the UK's standing among Washington lawmakers (Hall Hall, 2022). But the initial US reaction to the Windsor Framework suggested the possibility of improvement.

Vinjamuri and Kundnani (2021) suggested that the US might find the UK a more congenial partner than the EU for its anti-China policy. In fact politically the Biden administration has seen the EU as a more powerful player in the world divided between liberal democracies and autocracies.

Towards quadrilateral dimension?

It seems that 'Indo-Pacific' is emerging as a new geostrategic international factor that may affect the UK-US relation in the future. 'Indo-Pacific' is a concept that the US and its allies (e.g. Australia, Japan and India) have been promoting in the geopolitical strategic context from the middle of 2000s (Wilkins and Kim, 2020) before the UK started to introduce it in its diplomatic concept. Sino-US geostrategic competition and formation of economic and security alliance networks to attenuate China are the critical concepts behind (Pan, 2014).

On the UK side, since Brexit, the UK is geopolitically shifting its diplomatic pivot from the EU towards the Indo-Pacific region, framed as an 'Indo-Pacific tilt' in its Integrated Review in 2021 (HM Government, 2021). The UK government aims to strengthen economic and security relations with the region using bilateral and plurilateral policy actions. In the area of trade, the UK is actively engaged in creating trade deals with Indo-Pacific countries, such as new bilateral FTAs with Australia and New Zealand and digital economy agreement with Singapore in 2022. The UK government also aims to join the Comprehensive and Progressive Agreement for Trans-Pacific Partnership (CPTPP) by 2023. And the FTA negotiation with India has started in 2022. The UK continuously places the US as the most important strategic ally (p60 in HM Government, 2021) while creating trade deals with Indo-Pacific countries. The UK's ambitions are clearly to reorient towards an 'Indo-Pacific' alliance, but this is subject to the US strategy in this area.

The Biden administration has presented the 'Indo-Pacific Economic Framework (IPEF)' as a way to rebuild its economic and diplomatic engagement in the Indo-Pacific region. Whereas the IPEF provides a forum to discuss policies that strongly reflect US's worker-centred trade policy agenda, it is not a negotiating framework towards a trade deal (Goodman and Reinsch, 2022) nor a political base to maintain free and open trade order in the region. The significance of IPEF lies in the US strategy of enhancing cooperation among like-minded countries in the region to counter China's emerging power and regional security.

Although the UK is a bystander of the IPEF, the UK shows strong alignment with the US by taking a tough stance on China (Vinjamuri and Kundnani, 2021). The UK-AUS-US defence deal is a perfect example of how the current UK government would see its relations with the US and Asia-Pacific evolving but it is somewhat exceptional. But will the US seek to join the CPTPP or try to negotiate revised TPP, and what difference might this make to UK ambitions? Perhaps if an old fashioned Republican free trade administration were returned, they might want to take an export-oriented approach, trying to push US style regulations on to CPTPP members including the UK.

However, once again we need to remind ourselves that this is not the only way the global system might evolve. We cannot project forward from the current situation: we can merely identify the forces that need to be researched. There could be a change again in the balance of economic interests over ideology. And new technology (e.g. 3D printing) could change the impact of economic forces such as distance. Biden could be succeeded by a Trump or equivalent. The impact of the Ukraine crisis is unknown at the time of writing. The shape of geostrategic pressures could pull the UK in a variety of different directions in terms of trade and investment and its relationship with the US.

Conclusion and future research implications

As we have argued, nothing is predictable. Ten years ago, one would have been able to point to the UK's good relations with China as offering a unique basis for trade and investment relations. UK energy and telecoms infrastructure was subcontracted to China. And the UK seemed to offer a bridge between China and the EU as it had been for the US. No longer though. Brexit seemed to offer an opportunity for a radical realignment with the US, and when the direct attraction of that faded, alignment with the Indo-Pacific region including the US came in. Perhaps distance might matter less. But politics, COVID-19 and Russia's war with Ukraine have disrupted the landscape totally. History and geography are returning to the stage even if they are wearing different clothes.

There is a need for further research on issues including the details of how regulatory systems interface. The hope that mutual recognition would allow UK firms to trade freely anywhere with no need for commitments to regulatory alignment has not come about. There is increasing acceptance, especially in the US, that simple globalisation will not and should not proceed as it has in the past even if the latest analysis suggests globalisation has changed its character rather than been reversed. Some economists fear the costs of policies for 'friendshoring' to increase 'resilience' of supply chains may be high, but the political pressures are there. We do not know how digital technologies will ultimately affect this and what choices the UK will be forced to make on digital regulation. At the moment of writing, the signs are that the UK is not easily going to be sailing out of European waters to join – let alone lead – the US fleet on a journey to the Indo-Pacific.

Notes

* Our special thanks go to Guillermo Larbalestier, Research Assistant in International Trade at the University of Sussex and Fellow of the UKTPO, for working on economic data.
1 For more on trade and investment opportunities, see Holmes and Larbalestier (2021). See also Heron, Siles-Brugge (2021) and Niblett (2022).
2 https://uk.usembassy.gov/our-relationship/policy-history/special-relationship-anniversary-1946-2016/
3 G. Lanktree March 5 2023 "Biden rebuffs UK bid for closer cooperation on tech" https://www.politico.eu/article/biden-united-kingdom-technology-rishi-sunak-cooperation-trade/
4 HM Government (2021).
5 https://www.gov.uk/government/speeches/pm-speech-in-greenwich-3-february-2020
6 https://www.whitehouse.gov/briefing-room/statements-releases/2021/06/15/u-s-eu-summit-statement/
7 https://ustr.gov/about-us/policy-offices/press-office/press-releases/2022/march/joint-statement-usuk-dialogues-future-atlantic-trade
8 See the chapter by Young, A. in this Handbook.
9 For example, The UK remains part of CEN and CENELEC; https://www.cencenelec.eu/news-and-events/news/2021/pressrelease/2021-11-25-bsi-membership/
10 As for the EU-UK digital trade relations, see chapters by Maria Tzanou; and Elaine Fahey and Fabien Terpan in this book.
11 USTR (2022).
12 https://internationaltradetoday.com/news/2022/03/22/ustr-says-ftas-are-20th-century-tools-2203220070
13 UK & US launch transatlantic dialogues to boost £200 bn trade relationship – GOV.UK (www.gov.uk).
14 Joint Statement on the U.S./UK Dialogues on the Future of Atlantic Trade | United States Trade Representative (ustr.gov).
15 Memorandum of Understanding on economic cooperation and trade relations between Indiana and the United Kingdom - GOV.UK (www.gov.uk) and Memorandum of understanding (MOU) on cooperation and trade relations between the US state of North Carolina and the United Kingdom - GOV.UK (www.gov.uk).
16 https://www.euractiv.com/section/uk-europe/news/ni-protocol-the-main-barrier-to-trade-deal-says-us-official/
17 US urges compromise on Britain and EU over Northern Ireland trade deal, *Financial Times*, https://www.ft.com/content/6494947f-feba-4d86-ad8a-cfa4c115262e

References

Baldwin, R., (2022). *The Peak Globalisation Myth*: Part 1, VOXEU COLUMN, 31 August 2022; https://cepr.org/voxeu/columns/peak-globalisation-myth-part-1

Balls, E. et al. (2018). On the Rebound: Prospects for a US-UK Free Trade Agreement, May 2018, M-RCBG Associate Working Paper No. 89, https://www.hks.harvard.edu/sites/default/files/centers/mrcbg/working.papers/USUK%20FTA%20516%20FINAL.pdf

Berge, E. T. and Bigart, A. E. (2020). Challenges in Expanding Financial Services to the U.S. Market, Venable LLP, February 27, 2020; Challenges in Expanding Financial Services to the U.S. Market | Insights | Venable LLP.

Brown, M. (2022). Data reform: A harbinger of efficiency or complacency? | BSI (bsigroup.com)

Chaney, T. C. (2018). The Gravity Equation in International Trade: an Explanation, *The Journal of Political Economy*, vol. 126, no. 1, 150–177.

Clift, C. (2019). The NHS is not for sale -But a US-UK trade deal could still have an impact, Chatham House, November, 2019. The NHS Is Not for Sale – But a US–UK Trade Deal Could Still Have an Impact | Chatham House – International Affairs Think Tank.

Department for International Trade (2020). UK-US Free Trade Agreement, March 2020; UK and US Free Trade Agreement (publishing.service.gov.uk).

Foreign & Commonwealth Office (2014). Review of the balance of competences, December 2014; https://www.gov.uk/guidance/review-of-the-balance-of-competences

Garcia Bercero, I. et al. (2018). EU-US Engagement on Regulatory Issues: Lessons Learnt, Notably in the Context of the TTIP Negotiations, *European Foreign Affairs Review*, vol. 23, no. 2, 149–165.

Goldstein, J. (1988). Ideas, Institutions, and American trade policy, *International Organization, Co.* vol. 42, no. 1, 179–217.

Goodman, M. P. and Reinsch, W. (2022). Filling In the Indo-Pacific Economic Framework, January 2022, Center for Strategic & International Studies; Filling In the Indo-Pacific Economic Framework | Center for Strategic and International Studies (csis.org).

Hall, A. (2022). What America's security and foreign experts really thing about Boris Johnson's Brexit Britain, BYLINE TIMES, 4 May 2022: https://bylinetimes.com/2022/05/04/what-americas-security-and-foreign-experts-really-think-about-boris-johnsons-brexit-britain/

Henig, D. (2018). ECIPE, Assessing UK Trade Policy Readiness, Policy Brief No. 4/2018; https://ecipe.org/wp-content/uploads/2018/04/ECI_18_UKTradePolicy_4_2018_LY03.pdf

Heron, T. and Siles-Brugge, G. (2021). UK-US Trade Relations and 'Global Britain', *The Political Quarterly*, vol. 92, no. 4, October-December 2021.

HM Government (2021). Global Britain in a competitive age -The Integrated Review of Security, Defence, Development and Foreign Policy Integrated Review, March 2021; Global Britain in a Competitive Age: the Integrated Review of Security, Defence, Development and Foreign Policy - GOV.UK (www.gov.uk).

HM Government (2014). Review of the Balance of Competences between the United Kingdom and the European Union Trade and Investment, February 2014; Review of the Balance of Competences | Trade and Investment (publishing.service.gov.uk).

Holmes, P. and Rollo, J. (2020). EU-UK Post-BREXIT Trade Relations: Prosperity vs. Sovereignty?, *European Foreign Affairs Review*, vol. 25, no. 4, 523–550.

Holmes, P. and Larbalestier G. (2021). Deepening and managing transatlantic economic relationships, UKTPO Briefing Paper 65, December 2021; Deepening and Managing Transatlantic Economic Relationships « UK Trade Policy Observatory (sussex.ac.uk).

Kimura, F. and Lee, H. (2006). The Gravity Equation in International Trade in Services, *Review of World Economics*, vol. 142, no. 1, 92–102.

Kundnani, H. and Vinjamuri, L. (2021). New UK-US alignment can reshape transatlantic cooperation, Chatham House Expert Comment, 2 March; New UK-US alignment can reshape transatlantic cooperation | Chatham House – International Affairs Think Tank.

Mycock, A. and Wellings, B. (2017). The Anglosphere: Past, present and future, 12 November, 2017, The British Academy; The Anglosphere: Past, present and future | The British Academy.

Morita-Jaeger, M. (2021). Accessing CPTPP without a national digital regulatory strategy? Hard policy challenges for the UK, UKTPO Briefing Paper 61, July 2021; Briefing-paper-61.pdf (sussex.ac.uk).

Niblett, R. (2022). Global Britain in a divided world - Testing the ambitions of the Integrated Review, Chatham House Research Paper, March 2022. At: 2022-03-29-global-britain-in-a-divided-world-niblett (chathamhouse.org).

Pan, C. (2014). The 'Indo-Pacific' and Geopolitical Anxieties about China's Rise in the Asian Regional Order, *Australian Journal of International Affairs*, vol. 68, no. 4, 453–469.

Reynolds, D. (1988). Rethinking Anglo-American Relations, *International Affairs*, vol. 65, no. 1, 89–111.

Schuyler, F. and Raymond, R. (2017). The US-UK 'Special Relationship' at a Critical Crossroads. Atlantic Council. http://www.jstor.org/stable/resrep03496.

Smith, I. D., MP, Villiers, T., MP, and Freeman, G., MP (2021). Taskforce on Innovation, Growth and Regulatory Reform, May 2021: FINAL_TIGRR_REPORT__1_.pdf (publishing.service.gov.uk).

Springford, J. and Lowe, S. (2018), Britain's Service Firms Can't Defy Gravity, Alas, Centre for European Reform, 5 February 2018; https://www.cer.eu/insights/britains-services-firms-cant-defy-gravity-alas

Sracic, P. (2021). Reauthorizing Trade Promotion Authority: The first trade test for the Biden administration, Hinrich foundation, March 2021: https://www.wita.org/wp-content/uploads/2021/03/Reauthorizing-Trade-Promotion-Authorityv2.pdf

Thorne, C. (1978). *Allies of a Kind: The United States, Britain and the War Against Japan 1941–45*. New York: Oxford University Press, p. 772.

USTR (2019). United States-United Kingdom Negotiations Summary of Specific Negotiating Objectives, February 2019; Summary_of_U.S.-UK_Negotiating_Objectives.pdf (ustr.gov)

USTR (2022). 2022 Trade Policy Agenda & 2021 Annual Report, March 2022; 2022 Trade Policy Agenda and 2021 Annual Report (1).pdf (ustr.gov).

Van Loon, A. (2018). Diverging German and British governmental trade policy preferences in the Transatlantic Trade and Investment Partnership (TTIP) negotiations, *Journal of Contemporary European Studies*, vol. 26, no. 2, 165–179.

Vinjamuri, L. and Kundani, H. (2021). New UK-US alignment can reshape transatlantic cooperation, Chatham House Expert comment, 2 March 2021; https://www.chathamhouse.org/2021/03/new-uk-us-alignment-can-reshape-transatlantic-cooperation

Which? (2021). Written evidence (CPT0049), House of Lords International Agreement Committee; House of Lords International Agreement committee. At: https://committees.parliament.uk/writtenevidence/40748/pdf/

Wilkins, T. and Kim, J. (2020). Adoption, Accommodation or Opposition? - Regional Powers Respond to American-led Indo-Pacific strategy, *Pacific Review*, vol. 35, no. 3, 415–445.

21

ANGLO-AMERICAN POWER IN THE WAKE OF BREXIT AND AMERICA FIRST

A Crisis at the Heart of the Liberal International Order

Inderjeet Parmar and Mark Ledwidge

CITY, UNIVERSITY OF LONDON

Introduction

New research reveals a growing interest in the role of the Anglosphere as a global power (Wellings and Mycock, 2019). Despite being difficult to define the Anglosphere – alliance, strategic partnership, network (Vucetic, 2021) – there is no question of its growing significance as the global distribution of power shifts towards the East, especially China. We argue that the Anglosphere is an *imperial transnational historic bloc* of powers rooted in nineteenth-century racialised Anglo-Saxonism, British imperialism and the white dominions of the Commonwealth. After 1945, the Anglo-American alliance forged in World War II consolidated in the 'rules-based liberal international order' (Vucetic, 2011; Elkins, 2022). The Anglosphere represents dense networks exclusive to its five core powers (Britain, the US, Canada, Australia, New Zealand) that cooperate in intelligence, immigration, counter-terrorism, military security, and so on. Historically, the networks have been inward-looking and operational, with indirect external effects. However, as the global hierarchies of power shift, the Anglosphere is increasingly active as a global force within existing multilateral institutions as well as towards strategic competitors such as China and Russia (Legrand, 2020). This is borne out by the recent barring or restricting from the Anglosphere's 5G roll-outs relevant technologies from China's Huawei.[1] The Anglosphere is, therefore, a security community, a cultural-linguistic English-speaking bloc with shared blood ties, rooted in empire, war, and the liberal international order (LIO). Its significance intensified in the President Trump and Prime Minister Johnson era – of Brexit and America First – as the LIO has loosened due to internal tensions and global power shifts (Vucetic, 2021).

DOI: 10.4324/9781003283911-26

We argue that realist and liberal-internationalist theories legitimise the liberal order, characterise the Anglosphere as a force for good, as an equally elite and mass-led hegemonic project, or a mixture of both. Our theoretical approach recognises those approaches but highlights the imperialistic, racialised, and hierarchical foundations of the Anglosphere. We underscore the growing interest in racial, colonial and class-based analysis of global politics. Significantly, our approach contributes to a deeper understanding of Anglo-American power, regarding their declining position in the global system, and their anxieties about decline that is prevalent in Anglospheric discourses about America First, Global Britain and attitudes to non-white powers like China, in addition to the European Union (International Strategic Analysis, 2020).[2]

The notion that the Anglo-Americans, the architects of the post-1945 order, are declining and have lost confidence in the LIO's ability to maintain their relative dominance over emerging non-western powers, is growing in its significance (Parmar, 2019). By extension, the Anglosphere's leaders seek to reassert their authority due to racial, security and economic challenges, in addition to Russia's invasion of Ukraine, which could lead to wider military conflict. Initiatives include the AUKUS trilateral military pact (between Australia, UK, and US), alongside the Anglosphere's 'Five Eyes' and related networks, the Quad (Quadrilateral Security Dialogue between the US, India, Australia, and Japan), and the Indo-Pacific Economic Framework (14 states including US, Australia, India, Japan, New Zealand, among other mostly Asian states) represents a major shift from broad 'congagement' of China to a more militarised and cyber-securitised policy designed to contain, rollback and subordinate China, whilst attempting to maintain economic, commercial and financial interdependency with China (Turner and Parmar, 2020). The chapter highlights the continuities and intensification of the racial and xenophobic attitudes of the Trump administration, mirrored by the Biden administration, and reflected by 'Global Britain'. We show that the Anglosphere's campaign to contain China's rise is not a new cold war, but is better understood in Gramscian-Kautksyian terms as a complex effort to 'manage enmity' and conflict, within the context of a competitive interdependent and racialised system. (Huo and Parmar, 2019). Overall, we argue that neither liberal nor realist theories explain the complexities of Sino-Anglospheric relations, nor do they correctly recognise the Anglosphere as a racialised global system, founded on historical, military, cultural, material and ideological power. The Anglosphere expresses enduring sentiment, kinship, trust, deep structures and interests (Wellings and Mycock, 2020).

The chapter begins with a description and analysis of the Anglosphere as a core aspect of transatlantic relations, and the LIO, as it relates to the distribution of global power. We will show how the Anglosphere coordinates its dense ecosystem of policy, security, military and intelligence networks through which funds, ideas, people and policies flow. We then evidence the economic-financial dimension of the Anglosphere, before highlighting 'Trumpist' and 'Global Britain's' orientation to the world and how elites infuse their ideas into policy outcomes. Finally, we challenge mainstream theoretical explanations of the Anglosphere by drawing on the work of Antonio Gramsci which emphasises the class, racial and imperial hierarchies, embedded in the Anglosphere (Hoare and Nowell-Smith, 1971; Kautsky).[3] Ultimately, we define the Anglosphere as an ultra-imperialist power paradigm, founded on a transnational historic but plastic global order, committed *to* globalising economies whilst maintaining an Anglo-led interstate system geared to absorbing China and an increasingly assertive EU.

Understanding the roots of the Anglosphere

At heart, the Anglosphere is a non-treaty-based association of English-speakers whose original migration from Britain created an enduring diasporic identity. Its core members consist of Britain, Australia, Canada, New Zealand, and the US. Although some scholars and government figures view the Anglosphere as a force for good, its history is much more sinister. The Anglosphere is considered a conduit of liberal internationalism, capitalism and democracy. However, the aforementioned is both narrow, historically inaccurate and fails to grasp the Anglosphere's continuing legacies (Malik, 2021). Essentially, the Anglosphere rests on a history of imperialism, colonial violence and exploitation of indigenous peoples (including genocide). Race, ethnic kinship and class represent key factors that underpin the transnational relationships which sustain the status of the Anglosphere. Indeed, within academia, elite attitudes regarding the British empire are often decoupled from the exploitative and militaristic roots championed by the British state and its mercantile class' acquisition of territories inhabited by non-whites. In short 'Whiteness' and 'race' are ignored by the Anglosphere's proponents (Gilroy, n.d).

While membership of the Anglosphere reputedly extends beyond its core states, we suggest that the empire's evolution into the 'Commonwealth' was a strategic neo-colonial move by Britain to retain control over colonial resources and to halt Britain's global decline. Domestically, all five nations (despite superficial changes) are led by white elites with a powerful grip on the state apparatus. The leadership and governance of the Anglosphere reflect its original elitist, racial and cultural foundations. Likewise, most Asian and African states are peripheral within the world's major governance structures – such as the International Monetary Fund (IMF), World Bank, WTO and G7. Indeed, it would seem that the equal inclusion of the non-white majority in the Anglosphere is not a priority. Rather, as Furedi shows, the West tries to obscure its racist past. The Anglo-Americans were forced to pursue reforms and public relations exercises to maintain their moral authority in the post-1945 world due to the emergence of independent Asian and African nations, and cold war competition with the USSR and China (Furedi, 1998; Dudziak, 2011; Ledwidge, 2013). These post-1945 domestic and international reforms represented strategically managed change as opposed to uprooting the mentalities, structures and networks of the racialised-class system. Paradoxically, in regard to China, whose rise and continuous growth threatens Western hegemony, whilst also creating opportunities, drives the Anglosphere to 'congage' China (Huo and Parmar, 2019).

Given that the Anglosphere is rooted in British but particularly English cultural, linguistic, economic and racial expansionism (Virdee and McGeever, 2018), it was designed to promote the power and interests of the British diaspora through limited assimilation but continued hegemonic control. As previously stated, the aforementioned changes in the global and domestic landscape prompted shrewd politicians across and beyond the Atlantic to refashion and reformulate their rhetoric on race and culture (after successive challenges from people of colour both domestically and internationally) which witnessed the alleged emergence of an egalitarian and inclusive international system that touted the rule of law, good governance, free trade, racial equality and capitalism (Parmar, 2016; Morey, 2021). Shifts in domestic and international politics forced the transnational Anglo-American elite to reconstruct their image and language in order to direct their attention towards the USSR. Thus, the post-1945 speeches of Churchill and other anglophile internationalists presented the Anglosphere as a bulwark against the totalitarianism of the Soviet Union (Vucetic, 2017). To summarise, the Anglosphere was never truly disconnected from the staunch racial hierarchy derived from Anglo-Saxonism that, despite some nuances, was akin to Nazi 'herrenvolk' theory. Arguably the contradictions and continuing legacies of race, class and cultural hegemony are still interwoven into the domestic and foreign policies of 21st-century Britain and America. The Anglosphere then stood for the following and still does:

1 White supremacy or cultural hegemony
2 The alleged civilisational superiority of English-speaking whites which legitimised colonialism and continues to validate their standing in the global hierarchy
3 The belief that the English have played a profoundly important and benign role in international affairs via capitalism, diplomacy, and military power
4 That English exceptionalism has made them naturally suited to wielding global power

Those characteristics explain why the settler outposts of Australia, New Zealand, Canada and the US engaged in the large-scale cultural and physical eradication, and subjugation, of 'their' native populations. It is impossible to separate White supremacy from the historic construction of the Anglosphere nations, just as it is impossible to separate their contemporary foreign and domestic policies from the current 'culture wars'. Although the Anglosphere is Eurocentric, it is specifically British or English, which explains both Brexit and the Brexiters' frustration with the EU due to their inability to leverage the EU to promote British interests (Virdee and McGeever, 2018). This indicates Britain's historic desire to create an alternative transnational Anglocentric global power bloc. It would be naïve to ignore the divergent historical and contemporary tensions that currently reflect the specific interests of the Anglosphere's states. The racial and ethnocentric model of Anglophile power politics suggests that cultural, economic, political and military challenges to Western racial hegemony are prioritised as *threats to the old*, English-speaking power bloc because they are deemed as *antithetical to the current international order.* Here, the rise of non-white nations is perceived as problematic because their divergent racial and cultural identities challenge historical norms (Barder, 2021). Note, the ascendance of America or other European powers is considered more palatable than the rise of China whose rise has been characterised as the 'yellow peril' (Turner, 2016). Additionally, Russia, Iran, Pakistan and India are similarly viewed as threats to the old order firstly as a possible alternative power bloc, and secondly due to their non-white credentials, which threaten the established order. Demographic factors such as declining birth rates among whites in contrast to the population growth of non-white populations in the world are seen as problematic. The aforementioned is exemplified by US white nationalists' fixation regarding 'replacement theory' and the 'swamping' metaphors employed in discourses on immigration. This, coupled with the increasing strength of the BRICS' economies, has provoked overt and covert fears for the survival of the post-1945 Western hegemonic system.

So, rather than assuming that the Anglosphere is a force for good, international relations (IR) scholars should be more critical of the Anglosphere's conceptual frameworks, institutional logic and the identity profiles of its global networks. Scholars should show how the Anglosphere's hidden or overt world view and narrow identity profile impacts on its domestic and foreign policy, and a variety of other issues, such as immigration, race relations and the neo-colonial exploitation of weaker nations. Such issues are reflected in the contemporary ideological conflicts related to race, class and the Left-Right schisms in Western politics. All of the aforementioned have found expression in Brexit and the right-wing white nationalism peddled during the Trump presidency. Trump's anti-immigrant statements regarding Africans and Mexicans rest on the foundational racial and cultural logic of the Anglosphere. This attitude was crudely displayed by the Western media's coverage of Ukrainian refugees in the wake of the Russian attack of 2022 – whom they referred to as 'blond, blue-eyed, relatively civilised, European', and not Syrian or Iraqi or other (Parmar, 2022). Here, the global challenges to Western hegemony might explain why the Anglosphere has gained more political and conceptual currency in recent years (Wellings and Mycock, 2020; Lo, 2021).

Given that mainstream IR theories generally ignore the significance of race and colonialism in global politics (Ledwidge, 2013), the Anglosphere provides an opportunity to understand this highly significant international phenomenon, which allows further theorising regarding the synthesised influence of neglected transnational ideas, experiences and practices. The Anglosphere then represents a system of comprehensive and securitised power – an imperial transnational historic bloc – which quite possibly attained full spectrum dominance in the past. It is hard to define, there are disagreements over its membership – over its aims or whether it can survive in our new world disorder, but the Anglosphere is alive as an idea, material reality and operational in both formal and informal transnational elite networks. Whether it is an imagined community or not its historical pedigree and world-historical influence, make it a powerful international entity.

Still, despite 'shared 'blood ties' and (Anglo-)American liberal-internationalist traditions, Trump's 'America First-ism' and, PM Johnson's post-Brexit Britain, and the Indo-Pacific region's security framework, challenged the Anglospheric alliance. However, irrespective of challenges, adherents and critics suggest that what the core powers of Anglosphere 'do' is wage and win wars and build the governing structures that 'order' the world, echoing the work of Mead's *God and Gold: Britain, America, and the Making of the Modern World* (2007).

We suggest that racial Anglo-Saxonism is the hidden 'ghost in the machine', not necessarily intended to be up front and centre due to its controversial hierarchical political character. And that pragmatic, softly spoken Anglospherism is powerful and consequential, but quintessentially English and outwardly genteel. It is Nye's (2004) soft, hard and smart power rolled up into one multi-dimensional force. The Anglosphere is an almost perfect embodiment of the intangible, institutional, coercive and consensual combination that Gramsci calls 'hegemony' (Hoare and Nowell-Smith, 1971).

Here the longevity of Anglospherism is its promise of opening its membership to *acculturated* Anglo-Saxons which is expressed in the American exceptionalist 'melting pot' theory of American society and the outward multi-raciality of Britain and the British commonwealth of nations. For example, the rise of Rishi Sunak and the cohort of non-white Conservatives suggest that anyone can eventually become an Anglo-Saxon (Parmar, 2016), even if enduring systemic racism helps perpetuate the structures of white hegemony.

The Anglosphere – its operational system of security, intelligence and policy networks

Legrand (2020) highlights 36 operational networks within the Anglosphere that convene regular meetings and conferences led by senior elected and civil service officials. These networks preside over policing, social welfare, internal affairs, cyber-security, infrastructure, education, borders, immigration and finance. Their discussions are based on a Memorandum of Understanding – which is neither formally nor legally binding but based on mutual trust. They infrequently issue public reports, court publicity, and are exclusive to the five core states. They transcend the nation-state, operate as transnational ruling elite collaborations, cut across notions of soft and hard power, *securitise* practically all aspects of governance and develop the basis of shared understandings and approaches to global issues, problems and challenges (Vucetic, 2021).

In addition to the Five Eyes intelligence-gathering and sharing programme, officially known as the Technical Cooperation programme, there is a *Quintet of Attorneys-General* that meets annually. The latter hosts the *Five Eyes Law Enforcement* group that is in permanent conference. A *Five Country Conference* brings together immigration and customs officials, encompassing the *Migration 5* and *Border 5*. The *Five Country Ministerial* consists of ministers responsible for national security, transnational crime, terrorism and 'radicalisation'. It has several sub-networks including the *Critical Five* and the *Aviation 5* that manage critical infrastructure and aviation security matters. The Critical 5 plays a key role in 'developing "shared narratives" of security' (Legrand, 2020).

In addition, the Technical Cooperation programme brings together the Anglosphere's military-scientific communities, ABCANZ promotes the interoperability of its armies, AUSCANNZUKUS coordinates its navies, ASIC its air and space interoperability capacities. At the same time, the Anglospheric core powers also collaborate with and maintain interoperability with their NATO allies.[4] Leading Anglospherists, in the wake of Brexit, also proposed to form CANZUK as the basis of the third pillar of western civilisation alongside the US and EU (Bell and Vucetic, 2019).

Legrand shows how the various Anglosphere groupings express their common identity, traditions, concept of 'cohering global trends and threats' and strong sense of 'Anglospheric solidarity' (Legrand, 2019). Anglosphere identity is based on wartime solidarities from World War II onwards, as well as twenty-first-century threats. That shared history of solidarity extends into valuing human rights, the rule of law and trust-building across the Anglosphere. It is clarified in these interactions and rare publicly-available communique that the central role in balancing security against rights lies with senior officials. It presents the basis on which soft powers and values become embedded in the language of security – become securitised, blurring the line between hard and soft power, material and cultural forms. This is further evidenced when the Anglosphere is described by officials as a globally interdependent formation facilitating legitimate trade and movement of peoples, in a world of threats, which further binds the bloc. According to Legrand, the threats facing the Anglosphere are, 'global, new and urgent', requiring deeper and greater cooperation and solidarity (Legrand, 2020, 73).

Legrand (2020) shows the Anglosphere has consciously developed a 'two-level strategy that mobilizes a concerted Anglosphere axis of global action for economic or political gain'. The first level is via concerted action within multilateral international organisations, such as the UN or WTO. The second is as 'a polylateral international organization to develop regulatory standards and conditions for finance and technology firms and exert global pressure independent of the diplomatic horse-trading and stalemates found in IOs [international organisations]'. Hence, numerous initiatives emerged focused on Anglosphere members of multilateral organisations and post-Brexit international trade agreements. As the US state department noted, the Anglosphere states have 'combined central government spending of more than USD 600bn in 2017 … [enabling] … significant financial leverage and policy options]' (Legrand, 2020).

The Anglosphere states are also united in exerting 'political pressure on rogue states – prominently China and Russia – outside of the political stalemates in traditional IO forums, and second to produce autonomous trade regulation' (Legrand, 2020). For example, Anglosphere foreign ministers released a joint statement against China's Hong Kong security law, while Anglosphere ambassadors condemned Russia's stance on LGBTI rights. Anglosphere pressure is set to intensify especially as 'a counter to China's growing influence in telecommunication technology via Huawei and potentially their dominance in energy too'. Hence, by 2022, Huawei had been barred or restricted on security grounds by the Anglosphere.

There is a 'strategic shift' towards an 'externalized' attitude 'attempting to set the terms of global trade, security and governance. Though these trends are developing, they augur an Anglosphere axis based on international consensus where the group of five can achieve it and contestation where it cannot' (Legrand, 2020). Vucetic adds that China has threatened to 'blind' the Five Eyes should they encroach its sovereignty, while Japan has mentioned adding 'more eyes' to the traditional core 5 (Vucetic, 2021).

Anglosphere as an economic and financial force

The Anglosphere is also a major global commercial, and financial force, with structural power. Although the level of intra-Anglosphere trade has decreased from around two-thirds to one-third of their total trade, it remains vast in world terms (Ravenhill and Huebner; Wellings and Mycock, 2020, p. 99). Fichtner argues that the Anglosphere plays a key role in promoting the neoliberal model of political economy through its robust and early support of globalisation. Global finance is also dominated by the Anglosphere, especially the Wall Street City of London powerhouses, and intra-Anglosphere financial ties (particularly Anglo-American) which constitute the world's largest bilateral financial group. Their value stood at US$4.7 trillion in 2016, which Fichtner calls 'persistent structural power'. While New York and London are financially intertwined, the Australian and Canadian systems constitute the Anglosphere's 'outer layer' that helps sustain Anglo-American dominance. The Anglosphere's share of global gross domestic product (GDP) is down, however, from 40% in 2009 to 33% in 2015. Conversely, its share of global financial wealth increased from 46% to 54% since 2009 (Fichtner, 2015; 2016).

The interconnections and linkages of Anglosphere economies with China are also highly significant. For example, British-China total trade in 2020 stood at US $93.4 billion while the value of foreign investment between them stood at US$3.5 billion. Total Chinese investment in the UK tops US$143 billion. There have been discussions regarding British and Chinese membership of the CPTPP as well as a free trade agreement between them (Jiang, n.d). Australia-China trade is highly significant: between 35% and 40% of Australia's exports go to China and 20% of its imports are from China (Das, 2022). China's investments in Australia quadrupled from US $19 billion in 2010 to US$87 billion in 2016 (Deloitte Access Economics, 2017).[5] US FDI in China in 2020 alone equalled over US$120 billion, an increase of 9.4% over 2019, while China's investments in the US in 2020 totalled US$38 billion (USTR, 2020).

The Transatlantic economy remains fundamental to the world economy, generating US$5.5 trillion in total commercial sales annually, employing around 15 million workers, and accounting for over 35% of world GDP in purchasing power terms. While transatlantic trade equals 25% of global exports, the US and Europe account for 70% of the outward and 60% of the inward stock of FDI. Nevertheless, China's importance for US commercial sales has grown in significance, although at US$293 billion in 2013, they remained less than the equivalent in Ireland (US$313 billion). But US affiliate income levels in China (US$7 billion dwarfed those for Spain, Germany and France, individually (Hamilton and Quinlan, 2016).

The Anglosphere is clearly a full-spectrum global entity with various types of 'capital' or power – in the Bourdieusian sense – which is highly valued as an attractive and coercive means of compelling compliance. However, scholars often pay little attention to Anglospheric soft power and its maintenance of the LIO. We argue that aside from military conquest, the Anglosphere's greatest strengths are its cultural, economic, linguistic, civilisational, racial and ethnic power which undergird its global security. We use the term 'capital' to represent both an idea or material force that may be leveraged in both symbolic and material ways. Our use of 'capital' corresponds to and is derived from the work of Bourdieu: 'The gaining of control over resources depends upon agents' capital and the skill (or fortune) with which they invest it'. Again, 'capital' is not an exclusively material resource (such as financial wealth) but is also symbolic (degree of prestige or honour) and cultural (Mambrol, 2017).

Trumpist and global Britain attitudes

According to Rachman, China's increasingly aggressive behaviour triggered retaliatory action from the Anglosphere, especially from the Trump administration but with the support of Britain, Canada and Australia. The aforementioned set the stage for the Biden administration to continue the confrontation – via 'extreme competition' – despite the reservations of the EU. The EU signed a major investment deal with Beijing in December 2020 over US objections while Franco-German leaders warned of the dangers of anti-China rhetoric. But the Anglosphere states 'are more inclined to take the American view that a rising China is a threat that must be countered' (Rachman, 2021). Yet, Russia's war on Ukraine has pushed the Anglosphere and EU closer together, regarding China's role, still although the EU does not fully align with the Anglosphere, particularly over energy imports from Russia, or China's possible honest broker role in the Ukraine war (FT, 2022).

Ironically, despite his 'isolationist' and transactional rhetoric, President Trump's administration operated within Anglospheric norms and expectations. Vucetic (2021) argues that the Trump years saw a remarkable increase in the bloc's media visibility, as well as its openness to 'diplomatize' and 'politicize' the Five Eyes partnership. Trump was aggressive towards China over economic and trade practices, labelled it a 'strategic competitor', and condemned its state-driven protectionist policies that allegedly harm US companies, violate international norms, and pollute the environment (White House, 2020 'Strategic Approach to the People's Republic of China' (White House, 2020).

Indeed, Trump started a prolonged trade war, claiming to decouple their economies, prohibiting technology transfer, blacklisting Chinese high-tech companies and tightening export controls on sensitive technologies to end users in China. Despite being critical of Trump's failures, Biden continued with similar policies and rhetoric and has yet to remove Trump's trade tariffs. 'America First' and 'Extreme Competition' may not differ fundamentally after all (Yin and Parmar, 2021).

Trump simultaneously intensified Sino-US rivalries and rhetoric regarding a 'new cold war' over freedom of navigation in the Indo-Pacific and the alleged Wuhan lab leaks in relation to the Covid-19 virus. Underpinning this was Trump's racial-civilisational attitudes to China (and the non-white world) which stoked Sinophobia on a large scale. COVID-19 was labelled the 'Chinese virus' to delegitimise China and global institutions, highlighting its culpability in suppressing information and hoarding medical equipment (Nast, 2021). The World Health Organization (WHO) was criticised as 'China-centric', and defunded. Trump also backed 'medical/vaccine nationalism' aimed at developing the first coronavirus vaccine and controlling supply's and boosting corporate profits and strengthening US geopolitical interests. The administration deployed rhetoric about COVID-19 and China to narrate a 'clash of civilizations' (Parmar and Furse, 2021). Kiron Skinner, as director of the US state department's policy planning staff, argued that the 'clash' was predicated on racial-civilisational criteria because 'it's the first time that we will have a great power competitor *that is not Caucasian*' [emphasis added]. Skinner noted that 'when we think about the Soviet Union and that competition, in a way it was a fight within the Western family. Karl Marx was a German Jew who developed a philosophy that was within the larger body of political thought … that has some tenets even within classical liberalism. … That's not really possible with China. This is a fight with a really different civilization' (Denmark, 2019). This perpetuated 'yellow peril' myths, justified anti-China policies and denied findings of China scholars (Brown, 2021; Pu and Wang, 2018). The administration co-opted human rights discourse, selectively defined China as oppressive in contrast to the West and cast Trump as a *defender and reformer* of the American-led LIO. The 'clash of civilisations' narrative linked to Trump's neo-mercantilism by reframing free trade and multilateralism as Western weakness. Trump's withdrawal from the Trans-Pacific Partnership, imposition of tariffs and various hawkish appointments, blended protectionism and anti-elitism, linking a strategy of industrial consolidation with anti-immigrant sentiment.

But in reality, the US remains interlocked as an economic power, financially interdependent with China. China has the world's largest holdings of foreign currency reserves (over US$3 trillion), the majority of which are in US dollars, and over 20% of US treasury securities (Salidjanova, 2014). US corporate relations with China continued to increase during 2016–2020 despite Trump's anti-China rhetoric and policies which were, partly, motivated to 'open up' China, rather than destroying it. Phase One of Trump's US-China trade deal highlighted the contradictory conflictual and cooperative relations between US corporate interests, the Trump administration and Sinophobia on the US far-right.

Space prohibits an extensive analysis of Global Britain narratives steeped in imperial nostalgia, and the recovery of past glories to strengthen British nationalism and the projection of post-Brexit greatness (Cabinet Office, 2021). There are clear anti-China undertones, as well as ambivalence about the EU's capacity to assert itself on the global stage behind Anglo-American congagement strategies (Turner, 2019). (Former) UK Prime Minister Johnson's racialised attachments to the Anglosphere are evident, despite coded language that simultaneously 'others' non-white Commonwealth peoples (Namusoke, 2019). This 'othering' of the non-white Commonwealth is strongly indicated in Johnson's vision of Global Britain in the 2021 Integrated Review. In it, Australia, New Zealand and Canada are discussed separately from the broader Commonwealth countries, although the US is mentioned in that very section, as united by a shared history and the Five Eyes programme (*Cabinet Office,* 2021, 69–70). Johnson and US President Biden signed a grand declaration called 'The New Atlantic Charter' in 2021 that claims continuity with the original 1941 Atlantic Charter signed by President Franklin Delano Roosevelt and PM Winston Churchill. Note the original Charter enshrined the right to self-determination to white Europeans states – excluding colonised Africans and Asians. The new Charter commits to upholding the rules-based order and human rights, opposing external interference in the internal affairs of nations, and threats to 'freedom of navigation and overflight and other internationally lawful uses of the seas' (Biden and Johnson, 2021). The latter is clearly directed at China's claims in the region.

The America First and Global Britain approach towards the EU differs significantly from their approach to China but remains ambivalent about the EU: issues regarding trade, EU disagreement over the relationship with China, the bloc's over-reliance for its security on the US, and disagreements over Russia's role in security and energy terms. The EU is seen as an irritant and competitor (Le Corre, 2022; FT, 2022), especially since the war in Ukraine.

In foreign policy, despite coercive rhetoric, interpenetrations with China – trade, investments, students – are dense, enduring, even if under pressure from specific administrations (Cabinet Office, 2021, 28–32; 70–76). The Anglosphere states don't want China's collapse – unlike the goals of the anti-Soviet cold war – they would rather maintain but subordinate China to western power. Clearly the world is transcending the liberal post-war arrangements. The issue is on what or whose terms, and which political and economic approach, will assume a dominant role in the interlocking world system. Anglospherists are committed to perpetuating their own power and diminishing China's (HJS (n.d.)).

Gramscian-Kautskyian analysis versus dominant frameworks

The question is what theories or concepts should we use to determine the Anglosphere's role in world politics? Though realist and liberal theorists' arguments have some traction, neither accurately teases out current or future dynamics and trajectories. Realists' principal, and timeless, argument suggests near-inevitable inter-hegemonic war between the US and China (Allison, 2017). Meanwhile, liberals categorise the US-led regional order as largely positive-sum 'benign' and collaborative. Yet, liberals fail to highlight the changes within in the global power dynamics, and the existing levels of social inequality within societies, which are partly fuelled by capitalist globalisation (Huo & Parmar, 2019). Finally, liberals and realists fail to acknowledge that the LIO and its Anglosphere core is capable of hierarchically-co-opting and integrating emerging powers, enabling them to challenge, and potentially re-shape, rival forces.

We argue that the Anglosphere is, an imperial transnational historic bloc, a formulation derived from Gramscian hegemony theory, but combined with Kautksy's concept of 'ultraimperialism. Kautsky's approach denotes transnational ruling elites' and classes' collaboration based on shared interests even within a competitive and conflictual system and expresses the complexities of global transitions that witness simultaneous selective collaboration, accommodation, competition and simmering underlying conflicts of interests. Such transnationalism, however imperfect, is consequential in diminishing the chances of outright great power military conflict. The common market/EU is an excellent example of this, forged in the aftermath of two bloody World Wars caused by European states. This is, in essence, what the 'Long Peace' since 1945 refers to. We argue that the Anglosphere should be viewed in a similar way. It is an 'extraordinary partnership', embedded within it an enduring, probably permanent, transnational historic bloc (a hierarchical but unified diverse ruling coalition). It combines multiple states and political parties, elite knowledge networks of think tanks and academic institutions, corporate networks, and strong levels of civil society support. This constitutes deep, enduring, strategic, cultural and racial power relations.

Global interpenetrations within the Anglosphere also encompass broad aspects of the LIO, and non-Anglosphere states and economies, including the EU and, importantly, China, as detailed earlier. China's opening up to the world was a Chinese elite project that was fully supported by American, British, German and other states, multilateral institutions, and private corporations and corporate foundations (Huo and Parmar, 2019). It was US and Chinese recipients of public funds and private foundation grants, from the late 1970s to the present, who formed transnational networks to open up opportunities for exchanges of people, money, and ideas. The debate over 'ideological' differences between neoliberal Anglosphere and Chinese ideas about state-economy relations hardly rivals the contradictions of western capitalism in regard to the communist USSR. Neither does China have anything resembling a military alliance like the Warsaw Pact, let alone NATO, and no network of pro-Chinese political parties across the world. This is not a cold war (Walt, 2018).

Gramscian elite knowledge networks blend well with the Kautskyian conception of 'ultra-imperialism' and provide a more exact explanation regarding the recent and future trajectories of regional and China-Anglosphere relations. Kautsky's concept contends that to exploit the world's people and resources, ruling classes form international class-based alliances (Kautsky, 1914). Those alliances lead to co-operation across a range of domains as determined by the balance of power between dominant states. While competitive, they promote regulated competition via common rules, and official and unofficial diplomacy. Understanding Anglospheric hegemony as consisting of transnational elite knowledge networks, in which are embedded key elements of the power elites of other great powers, best explains Sino-Anglosphere relations' 'ups and downs' as interdependent and interpenetrated powers jostling for position while cooperating on several fronts. It also explains the domestic sources of class-based resistance and turbulence in the relationship, as imperial transnational elites try to manage popular opposition to the effects of globalised interdependence and the redistributions of work that led to economic change, and rising inequalities.

Conclusion

We have shown that the Anglosphere is a self-conscious, broadly united, historically-rooted, heavily institutionalised, and racial and cultural association of English-speaking powers at the heart of the LIO and the world's political economy. That is been challenged by the 'rise' of Asia and the BRICS, especially China, and from domestic political resistance to inequality, declining living standards, rise of ultra-nationalism and domestic political instability. The Anglosphere defines as threats a number of factors and forces and is intensifying its unity and power projections through new agreements like AUKUS, renewing existing bodies like the Quad, and militarising and securitising strategies and rhetoric. This is aimed at exerting pressure on China and other perceived 'revisionist' powers, via racialised-civilisational messaging and mobilisation that has numerous effects, including restrictions on non-white immigration and rising violence against Asians, (Elias, et al., 2021), as well as US and other government programmes, such as the China Initiative, that target Chinese nationals (Lewis, 2021; Daly, 2022). Such tendencies are deeply rooted in the British empire, Anglo-Saxonism and white supremacist ideologies that criss-cross the Anglosphere (Barder, 2021).

The world and interstate relations are in a transitional phase, an organic crisis destabilising established institutions, norms and their liberal ideology. This suggests that the major crises of order, although attributable to hyper-globalisation, are largely domestic in character, which spills-over into international politics. These structural-level sources of instability and resistance are only partly replicated at the global level due to the elite lead unequal interpenetrations and interdependencies characterising intra-Anglosphere relations, Anglosphere relations with the EU and China, not to mention a broader range of powers (e.g. Japan, South Korea and India) embedded in security, economic and financial relationships. Therefore, and with due regard to the many sources of global turbulence, we conclude via Gramscian-Kautskyian theory that the probabilities of outright military conflict among great powers are low due to the range of interdependencies and interpenetrations between the rival powers. Rather, the greater dangers lie within nation states.

Notes

1 https://www.npr.org/2022/05/20/1100324929/canada-bans-chinas-huawei-technologies-from-5g-networks.
2 https://www.isa-world.com/news/?tx_ttnews%5BbackPid%5D=1&tx_ttnews%5Btt_news%5D=575&cHash=4527ce6f1a6634cbec0f2c26d6f7f00e
3 'Ultra-imperialism,' *Die Neue Zeit*, 1914; https://www.marxists.org/archive/kautsky/1914/09/ultra-imp.htm
4 https://web.archive.org/web/20091112150228/http://www.abca-armies.org/History.aspx
5 https://www2.deloitte.com/content/dam/Deloitte/au/Documents/Economics/deloitte-au-economics-benefits-chinese-investment-in-australia-130617.pdf.

References

Allison, G. (2017). *Destined for War.* Scribe Publications.
Barder, A.D. (2021). *Global Race War.* Oxford University Press.
Bell, D. and Vucetic, S. (2019). Brexit, CANZUK, and the legacy of empire. *The British Journal of Politics and International Relations*, 21(2), 367–382.
Biden Jr., Joseph. R. and Johnson, Boris. (n.d.). *The New Atlantic Charter* 2021. https://www.gov.uk/government/publications/new-atlantic-charter-and-joint-statement-agreed-by-the-pm-and-president-biden/the-new-atlantic-charter-2021.

Brown, K. (2021). *Kerry Brown, the academic defending the Chinese perspective.* https://qz.com/2005978/kerry-brown-the-academic-defending-the-chinese-perspective/.

Cabinet Office (2021). *Global Britain in a Competitive Age.* https://www.gov.uk/government/publications/global-britain-in-a-competitive-age-the-integrated-review-of-security-defence-development-and-foreign-policy/global-britain-in-a-competitive-age-the-integrated-review-of-security-defence-development-and-foreign-policy.

Corre, P.H. (n.d.). *Russia's Invasion of Ukraine Has Jeopardized the China-EU Relationship.* https://carnegieendowment.org/2022/05/10/russia-s-invasion-of-ukraine-has-jeopardized-china-eu-relationship-pub-87107.

Daly, C. (2022). *That hostility to China was orchestrated* | https://www.tellerreport.com/news/2022-01-19-mep-claire-daly--that-hostility-to-china-was-orchestrated.B1xX-fUBTK.html.

Das, S. (2022). *The Guardian. The sheer size of the China trading relationship is why Australia has to share its feasts and famines with Beijing* https://www.theguardian.com/commentisfree/2022/may/31/the-sheer-size-of-the-china-trading-relationship-is-why-australia-has-to-share-its-feasts-and-famines-with-beijing.

Denmark, A. M. (2019). *Problematic Thinking on China from the State Department's Head of Policy Planning.* https://warontherocks.com/2019/05/problematic-thinking-on-china-from-the-state-departments-head-of-policy-planning/.

Dudziak, M.L. (2011). *Cold War Civil Rights.* Princeton University Press.

Elias, A. and Ben, J. (2021). Racism and nationalism during and beyond the Covid-19 Pandemic. *Ethnic and Racial Studies*, 44(5), 783–793.

Elkins, C. (2022). *Legacy of Empire.* Vintage

Fichtner, J. (2015). https://www.duckofminerva.com/2016/08/the-anglosphere-dominance-in-global-finance-and-the-consequences-of-brexit.html

Fichtner, J (2016). Perpetual decline or persistent dominance? *Review of International Studies*, 43, 1.

Financial Times (2022). Europe's fight to stay united over war in Ukraine. https://www.ft.com/content/de9056bf-9121-4b17-b569-f5e889e4eff0

Furedi, F. (1998). *The silent war.* Rutgers University Press.

Gilroy, P. (2020). *Toward a Global History of White Supremacy.* https://www.ucl.ac.uk/racism-racialisation/transcript-toward-global-history-white-supremacy

Hamilton, D.S. and Quinlan, J.P. (2016). *The transatlantic economy 2016.* Washington, D.C.

HJS. (n.d.). *Breaking the China Supply Chain.* https://henryjacksonsociety.org/publications/breaking-the-china-supply-chain-how-the-five-eyes-can-decouple-from-strategic-dependency/.

Huo, S. and Parmar, I. (2019). 'A new type of great power relationship'? Gramsci, Kautsky and the role of the Ford Foundation's transformational elite knowledge networks in China. *Review of International Political Economy*, 27(2), 234–257.

Hoare and Nowell-Smith, G. (eds.) (1971). *Selections from the Prison Notebooks of Antonio Gramsci.* London: Lawrence and Wishart.

International Strategic Analysis. (2020). https://www.isa-world.com/news/?tx_ttnews%5BbackPid%5D=1&tx_ttnews%5Btt_news%5D=575&cHash=4527ce6f1a6634cbec0f2c26d6f7f00e

Jiang, E. (n. d.). UK-China investment and trade. https://www.ibanet.org/dec-21-uk-china-investment.

Ledwidge, M. (2013). *Race and US Foreign Policy.* Routledge.

Lewis, M. (2021). Criminalizing China. *Journal of Criminal Law and Criminology*, 111(1), 145.

Legrand, T. (2020). The past, present and future of Anglosphere Security Networks. In Wellings and Mycock.

Lo, A. (2021). *South China Morning Post. A desperate call for an 'Anglosphere' against rising China.* https://www.scmp.com/comment/opinion/article/3121169/desperate-call-anglosphere-against-rising-china.

Malik, K. (2021). *The Guardian. We should not allow the Anglosphere to distort the history of liberty.* https://www.theguardian.com/commentisfree/2021/sep/25/the-anglosphere-is-just-a-cover-for-the-old-idea-of-white-superiority.

Mambrol, N. (2017). *The Sociology of Pierre Bourdieu.* https://literariness.org/2017/05/09/the-sociology-of-pierre-bourdieu/.
Morey, M. (2021). *White Philanthropy.* UNC Press.
Namusoke, E. (2019). The Anglosphere, race and Brexit, in Wellings and Mycock.
Nast, C. (2021). *Biden's COVID-19 Origins Report Leaves the Lab Leak on the Table. Vanity Fair.* https://www.vanityfair.com/news/2021/08/bidens-covid-19-origins-report-leaves-the-lab-leak-on-the-table.
Nye, J.S. (2004). *Soft Power.* Public Affairs.
Office of the United States Trade Representative (2020). *The People's Republic of China.* https://ustr.gov/countries-regions/china-mongolia-taiwan/peoples-republic-china.
Parmar, I. (2016). Racial and imperial thinking in international theory and politics. *British Journal of Politics and International Relations*, 18 (2) 2016.
Parmar, I. (2019). Transnational elite knowledge networks. *Security Studies*, 28 (3), 532–564.
Parmar, I. (2022, forthcoming). A humane analysis of a violent international order. Forum on "Putin's Ukraine Aggression", *International Politics.*
Parmar, I. and Furse, T. (2021). The Trump administration, the far-right and world politics. *Globalizations.*
Pu, X and Wang, C. (2018). *What does China think about China's rise?* https://medium.com/international-affairs-blog/what-does-china-think-about-chinas-rise-26ce67b1cffb.
Rachman, G. (2021). Why the Anglosphere sees eye to eye on China. *Financial Times.* 8 Feb. https://www.ft.com/content/ed2d9c00-c8df-4efc-a1ad-63bc8e97bd25
Salidjanova, N. (2014). *China's foreign exchange reserves and holdings of U.S. securities.* Washington, D.C.: U.S.-China Economic and Security Review Commission.
Turner, O. (2016). *American Images of China.* Routledge.
Turner, O. (2019). Global Britain and the Narrative of Empire. *The Political Quarterly.*
Turner, O. and Parmar, I. (eds.), (2020). The United States in the Indo-Pacific. Manchester University Press.
Virdee, S. and McGeever (2018). Racism, Crisis, Brexit. *Ethnic and Racial Studies*, 41, 10.
Vucetic, S. (2011). *The Anglosphere.* Stanford University Press.
Vucetic, S. (2017). "The Fulton address as racial discourse," in A.P. Dobson and S. Marsh, eds., *Churchill and the Anglo-American Special Relationship.* Routledge.
Vucetic, S. (2021). *More than a Spy Alliance? Centre for International Policy Studies.* https://www.cips-cepi.ca/more-than-a-spy-alliance-the-five-eyes-today/.
Walt, S.M. (2018). *I Knew the Cold War.* Foreign Policy. https://foreignpolicy.com/2018/03/12/i-knew-the-cold-war-this-is-no-cold-war/.
Wellings, B. and Mycock, A. (2019). *The Anglosphere: continuity, dissonance, and location.* Oxford: Oxford University Press.
White House (2020). Strategic Approach to the People's Republic of China. https://trumpwhitehouse.archives.gov/wp-content/uploads/2020/05/U.S.-Strategic-Approach-to-The-Peoples-Republic-of-China-Report-5.24v1.pdf
Yin, S. and Parmar, I. (2021). *The Wire. Under Biden, the Fundamentals of Sino-US Relations Will Remain the Same.* https://thewire.in/world/joe-biden-fundamentals-sino-us-relations-remain-donald-trump

22

THE MEASUREMENT, STRUCTURE AND DYNAMICS OF THE TRANSATLANTIC CURRENT ACCOUNT

Martin T. Braml and Gabriel J. Felbermayr

General misconceptions on transatlantic trade

International trade relations, often summarized by the sign of bilateral trade balances, have played a major role in US politics over the past years. In the economics literature, a new strand of empirical work following Autor et al. (2013) has shown that 'trade shocks' like China's joining of the World Trade Organization (WTO) have yielded adverse economic and political outcomes for US counties with increasing trade deficits.[1] Similarly, in the European Union (EU), whether trade policies are deemed successful or not is often simply measured by growth of exports – as if imports were something suspicious or deplorable, or both. This *mercantilist bias* in political debates, which ignores falling consumer prices and an increase in the availability of imported goods (often of higher quality), is present almost everywhere in the world.

In case of trade relations between the United States and the EU, hereinafter referred to as transatlantic trade – apologies to Canada, the UK or Switzerland – another bias complements this common misunderstanding: the almost exclusive focus on goods trade, which has proven to be the root cause of trade tensions in recent years. This *goods trade bias* may have to do with the tangible nature of goods and is just another expression of overemphasizing agricultural and manufacturing production while neglecting services despite their paramount economic significance.[2] This bias also distracts from foreign direct investments, which are fundamental for the transatlantic economic relationship, too.

As outlined in Braml and Felbermayr (2018), a third conceptual misunderstanding of the transatlantic current accounts comes with respect to the institutional setting of the EU: trade balances between the United States and any EU member state such as Germany are (almost) as meaningless as, say, France's balance with

DOI: 10.4324/9781003283911-27

California. Member states of the EU are part of a customs union, pursue a uniform foreign trade policy, constitute an ever more integrated internal market – most comprehensively for manufacturing industries – and most of them even share a common currency, meaning that they do not individually control the external value of their money. Just as US states do. Therefore, the EU as trade-bloc, and not its member states, is the right addressee for US concerns over EU trade policies or the size and structure of transatlantic economic transactions.

The transatlantic current account

Against this background, Figure 22.1 updates findings in Braml and Felbermayr (2019). It depicts the evolution of the current account balance (solid line) and its sub-balances (bars), that is, goods trade, services trade, primary income and secondary income, from 2003 to 2020. The figure shows the US perspective, meaning that positive balances represent US surpluses and negative balances US deficits. It stands out that the United States continuously runs a deficit in goods trade vis-a-vis the EU. It's neither excessive (0.4% of US GDP in 2021), nor has it grown significantly relative to US income between 2014 and 2020 and vice versa, the United States has run surpluses in both services trade and primary income (more details

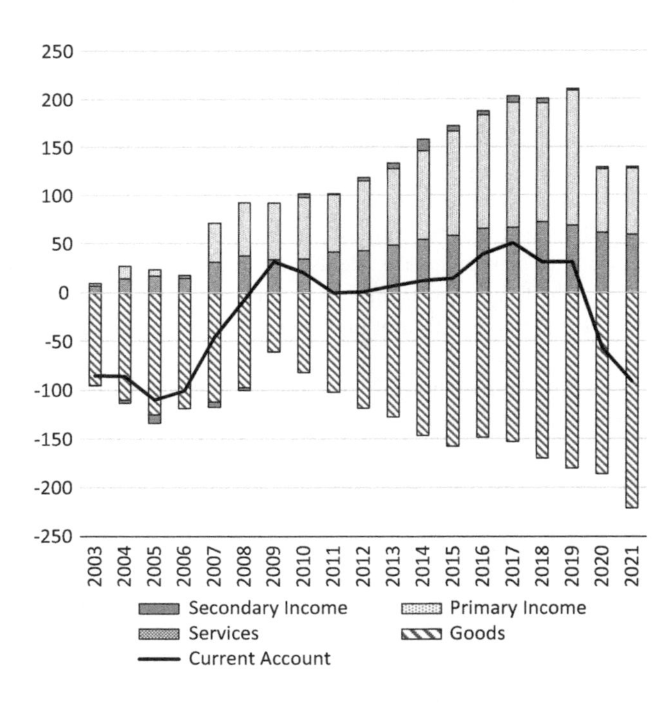

Figure 22.1 The transatlantic current account 2003–2020, balances, US perspective, bn USD[3]

Source: Bureau of Economic Analysis, 2022. Author's illustration.

below). For a decade between 2009 and 2019, these surpluses have more than offset the goods trade deficit leading to a relatively balanced but positive overall current account balance. The significant drop in US primary income in 2020 is attributable to Brexit as substantial US investment is 'located', or put more precisely, managed by companies located in London. Accordingly, the overall current account turns negative in 2020. The secondary income account, which in case of the EU-US relations mainly consists of fines and penalties for corporates, migrants' remittances or development aid, is, grosso modo, economically irrelevant for the transatlantic relations and will, therefore, not be discussed further.

What's the economic interpretation of these differently shaded bars and why does only the overall balance really matter? Adding services and goods trade, in this respect, appears relatively straightforward. The different signs of the balance – US goods trade deficit and services exports (and EU positions vice versa) – are simply an expression for the structure of comparative advantages of the economies. Apparently, Americans are more efficient in developing software, producing movies and providing financial services, while the Europeans are more efficient in assembling cars, making wine and inventing machinery. This is, in brief, the logic of international trade as David Ricardo has envisioned it 200 years ago.

The substitutability of exports and FDI

But how does investment income complement the exchange of goods and services? Primary income accounts measure the compensation of domestic production factors located in foreign countries. As cross-border commuting of workers is almost impossible geographically, transatlantic primary income accounts consist almost entirely of investment income, that is, dividends, interest payments, rents et cetera. The pattern of balances in the sub-accounts, foreign direct investment (FDI) income and portfolio investment (PI) income, is quite telling: the United States runs a surplus of USD 105 bn in FDI income and a deficit of USD 38 bn in PI income in 2020. This exemplifies that US firms choose a different approach in serving the European market than Europeans do in the United States; instead of engaging in cross-border trade, US companies establish subsidiaries in the EU and provide their services via them. In fact, the famous Heckscher-Ohlin trade theory, according to which trade between countries is the result of differences in relative endowments with production factors, implies that exports and imports are substitutes: instead of employing relatively abundant factors domestically and utilize them in the production of goods that are subsequently shipped to foreign countries, one can also directly re-locate these factors of production to the destination country and utilize them on site.

This investment-to-exports substitution depends to a significant extent on transaction costs: when the costs of physical shipments (e.g. transportation and tariffs) are low, exporting is attractive relative to FDI; when production factors are easily mobile internationally, FDI becomes more profitable. These considerations apply very well to the patterns of transatlantic trade: as shipment costs for goods have gradually fallen over the last decades (Baldwin, 2006), Europeans have supplied the

US market with direct exporting of goods. In contrast, in many industries, US services exports depend on intellectual property (IP) such as patents, and thus on highly mobile production factors. Provided existing differences in corporate tax rates across countries, US firms optimize their corporate tax planning by locating their IP in European tax havens with a tax-friendly treatment of IP income. This is what brought the headquarters of Alphabet and Apple to Ireland or Starbucks to the Netherlands (and many more US firms, of course, as well). The trade implications of such legal structures are quite interesting: US services exports to the EU are artificially converted into FDI income – with no difference compared to direct experts regarding their fundamental drivers and the generated incomes. For exactly this reason, the current account captures them both.

On the one hand, the substitution between FDI and direct exporting faces more severe restrictions for manufactured goods than for IT-based services: scale economies make FDI profitable only for a few, very productive firms; physical capital bound by factories and production facilities is less mobile than IP and therefore commonly concentrated around historical clusters; labour as a factor of production matters, too, for the production of specialized products while the mass of labour force is even less mobile than physical capital; finally, there are no comparable tax loopholes benefitting the re-location of manufacturing firms.

On the other hand, recent political events might strengthen the case for FDI-based manufacturing exports as trade costs can be expected to increase: the COVID-19 pandemic has led to significant interruptions of international logistics and to rising shipment cost, threatening not just global value chains but also the supply of final products. Natural disasters such as a volcanic eruption in Iceland in 2010, or the blocking of Suez Canal in 2021 have demonstrated the potential fragility of important trade routes; climate change could make such events more likely. An increased emphasis of risk assessment and the reinforcement of delivery capability could therefore result into more diversification of production facilities and shorter supply chains.

Moreover, deliberate political decisions increasingly contribute to rising trade costs: during the Trump era, additional trade restrictions in the form of higher tariffs have become en vogue and might, in a geopolitically more fragmented world, become even more frequent. The EU proposal to establish a carbon border adjustment mechanism,[4] which, in essence, will tax imports based on their carbon content, makes direct exporting more costly. This is particularly the case, if such measures are misused for protectionist purposes and not just to neutralize adverse effects of domestic carbon prices. Provided that shipment-related emissions fall under such a carbon pricing scheme adds another source of additional trade cost. Finally, the United States is lacking a domestic carbon pricing scheme and is not intending to introduce one in the foreseeable future. Thus, it cannot expect being granted any rebate on the EU's new carbon import tariff. Moreover, the EU intends to pass a law that requires firms to perform a supply chain due diligence when importing to Europe.[5] Altogether, these developments constitute trade cost shocks that could make FDI-based exporting more attractive in the future, with important consequences for the current account.

The Heckscher-Ohlin trade theory provides a simple and reasonable explanation for trade pattern observed between the United States and the European Union. However, there are competing theories that come to different conclusions about the export versus FDI nexus. If trade patterns are driven by technological differences or increasing economies of scale, certain regions can be both hubs for export and FDI.[6] In Melitz-type heterogenous firm models, only the most productive firm enter foreign markets by direct investment. Less productive firms 'just' export, whereas the least productive firms do not engage in international trade relations at all. This follows by differences in firms' productivity and different sorts of costs assumed to exports and FDI, of which the former is a variable cost, and the latter a fixed cost. Thus, according to Helpman et al. (2004), the different trade pattern between US and European firms could result from higher productive firms in the United States. Notwithstanding the presence of tax shifting practices, firms such as Alphabet, Apple, or Meta are highly productive.

Do bilateral balances matter at all?

Having established that the current account contains the proper measures of bilateral economic ties between countries, let us now turn to Figure 22.1 again. It illustrates that the United States has run a current account surplus vis-a-vis the EU for one decade, which eventually reversed into a deficit in 2020. We argued that this is due to Brexit, but how can we be sure of this? As the United States publishes bilateral US-UK current account figures, one can easily construct figures that remove British-US transactions from the overall EU current account for periods prior to Brexit. How would the EU-US current account have looked like if the UK withdrew from the EU already in 2019? Applying this thought-experiment, one can demonstrate that the drop in the current account in 2020 is consistent with the UK's contribution to the EU-US current account. The United States ran a surplus with both the EU and the UK in 2019 worth 31 and 69 bn USD, respectively. Thus, by assuming that the UK were no part of the EU even prior to Brexit, the United States would have run deficits with the EU. Apparently, further distortions related to the Corona pandemic in 2020 and 2021 did not translate into severe changes of these net positions.[7]

With respect to its implications for the transatlantic current account, Brexit marks an interesting event: for the United States, nothing of substance has changed because of Brexit, except that transactions between the United States and the United Kingdom are no longer subsumed under the US-EU account. The bilateral US current account deficit with the EU following Brexit has no impact on the total US current account balance. Bilateral accounts might change but what matters for US welfare is the overall current account balance whose sign has a meaning: a surplus means that consumption falls behind production and, therefore, translates into an accumulation of net savings abroad. Vice versa, a deficit in the current account shifts future consumption into present periods (which, if being done excessively, can lead to balance of payments/ international debt crises). However, bilateral positions are, to some degree, artificially apportioning the overall balance into bilateral pieces. Provided this background, intuition for the transatlantic relationship based on standard textbook two-country trade models featuring only 'home' and 'abroad' are too simplistic.

Having said this, there are two important situations in which bilateral positions would indeed matter. First, in times of trade-related or geopolitical conflicts and, second, if overall surpluses/deficits are so high that they cause severe distortions elsewhere. In the former case, the sign of the bilateral balance is a rough but informative measure which party (of roughly equal economic size) has more to lose if sanctions were introduced, trade-financing were stopped, or embargoes were imposed. In the latter case, if a given country's objective is to reduce/increase the overall balance, bilateral positions might indicate where to find a point of leverage. Arguably, these two issues are not overly relevant for the economic relations between the EU and the United States, but when the Trump administration initiated what could have become a full-scale trade war in 2018, the European Union has intensified discussions about a digital services tax.

The taxation of goods trade via tariffs and duties is a traditional source of government income. even if nowadays its fiscal relevance is almost negligible in advanced economies, Border institutions such as custom offices are capable of recording and classifying all goods entering the customs jurisdiction. The collection of tariff revenues is, thus, relatively cost efficient and less prone to fraud compared with other ways of raising taxes. By contrast, services and FDI are not affected by border taxes such as tariffs. FDI activities deserve national treatment, and for services, due to their intangible nature, customs officers cannot record physical transactions. This means that the United States has had more leverage to harm the EU with classical trade policy measures, as the scope for the EU to retaliate was limited. Hence, the European threat to *legally* impose a non-discriminatory tax on large service providers (that would have been equally applied to EU domestic providers, too) was *effectively* a threat to target US firms with tariff-like measures.

Are we sure about the data we use?

Obviously, a quantitative assessment of transatlantic trade relations inevitably stands and falls with the quality of the underlying data. Braml and Felbermayr (2019) analyse the transatlantic account relying both on US data and its so-called mirror data provided by official EU sources. This reveals noticeable discrepancies: According to Eurostat, the transatlantic current account follows a different pattern that what the US data published by the Bureau of Economic Analysis (BEA) shows. Over the period 2009 to 2017, according to the BEA, the United States reported a cumulative current account surplus of USD 113 bn. For the same period, Eurostat also claimed a current account surplus but not for the United States but for the EU. And the cumulative figure, according to the EU, stands at USD 957 bn; an enormous gap of about USD 1,070 bn accumulated over nine years.

Logically, it is strictly impossible that both sources are right. A surplus of one party must necessarily be reflected by a deficit of the other party. Tertium non datur. In an ideal world with perfect data reporting, the sum of these two figures must equalize to zero. But apparently there exists a current account discrepancy worth US 1.070 bn over nine years. This discrepancy even increased such that it amounts to USD 180 bn in 2017. Braml and Felbermayr (2019) break down the EU current account into Member States contributions and find that, while French and German data nearly perfectly mirror US data, the Netherlands and the UK contributed most significantly to this data miracle. Thereby, it stands out that predominantly services accounts (UK) and primary income accounts (Netherlands) mattered for such obviously contradicting pattern. The latter case, the analysis concludes, is linked to the Dutch role as tax haven for investment income. Overall, the BEA data appeared to provide a more concise and accurate picture of the actual economic relations between the United States and the EU.

Transatlantic ups and downs in trade policy

The United States and the EU look back at a long history of trade disputes – think of Airbus vs. Boeing WTO trade dispute settlement cases or the disagreement over the EU's arbitrary import ban on US hormone-treated beef. At the same time, transatlantic trade has been at the centre of establishing a rules-based trade order after World War II by reaching the General Agreement on Tariffs and Trade (GATT) in 1948, which eventually evolved in the creation of the WTO in 1995. Beyond these multilateral efforts to liberalize world trade, the EU and the United States engaged in bilateral negotiations over a free trade agreement since 1990: while in the 1990s, this objective – then labelled as 'TAFTA' (transatlantic free trade area) – had ultimately not been realized, the idea was revitalized after the collapse of the Doha Round, a WTO-members-led initiative for multilateral tariff cuts. By that time in the late 2000s, the nature of world trade has changed some remarkable respects: as Lamy (2015) points out, this what he describes as a 'new world of trade' is characterized by the fact that businesses are pro-trade liberalization, whereas consumers oppose them. As for advanced economies, tariffs on merchandise products are historically low – except certain products mostly in the agricultural sector – trade liberalization implies the reduction of non-tariff trade barriers (NTBs). These include but are not limited to the harmonization of product safety regulations, sanitary and phytosanitary measures, product conformity assessments and, increasingly, the fulfilment of social and ecological standards. Accordingly, the political economy of trade policy is upside down compared to traditional patterns. In earlier times, consumers lobbied for free trade in their desire for lower consumer goods prices. Businesses, by contrast, were in favour of protectionism to limit competition and to sustain their market power. Today, a reduction in NTBs reduces production costs and provides better opportunities for scale economies. Thus, industry representatives became advocates of free trade agreements that facilitate production in complex and internationally integrated supply chains. On the other hand, consumers and consumer protection lobby groups, fear an erosion if not a race to the bottom with respect to of safety, social and environmental standards. Accordingly, consumers consider themselves not winners of trade liberalization but losers. This is consistent with empirically observed pattern for individual free trade attitudes (Braml and Felbermayr, 2021).

In the late 2000s, transatlantic trade talks – re-labelled as 'TTIP' (Transatlantic Trade and Investment Partnership) – tried to address not only the importance of NTB reductions but also the growing relevance of trade in services. The latter is particularly relevant for the services-oriented US economy, whose comparative cost advantages are in exactly those sectors, whereas Europe's advantage is in manufacturing products as shown above. By this, the agreement became increasingly comprehensive and complex. Because of a missing EU-US investment protection treaty (the EU and the United States are party of many such treaties with third countries but not with each other), the goal of TTIP also was to contain a chapter on investment protection. As the substitutability between FDI and direct exports indicates, this attempt was rational from a purely economic standpoint. From an institutional point of view, it implied that the agreement was no longer considered a pure trade agreement and, therefore, did no longer fall under the exclusive legislative power of the European Union. EU member states became parties of the treaty (if it had been reached) leading to additional political frictions. On services, the agreement was far-reaching, too, thereby exceeding the degree of harmonization even within the EU in certain aspects.

Growing resistance in Europe, including mass protest, have diminished political support for the TTIP. Ultimately, the election of Donald Trump for US President in 2016 made any further trade talks obsolete. Interestingly, in Eurobarometer survey data, the public support for TTIP has just increased after the United States under President Trump has withdrawn from the trade talks. The following years were characterized by trade disputes over steel and aluminium tariffs imposed by the United States in 2018, which the EU has retaliated by retorsion tariffs. Also the disputes over subsidies in the aviation sector have been brought forward by WTO dispute settlement. However, the dimension of these trade disputes has been very limited compared with those the Trump administration has initiated against China (Braml, 2020).

Transatlantic protectionism is ongoing

The Global Trade Alert project[8] collects data on policy interventions affecting international trade, thereby differentiating between trade liberalizing and protectionist ('harmful') interventions. A comparison between the European Union and the United States suffers from the fact that that EU member states' interventions cannot easily be aggregated.[9] However, to compare dynamics and pattern of government interventions, we proxy the EU by Germany, the largest member state and most important trading economy. Figure 22.2 shows the number of policy interventions by the United States vis-a-vis Germany/the EU (left panel) and vice versa (right panel). It stands out that in every year since 2009, when the data collection began, the number of harmful interventions exceeded those of liberalizing interventions on both sides. Whereas the absolute number of liberalizing interventions is roughly comparable (average per annum: 19 (United States) and 16 (Germany), respectively), the United States imposes by far more protectionist measures (202) than Germany (63) on average. Interestingly, this number was lowest (188) – despite the Covid Peak in 2020 – during the presidency of Donald Trump from 2017 to 2020. However, the sole number of interventions provides only an indication on the state of bilateral protectionism, not accounting for the severity and significance of such policy interventions.

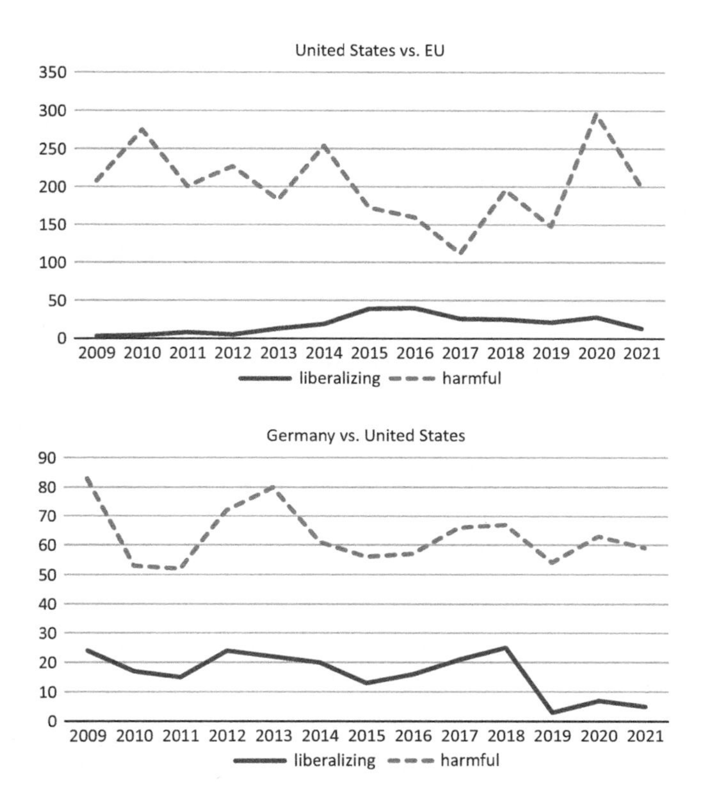

Figure 22.2 Bilateral trade policy interventions, annual, unweighted count
Source: Globale Trade Alert, 2022.

When the United States is targeted with protectionist measures, the most often affected sectors are aircraft and spacecraft, machinery and basic chemicals. Vice versa, the United States targets metals products, iron and steel and products thereof, as well as the aviation sector. Hence, either side chooses its harmful interventions on sectors in which both the parties are relatively productive. The pattern, thus, is not to protect comparative disadvantaged sectors but to strengthen the competitive position of productive industries. This might indicate that organized industry groups lobby for this sort of protectionism, and that protectionism on both side of the Atlantic is 'for sale' (Grossman and Helpman, 1994; Gubbay et al., 2020; Bombardini, 2008; Bown et al., 2021; Gawanda and Bandyopadhyah, 2000).

The transatlantic technology council

The Biden administration brought relief for transatlantic trade tensions: the EU and the United States agreed on a full removal of tariffs and counter-tariffs related to the aviation industry. Additionally, while negotiations on a free trade agreement a la

TTIP continue to be on freeze, both parties agreed on establishing the Trade and Technology Council (TTC) in 2021. The focus of the TTC is not in the core field of trade policy: as the TTC does not fulfil the requirements the GATT sets on preferential trade agreements (to liberalize 'substantially all trade'), tariff rate cuts and removals of quantitative import restrictions, so-called import quotas, are not addressed. By contrast, the TTC aims at harmonizing of product and process standards, defining such standards fore frontier technologies such as digital applications and green technologies, and enhancing competitiveness and defending the EU-US technological leadership.

Joining forces of the two largest economic blocs follows a clear geostrategic focus, directed at the limiting the powers of autocratic adversaries such as China and Russia. These recent developments indicate that transatlantic trade policy has become an instrument of foreign and security policy, whereas in the past, trade policy was shaped by economic rationals. This is a remarkable change and reminds of the Coordinating Committee on Multilateral Export Controls (CoCom) during the cold war, an institution that defined export restrictions of western cutting-edge technologies to the communist east. What is the outlook of the TTC?

In light of Russia's war of aggression against Ukraine starting in February 2022, the TTC plays no role in coordinating economic sanctions against Russia, as sanctioning countries also include Australia, Canada, Japan, Korea, Norway, Switzerland and the United Kingdom. These like-minded democratic countries may use their economic power – their combined GDP exceeds Russia's 33 times – not just to punish the Putin regime but also to deter China from similar aggressions. An export ban of modern semiconductors to China is also a top priority for the United States, whereas the European Union seeks to reach strategic sovereignty, that is, some sort of a decoupling from China. In the medium-term perspective, the TTC may be joined by some of these US-/EU-allied countries and increases its leverage in geopolitical conflicts. Trade liberalization between the US and the EU is then, once again, no longer a political objective.

G3 Trade – how interdependent are the major powers?

While both the EU and the United States endeavour to greater independence from China, also the People's Republic pursues a policy towards more self-sufficiency and import substitution. Such an economic de-coupling in a discriminatory way not only poses a risk to the global trade order – as it stands at odds with the most favoured nation principle, which is at the core of GATT/WTO trade rules; de-coupling also comes with economic costs for all three major economies; these costs can are approximately proportional to the volume of bilateral trade.

Figure 22.3 illustrates the EU's current account positions vis-à-vis the United States and China, respectively. Total EU exports to the United States double those to China and also its imports from the United States outnumber Chinese imports by 45%. While EU exports and imports consists only to 48% and 27% of merchandise products, respectively, EU-China trade is extensively dominated by goods trade indicating a less balanced and diversified portfolio of economic exchange. Overall,

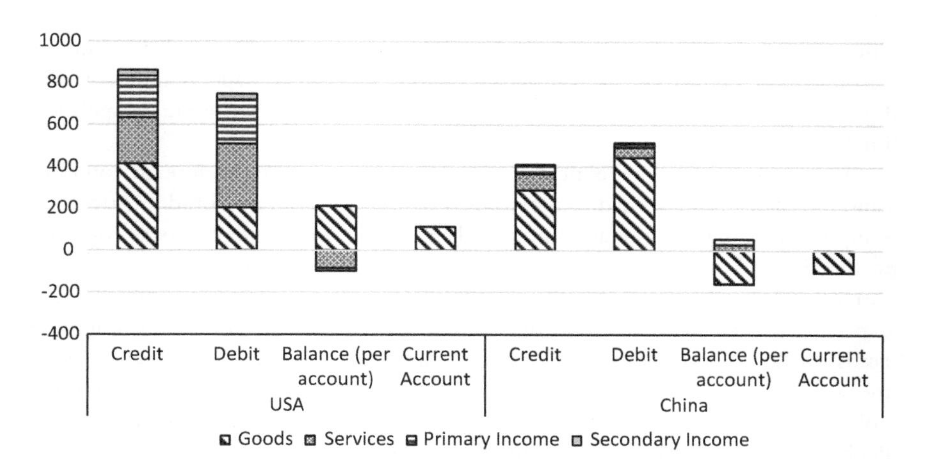

Figure 22.3 EU current account, balances and totals, bn EUR, 2021

Source: Eurostat, 2022.

the bilateral current account figures of the EU with the United States and China suggest a significantly higher degree of transatlantic economic integration than the EU has established with China.

Figure 22.4 shows the same comparison of trade partners from the perspective of the United States. The EU ranks first as destination for US exports, exceeding to those to China more than threefold. The United States also imports 53% from the EU than from China. Again, US-China trade is also dominated by merchandise products, whereas primary income and services trade plays only a negligible role. As

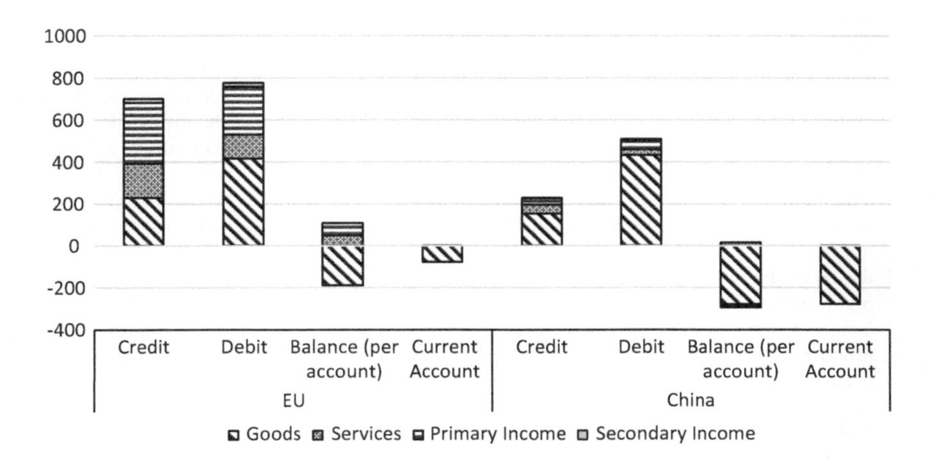

Figure 22.4 US current account, balances and totals, bn EUR, 2021

Source: BEA, 2022.

discussed previously, transatlantic trade is fairly balanced with a small US current account deficit vis-à-vis the European Union. US-China trade is different: the United States runs a deficit of 277 billion Euro. This has some geopolitical implications.

When it comes to geopolitical tensions, restraining exports to foreign countries causes welfare losses abroad (exports are not directly relevant for domestic consumption and, thus, do not account to welfare). Vice versa, imports expose countries to the risk of becoming subject to such export restraints by others. Hence, export surpluses ultimately provide an advantage when it comes to situation in which trade is expected to collapse completely, for instance, in wartimes. By contrast, as imposing tariffs on US imports from China by the Trump administration has shown – these measures are still maintained by the Biden administration – the United States can apply policy measures to a far greater number of imports than vice versa. If such tariffs are set deliberately as optimal tariffs – tariffs that are paid by foreign producers and not domestic consumers because import demand is rather price-elastic and export supply is rather price-inelastic – the United States is potentially able to extract more economic rents from such tit-for-tat tariff setting as long as China does not entirely withdraw from trade with the United States.

All in all, the implication for political alignment is that each party, when it had to choose between China and the United States/EU, must assess transatlantic trade more important than trade with China. Thus, from a trade perspective and in line with other policy areas (defence, history, culture), if world trade partially falls apart into trade blocs, the EU and the United States are unlikely to be divided.

Notes

1 In this respect, a large body of literature has evolved including replication studies for other countries such as Dauth et al. (2014) for Germany. For an article studying the effect of trade in value add instead of gross trade, see Jakubik and Stolzenburg (2021), who identify quite different regional patterns than Autor et al. (2013).

2 According to WTO figures for 2019, world trade equals 28% of global income and 7 percentage points thereof is attributable to services trade. Ignoring trade in services, thus, would underestimate trade by one fourth; however, for technologically advanced economies such as the EU but even more so for the United States, service trade shares are even larger.

3 This figure comprises US current account position vis-à-vis the EU in its current composition, which has changed in 2004, 2007 and 2013 because of Eastern Enlargements, and in 2020 because of Brexit.

4 the increasing effectiveness of the EU's internal carbon pricing scheme and, consequently, higher prices for carbon dioxide emissions, have substantially increased the risk of *carbon leakage* has evolved as well. The EU Emissions Trading Scheme (ETS) captures only production-related emissions for industrial, energy and domestic aviation industries. This means, that imports are not subject to such carbon prices, which have reached heights beyond 100 USD per tonne of CO2 in January 2022. The fear is that production of tradeable, energy-intensive goods relocates to countries with no such carbon prices. To avoid adverse import competition, the EU is now considering introducing a border tax to neutralize the ETS price effect on domestic production. For more details, see European Commission (2021).

5 Several EU Member States established so-called supply chain acts thereby obliging firms to set up surveillance measures and conduct due diligences of their supply chains, mostly to strengthen compliance with universal human rights on workplaces. For the sake of the EU's internal market integrity, the EU Commission seeks to establish such a mandate EU-wide. For more details, see European Commission (2022).
6 Empirical research has identified that exports and FDI often even constitute complements and no substitutes. Hence, FDI even facilitates exports and so do exports vice versa. This is intuitive in some case, e.g. establishing sales and distribution affiliates can be seen as prerequisite for the market-entry. Markusen (1998) reviews theoretical literature that can encompass both FDI and exports as substitutes and as complements.
7 This implies that, despite a reduction in gross trade volume, both US and EU exports have fallen more or less symmetrically.
8 See https://www.globaltradealert.org/, accessed on September 14th, 2022.
9 If all 27 member states, e.g., adjust national law according to EU Directives, the data would count 27 interventions, although only one EU-wide intervention is implemented.

References

Autor, D. H., Dorn, D., & Hanson, G. H. (2013). The China syndrome: Local labor market effects of import competition in the United States. *American Economic Review*, 103(6):2121–2168.

Baldwin, R. E. (2006). *Globalisation: the great unbundling (s) (No. BOOK)*. Economic council of Finland.

Bombardini, M. (2008). Firm Heterogeneity and Lobby Participation. *Journal of International Economics*, 75:329–348.

Bown, C. P., Conconi, P., Erbahar, A., & Trimarchi, L. (2021). *Trade Protection Along Supply Chains*. Mimeo.

Braml, M. T. (2020). Beggar-thy-Neighbor or Favor thy Industry? An Empirical Review of Transatlantic Tariff Retaliation. IFO Working Paper No. 326.

Braml, M. T. & Felbermayr, G. J. (2018). Trump economics lesson: he misunderstands the current account. *The International Economy, Summer 2018*. http://www.international-economy.com/TIE_Su18_BramlFelbermayr.pdf

Braml, M. T. & Felbermayr, G. J. (2019). What do we really know about the transatlantic current account?. *CESifo Economic Studies*, 65(3):255–274.

Braml, M.T. & Felbermayr, G.J. (2021). The EU self-surplus puzzle: an indication of VAT fraud?. *International Tax and Public Finance.* 10.1007/s10797-021-09713-x

Dauth, W., Findeisen, S., & Suedekum, J. (2014). The rise of the East and the Far East: German labor markets and trade integration. *Journal of the European Economic Association*, 12(6):1643–1675.

European Commission (2021). Proposal for a Regulation of the European Parliament and of the Council establishing a carbon border adjustment mechanism. https://eur-lex.europa.eu/legal-content/EN/TXT/?uri=celex:52021PC0564

European Commission (2022). Proposal for a Directive of the European Parliament and of the Council on corporate sustainability due diligence and amending directive. https://eur-lex.europa.eu/legal-content/EN/TXT/?uri=CELEX%3A52022PC0071

Gawande, K. & Bandyopadhyay, U. (2000). Is Protection for Sale? Evidence on the Grossman-Helpman Theory of Endogenous Protection. *Review of Economics and statistics*, 82(1):139–152.

Grossman, G. M. & Helpman, E. (1994). Protection for Sale. *American Economic Review*, 84(4):833–850.

Gubbay, M. B., Conconi, P., & Parenti, M. (2020). *Globalization for Sale (No. 2020-08)*. ULB--Universite Libre de Bruxelles.

Helpman, E., Melitz, M., & Yeaple, S. (2004). Exports versus FDI with Heterogeneous Firms, *American Economic Review*, 94(1):300–316.

Jakubik, A. & Stolzenburg, V. (2021). The "China Shock" revisited: insights from value added trade flows. *Journal of Economic Geography*, 21(1):67–95.

Lamy, P. (2015). The New World of Trade. *Introduction to the The Third Jan Tumlir Lecture.* https://ecipe.org/publications/new-world-trade/

Markusen, J. (1998). Multinational firms, location, and trade. *The World Economy*, 21(6):733756.

23

ASYMMETRY AND CIVIL SOCIETY BACKLASH

Changing European Calculations in Trans-Atlantic Investment Relations from CETA to TTIP and Beyond

Robert G. Finbow

DALHOUSIE UNIVERSITY

Overview

This chapter examines the recent history of EU's transatlantic investment relationships with Canada and the United States. It will compare the provisions in the Canada-European Union Comprehensive Economic and Trade Agreement (CETA) with the European Union's proposals for a Transatlantic Trade and Investment Partnership (TTIP) with the US. It is based on background interviews, official policy statements, ratified agreements, draft texts and academic analyses. It will consider stakeholder and official views of the benefits, costs and controversies of an investment chapter. It will assess how CETA, particularly its proposed investor-court system (ICS), was influenced by civil society backlash against investor state disputes settlement (ISDS) in TTIP. While CETA initially inspired less concern in Europe, the asymmetrical character of the relationship with the US lead to civil society fears that American firms could use ISDS to challenge EU social and environmental regulations. Despite originally proposing a conventional ISDS arbitral system in TTIP, the EU changed course in response to this political backlash.

This differential civil society concern and politicization of investment relations in TTIP (and eventually by extension in CETA) reflects differential EU economic relationships with Canada and the US. While in a strong position in asymmetrical trade and investment flows with Canada, the EU is in a somewhat weaker asymmetrical relationship with the US. Because of this relative weakness, TTIP generated heightened civil society concern and lobbying activities and prompted member states reconsideration of the risks of investor state provisions, particularly the potential for

DOI: 10.4324/9781003283911-28

US corporate plaintiffs to bring disputes arbitrations affecting EU or member states' laws and regulations. This put the EU's somewhat 'stealthy' (Meunier, 2017) takeover of competence in international investment to the test, as some member states rejected this approach. In response to adverse politicization, the EU proposed an investor-court system (ICS) in TTIP and CETA, to replace private arbitration panels to address civil society criticism and member state vulnerabilities in deals with stronger, developed state partners.

The implications for the future of investor state provisions in these two trans Atlantic economic and trade relationships will be assessed. Several core themes will be addressed: (1) asymmetry and its implications for the EU, as the slightly weaker partner in trade relations with the US in TTIP vs substantially stronger partner with Canada in CETA; (2) emergence of civil society concerns in Europe about investor-state disputes settlement (ISDS) measures in economic agreements with the US and Canada; and 3) EU's proposed adjustments to ISDS, adoption of ICS in CETA and the difficult road to accommodation with the US. The chapter will conclude with the impact of populism and withdrawal from TTIP on the future of investment relations between the EU and US as discussed in other chapters in the collection.

Politicization of investor-state dispute settlement proposals

Investor-state dispute settlement (ISDS) has become an entrenched aspect of many bilateral investment treaties (BITs) and multilateral economic agreements. ISDS mechanisms create processes whereby states can be challenged directly by actual or potential investors over loss of real or anticipated profits. Under such arrangements, the state agrees to arbitrate breaches of investment obligations under international arbitration rules using international arbitration systems. Most important is the system used from the World Bank's International Centre for Settlement of Investment Disputes (ICSID) (Elkins et al., 2006). If a case is brought by an aggrieved investor, an ad hoc tribunal of three arbitrators determines if state has breached its investment obligations; the arbitrators are chosen by investor and state, and they choose a third party. This tribunal can award damages, costs and interest totaling millions of dollars. Generally, the process is closed with little transparency over procedures and no setting of precedent, allowing for variable outcomes from similar complaints and behaviours. In most cases, there is no routine appellate system: in some cases, the arbitral awards can only be reviewed on very limited procedural grounds (Dullien, 2015). In most of these arrangements, the members of the ad hoc tribunals are drawn from a closed set of legal professionals who get to determine if a state has breached investment obligations; they can decide on damages and impose costs and penalties with limited possibility for review and limited transparency and without releasing any justification for decisions. The pacts can be used to impose settlements, which domestic courts may enforce, but in the absence of compliance by a respondent state, international law may be used under the New York Convention on arbitration settlements to enforce judgements. Evolving jurisprudence in the U.S. and other jurisdictions may permit claimants aggrieved at national or provincial policies to sue in foreign courts and have assets of those entities seized as compensation if they do not enforce arbitrations and decline to pay penalties (Van Harten and Loughlin 2006). Supporters of such provisions suggest they protect investors and clarify investment rules and ensure that investors can obtain redress for laws or regulations which erode profit potential. After the Lisbon treaty transferred competence, most aspects of investment treaties are now dealt with by the European Commission (Bungenberg, 2010). This created debates between states like Germany and France and Commission actors over whether to include such measures in agreements with Canada and the US. And it revived member states questions about EU competence in international representation (Gatti and Manzini, 2012), leading to court challenges and forcing to Commission to acknowledge mixed competencies on investment agreements.

Critics complain that ISDS provisions impose restrictions on state decision-making which runs against the democratic accountability of government. The closed non-transparent system, with arbitrations by for-profit firms, leads to frivolous lawsuits to secure payouts for investors and their specialized legal teams. European states have begun to face such challenges, with Sweden fighting claims respecting worker rights and Germany challenged for its post-Fukushima move away from nuclear power. Environmental regulations are often a concern, with governments facing challenges to their limits on harmful practices. For Europe, being on the receiving end of such actions could happen more frequently with TTIP would be novel. EU member states led by Germany were the principal architects of and users of ISDS over the years in a plethora of bilateral investment deals mostly with developing and emerging economies in which those states benefitted from asymmetry. The negotiation of deals where the EU might be the weaker partner, especially TTIP, generated politicization around ISDS in civil society which eventually induced changes to the EU model on ISDS. After extensive civil society consultations (including sessions attended by the author and several interviewees) the EU proposed reforming ISDS. Its revisions provided clearer standards and transparency for arbitral proceedings, appointment of public arbitrators and protection of governments 'right to regulate' including a limited definition of indirect expropriation and a bilateral (and potentially international) investment court (European Commission DG Trade, 2015a).

Asymmetry in transatlantic economic relationships

Since new economic powers in the South challenged the post-war global trading order, the World Trade Organization (WTO) talks have stalled. This is largely because of core states' unwillingness to accept more balanced trade and investment arrangements. This led to a shift towards more bilateral trade and investment instruments on the part of the US and EU, which presents problems for all but the most robust emerging economies. 'Unequal conditions are even greater in bilateral or inter-regional trade processes than in multilateral processes' (Tussie and Saguier, 2011). The EU network of preferential trade agreements, bilateral and multilateral, is the largest in the world. Up until the Lisbon Treaty, investment remained member state competence, so this web of agreements involved bilateral investment treaties between EU members and other states. Core EU states like Germany, UK and the Netherlands have employed BITs usually in relationships with important trade and investment partners where they have been clearly the core to another state's periphery in the asymmetrical relationship. Half of the first 40 BITs signed between 1959 and 1965 were by Germany, with the other half a mixture of other Western European trading states – the Netherlands and Switzerland, with eventual action by Italy and Sweden. Moreover, at the outset, the differential in gross domestic product (GDP) between the Europeans and their developing world partners was high, easing slightly by 1980 and narrowing somewhat more by 2000 (Elkins, Guzman, and Simmons, 2006, 817–818). The EU could usually dictate economic terms and partners were forced to be takers with fewer long term economic benefits.

Usually, asymmetrical regionalism in economic and trade relations has been assumed to be North-South, and the EU has been at the forefront – both via individual states pre-Lisbon and the EU institutions post Lisbon – in pursuing a wide range of advantageous bilateral trade and investment arrangements with less developed and newly industrialized emerging states. But as scholars remind, asymmetry in economic and trade relations is 'fluid'; 'asymmetry must not be viewed as static. Form and content suffer tortuous twists and remain in constant flux' (Tussie and Saguier, 2011). Emerging economic powers in the BRICS are changing the balance, especially with the rise of Asian states 'exacerbated by the relative decline in the established trans-Atlantic nexus whether narrow, bilateral Anglo-American or broader multilateral EU-NAFTA' (Shaw, 2011). But while new players like China change the terms of regional economic systems around the world, some longstanding partnerships among developed states are clearly asymmetrical in nature, such as those within NAFTA and CUSMA between the US, Mexico and Canada.

Since Lisbon transferred investment competence, the EU has been engaged primarily in agreements in which it, as the largest such agreement currently in place, is in a powerful position relative to the trade partners involved. This confidence remained evident as CETA and TTIP negotiations commenced: 'With its global economic weight, the EU is in a strong position to convince its trading partners of the need for clearer and better standards' including definitions of indirect expropriations and fair and equitable treatment, clarification of the right to regulate, improved transparency and a code of conduct in arbitral proceedings and so forth (European Commission, 2013). However, the EU in relation to North America finds itself in complex and differentiated relationships This reflects an interesting – though expected – reaction to the alteration of the EU's position in relation to the two agreements, an instance of asymmetrical regionalism. This complicated decision-making within the EU as member states confronted the costs of delegating investment competence to Brussels and balked at this as CETA and TIIP talks prompted civil society backlash.

Since the 1960s, Canada sought more trans-Atlantic trade to offset its heavy dependence on economic ties with the US. Prime Minister Pierre Trudeau proposed a so-called Third Option or contractual link with the European Community in the 1976 Framework Agreement for Commercial and Economic Cooperation to balance US dominance. For the most part, the Third option was stillborn. Overall, rather than increase, Canadian trade with the European Common Market declined relative to US trade. The Transatlantic Declaration of 1990, the Canada-European Union (EU) Political Declaration and Action Plan of 1996 and the Canada-EU Partnership Agenda of 2004 led to collaboration on crisis management, customs, education, training, energy, fisheries, health, science and technology, competition, social security and the environment (Finbow 2010). The 2005 talks on a Canada-EU Trade and Investment Enhancement Agreement (TIEA) faltered. Spurred by global recession, in May 2009, Canada and the EU launched negotiations towards a CETA, provisionally in force since September, 2017. This included elimination of tariff and non-tariff barriers, access to procurement at all levels of government, access to raw materials, regulatory convergence, dispute settlement measures, skilled labour mobility and mutual recognition of professional qualifications. The agreement covered trade in services (finance, environment, engineering, architecture etc.), extended protection for intellectual property (covering patents, copyright, trademark, industrial design) and opened telecommunications and electronic commerce (Finbow, 2022).

While CETA is portrayed as a deal between two advanced, equitable partners, the EU negotiated from a position of relative strength since the EU is Canada's second-largest trade partner while Canada is only the EU's 11th-largest partner. When CETA was proposed, Canada had sizeable trade deficits with the EU, as much as $20 billion in goods and services. Canada's largest exports were raw or semi-processed goods, led by diamonds valued at over $3.2 billion, and wood pulp exports around $1.3 billion. EU exports to Canada featured high-value-added products like chemicals and machinery, giving Europe an advantage in terms of trade as these promote more advanced production (Byrd, 2006). Canada was hard pressed to secure beneficial arrangements or concessions, and critics suggest it conceded to EU positions on some key issues. Trade with Canada was negatively impacted by the pandemic. By the end of 2021, the monthly totals had improved to €23.4 billion for imports from Canada versus €37.3 billion in exports, for a EU surplus of €13.8 billion (Eurostat, 2022b). Investment flows were substantial but limited compared to the US-EU total. By 2022, Canadian direct investment in the EU reached $229.1 billion, while EU direct investments in Canada totalled about $262.5 billion, almost a quarter of FDI in Canada (Canada, Global Affairs, 2022).

The Transatlantic Declaration on EC-US Relations of 1990 (EU-US 1990) pledged 'further steps towards liberalization, transparency, and the implementation of GATT and OECD principles concerning both trade in goods and services and investment'. The New Transatlantic Agenda (NTA) of 1995 (EU-US 1995) furthered this collaboration. Both parties were primary movers of the creation of the WTO and the Multilateral Agreement on Investment (MAI), until the stalemate created pressure for bilateral responses. Simmering disputes on investment vexed the relationship and limited effective collaboration on issues like the MAI (Hufbauer, 2002). By the mid-2000s, negotiators sought to pursue greater economic collaboration especially removal of obstacles for investment. Concerns were expressed about trade barriers often invoked on vaguely defined national security grounds. EU negotiators sought a comprehensive economic agreement encompassing investment disputes measures as it was perfecting in agreements with Canada, South Korea and elsewhere. (European Commission, 2014).

The EU began TTIP talks with a similar ambitious agenda, including incorporation of conventional ISDS arbitration. While ISDS could put EU standards and regulations under review, European negotiators wanted TTIP to set an example of comprehensiveness on investment matters against new challengers such as China. This disregarded the relative position of the EU whose prior BITs were with less economically powerful partners. 'While in former agreements with mostly developing states, the European partners were in a more powerful negotiating position and could, to a great extent, determine the terms of the agreement, this would be unthinkable with an agreement with the US' (Koeth, 2016, 5). The EU relationship with the US is one of the largest bilateral trading relationships on earth. The EU is more dependent on the relationship, with positive balances in exports of goods and services and a substantial greater exposure in outward investment flows (EU Business, 2011; European Commission, 2013). While current account balances overall are complex (Braml and Felbermayer, this volume), the EU carries a sizeable goods trade surplus with its larger North American partner. While disrupted by the COVID-19 pandemic, trade volumes recovered substantially by end of 2021. The EU imported €232 billion worth of goods from the US, while exporting €339.4 billion for a surplus of over €167 billion (Eurostat, 2022a).

Despite this sizeable exchange of goods, per the Commission, 'EU and US investments are the real driver of the transatlantic relationship, contributing to growth and jobs on both sides of the Atlantic' (European Commission, 2022). As TTIP negotiations commenced around 2012, US FDI in Europe was valued at $2,236,265,000,000 while incoming investments from Europe totalled $1,642,107,000,000. This accounted for 20% of FDI driven projects in Germany. By 2018 before the pandemic, the investment totals bilaterally had increased with the EU having €2.2 trillion in outward invested in the US (European Commission, 2022). Hence the stakes for the EU as potential respondents in ISDS cases are much greater than in prior EU agreements. Additionally, per Braml and Felbermayer (this volume), the US preference for FDI means many US branch plants and subsidiaries operated in Europe, creating potential for claims based on EU politics and regulations. The US has included robust ISDS measures in all its economic external agreements, and a well-tested US model is generally a requirement for any such deal. While the US may have less legal concerns in most of the EU, new markets in Central and Eastern Europe are cited to justify an investment arbitration system, as legal protections are less tested in those EU member states.

Civil society resistance and proposed changes to ISDS

The initial EU proposals in TTIP incorporated the standard ISDS arbitration model, based on existing EU BITs with the expectation that Lisbon gave the Commission unilateral right to negotiate such provisions. ISDS has been plagued by claims for vaguely defined indirect expropriation including requiring compensation for lost potential profits based on domestic public interest regulations which results in 'regulatory chill' (Malakotipour, 2020). Also cases are decided by ad hoc panels in secret, in costly processes available to foreign firms, not local ones. Fabry and Garbasso (2015) note that large ISDS claims made some states question their impact on sovereignty and consider withdrawal or avoidance of proposed new pacts to avoid negative political fallout. From the outset of CETA talks, based on experiences with ISDS challenges under NAFTA's Chapter 11, Canadian civil society groups challenged this conventional ISDS system. Allied EU civil society groups networked but with lower urgency at the outset.

However, they feared a TTIP with the larger American economy meant greater potential impact of ISDS on EU members and reduced regulatory space. As the earlier-given data illustrates, the differential importance of the investment relationship between the EU with Canada and with the US is significant. Having pioneered the technique in dealings with developing states, European countries became concerned about potential American firms' use of the investor-state disputes process and attendant penalties. The Lisbon provisions were tested with resistance to a common EU position by members states. Countries like Germany, where a dominant position in BITs was taken for granted, faced novel challenges and heightened civil society resistance. EU civil society and member states feared being on the receiving end of US corporate claims. As TTIP talks advanced, civil society pressure led to heightened politicization and member state recalcitrance, prompting a transformation in approach by the Commission in both CETA and TTIP.

Much of the concern was expressed by civil society and labour organizations who this author engaged with in interviews and consultation processes.[1] The UK's Trade Union Congress feared that ISDS in CETA and TTIP. would it put public services at risk: 'health and education are particularly under threat from ISDS due to the extent of American investment in these areas' (TUC 2014). EU negotiating policy met with increased resistance, with progressive critics and populist nationalists challenging the liberalized model. Notably, "European consumers rebelled at what they perceived as Big American Business undermining their social protections, including through investor-state dispute settlement (ISDS)" (Chase, 2021). By contrast, business representatives consulted by the author were enthusiastic about TTIP. While both partners had well-developed systems of investment protection; an improved ISDS needed to be included to handle outliers and as an example to the rest of the world (Business Europe, 2015).

European NSMs gained support and political leverage, sometimes using Canadian critiques used as a model. While business access remained stronger, the civil society dialogue in the EU did provide some influence. Under pressure from civil society and member states, the EU created a consultation process on TTIP and CETA. The Commission received 250,000 plus submissions, many of them critical. Then trade commissioner Cecilia Malmström insisted the consultations were not a referendum on how to proceed but eventually proposed revisions to ISDS in CETA and TTIP. While biased towards inclusion of ISDS with minor tweaks, the EU had to revise its approach to address increased politicization of the trade negotiation process (Young, 2017). Even supportive groups recognized that 'the planned ISDS provisions are problematic and … their benefits are far from clear. Because of this, ISDS will be a highly contentious issue not only in the negotiations, but also in the ratification process' (Dullien, 2015). The Commission risked damage to its reputation if a contentious case forced a member state to make a costly settlement with a US-based firm.

The EU's 2015 'Trade for All' strategy (European Commission, DG Trade 2015) was a partial response to politicization and opposition to liberalizing elements of CETA, TTIP and other deals, especially investment disputes settlement. Responding to criticisms of weak commitment to the social dimension, the EU promised open transparent negotiations; worker and small business protections; and the promotion of sustainable development, human rights and good governance (European Commission, 2015). The EU proposed an investment court system (ICS), with bilateral courts with permanent highly qualified investment judges to replace the panel of appointed ad hoc arbitrators used in international forums. A First Instance Tribunal and an Appeal Tribunal would allow for reconsideration of the court's decisions. The court would operate based on similar principles to the WTO Appellate Body. Proceedings would be transparent, hearings open and comments available online with a right to intervene for parties with an interest in the dispute. Also "forum–shopping" by companies to seek the most lenient, favourable jurisdiction for arbitration would be banned and frivolous claims used to seek lucrative settlements from hard pressed governments would be dismissed. "The ability of investors to take a case before the Tribunal would be precisely defined and limited to cases such as targeted discrimination on the base of gender, race or religion, or nationality, expropriation without compensation, or denial of justice" (European Commission, 2015a). Governments' right to regulate would be guaranteed in the provisions of the trade and investment agreements.

The Canadian government of Justin Trudeau agreed to include the ICS in CETA. The Commission announced that the deal "is a clear break from the current ISDS system and shows the commitment to work together to establish a multilateral investment tribunal" (European Commission, 2016). This provided a "high level of protection for investors while fully preserving the right of governments to regulate and pursue legitimate public policy objectives such as the protection of health, safety, or the environment" (European Commission 2016a). Both parties adopted a Joint Interpretive Instrument (JII), which affirmed the break with past practices on ISDS to address concerns about transparency, impartiality, favouritism to foreign investors through creation of a judicial level body to arbitrate investment disputes. The two parties highlighted the success of the renegotiation as an example of the open, transparent negotiation process: "We have responded to Canadians, EU citizens, and businesses with a fairer, more transparent, system" (Canada-EU Joint Statement, 2016).

The Commission claimed CETA demonstrated its new commitment to social responsibility in trade matters: "the Commission has taken social considerations into account in all policies, including its foreign trade policy – the Comprehensive Economic and Trade Agreement with Canada is an example thereof" (European Commission, 2017). But some civil society actors remained skeptical of these changes which they believed constituted minimal adjustments. The alteration in the balance between the new supranational ICS and domestic jurisprudence on investment created significant complications for the ratification of CETA in the EU. Some five years after provisional implementation, many EU member states had yet to ratify CETA based largely on its investment provisions (Finbow, 2022).

US resistance to the EU approach

Even before the Obama administration was replaced by the populist Trump administration, differences over investment disputes regimes threatened to prevent agreement on TTIP. Since the Reagan administration, the US developed bilateral investment treaties, sparked in part by European success in such arrangements with developing states (Ruttenberg, 1987, 122). The United States negotiated far fewer BITs than Europe but built investment provisions into its multilateral regional trade and economic frameworks. The purpose of this effort was distinctly liberalizing and designed to protect American investors who remain dominant players in foreign direct investment and frequent users of the arbitral system. According to the USTR, BITs aimed to protect investment abroad in countries where investor rights are not already protected through existing agreements (such as modern treaties of friendship, commerce, and navigation, or free trade agreements); to encourage the adoption of market-oriented domestic policies that treat private investment in an open, transparent, and non-discriminatory way; and to support the development of international law standards consistent with these objectives (USTR, 2022).

The Model of NAFTA Chapter 11 briefly became the US norm and influenced subsequent bilateral investment treaties. These included core guarantees for investors prohibiting 'discrimination, actions tantamount to expropriation, money transfer bans, performance requirements and violations of the minimum standard of treatment'. Moreover, to 'ensure compliance with these substantive obligations, they entitle investors of signatory nations to binding arbitration actions against a host government (investor–state provisions)' (Gagne and Morin, 2006, 358). But fears grew that claims could erode sovereignty and frivolous claims against governments could potentially created a brake on regulation and legislation in areas which might affect investor rights and profits.

The 2004 BIT was adopted after a year long consultative process and aimed to redress several significant concerns which developed in reaction to NAFTA Chapter 11 and similar BIT models. The revisions for BITs going forward 'clarified and narrowed the definition of covered investments; added language to explain and constrain the meaning of the "minimum standard of treatment' and expropriation obligations and closely guide arbitral tribunals' 'interpretations of those provisions'". The new model added "language expressly giving investor-state tribunals authority to accept submissions from amicus curiae and language providing for public disclosure of information regarding the disputes". To address concerns respecting regulatory chill, it added "articles on labor rights and environmental protection and text in the preamble clarifying that investment protection aims to improve living standards". Finally, "arbitration should be consistent with the protection of health, safety, and the environment, and the promotion of internationally recognized labor rights" (Johnson, 2012).

The current Model BIT, developed with only modest adjustments after a consultative process in 2012, did include adjustments on a few key points, including measures that impose additional burdens and restrictions on host states in order to facilitate and protect foreign investment; provisions that add slight protections for government authority in the area of financial services regulation; and new language on environmental and labor issues that may better address and help avoid some of the possible negative effects that can be associated with foreign investment (Johnson, 2012).

The model BITs are designed to serve the outward investment requirements of US firms, an outward projection of US corporate interests in imposing limits on host state actions considered harmful and limiting the need to proceed via host state judicial procedures. The US model remained a "traditional" approach to investment arbitration, which has been criticized for its "a lack of legitimacy, transparency, fairness and coherence" (Butler, 2016, 3). Having consulted extensively on these BITs, the US now uses them as the model for trade and investment treaties and expected this private arbitral ISDS system in TTIP. This generated an impasse as even EU proposals on transparency and arbitrator conduct and core definitions of expropriations were rejected by President Obama's USTR team, let alone the transformative shift to the ICS model used in CETA.

Initially, the TTIP negotiations seemed like an opening to permit improvement of ISDS provisions to balance investor protection from arbitrary host county impositions with a guarantee of states' right to regulate for legitimate purposes (Quick, 2015). Weaver (2014) suggested that the initial US and EU draft proposals contained the seeds for reconciliation, with transparency, third-party participation and appellate mechanisms. Critics suggested the existing legal protections in each of these parties made any ISDS mechanism redundant and an intrusion on democratic governance, though the US felt the need for BIT protections in Eastern and Central Europe as post-communist states there adjusted to liberalized investment and capital flows (Propp, 1992). But uncertainty in major EU member states, based on fears of the impact of ISDS in the asymmetrical investment relationship with the US, prompted the consultative process and adoption of a far-reaching proposal for an international investment court which pushed the parties further apart.

Some academic observers suggest that the boldness of the EU investment court plan has been overstated, that on examination it is a narrow gap between ICS and the US model BIT (Butler, 2016). But US responses to the EU proposal for an investment court made such reconciliation elusive. And public backlash pushed the EU to solidify its position on the ICS which it projected as a template for a future Multinational Investment Court. This did not meet the US vision for the future investment regime. The final report on TTIP rounds in late 2016 and early 2017 included no mention of progress on an investment chapter (USTR and European Commission, 2017). The ICS system adopted provisionally in CETA was at odds with US proposals and practices in its model bilateral investment treaties, including the Trans-Pacific Partnership (TPP). Thus, no agreement was possible even before Trump's populist rejection of multilateral trade deals; the US instead halted TTIP and TPP and rejected ISDS with developed states as in the revised US Mexico Canada agreement where ISDS was eliminated respecting Canada.

Conclusion: Divergent paths on investment relations

While waiting for ratification, CETA partners have moved forward on plans for implementation of the ICS. They have developed rules on the appellate process, a code of conduct for judges and rules for mediation and binding interpretations (Finbow, 2022, 314). But as designated mixed competence, the ICS depends on ratification by member states which may not be forthcoming (17 of 27 members had ratified by Spring 2022). So this model remains for the moment on paper only, though the partners still expect to employ it at some point (Finbow, 2022). It may be the last of its kind though as the EU moves to separate investment and trade agreements in future deals to avoid the problem of mixed competence and member state recalcitrance (European Council, 2018). Despite the appearance of success, it remains in limbo pending ratification and may be problematic if implemented as the procedures for enforcing judgements against EU states remains unclear (Butz, 2020).

Relations with the US moved in the opposite direction after abandonment of TTIP in 2017. Trump's populist messaging included rejection of multilateral institutions such as trade agreements in pursuit of 'America First' (Blendon et al., 2017). This created a significant challenge for EU-US economic relations (McNamara, 2017). His administration adopted a more 'aggressive approach', eschewing multilateral, global or regional negotiations and instead used 'all possible leverage' in bilateral talks to pressure individual countries to make concessions to American concerns (USTR, 2017). Above all, TTIP was abandoned and arbitrary, politicized tariffs and quotas marked that regime's attitude towards Europe. Most notably, the renegotiation of NAFTA lead to omission of Chapter 11 ISDS provisions for US-Canada trade, marking a reversal of the US BIT approach (though some elements were kept in the more asymmetrical relationship with Mexico). This reflected a populist nationalist backlash against measures perceived to intrude on US interests, notwithstanding American success in most Chapter 11 claims under NAFTA. This precedent will likely apply to any American trade and investment agreement with developed states, including future US-EU discussions on investment. As discussed in more depth in other chapters, the relationship with the EU has revived to a degree under President Biden, though some issues like steel tariffs remain challenging and reconfiguring relations with the UK post Brexit is also problematic. (See Holmes and Morito-Jaeger this volume.) There is reluctance on both sides to retreat to a form of TTIP light. But there appears to be a consensus that, as the EU has done in recent negotiations, contentious issues like ISDS should be set aside to focus on politically achievable results. For proponents, this is not because ISDS provisions are inherently negative. But given civil society resistance, politically exclusion of ISDS makes achievement of a cooperation agreement more likely.

While a return to a full TTIP cannot be envisioned, revived collaboration under the Biden administration included a new EU-US Trade and Technology Council which held initial meetings in 2021. As Braml and Felbermayer suggest (this volume), geopolitical concerns such as the looming rivalry with China will influence these new directions more than past liberalization foci. One of the main elements of this will be a focus on investment screening to collaborate on security grounds against potential undesirable foreign takeovers involving sensitive technologies (see Egan chapter, this volume). This remains a work in progress and with the 2022 midterm elections producing a populist, nationalist revival in Congress, gridlock and inaction or even retreat might be possible on transatlantic issues. At the very least, ISDS is unlikely to be revisited between the US and EU, though the parties have committed to promoting 'shared principles, such as non-discrimination between foreign investors and transparency of rules' and 'exploring ways of intensifying engagement with stakeholders' on investment matters (EU-US, 2021). Even American pro-market advocates have retreated from support for ISDS, given the political risks and the lack of need in these jurisdictions with relatively strong domestic protections for foreign investors. The benefits – increased investment flows, precedent for future deals and springboard for transnational investment regime – are insufficient to justify the risks with developed partners.

Note

1 In researching projects on CETA and TTIP in 2015-16, the author conducted numerous confidential interviews with civil society actors, business associations and officials on both sides of the Atlantic.

References

Blendon, R.J., Casey, L. S., & Benson, J. M. (2017). Public Opinion and Trump's Jobs and Trade Policies. *Challenge (White Plains)*, *60*(3), 228–244. 10.1080/05775132.2017.1308763

Butler, N. (2016). The EU Investment Court Proposal in TTIP: ISDS 2.0. *Policy Briefing* University of Manchester. Available from http://documents.manchester.ac.uk/display.aspx?DocID=28671 [Accessed August 10, 2022].

Business Europe. TTIP Should Include Fair Investor-state Dispute Settlement. Press release 9 September, Available from https://www.businesseurope.eu/news/ttip-should-include-fair-investor-state-dispute-settlement [Accessed July 12, 2022].

Bungenberg, M. (2010). 'Going Global? The EU Common Commercial Policy After Lisbon'. in C. Hermann and J. P. Terhechte (eds.), *European Yearbook of International Economic Law*, pp. 123-151.

Butz, L., (2020). Beyond the Pledge-The Imperfect Legal Framework for Enforcing Awards of the CETA Investment Court against the European Union. *McGill Journal of Dispute Resolution*, 7, 88.

Byrd, C. (2006). Canada's Merchandise Trade with the European Union: 1995 to 2004. International Trade Division, Statistics Canada. Available from https://www150.statcan.gc.ca/n1/pub/65-507-m/65-507-m2006006-eng.htm [Accessed July 12, 2022].

Canada, Global Affairs (2022). Canada and the European Union: Trade and investment. Available from https://www.international.gc.ca/world-monde/international_relations-relations_internationales/eu-ue/index.aspx?lang=eng#a3 [Accessed August 17, 2022].

Canada EU, (2016). Joint statement by European Commissioner for Trade and Canada's Minister of International Trade on Canada-EU trade agreement.

Chase, P. (2021). Enhancing the Transatlantic Trade and Investment Relationship. Transatlanic Series, Wilson Centre. Available from https://www.wilsoncenter.org/article/enhancing-transatlantic-trade-and-investment-relationship [Accessed May 12, 2022].

Dullien, S. (2015). Why we Favour Ditching Investment Protection in TTIP. European Council on Foreign Relations Commentary February, 11. Available from http://www.ecfr.eu/article/commentary_why_we_favour_ditching_investment_protection_in_ttip422 [Accessed July 15 2022].

Elkins, Z., Guzman, A. T., and Simmons, B. (2006). Competing for Capital: The Diffusion of Bilateral Investment Treaties, 1960-2000. *International Organization, 60*(4), 811–846.
EU Business, (2011). "The EU's Trade Relationship with the United States" Available at www.eubusiness.com/topics/trade/usa
European Commission, DG Trade, (2014). Factsheet: Transatlantic Trade and Investment Partnership (TTIP). Accessed May 8, 2023. https://trade.ec.europa.eu/doclib/docs/2015/may/tradoc_153471.pdf
European Commission (2013). Investment Protection and Investor-to-State Dispute Settlement in EU agreements. At http://www.sice.oas.org/tpd/USA_EU/Studies/tradoc_151916__Investment_e.pdf [Accessed May 16 2022].
European Commission, DG Trade (2021). EU-US Trade and Technology Council Inaugural Meeting 29 September 2021 Pittsburgh, United States. Available from https://trade.ec.europa.eu/doclib/html/159846.htm [Accessed 17 May, 2022].
Eurostat (2022a). USA-EU - international trade in goods statistics. *Eurostat Explained*. Available from https://ec.europa.eu/eurostat/statistics-explained/index.php?title=USA-EU_-_international_trade_in_goods_statistics#Recent_developments [Accessed 9 May, 2022].
European Commission DG Trade (2022) EU trade relations with the United States. Facts, Figures and latest developments. Available at https://policy.trade.ec.europa.eu/eu-trade-relationships-country-and-region/countries-and-regions/united-states_en [Accessed 12 July 2022].
European Council (2018). EU-Singapore: Council Adopts Decisions to Sign Trade and Investment Agreements. Available from https://www.consilium.europa.eu/en/press/press-releases/2018/10/15/eu-singapore-council-adopts-decisions-to-sign-trade-and-investment-agreements/ [Accessed 12 July, 2022].
EU-US (1990). Transatlantic Declaration 1990. Available from https://www.europarl.europa.eu/cmsdata/124320/trans_declaration_90_en.pdf [Accessed 10 May, 2022].
EU-US (1995). New Transatlantic Agenda. Available from https://www.europarl.europa.eu/cmsdata/210469/New-Transatlantic-Agenda_EN.pdf [Accessed 5 May, 2022].
Eurostat, (2022b) Canada-EU - international trade in goods statistics [WWW Document], n.d. https://ec.europa.eu/eurostat/statistics-explained/index.php?title=Canada-EU_-_international_trade_in_goods_statistics accessed 7 March, 2023.
European Commission DG Trade (2015a). Press release: Commission proposes new Investment Court System for TTIP and other EU trade and investment negotiationsBrussels, 16 September, Accessed http://europa.eu/rapid/press-release_IP-15-5651_en.htm
European Commission DG Trade (2015b). *Trade for all: Towards a more responsible trade and investment policy*. Brussels. Available from http://trade.ec.europa.eu/doclib/docs/2015/october/tradoc_153846.pdf [Accessed 5 May 2022].
European Commission DG Trade (2015c). Press release: EU finalises proposal for investment protection and Court System for TTIP. Brussels, 12 November. Available from http://europa.eu/rapid/press-release_IP-15-6059_en.htm [Accessed 5 May 2022].
European Commission DG Trade (2016). Press Release: CETA: EU and Canada Agree on new approach on investment in trade agreement. Brussels, 29 February. Available from http://europa.eu/rapid/press-release_IP-16-399_en.htm [Accessed 12 May 2022].
European Commission, (2016). Investment Provisions in the EU-Canada Free Trade Agreement (CETA). https://trade.ec.europa.eu/doclib/docs/2013/november/tradoc_151918.pdf
European Commission, 2017. Reflection Paper on the Social Dimension of Europe. Accessed 15 March 2021. https://ec.europa.eu/info/publications/reflection-paper-social-dimension-europe_en
Fabry, E. and Garbasso, G. (2015). ISDS in the TTIP The Devil is in the Details. Policy Paper No. 122 *Notre Europe* January 16 Jacques Delors Institute. Available from http://www.institutdelors.eu/media/ttipisds-fabrygarbasso-nejdi-jan15.pdf?pdf=ok. [Accessed 15 July 2022].

Finbow, R. (2010). "Progress and Obstacles on the Road to a Canada-European Comprehensive Economic and Trade Agreement"European Union Centres of Excellence Newsletter, 5, 1 Ottawa, https://carleton.ca/euce-network-canada/wp-content/uploads/V5-1-EUCE-Newsletter-Winter2010.pdf

Finbow, R. (ed), (2022). *CETA Implementation and Implications: Unravelling the puzzle.* Montreal: McGill-Queens University Press 2022.

Gagné, Gilbert, & Morin, Jean-Frédéric (2006). The Evolving American Policy on Investment Protection: Evidence from Recent FTAs and the 2004 Model BIT. *Journal of International Economic Law*, 9, 357–38210.1093/jiel/jgl006.

Gatti, M. and Manzini, P. (2012). External Representation of the European Union in the Conclusion of International Agreements. *Common Market Law Review*, *49*(5), 1703–1734.

Hufbauer, G. (2002). US-EU Trade and Investment: An American Perspective. Paper presented at a conference titled" Transatlantic Perspectives on the US and European Economies: Convergence, Conflict and Cooperation" Kennedy School of Government Harvard University Available from https://www.piie.com/commentary/speeches-papers/us-eu-trade-and-investment-american-perspective [Accessed 8 June 2022].

Johnson, L. (2012). The 2012 US Model BIT and What the Changes (or Lack Thereof) Suggest About Future Investment Treaties. *Political Risk Insurance Newsletter*, *8*, 1–5. Available from http://ccsi.columbia.edu/files/2014/01/johnson_2012usmodelBIT.pdf. [Accessed 12 November 2016].

Koeth, W. (2016). *Can the Investment Court System (ICS) save TTIP and CETA?*. European Institute of Public Administration Working Paper 2016/W/01. Available from https://www.eipa.eu/wp-content/uploads/2022/01/20161019072755_Workingpaper2016_W_01.pdf [Accessed 12 June 2022].

Malakotipour, M. (2020). The Chilling Effect of Indirect Expropriation Clauses on Host States' Public Policies: a Call for a Legislative Response. *International Community Law Review*, *22*(2), 235–270.

McNamara, K. (2017). Trump Takes Aim at the European Union. *Foreign Affairs* January 24. Available from https://www.foreignaffairs.com/articles/europe/2017-01-24/trump-takes-aim-european-union [Accessed 11December, 2019].

Meunier, S., (2017). Integration by Stealth: How the European Union Gained Competence over Foreign Direct Investment. *JCMS: Journal of Common Market Studies*, *55*(3), 593–610.

Propp, K.R. (1992, April). Bilateral Investment Treaties: The US Experience in Eastern Europe. In *Proceedings of the Annual Meeting (American Society of International Law)* (pp. 540–544). The American Society of International Law. Available from https://brill.com/view/journals/iclr/22/2/article-p235_5.xml [Accessed 12 September 2022].

Quick, R., (2015). Why TTIP should have an investment chapter including ISDS. *Journal of World Trade*, *49*(2). 199–209.

Ruttenberg, V.H., (1987). The United States bilateral investment treaty program: Variations on the model. *University of Pennsylvania Journal of International Law*, *9*, 121.

Shaw, T.M., (2011). Postscript: Asymmetric Trade Negotiations After the Turn-of-the-decade 'Global' Financial Crisis?. in *Bilal, Bilal, Sanoussi, Lombaerde, Philippe De, and Tussie, Diana. Asymmetric Trade Negotiations The International Political Economy of New Regionalisms Series*. Burlington, VT: Ashgate. pp. 181–192.

Tussie, D. and Saguier, M. (2011). The Sweep of Asymmetric Trade Negotiations: Introduction and Overview. in Bilal, B., Sanoussi, L., De, P., and Tussie, D. (eds). *Asymmetric Trade Negotiations The International Political Economy of New Regionalisms Series.* Burlington, VT: Ashgate. pp. 1–25.

Trade Union Congress (TUC), (2014). "TTIP threats and opportunities" Speech by Sally Hunt, TUC Delegate to the ITUC World Congress Berlin, May 2014. Available online athttps://www.tuc.org.uk/ituc-ttip-speech

United States Trade Representative (USTR) (2022). Bilateral Investment Treaties" Available from https://ustr.gov/trade-agreements/bilateral-investment-treaties [Accessed 16 May 2022].

United States Trade Representative (USTR) and European Commission (2017). U.S.-EU Joint Report on TTIP Progress to Date" (January 17). Available from http://trade.ec.europa.eu/doclib/docs/2017/january/tradoc_155242.pdf [Accessed 22 May 2022].

United States Trade Representative (USTR) (2017). *The President's Trade Policy Agenda Washington*. Available online at https://ustr.gov/sites/default/files/files/reports/2017/AnnualReport/Chapter%20I%20-%20The%20President%27s%20Trade%20Policy%20Agenda.pdf [Accessed 16 May 2022].

Van Harten, Gus, and Loughlin, Martin (2006). Investment Treaty Arbitration as a Species of Global Administrative Law. *European Journal of International Law*, 17, 121–15010.1093/ejil/chi159.

Weaver, M. (2014). The Proposed Transatlantic Trade and Investment Partnership (TTIP): ISDS Provisions, reconciliation, and future trade implications. Available from http://papers.ssrn.com/sol3/papers.cfm?abstract_id=2548830 [Accessed 23 June 2022].

Young, A. R. (2017). European Trade Policy in Interesting Times. *Journal of European Integration*, *39*(7), 909–923, 10.1080/07036337.2017.1371705

24

TRANSATLANTIC RELATIONS IN A CHANGING WORLD

Marianne Riddervold, Akasemi Newsome, and Albert Didriksen

Introduction*

The connection between the EU and the US appears to be stronger than ever, at least on the surface. At the time of writing, the two parties have provided a powerful and well-coordinated reaction to Russia's invasion of Ukraine. But does this suggest that transatlantic relations have returned to normal after the turbulent years of the Trump administration and the US pivot to Asia? Will we see a continuation of this relationship's strength in the years to come? Or, is there evidence to suggest that the Ukraine crisis is less representative of the more comprehensive picture and that we instead observe a longer-term weakening of EU-US relations? This chapter seeks to address these questions, with a particular focus on identifying the factors that serve to stabilize or weaken the relationship. To do this, we discuss the findings in this volume together with the findings that emerged from our recent research project titled 'Transatlantic relations in times of uncertainty. Drivers and mechanisms of EU-US relations' (TRANSAT; see Newsome and Riddervold 2022; Riddervold and Newsome 2018 and Riddervold and Newsome 2022).

We concentrate our attention primarily on two significant concerns spanning the two main thematic areas of transatlantic relations: relations between the EU and the US inside formal and informal institutions and EU-US collaboration on matters of security and defense.

On the one hand, we find that EU-US relations are robust in many contexts and settings. We also identify several mechanisms that help explain why this stability exists, including the presence of common institutions, soft institutionalization through shared feelings of commonality, the engagement of non-state actors such as expert communities and members of parliament, and the extent to which the US takes the lead in the face of serious crises. It is obvious that the

DOI: 10.4324/9781003283911-29

Russian invasion of Ukraine has helped to enhance relations between the allies. However, structural and domestic considerations predict that the EU-US relationship nonetheless might become weaker over time. The emergence of China, a more uncertain geopolitical environment in parallel to what Smith (2022) refers to as a crisis of multilateralism, are the essential structural components, while populism and anti-globalisation trends – particularly in the US – create domestic challenges.

We have structured the chapter as follows: We give some context by analyzing the long-term stability of the relationship, including the shifts that have occurred in more recent times. We thereafter construct our analytic framework by identifying five distinct factors of the relationship that have the potential to influence its degree of strength (Riddervold and Newsome 2022). Part four discusses findings across the cases, first exploring formal and informal institutional settings before moving to a discussion of EU-US security and defense cooperation.

Background

The term *transatlantic relations* can be defined as 'the overall set of relations between the EU and the US, within the broader framework of the institutional and other connections maintained via NATO and other institutions' (Smith 2018, p. 539). Since the end of the Second World War, these relations have been an essential pillar of international relations, in many respects defining the structure and content of the 'International Liberal Order' (see, e.g., Hill et al. 2017; Ikenberry 2018). Today, after decades of continuous cooperation and as the EU member states have moved closer together in the EU, no other parts of the globe have stronger economic, security, and political ties than Europe and the US (see, e.g., Alcaro et al. 2016; Fernández Sola and Smith 2009).

However, as a result of the US' shift to Asia and the unorthodoxy of the Trump administration, academics and analysts havebegun to question the durability of this partnership. Trump brought about the realization that the steady relationship with the US could no longer be taken for granted (see, e.g. Anderson 2018; Riddervold and Newsome 2018; Rose 2018). In fact, President Trump signaling that 'the very basis of the relationship with Europe no longer fits with US values, needs, and interests' (Anderson 2018 p. 27) caused some academics to speculate that the EU-US relationship is on the verge of 'breaking down.'

The relationship changed again with the election of Joe Biden. When Russia invaded Ukraine in February 2022, Europe and the US quickly joined together in a strong and coordinated response, involving all means except direct military confrontation with Russia. The EU member states have again proved able to unite in crisis (Riddervold, Trondal and Newsome 2021), and NATO and the EU have been coordinated in their response, so far avoiding the scenario some have feared might follow as the EU grows stronger in the foreign and security policy domain. When push really came to shove, it seems like the transatlantic relationship stood to the test. But how telling is the Ukraine crisis response for longer-term trends in transatlantic relations?

Framework: drivers and mechanisms

The transatlantic relationship is intricate and multifaceted and is affected by several factors, many of which interact with one another. To tease out a comprehensive picture of EU-US relations, we draw on diverse theoretical perspectives and earlier research to develop a framework that differentiates across five aspects that help explain a weakening or stable/strengthening connection across cases. Three factors are consistent with the main explanations of the transatlantic relationship, which centers around interests, security, and institutions. To get a better picture also of other factors potentially affecting the relationship, we, however, also build on cleavage theory and a constructivist crisis perspective to develop two additional explanations of EU-US relations. These explanations focus on the significance of domestic support and the extent to which the relationship is perceived to be in a crisis.

First, a *liberal intergovernmentalist perspective* regards the transatlantic relationship as a transactional relationship affected mainly by the actors' economic interests and interdependencies (Krasner 1999; Moravcsik 1998). If their interests coincide, and if each believes that a strong partnership may help them advance those objectives, one would anticipate continued strong EU and US relationship, in spite of other challenges. As argued by Ikenberry and others (Ikenberry 2018), globalization, interconnectedness, and a shared interest in open and well-functioning markets create a drive for cooperation in the quest for effective solutions to shared global problems. Such interdependencies are, moreover, dynamic relationships that, once established, incur high costs to terminate (Keohane and Nye 2012).

On the other hand, the relationship may weaken if independencies are reduced, if one or both do not see the economic gain of a strong relationship, or if other relationships are seen as more valuable. We have, for instance, already seen that the EU reacted to US protectionism under Trump by increasing economic ties with Japan and China. Trade is also increasingly securitized, and it is increasingly difficult to differentiate between economic factors and strategic issues, particularly in technology. The EU and the US also disagree on a number of trade matters, including how to tax and regulate (typically American) technology companies, or how to reform the World Trade Organization (WTO).

Also, a *neo-realist* perspective perceives interstate relations as transactional. However, rather than focusing on economic interdependencies, it links the strength of the relationship to geopolitical trends and the actors' strategic objectives, arguing that EU-US relations are determined by relative power hierarchies and shifting geopolitical dynamics (Mearsheimer 2014; Waltz 1979). The relationship may thus strengthen if the EU and the US enhance their partnership to counterbalance the threat posed by other growing powers. Scholars have already suggested that the ongoing conflict with Russia may lead to a new cold war between the West, on the one hand, and Russia and China, on the other, with the degree to which China decides to support Russia largely determining whether a new cold war will break out (Beckley and Brands 2022). The two might also agree on a division of labor where the US supports Europe on Russia, and the EU is loyal to the US in its dealing with

China (Cross and Karolewski 2017; Riddervold and Rosén 2018). Broader structural changes may, however, also weaken the relationship. The rise of China and the parallel weakening of Europe may soon cause the US to turn its attention back to Asia rather than Europe. This might eventually lead to a worsening of ties between the two continents (Schwartz 2022; Smith 2022). In consequence, the EU may also seek to increase its power and independence globally, including in relation to the US.

A *third possible set of factors* starts from the ontological assumption that other components, such as norms and institutions, can influence foreign policy and, as a result, the strength of the relationship between the two actors (Checkel 2007; Kratochwil 1989; March 1998; Risse 2016). *Institutionalist theories* link a putative strong or stable relationship to well-established patterns of cooperation in numerous pre-existing institutions. Institutions are 'persistent rule structures that prescribe appropriate behavior and enable or constrain behavior' (Risse 2016, p. 24) and can be formal (like NATO or the EU) or more soft and informal (such as well-established modes of collaboration). Within these institutions, policymakers make decisions based on preexisting path-dependent routines and established behavioral norms (March and Olsen 1998). Customs, anticipations, and duties that have gradually become institutionalized and ingrained within the transatlantic community may thus lead to continued, almost automatic cooperation.

These roles may be triggered in times of crisis, when shared perceptions and world views come to the forefront. The EU and NATO have recently been very clear not only about the strategic danger posed by Russia but also aboutthe importance of protecting international law and core values such as sovereignty and human rights. However, crises may also have the opposite effect. When confronted with crises and difficulties, existing governance arrangements and 'long-cherished beliefs' in existing solutions, such as the relationship between the US and Europe, may be called into question (Lodge and Wegrich 2012, p. 11). Crises may also produce critical junctures that generate 'windows of opportunity' for a major shift in the direction of policy (Kingdon 1984). During the Trump-crisis (Anderson 2021), for example, preexisting frameworks and routines that are usually taken for granted were shaken up, and may, over time, not least with a new Trumpist administration, lead to a more significant weakening of the EU-US. To get a better picture of the connection between the EU and the US, we therefore consider two additional factors linked to perceptions, trust, and domestic support.

Our fourth consideration is based on the core *social constructivist principles* and suggests that the stability of the transatlantic relationship depends on the various players' perceptions of the robustness of and trust in this relationship (Cross 2022; Kratochwil 1989; Risse 2016). In her study of the social construction of crises in the EU, Mai'a Cross (Cross 2021, p. 199) holds that crisis is a constructed phenomenon: 'Crises must be seen to threaten whatever defines the current order of things. (...) It takes opinion-makers (...) and various other social actors to construe an event as a crisis in order for it to be recognized as such.' This logic may also be relevant for understanding the transatlantic relationship: On the one hand, if a crisis is regarded as a common crisis by actors from both sides of the Atlantic, it could draw them closer together in terms of similar reactions and shared role conceptions. If, on the other hand, the relationship itself is represented as in crisis or facing serious challenges, this may, over time, have consequences for their trust in the relationship and, consequently, their behavior toward each other. Even if the two traditional partners stand together in the face of the immediate and unparalleled risk to European security prompted by the Russian invasion of Ukraine, Trump's cut with conventional US foreign policies created a European mistrust in a long-term American commitment.

A fifth factor that may impact the stability of EU-US relations is linked to domestic politics, namely the degree to which voters and parties endorse transatlantic links and, more generally, international cooperation. We base this argument on Hooghe and Marks' post-functional cleavage theory (Hooghe and Marks 2018), developed to comprehend voters' perceptions of European integration. Following Hooghe and Marks, populism in Europe is the result of a collision between, on the one hand, the functional need for more European integration in reaction to common challenges and, on the other hand, local identities. Over time, this collision has led to the development of a new and increasingly prominent transnational party cleavage, referred to as the GAL-TAN cleavage, indicated by a systematic correlation between voters' perspectives on various political issues such as climate change, migration, and liberal values, on the one hand, and their support of trans-border cooperation and EU integration, on the other. Similar patterns have been found in studies of polarization in the US, suggesting a new and increasingly substantial division between voters who are considered the losers and the winners of globalization (Peterson 2018; Zürn 2018). This is an observation that bears an obvious connection to the EU-US ties as well: After all, '(d)omestic politics affects all aspects of foreign policy' (Eliasson chapter 14, this volume), suggesting that 'the fate of the liberal international order begins at home' (Peterson 2018, p. 649).

Still going strong?

EU-US relations in formal and informal institutions

First, what trends are evident in formal and informal institutions? Are transatlantic ties still strong, or is there evidence to suggest a longer-term weakening of the relationship?

On the one hand, some of the studies in the aforementioned project and in this volume find evidence to suggest that institutional relations remain stable or even grow stronger, due to factors such as economic and financial independence, common values and structures of more informal institutionalisation, and in response to the Russian war on Ukraine. Others, however, point to how these factors are increasingly challenged due to geopolitical structures, diverging interests, and domestic political trends.

David O'Sullivan (chapter 2, this volume) writes about the transatlantic space between shifting administrations, and how the Ukraine war – at least temporarily and depending on the upcoming US election – has strengthened EU-US relations. The Trump administration questioned not only the foundation of the transatlantic relationship, but also the value of the liberal order as such. Biden soon renewed the security guarantee and returned to several key international agreements. But he continued many of Trump's foreign policies, with its two main goals being to balance China and conduct a 'foreign policy for the middle class.' In O'Sullivan's words, the Ukraine war, however, became a game changer, with the Biden team quickly seeking a unified approach with the EU. Acknowledging the important role the EU plays in coordinating sanctions and other foreign policies, an active Biden administration engaged in what he describes as an 'unprecedented degree of transatlantic consultation and coordination' by which they 'managed to build a coalition of support for Ukraine, through sanctions and other measures.'

Contributing to a stable relationship over time, several authors find that feelings of commonality and shared foreign policy values between actors in Europe and the US create what Dunne (chapter 1, this volume) refers to as a soft institutionalization of EU-US relations. In his study of The European Parliament Liaison Office in Washington DC (EPLO). Dunne finds that EU-US parliamentary cooperation is characterized by positive mutual perceptions and shared perspectives on the importance of international cooperation on key global issues, something that serves to uphold a strong relationship between the two – including in periods of more turbulent political relations. The very purpose of the EPLO is to facilitate dialogue and interaction between the US and the EU parliaments, and thus also adds a 'hard institutional' dimension to this already-existing softly structured relationship. Dunne also argues that this cooperation is likely to become stronger in the future: With the EU taking a bigger global role not only in response to Ukraine but also in areas such as climate, tech regulation, and privacy rights (often referred to as the EU's global regulatory power), Congress has come to realize the importance of having good relations to an actor that plays a decisive part in many of the EU's decision-making processes.

According to Fahey and Terpan (chapter 16, this volume), these types of mutual positive perceptions characterize not only particular cases but also the broader EU-US relationship as such, making it very different from other regions of the world. In addition to the many formal agreements between the EU and the US, as well as between the US and various member states, political and other EU and US actors continue to share a sense of commonality and empathy toward each other that is key for understanding strong transatlantic links. These sentiments also seem to survive political disagreements and proclaimed anti-globalization sentiments such as those expressed by Trump.

Another example of how ideas and softer forms of institutionalization continue to underpin the relationship is linked to the EU's and the US' promotion of human rights promotion in third countries. As Poli (chapter 7, this volume) notes, only Western states have developed and implemented global human rights sanctions regimes as part of their foreign policies, and the EU and the US, together with the UK and Canada, continue to be the main promoters of such values externally. The EU and the US also play a common important role in upholding these values, since silence over serious or even gross human rights violations would be tantamount to considering similar breaches acceptable (Poli, chapter 7, this volume). There is some coordination between the four when listing individuals and entities in breach of human rights, but not much and not within formal institutional structures, suggesting instead that similar policies are based on shared values and perceptions.

A number of studies, however, also find evidence to suggest a weakening of the relationship – a trend that perhaps is more surprising in light of the historically strong ties and the impact of an ongoing war in Europe.

Also exploring the role of values and perceptions, Petersmann (chapter 9, this volume) challenges the notion that there is a strong normative consensus or shared value base in the EU-US relationship. On the one hand, we have indeed witnessed a strong transatlantic democratic alliance in response to the war in Ukraine, with partners on both sides of the Atlantic largely driven by principled concerns linked to legal international principles such as the UN charter, the Geneva conventions, and international human rights. US and European leaders have also underlined how this is a fight not only between Ukraine and Russia but also between democracies and autocracies. At the same time, however, the Trump administration, Brexit, and the financial crisis have revealed an increasing number of transatlantic differences over how to regulate international relations. According to Petersmann, path-dependent value-conflicts and ideological differences between EU's and the US' approaches to international rules and organizations are likely to persist. In the long run, these disagreements moreover 'disrupts UN and WTO governance of the universally agreed sustainable development goals (SDGs) and risks impeding transatlantic and global trade, investments and environmental cooperation' (Petersmann chapter 9, this volume).

Raube and Vego Rubio (2022) are also sceptical to the extent to which common values will uphold a strong relationship in the face of diverging strategic priorities. On the one hand and in line with Poli's argument, Raube and Vega Rubio find that shared values continue to be important aspects of a stable EU-US relations: In cases where shared values and the EU and US' shared identity as liberal actors come to the forefront, as in the case of human rights sanctions, they are likely to act coherently. Increasingly diverging interests due to changing global power relations, however, challenge this coherence, not least due to the US' pivot to Asia. When faced with choices affecting its core strategic interests, as was the case with AUKUS, US strategic interests trump a joined EU-US approach. A future US administration that is less focused on the promotion of liberal values or more concerned with China may hence contribute to weakening the relationship further.

Peter Van Elsuwege and Viktor Szép (chapter 6, this volume) share the view that the war and the US' response have prompted unprecedented EU-US coordination, both bilaterally, between the US and various EU member states, and vis-a-vis other states, in the G7. Sanctions is a tool that, in general, is increasingly applied by both, and coordination with likeminded states is seen to increase their impact. However, as in many other areas of transatlantic relations, EU-US coordination on sanctions is, however, not based on formal legal or institutional structures but is essentially informal and political. As the US sanctions on Iran illustrate, this makes them more sensitiveto changes in different administrations' policy decisions and reminds us that challenges remain, in particular over the extraterritorial application of US secondary sanctions. Domestic political contexts in the EU and the US may thus determine the future scope for cooperation and the extent to which unilateral sanctions regimes converge.

Moving instead to studies of financial and economic relations between the two sides of the Atlantic, Hjertaker and Tranøy's (2022) analysis of the US rescue of European banks in 2008 reveals evidence of strong and even advancing transatlantic financial ties, in which the US's dominance at the top of the hierarchical structure leads to increased collaboration between European and US banks – a trend further substantiated by the COVID-19 pandemic response. Both during the financial crisis in 2008 and during COVID, in line with a liberal internationalist perspective, the US central bank's view on the economic and financial interdependencies between the EU and the US was crucial for understanding why it decided to rescue European banks. As long as the US dollar continues to be the world reserve currency, the US will thus continue to play a dominant role in EU-US relations and in various financial regulatory groups.

Given the traditional importance of their trade relations and the strong economic interdependencies that exist between the US and the EU, it is not surprising that several authors, both in this volume and in the TRANSAT project, explore EU-US trade relations and discussions in the World Trade Organization (WTO) and related organizations. In his analysis of labor rights, trade defense instruments, and discussion on reforming WTO, Eliasson (chapter 13, this volume), finds that, although differences remain, the EU has, in fact, moved closer to America's position on many issues. As a consequence, it is easier for the two to form common positions in multilateral organizations, and vis-a-vis other actors. Domestic political developments, however, have a strong impact on transatlantic trade cooperation, and different perspectives across the Atlantic challenge the strength of the relationship. In particular, while the EU and the US are moving closer together in their view on protecting labour rights and the EU increasingly is joining the US in its attempts to balance China, key differences remain on WTO reform, as also by several other authors in the volume. As a consequence, 'differing domestic preferences on multilateralism, and an EU far less comfortable with power politics than the US, may continue to hinder coordination on significant WTO reforms for the foreseeable future' (Eliasson chapter 13, this volume; 10).

Kerremanns (2022) also find that the EU and the US are facing severe challenges in their trade relations, in particular in the WTO and on issues linked to WTO reform. While Europe's judicial system has developed with the acceptance that national law in many areas is subordinated to international legal authorities (the primacy of EU law), US legal and judicial professionals oppose giving international organizations precedence over US law. As a consequence, the EU sees the WTO as an international anchor supportive of international commerce, while the US has been wary of having to abide by WTO decisions. With an increasing perception that the WTO no longer serves the US' agenda, it has stopped backing the WTO dispute settlement system. Domestic politics serve to further cement more difficult transatlantic trade relations. In the US, the electorate's increasing politicization of the WTO as a threat to national sovereignty has alarmed US political leaders. In Europe, the WTO has not been the focus of anti-globalization activism.

Transatlantic differences are also reported by Tzanou (chapter 18, this volume) and Kendrick (chapter 16, this volume), in their analyses of EU and US' perspectives on data privacy and on the reform of international legal taxation norms and regulations. In the data privacy space, the EU has, with its General Data Protection Regulation (GDPR), de facto developed almost global standards. Tzanou, however, finds that cooperation in this area is complex and multifaceted, leading to challenges in the transatlantic relationship, underpinned by both political and legal issues. On a more positive note, however, although not all problems related to this seem resolvable, Tyanou also points out that a lot can be fixed, given genuine commitment based on mutual trust, mediation, and substantive legislative reform. Similarly, following Kendrick, there is a transatlantic consensus that the international tax system must be transformed and harmonized to better deal with digitalization and multilateral companies. However, the EU and the US disagree on how to revise it, since they both want their own agendas and systems to become the basis of the new norms. Although presenting very different solutions, both moreover claim that their suggestions will be the fairest international regulatory system, suggesting that agreement nonetheless might be difficult to reach.

As Propp (chapter 3, this volume) explains, the particularities of the functioning of the EU in external and foreign affairs also affect the EU-US relationship since it influences the role of the EU and the member states in various international negotiations. While having full competencies in some areas, making the Commission the sole negotiating partner, other policy areas are so-called mixed competencies and require EU coordination as well as member state signatories. On top of this, both the European Parliament and the EU court actively influence and control EU external relations – a reality that is often difficult to grasp and handle for American policymakers. Hence, Propp concludes, while Washington may often be a difficult partner for the EU in reaching international agreements, the EU also is no ordinary sovereign for the US to face across the table.

Focusing mainly on structural dynamics and actors' limited ability to affect them, Smith (2022) and Schwartz (2022) paint the perhaps least gloomy picture of the future, arguing that the impact of such factors in the longer term will necessarily lead to a weakening of EU-US relations. According to Schwartz (2022), the asymmetrical and hierarchical nature of EU-US relations is weakening transatlantic relations in global trade and economic development. As international trade and industrial relations change, EU-US relations will change as well. And with a more powerful China and a more polarized US, the rules of international relations will no longer be determined by the US. At the same time, the US geostrategic attention is likely to remain focused on the Indo-Pacific region, facing the EU with difficult choices to make. On the one hand, the US still needs its allies to help contain China, and the Ukraine war has revealed Europe's profound security dependence on Russia. But on the other, the EU relies heavily on both US and Chinese markets. As Schwartz (2022:195) ends his article, 'The subtle difference here, however, is that US exports compete with Europe's future production, while China's exports compete with current European production.' Smith (2022) shares the view that geopolitical and economic structures will largely determine the long-term relationship. In spite of still-existing economic interdependencies and soft, value-based common structures and perceptions, the rise of China and corresponding US strategic priorities, the relative economic and strategic decline of Europe and what he refers to as the crisis in multilateralism all serve to weaken the relationship. Adding to this, also the fifth factor discussed earlier, namely domestic developments, will add further to this weakening, as not only increased polarization in the US but also what he sees as increased internal EU tensions will challenge the unity of each of the partners and their future commitment to maintaining a strong relationship.

Foreign and security relations

While not the main focus of this edited volume, security relations between the US and Europe form another core aspect of transatlantic relations. Drawing on realist theory, Olsen (Olsen 2022) looks at four instances of transatlantic security cooperation: the NATO alliance; the US pivot to Asia; the war in Afghanistan; and the sanctions against Russia. In all cases, in spite of different US security doctrines and US administrations, there is evidence to suggest that the transatlantic relations have remained stable. US President Trump's public criticism of NATO did not change the US interest in retaining NATO, and both the US and the European NATO members continued to uphold their obligations to the US-led defense alliance. Similarly, the EU replicated a tougher US approach to China by putting a halt to future negotiations on the 'EU-China Comprehensive Agreement on Investment' and by making statements referring to China as a 'strategic competitor.' While the US unilateral withdrawal from Afghanistan and AUKUS deal left the Europeans wondering about the US commitment, the US reaction to Russia has, according to Olsen, been convergent since the US election in 2020. Russia's 2022 war on Ukraine further consolidated the alliance.

Bolstad and Friis (chapter 8, this volume) share Olsen's view that security relations in NATO remain strong, in spite of the Trump administration's questioning of US commitments and the US orientation toward China. In line with several other authors in this volume and the TRANSAT project, they argue that the transatlantic defense alliance traditionally is built not only on common interests but also on softer institutional structures such as common values and trust. After all, they write, without trust in the parties' political commitment, the alliance cannot be taken for granted in a crisis or war situation. The main reason why NATO has remained relevant despite its many historical challenges is, however, foremost a strong and credible US leadership and the common nuclear deterrent. This, together with a shared threat perception, is also what has made NATO so relevant in response to Russia's war in Ukraine. Like most other authors, they, however, also warn that challenges lie ahead, not least the European fear that the US will soon continue its pivot to Asia. Less trust in the US' commitments, and what Knutsen (2022) and Smith (2022) refer to as internal EU disagreements on how to fill the void, may thus contribute to weakening the relations in the longer term.

Also arguing that the security relationship remains strong, Cross (2022) looks at how the EU and US interact in the increasingly significant field of space. In line with

Olsen and Bolstad, she argues that the transatlantic relationship remains intrinsically solid. Cross emphasizes that despite the US's political shift in focus and preferences toward China and its propensity to take the transatlantic alliance for granted, the two countries continue to be bound by deeply ingrained and potent strategic, economic, and political links. Furthermore, Cross demonstrates how shared norms and perceptions and informal cooperation, between non-state actors at the sub- and transnational levels, as in many other policy areas discussed earlier, have supported a robust relationship across the Atlantic. These socially constructed transatlantic networks are also key to understanding why space has remained calm, in spite of geopolitical conflict elsewhere.

Rieker's (2022) investigation into EU-US security ties in Africa also finds evidence that the alliance is still strong, albeit the image is less clear than what is argued by the articles discussed earlier. On the one hand, Rieker finds that structural changes have increased the gap between security interests on both sides of the Atlantic, with the US since 2010 having primarily focused on China and Europe concentrating on its near abroad, that is, Russia and Africa. Moreover, while the EU is heavily involved in numerous missions and actions, there is little direct bilateral cooperation between EU and the US, and little NATO engagement. Nonetheless, Rieker demonstrates that there are strong transatlantic due to the US and France's close collaboration in the Sahel. The US' participation and willingness to support France and Europe in Africa moreover demonstrates that this collaboration is supported less by shared interests than by a shared set of principles or practices. Echoing several other contributions, Rieker asks whether this support will continue under a new US government.

Finally, Knutsen (2022) instead believes that the US withdrawal from Afghanistan is indicative of the now-deteriorating ties between the US and the EU in the domain – a trend that will continue, also after Ukraine. US leadership has been key to upholding strong transatlantic ties, and with the US over time becoming less concerned with Europe as it pivots to Asia, Europe is struggling to agree on the scope and content of EU foreign and security cooperation. In particular, and in line with Smith's (2022) observation that there are internal disagreements in the EU, the lesser concern with European security has also sparked increased intra-European disagreements among European states over how NATO and deeper military EU integration fit together.

Concluding remarks

This chapter set out to give a broad overview of whether EU-US relations are weakening, in particular seeking to identify the factors that contribute to a stable or changing relationship. For this purpose, it described a framework developed by Riddervold and Newsome (2022), and applied this in a discussion of findings from the different chapters in this book as well as in a previously conducted project on transatlantic relations (TRANSAT-see Newsome and Riddervold 2022; Riddervold and Newsome 2018, 2022).

Our discussions show that several factors contribute to a remarkably long-lived economic, strategic, cultural and institutional relationship. Authors find evidence to suggest that several of the factors we identified – including strategic and financial interdependencies, various non-state actors such as experts and members of parliament and common institutions – help stabilize and uphold a relationship that is still going strong, in spite of the increasing number of challenges it has faced during the last decade. Several authors also point to how not only formal institutionalization but also softer types of institutionalization, such as shared feelings of commonality and empathy, are important for understanding the still comparably strong relationship.

At the same time, we also find that the EU-US relationship is facing more severe challenges than at any previous time since the Second World War. At a difference to previous periods in the relationship, both domestic and structural factors suggest a longer-term weakening of the relationship. Authors focusing on structural factors suggest that the rise of China and the US' corresponding pivot to Asia, changes in the economic relationships, and the parallel increasing contestation of the norms and values that underpin the liberal international order may challenge the coherence of the contemporary relationship. The EU increasingly uses its newly won regulatory power, at times in opposition to US preferences, and the two have many diverging perspectives on issues such as trade and tax regulations and the reform of key multilateral organizations. Many authors also discuss the influence of domestic factors, in particular the impact of an increasingly polarized US.

Structural and domestic factors may thus also be key to understanding the future developments of EU-US relations. In structural, geopolitical terms, the relationship may remain strong if the European states decide to join the US as a junior partner in its global competition with China, while also taking more responsibility for its own regional security. After all, on top of much else, Ukraine also proved to the Americans that Russia is a regional power and not a global threat to the US. How much and how long the US needs its European partners, however, remains to be seen – AUKUS and the unilateral withdrawal from Afghanistan both suggest that this is not something the Europeans can take for granted. Domestic factors may, moreover, be more difficult to address for the Europeans. As several authors in this volume underline, American foreign policies start at home. And although a majority of Americans support the US engagement in Ukraine (Smeltz and Sullivan 2022), we can only speculate what the US and hence transatlantic policies would have looked like with a Trumpist President, or what it will look like after the next election.

All of these issues will need much more research in the years to come. What we can conclude is, however, that at the very least, transatlantic relations are changing, and that most of the studies explored in this chapter suggest that it is or may be weakening. Although many factors still serve to stabilize the relationship, structural and domestic trends are particularly likely to continue to impact the relationship also in the years to come.

Note

* This chapter is based on a framework developed by Riddervold and Newsome (2022), and combines findings from Newsome and Riddervold (2022) with findings from other chapters in this volume.

References

Alcaro, R., Peterson, J., and Greco, E. (Eds.), 2016. *The West and the global power shift: transatlantic relations and global governance, Palgrave studies in EUpolitics*. Palgrave Macmillan imprint is published by Springer Nature, London.

Anderson, J.J., 2018. Rancor and resilience in the Atlantic Political Order: the Obama years. *Journal of European Integration* 40, 621–636. 10.1080/07036337.2018.1483841

Anderson, J. J. 2021. A Series of Unfortunate Events: Crisis Response and the European Union After 2008. The Palgrave handbook of EU crises, Palgrave studies in Eu politics, 765–790. Palgrave Macmillan, Cham, Switzerland.

Beckley, M., Brands, H., 2022. *The return of Pax Americana? Putin's war is fortifying the democratic alliance*. Foreign Affairs.

Checkel, J., 2007. Constructivist Approaches to European Integration, in: *Handbook of EUPolitics*. SAGE, London.

Cross, M.K.D., 2021. Social constructivism, in: *The Palgrave Handbook of EU Crises*. Palgrave Macmillan, Cham, Switzerland, pp. 195–2011.

Cross, M.K.D., 2022. Space Security and the Transatlantic Relationship. *PaG*, 10, 134–143. 10.17645/pag.v10i2.5061

Cross, M.K.D. and Karolewski, I.P., 2017. What Type of Power has the EU Exercised in the Ukraine-Russia Crisis? A Framework of Analysis: Europe's Hybrid Foreign Policy. *JCMS: Journal of Common Market Studies* 55, 3–19. 10.1111/jcms.12442

Fernández Sola, N. and Smith, M. (Eds.), 2009. *Perceptions and policy in transatlantic relations: prospective visions from the US and Europe*. Routledge, Milton Park, Abingdon, Oxon; New York, NY.

Hill, C., Smith, M., and Vanhoonacker, S. (Eds.), 2017. *International relations and the European Union*, 3rd ed. Oxford University Press, New York, NY.

Hjertaker, I. and Tranøy, B.S., 2022. The Dollar as a Mutual Problem: New Transatlantic Interdependence in Finance. *PaG* 10, 198–207. 10.17645/pag.v10i2.5028

Hooghe, L., Marks, G., 2018. Cleavage theory meets Europe's crises: Lipset, Rokkan, and the transnational cleavage. *Journal of European Public Policy* 25, 109–135. 10.1080/13501763.2017.1310279

Ikenberry, G.J., 2018. The End of Liberal International Order? *International Affairs* 94, 7–23. 10.1093/ia/iix241

Keohane, R.O. and Nye, J.S., 2012. *Power and interdependence*, 4th ed. Longman, Boston.

Kerremans, B., 2022. Divergence Across the Atlantic? US Skepticism Meets the EU and the WTO's Appellate Body. *PaG* 10, 208–218. 10.17645/pag.v10i2.4983

Kingdon, J.W., 1984. *Agendas, alternatives, and public policies*. Little, Brown, Boston.

Knutsen, B.O., 2022. A Weakening Transatlantic Relationship? Redefining the EU–US Security and Defence Cooperation. *PaG* 10, 165–175. 10.17645/pag.v10i2.5024

Krasner, S.D., 1999. *Sovereignty: Organized hypocrisy*. Princeton University Press, Princeton, N.J.

Kratochwil, F.V., 1989. *Rules, norms, and decisions: on the conditions of practical and legal reasoning in international relations and domestic affairs, Reprint. ed, Cambridge studies in international relations*. Cambridge Univ. Press, Cambridge.

Lodge, M. and Wegrich, K. (Eds.), 2012. *Executive politics in times of crisis, Executive politics and governance*. Palgrave Macmillan, Houndmills, Basingstoke, Hampshire; New York.

March, J.G. and Olsen, J.P., 1998. The Institutional Dynamics of International Political Orders. *International Organization* 52, 943–969.

Mearsheimer, J.J., 2014. Why the Ukraine Crisis Is the West's Fault: The Liberal Delusions That Provoked Putin. *Foreign Affairs* 93, 77–84.

Moravcsik, A., 1998. *The choice for Europe: social purpose and state power from Messina to Maastricht*. Routledge, Taylor & Francis Group, London New York.

Newsome, A. and Riddervold, M., 2022. Conclusion. Out with the old, in with the new? Explaining changing EU-US relations. *Politics and Governance*, 10(2), 229–234.

Olsen, G.R., 2022. "America is Back" or "America First" and the Transatlantic Relationship. *PaG* 10, 154–164. 10.17645/pag.v10i2.5019

Peterson, J., 2018. Structure, agency and transatlantic relations in the Trump era. *Journal of European Integration* 40, 637–652. 10.1080/07036337.2018.1489801

Raube, K., & Vega Rubio, R. (2022). Coherence at Last? Transatlantic Cooperation in Response to the Geostrategic Challenge of China. *Politics and Governance*, 10, 176–185. 10.17645/pag.v10i2.5022.

Riddervold, M. and Newsome, A., 2018. Transatlantic relations in times of uncertainty: crises and EU-US relations. *Journal of European Integration* 40, 505–521. 10.1080/07036337.2018.1488839

Riddervold, M. and Newsome, A., 2022. Introduction. Out with the old, in with the new? Explaining changing EU-US relations.*Politics and Governance*, 10(2), 128–133.

Riddervold, M. and Rosén, G., 2018. Unified in response to rising powers? China, Russia and EU-US relations. *Journal of European Integration* 40, 555–570. 10.1080/07036337.2018.1488838

Riddervold, M., Trondal, J., and Newsome, A. (Eds.), 2021. The Palgrave handbook of EU crises, *Palgrave studies in EUpolitics*. Palgrave Macmillan, Cham, Switzerland. 10.1007/978-3-030-51791-5

Rieker, P., 2022. Making Sense of the European Side of the Transatlantic Security Relations in Africa. *PaG* 10, 144–153. 10.17645/pag.v10i2.5048

Risse, T., 2016. The Transatlantic Security Community: Erosion from Within?, in: *The West and the global power shift: Transatlantic relations and global governance*. Palgrave Macmillan, London, pp. 21–42.

Rose, G., 2018. Letting Go. Trump, America, and the World. *Foreign Affairs* 97, 1–192.

Schwartz, H.M., 2022. The European Union, the US, and Trade: Metaphorical Climate Change, Not Bad Weather. *PaG* 10, 186–197. 10.17645/pag.v10i2.4903

Smeltz, D. and Sullivan, E. 2022. Americans Support Ukraine "As Long As It Takes", https://www.thechicagocouncil.org/research/public-opinion-survey/americans-support-ukraine-long-it-takes

Smith, M., 2018. The EU, the US and the crisis of contemporary multilateralism. *Journal of European Integration* 40, 539–553. 10.1080/07036337.2018.1488836

Smith, M., 2022. How Much of a New Agenda? International Structures, Agency, and Transatlantic Order *PaG* 10, 219–228. 10.17645/pag.v10i2.4985

Waltz, K.N., 1979. *Theory of international politics*, 1st ed. ed. McGraw-Hill, Boston, Mass.

Zürn, M., 2018. *A theory of global governance: authority, legitimacy, and contestation*, First ed. Oxford University Press, Oxford; New York, NY.

INDEX